WASHOE COUNTY LIBRARY
3 1235 01014
P9-CJI-934

VIRGINIA WOOLF

By the same author

WILLIAM COWPER: A BIOGRAPHY
INTERIOR LANDSCAPES: A LIFE OF PAUL NASH
THE LAST MODERN: A LIFE OF HERBERT READ
WILLIAM BLAKE: HIS LIFE

co-editor:

THE LETTERS AND PROSE WRITINGS OF WILLIAM COWPER
WILLIAM COWPER: SELECTED LETTERS

VIRGINIA WOOLF

James King

W · W · Norton & Company
NEW YORK · LONDON

First American Edition 1995

Printed in the United States of America

Manufacturing by the Haddon Craftsmen, Inc.

ISBN 0-393-03748-7

W. W. Norton & Company, Inc.
500 Fifth Avenue, New York, N.Y. 10110
W. W. Norton & Company Ltd.
10 Coptic Street, London WC1A 1PU

1 2 3 4 5 6 7 8 9 0

TO
VANESSA KING

Contents

CONTENTS

PART FIVE
THE OUTSIDER

List of Illustrations

Between pages 236 and 237

In-text illustrations

Acknowledgements

For permission to quote from Virginia Woolf's letters and diaries, I am much indebted to Quentin Bell and Angelica Garnett, the Executors of the Estate. I am deeply grateful to Trekkie Parsons, Frances Partridge and George Rylands for talking with me about Virginia Woolf. I learned a great deal from them, as I did, years before, from Lord David Cecil, who spoke with candour about the marriage of Leonard and Virginia Woolf.

I am grateful to the staff of various institutions for access to material in their possession and for their kind assistance: Stephen Crook at the Berg Collection, New York Public Library; the Tate Gallery Archive; Elizabeth Inglis at the University of Sussex Library; Dr Michael Halls at King's College, Cambridge; Valerie Thomas at Mills Memorial Library, McMaster University. John Bicknell, Jean O. Love and S. P. Rosenbaum have given me the benefit of their expert knowledge on various aspects of Virginia Woolf's life.

When I began work on this book six years ago, I soon became familiar with the considerable scholarship which has been devoted to Virginia Woolf. This work is of three kinds. There is the splendid textual work of Anne Olivier Bell, Nigel Nicolson, Joanne Trautmann Banks, Susan Dick, Mitchell A. Leaska and Andrew McNeillie. Virginia Woolf and her circle have been given careful attention by biographers such as Quentin Bell, Phyllis Rose, Lyndall Gordon, Jane Dunn, Frances Spalding, Michael Holroyd, Victoria Glendinning and Peter F. Alexander; there are also important books devoted to the historical understanding of Virginia Woolf and Bloomsbury by Edward Bishop, S. P. Rosenbaum, John Mepham, Grace Radin, Roger Poole, Brenda Silver and Louise DeSalvo. Then there is the third branch of scholarship: those books and articles which remind the reader that the feminist context of Woolf's writing is central to any genuine understanding of her and her work. In this regard, I am particularly indebted to the work of Carolyn G. Heilbrun and, especially, Jane Marcus.

For generous financial assistance, I should like to thank the Social Sciences and Humanities Research Council of Canada. Susan Clarke, my research assistant, did everything I asked of her with great precision and abundant cheerfulness. Edward Bishop, John Covolo and Anthony Goff read drafts of this book, and I am grateful to them for many valuable suggestions and comments. At Hamish Hamilton, I am much indebted to Caroline Hartley, Keith Taylor and, especially, my editor and publisher, Andrew Franklin. Lesley Levene copy-edited this book with exceptional precision and sensitivity. I also wish to thank my wife and children for giving me, at their expense, the space and time in which to write this book.

Introduction

Virginia Woolf is one of the quintessentially great writers of our century, always attuned to the contradictory nature of what it is to be alive now. She is one of us. Never satisfied with easy answers, she asked – and continues to ask – many troubling questions about parents and children, men and women, love and friendship, husbands and wives, reason and passion, life and death. Life, she tells us, is always transitory and frequently tragic, but it is all we have. We must, she urges, love this world, even though we may be attracted to death.

Virginia Woolf is ours because she speaks to us of life as we experience it. She tells us of our hopes, aspirations and fears in language of unmistakable radiance and poignancy. The great writers embrace life in all its complexities; we find ourselves and each other in their pages. Virginia Woolf is among this select company. In her books, the great joy and sorrow she took in life are immortalized. This biography, in large part about the joys and sorrows of her existence, explores her inner landscape, the abundant source of her creative genius.

In her vision, life may be fluid, but it is filled with moments of sacred beauty. She wanted to capture the illusive 'it' of existence, to create a sonorous, delicate prose to accomplish this difficult task. Virginia Woolf frequently felt that she was too ambitious, that she might have to pay the price of oblivion for having had the courage to invent a language which could tell the truth of modern life. She was painfully aware that – despite Austen, the Brontës and Eliot – women remained outsiders to the literary tradition.

'Can there be Grand Old Women of literature,' she once sarcastically asked, 'or only Grand Old Men? I think I shall prepare to be the Grand Old Woman of English letters.' This biography explores the relationship between her life and the various writings – the novels, essays, book reviews, letters and diaries – which have made her one of the most celebrated authors in the English language.

Surprisingly, this is the first full-scale literary biography of Virginia Woolf. By design, Quentin Bell's splendid biography of 1972 pays limited attention to her writings. Other lives tend to be specialized. Phyllis Rose's excellent *Woman of Letters: A Life of Virginia Woolf* (1978) demonstrates how she attempted to create a literature which is both modernistic and feminine. Lyndall Gordon's moving and compassionate *A Writer's Life* (1984) is meditative and thematic, much of it being given over to *To the Lighthouse* and *The Waves*, which she considers Virginia Woolf's masterpieces.

In this book I consider the starting points of all her major works, their relationship to her life, their composition and their critical reception. My discussions of her writings are centred on their relationship to her life, though I realize that there are other equally valid critical approaches to her texts. The task of a literary biographer is to show the relationship between life and art, but such an approach, even to a major writer, can in some cases capture only a part of the subject's life. This is not so with Virginia Woolf, because her career was the central fact of her existence and her fictional writings are so deeply autobiographical.

This biography of Virginia Woolf is certainly longer and more leisurely than previous treatments of her life, and the resulting book is a great deal more intimate, especially in its treatment of her marriage, friendships, mental instability and sexuality.* At its heart, centred on the subject's two favourite things – books and friendship – is Virginia Woolf's greatest creation: herself.

To portray a person rather than an icon means that this book must take a stand on many contentious issues. In recent years,

* Through the publication of her diaries and letters, the facts of Virginia Woolf's life are, in the main, well documented. However, this book does contain important new information about, for example, her childhood illnesses, her sexual involvement with her sister and her attempt, during her 1904 breakdown, to obtain a baby.

much has been written about the Duckworth brothers' incestuous behaviour and its tragic effect on their half-sister's life. In the main, I agree with this position, but Virginia Stephen was a constitutionally vulnerable child and there is convincing evidence that many members of the Stephen family suffered from bipolar disorders. The crucial incident in her early life, however, was the death of her mother, Julia, when she was only thirteen. In my opinion, Virginia Woolf's frequent depressions and rare bouts of psychotic breakdown derive from a mixture of frailties, not a single source.

After the death of her mother, Virginia found solace in close friendships with women. In the case of Vita Sackville-West this was expressed physically, but the quest was always for a warm, caring mother. Virginia was very well aware of the real nature of this search. She was never very interested in the sexual expression of her needs, although she was fascinated by the sexual behaviour of others. She distanced herself from what she called 'these Sapphists' and was, at various times, physically attracted to Clive Bell and T. S. Eliot. Her sexuality – very much a composite one – cannot be encapsulated in a simple term or catch-phrase.

In marrying Leonard Woolf, Virginia had found a husband of a 'lower' station who, because of his Jewishness, was an outsider like herself. However, the stereotypical roles were reversed: Leonard 'nursed' Virginia and took on many of the nurturing duties usually associated with women. This relationship worked well because the couple were able to discard so many conventional trappings, but despite this Leonard often acted in an unduly controlling way. Extremely attracted sexually to Virginia, he was bitterly disappointed by her reserve. His resentment seeped through in the ways he became at times too harsh and punitive a caretaker of his fragile wife. But Leonard was neither an angel nor a devil. This was a marriage which succeeded on its own carefully regulated and unconventional terms.

Although from childhood she was bewitched by literature and anxious to find her own niche as a writer, the difficulty with such a profession for Virginia Woolf was that she would thus share a 'common shop' with her father, whom she both revered and loathed. One reason why her gestation as a writer was so lengthy and so painful is that she was entering terrain in which this austere, difficult man had been remarkably successful. In so doing, she faced two major hurdles: she felt compelled to write about dour, anxiety-ridden Hyde Park Gate, where she was born, while, at the same time, she emulated the patriarch of that troubled household.

Once she had overcome those formidable obstacles in her first two novels, Virginia not surprisingly came to see that the forces which threatened her were masculine and could be fought against only by employing a new conception of the female self, one which had not been assimilated into male culture. The results of such daring can be seen in *Jacob's Room*, *Mrs Dalloway*, *To the Lighthouse*, *Orlando*, *The Waves* and *Between the Acts*, and in two crucial book-length essays, *A Room of One's Own* and *Three Guineas*. Thus she searched for new forms in fiction and non-fiction that allowed her to eschew the masculine, which for her was connected to the death instinct. In this way she attempted to stay alive as a person and a writer. In reinventing herself she redesigned English literature.

Since my biography of Virginia Woolf entails a total revaluation of her as a writer, I look closely at how her novels and other writings reflect the search for a distinctly feminine aesthetic, one in which the intuitive parts of the self are dominant. Virginia's early years were spent in an atmosphere where women nursed men (Julia Duckworth Stephen's only published book was on nursing) and where women were seen as playthings by men. To a degree, the genesis of her notions of feminism derives from a rejection of the standards set for women in Leslie Stephen's household. She once claimed, 'I am more & more attracted by looseness, freedom & eating one's dinner off a table anywhere.' In labelling herself an outsider, she extended her view of herself to the place of all women in society and ultimately to all of society's outcasts.

Her entire life was dominated by depression and sadness – powers which threatened to overwhelm and annihilate her. In many ways, her writings were attempts to run counter to those forces and to grasp at the healing aspects of life. Valiantly she fought to escape 'the fin in the waste of water which appeared' to her one day over the marshes out of her window; she tried to put aside the sharp, penetrating feelings of self-loathing, as when she described herself on 28 September 1926 as an 'elderly, dowdy, fussy, ugly incompetent woman; vain, chattering & futile'. This is one of her central reasons for writing: to investigate and in so doing contain her fascination with death. Through her writing, she sought to capture the vitality of existence. The paradox is that the search for affirmation inevitably brought her back to the subjects she knew best: the destructiveness of men, the burdens of the past, and the fragility of life.

If there were many unresolved conflicts at the core of her being, though, there was also considerable merriment. Virginia boasted of tossing off her letters like omelettes, and friends and acquaintances were given places in a bestiary: the ballerina Lydia Lopokova had the 'soul of a squirrel', Rebecca West was a shaggy dog and Beatrice Webb a moulting eagle. At various times, Virginia dubbed herself the Goat, Potto the Lemur and Mandrill the baboon. Overall, she was a much funnier, stronger, more roguish and sly person than is usually perceived, one who put up a mighty struggle against death. Writing was her way of doing battle. She strove to find words with roots which would connect her with the transcendent but transient beauty of human existence: pure, happy, radiant points of time.

Writing gave Virginia Woolf great pleasure and great anguish. It also unleashed her incredible sense of boldness. Like James Joyce, she was an intrepid experimenter, one who was anxious to snare the 'real thing', to pen a novel which encapsulated the very essence of life itself. A remorseless self-critic, she was never satisfied with her efforts. So she was always trying something new. In large part because of the resultant, enormous variety in her work, she has unjustly acquired the reputation of being difficult or forbidding. In this book, I have tried to show that the opposite is true.

I have also endeavoured to provide a complete portrait of this daring, impetuous, tormented person, the woman who strove relentlessly to find the right words. While working on this book I became more and more aware of just how much of a fight each day of Virginia Woolf's existence had been. Perhaps more than any of the other great writers, she was desperately aware of life's insubstantiality, of conflicts which could not be resolved. She wanted to live, but at the very same time she was entranced by death. As I confronted her magnificent battle against the powers of extinction, I constantly asked myself, doesn't her struggle to stay alive – and to be fully alive – constitute another kind of greatness, a heroism which exists apart from her considerable achievement as a writer?

Part One

A BORN WRITER

Chapter One

STRANGE SOLEMN MUSIC

(1877–8)

'How did father ask you to marry him?'[1] little Virginia Stephen once playfully asked her mother. Julia gave her customary little laugh, half surprise, half shock. She did not answer the question, but her mind must have drifted back to February 1877 and a dinner party at the home of Leslie Stephen, her neighbour. As she was departing, she was startled when her host thrust into her hands a letter that both dismayed and moved her:

> I am forced to say something to you which concerns me much – and you very little. It was revealed to me a little while ago that I love you – as a man loves the woman he would marry . . . Now a sure instinct tells me that you have no such feelings for me. *I have not the slightest illusion about this.* I feel certain too that you will never have such a feeling for me. Nay, I am convinced that even if you love me, I could hardly make you happy as my wife.[2]

In confessing his love to Julia, Leslie mixes passion with desperation. He is sexually attracted to her, is sure that she does not reciprocate and is certain that, even if she loved him, he could probably not make her happy as his wife. Nevertheless, he assures her, 'I shall love you . . . as long as I live.' Thus began a year-long courtship by forty-four-year-old Leslie Stephen, a widower since 1875, of thirty-one-year-old Julia Duckworth, herself a widow since 1870.

Leslie's habitual, consuming sense of himself as a failure is evident in this letter. Julia was not deeply stirred by its declaration. However, she was a person who habitually placed the needs of others above her own. Upon reading this message, she returned to Leslie's house, where widow and widower closeted themselves in his study. Julia tenderly patted Leslie on the shoulder and told him that he had rightly divined her feelings. Marriage was out of the question, but she agreed, as Leslie recalled, that they should not go further apart from each other. They were to be the closest of friends but 'never upon closer terms'.[3]

In Leslie's make-up, low self-esteem was accompanied by persistence. A tall, silent man wrapt in gloom, he became a shadow whose melancholic presence accompanied Julia everywhere. As he himself knew full well, he had come to live among phantoms, his entire existence reduced to 'a dingy, idiotic white brown, with no vivid colour in it'. He did not seem quite real even to himself. 'Life has been a queer sort of dream to me,' he confessed to Julia. But when she was near, he assured her, the dream had substance to it. He no longer felt like a 'mere formless ghost'.[4]

A man who saw himself as desperately ill, Leslie needed a tender nurse to restore him. The challenge appealed to Julia and eventually overcame her reservations. Two months after he first proposed, Leslie suggested a secret, legal marriage with neither of them changing residences or outward modes of life. Julia rejected this on the grounds of practicability and propriety. She had also become frightened that she made Leslie restless and hinted that their special friendship might best be terminated.

Leslie was stung: 'You treat me like a baby.' Reluctantly, though, he admitted that his behaviour was infantile and promised to reform himself. Then, having given this assurance, he proceeded to complain bitterly: 'I am not a person to whine for what I can't get; or to let my life become fretful and peevish and unsettled.' A bit improbably, he added: 'I have more courage than that could imply.' Should he be deprived of bread and water, he asked, simply because he had asked for cake and wine? If she did abandon him, he threatened to overwork himself and thus ruin his health.[5]

Julia became increasingly convinced that she could wound rather than heal her would-be lover. Only two years before, her eyes full of tears, she had asked an aunt to pray that she might die.

However, their talks and spats gradually drew Julia and Leslie together. Never, Leslie implored her, was she to write that her affection did him harm. She should voice such sentiments only in person – so that he could immediately contradict her. Leslie remained painfully aware that Julia's unwillingness to love him provided yet another kind of torment.

In spite of herself, though, Julia was drawn to Leslie and gradually convinced herself that she could love him with her whole heart, although it seemed to her a poor dead heart. She began to cling to, rather than shrink from, intimacy with him. At the very same time that his pleas were beginning to be favourably received, Leslie's letters to Julia became filled with recriminations and, in turn, Julia upbraided him for the ready ways in which he manufactured litanies of disappointments. He grumbled when he had to stay in lodgings while travelling; she assured him that she had patiently borne such deprivations for years. He lamented his solitary existence; she told him that he would be unhappy if he did not have four or five hours a day to himself.

Julia's reluctance to marry Leslie was overcome as it became more and more apparent to her that he desperately needed someone to look after him, a task abandoned by his sister-in-law, Anny Thackeray, when she married Richmond Ritchie in August 1877. An observer at that wedding noted that Leslie looked deplorable and that Julia's thick black velvet dress and veil gave her a gloomy, tragic aspect.

By December 1877, Julia was reduced to painful indecision. Just then, Leslie perversely informed her that he was so poor a creature that she might do well to decline him. He compared himself and Julia to battered hulks leaving the comfort of a harbour for the certainty of a maelstrom. Spiritedly, Julia assured him that she did not see the prospect of marriage to him as setting out in a storm, although she hardly expected a smooth passage. When she mentioned to her mother, Maria Jackson, the possibility of marriage to Leslie, Julia burst into tears. She told her that thoughts of marriage unsettled her now customary tranquillity. Somewhat guardedly, her mother assured her that such an alliance would not necessarily be a dreadful thing. Still, as she confided to Leslie, Julia was inclined to let herself sink rather than attempt to save herself from drowning.

This impasse went unresolved until 5 January 1878, when Leslie was visiting Julia. He repeated his arguments in favour of marriage, met with little response and rose to depart. Julia, sitting in her armchair by the fire, suddenly met his eyes and perfunctorily declared: 'I will be your wife and will do my best to be a good wife to you.'[6]

Despite their differences, the newly engaged couple shared a bitter emotional heritage. Both had lost spouses to whom they were deeply attached. Until they found each other, life had offered them little. Leslie was filled with self-doubt and Julia's self-esteem was fragile, centred as it was on caring for others. In this alliance, there was more than a dash of desperation. Immediately after the announcement of her forthcoming marriage, Julia went away to nurse her ailing uncle Thoby Prinsep, and remained there for most of the engagement. Her very mixed feelings can be discerned in that decision. For his part, Leslie was ecstatic:

> All doubts vanished like a dream. She writes to me ten days later . . . 'My darling one. I feel most commonplace and quiet. The only thing I can't quite believe is that we are not married. Perhaps when I see you, you will go a little further off. Just now we seem part of each other and I feel as if it were all such an old thing that I need neither talk nor think about you!'[7]

When providing this account, Leslie did not mention that in the very same letter Julia had told him she felt horribly unsentimental about her engagement. She also informed him that when her dying uncle had asked her if Leslie would make a good husband she had assured him he would not. Nevertheless, as Leslie complacently put it, Julia 'yielded absolutely when she had once felt yielding to be right'. The couple were married in Kensington on 26 March 1878.

Julia's haunting otherworldly beauty impressed itself on everyone who met her. One of Virginia's first memories was of a Pre-Raphaelite madonna in a white dressing gown on a balcony surrounded by passion flowers. Julia had full features, but her large eyes, nose and mouth threatened to overwhelm her delicate cheekbones, profile and long neck. Her face was stunning in the contrast between forbidding remoteness and inviting sensuousness.

Julia derived her exotic good looks from her mother. Maria Jackson was one of seven Pattle sisters, a family whose blend of attractiveness and eccentricity led to the quip that there were three sexes: men, women and Pattles. According to the novelist Thackeray, matriarchal 'Pattledom' was simply a state of being. The ancestry of this family stretched back to the Court of Versailles and one Chevalier Antoine de l'Etang, who was a member of the household of Marie Antoinette. A superb horseman, he was handsome, elegant, extravagant – and available. According to a family legend, either he or the Queen possessed a roving eye. In any event, he was exiled to Pondicherry in India, where he entered the service of the Nawab of Oudh. In 1788, at the age of thirty-one, he married Mlle Thérèse Blin de Grincourt and became the father of one son and three daughters, Julie, Adeline and Virginie.

Adeline de l'Etang, Virginia's great-grandmother, perhaps in search of a husband with even more panache than her father, married James Pattle, renowned for extravagant wickedness. This man, nicknamed the 'King of Liars', drank himself to a justly celebrated death in 1845. He was packed off to England in a cask of rum which unfortunately exploded, shooting out his corpse before the grieving widow's eyes. This event understandably drove Adeline mad – and also set the ship on fire. The vessel was stranded in the Hooghly and, according to Virginia Woolf, the sailors later drained the cask long before the re-encased body reached England.

What seems a bit more certain is that five years earlier Adeline Pattle had travelled to England with her seven daughters – Adeline, Julia Margaret, Sara, Maria, Louisa, Virginia and Sophia. According to Ruskin, they had 'Elgin beauty with dark eyes'.[8] Virginia, whose comeliness was celebrated, married Charles Somers-Cocks and became Countess Somers. According to the painter G. F. Watts, Julia Margaret, a 'woman of noble plainness', was intractably bossy and interfering. Once, when visiting friends whose taste did not meet her high standards, she stayed up after her hosts had retired for the night in order to surprise them the next morning with a redecorated room. On another occasion, she sent the ailing Hallam Tennyson a pair of loose purple and gold Oriental trousers, a Japanese teapot and cups and a roll of flannel. Her eccentricity is the stuff of legend. One day, she was spotted, dressed in flowing red velvet, walking towards the railway station at Putney, a tea cup in one hand and a teaspoon in the other.

Julia Margaret, who married Charles Hay Cameron, found the fullest expression of her talents at the age of fifty, when her daughter, also Julia, gave her a camera. No other Victorian photographer was as gifted as she soon became in evoking a twilight, mythological world of pure innocence blended with ripe sexuality. Her poets (Tennyson, Browning), celebrities (the explorer Captain Speedy with the Prince of Abyssinia), literary subjects ('The Passing of Arthur', 'Hetty and Adam Bede') and women (Lewis Carroll's Alice Liddell as 'Alethea') emerge boldly from thick Venetian chiaroscuro. Their eyes, usually turned away from the viewer, are filled with unspeakable sorrow.

Virginia Woolf, who was well aware that her own creative impulses were derived in part from Julia Margaret, later pointed a satirical but loving finger at her great-aunt in the play *Freshwater*, named after the artists' colony on the Isle of Wight founded by the Camerons. At one point, Julia Margaret reflects on the difficulties involved in finding suitable people to sit for her:

> What is the use of a policeman if he has no calves? There you have the tragedy of my life. That is Julia Margaret Cameron's message to her age! All my sisters were beautiful, but I had genius. They were the brides of men, but I am the bride of Art. I have sought the beautiful in the most unlikely places. I have searched the police force at Freshwater, and not a man have I found with calves worthy of Sir Galahad . . . If a burglar came

> and he were beautiful, I should say to him: Take my fish knives! Take my cruets, my bread baskets and my soup tureens. What you take is nothing to what you give, your calves, your beautiful calves.[9]

Next to Julia Margaret, her sister Maria, Virginia Woolf's grandmother, seems an inconsequential figure, a devotee of hypochondria rather than art. In about 1835, the seventeen-year-old married John Jackson, fourteen years her senior. He was a physician who practised in India. Although family mythology claimed that he had a commonplace understanding and worshipped respectability, he became the first professor of medicine at Calcutta Medical College and was the author of a book on tetanus.

John and Maria had three daughters, Adeline (b. 1837), Mary (b. 1841) and Julia (b. 1846), all of them probably born in India. By 1848, Julia's two sisters had left the subcontinent and were living in England with their aunt Sara and her husband, Henry Thoby Prinsep. In that year, Maria and Julia returned to England. From then until 1855, mother and daughters lived in a variety of places, including Well Walk in Hampstead. John Jackson returned to England in 1855, at which time the family settled at Brent Lodge, Hendon, where he continued to practise medicine. They moved in 1866 to a house named Saxonbury in Frant, near Tunbridge Wells, so that Maria could be close to her idol, the poet Coventry Patmore.

In addition to beauty and eccentricity, the Pattles were celebrated for their inordinate interest in illness. Lady Somers, who lost a child to diphtheria, was obsessively concerned with the health of her two remaining daughters, as her constant queries in letters make clear: 'Do you feel *very well*? Are you sensible of feeling much stronger for Brighton air? Does your throat look better? Do you ever have backache? Is your appetite good?'[10] In Maria Jackson, this neurosis reached its apogee. She cultivated headaches, rheumatism, giddiness and indigestion, which she treated with morphia and chloral. Relentlessly, she catalogued the maladies of her daughters, sisters, cousins, nieces and nephews. She had a corresponding interest in another aspect of health – the retention of beauty. Her existence was centred on the preservation of the flesh in all its guises.

Julia, undoubtedly Maria's best-loved child, was taught French, which she spoke with a good accent. She could play the piano, pronounced De Quincey's *Opium Eater* her favourite book and knew *Hamlet* sufficiently well to jump when 'sliver' was misread as 'silver'.[11] So great was Julia's share of Pattle beauty that Maria attempted to protect her from admiring looks by not allowing her out alone. Even as a youngster Julia nursed her frequently invalid mother. Later, from her early teenage years, she became her mother's companion on pilgrimages to various spas. The search for health was a shared enterprise and in the process Julia became an excellent nurse, attuned to the slightest fluctuations in the well-being of her beloved patient. Mother and daughter considered themselves so expert in their diagnoses that they never conferred with Dr Jackson, who was seldom ill. Sometimes he was allowed to relate tall tales of shipwrecks and pirates. Overall, the old man with an astonishing mane of white hair that stood out like a three-cornered hat round his head was excluded from the medicinal fairyland of his wife and daughter.

On visits to Freshwater, Julia inhabited a different world. There, she was in touch with some of the best-known writers and painters of the day: Tennyson, Thackeray, Watts, Holman Hunt and Burne-Jones. However, Julia's sentimental education took place in the 1860s at Little Holland House, the London home of her aunt and uncle, the Prinseps. When Sara Prinsep wanted a house large enough to hold a salon, it was Watts who suggested the old, rambling farm dwelling, some 500 yards from Kensington High Street, which had stood empty since the death of its owner in 1845. Adorned with a flurry of chimneys and gabled roofs, the quaint, old-fashioned building had an informal garden bordered by rose-bushes and poplars. With the arrival of the Prinseps in about 1850, the house returned vigorously to life. The long corridors and large, low rooms were filled to bursting. The walls were painted green, the ceilings a dusky blue. Watts had a studio in the house to which visitors were admitted as long as they admired the pictures. That painter's fascination with the richest tints of Venetian colour further enhanced the house's décor.

Little Holland House was at its liveliest on Sundays in the summer, when the at-homes were held. The pleasant clicking of mallets hitting balls could once more be heard from the croquet lawn. Meals were served at irregular times, but Sara's hospitality was outlandishly charming. 'It is a nest of proeraphaelites [*sic*],' George du Maurier claimed, 'where Hunt, Millais, Rossetti, Watts, Leighton, etc. Tennyson, the Brownings and Thackeray etc., and tutti quanti receive dinners and incense, and cups of tea handed to them by these women almost kneeling.'[12] Some thought Sara particularly adept at curries but her interests obviously ranged beyond the domestic.

At-homes were commonplace in Victorian life, but convention was not cultivated by the new regime at Little Holland House. Uncle Thoby, a former Anglo-Indian administrator who had been a member of the Council of the East India Company, was his wife's helper in the collecting of artists, writers and politicians. One notable acquisition was Burne-Jones, whom, when she heard he was ill, Sara whisked away from his home in Red Lion Square. He afterwards called her 'Aunt' and described her as the nearest thing to a mother that he ever knew.

The more sedate comeliness of Julia Jackson soon attracted the attention of the artists who frequented or lived at Little Holland House, for whom she became a model: Watts, Burne-Jones, Marochetti, Clifford, Lisa Stillman. There were proposals of marriage from Burne-Jones and Thomas Woolner, the sculptor. When she was twenty, Leslie Stephen first saw her at a picnic in Abinger Hatch. She was dressed in white with blue flowers in her hat. As he later recalled, he 'saw and remembered her, as I might have seen and remembered the Sistine Madonna'.[13]

In her evocation of her mother's youth, Virginia pictured Julia on a bright summer afternoon as one of a throng of women stepping out of the long windows at Little Holland House on to the lawn. She was dressed in a striped silk dress, buttoned at the throat, with a flowing skirt. This vision was accompanied by the enticing sound of music coming 'from those long low rooms where the great Watts pictures hang; Joachim playing the violin; also the sound of a voice reading poetry'.[14]

A much more secular likeness of Julia is captured a year later in 1867 by her aunt Julia Margaret Cameron. Julia's entire face is lit up with a radiance absent from all other portraits. The photograph reveals a countenance alive with pure feeling. As such, it enshrines Julia's love for Herbert Duckworth, whom she first met in Italy in 1862. The couple became engaged in February 1867 and married on 4 May 1867.

According to Virginia Woolf, the atmosphere of Little Holland House 'cast over the figure of [Julia's] bridegroom all the golden enchantments of Tennysonian sentiment'.[15] He was, as it were, a sleeping prince kissed back to life by a beautiful woman. There was a fairy-tale element in their romance, but for Virginia her mother's first husband was but a cipher who represented the ultimate in propriety. She felt that he was Julia's inferior in all ways. Leslie Stephen, another biased witness, was also suspicious of Duckworth, although he considered him a gentleman: 'A man of honour, of fair accomplishments and interest in books, he was fitted to take his place in any society, without being the least of a dandy or a fop: simple, straightforward and manly. But, besides this, he was, as everyone could perceive who knew him, a singularly modest and sweet-tempered man.'[16] There is more than a hint of condescension in Leslie's words of praise. The question is worth asking: how could Julia have chosen such a commonplace person?

At the age of twenty, Julia might have wanted to escape the confined, hypochondriac world of her mother, preferring, for a change, to find someone to look after her. There might have been a touch of her quiet, gentlemanly physician father in Herbert. Temperamentally, she might not have fitted into the bohemian world of the Little Holland House set; this unconventionally raised young woman might have prized the exceedingly conventional. Herbert Duckworth, who was educated at Trinity College, Cambridge, and joined the Northern Circuit as a barrister, was an amiable, pleasant – perhaps dull – person. He was also exceedingly handsome and virile-looking, and Julia adored him. The couple obviously shared a strong sexual attraction – and that affinity is caught in Julia Margaret Cameron's photograph of her niece. The couple, who settled at Bryanston Square in London, already had two children, George (b. 1868) and Stella (b. 1869), when on 19 October 1870 Herbert died suddenly of an undiagnosed abscess which burst as he reached up to pick a fig. Six weeks later, Julia gave birth to a third child, Gerald.

Herbert Duckworth's death irrevocably changed Julia's subsequent existence. She had become habituated to happiness and suddenly it was snatched from her. Her spouse's death was, as Virginia Woolf later reflected, 'a disillusionment as well as a tragic human loss'.[17] Like Mrs Ramsay in *To the Lighthouse*, Julia now asked: 'How could any Lord have made this world?' She not only lost her faith; she became anti-religious. For her, there was no longer any 'reason, order, justice . . . There was no treachery too base for the world to commit . . . No happiness lasted.'[18] The joyful bride was thrust into a nightmarish existence where nothing seemed to matter. She had been shipwrecked, but she had to continue: 'I knew that I had to live on and on, and the only thing to be done was to be as cheerful as I could and do as much as I could and think as little. And so I got deadened.'[19]

Through her marriage to Herbert Duckworth, Julia had kept well within the upper-middle-class preserves of the Jacksons, the Camerons and the Prinseps. The Duckworths had been established for so long in Somerset that they were reckoned gentry. Julia herself was the cousin of the Duchess of Bedford. She came from a family which depended upon influence and patronage and could, in turn, bestow those valuable commodities. The Stephens were not so well established. As a clan they had had to battle for their entrée to that level of society the Jacksons took for granted. All his life Leslie felt precariously poised among the intellectual gentry.

The origins of the Stephens were cloaked in romantic mist of a Scottish variety. James Stephen of Ardenbraught in Aberdeenshire died in about 1750, leaving seven sons and two daughters. His son, also James, was trained as a lawyer but became a merchant sailor and was shipwrecked off the Dorset coast. A man of indomitable courage and exceeding charm, he rescued himself and four companions. The party soon found themselves on the Isle of Purbeck, where they were assisted by Mr Milner, the Collector of Customs. With Mr Milner's assistance, James salvaged much of his cargo – and also won the heart of Sibella Milner, whom he secretly married.

Unfortunately, James's later picaresque adventures went badly for him. His business failed and he found himself in the King's Bench Prison. Not a man to bend to authority, he mounted a defence, published in 1770: 'Considerations on Imprisonment for Debt'. In it he argued that incarceration on such grounds was a barbarous custom, but ultimately he owed his release to his creditor rather than his rhetoric. His appetite for law having been rekindled, James attempted without success to enter the Middle Temple. A man who never took no for an answer, he became the partner of a solicitor under whose name he practised, but his clients turned out to be scoundrels, much of his work being done in public houses. He lost money, reputation and health and died a broken man in 1779, at the age of forty-six. His wife had died four years before him, leaving six children.

Virginia's great-grandfather James, the second of these six, shared his father's indomitable will. When he was a student at the Marischal College, Aberdeen, the often sickly young man found his way ostensibly barred by an examination to be conducted in Latin, a language in which he had little proficiency. He managed to get round the regulation, and this remained his attitude towards life: if a rule barred your way, circumvent it. Eventually, he became a Member of Parliament and a Master in Chancery. He never felt alone, having the comfort and support of a benign God who steadily guided his fortunes – even while he was engaged to one woman and had impregnated another.

As a young man, James went to the West Indies. There he practised as a lawyer, witnessed the French and American disregard for the British blockade and wrote his celebrated pamphlet, 'War in Disguise'. But James's outrage was more directed against slavery, the full brutality of which he witnessed in the West Indian courts. When he returned to England, 'Jem' became a staunch ally of Wilberforce, whose sister Sarah was to be his second wife. Thus he was steadily drawn into the Clapham Sect, a prosperous evangelical group dedicated to abolition. Devoutly religious and politically daring, these men and women were much more interested in social action than inner contemplation. Tinged with more than a dab of complacent superiority, they nevertheless acted as the conscience of the upper middle class.

James died in 1832, just before the abolition of slavery. His third son, yet another James, served in the Colonial Office, where his intrepid self-righteousness – even in the face of ministers – earned him the dubious sobriquet 'Mr Over-Secretary'. James reinforced his family's position within the Clapham Sect by marrying Jane Catherine Venn, whose grandfather wrote the Bible of that group, *The Compleat Duty of Man.* Although she maintained a household dominated by a strong puritanical strain, Jane Catherine had a lively sense of fun. Her husband did not. He once tasted a cigar and liked it so much that he resolved never to smoke another. Although a dynamic administrator and the author of numerous articles in the *Edinburgh Review*, James was filled with self-loathing. His imaginative boldness did not bolster him. He wanted to be a recluse and, behind the façade of public success, was a desperately reticent man. So convinced was he of his ugliness that he could not abide, like his granddaughter Virginia, looking in a mirror.

Unfortunately for him, Leslie, who was born in 1832, was temperamentally his father's son. As a young boy, he constantly measured himself against his brother James Fitzjames, who was three years older, and he did not like what he saw. Although the two boys were bullied when they first went to Eton, Fitzjames eventually became known as 'Giant Grim'; at Cambridge, he was nicknamed the 'British Lion'. As he boasted, he learned that to be weak is to be wretched, that the state of nature is actually a state of constant war. In contrast, Leslie remained deeply shy, convinced that he was not fully masculine.

Without doubt, Jane Stephen pampered Leslie to an excessive degree. She had good reason to do so: her eldest son, Herbert, sickly from birth, died in 1846, when Leslie was fourteen. She was perhaps too deeply attuned to what could go wrong with a frail child. Strangely, she was also an excessively demanding parent, one who saw no incongruity between concern for her son's health and desire for him to excel. When he was two, she noticed that he was easily frustrated; his violent temper and frequent crying also upset her. Yet she pushed him to begin his studies at the age of three. She marvelled that his nerves often got the better of him and prevented him from following her instructions.

By the time he was eight, Leslie switched from subject to subject, opting for Latin because it was boyish. However, he tended to get absorbed in poetry, seeming to lose touch with himself and his surroundings. A doctor was consulted: he prescribed school, fresh air and a rigorous abstinence from poetry.

Between Sir James and his second son there was an impenetrable wall, never to be breached. Caroline Emelia, Leslie's only sister, noted that he never stopped calling his father 'Sir' whereas boys from other families resorted to the slightly less formal 'Governor'. On occasion, James would propose long walks to Leslie and then become inarticulate and reserved. But Sir James did move his household to Brighton and its sea breezes when excitation at home was condemned by Leslie's physician and the boy was said to need 'to have the sugar taken out of him'. Later, when Leslie was nine and a half, James moved his household to Windsor, so that Fitzjames and Leslie could attend Eton as dayboys.

Very much in the tradition of the eldest son, Fitzjames became a prominent civil servant and was later the 1st Baronet Stephen. He made the transition easily from nervous schoolboy to successful bureaucrat. And Leslie, having inherited his father's wavering temperament and been mollycoddled by his mother, looked to Fitzjames as a model. In his teens and as a young man, Leslie devoted his existence to a relentless aping of his elder brother. He became, as he put it, wiry; he walked, he rowed, he ran, he transformed himself into an expert Alpine climber. He was Broad Church, a true specimen of muscular Christianity.

He remained, however, a divided man, profoundly aware that he was drawn to the world of letters even though this was a calling which smacked to him of the effeminate. He became a justly celebrated man of letters, but remained suspicious of any kind of aesthetic response. Another conflict surfaced when he had to find a calling suitable for a second son. When he was offered a fellowship at Trinity Hall, it was still necessary for fellows at Oxford or Cambridge to take holy orders. He did so in 1859, but three years later he had become convinced that the story of the Flood was a fiction. It is a measure of Leslie's integrity that he could no longer live what he considered a lie. Many of his colleagues, undergoing similar crises of faith, simply overlooked their inconvenient vows.

When he left Cambridge in 1862, Leslie was in search of a new career. Fitzjames helped him find work as a journalist and Leslie soon became attracted to the union cause in the United States, travelling there in 1863, in the middle of the Civil War. He interviewed Lincoln and made close friends with the Boston brahmins, James Russell Lowell, Charles Eliot Norton and Oliver Wendell Holmes. Back in London, Leslie settled in with his mother and sister at 19 Porchester Square, where he began his literary career in earnest, a career which led to the editorship of the *Cornhill Magazine* and eventually the *Dictionary of National Biography*.

As a writer, Leslie Stephen could boast of two outstanding achievements. He was the first English critic to elevate the novel to the rank of serious writing. With great eloquence, he described how social conditions shape literature. Later, he became the principal spokesman of Cambridge agnosticism, utilitarianism and scepticism. He was a proponent of individual freedom, the family as the mainstay of society and the eighteenth century, which he proclaimed the century of common sense, toleration and social and industrial development. He was not only an advocate of radical utilitarianism; he became that doctrine's historian.

Some philosophers who argue on behalf of the family as the

vital social unit can perhaps avoid putting theory into practice. Leslie could not. Either at his mother's table or at that of George Smith, the proprietor of the *Pall Mall Gazette*, he met Thackeray's daughters, Anny (Anne Isabella) and Minny (Harriet Marian), who lived together in a tiny house at 16 Onslow Gardens. In every sense, Anny was her late father's child, eventually becoming an enormously popular novelist. Once, during a luncheon at Porchester Square, Leslie and Anny were discussing novels and he observed that he liked old favourites best. When pressed by the sparkling, effervescent Anny, he admitted that *Vanity Fair* would be his particular choice. Anny may have been Leslie's intellectual equal, but it was Minny with whom he fell in love.

At a luncheon in Hampstead at the Smiths' house, Elizabeth Gaskell's observant eye caught an exchange between Leslie and Minny and she instantly knew that the two would marry. As Leslie recalled, it 'is probable enough that our mutual feelings were sufficiently transparent to a looker-on'. Yet, as he himself admitted, he moved slowly. In the summer of 1866, he had the perfect opportunity to propose at Zermatt, where he spent two or three days of exquisite happiness in Minny's company. 'I began to know that my fate was fixed. Yet, rather perversely, I chose to keep an engagement'[20] in Vienna. He remained troubled by doubts and diffidence, which he did not overcome until he heard that his dilatory conduct had offended one or both of the sisters. Finally, on 4 December, he steeled himself, took lunch at his club, considered the entire matter in a philosophical spirit and marched over to Onslow Gardens, where Minny quickly accepted him. They married on 19 June 1867.

Leslie had been strongly attracted to Anny and yet he had pursued Minny. This might account for his procrastination in approaching Minny and for the sparks which constantly flew between him and his sister-in-law, Leslie being a vociferous cataloguer of Anny's many extravagances. Years afterwards, when he wrote his memoir, the *Mausoleum Book*, he often began with thoughts of Minny, only to be led astray by his fascination with Anny.

Although she was Thackeray's daughter, Minny resembled one of Dickens's child-brides. She was warm, confiding and totally dependent on Anny. 'The relation between them might be compared,' Leslie accurately noted, 'to the relation between a popular author and his wife. My Minny, of course, played the part of wife in the little household.' Not surprisingly, a struggle for mastery over Minny erupted between husband and sister. Leslie once tartly observed that he liked Anny best when she was in the next room. When he speaks of his first marriage, Leslie presents himself as a David Copperfield happily entwined with his cherished Dora, Anny being a charming serpent in that domestic paradise.

After a miscarriage, a daughter, Laura, was born prematurely to Minny on 7 December 1870. The small family of three spent many happy hours in Leslie's beloved Alps, often gathering purple sweet-scented cyclamens from Primiero. Tragedy struck on the evening of 27 November 1875, soon after the desolate Julia Duckworth, their neighbour, called upon them. As she was getting ready for bed, Minny felt some discomfort and her maid was asked to sleep in a nearby room from where she could keep an eye on her. During the night, the maid summoned Leslie to his wife, who was experiencing severe convulsions. Twenty years later, Leslie could hardly write of what happened next: 'I remember only too clearly the details of what followed; but I will not set them down. My darling never regained consciousness. She died about the middle of the day, 28 November, my forty-third birthday. You know why I have never celebrated that day! I was left alone.'[21] Like Julia's earlier in 1870, his heart became deadened.

Immediately after Minny's death, the tensions between Leslie and Anny increased. Leslie was deeply irritated when Anny criticized Julia's conduct on the day of Minny's death. Tenderly, Julia had kissed Leslie and asked if he had kept many letters from her, the only genuine sources of comfort. Anny considered Julia far too restrained; she would have preferred a greater outpouring of emotion.

Whenever they were thrown together, Leslie and Anny baited

each other mercilessly. During time spent at Coniston, Leslie was displeased to see Anny make a conquest of Ruskin. Anny flaunted her high spirits and spendthrift ways and Leslie, who deeply feared bankruptcy (financial security always being a metaphor for him of psychic well-being), tried to find ways to counter her disregard for his worries.

The distraught in-laws moved to 8 Southwell Gardens, the interior of which had been decorated by Minny before her death. The house was large for Leslie, Anny and Laura, but its close association with his dead wife was what unnerved Leslie. Then 11 Hyde Park Gate South, which was owned by Anny, became vacant. Julia had shortly before moved into number 13. Her presence next door prompted the in-laws to move there.

When Leslie and Anny were not arguing about money, they fought over Laura. Although Leslie considered his daughter's German nurse, Louise Meincke, to be empty-headed, he encouraged her to resist Anny's authority. In 1877, at the age of seven, Laura was precocious. She was also reading well and Leslie began teaching her German. However, unseemly behaviour on Laura's part was frequently evident, as when she spat meat out at meals.

The frequent skirmishes between in-laws finally gave way to what Leslie considered a catastrophe in January 1877: 'To speak plainly, I came into the drawing-room and found Richmond [Ritchie] kissing Anny. I told her at once that she ought to make up her mind one way or other: for it was quite plain that as things were going, there could be only one result.'[22] The forty-year-old Anny accepted his ultimatum, announcing that afternoon her engagement to Ritchie, her junior by seventeen years and her godson. In her plain-spoken way, Julia informed Leslie that he was jealous of being put at a lower level in Anny's affections. Meanwhile, the prospect of being left alone with Laura loomed before Leslie and he pressed his sister, Caroline Emelia, into service. She quickly shrank from the responsibility.

A while later, Leslie went off to Switzerland for his first winter expedition to the Alps. Upon his return, he was walking past Knightsbridge Barracks when the thought struck him: 'I am in love with Julia!' He realized that Julia was no longer alarmed by his sometimes silent, cold and sarcastic exterior. Her own loss of faith was mirrored, he knew, in his Cambridge struggles and in his writings. She recognized him, he was sure, for what he was: a 'shy "skinless" man'. He felt revived: 'It seemed again that there was a music running through me, not altogether cheerful, very far from altogether unhesitating, but yet delicious and inspiring. Julia was that strange solemn music.'[23] And so Leslie pursued her.

Chapter Two

GHOSTS IN THE NURSERY

(1882–95)

After their wedding in March 1878, Leslie and Julia spent several weeks at Eastnor Castle, near Ledbury. Then, together with George, Stella, Gerald and Laura, they settled in at Julia's house, 13 Hyde Park Gate South (which became 22 Hyde Park Gate in 1884). This was a five-storey house of countless small, oddly shaped rooms to which additions, including two further storeys, were added by the Stephens in a slapdash manner: 'now a storey would be thrown out on top, now a dining room flung out at bottom'. The two families poured in their possessions. Old letters filled dozens of black boxes. One opened them, Virginia observed, and 'got a terrific whiff of the past'.

The house was dark because the street was incredibly narrow. A neighbour, Mrs Redgrave, could sometimes be seen washing her neck in a bedroom across the street. The rooms at the front were made even more gloomy in summer by Virginia creeper. The inhabitants felt completely cut off from the bustle of London. Occasionally, a hansom or butcher's cart would trundle by. The eerie stillness of the street would be broken only by the tapping of footsteps.

The Titianesque interior decoration, in the mode of Little Holland House, added to the pervading sense of otherworldliness. The drawing room was divided by black folding doors picked out with thin lines of raspberry red. The furniture was covered in red velvet and the woodwork was painted black with gold lines serving as a further embellishment. In addition, there were busts draped in crimson velvet. The bold contrast between red and black was both intoxicating and overpowering. For one inhabitant, the young Virginia Stephen, the place seemed tangled and matted with emotion: 'The walls and the rooms had in sober truth been built to our shape. We had permeated the whole vast fabric.'[1] Some visitors found the house a place of overly serious refinement which manifested itself in a curious, hidden way, for few of the items of furniture or paintings were in themselves beautiful or even tasteful.

The newly constituted family kept seven maidservants but no manservant. They travelled third-class by rail and by red bus in London. On occasion they took hansoms by night, but they considered it frivolous to use one during the day. They were in a precarious position: they belonged to the lower division of the upper middle class. (The Duckworths, however, had pretensions to the higher reaches of society and this would ultimately be a cause of much friction.) At one time, seventeen or eighteen people lived at 22 Hyde Park Gate, sharing one bathroom and three water-closets.

Gradually, the two families merged into one. George, who bore a striking resemblance to his father, was especially keen to please his mother. Gerald was thinner and more delicate and babyish. In looking at the two boys, Julia could see their father brought momentarily back to life. Stella's beauty was a mirror of her mother's and, in part, this may explain why Julia was excessively demanding of her. Both Leslie and Anny also noticed that Julia was rather stern with her. When Leslie reproached his wife, she replied that she did not love the boys more than Stella but that Stella seemed to her more a part of herself. Julia was the sun, Stella the moon, 'reflecting and satellite'.[2] As such, Julia could extend her strong dissatisfactions with herself to her daughter.

Without doubt, Julia valued sons more than daughters. For her, women found their truest selves by becoming wives, mothers and hostesses. Although women were then beginning to attend Oxford and Cambridge, neither Julia nor Leslie set any store by formal education for their daughters. Many years later, Virginia bemoaned that attitude: 'was I clever, stupid, good looking, ugly, passionate, cold – ? Owing partly to the fact that I was never at school, never competed in any way with children of my own age, I have never been able to compare my gifts and defects with other people's.'[3] Stella, Vanessa and Virginia were expected to make do with leftovers, bits of learning bestowed on them by their father and brothers.

In general, Julia was also much more critical of women than men. Her friend Elizabeth Robins, the actress, remembered that she never 'confided. She would suddenly say something so unexpected, from that Madonna face, one thought it *vicious*.'[4] For example, although it was obviously expressed with some affection in her voice, Julia often referred to Stella as the 'Old Cow'. Leslie was the *obvious* domestic tyrant whose explosions were public and to some extent predictable; he was a deeply unsure person who compensated for such feelings by acting as a bully. His fragility was palpable. Julia was even more vulnerable, but her bullying side was more hidden and thus intangible; as a result, she was more difficult to deal with. She had depths of sorrow of which even Leslie was ignorant.

The gloom of Hyde Park Gate was dispersed by visitors, especially on alternate Sunday afternoons, when the oval tea-table was full of spiced buns. Then General Beadle would lament the Indian Mutiny and Frederick Gibbs, once tutor to the Prince of Wales, would try Leslie's patience. To this same table came Julia's sisters with their husbands and children. Adeline and Henry Halford Vaughan, who married in 1856, had four daughters and one son, whereas Mary and Herbert Fisher, married in 1862, had eleven children. According to Virginia, the puritanical Fishers would have made Eden unhabitable. Like Julia, Mary, also a beauty in the Burne-Jones tradition, had a tragic aspect, but she suppressed it with even more forced cheerfulness than her younger sister. As a result, her energy was thoroughly drained by her enormous family.

The domestic tragedy of the Vaughans obsessed Leslie. Halford Vaughan had been a professor of history at Oxford and a clerk of assize on the South Wales Circuit. At Oxford, he was celebrated as a brilliant teacher. In 1858, at the age of forty-seven, he resigned his professorship, abandoned his Hampstead home and retired to Upton Castle, an old ruin in Pembrokeshire. He wanted to devote himself to his *magnum opus*, a book on ethical principles, but his manuscript was torn up at intervals by, he suspected, some half-mad servant. He even printed a poster advertising a reward for anyone successful in detecting the malefactor. Leslie was quite certain that Vaughan himself was the culprit. This was a life of misapplied ingenuity, Halford's brother-in-law truthfully claimed.

Fidgety Caroline Emelia – Milly – Stephen was also a visitor to Hyde Park Gate. Early in life, she had fallen in love with a young man who had not been responsive and had taken himself off to India. In Milly, Leslie saw a woman whose life had been destroyed by a broken heart. Although he recognized her kind intentions, he could not get along with her. If he mounted an argument in the hope of having it contradicted, she would perversely support his point of view. If he was sad, she would weep uncontrollably, thus deepening his misery. Leslie saw Milly as weak-willed and indecisive, but she was a dedicated philanthropist who wrote *The Service of the Poor* and became an ardent Quaker mystic – one of her other books was *Quaker Strongholds*. Her elder brother, Fitzjames, now a bulky, ponderous figure, appeared to be strapped into his frock coat when he visited Leslie and his family. The children remembered him as a man who, having lost all hope of paradise, clung 'instead to the wider hope of eternal damnation'.[5]

Despite the stale air of 22 Hyde Park Gate, Julia bestowed her love openly upon her three children. The births of Vanessa on 30 May 1879 and Julian Thoby on 8 September 1880 were sources of great happiness to both husband and wife and the first four years of their marriage were comparatively happy, although from the outset Leslie insisted that Mrs Jackson made too many demands on his wife. According to him, his mother-in-law needed managing rather than nursing, which was to be reserved for himself.

There were other domestic dramas. Leslie could be tetchy, as when he reminded Julia that her large nose flawed her otherwise perfect beauty. And he was fully aware that he could sometimes be a 'brutal wetblanket'. George complained that his stepfather saddled Julia with Laura, whose behaviour was becoming increasingly unnerving. She was now given to wild howling and shrieking. In turn, Leslie observed that Julia's remedy – putting Laura to bed as punishment – was ineffective; he wanted a way to be found which would control Laura's outbursts without inciting her to even more elaborate demonstrations of fury, which, on one occasion, led her to throw scissors into the fire.

Earlier, Caroline Emelia Stephen's firm but gentle regimen with her niece had worked well, but as Laura became older, she was more difficult to deal with. She was eventually labelled an idiot, but was probably suffering from childhood schizophrenia. Her 'lockjaw' way of talking, 'queer squeaking' and 'semi-stammering' point to this diagnosis.[6] Minny's death might well have exacerbated such tendencies. At the same time, in the early 1880s, Leslie was agitated about his future as a writer. In particular, he was preoccupied with his posthumous reputation – would he be a footnote or a paragraph in literary history? Should he take on the editorship of the *Dictionary of National Biography*?

For a variety of reasons, Leslie and Julia decided, when Julia became pregnant in 1881, to bring their family to a halt: 'Dearest,' he instructed her, 'whatever the difficulty, there must not be a successor to Chad [the name planned for the infant if it should be a boy]. It is hard to speak & write of such things; but of that I am more & more certain.'[7] Three months later, Adeline Virginia was born on 25 January 1882 at 22 Hyde Park Gate.

During the last six weeks of the difficult pregnancy, Leslie was away on one of his tramps. He was worried that Julia was laid low, suffered from a bad cold and should be resting to summon up her strength for the delivery. If Julia became ill, Leslie assured her, life would indeed become bleak for him. He was concerned that his 'selfish indifference'[8] – sexual demands – had possibly precipitated a tragedy. If this occurred, all his happiness would be destroyed. Much later, when Virginia imagined herself to have been cramped and cabined in the womb, she was simply expressing her feeling that from the outset her parents had been drained of the energy to sustain and nourish her. She was correct. By early April, an exhausted Julia decided that she could no longer breast-feed the baby, who would have to be 'bottled'. Julia had been afraid that Leslie would disapprove, but he assured her – a bit brusquely – on 9 April 1882: 'I would like you to nurse her as long as it does not hurt your health; but I could not really wish you to go on one moment after it became really trying. Now I must write some other letters.'[9]

However, Virginia was rosy and chubby. One of this child's first recollections was of the dark land under the nursery table, in a gloom encircled by firelight. There were the pungent odours of dead flowers, of leaves and of chestnuts. Virginia's other, fragmented memories were of white moths in the summer and of firewood being cut in the winter. She called herself a green-eyed brat.

Sometimes, this toddler had little wars with Nessa and Thoby, but her tranquil happiness was jarred by the 'others', the Duckworth children, who were possessed of knives. After Adrian's birth, the Stephen children referred to themselves as 'us four'. At an early age, Virginia wrote a satirical, highly inaccurate and now-lost 'History of the Duckworths', which began:

> One day when William Rufus was hunting in the New Forest he shot a duck. It fell into the middle of a pond and could not be recovered; but an active little page boy waded out into the water and recovered the bird. The king drew his sword and dubbed the lad saying: 'Arise Sir Duckworth, for surely thou art worth many ducks.'[10]

However, on occasion young Virginia could joke with George: 'I AM A LITTLE BOY AND ADRIAN IS A GIRL I HAVE SENT YOU SOME CHOCOLATES GOOD BYE VIRGINIA.'[11]

Virginia was almost two when Adrian was born on 27 October 1883, this pregnancy obviously being contrary to Julia's and Leslie's intentions. The sickly new baby, who, according to Virginia, had almost been annihilated in the womb, quickly became Julia's favourite (she called him 'My Joy') and there is a slight hint of resentment against her mother in Virginia's very first memory, that of pressing her head against her mother's lap and feeling the scratch of the beads on her dress.

The kingdom of the children consisted of two rooms on the third floor: the day nursery, where they had their meals, took lessons and played; and the night nursery, where the four Stephen children and their nurse slept. (Laura Stephen, who had her own attendant, was kept separate from these four.) One of Virginia's unhappy recollections was of the time she awoke in what she thought was the dead of night and heard strange, horrible music. She was so frightened that she crawled to the cot next to hers for sympathy. But the strongest memories were jubilant: the tinkle of Julia's bracelets as she came up to the night nursery, a shaded candle in her hand, to see if the children were asleep; the tiny drops in which her laugh ended: 'Ah – ah – ah'; gentle admonitions to sleepless children to think of rainbows and bells.

There were also the nearby pleasures of Kensington Gardens: the Broad Walk, the Round Pond and the Flower Walk. This urban paradise was entered by either of two gates – one opposite Palace Gate, the other opposite Queen's Gate. Each had an old lady who acted as its titular deity. The woman at Queen's Gate, Virginia remembered, was 'an elongated, emaciated figure with a goat-like face, yellow and pockmarked'. The other was round, squat and eminently toad-like.

> To her was attached a whole wobbling balloon of air-balls. She held this billowing, always moving, most desirable mass by one string. They glowed in my eyes always red and purple, like the flower my mother wore; and they were always billowing in the air. For a penny, she would detach one from the bellying soft mass, and I would dance away with it.

Within the park itself were even more wonderful sights. Vanessa and Thoby entertained – and horrified – Virginia and Adrian with their story of coming upon the corpse of a little black dog in the swamp below Flower Walk. This place 'must have been covered with reeds and full of pools . . . for we believed that the dog had been starved and drowned'.

The Broad Walk was not a proper hill, although it rose higher and higher as summer advanced. The four Stephen children took delight in scrunching the shells with which now and again Flower Walk was strewn. Often they would wander on the Speke Monument trail to the crocodile tree, its great root exposed: 'and the root [was] polished,' Virginia fondly recalled, 'partly by the friction of our hands, for we used to scramble over it'.[12] They would also wander off to a white house near Kensington Palace, where they bought sweets from a smooth-faced, pink-cheeked woman in a grey dress. They were naughty, as when they knocked their go-cart into an unsuspecting woman as she turned a steep corner or when they tied their dog, Shag, to a railing. This wicked act was reported to the keeper by some other children. Once, while in the park, Virginia lost her knickers. She retired behind a bush and loudly sang 'The Last Rose of Summer'. Such boisterous adventures earned her the sobriquet 'The Goat' or 'Billy Goat'. All her life, Virginia retained her exuberance. She was quite capable of dramatic displays of fancy and invention.

Ultimately Kensington Gardens became rather boring when compared to the more exotic beauty of St Ives in Cornwall. The steep little town was a pyramid of whitewashed granite houses which hugged the slope and had steps running up from the pavement; granite was the only building material which had any chance of withstanding the encroaching sea. Although the whitewash was a shade of cream, there was nothing mellow about St Ives, which was irregular, rough and uncultivated, filled with noises from the sea. And the smell of the ocean permeated everything.

In the spring of 1881, while on one of his tramps, Leslie came upon a 'pocket paradise' just outside the town where a gradually sloping moor of gorse was broken by masses of primroses and bluebells. The bay of St Ives and its sand hills were in the distance, all of this enclosed in air which seemed as soft as silk. So taken was he by this place that he inspected and took the lease of

Talland House. This large, square, solid white villa, built by the Great Western Railway in the 1840s or 1850s, was remarkable only for its flat roof and the railings with crossed bars which ran round it. It did, however, have a breathtaking view across the bay to Godrevy lighthouse. There was a path which led down to a sandy cove where, Leslie assured Julia, the children could swim safely.

The approach to the house was dramatic, up a carriage drive, its steep wall scattered with mesembryanthemums, which came to a lookout on the right. The view of the bay from here reminded at least one guest of Naples: large-lapped, many-curved, sand-edged, silver-green-coloured. The garden consisted of an acre or two up and downhill with small terraces divided by hedges of escallonia, a grape house, a kitchen garden and a so-called orchard. Julia and Leslie made a tennis lawn on the most level area and the children played cricket here in the evening. There were other special places: the 'loo corner' behind the grape house, the love corner where jackmanii grew, the coffee garden which was shaded by escallonia, the strawberry bed, the pond and the porch, from which husband and wife viewed the cricket. And there were excursions to Land's End and Gurnard's Head.

One of Virginia's fondest recollections was of lying half asleep, half awake, in bed in the nursery at St Ives. She was encased in a 'blue gummy veil' against which stood out the pale yellow blind, the green sea and silver passion flowers.

> It is of hearing the waves breaking, one, two, one, two, and sending a splash of water over the beach; and then breaking, one, two, one, two, behind a yellow blind. It is of hearing the blind draw its little acorn across the floor as the wind blew the blind out. It is of lying and hearing this splash and seeing this light, and feeling, it is almost impossible that I should be here; of feeling the purest ecstasy I can conceive.

'If life has a base that it stands upon,'[13] she claimed, her life was rooted to that memory.

Then another sensation, one more of rapture than of ecstasy, asserted itself. This time, she stopped at the top of the gardens, sunk beneath the road.

> The apples were on a level with one's head. The gardens gave off a murmur of bees; the apples were red and gold; there were also pink flowers; and grey and silver leaves. The buzz, the croon, the smell, all seemed to press voluptuously against some membrane; not to burst it; but to hum round one such a complete rapture of pleasure that I stopped, smelt; looked.[14]

To these radiant, intensely felt moments were added the changing colours of the sea: deep blue, emerald green, purple, silver. There were the ships streaming in and out of the harbour. Occasionally a white yacht would pull in. Every September the boats for catching pilchards would be hauled down to the shore, but, during Virginia's childhood, the fish always contrived to arrive (or depart) before the boats could reach them.

Trencromor, or, as the children called it, Trick Robin, was the usual destination of the Sunday morning walk. Both sides (St Michael's Mount and St Ives Bay) of the ocean were visible from this spot. The Stephens would scramble on to a loggan rock and be fascinated by a hollow in the rough lichened surface which had been made, they were told, to hold the blood of sacrificial victims. There were other rewards to be had on this arduous trek. 'Our knees were pricked by the gorse – the blazing yellow gorse with its sweet nutty smell,'[15] Virginia affectionately recollected. Some of the ferns were higher than the children's heads and so they walked on a wall beside them, peering down into the green skeletal shapes. Their nostrils would be filled with the scent of acorns and oak apples. There was also Halestown Bog, where they leaped from log to log and, eventually, went squelching into the brown water, which went up above their knees. They also became skilled lepidopterists, wonderfully adept at catching and preserving all manner of butterflies and moths. Then there were activities such as digging in the sand and buying boxes of tintacks, all the while breathing in the fishy smells and helping themselves to enormous portions of Cornish cream. There were funeral ceremonies for birds and mice. All the children played cricket and, as Thoby told Adrian, 'Gin can bowl a good deal better than some of the chaps.'[16]

Every ten days there would be expeditions by boat. The rampageous Thoby would be allowed to steer, Leslie reminding him to keep the sails full of air. 'Show them you can bring her in, my boy.'[17] Once the sea was full of pale jellyfish with streaming tentacles. Sometimes they fished. Eventually there would be a tug and out of the water would emerge a sparkling gurnard or mackerel. Virginia, 'the demon bowler', retained her passion for angling until Leslie sulkily observed: 'I don't like to see fish caught but you can go if you like.'[18] This was supposedly not a rebuke, simply a statement, but she knew a reprimand when she heard one. Not surprisingly, the desire to fish – one which was 'beyond words' – vanished.

Messy, pleasantly dishevelled Talland House held other memories, as of the lobsters, still blue, placed on the kitchen table by the fisherwoman, their great claws opening, closing, pinching. And once, wriggling on a hook in the larder, there was the long, thick fish which Gerald beat to death. The kitchen – unmistakably the kingdom of Sophie Farrell, the cook – was directly beneath the night nursery. The greedy children would lower a basket down to the window below, while the grown-ups were eating. Often the anglers would draw back their trap to find a treat from their elders' dinner. If they were out of favour with the querulous Sophie, the basket would be abruptly jerked and the string severed.

Visitors to Talland House provided many droll moments, as when old, brown, fat-cheeked and small-eyed Professor Wolstenholme arrived. Like a huge bird, the 'Woolly One' nested in a brown wicker beehive chair, which gave him perfect camouflage. There was another 'caricature', Justine Nonon, an old, frail retainer of the Thackerays who lived by herself at Shepherd's Bush in London. For Virginia, she was a semi-sinister character straight out of the Brothers Grimm: 'Little hairs sprouted on her long bony chin. She was a hunchback; and walked like a spider, feeling her way with her long dry fingers from one chair to another.'[19] Virginia would sit on her knee, but this was dangerous because that limb would eventually give out, tumbling the child to the floor.

Most of Virginia's memories were not quite so precarious. She had no recollection of her father throwing her naked into the sea (as reported to her years later by a St Ives resident). Her earliest extant letter was to Leslie, who had stayed back in London: 'WE HAVEENT BATHED YET WE ARE GOING TO TOMORROW WE SANG IN THT TRAIN YOUR LOVING VIRGINIA.'[20] For her, St Ives was a fusion of brilliant colour, carefree gambols, butterflies, ocean, waves and steep streets. It was also closely linked to the literary and art establishments. Virginia recalled John Addington Symonds's nerve-drawn white face; Watts in his frilled shirt and grey dressing gown, consuming bowls of whipped cream and minced meat; Meredith dropping rounds of lemon into his tea. Long afterwards, she could hear the roll in Meredith's voice and the hesitation, qualification, humming and hawing of Henry James's.

In taking her to Talland House, Julia and Leslie bestowed upon Virginia something invaluable. Nothing was ever quite so important to her as summers in Cornwall. There were drawbacks – the enormous distance from London meant that their time there was concentrated into two and a half months. Julia had to supervise the move of family, nurses, servants and children. The tremendous costs of such migrations disturbed Leslie, who from the outset had feared that the boiler at Talland House might blow up, rendering him liable for injuries to servants.

For Leslie, Virginia was, variously, 'Ginia', 'Ginnums', 'Ginny' and 'Jinny'. Without doubt, she was his favourite child, a mutual admiration plainly seen on the evening when the two young sisters were jumping about naked in the bathroom. Virginia asked Vanessa which parent she favoured. 'Mother,' Vanessa answered, whereas Virginia went on to explain why she, on the whole, preferred her father. As Leslie fondly recollected, two-year-old Virginia once delayed his departure for his study: 'Little Ginia is already an accomplished flirt. I said today that I must go down to my work. She nestled herself down on the sofa by me; squeezed her little self tightly up against me & then gazed up with her bright eyes through her shock of hair & said "don't go, Papa!" She looked full of mischief all the time. I never saw such a little rogue.'[21] A bit earlier, he recalled, she had sat on his knee, beseeching him for a kiss and placing her cheek against his. When the children visited their maternal grandmother at Brighton, Leslie instructed Julia to ask her mother to say honestly which child she preferred. He was confident that she would choose wisely. At the time Virginia turned two, Leslie was away in the Alps and wondered aloud in a letter to Julia why he and Virginia were so alike.

Why, indeed, was Virginia the chosen one? Thoby's aggressive, noisy masculinity disturbed Leslie, who disciplined him when he became truculent with the nurses. As a young child, Thoby was frail, in a manner reminiscent of his father. For Leslie, bad health was a sign of overall weakness; in Thoby, a child he loved very much, he discerned a reflection of his own unsteady youth – and was repulsed. When Julia insisted that the eleven-year-old boy be sent away to school, Leslie remembered his own isolation and loneliness from years before. 'You have taken my poor To,' he told his wife, 'to school today. I saw a calf going on a sledge to the butcher's & To rather reminded me of it. However, I have no doubt he will be fattened.'[22]

Once the little boy was rebuffed when he brought down his father's walking stick just as Leslie was setting out on one of his tramps. But Leslie, a deeply contradictory man, was touched by the boy's thoughtfulness and hoped that he had not hurt his feelings. When, at the age of five, Thoby went to his father's study for a chat, Leslie felt obliged to turn him out.

Adrian remained Julia's 'Joy' and could not be exclusively Leslie's – in 1884, he told his wife that all the children were beautiful except Adrian. Early on, Vanessa's ambition to become an artist separated her from her father, the man of letters. In selecting Virginia as his favourite, Leslie conferred his imprimatur on her obvious talents, but at the same time he singled her out. His benediction was wonderful but it also crippled Virginia, making her the inheritor of his thin-skinnedness and excessively self-critical regard. Since Julia saw a woman's life as consecrated to service, Leslie's blessing opened a gulf between her and her youngest daughter. From early on, Virginia was subjected to a seemingly unresolvable dilemma: how to be both a woman and a writer.

For a variety of reasons, Leslie's nerves were often frayed. In February 1887, he informed Julia that his fellow Alpine tourists rubbed his sensitive skin with sandpaper. Julia felt that he needed this holiday apart from her and the children, but he notified her that he would have 'tantarums' if he stayed away longer. Leslie had also become aware of how the remoteness of the Alps and of Julia were linked in his mind: 'The Alps make me feel better & yet have a touch of melancholy & storminess about them. They are inacessable [*sic*] or nearly so, very often. And in all that there is something of you.'[23] Despite their outwardly happy marriage, Leslie rightly divined that he and Julia were very separate from each other. He certainly remained a desperately lonely man.

A year earlier, Leslie had hinted that he would become 'tantarous' if he had to abstain from sexual intercourse. He complained about Julia's extended stays away from Hyde Park Gate to nurse ailing friends and relatives. When she was away, he would inflict greater loneliness upon himself by refusing dinner invitations. Once he told Julia that he intended to creep into a corner and snarl until she returned.

Gradually, Leslie became more and more saddened by his awareness that the days of his great feats on the river and on the mountains were over. To the end of his life he would speak of great climbers and explorers with a mixture of admiration and envy. In turn, Julia could survive only if she had breathing space from Leslie. She found it much easier to attend to the demands of relatives and friends than to those of her husband.

Despite the rapid fluctuations in his moods, Leslie, who was a more indulgent and whimsical parent than Julia, loved to play

Leslie Stephen. Pencil drawings of animals in a copy of George Meredith's The Egoist.

with the 'Ragamice', his nickname for the children, who became characters out of Uncle Remus: Vanessa was 'Tarbaby', Virginia 'Br'er Fox' and Adrian 'Br'er Rabbit', while naturally Thoby was the 'White Bull'. Sometimes, to the surprise of nursery maids and park-keepers as well as his children, Leslie would recite verse at the top of his voice as he went about the house or as he walked in Kensington Gardens. He was also a skilled draughtsman who drew beast after beast on the flyleaves of his books.

Husband and wife collaborated in about 1885 on a series of children's stories which Julia wrote and Leslie illustrated. The project seems to have been rejected by Routledge, but the manuscript survives. Literary influences are not hard to find in these narratives, which have touches of the Brothers Grimm, Hans Christian Andersen, Harriet Martineau, Frederick Marryat and Lewis Carroll. One ('The Black Cat or the Grey Parrot') has a setting in an animal hospital and another ('Cat's Meow') obliquely upbraids parents who spend too much time undertaking charitable acts outside the home – in this instance, Julia might have been reflecting on her own behaviour. Overall, children are indulgently depicted. In 'The Duke's Coal Cellar' Jim suffers for his excessive curiosity and yet his independence is praised. The rascally hero of 'Tommy and His Neighbours' is allowed to escape punishment. Another Tommy enters a magical world of speaking animals in 'Emlycaunt', but later cannot return to the enchanted kingdom. Gently, this story pushes children from the world of innocence to that of adult experience. However, the inquisitive nature of boys is more indulged than identical impulses in girls.

Leslie's accompanying visual menagerie, which includes monkeys, cats, pigs, bears, giraffes and fish, perfectly complements the whimsy of his wife's tales. Leslie, who was not a particularly good storyteller, could convey his impression of a person in a few words. And he often expressed opinions contrary to conventional wisdom. Like Virginia, he had a way of upsetting established reputations and disregarding received values. The more traditional side of Leslie was evident in the large stock of walking and Alpine stories with which he regaled company.

From her mother and father, Virginia imbibed an inclination to tell and write stories. She herself felt that her artistic bent derived from Julia, whose mother was part French and whose family was therefore, of necessity, frivolous and art-loving. Nevertheless, words did not come easily to her. Vanessa had a clear memory of her younger sister drumming impatiently for her breakfast and the little tyrant's lack of speech worried her elder sister. This state of affairs, however, did not last long, for words soon became Virginia's 'deadliest weapon'.

When she was without speech, Thoby and Vanessa had been able to make Virginia purple with rage. Then came the change. At two, Virginia asked Thoby for a toy in his safekeeping. He refused, whereupon she hugged him, calling him 'darling sweetheart boy'. He remained obdurate, whereupon she cuffed him and called him 'nasty, pigwash, horrid and usgusting'. Her powers increased suddenly and dramatically. She noticed that Vanessa was excessively compliant to the wishes of adults. 'How,' Vanessa asked, 'did she know that to label me "The Saint" was [a] far more effective [weapon against me than physical combat], quickly reducing me to the misery of sarcasm from the grown-ups as well as the nursery world.'[24]*

Story-telling became a nursery ritual. There was a seemingly endless serial about their next-door neighbours, the Rilkes, who suffered the collective shame of not being able to pronounce the letter r. The proceedings began when Vanessa, in an affected drawl, would proclaim, 'Clementé, dear child.' Leslie – who rather perversely became annoyed with the children when they insisted on identifying with the heroes rather than the villains in the tales he told them – was pleased when five-year-old Virginia declaimed a long, involved anecdote about a crow and a book. When her audience became restive, she would not stop – they had to cough her down. She told Leslie a story every night. Although it did not change much, he indulgently observed, she took great joy in relating it. There were London and St Ives stories. The best London one was of Jim, Joe and Harry Hoe, three brothers who had herds of animals with whom they became involved in a series of picaresque adventures. By definition, a London story was inferior to a St Ives one. The finest of the latter genre concerned Beccage and Hollywinkles, evil spirits who lived on the rubbish heap and disappeared through a hole in the escallonia hedge.

As an adult, Virginia remembered herself as 'a little creature, scribbling a story in the manner of Hawthorne on the green plush sofa in the drawing room at St Ives while the grown ups dined'.[25] In one of her earliest surviving letters, she told Julia a grisly news item-cum-moral fable which shows her ability to frame a lively story: Mrs Prinsep 'says that she will only go in a slow train cos she says all the fast trains have accidents and she told us about an

* In a letter of 1 January 1916 (MS Tate), Vanessa told Roger Fry of another aspect of her sibling rivalry with Virginia: 'It is always rather a joke that she advises every one to write – me, Adrian, every one who wouldn't excel her.'

old man of 70 who got his legs caute in the weels of a train and the train began to go on and the old gentleman was draged along till the train caute fire and he called out for somebody to cut off his legs but nobody came he was burnt up'.[26] This grim anecdote also reveals the young writer's awareness of how much of life was arbitrary as well as tragic.

From early childhood, the instinct to tell stories was dominating, as was Virginia's distinction between 'being' and 'non-being', between moments of being intensely alive and moments which simply passed. At St Ives there would be weeks of the cotton-wool of non-being. 'Then, for no reason that I know about, there was a sudden violent shock; something happened so violently that I have remembered it all my life.' Three such incidents haunted her. The first occurred during a fight with Thoby. She raised her fist to pummel him and then she wondered why she would want to hurt another person. 'I dropped my hand instantly, and stood there, and let him beat me . . . It was a feeling of hopeless sadness.' Then there was an instant in the garden at St Ives, when she stared at the flower bed by the front door. '"That is the whole," I said. I was looking at a plant with a spread of leaves; and it seemed suddenly plain that the flower itself was a part of the earth; that a ring enclosed what was the flower; and that was the real flower; part earth, part flower.' The third instance was deeply painful. She overheard her parents remark that Mr Valpy, a recent guest of theirs at St Ives, had killed himself.

> The next thing I remember is being in the garden at night and walking on the path by the apple tree. It seemed to me that the apple tree was connected with the horror of Mr Valpy's suicide. I could not pass it. I stood there looking at the grey-green creases of the bark – it was a moonlit night – in a trance of horror. I seemed to be dragged down, hopelessly, into some pit of absolute despair from which I could not escape. My body seemed paralysed.

In addition to her ability to see connections which others did not, Virginia – in two instances of 'despair', one of 'satisfaction' –

was stopped in her tracks: 'they seemed dominant; myself passive'. Such flashes gave her a token of some real thing behind appearances and the only way to capture this real thing was to put it into words. From childhood, the telling of stories gave her mastery and pleasure: 'we are the words . . . we are the thing itself. And I see this when I have a shock.' The link between the shocks and words was clear and gave her sustenance. As an adult she proclaimed, 'I feel that by writing I am doing what is far more necessary than anything else.'[27]

Concurrent with the shocks and the words to capture them was Virginia's sense of her mother living on an extended surface where 'she had not time, nor strength, to concentrate, except for a moment if one were ill or in some child's crisis, upon me, or upon anyone – unless it were Adrian'.[28] For Virginia, Julia was always in a room full of people. The child accepted her mother's beauty as the natural quality that a mother had by virtue of being a mother. However, Julia could be sharp, overly critical and unduly cautionary. When Virginia was nine, she told her of a woman who had unintentionally killed her baby by waltzing it around the room until its breath was gone. Julia also felt compelled to supervise. For example, she once looked at her husband relaxing, reading with one leg curled round the other and twisting a lock of hair. 'Go and take the crumb out of his beard,' she instructed Virginia.[29]*

Once, while at St Ives, Virginia saw Julia come up the path by the lawn, holding herself straight; just as Virginia was about to speak to her, she turned away and lowered her eyes. 'From that indescribably sad gesture I knew that Phillips, the man who had been crushed on the line and whom she had been visiting, was

* As an adult, Virginia had deeply conflicting feelings about her mother. This can be clearly seen in the contrasting portraits of Julia in her daughter's various memoirs. Julia Stephen is idealized in 'Reminiscences' (written 1907–8), whereas more realistic (that is, in part, harsh) depictions of her are contained in '22 Hyde Park Gate' (written 1920–21) and, especially, 'A Sketch of the Past' (written 1939–40), the latter begun well after she had 'exorcized' her mother by writing *To the Lighthouse*.

dead. It's over, she seemed to say. I knew, and was awed by the thought of death. At the same time I felt that her gesture as a whole was lovely.'[30] The gesture may have been beautiful, but Virginia was imbibing the tremendous sorrow in which her mother existed.

At night Virginia lay awake, longing for her austerely beautiful, melancholic mother to visit her. Sometimes she did not and the child, whose quest for intimacy with her was always being interrupted, began to fear for her mother's safety. 'I wait in agony,' Virginia said, recalling the past as an ever-present reality, 'peeping surreptitiously behind the blind for her to come down the street, when she has been out late the lamps are lit and I am sure she has been run over.'[31] On one such occasion Leslie offered comfort: 'You shouldn't be so nervous, Jinny.'[32]

As an adult, Virginia asked herself: 'Can I remember ever being alone with her for more than a few minutes?'[33] It was Leslie's ever-increasing demands which occupied much of Julia's time – and it was those demands which, as we have seen, drove her out of the house to tend others. In 1890, a very worried Maria Jackson had asked the Stephen children to be vigilant about their mother's health. The tragedy was that only away from home could Julia find any breathing space. Yet if she was prevented from partaking in a family activity, things quickly fell apart. In the summer of 1893, when Virginia was eleven, Julia stayed back in London to care for Stella, who had mumps. The supervision of the yearly migration to St Ives fell on Leslie's shoulders. When lemonade was spilled over the lunch Julia had packed, the children were repulsed by the soggy mess but were forced to eat it by their father. Vanessa escaped this torture by feigning motion sickness and burying herself in a book.

When Virginia turned eight in 1890, the balance of power in the nursery shifted. Thoby was sent away to school and Virginia replaced him in Vanessa's affections. Now, Adrian was rejected by his former comrade-in-arms. The sisters shared nerve-racking lessons, taught jointly by Julia and Leslie. Julia was a font of misinformation on the intricacies of Latin, French and history, but Leslie's instruction in mathematics was even worse. As Vanessa recalled, 'Virginia all her life added up on her fingers and I am very little better.' When Julia was away, the children were instructed by 'harmless, ordinary little governesses'.[34]

There were other lessons, taken with other children. The music mistress, the exceedingly religious Miss Mills, reduced the girls to complete inertia. She also provoked the atheistic – and teasing – side of the girls when she asked if any of her pupils knew the significance of Good Friday. A girl with the astounding name of Pensa Filly provided the correct answer, at which point Virginia had to be hurriedly banished from the room so loud were her shrieks of laughter. The same hapless Miss Mills asked Virginia why she hung up her stocking on Christmas Eve and could not have been terribly pleased to hear that it was to celebrate the crucifixion. Then there was the dancing class with Miss Wordsworth, who was always clad in black satin. 'She had a stick and a glass eye at which she dabbed perpetually with a lace pocket handkerchief, and she croaked like a raven and made all of the little girls jump up and down in a frenzy.'[35] The sisters were bored and retired to the WC for as long as they dared.

Virginia's loveliness and verbal brilliance were more successful than Vanessa's in attracting favourable notices from adults. She reminded her admiring elder sister of a sweet pea of a special flame colour, but Vanessa often felt intense dislike for her. For example, she resented the fact that Virginia, in a household of atheists, had a glamorous godfather, James Russell Lowell, the American ambassador, who, when he visited, gave threepenny pieces to each of the children except Virginia, who received sixpence. What really aroused envy was Lowell's gift to his god-daughter of a live bird in a cage. One of her first extant letters is to him:

MY DEAR GODPAPA HAVE YOU BEEN TO THE ADIRONDACKS AND HAVE YOU SEEN LOTS OF WILD BEASTS AND A LOT OF BIRDS IN THEIR NESTS YOU ARE A NAUGHTY MAN NOT TO COME HERE GOOD BYE

YOUR AFFECTE
VIRGINIA.[36]

From early on, Vanessa wanted to be a painter and Virginia a writer. As Vanessa remembered, it was 'a lucky arrangement, for it meant that we went our own ways and one source of jealousy at any rate was absent'.[37] For Virginia, Vanessa was always the eldest, someone who would nourish and protect her. Although Virginia mocked Vanessa for her tendency to enforce the regulations of the grown-ups, she also had the habit of fingering her elder sister's amethyst beads and enumerating on each the names of friends and relatives whose place in Vanessa's affections stirred her jealousy.

Photographs of Virginia as a child reveal a deeply observant girl, one who studies the faces of adults for clues to inner moods. This can be seen in the snapshot of her with her parents at Talland House. Hand on chin, she gazes intently at the couple, who are absorbed in their reading. For her the tragic lingered close below the surface of existence. Virginia was acutely sensitive, aware of being deprived of her mother's full attention and of being the favourite of a father who valued her in large part for her literary inclinations. She was also the offspring of parents who had been thwarted cruelly by the losses of their first spouses. From early on, this girl was aware of the sorrow which had blighted the lives of those adults. On some days at St Ives, while she was doing lessons at the long table in the drawing room, she could feel a blackness crossing the waves in the bay. Nevertheless, no matter how susceptible Virginia was to melancholia or the shifting propensities of grown-ups, the simple truth is that she was caught completely unawares at the age of six by eighteen-year-old Gerald Duckworth, one of the 'others' who inhabited her London and St Ives homes.

> There was a slab outside the dining room door for standing upon. Once when I was very small Gerald Duckworth lifted me onto this, and as I sat there he began to explore my body. I can remember the feel of his hand going under my clothes; going firmly and steadily lower and lower. I remember how I hoped

> that he would stop; how I stiffened and wriggled as his hand approached my private parts. But it did not stop. His hand explored my private parts too. I remember resenting, disliking it – what is the word for so dumb and mixed a feeling? It must have been strong, since I still recall it. This seems to show that a feeling about certain parts of the body; how they must not be touched; how it is wrong to allow them to be touched; must be instinctive.[38]

Another time, in talking of how much of life is sexual, she went back to this painful memory: 'I still shiver with shame at the memory of my half brother, standing me on a ledge, aged about 6, and so exploring my private parts. Why should I have felt shame then?'[39]

Any young girl would have been damaged by such a brutal intrusion into her privacy; Virginia was permanently wounded. Her suffering can be discerned in the change in her health. At about this time, the four Stephen children came down with whooping cough. On 20 April 1888, Leslie told Charles Eliot Norton: 'Three of [the children] have not been ill beyond the cough and are now nearly well; but the 4th, my little Virginia, has been very bad, & is only just beginning to improve. It is most piteous to see a sweet little girl trembling and moaning for an hour before the spasm comes on and then apparently suffering severely.'[40] As Vanessa recalled, the rest of the children quickly recovered, but Virginia had become different: 'She was never again a plump and rosy child and, I believe, had actually entered into some new layer of consciousness rather abruptly, and was suddenly aware of all sorts of questions and possibilities hitherto closed to her.'[41] Virginia's resilience vanished. Previously she had been a vulnerable child. Now, she felt utterly defenceless. The 'billy goat' side of her was no longer much in evidence.

This single incident with Gerald completely unnerved Virginia, who saw herself as violated – and marked. One sharp memory of this time was standing tiptoe to look at herself in a mirror at

Talland House: 'When I was six or seven perhaps, I got into the habit of looking at my face in the glass. But I only did this if I was sure that I was alone. I was ashamed of it. A strong feeling of guilt seemed naturally attached to it. But why was this so?'[42] Because she was a tomboy who played cricket, scrambled over rocks and climbed trees? Because she had inherited a streak of the puritan from the Clapham Sect? These two possibilities suggested themselves to Virginia, who remained deeply ashamed of her own body. Gerald's coarse behaviour might have reinforced the child's low self-esteem. Or his conduct might have propelled her self-loathing to the surface, from where it was never dislodged. At about this time, Virginia had a terrifying experience which she connected with the looking glass:

> I dreamt that I was looking in a glass when a horrible face – the face of an animal – suddenly showed over my shoulder. I cannot be sure if this was a dream, or if it happened. Was I looking in the glass one day when something in the background moved, and seemed to me alive? I cannot be sure. But I have always remembered the other face in the glass, whether it was a dream or a fact, and that it frightened me.[43]

Whether fact or fantasy is irrelevant: Virginia had been terrorized, and the shadowy 'it' and 'something' were connected to invasive male brutality.

For the remainder of her life Virginia saw a rift between the sexual side of existence and her own life. In October 1940, she remembered her parents' bedroom as the 'sexual centre' of the house: 'in that bed we four children were begotten'. In contrast, her own bedroom was – and remained – spartan and lonely. She felt a deep conflict between the sleeping and living portions of the house: 'And how they fought each other: how often I was in rage & in ecstasy; & torn between all the different forces.'[44] She was torn because she was made to feel guilt and shame, and she was powerless to understand how and why those emotions invaded her at the age of six.

The eccentric behaviour of her first cousin, J. K. Stephen,

Fitzjames's son, also frightened her. Jem, as she recalled, had broad shoulders, a deep voice and intense blue eyes. In 1886, while at Felixstowe, he injured his head. From that time onwards, his behaviour became erratic and uncontrolled. One day he rushed into the nursery at Hyde Park Gate and plunged a sword into some bread. On another occasion he carted Julia and Virginia off to his rooms in De Vere Gardens so that Virginia could pose for him. Then he decided that he was in love with Stella and must have her. In a letter of 2 November 1890, he pleaded with her: 'Love me a little, Stella.'[45] Leslie wanted to bar the way to his nephew but Julia was adamant: 'I cannot shut my door upon Jem.'[46] And so, this disturbed young man, almost always in a state of euphoria, continued his unwelcome advances.*

There were other terrifying events. At Hyde Park Gate both Stephen sisters witnessed a man exposing himself.† A measure of

* In recent years, Michael Harrison and David Abrahamsen have argued that there is sufficient evidence to suggest that Jem was Jack the Ripper or, at the very least, directly linked to the Ripper murders. See Abrahamsen, *Murder & Madness: The Secret Life of Jack the Ripper* (New York: Donald I. Fine, 1992). Dr Abrahamsen's accusations are open to question, but he does provide some fascinating documentary evidence on Jem's brief life.

Of one thing there can be little doubt: Jem's *Lapsus Calami and Other Verses* (Cambridge, 1898) is full of misogynistic sentiments.

> If all the harm that women have done
> Were put in a bundle and rolled into one,
> Earth would not hold it,
> The sky could not enfold it,
> It could not be lighted nor warmed by the sun;
> Such masses of evil
> Would puzzle the devil . . .
>
> I should not mind
> If she were done away with, killed, or ploughed.
> She did not seem to serve a useful end:
> And certainly she was not beautiful.

† This incident and the one with Gerald were mingled by Virginia in *The Years*. One evening, the child Rose is accosted by a man who emerges suddenly from under a gas lamp. He almost catches her, but she evades him.

Virginia's increasing state of anxiety can be discerned in an incident at Kensington Gardens when an 'idiot boy . . . mewing, slit-eyed, red-rimmed'[47] – sprang up before her with his arm outstretched. Without saying a word but transfixed with horror, Virginia poured into his hand a bag of Russian toffee. The boy was threatening because she identified his visible defects as somehow identical to her own inner ones. The same fragility is displayed in her response to Laura, whom she refers to as 'an idiot'[48] and as 'Thackeray's grand-daughter, a vacant-eyed girl whose idiocy was becoming daily more obvious.'[49] By labelling Laura Thackeray's granddaughter, Virginia is denying Leslie's connection to her and the fact that she is her own half-sister.* In reality, Laura was granddaughter and daughter of two celebrated men-of-letters. Virginia afterwards wondered whether the profession of writer was not a dangerous one.

Although Virginia had trouble attracting Julia's attention, she remained the focus of Leslie's. By 1893 he had determined that his eleven-year-old daughter was to be a writer of some sort: 'Yesterday I discussed George III with Ginia. She takes in a great deal and will really be an author in time; though I cannot make up my mind in what line. History will be a good thing for her to take up as I can give her some hints.'[50] 'Ginia', her father once playfully complained, devoured books faster than even he liked.

As early as 1885 Leslie had concluded that sixteen-year-old

Then she sees him again: 'He was leaning with his back against the lamp-post, and the light from the gas lamp flickered over his face. As she passed he sucked his lips in and out. He made a mewing noise. But he did not stretch his hands out at her; they were unbuttoning his clothes' (Oxford: Oxford University Press, 1992, 28).

* Laura left 22 Hyde Park Gate in 1887, when Virginia was five. For two years she was placed in temporary accommodation in the country; in 1891 she was sent to an institution, though for the next two summers she continued to join the Stephen family at St Ives. She died in an asylum in York in 1945.

Stella should not write essays. Like her mother, she would become an excellent nurse. Eight years later, his opinion remained the same: nursing would be much 'more useful than . . . would be writing articles. That, I suppose, will be Ginia's line unless she marries somebody at 17.'[51] In 1891, as he had done earlier, Leslie rejected the idea that Thoby should become a writer: 'That is a thing for ladies & Ginia will do well in that line.'[52]* Leslie's identification with Virginia had more than a touch of narcissism in it, but it was imbued with wonder at her exuberant vitality: 'Today is Ginny's [ninth] birthday – she is certainly very like me, I feel, though I cannot say how – but much more life in her than I had at her age.'[53] When he made this moving declaration to Julia, he could not resist adding: 'I am glad she does not remind me of some other members of the family about the nose.'

From February 1891, Virginia was the driving force behind *Hyde Park Gate News*, the family newspaper of the Stephen children. Virginia, as Vanessa recalled, used the *News* to gain Julia's attention.

> I remember putting the paper on the table by my mother's sofa while they were at dinner, and then creeping quietly into the little room to look through the window and hear the criticism. As we looked, [Virginia] trembling with excitement, we could see my mother's lamplit figure quietly sitting near the fire, my father on the other side with his lamp, both reading. Then she noticed the paper, picked it up, began to read. We looked and

* From early on, Virginia was precise in what she considered the correct use of words. Virginia's childhood friend Susan Grosvenor (later Susan Tweedsmuir, Lady Buchan) remembered this conversation with Leslie: 'I can only recall that he often talked of his children and that one day he said to me, "My daughter Virginia is a great purist about language, she does not like us to use the word 'wire'. We always have to say 'telegram'." Years afterwards I told Virginia this story of her father and her comment was "What a shocking little prig I must have been" '(letter to Elizabeth Bowen about Virginia Woolf, May–September 1952, printed in Susan Tweedsmuir, *A Winter Bouquet*, 77).

> listened hard for some comment. 'Rather clever, I think,' said my mother, putting the paper down without apparent excitement. But it was enough to thrill her daughter; she had had approval and been called clever, and our eavesdropping was rewarded.[54]

Never, Virginia later observed, could she forget such extremities of pleasure: 'it was like being a violin and being played upon'.[55] This was when Julia sent one of Virginia's stories to a relative with the spare recommendation that it was 'imaginative'. So acute was Virginia's need for her mother's commendation that even a cursory word of praise was leaped upon.

The search for approbation is strong throughout *Hyde Park Gate News*.[56] The issue of Monday, 7 February 1895, contains a potted biography of one Miss Smith. At twelve she adored Virgil, by fourteen she wrote sonnets and by twenty protested that society must be entirely reorganized. 'The position of men and women towards each other was altogether disgraceful. She wrote the most remarkable essays upon Woman's Rights, and declared herself to be a Temperance lecturer.' Miss Smith's hubris almost leads to spinsterhood; only when she has 'thought bitterly of her former self and prepared to live alone' does she finally acknowledge the need of someone stronger and wiser than herself: 'At 30 she had deserted Woman's Rights and Temperance, was settling down into a mild hobby . . . It was just about this time, when she with many pangs allowed herself to be only a woman that a gallant gentleman appeared.' There is a curious tension in this sketch between the impetuous daring of young Miss Smith and the conventional ending to her experiments, as if a contrast is being made between an adolescent girl's desire for independence and her fear that such a quest might ostracize her from the family circle. Julia Stephen had decidedly conservative opinions on female independence and this piece of prose concludes with sentiments she would have applauded.

There are also adventure and love stories, as well as bulletins on the activities of the Stephen children. On 1 February 1892 'The

Midnight Ride' appeared, describing how a boy has to journey 'through a dangerous North American bog to see his brother, who lies ill at school'. A bit later there is a story of a lovers' quarrel. Mr John Harley accuses Miss Clara Dimsdale of having jilted him most shamefully. She curtly replies: 'As I never kept your love-letters you can't have them back. I therefore return the stamps you sent.' On 12 September 1892 there is a snippet about a trip to Godrevy lighthouse: 'On Saturday morning Master Hilary Hunt and Master Basil Smith came up to Talland House and asked Master Thoby and Miss Virginia Stephen to accompany them to the light-house.'

The most adventurous and sustained piece in *Hyde Park Gate News* is 'A Cockney's Farming Experiences' and its sequel, 'The Experiences of a Pater-Familias', which appeared in August 1892. Although the authorship may have been divided between Virginia and Thoby, the farmer's reference to going back to his room in order to change his dress suggests that ten-year-old Virginia may have been the principal author. The story concerns a newly married couple who, knowing nothing of farming, decide to purchase a small farm in Buckinghamshire. Out of London, the cockney proves to be completely inept. Soon he and his wife, Harriet, quarrel about this and the resulting lack of money. An 'odius' man, Buskin, hangs about the house, trying, the cockney thinks he hears, to arrange an assignation with Harriet. The newly-weds' problems seem to vanish when the cockney's aunt Maria dies, leaving him a 'jolly lot of money'. The longer, unfinished sequel takes place three years later in a little house 'on the boarders [*sic*] of London which goes by the name of Oak Lodge'.

This piece of writing begins abruptly: 'My Wife a month ago got a child and I regret to say that I wish he had never been born for I am made to give in to him in every thing.' The tension in this narrative is quickly established: 'I now look upon the nursery as a cage where I am made to perform compulsory tricks and therefore I avoid it as much as possible.' Throughout the story, the cockney continues to show scant interest in the fate of little

Alphonso, whose sash he attaches to a branch of a tree, leaving him dangling there while he continues on a walk. The cockney remains blissfully unconcerned about Alphonso's plight and this leads Harriet to pretend that the baby has indeed been lost. She wants to find out if her husband is really as brutal as he appears. This conflict eventually ends on a positive note as the couple become 'more amiable towards one another'.

In these interlocking stories, many of Virginia's real-life preoccupations become abundantly clear as she attempts to understand and come to grips with adult turmoil. Conflicts between husband and wife often centre on money, men may feel trapped by parenthood, although it is the wife who is really caged in, and the rustic (St Ives) only initially offers a respite from the difficulties of urban life. In Virginia's daily life, Leslie constantly fretted about money, Julia was often away and sex was something she had come to dread. Virginia's sense of being displaced by Adrian surfaces in the cockney's anger at Alphonso. Sex is associated with the vigorous servant class. Although there is an element of sexual tension in 'Experiences', the wife has – seemingly unaided – 'got' a child in 'Pater-Familias'.

Virginia's writings are always imbued with strong autobiographical touches and here her young observant eye gazes upon a wide spectrum of confusing grown-up behaviour. The two pieces are comic, but in a downbeat way. In any event, emboldened by her successes in *Hyde Park Gate News*, Virginia sent a short story to *Tit-Bits*, a magazine which the children often bought. This piece, which was refused, was a romantic account of a young woman on a ship (in miniature, this lost story contained the seeds of *The Voyage Out*, Virginia's first novel). Other early – also lost – attempts at writing included a piece of fiction in the manner of Nathaniel Hawthorne, a long piece in Elizabethan style called 'Religio Laici' and even 'A History of Women'.

On 4 March 1895, the *Hyde Park Gate News* ominously observed: 'For the last fortnight Mrs Leslie Stephen has been in bed with influenza.' Two weeks later, readers were assured that her condition had improved. On 8 April, the departure of George, Stella and

Gerald Duckworth for the Continent was mentioned in a brief news item.

That April, Julia assured her eldest daughter that she was making a satisfactory recovery. Of course Stella need not trouble to stay behind to nurse her. Much earlier, George had complained that Leslie had saddled Julia with the onerous task of taking care of Laura. In the last months of 1894, it was Stella's turn to upbraid her stepfather for taking advantage of her mother.

The family had undergone many crises in the early 1890s. In April 1891, Leslie had finally given up the editorship of the *Dictionary of National Biography*, a responsibility which had bothered him for the previous nine years. In about 1890, William Rothenstein made a portrait sketch of Julia in which she looks utterly worn out. The whole family was upset by this likeness; Maria Jackson rang for a stick in preparation for giving the impudent young artist, who was paying a call, a piece of her mind.

For a long time, then, the Stephens and Duckworths had existed in a state of 'anxious growth' in which 'the future was always too near and too much of a question of sedate self-expression'. The air was charged with conflicting emotions. Above such discord was the calm, reassuring, if remote, presence of Julia, who orchestrated all the varying notes into a semblance of harmony. Julia was obviously overworked by her husband, but she was driven to overextend herself, even though she had an intimate awareness of the deep futility of all effort. She had never really ceased to be the desperate widow who had lain inconsolably upon Herbert Duckworth's grave at Orchardleigh.

On 30 March 1895, Henry James told a friend of Julia's influenza: 'Mrs Stephen having had it severely, but having looked so intensely beautiful on her sofa in her longish convalescence that one felt it to be a blessing in disguise'.[57] But Julia did not get better. As warm, lush weather established itself that April, her condition worsened. At the end of the month, Vanessa was instructed to inform Stella that a slight illness had indeed attacked her mother. 'But,' as Virginia later observed, 'with the strange and ghastly fantasy of one who plays a part to the end, she would insist that the truth' be withheld from Stella.[58] Finally, the Duckworths were summoned back. To the end Julia remained the diligent nurse, dedicated to others, as when she noticed Virginia slouching: 'Hold yourself straight, my little Goat.'[59]

In the last week of Julia's life, influenza gave way to rheumatic fever. Leslie hoped against hope that her life would be spared. But on the morning of 5 May George summoned him and he 'came down to see [his] beloved angel sinking quietly into the arms of death'.[60] He staggered from the bedroom. Virginia stretched out her arms to stop him, but he brushed past her, crying out something which she could not catch. He could neither comfort her nor accept the comfort she offered.

Later that day, Virginia, Vanessa and Adrian were led by George into the bedroom of their forty-nine-year-old mother. Their teeth must have been chattering for George gave them each a drop of brandy in warm milk and towels were wrapped around them. Sunlight flooded the room while candles burnt. There was the long looking glass, the wash-stand and the great bed in which the corpse of Julia lay. One of the nurses was sobbing and Virginia, who had no idea of how to respond, felt like laughing. She said to herself, as if to keep herself in check: 'I feel nothing whatever.' Then she stooped and kissed her mother's still warm face. The next day Stella took her into the room to kiss her mother for the last time. Again, the young teenager was afraid of not feeling enough.

> [Julia] had been lying on her side before. Now she was lying straight in the middle of her pillows. Her face looked immeasurably distant, hollow and stern. When I kissed her, it was like kissing cold iron. Whenever I touch cold iron the feeling comes back to me – the feeling of my mother's face, iron cold and granulated. I started back. Then Stella stroked her cheek, and undid a button on her nightgown. 'She always liked to have it like that.'

Later that day, Stella visited Virginia in the nursery in order to beg forgiveness. She was certain that she had given her younger sister a shock when she had bossily undone the button. Virginia burst into tears and confessed: 'When I see mother, I see a man sitting with her.' This disclosure frightened Stella. Afterwards, Virginia was confused – as she had been earlier by the sinister face in the mirror. 'Did I say that,' she asked herself, 'in order to attract attention to myself? Or was it true?'

She wanted to love her dead mother but, as so often before, she was thwarted. Julia remained 'distant, hollow and stern' and the corresponding image is metallic. Virginia's other strong memories were of the heavy, musky smell of flowers penetrating the front hall and of the family clad in unbroken black. Above all, there remained the discrepancy between the luxuriant weather and their tear-stained hearts: 'I see us emerging from Hyde Park Gate on a fine summer afternoon and walking in procession hand in hand, for we were always taking hands – I see us walking – I rather proud of the solemn blackness and the impression it must make – into Kensington Gardens; and how golden the laburnum was.'[61] And they sat under the trees, wrapped uncomfortably in a stifling silence.

The memory which haunted Virginia all her life was of the morning of 5 May, just after Julia died. She looked out of the nursery window, and saw David Seton, the family doctor, walking away with his hands behind his back, as if to say, 'It is finished.' Then doves descended to peck in the road and, in their graceful, diving movements, she glimpsed an infinite peace. Despite the melancholia which invaded her, there was for this precocious thirteen-year-old another moment of great beauty, when she accompanied George and Vanessa to fetch Thoby from Paddington, where his train from school was arriving.

> It was sunset, and the great glass dome at the end of the station was blazing with light. It was glowing yellow and red and the iron girders made a pattern across it. I walked along the platform gazing with rapture at this magnificent blaze of colour, and the train slowly steamed into the station. It impressed and exalted me. It was so vast and so fiery red.

The contrast between the blaze of red and the desolate blackness of Hyde Park Gate was intense, making Virginia aware in a moment of the fullness of human life, of its joys and sorrows, of how it is a fusion of the comic and the tragic. Her mother's death was a moment of being which 'unveiled and intensified' her perceptions. It was, she said, 'as if a burning glass had been laid over what was shaded and dormant'. In this particular violent shock, the young writer saw all the strands holding life together. A pattern was revealed. But, she well knew, 'the grown-up world into which I would dash for a moment and pick off some joke or little scene and dash back again upstairs to the nursery was ended'.[62]

Chapter Three
A BROKEN CHRYSALIS
(1895–9)

Julia's death ravaged her youngest daughter, who felt that her life was now a part in an inconsequential play; she had to speak lines and assume postures which she did not feel. Other members of the household, particularly George and Gerald, wanted the family to draw closer together, but Virginia existed in an underworld of numb desolation. As she recalled, life was reduced to a chronic state of confusion: 'We were quite naturally unhappy; feeling a definite need, unbearably keen at moments, which was never to be satisfied. But that was recognizable pain, and the sharp pang grew to be almost welcome in the midst of the sultry and opaque life which was not felt, had nothing real in it, and yet swam about us, and choked us and blinded us.'[1] The miasma of despair invaded everything. This dull sense of gloom obscured the living and the dead. In place of her mother, Virginia was haunted by an unlovable ghost.

Strangely enough, the real impulse to see the family break free from the burden of despair often came from Leslie. On a walk, he would suddenly brush aside convention and rhapsodize about the beauty of life, but his offspring were not touched by such momentary exaltations. They remembered all too well his fluctuating moods, his habitual tendency to be impatient.

Leslie's 'eccentric storms'[2] were modified by Stella's assumption of Julia's place within the household. She, by sheer beauty of character, did all that she could, but she performed her tasks as if she were an automaton. Filled with a sense of the loss of the person for whom she had cared most, she struggled to keep 22 Hyde Park Gate running. This was a painful and bewildering task and she was unsure of herself. Although she did keep things together, her lack of enthusiasm was often apparent. As Virginia recalled, 'like some creaking old waggon, pitifully rusted, and yet filled with stirring young creatures, our family once more toiled painfully along the way'.[3]

Stella, who came to resemble a white flower in a steam-filled hothouse, became attached to sixteen-year-old Vanessa. In her younger sister, Stella felt that 'curiously intimate pride which a woman feels when she sees womanly virtues beautifully expressed by another, the torch still worthily carried'.[4] The bond between the two Stephen girls was still strong; Virginia remained 'The Goat' or 'Billy Goat' to her elder sister, whereas Vanessa was now 'William' or 'Maria'. Nevertheless, the newly forged closeness between Vanessa and Stella, who shared the same birthday, obviously excluded Virginia, who felt that Stella had extremely limited intellectual capacities. The contrasting personalities of the three sisters are captured in a photograph of 1896. Stella looks primly away from the viewer's gaze; Vanessa meets the eye of the spectator; Virginia stares into space. Stella's countenance is delicate but full; Vanessa's hooded eyes betray her sensuous nature; Virginia's face, which possesses the most delicate bone structure of the three, is drained of animation and colour. Virginia, who was incapable of carrying a torch, was younger and perforce more childish than her older sisters. Virginia needed Vanessa, and the new intimacy between Stella and Vanessa heightened the sorrow which overran Virginia in May 1895.

For Virginia, Stella remained the remote elder half-sister. 'Among my earliest memories,' she recalled, 'is the memory of going out with her; perhaps to shop, or to pay some call; and, the errand done, she would take me to a shop and give me a glass of milk and biscuits sprinkled with sugar on a marble table . . . But she lived, of course, downstairs in the drawing room.'[5]

Virginia's menarche probably occurred in October 1896. This fact can be gleaned from Stella's pocket diary, in which she inscribed many of the tasks she undertook on a daily basis.* As that document makes clear, purchasing sanitary towels was also one of Stella's chores. She handled these responsibilities with remarkable energy and patience, but she was not able to help her motherless youngest sister to handle the onset of menstruation. Virginia usually retired to bed on the first day of her periods and, in 1924, confessed that for ten years of her life she had made sanitary towels out of kapok rather than have to ask a shop-girl for them and admit, 'I too am a woman.'[6]

At about this time, Virginia began to perceive the world from two vantage points: the perspective of her observant, satirically oriented self and that of 'Miss Jan', the name she gave to the outwardly conforming, conventional, painfully shy side of herself. The adoption of the persona of a timid adolescent who embodies society's stereotypical views made it possible for Virginia to control and thus keep sorrow at bay. Such a role also allowed her to exhibit the side of herself of which Stella approved. In that way, she held herself together, but ultimately this effort was doomed to failure.

Ever afterwards, Virginia found it difficult to describe the torpor into which she descended during her first breakdown in the summer of 1895 at Freshwater on the Isle of Wight. Her few words on the subject seem deliberately illusive: 'and the heat there in the low bay, brimming as it seemed with soft vapours, and luxuriant with lush plants, mixes, like smoke, with other memories of hot rooms and silence, and an atmosphere all choked with too luxuriant feelings'.[7] The heat and her own feelings were 'luxuriant' in the sense that they were warm, ripe and impossible to decipher. This is all that is known of Virginia's first breakdown, but 'choked'

* Stella's pocket diary for 1896 is in the Berg Collection, New York Public Library. She used an X to indicate the beginning day of the periods of Vanessa, Virginia and herself. The first such mark for Virginia is recorded on 16 October (a Friday) and subsequently 16 November (a Monday). There is no such mark against Virginia's name in the multitudinous entries from January to June; there are almost no entries from 2 July until 19 September; there are no entries for December.

is exactly the right verb to describe her emotional state. She felt overwhelmed, as if an enormous force had stifled her, robbing her of air.

Not surprisingly, Leslie's demands upon Stella increased. To him, she gave indiscriminately. This was because she doubted her ability to bestow anything worthwhile, but Leslie greedily consumed all she offered. He continued to reel, like a Milton staggering blindly. He asserted that he wanted to die and Stella was the principal, hapless witness to his despair. He worried that he had never told Julia of the depths of his love for her. Some nights Stella would sit alone with him in the study, hearing again and again the bitter story of his loneliness. Had he been too selfish, too self-absorbed to notice Julia's fading health? 'I was not as bad as Carlyle, was I?' he once asked her. 'Stella perhaps knew little of Carlyle,' Virginia pointed out, 'but her assurance came over and over again, tired but persistent.'[8]

Despite the despair which threatened to overwhelm him, Leslie continued to oversee his youngest daughter's ripening appetite for literature. In 1897, her reading included Lockhart's *Life of Sir Walter Scott*, *A Tale of Two Cities*, *Silas Marner*, Anthony Hope's *The Heart of Princess Osra*, three volumes of Pepys, *Barchester Towers* and at least five volumes of Carlyle. 'Gracious child, how you gobble!' Leslie teased her.[9] Before, he had issued books to her. At about this time, he gave her the freedom of his library, although he rather primly suggested that there were certain books – such as George du Maurier's *Trilby* – best avoided.

At the same time that Leslie granted greater liberty to Virginia, Stella sought her escape when lean, threadbare and determined John Waller Hills, who had been courting her for some time, renewed his claim for her hand. To Virginia, he resembled a tenacious wire-haired terrier. Vanessa, now Stella's confidante, liked this faithful retainer and Stella's own standards became, according to Virginia, far from exacting. Although Jack was, like Leslie, demanding, Stella came to see the prospect of a life with him as attractive. She yearned for an independent existence, where she could be the centre of another person's life. Ultimately, Jack offered Stella the prospect of a revolt against Leslie's dominion.

At times, Virginia saw Jack as the plucky 'English country gentleman type'.[10] He was not the most prepossessing of men, although he had limpid brown eyes. His most remarkable features were his nose, with an obstinate knob at the end of it, the wrinkles which crisscrossed his countenance, a retreating chin and a decided stammer. Years later, however, it was his earthiness which, Virginia realized, had impressed itself upon her: 'He opened my eyes on purpose, as I think, to the part played by sex in the life of the ordinary man. He shocked me a little, wholesomely. He told me that young men talked incessantly of women; and "had" them incessantly.'[11] In 1895–6, without being fully aware of Jack's strong sex drives, Virginia was moved by his and Stella's mutual adoration:

> Certainly he was passionately in love; she at first passively. And it was through that engagement that I had my first vision – so intense, so exciting, so rapturous was it that the word vision applies – my first vision then of love between man and woman. It was to me like a ruby; the love I detected that winter of their engagement, glowing, red, clear, intense. It gave me a conception of love; a standard of love; a sense that nothing in the whole world is so lyrical, so musical, as a young man and a young woman in their first love for each other.[12]

Stella's body became incandescent and Virginia, when she discovered one of Jack's love letters, was reduced to a quiver of ecstasy at being a witness to passion.[13] However, her feelings about Jack were very mixed. He was a prosaic, businesslike man who wanted to spirit Stella away; on the other hand, he was a virile man whose sexual appetite was blended with a courtly devotion to Stella.

Much of Virginia's irritation with Jack was vented on his parents. Judge Hills – known as 'Buzzy' – was commonplace, little and round. Anna Hills was a snobbish, overly decorous person, who was inordinately relieved that she had given birth only to sons. Of those three, Jack was the one she cared for least and Julia, a few years before her death, became for Jack a substitute mother – a situation which a friend once mentioned to Virginia: 'For instance, how could Mrs Hills have liked it – Jack treating your mother as if she were his?'[14] In a sense, Jack and Stella were siblings, tied to the same mother. There was more than a tinge of incestuous feeling in their love.

Before Julia's death, Leslie had been sufficiently concerned about the courtship to read one of Jack's letters, as he informed his wife on 2 August 1893: 'I enclose a letter from Jack Hills. I opened it from curiosity, not knowing the hand. Poor boy – it is pathetic & I am very sorry for him: but I suppose that it is all over & that he will recover by degrees.'[15] In 1896, the pathos of the situation had turned against Leslie, who depended upon Stella to run his household and to bolster his fading sense of self-worth. Now the name Jack sounded like the crack of a whip.

Stella had refused Jack before Julia's death, and did so once again in 1895 or 1896. But Jack knew exactly what he wanted when he bicycled on 22 August 1896 to Hindhead House, Haslemere, where the Stephens were on holiday. That black and silver night, the overpoweringly humid air added to the tension building between the two lovers, who slipped away into the garden. Virginia and the other children used the pretext – on a moonlit evening – of catching moths to keep tabs on the couple, who evaded their net. Virginia heard whispers and the rumpling of clothing – or thought she did. There were glimpses of the runaways, hastening round corners. Then Leslie, who had become restless, sent his children to bed. The four, now deeply anxious, gathered in Adrian's room. Then there was a noise. The ever-fearless Thoby ventured outside and discovered a tramp, whom he dispatched with boisterous eloquence. Still, nothing happened. Leslie paced the terrace.

Virginia had two distinct recollections of the outcome. In one, Stella, a resplendent Eve, walked back to the house that evening, arm in arm with her Adam: 'we ran to our rooms, and in a few minutes Stella came up herself, blushing the loveliest rose colour, and told us – how she was very happy'.[16] Later, Virginia told the story differently: 'Nessa and I sat up in our bedroom waiting; and Stella never came; and at last in the early morning she came and told us that she was engaged.' At breakfast, Leslie, discovering one of his children in tears, commanded: 'We must all be happy, because Stella is happy.'[17] George and Gerald seemed enthusiastic and arranged that Jack and Stella be left alone together. Soon, however, they made it clear that there would be difficulties if Jack came too much to Hyde Park Gate.

While settling into her engagement, Stella, under the supervision of Dr Seton, kept a watchful eye on Virginia. David Elphinstone Seton, long the Stephen family physician, prescribed a regimen then common in the treatment of female patients who were considered unduly irritable or excitable. According to the current theory of psychology, reading, writing or studying drained energy from the reproductive system of such women. Thus such harmful activities had to be curtailed until the patient regained her equilibrium.

Virginia's breakdown in 1895 signalled such an imbalance to Seton. While men were sometimes subjected to similar treatments, there can be little doubt that many medical practitioners were wont to see a link between female independence and so-called hysteria. Sir George Savage, who treated Virginia later, claimed: 'If a . . . promising girl is allowed to educate herself at home, the danger of solitary work and want of social friction may be seen in concert developing into insanity.'[18] In 1894, the year before his mother's death, Thoby Stephen had, during a bout of influenza, become delirious and attempted to throw himself out of a window; a month later, he had a similar attack at home. Soon after, he went back to Clifton College, where his masters could closely supervise him. Women were seen to be more fragile than men and thus in need of more extended care.

A racing pulse was Virginia's principal symptom: 'It beat so quick I could hardly bear it.' She felt what she labelled 'the excitement and the depression of the bodily state'. Years later, she wondered, 'Can I therefore be a good witness? Am I not getting everything queered?' What Virginia painfully remembered was that the desire to write left her: 'Never wrote a story or an essay: never wished to'. But, at the very same time, 'the experiencing power'[19] was intense, although it was, she recalled, spasmodic, jaundiced and erratic. On 13 October 1896, Stella took Virginia to Seton because she had an 'anxiety attack';[20] eight days later, at another consultation, Seton instructed Virginia to give up lessons entirely until January at the earliest and to spend four hours each day outside the house.

The heavy responsibilities which Stella shouldered eventually aroused a grudging devotion in Virginia. But Stella remained remote: 'Perhaps one would come into a room unexpectedly, and surprise her in tears, and, to one's miserable confusion, she would hide them instantly, and speak ordinary words, as though she did not imagine that one could understand her suffering.'[21] Lukewarm veneration was only half of Virginia's response to Stella. She also saw her as an unimaginative and overbearing caretaker who subjected her almost daily to an 'inquisitive hour', during which Stella systematically questioned Virginia about her mental health.

The only break in Virginia's oppressive London routine was a trip to northern France in November with Vanessa, George and his aunt Minna Duckworth. That year, Adrian entered Westminster, Vanessa began drawing lessons, Thoby continued at Clifton College and George and Gerald worked at establishing themselves in London society. And thus Stella and Leslie focused their attention on Virginia, who was forced to do nothing.

At the beginning of 1897, Virginia began a diary in which she recorded the daily life of herself and Miss Jan. When, during a visit to some friends, Virginia dropped her umbrella, she came to the conclusion 'that what ever talents Miss Jan may have, she does not possess the one qualifying her to shine in good society'.[22] Despite her keen sense of herself as a gawky adolescent, she began writing fiction again on 5 February: the no longer extant 'The Eternal Miss Jan'.

That February an announcement was made which irritated Virginia: she and Vanessa were to accompany Jack and Stella to Bognor. Their marriage had been briefly postponed because Jack had undergone a minor operation that January and needed a few days at the seaside to convalesce. This request became a horrible fix which put Virginia in a dreadful temper. 'Poor Miss Jan [was] bewildered.' In part, Virginia's discomfort arose because she did not wish to be a witness to the strong sexual attraction which the couple expressed for each other. She lamented: 'Impossible to be alone with those two creatures, yet if I do not go, Stella will not . . . goodness knows how we shall come out of this *quandary*.'[23] Predictably, the trip, from 8 to 13 February, was not a success.

Back in London, Virginia made brief notes in March on the almond trees and crocuses on the verge of blooming in Kensington Gardens and woefully reflected on her own seemingly perpetual dormant state. Earlier, in mid-February, she was allowed to resume her lessons, but much of her time was consumed in visiting, shopping, ice-skating and bicycle riding. There were trips to Battersea Park, London Zoo, the Serpentine, the Round Pond, the National Gallery, the National Portrait Gallery and Carlyle's House. In June, she saw Queen Victoria on the day commemorating her Diamond Jubilee. The frail monarch had to be told to look up and bow, whereupon she smiled and nodded her poor tired head.

When a well-meaning friend sent him a *Thesaurus*, Leslie was insulted and accordingly, Virginia recalled, 'handed it over to me – and I have been trying to make use of it'.[24] On 27 February, as Virginia gratefully recorded, Seton had determined that 'I may do some Latin with Nessa in the mornings, but as far as I can make out, nothing else'.[25] Virginia's mental health was slowly improving, but she remained acutely aware of the fragility of existence, as she told her diary on 26 March:

> As we were coming home, we saw a poor young lady byciclist [*sic*] run over by a cart – she was coming up Gloucester Road with another lady – and tried to turn round to the right, and ran straight into the cart. The cart was coming slowly, and there was nothing else in the road, so I cannot understand how it could have happened.[26]

And in late January, Virginia caught a reflection of her own inner desolation in a house on Grosvenor Street destroyed by fire: 'The windows were all broken, and we saw into black empty rooms; the roof was off, and everything was burnt and blackened.'[27]

Stella's approaching nuptials were for Virginia the beginning of the end. The only good Virginia could envisage was that Stella's removal from 22 Hyde Park Gate meant she could finally have a room of her own. She would not have to retreat to the glazed room at the back of the house or an armchair in the day nursery. Virginia and Vanessa tried to remain calm, as if Stella's marriage did not touch them. The marriage ceremony on 10 April was half dream, half nightmare. The two desolate sisters acted as bridesmaids and were rewarded with pendant gold watches from Dent's in Pall Mall. Part of the nightmare was that Stella would no longer be at Leslie's beck and call, although Stella and Jack had taken a house a few doors away. Meanwhile, the newly-weds honeymooned in Florence and the Stephen family holidayed at Hove.

When the Stephens returned to London on 28 April, they were met at Victoria Station by George, who gave them ominous news: Stella had returned from Italy 'with a bad chill on her innards'. Soon afterwards, Dr Seton assured them that Stella was on her way to a speedy recovery. Nevertheless, the entire family was miserable and the atmosphere of both households was filled with tension. 'Oh dear,' Virginia reflected, 'how is one to live in such a world, which is a Miss Janism, but very much my mind at present.'[28]

Things became even more frightening when the diagnosis of gastroenteritis was suddenly changed to peritonitis. Stella was to be kept quiet. Another nurse was hired and straw was put down on the road to make the already quiet street deathly still. Stella seemed to make a rapid recovery. Although relieved, Virginia was 'unreasonable enough to be irritated'[29] with her half-sister, whom she had not seen since the wedding and whom she did not visit until May. At that meeting, Stella looked better than Virginia expected and gave her a pencil bought in Paris.

Meanwhile, Virginia was eager to resume her education and decided, in consultation with Leslie, to begin classes at King's College in the autumn, 'if', she added ominously, 'I begin at all'.[30]

She realized that she had to venture out from 22 Hyde Park Gate and take an active hand in forging her own destiny. Although she perceived her writerly inclinations as derived in large part from her mother's side, she knew that Julia had not really approved of such a profession for women. Leslie wanted her to be a writer, but for different reasons from his wife did not see the necessity of a literary woman obtaining a formal education. On this basis, Virginia pressed on, very much alone. Nevertheless, independence remained a fraught issue. Lingering anxiety can be glimpsed in her account of two accidents she witnessed on 8 May: 'we saw a hansom overturned in Piccadilly – I saw it in mid-air – the horse lifted from its legs, and the driver jumping from the box. Luckily neither horse nor driver suffered though the hansom was broken – Then again, I managed to discover a man in the course of being squashed by an omnibus.'[31] Five days later, while inside a bakery, she heard a stampede on the street and beheld one horse on the ground and a second prancing madly above it. Then, an infuriated steed appeared at the door, pushing it with its nose. He was soon captured.

Virginia's fascination with accidents – admittedly the streets seem to have been dangerous – was a metaphor for her sense of her own life being subject to unpredictable forces which might maim or crush her. She was almost pleased when she encountered such catastrophes, as if they proved graphically just how tragic life could be.

When, on 16 May, she visited Stella, who had announced by this time that she was pregnant, Virginia was extremely gruff and unpleasant. She ascribed this to the effect of hot weather on her nerves rather than to her displeasure at Stella's catechizing. Shortly before, Leslie had decided, in light of Seton's advice, that Virginia should work outdoors. She was to reclaim the back garden and accordingly a fork, spade, hoe and rake were ordered. At the same time, she was delightfully preoccupied with the antics of a new pet, Jacobi the mouse, who stealthily visited her in the night. Sometimes they chased each other around the room. There was an evening of uproarious joviality on 30 May, in celebration of Stella's twenty-eighth birthday and Vanessa's eighteenth. 'Georgie' gave Stella an opal necklace, which became both Virginia's envy and delight.

Despite her attachment to Stella, Virginia, a teenager caught between the extremes of dependence and independence, was often furious with her. On 12 June, she informed her diary: 'she ... irritated me extremely by saying that I should have to go with her when she goes away, which I with great vehemence, declared to be *impossible*'.[32] When a relative asked her the invariable 'How is Stella?', she realized just how much she 'hated poor Stella & her diseases'.[33] As far as Virginia was concerned, Stella remained a warden who monitored and reported on the condition of her soul.

On 11 July, Virginia became feverish and ill while visiting Jack and Stella and was put to bed at their house. On 14 July, Stella sat up well into the night to soothe her. The following morning, Stella came to see her before breakfast. She stayed only a moment. On the following day, she called out to Virginia through her open door to ask how she was. That disembodied voice was Virginia's last encounter with Stella, who died three days later following an emergency operation. For Virginia, the impossible thing had once again happened, an event which, at the time, was understandably unimaginable to write of: 'as if it were unnatural, against the law, horrible, as a treachery, betrayed – the fact of death. The blow, the *second* blow of death, struck on me: tremulous, creased, sitting with my wings still stuck together in the broken chrysalis.'[34] Guilt was intertwined with loss, since Virginia was acutely conscious of having rebelled against Stella's strictures. She was the only parental figure against whom Virginia had felt free enough to rebel.

Mixed with these conflicting feelings was an uneasy sense that Stella's sexuality had brought about her untimely death. There was gossip at the time that Jack had somehow injured Stella on their honeymoon. According to Violet Dickinson, later a close friend of Virginia, Stella had some inner malfunction which made sexual intercourse arduous. Something – Violet supposed it was the uterus – that should have been convex was actually concave. At the least, Jack had been, Violet reported, a rapacious, overdemanding lover.[35]

Virginia was the likely conduit of this gossip to Violet. Rightly or not, Virginia would have once again seen male sexual aggressiveness – as with Gerald almost ten years before – leading not only to a sense of unwarranted intrusion but also, in the case of Stella, to death. Earlier, Virginia had been entranced by the rhapsodic love between Stella and Jack, but such nascent feelings were strangled by Stella's demise. Significantly, Stella was also pregnant when she died and Virginia thus perceived a link between pregnancy and death.

Neither Virginia nor Vanessa attended the funeral service at Highgate on 21 July, but they did accompany Jack to visit the grave three days later. At that time Leslie complacently informed a friend that 'My Vanessa' was taking Stella's place as mistress of the house very calmly and would prove invaluable. Leslie's attention was now firmly focused on Vanessa. It was her turn to deal with his outbursts when the account books were placed before him every Wednesday. According to him, bankruptcy was nigh; the family was 'shooting Niagara to ruin'. Vanessa became responsible for such a highly unlikely event and had to curb the seemingly runaway household expenses. Unlike Julia and Stella, 'The Saint' did not pretend sympathy and understanding. Instead, she listened in reserved, angry silence to her father's imprecations.

Although Vanessa now occupied Leslie's regard, Stella's death soon took its toll on Virginia's writing, as she reflected on 9 August, when she and the other members of the Stephen family were staying at Painswick Vicarage, Gloucestershire: 'This poor diary is in a very bad way, but, strange though it may seem, the time is always so filled up here, that I get very little time for diarizing – even if I wished to, which I don't, having taken a great dislike to the whole process.' Nine days later, the diary was completely neglected and by 14 September it was 'lingering on indeed, but death would be shorter & less painful'.[36] For the remainder of 1897, it was reduced to a perfunctory record of appointments.

During this setback, Virginia began classes in Greek and history that October at King's College. Life, she increasingly realized, was a 'hard business – one needs a rhinirocerous [*sic*] skin – & that one has not got'.[37] As 1897 came to an end, her spirits rose as she thought of her neglected diary: it was a 'volume of fairly acute life (the first really *lived* year of my life) ended, locked & put away'. In a very real sense, the life was *lived* because, despite the sorrow she had encountered, she had confronted tragedy by writing about it and exploring beyond the confines of 22 Hyde Park Gate. Nevertheless, the years ahead seemed long and arduous: 'Nessa preaches that our destinies lie in ourselves, & the sermon ought to be taken home by us. Here is life given us each alike, & we must do our best with it: your hand in the sword hilt – & an unuttered fervent vow!'[38] This bravery went hand in hand with gnawing anxiety, as in Virginia's description of a little pugnacious brown mongrel, long a neighbourhood pest: 'A cab slowly passed over its middle: we were watching and saw it get up and run about as though it was not hurt. But that night it became unconscious and died.'[39] Although battered by life, it was possible to appear normal. But the façade of well-being could quickly crumble.

Just after she took up diary-writing in 1897, Virginia agreed to type her cousin Dorothea's poems. These were very long, watery effusions, with which Dorothea Stephen intended to 'invade the magazines'. Throughout her long career, Virginia would carefully measure herself against other women writers, usually *vis-à-vis* public recognition. The pious, overweight Dorothea was in 1897 labelled, somewhat rancorously, a 'great carcase'.[40] Even Dorothea's singing voice was subject to attack: it was high, shrill and completely out of tune. So infused was Virginia with her cousin's conversation that she became afraid lest she begin to write exactly like her.

Meanwhile, still faithfully tending the garden at 22 Hyde Park Gate, Virginia also diligently sought women who had attempted to carve out professions independent of husbands and homes. One of the first of these was the very white and shrivelled Clara Pater, who taught Greek and Latin at King's College. Earlier, she had been the first classics tutor and eventually Vice-President of Somerville College, Oxford. Very little of the decadence of her famous brother Walter's aesthetics touched her everyday life. Virginia saw Clara and her sister Tettie as 'most pathetic, growing old together, and one of them will drop off, and the other will be left. They seem so desolate.'[41] If Virginia had serious reservations about sexual involvement with men, she remained deeply frightened at the prospect of being a single woman.

January 1898 was enveloped in a deep yellow fog which necessitated candles at 3.30 in the afternoon. Virginia took Greek with G. C. W. Warr, but most of her time was devoted to the usual routine of reading, gardening, walking and shopping. The Easter holidays were spent at Hove. In May, the sisters stayed with their aunts at Cambridge and Godmanchester. There was a visit to Thoby at Clifton College in June and the following month they went to the Fens in pursuit of moths. Later, the family spent August and September at the Manor House, Ringwood, before returning to London, at which time Virginia studied Latin with Miss Pater and Greek with Dr Warr.

Early in 1898, Virginia began to correspond with her cousin Emma Vaughan, whom she almost always addresses as 'Dearest Toad'. The twenty-five-year-old Emma, whose mother had died in 1881 when she was eight, was sensible, restrained, highly whimsical and, except for her devotion to music, unduly conventional and lumpish. Virginia, eight years her junior, speaks to her as if she is the elder and, in turn, instructs, shocks and confides in 'Toad'. Frequently, Virginia directs mischievous sallies in her direction, as when she comments on their cousin Cordelia Fisher: 'Sometimes her face does not light up, as it should, and she refused to dance with "horrible undergraduates" in a manner which reminded me slightly of you.' And Emma and Virginia certainly shared an unease with men and sex, as can be seen in Virginia's sharp comment on Charlotte Leaf, one of John Addington Symonds's daughters: 'She is *enormous*. As for her body, I never saw such a shape save in those who are doing business with Infants – and surely she can not already be advanced to such a degree.'[42]

The letters to 'Dearest Toad' prepared Virginia for her next extended piece of writing, the diary she kept in August–September

1899, when the Stephen family was on holiday at the rectory at Warboys, within easy reach of Godmanchester and their Stephen cousins. This diary was glued into and between the pages of a copy of Isaac Watts's *Right Use of Reason*. Virginia tartly observed: 'Any other book almost, would have been too sacred to undergo the desecration that I planned.'[43]

At first, Virginia had been doubtful about an extended stay in the country. The landscape which they passed through on the train was certainly dull in the extreme. But, soon after they arrived, they were bathed in a delicious golden light. Immediately, Virginia began to write at a rate which threatened to use up her allotted space. Presciently, she reflected, 'the fever will not last – I know the disease will'. She thought that details might swamp the diary, which would have to undergo radical changes. Nevertheless, she was again aware of how writing was an essential part of her self: 'I find I write with greater ease than I talk sense or nonsense.'[44] Still she remained unsure of this talent.

This trip to the Fens sharpened Virginia's powers of observation, which now extended to a delicate albeit diligent account of the capture of a red underwing: 'By the faint glow we could see the huge moth – his wings open, as though in ecstasy, so that the splendid crimson of the underwing could be seen – his eyes burning red, his proboscis plunged into a flowing stream of treacle. We gazed one moment on his splendour, & then uncorked the bottle.'[45]

The telegraphic topic sentences which concluded the 1897 diary have given way to poignant, detailed, atmospheric and lush pieces of writing, as in this observation on a Fen funeral:

> As we passed them, a boy looked down at us very sullenly & with the peculiar sodden depressed look that Fen men & women have; they were absolutely silent; & the procession went on to the heart of the Fen. I dreamt most vividly of this last night; how I looked into the women's faces; & the carts passed on & on into the night. They were going back to some strange dark land.[46]

Also embedded in the Warboys journal is 'A Terrible Tragedy

in a Duckpond'. The disaster was simple enough. While Emma was visiting Warboys, she, Virginia and Adrian went punting by moonlight on 23 August. The threesome, frolicking noisily and recklessly, capsized the boat and were forced to swim ashore. In the journal, relatively straightforward fact is metamorphosed into sophisticated fiction: 'The angry waters of the duck pond rose in their wrath to swallow their prey – & the green caverns of the depths opened – & closed – The cold moonlight silvered the path to death – & perhaps tinged the last thoughts of the unfortunate sufferers with something of its own majestic serenity.'[47]

This comical tale – showing an obsession with water as an instrument of death and treating accidents in a facetious manner – demonstrates that Virginia's ability to see everyday events as the stuff of art had returned. As she realized, 'the most ordinary object is possessed with strange fascination for me'. And since 'we are a world of imitations, all the Arts . . . imitate as far as they can the one great truth that all can see. Such is the eternal instinct in the human beast, to try & reproduce something of that majesty in paint, marble or ink.'[48]

Chapter Four

SHELL-LESS

(1899–1904)

A much more poised Virginia Stephen accompanied her family back to London on 21 September 1899, but her growing self-assurance was quickly dissipated by the divergences within 22 Hyde Park Gate. Upstairs was the intellectual domain of her lonely, despotic father, whereas downstairs was filled with the banal society gossip of the Duckworth brothers. In particular, George, who had assumed the role of head of the family, wanted his sisters to ape every twist and turn in fashion among the English aristocracy and, in the process, made both of them deeply suspicious of that stratum of society. George's mindless devotion to convention may have been repulsive, but the sensibility of Leslie Stephen, the man of letters, had simply atrophied. 'He had,' Virginia recalled, 'so ignored, or disguised his own feelings that he had no idea of what other people were. Hence the horror and the terror of those violent displays of rage. There was something blind, animal, savage in them . . . He did not realize what he did. No one could enlighten him.'[1] He suffered. Everyone in the family suffered. There was no possibility of communication. He shouted. Everyone else was reduced to uneasy silence. Virginia had to choose between two kinds of tyrannies and she found both repulsive. More than a year later, on 22 January 1901, the day of Queen Victoria's funeral, she asked Jack Hills: 'do you think I shall ever commit suicide?'[2]

As before, Virginia was left very much to her own devices. In October 1899, Thoby went up to Trinity College, Cambridge, where he quickly became friends with Clive Bell, Lytton Strachey, Saxon Sydney-Turner and Leonard Woolf. Vanessa took refuge in her drawing lessons and entered the Royal Academy Schools in

September 1901. Adrian was off early in the morning to Westminster. Virginia was left alone at 22 Hyde Park Gate. Her father shut himself in his study on the top floor, the housemaid polished brass rods, the dog Shag slept on his mat and Sophie took in provisions from the tradesmen who called at the back door. Virginia mounted to her room, spread her Greek dictionary upon a table and translated Euripides or Sophocles.

Increasingly isolated from her brothers and sister and caught between two types of masculinity which repulsed her, Virginia became more and more attracted to the comforts of female friendship. One of these women was Madge Symonds, a daughter of John Addington Symonds. She had once spent a winter at Hyde Park Gate when Virginia was seven. Thereafter, she was known as 'The Chief' to the Stephen children. In July 1898, she married Virginia's cousin William Wyamar Vaughan, headmaster successively of Giggleswick, Wellington College and Rugby. Madge, who had grown up in the Swiss Alps, was a writer deeply tinged with melancholy. Thirteen years older than Virginia, she had been desolated by her father's death in 1893. Although she was able to mask her many sadnesses and carried out her numerous responsibilities as headmaster's wife and mother with great panache, her character was an uneasy blend of her father's sophisticated aesthetics and her mother's austere puritanism. There was also another side to her: when upset or startled, Madge would become incoherent and 'swoop' the air with flailing hands.

Although Virginia had a crush on Madge, it was in her letters to Emma Vaughan that she began to speak freely of her growing interest in a world – a chaste one – of music, books and pictures. 'I am going to found a colony where there shall be no marrying,'[3] she primly informed her cousin. Upon spinsterish 'Toad', who went for a time to Dresden to study music, Virginia further unleashed her comic, teasing side: 'I know that in time you will rave about Dresden, and discover some perfect Dresdenite – of the other sex.'[4] Virginia's own lack of interest in men and polite society is captured in a remark of August 1901: 'we can't shine in Society. I don't know how it's done. We ain't popular – we sit in corners and look like mutes who are longing for a funeral.'[5] Significantly, the existence she envisaged for herself was one where there would be no 'human element at all, except what comes through Art'. And Virginia was again uncomfortably aware of her own precarious mental state: 'This world of human beings grows too complicated, my only wonder is that we don't fill more madhouses: the insane view of life has much to be said for it . . . My spring melancholy is developing in these hot days into summer madness.'[6]

Just as Virginia had earlier come to perceive Jack Hills as a man whose emotional needs were in part tender, Thoby, once an explosive and frail little boy, became for his sister the lone male who mixed mastery with sensibility, friendliness with composure. Hardened by his father's earlier harsh treatment, Thoby never allowed a word of feeling to escape him. 'And beneath this reserve, when he was with us, I felt, though he could not say a word ever about his feelings, a dumb affectionateness, a pride in us, and something melancholy too – perhaps the deaths of mother and Stella made him older than his age.'[7]

At Cambridge, this reserved young man was nicknamed the 'Goth' in recognition of his huge, splendid physique and his amplitude of mind. Although he shared his Duckworth half-brothers' excessive concern with propriety and urged his sisters to follow the dictates of convention, Thoby remained a mysterious figure, one who blended a freely expressed masculinity with the intuitive. He was also, like his sisters, an intellectual with a rebellious streak, which can be discerned in his pamphlet 'Compulsory Chapel. An Appeal to Undergraduates on Behalf of Religious Liberty and Intellectual Independence': 'To take a firm stand in this matter is not only to free yourselves from the burden of a discipline that is inconvenient and degrading, but to strengthen the cause of religious liberty in the last English stronghold of religious intolerance.' Very much his father's son in this piece of writing, he hoped that he was pointing to 'no forlorn hope, no quest for the impossible. The prize is ready to the hand of all but the sluggard and the craven.'[8]

Virginia was quite certain that her brother saw her as a 'shell-less little creature'.[9] If he did, it was probably because he shared with her a similar constitution but had learned to adopt protective colouring. They had heated arguments about Shakespeare. He told her of life at Clifton College and Cambridge. Through him, she became fascinated with the classical world, especially the Fall of Troy.

Virginia found substantial consolation from Madge, Emma, Thoby and Vanessa, but from 1902 Violet Dickinson was her closest friend. When her mother died, Violet had been taken under Julia Stephen's protective wing, but Virginia first met her when she came to take tea with Stella on 3 June 1897. At that time, Violet noticed that Virginia was furtive and especially nervous at crossing the road. Five years later, in the summer of 1902, Virginia reacted rapturously to Violet:

> She came down to dinner in flowing & picturesque garments – for all her height, & a certain comicality of face, she treats her body with dignity. She always wore suitable & harmonious clothes – though she made no secret of the fact that they had lived through more seasons than one. Indeed she was singularly unreserved in many ways; always talking & laughing & entering into whatever was going on with a most youthful zeal. It was only after a time that one came to a true estimate of her character – that one saw that all was not cheerfulness & high spirits by any means – She had her times of depression, & her sudden reserves; but it is true that she was always quick to follow a cheerful voice . . . She has a very wide circle of acquaintances, mostly of the landed & titled variety in whose country houses she is for ever staying – & with whom she seems to be invariably popular. She is 37 – & without any pretence to good looks, – which she knows quite well herself, & lets you know too – even going out of her way to allude laughingly to her grey hairs, & screw her face into the most comical grimaces. But an observer who would stop here, putting her down as one of those cleverish adaptable ladies of middle age who are

welcome everywhere, & not indispensable anywhere – such an observer would be superficial indeed.[10]

In this portrait (written in 1907) Virginia displays her admiration for Violet's ability to blend cheerfulness with an acute awareness of the sorrow of life. She herself was struggling to do exactly this.

Violet, born in 1865 and thus seventeen years older than Virginia, was the daughter of Edmund Dickinson, a Somerset squire; her mother was the daughter of the 3rd Lord Auckland. Violet was, as Virginia suggests, extraordinarily tall for a woman – 6 feet, 2 inches – and she had the stooping demeanour which height often brings. But her awkwardness did not extend to the management of her own affairs. In 1902, this strong, self-reliant person designed and supervised the building of Burnham Wood, her cottage at Welwyn, Hertfordshire. Leslie responded warmly to Violet, whose only fault, according to him, was her height. He noted with pleasure that she had taken 'a great fancy to the girls, who went about with her all day & discoursed upon literary & other matters continuously – Miss D. told me many pleasant things about the two and admires Ginia's intelligence greatly.'[11]

From the outset of their intimacy, Violet was for Virginia 'My Aunt', 'My Child' and, most importantly, 'My Woman'. In one photograph, Violet and Virginia pose for the camera; the younger woman, nestled in the protective arms of the other, looks like a timorous child being embraced by a tender, maternal giant. Virginia's penchant for nicknames was released anew in the aliases she created for herself in the valedictions to her letters to Violet: 'Kangaroo' and 'Wallaby' were often employed. She once told Violet: 'I wish you were a Kangaroo and had a pouch for small Kangaroos to creep to.'[12] Even more pervasive is the signature 'Sparroy' (sparrow + monkey). In Virginia's make-believe bestiary, a monkey is a rapacious, inquiring creature, whereas the sparrow is a timid bird, often searching desperately for a crumb of food.

'Sparroy' embodies the paradoxes in twenty-year-old Virginia, who valued independence but was deeply unsure of her ability to make use of it once it was found. There is also a contrast between the highly developed sexuality of the monkey and the shyness of the sparrow. The contradictions can be seen in this query in Virginia's letter of 12 December 1902: 'Have you a real affection for the Sparroy? She folds you in her feathery arms, so that you may feel the Heart in her ribs. Rather mild, but these emotions are very upsetting.'[13] The emotions were unsettling because the need for Violet's affection and approval was commingled with a nebulous sexual interest in this older woman, who had a strong dash of 'masculine' decisiveness in her make-up. 'It is astonishing,' Virginia told her in July 1903, 'what depths – hot volcano depths – your finger has stirred in Sparroy – hitherto entirely quiescent.'[14] Who was Violet – a maternal figure or a possible sexual partner? The realization that Violet might be both led Virginia to tell her new friend in the autumn of 1902: 'You're a blessed hell cat and an angel in one. What a squalling and a squeaking there must be inside you.'[15]

Virginia's friendship with Violet prospered – and grew markedly stronger – in direct proportion to Virginia's fear that the abdominal cancer which overtook Leslie in the spring of 1902 would be fatal. It was as if Virginia had to find a substitute mother who could nurse her through the expected loss of her father. Although Virginia was obviously not as involved as Vanessa in ministering to Leslie, she participated in some of his activities: for example, she accompanied him and Vanessa in November 1901 to Oxford, where he received an Hon. D.Litt. In a letter to Violet of February 1903, Virginia draws a direct connection between her father's illness and her own need for the affection of women: 'Father is a fraud, only an invalid for the sake of his ladies. I wish I could be an invalid and have ladies. I am so susceptible to female charms, in fact I offered my blistered heart to one.'[16] As this passage shows, Virginia even had the power to make – and the pleasure of making – Violet jealous. And in a letter of March 1903 Virginia poignantly depicted a moment of intimacy in the all-encompassing friendship between herself and Violet: 'Sparroy only flaps her warm blooded paw, and says she has tender memories of a long embrace, in a bedroom.'[17]

At the very same time that Virginia was being so flirtatious with Violet, she may have been involved in a lesbian relationship with Vanessa. This can be glimpsed in Vanessa's letter to Virginia of 13 April 1905, which seems to be recalling events of two or three years before. Vanessa realizes that Virginia is 'pining for a real petting', presumably something which was once customary: 'perhaps – *if you* have been good – there's no saying but you may get it'. She also told her: 'As long as the ape [Virginia] gets all he wants, does not smell too much, and has his claws well cut, he's a pleasant enough bed fellow for a short time!' In October 1916, Virginia spoke of the pleasure of stealing kisses from her sister's 'most secluded parts'.[18] Both girls, exceedingly lonely since the death of their mother, eroticized their loss by seeking physical comfort from each other. Virginia's amorphous, low-key sexual impulses always remained more aroused by women than by men. Such inclinations were triggered by a psychic search for the dead mother, who, when alive, had never had much time for her youngest daughter, and by the conviction that the sexual demands of men were dangerous.

Meanwhile, in the early 1900s, Jack Hills and George Duckworth were drawn to Vanessa. Unfortunately for her, she bore an uncanny resemblance to Stella and quite soon Jack was smitten. This discomforted George, who asked Virginia to intervene. He reminded her that it was illegal for a widower to marry his wife's sister, such a union having obvious incestuous undertones. Later, Virginia could not recall what she said to Vanessa, only Vanessa's rather bitter answer: 'So you take their side too.' George had approached Virginia as a last resort, Leslie having bluntly told him he would not interfere. And so Virginia 'wobbled' at once from George's side to her sister's.

George's resentment of Jack Hills was fuelled in part by his desire to mould Vanessa into an acceptable model of upper-class Edwardian womanhood. By the time he was thirty, in 1898, George, who had a considerable private income, served as the unpaid private secretary of Austen Chamberlain, the Postmaster-

General. George's dark curly hair, deep-set eyes and handlebar moustache made him the epitome of ostentatious virility. Despite this façade, he was deeply insecure. He sometimes cried when he could not get his own way. If his half-sisters argued with him, he would seize them in his arms and assert vociferously that he could not quarrel with those he loved. 'Kiss me, kiss me, you beloved,' he would shriek. As Virginia recalled, 'Everything was drowned in kisses. He lived in the thickest emotional haze . . . one felt like an unfortunate minnow shut up in the same tank with an unwieldy and turbulent whale.' In George, great sentimentality and great cruelty resided uneasily side by side. His father's early death had left its mark and he had been inordinately attached to Julia. He had not been pleased by Stella's marriage and, after her death, looked to his two half-sisters for affection.

His principal way of coping with his sense of inadequacy was to concentrate his energies on marrying into the highest echelons of society. Not surprisingly, George felt that Vanessa should share his ambitions. So he attempted to instil such aspirations by giving her opals, amethysts, and an Arab mare which she rode every morning before breakfast down the Ladies' Row in Rotten Row. When Vanessa threatened to refuse an invitation, George would resort to emotional blackmail.

The balls, levees, state dinners, garden parties, concerts, operas and theatre trips which filled George's engagement book did not hold much fascination for a young woman whose real interest was in the bohemian artistic world. 'Underneath [Vanessa's] necklaces,' observed her sister, 'was one passionate desire – for paint and turpentine, for turpentine and paint.' Vanessa endured many outings to the homes of the likes of the novelists Mrs Humphry Ward and Mrs W. K. Clifford. In particular, she came to despise Lady Arthur Russell: 'a rude tyrannical old woman, with a bloodstained complexion and the manners of a turkey cock'. A further invitation by that lady to her house in South Audley Street infuriated her. When they arrived, George refused to make an entrance with his half-sister in a temper. The carriage drove round the park and arrived once more. This time, George was in tears and Vanessa was understandably reluctant to enter the house. Vanessa's defection meant that George turned his attention to Virginia, who was obviously even more unsuitable than Vanessa to act as his companion.

The very morning after the débâcle with Vanessa, George arrived at Virginia's room bearing a piece of jewellery. His face was sallow and heavily lined. He told his side of the story: he had seen a look in Vanessa's eyes which positively terrified him; it should never be said of him that he made her do what she did not wish to do. Then he quivered, but quickly checked himself. He made a series of claims: he was only acting towards his half-sisters in the way that he knew their mother would approve; the two of them were the most precious things that remained to him; they were driving Gerald from the house, whereas he himself had, up to this time, been content to live at home. If he could not bring his friends to the house, he would 'be forced into the arms of whores'. Virginia, in her 'virgin consciousness', could only dimly conjure up 'horrible visions of the vices to which young men were driven whose sisters did not make them happy at home'.[19] Of course, George's language suggests that his affection for the half-sisters was, in strong part, incestuous. Nevertheless, Virginia promptly agreed to accompany her half-brother to the ball of the Dowager Marchioness of Sligo.

Now it was Virginia's turn to be thrown into the whirlwind round of soirées, parties and entertainments. Despite her retiring demeanour, George praised her first outing warmly and assured her that she needed only a little practice to be a great success. She was then invited, on a hot June evening in 1903, to the home of the Dowager Countess of Carnarvon, who, although she had been Vice-Reine of Canada and of Ireland, was, according to George, simplicity itself. At this time, as Virginia told Violet, George was considering the possibility of marrying the Dowager Duchess. He was 'weighing the worth of a somewhat elderly, but quite untarnished, Coronet'.[20]

At dinner, Virginia, very much in the manner of Violet, made a terrible gaffe when she chose to talk about the need to express emotions openly. That, she claimed, was the great lack of modern life. Virginia was sure that she had held the other guests at dinner spellbound and earned George's eternal gratitude. A bit later she noticed that the Countess was twitching and her half-brother was blushing crimson. Immediately after dinner, George drew Virginia aside and informed her that the company was not used to young women saying *any*thing. Then, as if to apologize for his wayward half-sister, he withdrew behind a pillar with the Countess, whom Virginia heard him kiss.

After dinner, the Countess, a Mrs Popham, George and Virginia went to a theatre where a French farce was playing. Snubbed, shy, angry and upset, Virginia found her attention wandering from the play. All of a sudden, she noticed people squirming in their seats. The hero was chasing the heroine round the stage. 'As the pursuit continued, the ladies beside me held to the arms of their stalls with claws of iron. Suddenly, the actress dropped exhausted upon the sofa, and the man with a howl of gratification, loosening his clothes quite visibly, leapt on top of her. The curtain fell.' The entire audience was shocked by this example of Gallic forwardness.

As if in a post-coital depression, the party of four filed dispiritedly out of the theatre. Not one word about the play was uttered. The Countess and Mrs Popham returned by carriage to Bruton Street, whereas George secured a cab to take Virginia and himself to the Melbury Road home of Holman Hunt. 'It's quite early still,' he petulantly informed her. 'And I think you want a little practice in how to behave to strangers. It's not your fault of course, but you have been out much less than most girls of your age.' Because the company at the famous painter's house was shabbier than that at Lady Carnarvon's, Virginia was more at ease and soon attached herself to a little covey of Kensington ladies. George, who acted as if he were a prince slumming it, tried unsuccessfully to ingratiate himself with Holman Hunt. At long last, the evening was over.

Back home and in bed, Virginia's mind was racing with various things, including diamonds, countesses and copulations on stage.

> Sleep had almost come to me. The room was dark. The house silent. Then, creaking stealthily, the door opened; treading gingerly, someone entered. 'Who?' I cried. 'Don't be frightened', George whispered. 'And don't turn on the light, oh beloved. Beloved -' and he flung himself on my bed, and took me in his arms.
>
> Yes, the old ladies of Kensington and Belgravia never knew that George Duckworth was not only father and mother, brother and sister to those poor Stephen girls; he was their lover also.[21]

This was Virginia's version in '22 Hyde Park Gate', which was read to the Memoir Club between March 1920 and 25 May 1921. Near the end of 1921 or in 1922, she took up the story in 'Old Bloomsbury', where she hints that George forced himself on her on successive occasions.

> It was long past midnight that I got into bed and sat reading a page or two of *Marius the Epicurean* for which I had then a passion. There would be a tap at the door; the light would be turned out and George would fling himself on my bed, cuddling and kissing and otherwise embracing me in order, as he told Dr Savage later, to comfort me for the fatal illness of my father – who was dying three or four storeys lower down of cancer.[22]

Taken together, these two accounts suggest that George fondled or petted his half-sister in a grossly inappropriate manner. Virginia could be very loose in terminology: 'lover' does not have to be taken to mean that George forced Virginia to have intercourse.

George was obviously sexually attracted to both his half-sisters; they resembled Julia, to whom he had been overly attached. He was jealous of Jack Hills, who had married one sister and wanted to marry another. George wanted to rule his half-sisters, to force them to conform to his own notions of polite behaviour. He may have been aware (or, more likely, suspected) that they had lesbian inclinations. Perhaps Virginia's behaviour early that evening made him especially anxious to exert control over her and the pornographic edge of the French farce might have further inflamed him.

Like his brother years before, George infixed a deep wound on Virginia's heart and soul. Her suspicions about how dangerous and devious men could be had been rekindled by Stella's death and here again she saw how male sexual aggressiveness could callously invade female privacy. Virginia was twenty-one in 1903 and not a willing participant in her half-brother's activities. The house in Hyde Park Gate was full of unresolved tensions and it is very likely that she did not cry out on that hot summer night – and the nights that followed – from a wish not to escalate the constant turmoil in which the Stephen and Duckworth families existed.

At about the same time as the incident with George, Virginia began the Hyde Park Gate diary. This journal of 157 entries is comprised mainly of thirty unpublished essays and writing exercises, on topics as varied as 'A Garden Dance', 'Stonehenge', 'The Wilton Carpet Factory', 'An Expedition to Hampton Court' and 'The Beginning of the Storm'. It is very much like the Warboys diary in that Virginia attempts to transform events in her daily existence into the stuff of art. Her disdain for society is evident, but in a passage which anticipates *Mrs Dalloway* she says that a hostess may appear 'heartless, but surely she does more good making the world laugh than by sitting at home & weeping over her own sorrows. The truth is, to be successful socially one wants the courage of a hero – there is nothing really so desperately difficult, I am sure, as laughter.'[23] But, once again, Virginia describes herself as an outsider in such gatherings: 'It was characteristic of our tête à tête that we confessedly chose seats from which we could watch the rest of the party.'[24] Virginia saw her position as a loner as reflective of the position of *all* women in society: 'we have this in common with the women of the world – we are equally at home everywhere – (not at all, that is to say)'.[25] From that vantage point she would later create some of her most successful pieces of writing.

Janet Case, who became Virginia's Greek teacher early in 1902, is the subject of one of the essays. Miss Case, who lived with her sister Emphie and supported women's and pacifist causes, was more professional than Clara Pater and her world of blue china, Persian cats and William Morris wallpaper. Although at first Virginia found her too remote, she soon discovered in her new teacher a person of ardent theories which she could express fluently. At their initial meeting, Miss Case became convinced that Virginia had not established a good foundation and accordingly obtained a grammar for her and made her start with the first exercise. Miss Case's fine human sympathy even extended to the interpretation of literary texts: 'She was always expounding their "teaching" and their views upon life & Fate, as they can be interpreted by an intelligent reader. I had never attempted anything of this kind before, & though I protested that Miss Case carried it too far, yet I was forced to think more than I had done hitherto.'[26] Virginia Woolf, the embryonic literary critic, learned a great deal from the opinionated and resourceful Miss Case, herself a prototype of the common reader. Quite soon, Virginia had a crush on her, going hot and cold as she journeyed to the Case house in Windmill Hill, Hampstead.

Another type of woman is prominent in 'An Afternoon with the Pagans'. Although Virginia avoided the company of aristocratic women, she remained bewitched by their beauty and glamour. This preoccupation reflects her curiosity about an aspect of her mother – and of her own femininity – from which she felt alienated. She once confided in Violet: 'they are all the things we poor writers try to write – and can't'.[27] In this essay she attacks the happy, luxurious, lazy pagan women whose lives fascinated George Duckworth: 'They have no reason to doubt; haven't the Gods provided them excellently well? They shut their eyes & suck down their sugar plum.'[28] Society women were often brilliant hostesses and an important side of Julia had been her tremendous capability as such. But in Virginia's mind this was linked to being an angel of the house, Coventry Patmore's term for a woman whose sole purpose in life was to minister uncomplainingly and invisibly to the needs of the males of a family.

In particular, Virginia was suspicious of Kitty Lushington, who married Leopold Maxse. Kitty was many things Virginia was not:

poised, worldly, adept in social gatherings. She could be icy, especially when too much emotion was displayed. 'Once,' Virginia recalled, 'I called Kitty "darling" in a telegram! and we have never been on good terms since.'[29] In comparison, Madge Vaughan and Violet Dickinson were superb nurses and hostesses, but they were deeply sympathetic to the notion of women as writers and artists. In these friendships, Virginia attempted to conjoin her femininity and her literary aspirations. She also found much happiness in the company of the daughters of Lady Bath, Beatrice and Katherine Thynne (who married Lord Cromer), and, especially, of Nelly Cecil, who in 1889 had married Lord Robert Cecil, third son of the 3rd Marquess of Salisbury.

The saddest and most solemn moment in the Hyde Park Gate diary is in 'The Serpentine', where Virginia describes how chilled she was by 'A Suicide's pathetic letter' in the *Evening News and Evening Mail* of 23 September 1903.

> Yesterday morning then, the first Park Keepers saw something afloat in the Serpentine – *What* it needed little looking to tell. Bodies in the Serpentine are not uncommon in the early morning. They drew it ashore & found that it was a woman who had been drowned, drowned herself presumably some hours before . . . A scrap of paper was found pinned to the inside of her dress as though she had meant to keep it from the water as long as possible. It was blurred but the writing was still legible. Her last message to the world – whatever its import, was short – so short that I can remember it. 'No father, no mother, no work' she had written. 'May God forgive me for what I have done tonight.'

Then Virginia shifts ground, as she begins to explore the motivation of the poor wretch. 'It was for her father & mother that this middle aged woman yearned – a father & mother, maybe, who died when she was a child.' There is a further change in direction, as the reader enters the mind of the dead woman: 'Without husband or children, I yet had parents. If they were alive now I should not be alone. Whatever my sin my father & mother would have given me protection & comfort.' Then Virginia imagines the magnitude of the woman's loss: 'For the first time in her life perhaps she weeps for her parents & for the first time knows all that they were, & her loneliness without them.' As she wrote these poignant words of empathy, Virginia was aware of Julia's death eight years before and of Leslie's impending demise: 'if your father & mother die you have lost something that the longest life can never bring again.'

She realized how much the plight of the suicide resembled her own. In addition, she had recently been wounded by George Duckworth's outrageous behaviour. And yet she was able to draw back from complete identification with the dead woman: 'But there was one thing left which might make life endurable – . . . & that was work . . . by work she meant bread & butter, but she also meant something nobler.' That something nobler was the self-respect and 'blessed peace' which comes from dedicating the self to a cause or a task beyond mere ego. As the Hyde Park Gate diary demonstrates, Virginia was becoming more and more aware of her own powers as an artist, and thus she could identify with and yet disentangle herself from the anonymous woman, upon whom she pronounced this blessing: 'Whoever she is that sleeps tonight in a grave without a name, may she sleep well, as surely the tired have right to sleep.'[30]

The solace which Virginia took from reading and writing was essentially solitary. On that score, she was keenly aware that her brother Thoby's existence was very different from her own. She informed him: 'I have to delve from books, painfully and all alone, what you get every evening sitting over your fire and smoking your pipe with Strachey, etc.' She was reduced to 'grubbing along'.[31]

At times, she was jealous of the hold other ladies – particularly society ladies – might have over Violet. She even invented an imaginary, demanding husband for her friend. The continual presence of Nurse Traill, who looked after Leslie, made Virginia keenly aware of just how good a nurse Violet was: 'The London hospital haunts me. I dream I'm a nurse there – which is of all likelihoods the least likely.'[32] A bit later, she confessed: 'Sparroy thinks of nothing but self cultivation, never does a practical stroke for anyone else. Do you think that's true, my Violet? Don't say so, if you do.'[33] Not surprisingly, Virginia sent the Hyde Park Gate diary to Violet that autumn. This was entirely appropriate. Violet was the muse of these miscellaneous writings, for it was her love that sustained the author and thus made it possible for Virginia to create them.

Conflicting emotions jostled Virginia as she became more aware of her father's worsening condition: 'He feels, I think, that we are just grown up, and able to talk to him – and he wants to see what becomes of us. In that way it's hard – for him.'[34] And there were the relatives who swarmed to see Leslie. Virginia likened them to parasites. Virginia's sense that her father's impending death would splinter the family even led her to think of George in a new light:

> I hope as the weakness increases he will worry less about money and his own helplessness . . . Gerald says he's going to leave us, and George says he's going to stay whatever happens – and they both agree that Bloomsbury is the best place. George has been so extraordinarily understanding and feeling about all this that one forgets his irritating ways, and I believe we shall all get on very well together.[35]

One way to cope with impending disaster was to search for a house to move to after Leslie's death. It was the terrible anticipation of death that consumed her, and in such moments her need for Violet was at its peak, as when she complained that her friend's letters were a little perfunctory: 'You are a Carping Rake . . . Anybody can write half a sheet, but can anybody cram in the amount of pure hot affection that I do? And it's not appreciated, only imitated and ridiculed, typical of so much in my life . . . I will lick you tenderly.'[36]

In December 1903, Virginia supposed that her family would somehow come through, but the way ahead was arduous. On Christmas Eve, Leslie was too weak to recite Milton's *Nativity*

Ode, a family tradition of many years' standing. And Virginia retained the capacity to blind herself to the direst realities: 'We are the sanest family in London and talk and laugh as though nothing were happening.'[37] By February 1904, the waiting had become intolerable. Violet's love maintained her and yet Virginia could become deeply angry with her:

> Don't think me a crazy tempered Beast for the way I growl. With no one else should I dare to behave so badly. But this is devilish hard, and I believe he is very bad. Nurse thinks this may be the beginning of unconsciousness – he is wandering a little tonight. However, there's nothing to be said – but that at all times you are the comfort.[38]

Virginia remained uncomfortably aware of her resentment towards her father, but his death on 22 February put her back in touch with the kind and generous side of him. Now, devoured by guilt, she wanted him every moment of the day. Later that month, the Stephen children and George spent about four weeks at Manorbier, on the south Pembrokeshire coast. The craggy Welsh landscape reminded Virginia of St Ives and those idyllic summers which had ceased ten years before: 'The dreadful thing is that I never did enough for him all those years. He was so lonely often, and I never helped him as I might have done. That is the worst part of it now. If he had only lived we could have been so happy.'[39] Her moods changed rapidly and she was in what she termed an animal state. On 8 March, she was delighted that George had gone back to London. 'He never lets one alone a moment. Very well meant, but wearisome.'[40] During that bleak time, Virginia sustained herself with the certainty that she somehow knew all that was necessary for writing a book. That vision came to her with brilliant clarity at Manorbier as she walked along the cliffs by the sea.

Virginia had become sure of her future as a writer and this certainty gave her the courage to do battle with the dark forces of death. Nevertheless, her self-confidence would be easily shattered. She was writing to prove to herself that her mental faculties were intact, but she was beginning to fear they were not. A measure of her ability to distort reality – and of her skill in righting herself – can be seen in her description of the much-cherished emerald ring given to her by her father. According to the jeweller who was asked to repair it, she had ruined it. 'It [returned] rather a better colour, but full of odd cracks, and marks, as it was before.'[41] Shortly thereafter, she reflected: 'Since I wrote my ring has improved wonderfully. I can't think why, unless its being in the light that does it – but it has got much cleaner and a better colour.'[42]

However, her anxiety increased markedly. This alone might have assisted the decision of the family to go to Italy. In any event, Gerald was scheduled to visit Venice and, most importantly, Violet was planning a trip to Florence. The two-day journey by rail and boat was exciting but seemed endless: a snowstorm in the St Gotthard Pass, the pure crystal blue of the Italian lakes and the dubious pleasure of the company of the Humphry Wards on the train. The Stephen–Duckworth party reached Venice at midnight on 5 April – Easter Sunday. At first they were told that there was no accommodation to be had. Finally, they settled into three very dingy rooms in a dirty little place off the Piazza San Marco.

Virginia, who had never before been further afield than Boulogne, at first found Venice amusing and beautiful. Soon, Gerald was bored and forbade them to explore the back streets. They had to go everywhere by gondola. Although Virginia was certain they were cheated all the time, the Italians were delightful and the four Stephens rapidly approached a state of general benevolence. However, the brightly coloured city began to grate: 'Venice is a place to die in beautifully; but to live in I never felt more depressed.' Virginia felt like a bird in a cage. In particular, the obvious sexuality of ubiquitous honeymooners disturbed her: 'All the world seems to be coupling itself.'

Two weeks later, the usually soothing presence of Violet did not make Florence, Prato, Siena or Genoa any more acceptable than Venice: 'There never was a *beastlier* nation than this.' She confessed to Emma Vaughan: 'My dear Toad, where is a decent woman to look sometimes?' The innumerable small boys and cripples who set upon them were an annoyance. She had also noticed a strange race of gnome-like women who haunted hotels. These creatures came out in the dark. In addition, their hotel became 'a sort of black cave'.[43] The nightmare did not recede when they reached Paris. To Violet, who was now back in England, Virginia pleaded: 'if you could only find me a great solid bit of work to do when I get back that will make me forget my own stupidity, I should be so grateful.'[44] In contrast, Paris offered Vanessa the visual and spiritual freedom for which she longed: there were visits to the studios of Rodin and Gerald Kelly and an encounter with Clive Bell.

Virginia felt cut off, friendless. She distrusted Vanessa, whose alliance with her had weakened in direct proportion to the elder sister's resentful conviction that she had to mother her mercurial sibling. Not surprisingly, Virginia in turn saw her childhood confidante transformed into yet another bossy caretaker. Her grief for her father remained overwhelming. She had been the favourite child, the chosen one, but she had come to dislike the man she resembled in many ways. Virginia returned home despondent, keenly aware of how isolated she was. The oppressive psychic forces which had been intermittently pressing upon her now began to dominate. Her pulse started to race uncontrollably. She heard voices which urged her to commit suicide. She became convinced that these utterances originated from overeating and decided to starve herself. Her sense of guilt was so strong that she became convinced that she had murdered her father.

The words 'mad' and 'insane' (although she did employ them to describe herself) are not of much help in describing Virginia's bouts of depression, acute anxiety and psychosis; in fact, they are misleading, uninformative and, ultimately, condescending. Ascribing a medical-sounding diagnosis to her mental illness also achieves little. Although there is evidence that some members of the Stephen family suffered from bipolar (manic-depressive) disorders and that Virginia may have inherited such a tendency, all the acute episodes of mental illness in her life tie in with fairly well-documented external events. Therefore, it is more useful to look at the causes of distress and the ensuing ways in which anxiety and depression were expressed.*

In the summer of 1904, Virginia was placed in the care of Sir George Savage, a prominent specialist in the treatment of mental illness and a friend of her father, and three nurses she considered loathsome. Then Violet Dickinson volunteered to take care of her at Burnham Wood, where despite the additional comforting presence of Nurse Traill, who had attended Leslie, Virginia made an attempt at suicide by throwing herself from a window which was fortunately not high enough from the ground to cause serious injury. Here, the birds sang in Greek and Edward VII, speaking in the foulest imaginable language, lurked in the azaleas. A few months later, she remembered that the voices instructed her to do 'all kinds of wild things.'[45] Virginia became obsessed with the idea of having – or looking after – a baby, almost as if she wanted to nurse or mother the wounded child within herself. Violet tried to find a suitable baby but was unable to do so. Unfortunately, no other information survives about this crucial incident.†

In early September, a considerably improved Virginia, accompanied by Nurse Traill, was able to leave Hertfordshire and join her family, who were staying at Teversal in Nottinghamshire. Savage insisted that Virginia live very quietly, if possible outside London. She must, he ordered her, endure the life of a valetudinarian for the next year. Gradually, Virginia felt that she had come to grips with the loss of her father; such sorrow, she now realized, 'is soothing and natural, and makes life more worth having, if

* The most elaborate examination of Virginia Woolf's bipolarity is contained in Thomas C. Caramagno, *The Flight of the Mind: Virginia Woolf's Art and Manic-Depressive Illness*.

† This information is contained in an undated fragment (*c.* 1943–5) of a letter by Violet Dickinson to Vanessa Bell at the Tate Archive. In this missive, Violet comments on Virginia's stay with her in 1904: 'I was terribly fussed over the Goat being ill that I brought her down; & she remained here for months. I went to Dr Schrwalback [*sic*] with Mrs Crum to try & get her a baby!' A few years later, Virginia was to be obsessed once again with the idea of having a baby.

sadder.[46] She now felt herself a recovered bird: 'I think the blood has really been getting into my brain at last. It is the oddest feeling, as though a dead part of me were coming to life.'[47]

Virginia returned briefly to London in the autumn, but it was felt that she should not take part in all the turmoil involved in moving from Hyde Park Gate to 46 Gordon Square. She went to stay with Caroline Emelia at her small house, aptly called The Porch, in Cambridge. Here, she could see Adrian, who was at Trinity (Thoby had gone down that summer). Soon, Caroline got on her niece's nerves: 'I hear the Quaker trumpeting like an escaped elephant on the stairs, which means that it is near lunch time, and Quakers don't like to be kept waiting for their meals!'[48] Leslie and his sister had never really got on well and Virginia was an uneasy witness to the relentless fidgeting of the elderly woman: 'I quite understand – only too well – Father's point of view about her. I don't know what it is, but I can sometimes hardly sit still, she irritates me so. She is perpetually flowing with rather trivial talk . . . Also I disagree entirely with her whole system of toleration and resignation, and general benignity, which does seem to me so woolly.'[49]

In addition to putting up with her aunt, Virginia missed her books and pictures and pleaded with Vanessa to allow her, contrary to Savage's advice, to return home to London. Understandably, Vanessa took the exasperating view that Savage's orders should be obeyed. 'My own baby,' she instructed her on 22 October, 'you must be well cosseted for a year.'[50] Then another cause of friction between the two sisters surfaced. F. W. Maitland, who had been chosen by Leslie to write his biography, asked Virginia if she would peruse some of her father's personal correspondence before he looked at it; he also requested a few pages about Leslie as a parent. Virginia agreed, but then Jack Hills, learning of Maitland's request, instructed her: 'Whatever you do, *don't* publish anything too intimate!' Virginia felt that Jack, who had no more sense of what a book should be 'than the fat cow in the field opposite', had overstepped himself.[51] Vanessa, who had a very soft spot for her brother-in-law, took his side.

Sisterly enmity between 'Billy Goat' and 'Maria' was resolved by a compromise: Virginia was to spend ten days at the new house in London and then stay in Yorkshire, from mid-November, with Madge and Will Vaughan at Giggleswick, where Virginia had deftly invited herself. That November, her newly buoyant spirits gave her the courage to launch herself, at long last, as an author. Violet provided her with the introduction to her first publisher, Mary Kathleen Lyttelton, the widow of Bishop Arthur Lyttelton and the mother of Violet's friend, Margaret. Mrs Lyttelton was the editor of the Women's Supplement of the *Guardian*, a weekly journal for the clergy. As Virginia confided to Violet, she was desperately eager to earn money: 'I don't in the least want Mrs L's candid criticism; I want her cheque!'[52] Mrs Lyttelton rejected the article on Manorbier – probably similar in content and style to the essays comprising the 1903 diary – which Virginia sent her, but within a month accepted two other pieces.

The die was cast. Virginia had become more aware of the immense strengths residing within her and knew that they must be expressed in writing. She told Violet of this inner explosion in September 1904: 'I am longing to begin work. I know I can write, and one of these days I mean to produce a good book. What do you think? Life interests me intensely, and writing is I know my natural means of expression.'[53] In the process of giving voice to her real self, Virginia was drawn back to her father and his career. She realized that she would have to become a very different kind of writer. At the same time, her obsession with Violet diminished considerably. Although orphaned, she had found her vocation.

Part Two

INNER PASSIONS

Chapter Five

AN INNER WOMAN

(1904–6)

'My poor little Monkey. I hope I wasn't too dictational to you?'[1] Vanessa asked Virginia in October 1904. Concerned about her role as substitute mother to Virginia, Vanessa relied increasingly on Sir George Savage's advice. His hold on Vanessa increased markedly when he informed her that he could take no fees for treating Virginia. As Vanessa informed the patient, she had objected in vain. Savage piously pointed to a photograph of Leslie and said that he was proud to do anything for his late friend's child. His sole concern was that Virginia should get well.

That month, Vanessa was in the midst of supervising the move to 46 Gordon Square in Bloomsbury,* a neighbourhood which adjoined working-class districts but was beginning to attract upper-middle-class professional families. For some of the Stephens' friends, this change was unseemly, especially when the four were abandoning the semi-pastoral delights of Kensington. The exceedingly proper Kitty Maxse, who lived in Knightsbridge, was shocked. Gerald decided to set up his own bachelor establishment. An inducement for George *not* to live with his half-brothers and sisters was the fact that, probably in the spring of 1904, Virginia had informed Savage of his sexual advances and the doctor had upbraided him. Before that, George, who was obviously thick-

* This area, bounded by Tottenham Court Road, Euston Road, Gray's Inn Road and, on the south, New Oxford Street, Bloomsbury Way and Theobalds Road, derives its name from Blemondisberi, meaning the 'bury' or manor of William Blemond, who acquired some of this land in the thirteenth century.

skinned, might have insisted on a place at Gordon Square. By now, though, having dropped his pursuit of the Dowager Countess Carnarvon, George had married the much younger Lady Margaret Herbert, daughter of the 4th Earl of Carnarvon. The wedding took place on 10 September 1904, while Virginia was still convalescing at Teversal.

The 'Gothic mansion', as Lytton Strachey dubbed the new house, was not dissimilar in size or plan to 22 Hyde Park Gate. There was an additional storey and slightly more space. The rooms were tall, elegant and decorated with cornices and elaborate ceiling roses. On the first floor were two main living rooms divided by folding doors, which could be thrown open to make a huge L-shaped room. Each sister had a sitting room and Thoby made the large ground-floor library into a study. They looked out on to trees and lawns, but the constant noise of cabs made them keenly aware of London. On some days, they were more conscious than they wished to be of 'interminable roar'. In a short story Virginia wrote in 1906, a young woman travels from her fashionable quarter of London to the area in which the Stephens had just settled:

> But if one lived here in Bloomsbury, she began to theorize waving with her hand as her car passed through the great tranquil squares, beneath the pale green of umbrageous trees, one might grow up as one liked. There was room, and freedom, and in the roar and splendour of the Strand she read the live realities of the world.[2]

Much later, in 1918, Virginia reflected that the gulf was one between the 'respectable mummified humbug' of Kensington and her new neighbourhood's 'life crude & impertinent perhaps, but living'.[3]

The reds and blacks of the Kensington house were replaced by lighter, airier colours: the walls were painted white, Oriental shawls were draped over the furniture and the chintzes were green and white. Vanessa tried to purge 46 Gordon Square of material and spiritual clutter. However, she rehung Watts's portraits of her parents and in the hallway displayed photographs of Victorian luminaries opposite a whole row of Julia Margaret Cameron's of her mother.

Virginia thought Vanessa a dictator because she insisted on adhering so rigorously to Savage's orders – which meant that Virginia had to curb her desire to return to London. She wanted to be part of the whirl of fashionable dissipation in which she imagined Nessa and Thoby now existed. Finally, by November 1904, she was allowed to settle in at Gordon Square.

At Giggleswick, Madge, who managed to squeeze in book-reviewing despite multitudinous domestic chores, had been so adept at encouraging Virginia's *Guardian* pieces that she became the young writer's 'foster mother'. Back in London, Virginia assured her that she accepted her flattery but was unsure of the extent of her talent: was it first-, second- or merely tenth-rate? In addition to book-reviewing, Virginia wrote a comic (now lost) life of Caroline Emelia and in December embarked on a companion piece (also lost) devoted to another aunt, Mary Fisher.

Virginia, who always had a soft spot for marsupials, took special delight that January in the London Zoo's 'wombatty wombat'.[4] The animal's shapelessness, obesity, short legs and waddle especially endeared him to her.

The four Stephens enjoyed being reunited and were elated to have been abandoned by the Duckworth brothers. Vanessa would read aloud from the silliest piece of fiction she could find and after dinner the four would sketch for an hour and a half. Adrian's efforts in this regard were mundane: he drew foxes. Thoby's sly sense of humour surfaced in a back view he made of God. Comicality was balanced with sobriety, as when Virginia reflected on the death of the thirty-three-year-old portrait painter Robert Brough in a railway accident: 'This carries out my theory that artists & people of gifts die earlier than the common herd. If he had been a Plumber, he would have recovered.'[5]

Virginia's uncertainty about the extent of her talent was not helped by Kitty Maxse, who provided a scathing list of objections to the short memoir of Leslie prepared for F. W. Maitland. As

Virginia told Violet, Nelly Cecil's comments were like lavender and cream after Kitty's. However, to her diary Virginia confided her disgust at the censure freely bestowed on her writing by Violet: 'I get nothing but criticism from Violet now – oh d—it, & this makes me determine to invite no more than is absolutely necessary . . . How I hate criticism, & what waste it is, because I never take it really.'[6] If Virginia was overly sensitive, she was also deeply ambitious, wanting to find a large-scale project to which she could devote the next ten years. She labelled herself 'a lady in search of a job'.[7]

When they met in January, Mrs Lyttelton, her first employer, was not a disappointment. She was a stolid person whom Virginia wished would 'pet' her. Teasingly, she informed Violet that the obviously maternal Mrs Lyttelton had distinct possibilities in that way. However, the young author saw herself as a little black goat who had been mistakenly welcomed into the fold of Guardianese, a state of being which combined the essence of governess, maiden lady and high-church parson. Virginia's first pieces for the *Guardian* show just how much of a black sheep she really was, for they are the work of a person with strongly held convictions.

This can be seen in her dismissal of one of the major tenets in W. L. Courtney's *The Feminine Note in Fiction*: 'Women, we gather, are seldom artists, because they have a passion for detail which conflicts with the proper artistic proportion of their work. We would cite Sappho and Jane Austen as examples of two great women who combine exquisite detail with a supreme sense of artistic proportion.'[8] Women, she observes, have been held back because they have not had the same educational opportunities as men. In her very first review, a notice of William Dean Howells's *The Son of Royal Langbrith*, Virginia praises the American as the exponent of the novel of thought as distinct from the novel of action. Later, she herself would become one of the great explorers of the terrain of thought. Virginia also turned her hand to the personal essay in 'On a Faithful Friend', a miniature biography of Shag, the family's Skye terrier who died in December 1904. There is a certain amount of guilt in this piece. When he got older, Shag was deposed by Gurth, with whom he quarrelled fiercely. Shag was sent away, mysteriously reappeared and was then killed on the accident-filled London streets.

For this tenacious young writer 10 January 1905 was a red-letter day: 'Found this morning on my plate my first instalment of wages – £2.7.6. for Guardian articles, which gave me great pleasure.'[9] However, review-writing and translating Thucydides did not fill Virginia's days and she was thus intrigued by a proposal from Mary Sheepshanks that she should teach at Morley College, which had been set up as an adjunct to the Old Vic on the Waterloo Road in South London to run evening classes for working people. At first Virginia was doubtful: [she] 'wishes me either to hold what she calls a "social evening" or to teach *English grammar*!! I have had to tell her that I am not sociable, and I don't know any grammar.'[10] Mary Sheepshanks hoped Virginia could find the right combination of gossip, sympathy and pedagogical skills to entertain and instruct the pupils assigned to her. The opportunity to teach history was a strong inducement. The discipline which her father had thought might be her true calling continued to intrigue her.

Mary Sheepshanks was the daughter of the Bishop of Norwich and, although a resident of that city, she was effectively the principal of Morley College from 1899 until 1913.* She was large, kindly and able, though she could also be outspoken and demanding, as when she inquired of Virginia: 'Miss Stephen, do you ever think?' Even before she met the bishop's daughter, Virginia thought Sheepshanks the ideal surname for Violet, whom she also dubbed a 'longshanked reptile'.[11] The link she saw between Mary Sheepshanks and Violet is clear: both women's maternal instincts led them to dedicate themselves to serving others. Virginia, who had been deprived of a formal education by her parents and had

* Mary Sheepshanks's powers of persuasion were evidently enormous and extended well beyond Virginia to other members of the Stephen family and circle. Vanessa taught drawing, Thoby (and Clive Bell) Latin and Adrian Greek.

experienced a great deal of difficulty escaping the confines of 22 Hyde Park Gate, decided to extend her helping hand to workers, especially women. This was as close to being the angel of the house that she could become.

From January 1905 until the end of 1907, Virginia Stephen taught at Morley College. On 6 January she told her diary: 'I am to start a girls' club at Morley, & talk about books.'[12] She presumably offered a slightly less facetious explanation of her assignment to Sir George Savage on 14 January, the day on which he pronounced her cured and discharged her. He instructed Virginia to lead an ordinary life and to forget her illness. He even invited her to dine with him.

Although Virginia had a tendency to describe her duties at Morley College in a light-hearted fashion, she took the responsibility seriously. When, for example, she was preparing English history lectures in April, she read Edward Freeman's *History of the Norman Conquest of England*, A. S. Green's *Town Life in the Fifteenth Century* and A. V. Dicey's *Lectures on the Relations between Law and Public Opinion during the Nineteenth Century*. Thorough preparation, however, was not always a guarantee of success. Virginia's English composition class of four men and six women included a fifty-year-old socialist who wanted to introduce Marxist concepts into an essay on autumn, a Dutchman who was sufficiently confused to think he was taking a class in mathematics and anaemic shop-girls who did not have time to do justice to the assignments. Mary Sheepshanks attended one of these classes and manifested her impatience with the apprentice teacher.

Shy, reticent Virginia Stephen soon vanished. When Mary Sheepshanks had first made overtures to her, Virginia had had a glimpse of this side of herself: 'I'm sure I don't mind how much I talk, and I really don't see any limits to the things I might talk about.'[13] Novice though she was, she soon realized that in order to set such scenes properly she had to avoid lecturing; she then spoke from notes, which allowed her to be more spontaneous.

Mary Sheepshanks and her associates looked coldly on history when Virginia proposed it as a subject; it had always been taught poorly at Morley College. Virginia insisted on this addition to the curriculum and was not discouraged when her class dropped from eight to four: 'but then those four were regular attendants, & they came with one serious desire in common. The change then, was to my liking.' In one student, a Miss Williams, she caught a glimpse of her own literary aspirations – and of some of the difficulties that lay ahead. Miss Williams was a reporter on the staff of a religious newspaper, the editor of which instructed his over-worked subordinate not to read the books assigned to her for reviewing: she should simply select quotations at random and then string them together with connecting phrases. Miss Williams was a writing machine and this was literature 'stripped of the least glamour of art: words were handled by this woman as [another student] manipulated the bottles of a patent mouth wash.'[14]

In addition to unleashing her considerable skills as a teacher, Virginia the would-be writer learned to make the past live. When she was preparing a lecture on the battle of Hastings, she wanted her account to be so vivid that it would make her pupils' 'flesh creep'.[15] This was often a daunting, impossible task: 'I do not know how many of the phantoms that passed through that dreary school room left any image of themselves upon the women; I used to ask myself how is it *possible* to make them feel the flesh & blood in these shadows?[16] On one occasion she was scheduled to take a group to Westminster Abbey. Only one student showed up and her attention was riveted on the mummy of a forty-year-old parrot which, she assured her teacher, 'makes history *so* interesting, miss!'[17]

Virginia saw her time wasted. She realized that her charges had 'tentacles languidly stretching forth from their minds, feeling vaguely for substance, & easily applied by a guiding hand to something that [they] could really grasp'. She was willing to provide the guiding hand, but she also knew that the minds of her pupils had not been properly cultivated. She asked herself: '[what] will be the use of that? Eight lectures dropped into their minds, like meteors from another sphere impinging on this planet, & dissolving in dust again.'[18] Such disconnected fragments had little power of being received or applied by those whom society had already failed.

Virginia may have been shocked by Miss Williams's callous editor, but she herself was subjected to similar treatment by Mrs Lyttelton, when she was instructed that February to trim severely a review of Henry James's *The Golden Bowl*. This review had already cost her a lot of time and trouble, so insult was added to injury when she had with 'literal & metaphorical scissors'[19] to reduce the piece to 800 words. Two months later, the would-be historian was dismayed when the *Times Literary Supplement*'s Bruce Richmond rejected her review of Edith Sichel's *Catherine de Medici and the French Reformation* on the grounds that the piece was not in tune with the academic spirit of his journal.* But Virginia was philosophical: 'I am really thankful to have the beastly thing in my waste paper basket, though I did waste time over it, as it was bad, and I knew it. However, he's sending me more books, and is polite.'[20] Leo Maxse, the editor-owner of the *National Review*, commissioned 'Street Music', in which philistine attitudes towards art are dissected and roundly condemned:

> Artists of all kinds have invariably been looked on with disfavour, especially by English people, not solely because of the eccentricities of the artistic temperament, but because we have trained ourselves to such perfection of civilization that expression of any kind has something almost indecent – certainly irreticent – about it. Few parents, we observe, are willing that their sons should become painters or poets or musicians, not only for worldly reasons, but because in their own hearts they consider that it is unmanly to give expression to the thoughts and emotions which the arts express and which it should be the endeavour of the good citizen to repress.[21]

Here, Virginia is attacking an attitude towards art and literature which embodies many of the views of Leslie Stephen, who did not

* Virginia's first review for *TLS* was published on 10 March 1905.

wish Thoby to become a writer because it was unmanly. Musicians, she also points out, are viewed by society as a particularly suspicious lot, because their melodies incite something within the audience which is wild and primitive. In particular, Virginia's defence of street musicians displays a growing identification on her part with society's outcasts. She was also becoming more aware of the search for form which must be at the core of any work of art, as when she responded rhapsodically to the James McNeill Whistler memorial exhibition: 'Oh Lord, the lucid colour – the harmony – the perfect scheme. This is what matters in life'.[22]

But the mundane often got in the way. Violet did not like 'Street Music', and the Morley College girls showed a propensity to be bored by history and maps. Virginia's bedroom was so messy that it resembled a city in a state of siege. At times, she even had to spend time doing what she hated most: shopping. Her blood boiled when her essay in *Academy & Literature* was reduced to a hodgepodge by the editors. She also had to put up with George's earnest wife, Margaret. In her most sarcastic manner, she informed Emma: 'we see a certain amount of our dearly beloved and intensely respectable sister in law'. On balance, however, things were going well: 'I am realizing the ambition of our youth, and actually making money.'[23] This was crucial to her self-esteem and to her pocketbook. Although Leslie had left over £15,000, the funds from the estate had to provide for Laura; the Stephen children received the remaining amount, which was to be split four ways.* Although she did not have to work, Virginia wanted

* Leslie's effects were worth £15,715 and his personal estate £8,906. In her will, Julia had left her entire estate (valued at £5,483) to her husband. The only amount guaranteed in his will was a sum (amount not specified) in trust for Laura. Since no provision was made for the Duckworth children, Virginia presumably received a quarter of the monies remaining (22 Hyde Park Gate was not sold until 1928, at which time it realized almost £5,000). At the time of her marriage in 1912, Virginia's capital was £9,013 16s. 9d. (Leonard Woolf Account Books, 1906–1912, Monks House Papers, University of Sussex). The latter sum had been augmented in 1909 by £2,500, the amount left to Virginia by her aunt, Caroline Emelia Stephen.

to. In part, she measured her success by the amount of money an editor was willing to spend in exchange for her services.

The brothers Stephen provided their sisters with additional stimulation, amusement and irritation. On 16 March, Thoby held the first of his 'Thursday evenings' at Gordon Square. Technically, the very first such evening was on 16 February, with only solemn, withdrawn Saxon Sydney-Turner and Gurth the dog in attendance. In the main, the guests were Thoby's Cambridge friends, such as Clive Bell, Ralph Hawtrey, Walter Lamb, Robin Mayor, Desmond MacCarthy, Jack Pollock, Lytton Strachey, Leonard Woolf and Hilton Young. Thoby was reading for the Bar and simply wanted amusing company. So he was 'at home' to his friends. Virginia found all these men insufferably smug. They were definitely not amusing; in fact, they were not 'robust enough to feel very much'. In contrast, she reflected, 'women are my line and not these inanimate creatures'.[24] For Virginia, this first Bloomsbury group was filled with nonstarters who obviously did not wish to share any of their masonic secrets with women.*

Adrian's prankish side at least provided comedy and suspense. An inveterate practical joker, Adrian and some Cambridge friends dressed themselves as the Sultan of Zanzibar and his entourage and successfully hoodwinked the Mayor of Cambridge, who received them at the Guildhall. This led to a headline in the *Daily Mail* of 4

* Virginia's no-nonsense approach to her brothers and their friends can be seen in her unpublished review (MS Sussex) of *Euphrosyne* (1905), a privately published volume of verse to which, among others, Clive Bell, Lytton Strachey, Walter Lamb, Saxon Sydney-Turner and Leonard Woolf contributed. Virginia's commentary is dated 21 May 1906. If young men are badly taught at Oxford and Cambridge, Virginia observed, perhaps it is after all a good idea that women be educated at home. These young writers are, in her opinion, both prim and priggish. Her sarcasm is extremely heavy: 'But their most permanent & unqualified admiration is reserved for the works which, unprinted as yet, "unprintable" they proudly give you to understand, repose in the desks of their immediate friends. For it is characteristic of them, that they live closely in one "set", & made but few acquaintances outside it.'

March 1905: 'MAYOR HOAXED. CAMBRIDGE UNDERGRADUATES DARING TRIP. SUPPOSED ROYAL VISIT. IMPOSTERS RECEIVED WITH CIVIC HONOURS.' The group gave their nefarious selves away when, immediately after their appearance, they scampered off to the railway station.

A little more than three weeks later, Virginia and Adrian set sail from Liverpool to Oporto. Their ship, the *Anselm*, was white, clean and luxurious. Virginia liked the sensation of being cut off from ordinary life, but a pesky don was a constant source of irritation. If she took up a book, he still besieged her. Still, there were many pleasures, as when the foam of the ship spread like white lace on the dark waters. On the way to Portugal and Spain, the vessel docked for a day at Le Havre, from where the Stephens took the train to Rouen. There Virginia thought the most touching thing was the statue of Joan of Arc, placed (in the corner of the meat market) on the spot where she had been burnt. Although Joan of Arc's death was commemorated, Virginia considered the statues of her shoddy. The brave woman had not found a sculptor worthy of her achievements.

A few days later, somewhere off the coast of Spain, Virginia had the pleasant sensation of being cut adrift altogether from the world. Hers was a dreamy existence, but there was another side to this experience: 'I feel completely demoralized, as though I were going through a second rest cure.'[25] Virginia did not wish to recall or relive the events of 1904; she was also attached to her book-reviewing and teaching.

From childhood Virginia and Adrian had often not got along, but this trip was a shared sentimental journey, especially when compared with their stay in Italy the previous year. At Lisbon they let loose a caged bird that was singing by Fielding's tomb. The elephantine beauty of Seville Cathedral overwhelmed and disgusted Virginia, but she was enchanted by the Alhambra in Granada, and the intense lemon yellow of the Mediterranean sun became a source of consolation. Nevertheless, she was happy to return on 24 April to Gordon Square, where her own bed awaited her.

★

'Nessa and I have been arguing the ethics of suicide all the morning, as we are alone, and what is an immoral act.'[26] So Virginia informed Violet on 30 April, almost a week after her return from Spain and Portugal. The intimacy between the sisters had been renewed, although it was just beginning to be threatened by Vanessa's growing interest in Clive Bell, one of Thoby's Cambridge friends. Virginia was also unsettled as to the nature of her own literary inclinations. That May, she disclosed to Violet: 'By the way, I am going to write history one of these days. I always did love it; if I could find the bit I want.'[27] Her diary was threatening yet again to sink into a premature grave. Further doubts about her own future can be gleaned in her review of Elinor Lane's *Nancy Stair*, set in eighteenth-century Scotland:

> She is motherless, and her unusual gifts determine her father to give her a man's education, in spite of a friend's warning that women are not meant to be civilized, and that it is useless to attempt it . . . She realizes 'how little value verse-making holds to the real task of living', and understands the real task of living to mean, for a woman at any rate, marriage and motherhood. The genius for poetry seems to be incompatible with the duties of wife and mother, and, as the least important, Nancy has no hesitation in quenching it in order to marry and live happily ever afterwards.

Although he had not given his daughter a formal education, Leslie had encouraged his motherless daughter to become a writer. Having embarked on this profession, Virginia, unlike Nancy, had serious doubts about exchanging it for the duties of wife and mother: 'The prosaic mind may be tempted to suggest that the world might, perhaps, be considerably poorer if the great writers had exchanged their books for children of flesh and blood.'[28] Here, she states the dilemma in black and white terms; later she would see it as a far more complex, vexed issue.

Virginia had to 'splash' about in racing society. That was how she described the time she was forced to spend with George and Margaret Duckworth. That June she and Vanessa went to a dance

Virginia Stephen. Mrs Morris from the drawing by D. G. Rossetti, *1904*

at Trinity College, Cambridge. They picnicked on the Cam, dropped their lunch basket in the water and consumed wet sandwiches. Vanessa met up with Clive Bell and Virginia spoke with F. W. Maitland. In her letters to Violet, she accused her of being a dangerous woman who did not exercise the right kind of influence over young girls. When she dined that July with Sir George Savage, Virginia was tempted to ask him exactly what bee entered her bonnet when she wrote to Violet. The doctor, she was certain, would diagnose 'Sympathetic insanity'.[29]

Although her tone is light, Virginia remained fearful that the melancholia which had assailed her the year before would return. 'Why do I write all about suicide and mad people?' she wrote to Nelly Cecil that August. She asked this when she copied out for Nelly a piece of verse from the *Daily Chronicle*. The author, a char who had hanged herself, had simply been overwhelmed by her many burdens. As a result, this poem concludes, 'I'm going to do nothing for ever and ever.'[30] In order to keep herself together and to avoid such a fate, Virginia needed the distraction of work. Like Jane Carlyle – whose letters she reviewed that month –'she was very sensitive and had an inner woman to defend'.[31]

On 10 August, the four Stephens set off for Carbis Bay, near St Ives. Like children who eagerly expect to be transported by magic, they took their seats on the Great Western train: 'We would fain,' Virginia observed, 'have believed that this little corner of England had slept under some enchanter's spell since we last set eyes on it.' It was strange to behold the familiar shapes of land and sea appear before them, as if the same impresario had raised the curtain that hung between them and the landscape of their past. The visionary mood was enhanced by the dusk in which they were enveloped as the train arrived, providing, as it did, a layer between their early memories and the reality of the present. Under the protective covering of darkness, they made their way to Talland House and peered at it from behind the escallonia hedge. What they saw was both reassuring and also somewhat disturbing: the house was unchanged. In a sense, time had stood comfortingly still, but, they also realized, the house was no longer theirs. Their childhood had vanished. Often during that holiday they felt like disembodied ghosts.

The inhabitants of St Ives immediately remembered the four and frequently approached them, anxious to reminisce. One old woman had tender memories of Julia, particularly of her great beauty and resplendent charity. This deeply touched Virginia: 'And as I heard those humble words of the love that one woman felt for another, I thought that no acclamation of praise throughout the whole world could sound so sweet, or could mean so much.' However, Virginia did have serious doubts about this concept of womanhood. Here, momentarily, she is drawn to the side of Julia which gave to others and not enough to her own children.

Often Virginia spent her afternoon in solitary tramps. In her response to the landscape, her love of it became fused with her growing awareness of herself as a writer dedicated to form, as when she observed: 'The impetuous sweep of the large bay, curving round so that it half completes the circle, gives one an impression of beautifully curbed vitality.' This is also the perspective of an artist. A similar intensity of vision is found in her description of herself and her companions lost in a forest of ferns which bound their legs and brought them to their knees. They blundered along in the approaching darkness, only to find the road reduced to a vague white mist. Finally, they found their way home, feeling 'like creatures lately winged that have been caught & caged'. There were other expeditions, such as the sail in the bay the four of them had long promised themselves. On that voyage they saw a solitary shiny black fin performing cartwheels. Soon, they were surrounded by a whole school of dolphins, who put on a demonstration of marine gymnastics.

Virginia was struck by how much of herself was preserved at St Ives. She was again in touch with the intense beauty and grandeur of summers long past. She did not wish to abandon those bittersweet memories, but she also asked herself: 'is it possible that one has come to that age when partings are more serious & meetings less pleasurable?'[32] Did she regret that the past was no more or was she fearful that pleasures as wonderful as those of childhood were forever closed to her? Both possibilities terrified her.

That November, back in London, Virginia relayed Kitty Maxse's disapproval of Bloomsbury to Nelly. The wings of gossip had also conveyed Kitty's fears that a fate worse than death might be awaiting Virginia: she 'might marry an *author* and they always talk about themselves!'[33] Even more nefarious events were afoot. The second attempt at a salon at 46 Gordon Square had been Vanessa's, when she began the Friday Club. This group, which was to meet weekly, was centred on the fine arts. That July, the organizing committee began to quarrel, which Virginia rightly felt was a sign of life: 'one half of the Committee shriek Whistler and French impressionists, and the other are stalwart British'.[34] Vanessa's genius for organization was unleashed, but Virginia was glad that she was not responsible for such an assemblage. Not only would she have been, as she observed, bored to death; she could not have stood the resulting conflicts into which Vanessa fearlessly waded: 'Old Nessa goes ahead, and slashes about her, and manages all the business, and rejects all her friends' pictures, and [they] don't mind a bit.'[35]

Often the surface of Virginia's existence seemed prosaic, as when she went to a dance and retired to a corner to read Tennyson's *In Memoriam*. But the internal drama sparkles in her letters, as in this snippet: 'Don't think anything uncharitable of me; and try to come back an unspoilt virgin in spite of your widened mind.'[36] While at St Ives, Virginia issued this order to Violet, who, with Nelly Cecil, was just about to embark on a round-the-world voyage, including a stay in Japan.* Just before this, Virginia had been stung by what she considered Violet's unjustly severe criticisms of some of her book reviews and essays. In fact, Nelly, who was a closet writer, had also become fearful of Violet's overly observant eye. In July 1905, she lent Virginia her writings, with the proviso that they should not be shown to their mutual friend. Virginia assured her: 'I will keep the conditions faithfully . . . I feel always that writing is an irreticent thing to be kept in the dark – like hysterics.'[37] Whether art was or was not allied to insanity was ultimately irrelevant: Violet could no longer be completely trusted. Despite her reservations, Virginia still clung to her motherly friend, as can be seen in her letter to Violet of 27 August: 'I suppose you have permanently attached to yourself at least six fellow passengers, and that all the steerage wives bore their babies under your guidance.'[38] And she still retained warm feelings for Violet: 'I hear that you are *everything* to Nelly; nothing left for me then.'[39] For Virginia, 'nasty sarcasm'[40] remained a barometer of true friendship.

* In 1907, Virginia wrote 'Friendship's Gallery', which is a comic biography of Violet, together with an extended, fantastical account of her and Lady Cecil's trip around the world. In this piece, the strong, reliant aspects of Violet's character are emphasized. In addition, Violet and Nelly are depicted as 'Two Sacred Presences' who save Japan and become there the titular deities of motherhood.

While she was struggling, albeit comically, with the absence of Violet, Virginia began to see her aunt, Caroline Emelia, in a new light. In December 1904, Caroline Emelia warned Virginia not to sell her soul for gold; if she became a writer, she should be sure to dedicate herself to the 'beauty of hard work';[41] like Leslie, she wanted Virginia to become a historian. This was one writer speaking frankly to the other. Virginia felt that she had to begin as a journalist, a profession about which her aunt had serious reservations. Despite their differences, a new liveliness entered their dealings, as when Virginia told her aunt, who was fond of marzipan, that death from a surfeit of almond paste would not be a seemly end for the most prominent Quaker at Cambridge. When Virginia informed her aunt in November 1905 about her various projects, Caroline Emelia replied: 'When I asked what you were doing I meant writing.'[42] Virginia was mildly stung by the not excessively subtle point being made.

Eight months later, in July 1906, Virginia had become sympathetic to her aunt. On that occasion they

> talked for some 9 hours; and she poured forth all her spiritual experiences, and then descended and became a very wise and witty old lady. I never knew anyone with such a collection of stories – which all have some odd twist in them – natural or supernatural. All her life she has been listening to inner voices, and talking with spirits: and she is like a person who sees ghosts, or rather disembodied souls, instead of bodies. She now sits in her garden, surrounded with roses, in voluminous shawls and draperies, and accumulates and pours forth wisdom upon all subjects. All the young Quakers go and see her, and she is a kind of modern prophetess.[43]

Caroline Emelia also revealed to her niece that she looked forward to death because it would be so much better than life. Virginia may not have been religious, but she was – and remained – extremely mystical. During this encounter, Virginia saw the connection between the 'shocks' which dominated her conception of the art of words and the 'inner voices' which fascinated her aunt. Both women were obviously interested in the world beyond appearances, the landscape which could only momentarily be discerned by the inner eye.

Her aunt was both a writer and Leslie's sister. In her, Virginia saw what a female writer could accomplish: she could explore the plotless terrain of thought, often of little or no interest to men, who relied on an overly rigorous devotion to symmetry and closure. Virginia's sense of her new literary self can be gleaned from her comments of April 1906 on Elizabeth Barrett Browning:

> The vigour with which she threw herself into the only life that was free to her and lived so steadily and strongly in her books that her days were full of purpose and character would be pathetic did it not impress us with the strength that underlay her ardent and sometimes febrile temperament. Indeed, there is no questioning her deliberate and reasonable love of literature and all that the word contains. Not only was she a very shrewd critic of others, but, pliant as she was in most matters, she could be almost obstinate when her literary independence was attacked.[44]

Although Virginia was not physically disabled, she often felt mentally impaired. However, she discovered an occupation which gave her purpose and character. Despite her frailties, Virginia the writer had a strong, stubborn sense of purpose, one most consistently revealed in her evaluations of other writers.

The moors, stone walls and bleak stone houses of Yorkshire became yet again, in April 1906, a pleasant respite from London. Madge and Virginia continued to offer each other extended criticism, but Virginia, staying this time at the home of Mrs Turner, who took in lodgers, led a solitary life. She read, wrote, walked with Gurth, took tea with Madge and dined alone. There was, she observed, a Greek austerity about such an existence which could go straight into a bas-relief. She hardly ever washed or did her hair. Instead, she took giant strides on the moors, shouting the odes of

Pindar as she leapt from crag to crag. As she quipped, she had become 'Stephen Brontëized'. She was acutely conscious of how great a pleasure it was to write.

Virginia's critical side was unleashed when Madge took her to visit a young master and his wife. She hated everything about them; in particular, she recognized something artificial about their extremely self-conscious confusion of literature with life. The couple were followers of William Morris and the interior of their cottage was an arts and crafts confection filled with ungainly tables, green carpets and rush chairs. The rusticity was too studied. The emotional crudity of the couple was enhanced by the fact that they had written their creed in red ink on a strip of paper over the hearth. Virginia was also disgusted by the fact that they had named their son after Morris. The wife had attended Cambridge and this led to Virginia's sharp observation: 'raw Newnham let loose upon the moors; to grow crabbed and stiff, and call it originality.'[45]

There was at least one event at Giggleswick Virginia did not confess to her diary. However, she informed her sister of the mysterious episode in a letter that is no longer extant and with scarcely concealed humour Vanessa replied on 15 April, upbraiding her wayward sister: 'Naughty Billy – to get up a flirtation in the train. You really aren't safe to be trusted alone. I know some lady will get a written promise of marriage out of you . . . It was lucky you had Gurth to look after you.'[46]

At the time Virginia was playing the coquette, Vanessa was beginning to treat Clive Bell's overtures with a modicum of seriousness. Arthur Clive Heward Bell was a magnificent intellectual wolf in tweed clothing. Thoby once described him as a sort of mixture between Shelley and a sporting country squire. At Trinity College, he could be seen in full hunting gear, complete with horn, in the company of his whipper-in, plus whip. An intellectual with a fine and original turn of mind, he was decidedly at home in the field. He was born to a *nouveau riche* Wiltshire family whose fortune was derived from coal. They had no genuine interest in the arts, but at Marlborough Clive developed a passion for reading which set him apart from his family. Their money and his interests led him to Cambridge.

Clive dressed well and he had a shock of beautiful curls. Those curls had prompted a seemingly innocent compliment from a neighbour, Mrs Raven-Hill, who soon afterwards seduced Clive, then eighteen. All his life, he maintained an exuberant heterosexuality, in direct contrast to the homosexual propensities of many of his friends. His sensuality was warm, ripe, always ready to explode. His conversation was animated. At Cambridge his intellect was not judged to be of sufficient quality to allow him to become one of the Apostles (Cambridge Conversazione Society), an elite secret debating group founded in 1826. He had had to settle for membership of the 'Midnight' play-reading society. There is little doubt that he was fervently committed to friendship and that he was Thoby Stephen's greatest friend.

The various component parts of Clive Bell were brilliantly summarized by Lytton Strachey in July 1905:

> There is the country gentleman layer, which makes him retire to the depths of Wiltshire to shoot partridges. There is the Paris decadent layer, which takes him to the *quartier latin* where he discusses painting and vice with American artists and French models. There is the eighteenth-century layer, which adores Thoby Stephen. There is the layer of innocence which adores Thoby's sister. There is the layer of prostitution, which shows itself in an amazing head of crimped straw-coloured hair. And there is the layer of stupidity, which runs transversely through all the other layers.[47]

If, as Strachey observed, Clive was a mixture of great sensitivity and an equal amount of density, what was the layer of innocence connecting him to Vanessa? A clue can be found in Clive's letter to Lytton of 20 July 1905: 'My chamber is literally heavy with the scent of deep red roses; Vanessa dined here last night and it occurred to me that red roses would suggest the appropriate setting; I found armfuls at Covent Garden. I was absolutely justified. The something of duskiness which clings to her was more limpid and translucent than ever before.'[48] The rich, heavy scent of the full-coloured blooms was a reminder of Vanessa's sensuous nature, but, as in Dante or *Der Rosenkavalier*, the rose also denotes a love which is courtly and spiritual. In Vanessa, Clive saw a beautiful woman who encapsulated his own earthy nature and his great love of music, books and, above all, art. For him, she was Rossetti's Blessed Damozel come to life. He wanted to do all he could for her: he lectured to the Friday Club and in November 1905 even sent two paintings to its first exhibition.

At first, Vanessa was amused but not deeply attracted, although her long-standing affection for her brother-in-law Jack Hills found a new focus in a man who came from similar origins and had identical views on how men were attracted to women and '"had" them incessantly'. Since Vanessa was determinedly pursuing a career, she did not offer Clive encouragement. He first proposed in July 1905 and was turned down. A year later, she again said no. At about that time, Virginia, who was a far from disinterested party, told Violet that Clive had reacted well to the rebuff. About her own reactions, Virginia was far less certain:

> [He] looked and laughed and jerked his head: and in fact I think he must have made up his mind to think no more of it. Nessa is afraid of showing 'encouragement' – but I think it is much more sensible to get back on to easy terms; and he evidently wishes it . . . These affairs of the heart are so perplexing! I shall never understand Bell's; unless he has them written red across his shirt front . . . Madge tells me I have no heart – at least in my writing: really I begin to get alarmed. If marriage is necessary to one's style, I shall have to think about it.[49]

Virginia omits to mention that the second rejection was a difficult one for Vanessa. If marriage was simply a state of friendship, she implied that she would have accepted him. In this way, she gave her suitor hope.

Virginia had been pursued, mildly, for some time by Walter Headlam, the poet and scholar, who was a lecturer in classics at King's and sixteen years her senior. Julia had invited him to

Talland House and he enjoyed a great reputation as a Hellenist, a pursuit which would immediately have gained Virginia's admiration. He was obsessive and single-minded, but when he looked up from a book – which was often – he had a lively sense of fun. Violet called him a trifler and, in December 1904, Virginia defended his honour: 'he is a true artist in his way, which attracts me more than anything else in people. An artist is always so much more simple and sincere than anyone else, though he may be flirtatious too.'[50] Virginia is being extremely disingenuous here. She was well aware that Headlam's real sexual interests were *said* to be confined to little girls and she knew, from her already extensive experience, that artists were not more simple and sincere than anyone else. She may have encouraged Headlam because, in her own best flirtatious manner, she knew the relationship could not lead anywhere. But – and this now became an important question – what if marriage were necessary to give heart to her style?

In the midst of this dilemma, the persistence of Clive Bell threatened to do away with the equilibrium of Gordon Square. If Vanessa married, Virginia would lose her. Such a possibility was both dismaying and irritating. A part of Virginia was obviously hostile to the man who wanted to whisk her sister away. She had no trouble understanding Clive's love for her sister, but there was a portion of him she found difficult to read and thus interpret. The truth is that Virginia found Clive Bell physically and spiritually attractive. Like Jack Hills, his strong sexual feelings for women were good-natured and open. He was not furtive like the Duckworths, who were tied to their mother and to incestuous feelings for their half-sisters. In Headlam, Virginia glimpsed, however obliquely, the stale, fetid world of her unhappy past. In contrast, Clive displayed his feelings openly and thus represented the very antithesis of the hothouse repression which had ruled 22 Hyde Park Gate. He was uncharted territory.

Virginia had begun to wonder about the dangers of being unresponsive to the love of men: 'there is something indecent, to my virgin mind, in a maiden having that kind of heart'.[51] Virginia was still trying to sort out this predicament in August 1906 when she and Vanessa rented Blo' Norton Hall, a moated Elizabethan manor house in Norfolk on the Little Ouse river, about seven miles west of Diss. The house was something of a disappointment. According to Virginia, it was so obnoxiously antiquated that only Americans could revel in its medicinal virtues. There the sisters enjoyed, she said, 'a kind of honeymoon, interrupted . . . with horrible guests'.[52] These included Thoby, Adrian, Emma Vaughan and George Duckworth. Vanessa painted windmills and Virginia tramped, leaping ditches, scaling walls, and even, she claimed, desecrating churches. In this hideaway, Virginia revelled in writing stories.

'Phyllis and Rosamond' and 'The Mysterious Case of Miss V' were probably revised during this stay, whereas 'The Journal of Mistress Joan Martyn' was in large part inspired by Norfolk. Phyllis and Rosamond Hibbert are sisters who have been raised in accordance with the prescribed norms of society's expectations of women: they are to marry, have children and hold no ideas of their own. The principal event in this narrative is an encounter between the Hibberts and one of the Tristram sisters at the latter's Bloomsbury home. Although they, like Phyllis and Rosamond, have not been to college, Sylvia Tristram and her older sister have imbibed a spirit of freedom, which attracts and yet repels the visitors. According to Sylvia, the life of the Hibbert sisters is repulsive: 'My God. What a Black Hole! I should burn, shoot, jump out of the window; at least do something!'[53] As the story concludes, although Phyllis and Rosamond have glimpsed freedom, they have retreated back to their gilded cage. Here, the sour air of 22 Hyde Park Gate is unfavourably compared to the delectable licence of Gordon Square. Only someone who felt that she had escaped from gaol could have written this piece.

Miss V and her sister are inconsequential grey shadows in the London whirligig. Clara and Tettie Pater may have been Virginia's inspiration for the two Miss Vs, but the story is really a commentary on women in society. Are women simply shadows whose substance is never questioned?

In 'The Journal' a forty-five-year-old medievalist, Rosamond

Merridew, succeeds in gaining access to Joan Martyn's diary, a document not highly regarded by her descendant, John. Joan, who died at an early age before she could marry, had a great deal of affection for her mother but distrusted her view of the world. Instead, Joan is drawn to the romantic tales related by Master Richard and Elizabeth Aske. 'If I ever write again,' Joan says, 'it shall not be of Norfolk and myself, but of Knights and Ladies and of adventures in strange lands.'[54] The unresolved issue is why Joan does not realize that her own experience – which constitutes the bulk of the narrative – is completely valid subject matter. Is it because women have been taught to value certain kinds of narration which have little or nothing to do with their lives?

Virginia and Vanessa had only a week back in London before leaving, accompanied by Violet, for Greece on 8 September, Thoby's twenty-sixth birthday. Virginia packed a pair of Nelly's pyjamas, quizzing her: 'Don't you think this opens a very intimate and slightly bizarre chapter in our relationship?' Before they set off, George had warned them in the most dire terms that women should not travel alone. Virginia, who was 'fizzing' with excitement at the prospect of visiting the ancient temples and landmarks of the literature she adored, became in the process bad-tempered, as Vanessa and Violet frequently reminded her.[55] The sisters also ganged up on their elder friend, who was informed that she was acting like a stuffy old governess. The three women travelled through France and Italy, sailed to Patras and met up with Thoby and Adrian, who had ridden on horseback through Albania, at Olympia on 13 September. The party journeyed to Athens via Corinth, subsequently visiting, among other places, Epidaurus, Tiryns and Mycenae.

For Virginia, modern Greece seemed flimsy and fragile when set against the pageant which had passed so long before. She felt herself very much a belated pilgrim, since the builders and inhabitants of the shrines were long vanished. This did not stop her from responding enthusiastically to the dark purple of the hilly landscape and the sea of deepest blue. The landscape was 'always in a state of ferment & effervescence; every journey you take seems to lead through beautiful, or majestic or romantic country places. There is no rest; but a perpetual curve & flow, as if the land ran fluid & exuberant as the sea.'[56] A Baedeker was of limited use, since the eye had to 'spring like a creature set free' and discover spontaneously the beauty it craved. The taste of Homer was in her mouth.[57]

On the return journey from the Peloponnese in late September, Vanessa became ill at Corinth. She travelled with Violet to Athens, where she was again afflicted. It took two weeks of rest and four tumblers of champagne each day before she was well enough to be carried on a litter to the boat for Constantinople. Meanwhile, Virginia and her brothers went to stay with friends of Thoby's at Achmetaga, Euboea. On Sunday, 21 October, Thoby returned to England; the others met up with Vanessa and Violet in Constantinople, where Vanessa remained sickly. Finally, the dispirited group boarded the Orient Express on 29 October and arrived back in London on 1 November to find Thoby in bed with fever. Vanessa was shocked to discover her brother was also ill. She collapsed. Her illness was obviously a combination of physical breakdown, the nervous strain of looking after Virginia and agitation about Clive Bell. She could no longer cope and so Virginia had to look after her ailing brother and sister.

Margery Snowden, a friend of Vanessa from the Royal Academy Schools, arrived to supervise the nursing of both invalids. After a week, her patients seemed to be over the worst and she left. Then Thoby took a dramatic turn for the worse. His diagnosis of malaria was changed to one of typhoid fever. Clive Bell was often at the house, lending very much needed assistance. In the midst of this crisis, Virginia became jealous of Clive's increasing power over her sister. In particular, she was afraid that Vanessa's love of him would ultimately displace her: 'I look at him and think how one day I shall look him in the eye and say, "you're not good enough" – and then he will kiss me, and Nessa will wipe a great tear, and say we shall always have a room for you.'[58] Meanwhile, Thoby became delirious and incoherent. He was operated on and died three days later on 20 November.

Two days after Thoby's death, Clive proposed again and was accepted by Vanessa. Virginia thus suffered two cruel losses that November and, as with Stella, death and sex were again uneasily combined. Thoby had been for Virginia the embodiment of a masculinity which was both virile and tender. The sexual demands of Clive Bell, she felt, would exclude her from the intimacy she desperately wanted with Vanessa. Despite these awful setbacks, for the past two years Virginia had been discovering tremendous powers within herself and the events of that grim autumn did not overwhelm her. Thoby – his life and his death – would later find his way into her novels, especially *Jacob's Room* and *The Waves*.

She was understandably reluctant to set down her tormented reflections on these new, horrible twists of fate, but she realized that Violet Dickinson, who had also come down with typhoid fever and was herself in danger of dying, would become inordinately depressed if she knew that Thoby had succumbed. And so Virginia – in a series of letters from 20 November until Violet's accidental discovery of Thoby's death in a newspaper a month later – kept him very much alive:

23 November
There isn't much change. His temperature is up to 104 again this afternoon, but otherwise his pulse is good, and he takes milk well. The nurse is nice and quiet. The doctor hasn't been yet, but I write to catch the post.[59]

25 November
Thoby is going on splendidly. He is very cross with his nurses, because they won't give him mutton chops and beer; and he asks why he can't go for a ride with Bell, and look for wild geese. Then nurse says 'won't tame ones do' at which we laugh . . . And now that Thoby is out of danger things will go swimmingly: only my dear old furry one must heal up – and come to a festal dinner.[60]

29 November
Dear old Thoby is still on his back – but manages to be about as

full of life in that position as most people are on their hind legs. He asks daily after you, and whether you have sloughed yet, and how many spots you had, and what your temperature is. Shall he come and see you, or will you come and see him first?[61]

An obvious criticism can be made of Virginia's conduct: she told lies and should not have done so. This is irrelevant. These are splendid imaginary pieces of writing, skilfully combining biography with fiction, in which Virginia re-created her brother. In them Virginia indirectly asked herself whether the act of writing could become a bulwark against the armies of death.

She always experienced a great deal of difficulty in being the angel of the house, but this attempt at fiction was undertaken in order to nurse Violet back to health, to give her friend the confidence that she could beat a cruel disease and to keep her alive. These letters show a selfless person and a writer of considerable power. When the ruse was over, she asked Violet: 'Do you hate me for telling so many lies?' She truthfully answered her own question: 'You know we had to do it.'[62]

Chapter Six

PASSIONATE MAIDEN HEART

(1906–10)

'I feel perfectly happy about her,'[1] Virginia assured Violet, commenting on Vanessa's engagement on 18 December 1906. The underlining emphasizes the desperation in the sentence – and reveals Virginia's genuine feelings about losing her sister. She also tried to discover the 'unknown' Thoby by assiduously questioning his friends, Saxon, Clive and Lytton. In an attempt to hold things together, she was bold enough to invade previously inviolate male preserves. Having been forced to give up her sister, she wanted to recapture her mysterious elder brother.

Clive Bell occupied a dubious middle ground. He was taking Vanessa away, but he had been a close friend of Thoby. Despite indications to the contrary, was he, like Thoby had been, an embodiment of chivalrous manhood? On 20 December, in order to reach a decision on this vexed issue, Virginia demanded of Clive a description of himself. Archly, she assured him: 'The general opinion seems to be that no one can be worthy of her; but as you are unknown this is no reflection upon you.'[2] Without being fully aware of the consequences, Virginia was initiating an investigation which would eventually cause her a great deal of anguish.

Virginia's early judgement was that Clive was an inconsequential figure in comparison to her father and Thoby. When she beheld Clive 'twitching his pink skin and jerking out his little spasms of laughter,' she wondered 'what odd freak there is in Nessa's eyesight'.[3] Nevertheless, Virginia wanted to be generous because, as she well understood, 'any happiness is so rare that it must be treated tenderly at all costs'.[4]

Early signs of Clive's possible unworthiness could be discerned in his parents and their home, Cleeve House, Seend, Wiltshire, a Victorian pile masquerading as a Jacobean baronial mansion. Mr Bell could be outrageously bad-tempered and Mrs Bell, a rabbity-looking creature, constantly attempted to mollify him. Cleeve House was filled to bursting with hunting gear, as well as stuffed and live animals. The bucolic boisterousness of the inhabitants overwhelmed both Vanessa and Virginia. The inkpot – made from the hoof of a favourite hunter, whose name and date of death were inscribed upon a silver cartouche – placed on the table on which she wrote became for Virginia a symbol of the uneasy mix of connoisseurship and barbarity in Clive.

On New Year's Eve 1906, Virginia and Adrian joined Vanessa and Clive at Cleeve House. The Bells were exceedingly polite, but for Virginia they were rich, gauche and illiterate. At dinner, Clive's sisters wore pale-blue satin dresses. An additional touch was the satin bow adorning the hair of each woman. In Virginia's view, coyness was thus added to pretentiousness. On New Year's Day, she exploded at lunch and stormed out of the house. When she returned that evening, she was extremely embarrassed by her boorish behaviour and sought refuge in excessive charm.

In addition to Virginia's worry about losing her sister was her concern about whether she should consider marriage a viable option for herself. Violet and Kitty actively promoted this possibility and Virginia flirted with the idea. By such a move, she might gain financial and psychological security. She might even be able to overcome the coldness which she discerned in her work. Still, she found their advice crude and disgusting. On 3 January 1907 she was blunt with Violet: 'If either you or Kitty ever speak of my marriage again, I shall write you such a lecture upon the carnal sins as will make you fall into each other's arms . . . Ever since Thoby died women have hinted at this, till I could almost turn against my own sex!'[5]

Virginia felt herself uprooted. Some of her unease with her own writing can be seen in a January 1908 review of *The Sentimental Traveller* by Vernon Lee [Violet Paget], where she attacks a fellow woman writer for her impressionist technique. According to

Virginia, Lee 'lacks the exquisite taste and penetrating clearness of sight which makes some essays concentrated epitomes of precious things . . . Perhaps the most satisfactory essays in the book are those that treat of real people.'[6] She is able to dissect Vernon Lee so accurately because she was well aware of a similar propensity to avoid the real in her own work – and life. However, when Nelly Cecil invited her to her home, Gale Cottage, Chetwood Gate, Uckfield, she was quite frank about the reasons for her refusal: 'there are times when my company seems an infliction to myself, and therefore a curse to others; but whereas I can drug *it* (that is me) in a book, or an ink pot, you would have the creature crude and naked.'[7]

Who, she constantly asked herself, was the real Virginia Stephen? A cold-blooded person who, she improbably claimed, knew nothing about humanity? A woman of 'very little sexual charm'?[8] An impressionist writer who had no grip on reality? These were the numbing, anxiety-ridden questions she had to wrestle with at the time she suffered the loss of Thoby and Vanessa.

Vanessa's wedding took place at St Pancras Register Office on 7 February 1908. A few days before that, Henry James called on Vanessa to present her with a silver box. He was startled by the ripe eagerness for life he witnessed 'in that house of all the Deaths'. He could see nothing but the ghosts, 'on all of whom these young backs were, and quite naturally, so gaily turned'.[9] In this case, James may have mistaken the surface for the macabre inner reality of the situation. On the evening of 6 February the wedding party went to Covent Garden to hear the most appropriate of wedding operas, *Fidelio*. The next day, George lent his car and chauffeur for the occasion. However, the driver, not used to such low-life haunts, got lost on his way to St Pancras, making Vanessa and Virginia late for the ceremony. The same person caused the newly married couple to miss their train at Paddington. Vanessa used the delay to pen a note to Virginia, who had collapsed into a state of numb desolation.

Virginia was often able to conceal desperation with manic

outbursts of considerable wit and humour, as in the letter she wrote her sister the day before the ceremony:

Address of Congratulation
to our
Mistress
on her
Approaching Marriage.

This missive was signed by four of Virginia's personas: Billy, Bartholomew, Mungo and WOMBAT. These good-natured creatures express their sorrow that, despite their assiduous wooing, their mistress has chosen to marry another. This impediment aside, they hope to remain her lovers. In fact, they generously bestow a benediction upon the groom, the Red Ape: 'We have examined his fur and find it of fine quality, red and golden at the tips, with an undergrowth of soft down, excellent for winter. We find him clean, merry, and sagacious, a wasteful eater and fond of fossils. His teeth are sharp, and we advise that you keep him on Bones. His disposition is Affectionate'.[10] Perhaps, the writer is implying, things can stay the same. Perhaps apes can lie down with wombats.

There was an additional anxiety. Virginia had to find a place to live for herself and Adrian, since Vanessa and Clive were to settle at Gordon Square. Virginia, who had been in the midst of a severe depression during the previous house-hunt, was now left to do the foraging. This was no easy task. She wanted to be within easy walking distance of Gordon Square, but she did not wish to be too close to her sister's new home. They needed breathing space from each other. By 15 February, she was close to deciding in favour of 29 Fitzroy Square, the lease of which was owned by a former resident: Bernard Shaw. Even when Shaw had moved there in 1887, the interior of the building was a mess, though it boasted a handsome façade. In the intervening twenty years, things had gone from bad to worse. The house itself, which had electricity, could be remedied for £150. The real problem was the disreputable neighbourhood. Beatrice Thynne was shocked – and begged her friend to reconsider. Violet also had serious reservations. How much weight, Virginia wondered, should she attach to that most nebulous of entities, respectability? The surrounding streets were dingy but no worse than those around Gordon Square. If she hinted at even the slightest possibility of living in shabby surroundings, she knew that the Duckworths and Jack Hills would descend upon her and prevent her from taking the house. The police were consulted and gave their assurance that the environs were safe enough, but the final decision was wisely left to Sophie Farrell. That redoubtable person, with the considerable forces of persuasion at her command, urged Virginia to take the house. In fact, she went so far as to promise her mistress health, happiness, no repair costs and minimal housekeeping expenses.

The only genuine relic of grandeur in the neighbourhood was the beadle, in top hat and a tail coat piped with red cord and adorned with brass buttons, who marched around the square to keep children in line, although number 29's position on the south-west corner of the square did give a view of two stunning Adam façades. The ground floor was given over to Adrian's study and the dining room behind it. The first floor was entirely taken up by the beautifully proportioned drawing room, with long windows overlooking the square. This room had a clashing colour scheme: red brocade curtains and a green carpet. In the back part of this little-used room was a pianola, out of which Adrian would pump melodies by Beethoven or Wagner. When Lady Strachey paid her first visit to Virginia at the house, Hans the dog made a mess on the green carpet. Both women pretended not to notice.

Virginia's workroom was on the second floor. Books were arranged in untidy piles and the windows were doubled so that the noise of the square was reduced. The focal point of this room was the high table on which Virginia wrote standing, usually for two and a half hours in the morning.

Quite soon, Thursday evenings were extended to Fitzroy Square. The menu was the same – buns, cocoa and whisky – but a new sense of inquiry was apparent. Earlier, Clive and Virginia had hurled abuse at each other and Virginia sometimes spoke with great excitement. She had just begun to question the cloistered aridity of some of her male companions. Still, constraint reigned. The epiphanic moment may safely be assigned to an unknown date in 1908 when Lytton Strachey arrived and pointed his finger at a stain on Vanessa's white dress: 'Semen?' Can one really say it?, Virginia asked herself before bursting out in uncontrollable laughter.

> With that one word all barriers of reticence and reserve went down. A flood of the sacred fluid seemed to overwhelm us. Sex permeated our conversation. The word bugger was never far from our lips. We discussed copulation with the same excitement and openness that we had discussed the nature of good. It is strange to think how reticent, how reserved we had been and for how long.[11]

Virginia penned this recollection in 1921 or 1922. Her liberation from convention was not quite so immediate as she makes it sound. During 1907 and 1908, she was often a diffident, silent witness to what were still largely male conclaves. Duncan Grant remembered that at the outset Virginia was an unsatisfactory hostess: 'She appeared very shy and probably was so, and never addressed the company. She would listen to general arguments and occasionally speak, but her conversation was mainly directed to someone next to her.'[12] In particular, she was aloof and a bit fierce to the men, but more open to women friends, especially Clara Pater and Janet Case.

On 1 July 1909, Adrian witnessed his sister in a more assured but more perverse mood when a Miss Cole joined the group at half-past eleven that evening. Virginia paid her a compliment: 'Of course, you Miss Cole are always dressed so exquisitely. You look so original, so like a sea shell. There is something so refined about you coming in among our muddy boots and pipe smoke, dressed in your exquisite creations.' Miss Cole would have been exceedingly dense not to realize that she was being mocked, but when Clive pressed similar compliments on her, the poor woman's embarrassment became obvious. At this point Virginia interrupted: 'I think Miss Cole has a very strong character.'[13] The villainous in-laws continued to set traps for their victim, who remained the uneasy centre of attention until her tormentors were diverted. A very different Virginia, one who now actively collaborates with Clive Bell, can be glimpsed in this episode.

From early 1907, Virginia saw herself as an acolyte locked out of the temple that was Vanessa; she was the worshipper outside, while Clive had free access to the goddess, her sister. Of course, by making Vanessa into some sort of elemental figure, Virginia removed her from ordinary life and from emotions experienced by mere mortals. Once again, she made her elder sister into a 'Saint' whose needs did not have to be considered. Vanessa, as she informed Clive in June 1910, was fully aware of this idealizing process: 'Virginia since early youth has made it her business to create a character for me according to her own wishes & has now so succeeded in imposing it upon the world that these preposterous stories are supposed to be certainly true because so characteristic.'[14] If Vanessa did not have human feelings, Virginia did not have to worry about stamping on them.

In the first few months after the marriage, Virginia continued at Morley College and wrote reviews. In addition to the torment of exclusion, she felt like an errant child when she did not respond warmly to the overtures of George Duckworth and his wife, who made her feel ten years old: 'I always expect George to give me half a crown and Margaret to open a cupboard and bring out a box and take off the lid very slowly, and give me a large, rather nasty sweet . . . which I shall drop in the gutter on the way home.'[15] Quite soon after her marriage, Vanessa confessed to her sister that she had become painfully aware that the Bell and Duckworth families shared the same stupidities about money and propriety. Virginia's own worries centred on her career, and increased when she took tea with Henry James on 25 August 1907: 'My dear Virginia, they tell me – they tell me – they tell me – that you – as indeed being your father's daughter, nay your grandfather's grandchild – the descendant I may say of a century – of a century – of quill, pens and ink – ink – ink pots, yes, yes, yes, they tell me – ahm m m – that you, that you, that you *write* in short.'[16]

That August Vanessa was three months pregnant and experiencing morning sickness. In contrast, as she informed Violet, Virginia felt as fertile as a teapot which found it necessary to empty its brew, in the form of letters, on someone. A while later she asked the same correspondent: 'shall I ever bear a child I wonder?'[17] Here she is speaking metaphorically, publishing a book being equated with bearing a child. Three weeks later she observed that young men were so uninterested in her that she would spend her days as a virgin, an aunt and an authoress. Added to the loss of Vanessa was a corresponding feeling of jealousy at her sister's fecundity.

Ire was further aroused by a postcard from the now loathed Sheepshanks, summoning her to teach on Mondays. In turn, Virginia 'blasphemed'[18] her employer on a postcard and was promptly and curtly reminded that she herself had chosen that day of the week on which to offer instruction. So on 30 September she lectured to four working men on Keats: one had a bad stutter, one was an Italian who read English as though it were medieval Latin and another was a degenerate poet who ranted and blushed and almost seized her hand when they happened to like the same lines. By December, Virginia had had her fill and resigned from Morley College.

Her own writing made her blood run cold and she was also experiencing considerable difficulty in reading Clive's character: 'it will really be some time before I can separate him from'[19] Vanessa. As her language betrays, a part of her wanted to wreck the Bell marriage. Two other persons were making demands on Virginia. She and Nelly Cecil disagreed about the relationship between art and morality. In the face of her friend's strong opinions, Virginia maintained that there was no essential link between the two. Caroline Emelia's health was faltering and, when she visited her in December, Virginia was not impressed with the spouts of pure joy which her aunt felt emanating from her own entrails. She was deeply irritated when her aunt asked her if she felt this wondrous blessing: 'Ah God, I would as soon tell the butcher which was my jugular artery, or the thief which was my diamond ring. She hopes to suck blood and bread from me.'[20]

Virginia's overwhelming sense of being drained, as she well knew, was really centred on her worries about her writing and her sister. Mercifully, there were some diversions. In December a play-reading society was formed. This group – Clive, Vanessa, Virginia, Adrian, Lytton and Saxon – met alternately at Gordon and Fitzroy Squares. Their first performance was devoted to Vanbrugh's *The Relapse*. Naturally, Lytton was Lord Foppington.

At the time Julian Bell was born on 4 February 1908, Virginia was struggling to bring her first novel, *Melymbrosia*, to life.* She put this aside to write for her nephew a biography (*Reminiscences*†) of his mother. This piece was also written for Vanessa, to remind her that, although she had become a mother, she and Virginia shared a common, unhappy past. In turn, the subject assured her sister that she had got everything right. Julia, Stella, even Jack Hills were vividly evoked; blame was placed squarely where it belonged, on George's commonplace shoulders.

That winter and spring, Vanessa struggled with her feelings for Julian. She was sure that she played the part of the proud young mother even less well than she had acted the role of the engaged young lady. She missed the atmosphere of rarefied talk which had once been an essential part of her life and yet she found the bond linking her to the baby an increasingly powerful one. Although Clive liked the idea of babies, he was never the ideal father for new-borns. The mess and disruption of infants repulsed him. He had moved out of the bedroom he once shared with Vanessa. For the jealous Virginia, Julian was the 'very devil',[21] interrupting walks and conversations. That spring, Virginia was also grappling with the ghost of her father. She dreamt that she showed the manuscript of her novel to him; he snorted and dropped it on to a table.

* In the Monks House Papers (MS Sussex) are a fragment of an unfinished novel (*c.* 1904) and another manuscript (*c.* 1906) labelled 'Sympathy (first idea for an unpublished novel)'.

† This somewhat misleading title is derived from the inscription, not in Virginia's hand, on the envelope in which the manuscript was stored.

Virginia told this dream to Clive, at the very same time that she pointed out to him the futility of writing *Reminiscences*: 'seeing I never shall recapture what you have, by your side this minute.'[22] Her ambivalent relationship with Clive is enshrined here. He was a worthy confidant who could give her excellent advice in literary matters and at the same time he possessed the person she loved most deeply. On 17 April 1908, Virginia travelled to Cornwall by herself. A week later, she was joined by the three Bells.

> I had a fortnight at St Ives; Adrian and Nessa and Clive came for the last week. I doubt that I shall ever have a baby. Its voice is too terrible, a senseless scream, like an ill omened cat. Nobody could wish to comfort it, or pretend it was a human being. Now, thank God, it sleeps with its nurse . . . Clive and I went for some long walks; but I felt that we were deserters, but then I was quite useless, as a nurse, and Clive will not even hold it.[23]

Beneath this comparatively bland description (to Violet) lurks the beginning of what Virginia called her 'affair' with Clive and Vanessa. The real drama of the situation is found in a letter Virginia wrote to Clive on 6 May, less than a week after she arrived back in London, in response to some sort of declaration from him.

> Why do you torment me with half uttered and ambiguous sentences? my presence is 'vivid and strange and bewildering'. I read your letter again and again, and wonder whether you have found me out, or, more likely, determined that there is nothing but an incomprehensible and quite negligible femininity to find out. I was certainly of opinion, though we did not kiss – (I was willing and offered once – but let that be) – I think we 'achieved the heights' as you put it. But did you realize how profoundly I was moved, and at the same time, restricted, by the sight of your daily life? Ah – such beauty – grandeur – and freedom – as of panthers treading in their wilds – I never saw in any other pair. When Nessa is bumbling about the world, and

making each thorn blossom, what room is there for me? Seriously, nature has done so much more for her than for me. I shrank to my narrowest limits, and you found me more than usually complex, and contained. Chivalrous as you are, however, you took infinite pains with me, and I am very grateful.[24]

Clive and Virginia did not sleep together, but they betrayed Vanessa. Clive had become deeply attracted to a virginal woman who reminded him of his wife, now preoccupied with Julian. In Virginia, his twin passions for beautiful women and beautiful writing were perfectly conjoined. He was a Jupiter in pursuit of a Diana. During her walks with Clive, Virginia became momentarily aware of her ability to attract men, although she did not really believe that, like Vanessa, she had the powers of some bucolic goddess. Her self-assurance had momentarily been raised, but then guilt asserted itself. However, at long last, she claimed, her 'passionate maiden heart'[25] stood revealed.

To a large degree, Vanessa – the Ceres in this triangle – was aware of what was going on between her husband and her sister. She was sufficiently unsure of herself to choose not to speak directly either to Clive or to Virginia. Although betrayed by her sister, she agreed with her husband about her sister's charms and, what is more, she increasingly realized – as Clive failed as a husband – how much she needed her rival's companionship and love. Vanessa coped with an increasingly perilous situation by suggesting that her disorganized younger sister required someone to look after her: 'Oh Billy, how do you ever get about the world by yourself? I think you had really better marry a practical man who will pick up your leavings.'[26]

Walter Headlam's sudden death on 20 June 1908 at the age of forty-two evoked almost no response in Virginia, who was in the midst of trying to sort out the nature of her friendship with Clive and get work done on *Melymbrosia*. One cause of concern was the heroine's name. In August she was Cynthia, although Vanessa teasingly suggested that she consider calling her Belinda or, better still, Apricot. From 1 to 17 August, Virginia took rooms in Wells. She perceived an embryonic structure emerging from her now 100-page manuscript and hoped that a brief stay in Somerset would allow her to coax the right form into being.

At Wells, Virginia first boarded with Mrs Wall, the widow of a railway guard, at the Vicars' Close. These two rows of twenty-one houses were occupied mainly by theological students, to whom Mrs Wall was devoted. On 3 August Virginia told Clive of the attentions of one such clergyman, Mr Dallas, who had begged the landlady to act as intermediary. Would Virginia receive him, she inquired? Virginia, fearful of her landlady's disapproval, agreed to the request and quickly hid her books and cigarettes. When the young man appeared at her door, she pretended to be studying a map of Somerset. They were both excessively shy, but they managed to keep the semblance of a conversation going, on topics as various as Roman Catholicism, winter sports and Raphael. Obviously impressed by Virginia, he asked if she was the Miss Stephens who wrote for the *Tatler*. 'I spell my name without an s,' she coldly replied. When he took his leave shortly afterwards, Virginia, as 'meanly' as she dared, asked him to call again. She was not surprised the next day when he greeted her curtly. Much of the pleasure of this chaste encounter obviously lay in telling Clive about it.[27]

On 8 August Virginia moved to 5 Cathedral Green, situated on the north side of the cathedral. This lodging was run by Mrs Dorothy Oram, the wife of a verger. If she had hoped for a more congenial place to work, she was rudely disappointed. The two Oram children played all day long beneath her window and shrieked incessantly. When she awoke on the morning of 10 August, she 'imagined precisely what it is like to have a child. I . . . understood . . . the precise nature of the pain'.[28] If only, she observed, she could so envisage her novel in progress. But there was little rest to be had at Cathedral Green. On 13 August her two dogs, Gurth and Hans, were taken for a walk by a servant, escaped their keeper and were eventually imprisoned. Mr Oram fetched the animals, but he told Virginia that the constable wanted to interview her. The verger, who stuttered badly and referred to Hans as 'Miss Hans', also reminded her that the animals were without licences and she was therefore, in the eyes of the law, a criminal. Virginia was furious: 'I had to pretend that I was deeply moved. Do you think all the lower classes are naturally idiotic?'[29]

Virginia's own place was poised between the aristocracy and the upper classes on the one hand and the working and artisan classes on the other. She was a member of a small circle: the scholarly, book-loving upper middle class. She did not have a great deal of money, but she kept servants and, if exceedingly careful, did not have to work terribly hard for a living. In this and in similar instances, she is defining her own position in a carefully regulated but precarious chain of being. When her narrow perch was threatened by those above or below her, Virginia's snobbery was triggered.

Even though she realized that Virginia was beginning to find the appropriate form for her novel, Vanessa pointed out to her that she was nevertheless acting in increasingly 'bitchy'[30] ways. Virginia could certainly be surly, as when she commented on the life of Dorothea Beale, the educational reformer, she did not review: the subject was 'all committees and organizations – and what an ugly woman! She always allowed 2 hours to catch any train, and brushed away her breadcrumbs herself.'[31] And Vanessa would not have liked Virginia's facetious comments on one 'Dodo' [Antonia Booth Macnaghten], a family friend who had just given birth: 'Well, the rabbits of the field multiply, and replenish the earth with their bones.'[32] By 14 August, Virginia had decided to go to Manorbier, obviously in the hope that the craggy landscape there would prove a respite from the hurly-burly of a supposedly tranquil cathedral setting.

The Welsh cliffs were sometimes too rugged. One day she found herself slipping on a tiny ridge just at the edge of a red fissure. She had not remembered that the ridges came so near the path and realized that she did not wish to perish. She could, however, 'imagine sticking out one's arms on the way down, and feeling them tear, and finally whirling over, and cracking one's head'.[33] This grisly daytime fantasy was accompanied by relatively calm fireside evenings devoted to G. E. Moore's *Principia Ethica*. She 'split' her head over his concept of the good, 'feeling ideas travelling to the remotest parts of my brain, and setting up a feeble disturbance, hardly to be called thought'. In general, she found the philosopher deeply humane, despite his rigorous desire to know the truth.

Virginia also daydreamed about rising to the eminence of a popular lady 'biographist'. In more serious moments, encouraged by Clive, she saw clearly the great task which lay before her: 'I shall re-form the novel and capture multitudes of things at present fugitive, enclose the whole, and shape infinite strange shapes.'[34] Early that month, Clive had confided his sense of his own limitations to his sister-in-law: 'I am condemned all my life, I think, to enjoy through an interpreter; but then as the interpreter is art one must not complain too much.'[35] However, he had no such doubts about Virginia. He informed her that she was a true creator, one who could break the rules. She was, he kept assuring her, brilliant and inventive enough to enter uncharted waters.

Increasingly, Vanessa attempted to divert Virginia's attention from Clive by suggesting that she marry, even though she imagined her sister becoming something of a black widow who would inadvertently poison her spouse. That July, knowing that Lytton Strachey was supposedly on the verge of proposing, she encouraged his suit, even though she realized that this might not be a suitable match: 'I should like Lytton as a brother in law better than any one I know but the only way I can perceive of bringing that to pass would be if he were to fall in love with Adrian & even then Adrian would probably reject him.'[36]

Homosexuality – or buggery as it was called by Virginia and her friends – was obviously a major obstacle to a successful marriage. Virginia and Vanessa realized this, but they had also experienced, in the refreshing company of such men, an entirely different perspective on the world. At Hyde Park Gate, power and creativity had often seemed male preserves of a very narrow kind. Women had to become, as it were, little men in order to have any chance of literary or artistic success. At Thursday evenings the sisters had been exposed to a masculinity which welcomed – even embraced – the feminine and thus widened its definition of sensitivity, imagination and wit. In particular, whether they had read Moore or not, these homosexuals from Cambridge exposed the sisters to the philosopher's central notion: 'personal affections and aesthetic enjoyments include *all* the greatest, and *by far* the greatest, goods we can imagine'.

Nevertheless, Virginia's attitude towards male and female homosexuality was – and remained – extremely ambivalent. On 9 November 1939, she told a friend: 'I've seen so much of the nasty silly petty side of the homosexuals; which is obviously largely the result of secrecy.'[37] Homosexual practices as such did not offend Virginia; however, in addition to the secrecy, she intensely disliked what she considered to be effeminate demeanour on the part of some male homosexuals and, when she witnessed such behaviour, a homophobic edge enters her letters and diary. Her prejudice is based in large part on her uncomfortableness with her own contradictory sexual identity.

At first glance, Giles Lytton Strachey seemed an inappropriate disciple of Moore. He was a man of many sharp angles. Tall, exceedingly thin and willowy, he was known to harbour a rapier wit with which he could easily, and decisively, wound an opponent. In groups, he would often be silent for a considerable length of time, studying the situation intently before gathering himself together for an assault which would quickly destroy an antagonist. When he spoke, his voice was raspy and excessively muted, but the brilliance of his mind shone through. In 1908, he was four years away from the publication of his first book, *Landmarks in French Literature*; only in 1918 would come his first warts-and-all biographical study, *Eminent Victorians*.

Like Virginia, he was at this time very much a writer in embryo. After failing to get a fellowship at Cambridge, he worked in London as a journalist for the *Spectator*, the *Edinburgh Review* and the *New Quarterly Review*. Also like Virginia, he was a person who could appear to be unduly severe, demanding or self-centred; and also like her, he was essentially a sentimentalist – not a sensualist – in affairs of the heart. Although a lover of men's bodies, Strachey's strongest emotional attachments were to women, as in his liaison from 1912 with Dora Carrington, who can correctly be regarded as the great romance of his life. Vanessa's suggestion that Virginia should consider marrying Strachey was not therefore an entirely foolish one.

Could an alliance between a bugger and a half-inclined Sapphist have worked? Their marriage could have been dynastic, she making her mark with a new kind of novel, while he reformed the art of biography. The incompatibility between Virginia and Lytton was only partly sexual. They were very different prose writers: he was incisive, whereas she wanted to explore the nature of formlessness. The truth is that these two writers-in-waiting were deeply jealous of each other. Virginia told Clive on 9 August: 'I sometimes think that Lytton's mind is too pliant and supple ever to make anything lasting.'[38] Later that month she was upset when she heard that Clive considered Lytton's love poems almost as good as those of Catullus: 'Where are my works then? I shall have to alter my standard for judging Clive's praise.'[39]

Vanessa persevered in trying to find Virginia a husband. A measure of the resulting conflict this aroused in her can be seen in a comment she made that August. In imagining the day when Virginia's letters to her would eventually be published, she thought most people would think they had a 'most amorous intercourse. They read more like love letters than anything else – certainly I have never received any from Clive that you could compare with them.'[40] If Virginia was her lover, did Vanessa really want her to marry?

The emotions of Virginia, Vanessa and Clive remained unsorted and thus chaotic when they travelled to Italy that September, staying in Siena and Perugia and visiting Pavia and Assisi. Still bathed in Clive's wholehearted praise of her work, the static beauty of a fresco by the Renaissance painter Perugino prompted this reflection by Virginia on the fact that what she wanted to attain in writing was essentially the opposite of that artist's intentions: 'He saw [art] sealed as it were [whereas I want to] attain a different kind of beauty, achieve a symmetry by means of infinite discords . . . some kind of whole made of shivering fragments; to me this seems the natural process.' This was 'the flight of the mind'.[41]

At the beginning of the journey, Virginia penned a brief, incomplete portrait sketch of Clive. What is amazing about it is how much Virginia had come to idealize her brother-in-law. She had once been deeply suspicious of him. Now she glosses over exactly those traits which had annoyed her previously; even his family is handled kindly.

> It is important to remember Clive's birth & education when you consider his character. He is the son of a substantial country family, who are without culture or pretension, but spend their lives in the most sensible occupations, & are perfectly sure of their object. Not one of the arts, even in its baser forms, is suffered to disturb them, so that their views & conduct are of the most direct kind, & have probably a great deal of virtue in them.[42]

This is conversion, not simply transformation. The fragmentary outline and five paragraphs display just how serious her affair with Clive had become: she was attempting to come to terms with his fine skills as a critic and his aggressive heterosexuality. Could she fall in love with such a man, one so essentially different from Lytton?

Virginia also wanted to write with her mind as well as her eye. She yearned to 'discover real things beneath the show'. The diary she kept reveals that she was looking intently at other women and the options with which life presented them. There was the pretty young woman whose charms were directed to gaining a suitable husband so that she could become a wife and mother. 'Viewed in this light,' Virginia told herself, 'there is cause for alarm, & even for disgust.' But if that option was unacceptable, what about Miss

Poor, the spinster, who was just beginning to grow old? This poor wretch acted as if she knew a great deal of life and art, but if Virginia gazed at her silent countenance, it was 'difficult to detect any life in her. You seek it in the eye; it is dull & fitful; her skin is like folds of old leather; creases are in the very flesh.'[43] Virginia was obviously afraid of becoming such a grotesque.

In the midst of these reflections, Clive's frank sexuality overwhelmed her. Just before they set off for Italy, he apologized for his conduct in Cornwall: 'I wished for nothing in the world but to kiss you. I wished so much that I grew shy and could not see what you were feeling; that is what happens always, and one of the worst things in human nature.'[44] Italy might have conquered Clive's shyness – or Virginia might have simply been overwhelmed by the strain of being around a man who desired her and whom – against her own moral code – she was finding increasingly attractive. In any event, the in-laws quarrelled violently in Perugia and later in Siena.* Unfortunately, no information survives on the exact nature of the sparks which were flying. On 24 September, Virginia and the Bells returned to London by way of Paris, where they stayed a week. The adjectives in Virginia's letter of 4 October to Violet merely hint at inner turmoil: 'I liked Italy much better this time, except for the people. But the country was beautiful – all the grapes ripe, and the earth warm.'[45]

That autumn there was the welcome diversion of a new round of Thursday evenings and the play-reading society met again. Not surprisingly, Virginia's unresolved dealings with Clive and Vanessa kept her very much on edge. However, a large part of her depressive anxiety was focused, as she confessed to Madge Vaughan, on Thoby: 'It is just two years since he died, and I feel immensely old, and as though the best in us had gone. But what

* On 15 May 1935, Virginia sent Clive a postcard of the ramparts of Siena: 'It was on the spot now marked by a cross that Clive Bell quarrelled with his sister in law in Sept. 1908. I dropped memory's tear there today under the orange blossom.'

use is it to write? It is such an odd life without him.'[46] Although Clive assured her about her power of 'lifting the veil & showing inanimate things in the mystery & beauty of their reality'[47] in *Melymbrosia*, she struggled with the book, which she found increasingly difficult to bend to the correct shape. She was afraid that the novel as a genre, like a rare and elusive butterfly, would escape her net.

As far as Virginia was concerned, her reviews counted for nothing. Her evaluation of E. M. Forster's *A Room with a View* that autumn in the *Times Literary Supplement* was enthusiastic in an extremely diffused way. She admired the comedy, was sympathetic to the Emersons, the upstart father and son, but was offended by the fact that the sensibility of Lucy, the heroine, is moulded by the two men. Virginia had just returned from a trip to Italy during which she had been struggling with her feelings for Clive and with her plans for a novel which would also be about the English abroad. Her book would not necessarily have the crystalline clarity of Forster's and would be about a woman's desire to define her own destiny. These factors must be kept in mind when evaluating Virginia's gentle reprimand to Forster on his handling of Lucy: 'We care very much that Lucy should give up trying to feel what other people feel, and we long for the moment when, inspired by Italy and the Emersons, she shall burst out in all the splendour of her own beliefs.'[48]

Virginia very much wanted to 'burst out', but she was not really very sure in what she believed. Yet she knew that writing was her destiny and that she had to find the right angle in which to cast her vision. In another review from this time, she wrote with considerable admiration for Christina Rossetti, who 'was born with one genuine gift [her ability as a poet], and that in order to be true to it she must see the world consistently in a certain perspective'.[49] Consistency and perspective still eluded Virginia.

In mid-November, Virginia and Adrian spent a few days with Lytton at the Lizard peninsula in Cornwall and on Christmas Day she reported to Clive the not-astonishing news that she was not in love with Lytton, nor he with her. However, Lytton had told her the story of Adrian's thwarted homosexual attachment at Cambridge and this information was passed on to the Bells. Virginia complained to Clive that his wife had upbraided her: 'She said I never gave, but always took. In this case, as she must own, I have been forced to take.'[50] Virginia was obviously very much worried about being cold-blooded, about being a person who could never give to others. That January, as she celebrated her twenty-seventh birthday, she felt incredibly old, like a hoary grey tortoise which only comes out in the sun.

Late in 1908 Virginia met Ottoline Morrell, the daughter of General Arthur Cavendish-Bentinck and his wife, Lady Bolsover. In 1902 Lady Ottoline had married, very much on the rebound, Philip Morrell, the barrister and politician. One friend, David Garnett, described her as 'extremely handsome: tall and lean, with a large head, masses of dark Venetian red hair . . . glacier blue-green eyes, a long straight nose, a proud mouth and a long jutting-out chin'.[51] Others not quite so favourably disposed called attention to her piercing nasal voice, the exaggerated mahogany red of her seventeenth-century-style curls, the fish-like way in which she took air in through her mouth, the clashing colour schemes of her determinedly bohemian costumes and the deep crisscrossing lines with which her face was etched.

Nine years her senior, Ottoline was a consummate impresario and thus not really a rival to Virginia, who, after she dined with her for the first time, gave her the mildest of scratches: Ottoline 'has the head of a Medusa; but she is very simple and innocent in spite of it, and worships the arts.'[52] A hostess who very much wanted to find new habitués for her salon in Bedford Square, Ottoline ventured out to Bloomsbury's Thursday evenings and helped to cross-fertilize those gatherings. Eventually, Augustus John, Raymond Asquith, Winston Churchill, Gilbert Cannan and Bertrand Russell added a much-needed note of champagne, giddiness and heterosexuality to the sometimes mundane bitchiness and complacent superiority of Bloomsbury gatherings.

Quite soon after they met, Virginia and Ottoline were among

the participants, from late January to mid-March 1909, in what for Virginia was a very welcome diversion and frivolity: a short-lived experiment in creating a novel through correspondence, in which each participant adopted a fictional character. Ottoline was Lady Eastnor, Philip Morrell was Sir Julius, Virginia was Eleanor Hadyng, Lytton was Vane Hatherly, Clive and Vanessa were James and Clarissa Phillips. The experiment soon turned a bit sour, when Mr Hatherly cross-questioned Miss Hadyng on her dealings with the Phillips. Eleanor replied:

> So you've noticed it then? How clever you are, and how unkind! For don't you think that these 'extraordinary conclusions' you like so much may be rather uncomfortable for me and perhaps (though I really won't admit it) a little uncomfortable for Clarissa? We were not happy – no – and yet I know it's dangerous to imagine people in love with one, and so I told myself all the time.[53]

Lytton had obviously asked some painful questions about Virginia's affair with Clive, who continued to bolster Virginia's work on *Melymbrosia*.

Clive urged her not to sacrifice the magical qualities of the first draft to a mistaken notion of humanity and reminded her that the artist had an obligation to create without coming to conclusions. On 19 February, Eleanor Hadyng told James Phillips of her disdain for harpyish, middle-aged writers like herself: 'They remind me of those bald-necked vultures at the zoo, with their drooping bloodshot eyes, who are always on the look out for a lump of raw meat.'[54] Virginia's self-loathing was reinforced by the books selected by the *Times Literary Supplement* for her to review. At that journal, she was seen as a specialist in subtle and doubtful passions.

On 17 February, perhaps fired up by playing the role of the heterosexual Vane Hatherly, Lytton presented himself at Fitzroy Square, where at long last he proposed. Taken by surprise, Eleanor Hadyng said yes. There was a great deal of role-playing in this brief courtship, the principals certainly taking each other – and themselves – completely by surprise.

Dora Carrington. Pencil sketch of Virginia skating with Lytton Strachey

Then reality set in. As soon as Lytton had proposed, the impossibility of the situation asserted itself. There was even the disturbing likelihood that Virginia might kiss him. 'And how,' he later reflected, 'can a virgin be expected to understand? You see she *is* her name.'[55] At this time, his affair with Duncan Grant was over; the year before, Duncan and the economic wizard Maynard Keynes, who had become a close friend of Virginia at about this time, became lovers. Lytton wanted to escape his sexuality. Virginia, who was alternately alarmed and enthralled by Clive Bell, was presented with the possibility of a celibate marriage which could be fraternal and thus non-threatening to her fragile sexual identity. A few hours later, the gravity of what they had agreed to overcame both Lytton and Virginia. They met a second time that day. He withdrew his proposal and she assured him that she did not love him.

Virginia did not really want to marry Lytton, but she knew that her life had to change and marriage seemed a distinct possibility. There can be little doubt that this pseudo-proposal hurt her deeply. In now-lost letters, she told Vanessa of the event but otherwise she was uncharacteristically silent. Was a homosexual (or someone, like Walter Headlam, of dubious sexual proclivities) the only kind of man who would be interested in her? Of course, she was well aware that she did not have to marry, but the lonely existence of many single women, as we have seen, frightened her. Now Vanessa had gained the upper hand and there is a trace of mockery in her letter to Virginia of 10 March: 'I thought of you this afternoon . . . entertaining Lytton in Fitzroy Square. Did he ask you to marry him again or are you still Platonic?'[56]

Virginia's self-assurance was very much on trial when she reflected on recent events in a letter to Madge Vaughan of 21 March: 'life is certainly very exciting, but one would have to be a novelist to describe them. Oh how I wish I could write a novel!'[57] A month later, she linked her dissatisfaction with her career to even more intimate concerns: 'Virginia Stephen knows nothing about humanity.'[58] So despondent a figure had she become that a stranger who saw her at the Queen's Hall took pity on her and anonymously sent her a ticket to John Galsworthy's *Strife* at the Haymarket Theatre. He sat next to her, spoke to her and later asked for friendship. She was grateful but did not pursue the matter.

Caroline Emelia died on 7 April, leaving Virginia £2,500 (Vanessa and Adrian received only £100 each). In her obituary for the aunt she found extremely troublesome and deeply moving, she described how the elderly woman had chosen to dwell apart, among those things which are unseen and eternal. Virginia also praised her wonderful command of language and her desire to use it accurately. The question must have come back to haunt her: would her existence be merely a secular, more dreary version of her aunt's pursuit of the higher realities? Like her, was she remote and yet full of life?

In the midst of these agonies, Clive Bell openly declared his love:

> I was too shy to kiss you on Wednesday afternoon though I wanted to more than I care to say even in a letter. It's really odd my shyness with you; to be sure you gave me a chance of making a habit of kissing you, but that I found was not at all what I wanted. Perhaps I'm shy because you're so exciting in which case it's clearly for the best . . . God forgive me; Virginia

> forgive me; what a letter; never heed it; try to feel half the affection for me that I feel for you.[59]

In her reply four days later, Virginia flung the gauntlet down with an enticing rejoinder: 'Why should I excite you?'[60] She is asking Clive to justify his overtures while at the very same time implying that she is an unsuitable recipient of such affection.

Given the volatile nature of their relationship, the in-laws should not have travelled together to Italy on 23 April. Virginia's diary from that trip contains brilliant pen-portraits of a series of women, including Principessa Lucrezia Rasponi, Janet Anne Ross and Alice Meynell. The best is of Margaret Alice Murray, the Egyptologist and prolific writer on the occult: 'She was without humour, strained, & slightly elderly, & what imagination she had took this mystic form, which is imagination disembodied. And yet I think she was honest, unselfish, & clever above the average. I am never comfortable with these acute analytical minds.'[61]

Virginia was uncomfortable with herself and with the Bells. She played the coquette; Clive became further entranced and, of course, frustrated; Vanessa was caught in the middle – playing in turn the roles of jealous wife and envious elder sister. Any advance by Clive was repulsed by Virginia and Clive took his revenge by sleeping with his wife. This infuriated Virginia, who withdrew even more and, in the process, felt utterly unloved and unwanted. A trying situation quickly became an impossible one. Strained to the limit, all three became peevish and quarrelsome. After a fortnight, Virginia wisely cut short the holiday and returned to London.*

* At about this time, Clive resumed his affair with Mrs Raven-Hill. On 5 February 1921, Virginia reflected on this: 'This was a surprise to me. She coincided with his attachment to me then. But she was a voluptuary. He was not "in love".' In limiting herself to a distinction between chaste love and promiscuous sexuality, Virginia does not consider the possibility that her flirtatious behaviour might, in part, have contributed to Clive's unfaithfulness.

When Vanessa arrived back, she took a different tack with her difficult sister. In her own best flirtatious manner, she suggested that her sibling consider a different kind of love affair.

> Is Ottoline becoming my rival in your affections? I am suspicious. You will have a desperate liaison with her, I believe, for I rather think she shares your Sapphist tendencies & only wants a little encouragement. She once told me that she much preferred women to men & would take any trouble to know a woman she liked but would never do the same for a man.[62]

The recipient did not take this hint very seriously, although that summer she went, with Vanessa and Ottoline, to a fancy-dress ball. On that occasion, Virginia costumed herself as Cleopatra, the ultimate femme fatale.

Throughout 1908 and 1909, Virginia tried to focus her attention on *Melymbrosia*,* the plot of which had assumed a more or less definite shape by February 1909, when Clive Bell wrote his long, sustaining letter to the author. The story is centred on Rachel Vinrace, the twenty-four-year-old daughter of a ship-owner, who, with her father, Willoughby, and her aunt and uncle, Helen and Ridley Ambrose, sails on one of her father's ships, the *Euphrosyne* (Joy), for South America. Although Theresa, Rachel's mother, is dead, she is a central presence throughout. Early in the book, the omniscient narrator asserts: 'Nothing is stranger than the position of the dead among the living, and the whole scene was the work of one woman who had been in her grave for eight years.'[63]

On the sixth day of the voyage, Richard Dalloway, a former

* In order to distinguish between *Melymbrosia* and the published novel, *The Voyage Out*, I have referred to all early versions of the narrative as *Melymbrosia*, whereas I refer to the novel that was published in 1915 as *The Voyage Out*. However, *Melymbrosia* passed through at least four major revisions between its conception in or before 1908 and its arrival at the office of her publisher, Gerald Duckworth, in March 1913.

MP, and his wife, Clarissa, come aboard at the mouth of the Tagus. Mr Dalloway believes in a world of masculine values, to which his wife puts up a half-hearted resistance. During their brief stay, the Dalloways bicker pleasantly with the highly opinionated Helen, who distrusts the couple's hollow philanthropy and general falsity. In an unguarded moment, Richard, attracted to Rachel, gives vent to his feelings.

> 'You have beauty' he said. The ship lurched. Rachel fell slightly forward. Richard took her in his arms and kissed her. He held her tight, and kissed her passionately. She felt the hardness of his body and the roughness of his cheek. She fell back in her chair, with a tremendous beating of the heart. It sent black waves across her eyes. He clasped his forehead in his hands.
>
> 'You tempt me' he said. It was his voice that was terrifying. He seemed choked in fight. They were both trembling. Rachel stood up and went. Her head was cold; and her knees shaking. The physical pain of the emotion was so great that she could only keep herself moving above the great leaps of her heart. She leant upon the rail of the ship, and gradually ceased to feel, for a chill crept over her. The heart slackened. Far out between the waves little black and white sea birds were riding.
>
> 'You're peaceful' she said. She became peaceful too.
>
> A kind of exaltation dwelt with her.[64]

But the exaltation is momentary and that night Rachel has a horrible dream: 'Alone she walked a long tunnel; it grew dark and narrow; at length she saw a dim light, and found that the tunnel led nowhere, but ended in a vault, where a crouching man waited for her, gibbering, with long nails. The wall behind him dripped with wet.'[65] As the ship nears South America, Helen asks Willoughby to allow Rachel, who is scheduled to take a long voyage up the Amazon with him, to stay with her and Ambrose at their villa just outside Santa Rosa. He agrees.

Three months after they have settled in at the villa, Rachel and Helen stray into the grounds of the hotel at Santa Rosa, where a motley assortment of English tourists are lodged. Subsequently, aunt and niece become acquainted with their fellow countrymen. Rachel is attracted to Terence Hewet, a writer, and his friend, the acerbic but kindly St John Hirst, forms a platonic friendship with Helen. Rachel and Terence declare their love, but any display of sexual feeling is profoundly disturbing to Rachel, who tells Terence: 'Oh how I hate it – how I hate it!'[66] Later, Rachel tells Terence that her father's behaviour towards her mother was horrendous. 'I once heard him abuse her when she asked him for money. Feelings come in flashes like that and last all one's life.'[67] During this conversation, Terence reflects on Rachel's instability, on the fact that no conviction occupies her for long.

The two become engaged during an inland jungle expedition with some of the other tourists. During one of their conversations, she declares – in a seemingly illogical aside: 'O Terence. The dead! My mother is dead!'[68] Although Helen encourages the love affair between Rachel and Terence, she has ardent feelings for her niece, whom she pursues into the jungle.

> Suddenly Rachel stopped and opened her arms so that Helen rushed into them and tumbled her over onto the ground. 'Oh Helen Helen!' she could hear Rachel gasping as she rolled her, 'Don't! For God's sake! Stop! I'll tell you a secret! I'm going to be married!'
>
> Helen paused with one hand upon Rachel's throat holding her head down among the grasses.
>
> 'You think I didn't know that!' she cried.
>
> For some seconds she did nothing but roll Rachel over and over, knocking her down when she tried to get up; stuffing grass into her mouth; finally laying her absolutely flat upon the ground, her arms out on either side of her, her hat off, her hair down.
>
> 'Own yourself beaten' she panted. 'Beg my pardon, and say you worship me!'
>
> Rachel saw Helen's head hanging over her, very large against the sky.
>
> 'I love Terence better!' she exclaimed.

Although Helen gives way to Terence, she confesses her love to Rachel, adding: 'you're so like Theresa, and I loved her.'[69] In a later conversation, Rachel, in language charged with sexual passion, declares the joy and terror of her attachment to Terence: 'Loving you is like having iron thrust through one.'[70] Soon after they return to Santa Rosa, Rachel gets a headache, develops a fever, becomes delirious and, finally, dies.

Although set in South America, the landscape of *Melymbrosia* is really a composite one, manufactured from Virginia's firsthand knowledge of Spain, Italy and Portugal. The journey is based on her 1905 sea voyage from Liverpool to Oporto. Virginia's extraordinary shyness at parties is a trait shared by Rachel. Ambrose Ridley, the reclusive Greek scholar husband of Helen, is a mixture of Walter Headlam and, especially, Leslie Stephen. Lytton Strachey, Virginia's reluctant suitor, is sympathetically portrayed as St John Hirst. Virginia boasted that Clarissa Dalloway was Kitty Maxse and the aggressive Richard Dalloway bears some traces of George Duckworth. Helen is maternal very much in the manner of Vanessa and, like Vanessa, she has more than a passing interest in expressing her love of women physically.* Terence's character is idealized in a way which bears a strong resemblance to the portrait of Clive in the Italian diary of 1908.† Thoby, very much in the manner of Rachel, suffered delusions while dying.

* Vanessa did not recognize herself in the portrayal of Helen Ambrose, as can be seen in her letter to Roger Fry of ? April 1915 (MS Tate): 'I expect you're right in thinking Helen Ambrose like me in some way though I can't realize it – otherwise most of the minor characters seem to me more interesting than the principal ones.'

† For example, Hewet has an excellent understanding of how men attempt to dominate women: 'Consider what a bully the ordinary man is', he continued, 'the ordinary, hardworking, rather ambitious solicitor or man of business with a family to bring up and a certain position to maintain. And then, of course, the daughters have to give way to the sons; the sons have to be educated; they have to bully and shove for their wives and families, and so it all comes over again' (*The Voyage Out*, 196). Also, very significantly, Terence, as can be seen in this remark to Rachel, wants to write the kind of

Although many of its events and characters can be linked to Virginia's life, *Melymbrosia* is not so much autobiographical as it is a recapitulation of some of the central issues which dominated its author's existence. In particular, three events (the death of Julia, the sexual advances of George Duckworth and the 'affair' with Clive) which haunted Virginia are explored. Despite its eventual title, *The Voyage Out*, this book is concerned with the heroine's inner voyage, which is a deeply sad and tragic one. Rachel, a sensitive, fragile, well-read young woman, has never really been able to accept her mother's death; her melancholia stems from an inability to detach herself from Theresa. Although she is attracted to Richard Dalloway, she does not invite his amorous embrace, just as Virginia years earlier had not welcomed George Duckworth into her bedroom. In 1908 and 1909, Virginia was toying with the idea of falling in love with her brother-in-law, but she realized that such an alliance would ultimately alienate her from Vanessa.

Before the events described in the book, Rachel has experienced a great loss and is deeply distrustful of men. Richard Dalloway's behaviour reinforces those feelings. Rachel wishes to form an alliance with Terence, but her past holds her back. To a large degree, her confusion is sexual. She tells Helen that she loves Terence best, but she is not really sure of that assertion, since her suppressed sexual feelings for Helen provide her with a link back to Theresa.

Rachel's fatal illness is in large part derived from her realization that she can never truly overcome the deprivations of the past. In one of her final deliriums, she returns to the scene of her nightmare aboard ship and 'began to walk through tunnels with old women sitting in little archways playing cards'.[71] She sees one of them cutting a man's head off. In another passage, the dying heroine cannot conquer the surface of the sticky sea, the landscape of another frightening dream: 'She had long ceased to have any will

---

novel to which Virginia herself was increasingly drawn: 'What I want to do in writing novels is very much what you want to do when you play the piano, I expect . . . We want to find out what's behind things, don't we . . . Things I feel come to me like lights . . . I want to combine them' (206–7).

of her own in deciding what she did; she could not have escaped now if the faces had chased her. A wave seemed to bear her up and down with it; she lay on the top conscious only of pain.'[72]

Although *Melymbrosia* employs many of the set-pieces of a novel like *A Room with a View*, Virginia had serious doubts about the conventions which underpin such works of fiction. Like Forster, she can write with considerable humour and satire about the English abroad, but she is not able to come to similar, optimistic conclusions. Unlike Lucy, Rachel cannot become liberated by emulating a masculine vision of freedom. Rachel wishes to enter into a passionate relationship with Terence, but she cannot do so. In part, Virginia wrote a counter-vision to Forster's: if a woman looks closely at human life, she will uncover a web of falsity which men often have the ability – or determination – to ignore. She created a heroine who shared one of her worst suspicions: perhaps evil, not goodness, underpins all human activity.

Even though she wanted to create a work of fiction of classical beauty and perfection, the process of composition was violent:

> I am struggling with my work. (13 May 1908)
> I have been slashing at *Melymbrosia*! (May 1908)
> A page of *Melymbrosia* was strangled in the birth this morning. (9 August 1908)

Melymbrosia's parturition was such a terrible one because Virginia was exploring the extremely limited options with which life presented her while, at the same time, expanding the confines of fiction. Although this first novel is not as dramatically or as apparently experimental as many of her later books, it is an extremely subversive work which asserts, in essence, that human life is dominated by death.

Despite the nihilistic vision of *Melymbrosia*, that book is suffused with the author's affection for Clive Bell. At one point, St John Hirst tells Hewet, who wants to become an experimental novelist, that he envies him two things: his ability to avoid thinking and his considerable charm. However, Virginia did stand up to Clive's protest about her treatment of men: 'Your objection, that my prejudice against men makes me didactic "not to say priggish", has not quite the same force with me . . . Possibly, for psychological reasons which seem to me very interesting, a man, in the present state of the world, is not a very good judge of his sex.'[73] She did admit that she was perhaps too concerned about how others – male and female – might employ identical material, but she had to fight against this. Her boldness delighted, terrified and confused her.

In August 1909, Virginia reluctantly praised Laurence Sterne's ability to feel 'pain and joy acutely, and at the same time'.[74] Although the outward form of *Melymbrosia* appears conventional and certainly nowhere near as revolutionary as *Tristram Shandy*, the seeds of experimentation had been sown. The would-be novelist – who did not publish *The Voyage Out* until 1915 and would in the intervening years make many crucial changes to the book – was herself seesawing between extremes of pain and joy in both her writing and her everyday life. As *Melymbrosia* clearly shows, she was trying to find a middle ground between desire and solitude, but she had becoming increasingly despondent about her 'passionate maiden heart', the paradox at the core of her being.

Within a week after arriving back from Italy in May 1909, Virginia visited Cambridge, where she received a proposal in a punt on the Cam from Hilton Young (later Lord Kenet). Three years older than Virginia and the son of Sir George Young, he was the assistant editor of *The Economist*. As children, he and Virginia had bowled hoops together in Kensington Gardens. This old family friend was firmly declined; Virginia informed him that she could marry only Lytton. Suddenly Virginia was becoming something of an expert in dealing with suitors.

She was less able to deal with a dishevelled Madge Vaughan, who arrived at Fitzroy Square unexpectedly on the morning of 18 May, while she was taking a bath. Madge insisted on seeing her. This rattled Maud, the maid, who showed Madge to Virginia's bedroom and then summoned her mistress. Since March, Madge had been deeply worried about her six-year-old daughter Barbara, who had contracted a noxious and extremely disfiguring case of smallpox. Now it had become certain that Barbara would not survive. In her 'wild state', Madge lashed out at the girl's doctor. Then she blamed herself for having hired a new nurse. As Virginia informed Vanessa, Madge's language became increasingly muddled: 'It was mixed up with rhapsodies about fate, and God, and religion: she made swoops all the time, in her usual way, to explain things – and lay down the law. I think it has been ghastly. But I found it hard to say anything. Her mind goes off at such a tangent . . . She is like an excitable child, working itself into a passion.'[75] Virginia was sympathetic to the plight of the distraught mother, but she was a helpless bystander to such sorrow, almost as if she did not wish her friend's grief to touch her in any way. Virginia was never a cold or unfeeling person, but she saw herself as one of Madge's children. Since Madge was supposed to mother her, she could not find any words of consolation with which to comfort her.

Virginia did feel an obligation to care for Adrian, with whom she kept a cordial, if somewhat cool, relationship. From the outset, they had been rivals for Julia's attention and Virginia rightly felt that he had won that battle. As a child, he had defied Virginia and Thoby by producing competing newspapers (*Pelican News* and the *Corkscrew Gazette*) to the *Hyde Park Gate News*. Like Virginia, he had been deeply wounded by Julia's death when he was eleven. In the family circle, he was 'The Dwarf', and this nickname referred not only to his bony, nervous physique but also to his emotional immaturity. In 1903, Virginia referred to him as '15 years younger than all the rest of us'[76] and this is an acute observation, although by this time Adrian had become 6 feet 2 inches high (he grew 3 inches higher). At Westminster and later at Cambridge, he had been an indifferent but inquiring student, a person who did not necessarily go along with commonly held opinions. For example, he considered G. E. Moore a fraud and was not afraid to say so. Almost by serendipity, he fixed on law as a profession.

Despite the faults that Virginia readily perceived, and despite the fact that he was so much unlike Thoby, she and Adrian maintained an alliance, the weaknesses in which were papered over by banter. She had bouts of hysteria, he was obsessive; she enthusiastic, he mocking; she high-spirited, he phlegmatic. Opposites attracted, but things quickly fell to pieces if brother and sister were thrown together for long periods of time. Then they would fight at meals, throwing pats of butter at each other: the grease-spotted dining-room wall testified to these wars. Adrian's sceptical, often invisible personality carried over into the management of his sex life.

In June 1910, he somewhat academically discussed 'inversion' with Vanessa, who knew perfectly well that he was sleeping with Duncan Grant. She was shocked by the apparent lack of warmth he displayed towards his lover. Duncan, the only son of Major Bartle Grant, Lady Strachey's youngest brother, and Ethel McNeil, had been born in Rothiermurchus, Inverness, in 1885 but had spent his childhood in India, where his father was serving with his regiment. Although originally destined for a military career, Duncan was markedly unsuccessful in academic subjects while attending St Paul's School and Lady Strachey urged his parents to allow him to go to the Westminster School of Art. However, his unconventional though brilliant style of drawing meant he later failed to gain admission to the Royal Academy Schools.

Duncan was slovenly, dishevelled, inordinately self-centred and sometimes moody and withdrawn, but his charm and physical beauty could be overwhelming, as Strachey observed in 1905: 'His face is outspoken, bold, and just not rough. It's the full aquiline type, with frank gray-blue eyes, and incomparably lascivious lips.'[77] Duncan Grant became a member of Bloomsbury through his Strachey connection rather than the orthodox route of Cambridge. He did not speak the language of Moore and his anti-intellectualism immediately boosted him in Adrian's eyes. In 1905, the artist's ardent but fickle nature also appealed to a similar streak in the youngest of the Stephens.

Adrian was not lacking in emotion when playing or listening to music, particularly that of the High Romantics. There he discovered – and touched – feelings which evaded him in his everyday life. These sentiments were shared by the elusive, excessively silent

Saxon Sydney-Turner, alongside whom Adrian seemed positively bubbly. When he had first gone up to Trinity, Saxon was, as Lytton recalled, 'a wild and unrestrained freshman, who wrote poems, never went to bed, and declaimed Swinburne and Sir Thomas Browne till four o'clock in the morning'.[78] Then Saxon broke down; something in him was maimed or killed. Remnants of the boisterous freshman occasionally surfaced, as when he made a particularly brilliant observation but most of the time he presented an excessively dull, opaque face to the world. In public Saxon was a staid Treasury official, but a different side can be discerned in his career as a fanatical Wagnerian, alive to every nuance in the strife-ridden, highly charged music of *Tristan und Isolde* or *The Ring*. Saxon was not emotionally dead, but for him drama was lived out on a stage. For a time, he was considered a dark horse in the race to win Virginia's hand. This unlikely possibility receded even further when he confided to her that his sexual interests were, in part, sado-masochistic.

Since her visits to lush, sun-filled Italy with the Bells had not been a success, she chose to go to Bayreuth and later to Dresden with Adrian and Saxon in August 1909. At this time Virginia was open to Wagnerian splendour, particularly the way in which sexual and religious experiences are fused together – an accomplishment she felt was difficult to describe: 'Somehow Wagner has conveyed the desire of the Knights for the Grail in such a way that the intense emotion of human beings is combined with the earthly nature of the things they seek.' Her observations continue with an even more resplendent compliment: 'Like Shakespeare, Wagner seems to have attained in the end to such a mastery of technique that he could float and soar in regions where in the beginning he could scarcely breathe; the stubborn matter of his art dissolves in his fingers, and he shapes it as he chooses.'[79]*

* By May 1913, when she attended *The Ring* at Covent Garden, she had changed her mind: 'My eyes are bruised, my ears dulled, my brains a mere pudding of pulp – O the noise and the heat, and the bawling sentimentality, which used once to carry me away; and now leaves me sitting perfectly still.'

Virginia's admiration of Wagner did not extend to Bayreuth or the Germans she met there. The shrine was, she noted, very much like an English market town, although the souvenirs were cards and Holy Grails. The bourgeois appearance of the natives, particularly the women, appalled her: 'I haven't seen one German woman who has a face; they are puddings of red dough, and they dress in high art colours, with symbolical embroideries, rather like old Irish jewels, in their backs.'[80]

There were other problems. Throughout her life, Virginia was the despair of shopkeepers and their assistants. She found it difficult to make decisions, usually because she had an ideal in her mind beside which the items on display paled in comparison. At Bayreuth, Adrian was his sister's companion on several disastrous shopping expeditions. One was in search of a white parasol. All the articles of this description were presented to her. She then informed the assistant that white parasols had to have green lining. Apparently this was not the custom in Germany. Then she asked to see a coffee-coloured one. Finally, she bought the cheapest one on offer: a brown holland. There were further conflicts. Saxon found it difficult to make up his own mind about the simplest of things. When they were at a restaurant, his Prufrockian sensibility would reach a peak when he was presented with a menu. Adrian would then take charge and order for him.

Although confused by her dealings with Lytton, Clive and, to a lesser degree, Adrian, Virginia pressed ahead. By 1923, she understood better the challenges which her early life had presented and how she had faced them: 'never pretend that the things you haven't got are not worth having'. Significantly, she added: 'Never pretend that children . . . can be replaced by other things.' The real task of life she felt was to 'like things for themselves: or rather, rid them of their bearing upon one's personal life. One must throw that aside; & venture on to the things that exist independently of oneself.' Such an undertaking was, she knew, 'very hard for young women to do'.[81]

In mid-September, Virginia took a cottage at Studland, Dorset, near where the Bells were holidaying. During this stay, Virginia rented a 'bisexual' bathing costume and swam far out, until the seagulls played over her head, mistaking her, she claimed, for a drifting sea anemone. The three were re-evaluating their 'affair'. Virginia was becoming more aware of how dependent she was on her elder sister, of just how complete a human being Vanessa really was. With her Virginia could be more herself. And so there was a corresponding lessening of her ties to Clive. This change was aided by the unsubtle warning Vanessa gave her sister on 7 September, before she joined them in Dorset: 'You feel in doubt as to *my* mood – do you! . . . I am always only too ready to be calm & friendly. It is only your uncontrolled passion which disturbs the atmosphere so.'[82] Years later Virginia was painfully aware that she had been a sexual coward in her dealings with Clive.

When she returned to London that October, Virginia remained restless, uprooted and moody. Furthermore, Clive and Vanessa were seriously thinking of settling in Paris and Adrian had decided to give up the law and go on the stage. Both schemes were soon abandoned. When Adrian told her that an unknown woman, perhaps Violet, had smiled at him on the street, she asked her friend: 'was it you, or a prostitute?'[83] That November, Reginald Smith of the *Cornhill Magazine* rejected her story, 'Memoirs of a Novelist', which he felt was simply too clever by half: 'My feeling is that you have impaled not a butterfly, but a bumble-bee, upon a pin.'[84]

A measure of Virginia's anxiety can be seen in her sudden decision – much to Sophie Farrell's hysterical disdain – on Christmas Day to catch the train to Cornwall. In her typical fashion, Virginia, abetted by Maud, took her amethyst necklace but left behind a long list of necessities: handkerchiefs, watch, key, glasses, chequebook, a coat. She was fortunate that the weather in Lelant was warm and she experienced a delicious sense of satisfaction, the pure joy of which must have reminded her of the happiest days of her childhood. However, the dire reality of her present unhappiness was not far from her mind when, in a letter to Clive, she considered the possibility of settling in Cornwall and becoming a latter-day follower of Boadicea.

> Suppose I stayed here, and thought myself an early virgin, and danced on May nights, in the British camp! – a scandalous Aunt for Julian, and yet rather pleasant, when he was older . . . and wished for eccentric relations. Can't you imagine how airily he would produce her, on Thursday nights. 'I have an Aunt who copulates in a tree, and thinks herself with child by a grasshopper – charming isn't it? She dresses in green, and my mother sends her nuts from the Stores.'[85]

In letters and in conversation Virginia was capable of wild, exorbitant and dazzling imaginative leaps which often have a comical side to them. This is such a fancy, but there is a desperate loneliness too. She sees herself as an outsider, half human, half animal, who does not really know where she belongs. On 27 December, she apologized to Violet for not giving her a present. She had obtained a card for her but then handed it to Sophie. Having insulted her, she then assured Violet that only the delights of 'intercourse' made the prospect of being shut up in London tolerable. When was Violet free to take tea?

Early in the new year, Virginia did two uncharacteristic things. First, she volunteered to work for Women's Suffrage. In the office of that group, the young women were ardent and educated, the men brotherly. She spent hours writing names on envelopes and ruefully observed that the movement would never be successful if it had to depend upon the likes of her. Second, she participated on 10 February 1910 in the '*Dreadnought* Hoax', engineered by Adrian and Horace Cole; Duncan Grant, Anthony Buxton and Guy Ridley were the other accomplices. This group hoodwinked officials of the Royal Navy into believing that their party comprised the Emperor of Abyssinia and his court, who wanted to inspect the *Dreadnought*, then the most secret battleship afloat. They were allowed to do so, and the incident would have gone undetected had not Cole informed the *Daily Express* and the *Daily Mirror* of their success.

The repressed side of Adrian surfaced in his career as a practical joker, as it had done in the Zanzibar episode five years before in Cambridge. In 1910, Adrian had wanted to march a detachment of invading German troops into France in the face of impending hostilities, but he decided to settle for a tilt at the British Navy. An added inducement was a chance to hoodwink his cousin Billy Fisher, who was flag commander of the ship. Since the Emperor (Buxton) needed the semblance of a retinue, Adrian pressed Virginia into service. When Vanessa heard what was afoot, she warned Adrian and Virginia against the consequences of their childish behaviour, but they stood firm against her. For her supporting role, Virginia wore a turban, an embroidered caftan and a gold chain; her face was blackened with greasepaint and a handsome moustache was the *pièce de résistance*.

There were some frightening moments when the group thought they were on the verge of being unmasked, but the tour went very well. In his most pedantic and condescending manner, the captain explained the intricacies of guns, turrets and range-finders to the foreign dignitaries, who refused refreshments and a twenty-one-gun salute. When an exhausted Virginia arrived home that evening, Sophie was beside herself: 'Oh Miss Genia, Miss Genia!' Soon after Cole's leak to the newspapers, reporters had descended on 29 Fitzroy Square, having heard that one of the malefactors was a good-looking young woman with classical features. Newspaper headlines and questions in Parliament followed. Billy Fisher and some of his fellow officers abducted Duncan Grant to Hampstead Heath. Adrian and Virginia became the black sheep of the Stephen family.

Very much in need of a diversion, Virginia had willingly participated in Adrian's hoax. However, her firsthand glimpse of the military gave her additional evidence of male brutality and silliness. The joke had been, in part, a respite from troubling thoughts, but now her anxieties began to overwhelm her. Virginia's mental health deteriorated considerably that winter. In early March she stayed with the Bells in Cornwall. This pleasantly ramshackle holiday consisted, in part, of donkey rides, games of patience and servings of semolina pudding. When she returned to London, Virginia seemed better. Later, in the middle of June, she joined the Bells at Blean, near Canterbury. From there, she wrote to Saxon.

> Shortly before the rain began, three days ago, we had our windows prized open by a Smith. The decay of centuries had sealed them. No human force can now shut them. Thus we sit exposed to wind and wet by day; and by night, we are invaded by flocks of white moths. They frizzle in the candles, and crawl up my skirts to die, in the hollow of my knee. There is something unspeakably repugnant in the feel of creatures who have lost their legs.[86]

The insects invade, lose their legs and then crawl on to the bodies of their hosts. This is vivid, attenuated and sharply melancholic prose. Virginia was overreacting to the presence of the insects because, in a corresponding manner, she saw depression invading her, imprisoning her in its grasp. She feared that she was losing her mind.

Vanessa consulted Sir George Savage, who said that he would try to find a rest home which would take Virginia. She in turn told her sister of her worry about such a course of treatment and its cost. At the same time, she accused Vanessa of abusing her behind her back. When George Duckworth heard of this breakdown, he wrote to his wayward sister, who considered the possibility of intimating to him that she was pregnant. She was sure that he would suspect Saxon. On 28 June, Virginia was admitted to Burley, Cambridge Park, Twickenham, a rest home run by kind, religious and extremely gullible Jean Thomas.

For the next six weeks, Virginia was supposed to follow the regimen of such places: she was to rest in a darkened room and eat wholesome food. Shortly after her arrival, Virginia showed what a wonderfully unorthodox patient she could be. She once wandered in the garden clad only in a blanket; she threatened to escape to London. Vanessa, who was pregnant again (Quentin was born on 19 August), found it difficult to visit her sister and sent Clive as her proxy. When he arrived at Twickenham, he discovered that Virginia had completely won over Miss Thomas: 'Although Virginia was ill and intellectually and emotionally below normal her magic within a day or two had done its work. Miss [Thomas] was transformed. Nothing like this had happened before; suddenly life, which she had found drab and dreary, had become thrilling and precious.'[87] Certainly, Virginia's powers of seduction were unleashed. Vanessa was calmed to hear of her sister's progress, but she was not completely comfortable with the upper hand Virginia had taken over Miss Thomas and the other staff. She was certain that Virginia had corrupted the morals of the entire household: 'Perhaps you find massage conducive to lust?'[88] She then went on to joke that perhaps after all a marriage between Virginia the Sapphist and Lytton the Sodomite would be an ideal arrangement.

On 28 July, Virginia wrote to her sister, whom she addressed as 'Beloved, or rather, Dark Devil'. In that letter, Virginia describes some of the inmates incarcerated at Burley, hints at a conspiracy against her hatched by Vanessa, threatens to jump out of a window and outlines the limited appeal of chats with Miss Thomas: 'you can't conceive how I want intelligent conversation – even yours'. And she threatened: 'I feel my brains, like a pear, to see if it's ripe; it will be exquisite by September.'[89] Vanessa was exasperated. She thought that Virginia should be left to her own devices, even if it landed her in an asylum permanently. Then she backtracked. However, she told Virginia that she deserved a 'good blowing-up'[90] and asked an important question: who was hoodwinking whom?

In a chilling way, Virginia's life was beginning to become even more intertwined with Rachel Vinrace's. *Melymbrosia* was artifice, but in the process of writing it Virginia became even more poignantly aware of what life did not offer her. Her affair with Clive brought her into touch with the tempestuous, heterosexual side of her nature, but she found it impossible to put any lasting confidence in a man and, of course, she was unsure of her sexual identity. Simply put, she was not certain that there was any point in going on alone. Rachel's most sinister nightmare was of a tunnel, dripping wet, presided over by a sinister, crouching man. Could she, Virginia must have asked herself, escape that tunnel?

Chapter Seven

ALWAYS ALIVE, ALWAYS HOT

(1910–12)

'You might just as well be giving up the time to having babies as to having these attacks, as far as your brains are concerned,'[1] Vanessa advised Virginia in August 1910. She thought there was a slight chance that maternity would settle her younger sister down, but to her dismay Virginia seemed intent on remaining childless and childish. 'Did I tell you,' she asked Virginia, 'that [Jean Thomas] . . . seemed more enamoured than ever of you – in fact said that you were now her principal object in life? I believe she would like nothing better than to be taken on as your permanent attendant. Poor woman.'[2] Overall, Vanessa was relieved that someone else was assuming custodial duties and that her sister and Miss Thomas were about to embark on a two-week walking tour of Cornwall.

The beauty of that county worked its usual magic on Virginia, even though every scenic cliff seemed to be filled with passionate lovers. 'If,' she told Saxon, 'I am ever a lover, I shall try to convey to the world my great amiability. Even when clasped round the neck, I shall try to encourage timid maiden ladies to approach.'[3] During this tramp, Virginia became more and more content, although Jean Thomas's advice that insanity could be combated only by religion appalled her patient, who maintained that the self-conceit of Christians was unendurable. Her own increasingly high spirits led her to consider the possibility that marriage might bring her greater and more permanent bliss. 'I feel a great mastery over the world. My conclusion about marriage might interest you,' she told Clive. 'So happy I am it seems a pity not to be happier; and yet when I imagine the man to whom I shall say certain things, it isn't my dear Lytton, or Hilton either.'[4] There is a flirtatious edge to this letter, but there is also the growing certainty that marriage might provide the answer for her to many elusive questions.

Her brother-in-law's nerves were also frayed. That autumn, he squabbled bitterly with Lytton, who, he claimed, paid no attention to him or his opinions. Clive's objections were justified, but his anger was obviously fuelled by lingering resentment: despite the circumstances of his permanent bachelorhood, Lytton had been free two years earlier to propose to Virginia. The quarrel aroused Virginia's mischievous side, as she informed Ottoline: 'The plan is now to give a fancy dress ball, where Clive shall be a Guardsman, and Lytton a ballet girl, and they will embrace before they discover, and make it up.'[5]

Clive was further unsettled when he called upon Virginia at Fitzroy Square that November. That meeting was interrupted by a surprise visit from Mary Sheepshanks. Later he complained bitterly to his sister-in-law that she should have had the way barred: 'To see Sheep installed in my chair, doing what I ought to have been doing? To be ousted in fact. For I was ousted. It was a clear choice between a tête-à-tête with me or with Sheep, and Sheep won.'[6] As Virginia peremptorily informed Clive, she did not like to have Miss Sheepshanks inflicted upon her, but 'I'm certain that I shall never have the courage to turn people out when they're on the stairs – not [even] if I'm in my lover's arms!'[7]

Although Virginia was trying to loosen the considerable ties that bound her to Clive, she found it difficult to shake off the lingering effects of conspiracy and flirtation. On 12 January 1911, he confessed to her: 'In your black velvet coat and hat and red-pink carnations, you looked so lovely that I utterly lost my nerve and head for a time, and could only stumble through the end of a conversation and tumble silent into a taxi-cab.'[8]

A new area of shared interest between the in-laws concerned the nexus between literature and painting. These two pursuits had long been segregated by the sisters, but, as Virginia informed

Violet, 'now that Clive is in the van of aesthetic opinion, I hear a great deal about pictures'.[9] Virginia is referring to Clive's role in helping to select works for Roger Fry's seminal exhibition, 'Manet and the Post-Impressionists', which opened at the Grafton Gallery on 8 November 1910. The press view three days before made the show a *succès de scandale*. According to some, the exhibition was the tip of an iceberg, proving the existence of a widespread plot to destroy the whole fabric of European culture. Virginia could not understand why all the duchesses who attended were insulted by the show of work by 'a modest . . . set of painters, innocent even of indecency'.[10] She thought that the Post-Impressionists were like other painters, only better. Wisely, she thought such an opinion best kept to herself.

The chief conspirator was Roger Fry. Educated at Clifton College and King's, he had taken a first in both parts of the natural science tripos. From early manhood he had been torn between his desire to pursue a career in the arts and his Quaker father's wish that he become a scientist; the fine arts were a dubious commodity in the eyes of Sir Edward Fry, a judge. Without doubt, Fry's religious inheritance was inhibiting. Like Caroline Emelia Stephen, he retained a strong belief in the existence of universal truths hovering at the edge of reality, but his father's Quakerism was one which equated commercial success with spiritual goodness.

In 1891, at the age of twenty-five, Roger abandoned biology and went to Italy. His love of Italian Renaissance painting restricted his ability to paint in a modern idiom and he turned to criticism and connoisseurship instead. In 1905, he became Curator of Paintings and was subsequently European Adviser (head of acquisitions) at the Metropolitan Museum of Art in New York City, where he remained for five years. Then he quarrelled with the museum's chairman, the difficult J. Pierpont Morgan, and abandoned the United States. When he returned to England in 1910, at the age of forty-four, his life was in turmoil. That year he was refused the Slade Professorship at Oxford. More importantly, his wife, Helen, whom he had married in 1896, was suffering frequent bouts of severe mental illness. By the end of 1910, she was confined to an asylum.

From 1906, when he first saw a canvas by Cézanne, there had been a profound change in the way Fry viewed art. He became convinced that the French artist was deeply attuned to the underlying constructive design of Italian Renaissance paintings, whose strengths had been hailed in the eighteenth century by Joshua Reynolds, whom Fry greatly admired. Fry realized that Cézanne – together with Gauguin, Van Gogh, and Matisse – was the harbinger of a new order in the history of painting, a turning point which took into account the accomplishments of both Renaissance and Neoclassical art. Such convictions are apparent in this claim of 1912 on behalf of the Post-Impressionists: 'These artists do not seek to give what can, after all, be but a pale reflex of actual appearance, but to arouse the conviction of a new and definite reality. They do not seek to imitate form, but to create form; not to imitate life, but to find an equivalent for life.' Although his own canvases seem timid when compared to those of the painters who inspired him, Fry became the proponent in England of what was essentially an entirely new way of rendering the world. The fact that both his professional and personal lives were in disarray galvanized him into a truly radical act. He would expose the English to what was really contemporary.

Ultimately, Fry's relentless championing of experimentation helped to unleash parallel attempts in writing by Virginia. Clive Bell, who had earlier shown considerable understanding of the new directions in fiction-writing being taken by his sister-in-law, quickly joined Fry's cause and became in the process an important theorist concerned with the visual arts. Virginia asserted, truthfully, that she preferred books to pictures, but this exhibition made her aware of how much what she wanted to achieve as a writer was, like Post-Impressionist art, revolutionary.

Unlike the Impressionists, Manet and his associates were not so much interested in recording the shifting patterns of appearance as in stressing their individual responses to what they saw. However, they did emphasize an underlying, controlling structure. They thus felt free to select and rearrange reality in order to create the desired effects. Virginia, who always strove for organic unity, realized early on in her writing career that she wanted to move away from the established confines of fiction. In order to do this, she had to select and rearrange material in a manner markedly at variance with the practice of many of her fellow novelists. In December 1910, she told Clive: 'I should say that my great change was in the way of courage, or conceit; and that I had given up adventuring after other people's forms, as I used.'[11] Roger Fry's aesthetic doctrines were crucial at this turning point in Virginia's development as a writer, but his personal influence was more profound.

Fry, who had been away from England for five years, was a latecomer to Bloomsbury. He was sixteen years older than Virginia and for her he remained a benign paternal figure. He was tall, lanky and pleasantly unhandsome. He almost always had on a blue shirt and, as Clive Bell put it, he 'wore good clothes badly'. He could be a demanding taskmaster – there was certainly something of the entrepreneur in his make-up. Yet his craggy face was one of great charm – behind his glasses, his eyes twinkled constantly. Although deeply wounded by his wife's mental instability, he continued to hold love and friendship as life's true ideals.

As Virginia fondly recalled, Clive, who had made his acquaintance on the Cambridge train a short time before, introduced her to Roger:

> It must have been in 1910 I suppose that Clive one evening rushed upstairs in a state of the highest excitement. He had just had one of the most interesting conversations of his life. It was with Roger Fry. They had been discussing the theory of art for hours. He thought Roger Fry the most interesting person he had met since Cambridge days. So Roger appeared . . . he had canvases under his arms; his hair flew; his eyes glowed.[12]

Immediately, Virginia realized that Roger shared her brother-in-law's interest in the visual arts and his heterosexuality, but he was a very different kind of man, one who was gentler, less bluff, much more nurturing. Virginia was certainly sufficiently under his sway to appear, together with Vanessa, Adrian and James Strachey, as a South Sea savage *à la* Gauguin at the Post-Impressionist Ball at Crosby Hall in March 1911. She was dressed in Manchester African cloth and, as in the '*Dreadnought* Hoax', her face and limbs were blackened. She inquired of a friend: 'Was I less alarming as a savage – or as bad as ever?'[13]

Virginia continued to wrestle with *Melymbrosia*, which she now viewed as a fragment heap of 'love, morals, ethics, comedy, tragedy, and so on'.[14] Women's Suffrage had quickly become incredibly boring. She asked Janet Case: 'Do you ever take that side of politics into account – the inhuman side, and how all the best feelings are shrivelled?'[15] In addition, London was reduced in her mind to a place smelling of vice in stuffy rooms.

The landscapes of Cornwall and Wales had always offered her relief from the grimier aspects of urban life, but those places were not easily accessible from London. In December 1910, she went to Lewes in Sussex for a week and while there found a house to rent in Firle. This villa was raw, red and newly built, but it was near the country and thus could offer her a reprise of the happiest days of her childhood. Before that, she had been confined to the narrow 'strip of pavement'[16] of a London existence. Now, she would be able to take starlit walks upon the downs, where nibbling horses might possibly mistake her for a great white sheep. In sum, she was a bucolic goddess, one who could appropriately bestow the name Little Talland House upon her new retreat. By April 1911, under the influence of Vanessa, her co-tenant, the interior of the cottage was, Virginia joked, inconceivably ugly, 'done up in patches of post-impressionist colour'.[17] The countryside soon produced a new assortment of characters, including the clergyman who had possession of the head of Cromwell but was being persuaded to give it up. Virginia confessed that she had the greatest desire to see it – and even stroke it!

During the Post-Impressionist exhibition, Vanessa and Roger took several leisurely turns around the rooms. She was not sure that he had any real interest in women: 'Then sometimes I thought that underneath his possibly ascetic exterior there were hidden immense depths of passion and emotion – sometimes I thought he had been through too much and had become almost aloof and detached from that side of life.'[18] Sufficiently impressed by his connoisseurship and intrigued by his mysterious inner life, Vanessa agreed to accompany him, Clive and another friend, Harry Norton the Cambridge mathematician, on a trip to Turkey that April. Clive, who knew that his wife was not really in good health, was apprehensive. However, he wondered what would happen to Virginia in his absence: 'While we are apart, a good deal may happen; and I have an irrational foreboding that something will. Probably, I imagine, you will fall in love, or, at least, that someone will fall in love with you.' If such a change took place, Clive wanted his own spot in her affections: 'I assume, you see, I have a niche. But have I?'[19]

The trip did not start well. There was a strong gale at Dover and Clive was afraid lest a delay in the crossing might mean that he and Vanessa would miss the Orient Express (Fry and Norton had gone on ahead and were waiting for them at Brussels). He pleaded with her to turn back. She was steadfast and they arrived on schedule at Ghent. Once the party of four was together, Roger became the leader. Clive continued to fuss his wife, but she and Roger often wandered off together, sketching or painting. Clive and Norton had become superfluous accessories to the two artists.

After Constantinople, the party went via Greek steamer to Brusa, the original Ottoman capital at the foot of Mount Olympus. One day, while Roger and Vanessa were sketching, a Turk invited them to his home. There Roger painted the man's portrait while Vanessa made an oil sketch of his wife. Then the two visitors were taken into the garden to wash their hands. Vanessa sat on the ground, took off her rings and put them in her lap, but when she got up her engagement ring fell into the well. Despite the best efforts of their host, the ring could not be recovered. His wife became convinced that she was being accused of stealing the ring.

The only way Vanessa could console her hostess was to embrace her.

In a moment that was for her profoundly unsettling, Vanessa did what she customarily did: she offered help to another person. She also experienced the chilling sensation that something obscure but terrible had happened. Of course, the loss of her ring was symbolic of what had been happening for a number of years: she was losing her husband. A couple of days later, Vanessa miscarried. This brought on a complete physical collapse which was then followed by a mental breakdown. Clive was a hapless witness to his wife's distress, whereas Roger, who was accustomed to looking after his own wife, ministered to her. In fact, he insisted that she get better and he achieved his end by cajoling and bossing his patient back to health.

When Virginia was notified of her sister's grave illness, she thought that yet another tragedy was about to seize her. She set out for Turkey on 22 April and returned to England with the Bells and Roger on 29 April. Almost a month later, she asked Violet: 'Did you hear of our adventures in the East? . . . We had to get a litter made, and carry [Vanessa] stretched on it, through Constantinople and home by the Orient Express. It was the oddest parody of what we did five years ago.'[20] Although Vanessa was badly debilitated, she, unlike Thoby, survived. This shattering episode made Virginia aware of how much she loved and needed her sister. Also, she must have realized the full extent of the danger of losing Vanessa, a peril which she had courted in her affair with Clive. He had been virtually useless in Turkey, while significantly she saw firsthand in Roger Fry a person who understood that the role of nurse did not compromise male identity.

Vanessa's health was poor for the next two years and, almost inevitably, she drew closer to Roger. Having spent so much of her life caring for her younger sister, she had found someone who was willing and eager to look after her. Virginia's behaviour certainly weakened her hold on her elder sister, who was concerned lest Virginia attempt to destroy her relationship with Roger. On

5 September, she instructed her lover to exercise caution: Virginia, she assured him, was 'really too dangerous'. In particular, Virginia was provoking Clive by implying that his suspicions about Vanessa sleeping with Roger were true. Clive, an exasperated Vanessa told Roger,

> says that if she comes here he knows she will make mischief between you & him by making him think I am in love with you – Oh dear – what complications there are – I think we must be careful with her & give her no possible excuse for being able to say anything . . . It's true that she has in almost every letter (which she knows I read aloud for the most part) said something about you & my staying with her, implying that I do want to go there with you especially, which does naturally irritate Clive. I try to skip but it's not easy. I can't think why she does it & must try to stop her.[21]

Vanessa's affair with Roger made Clive more attentive to his wife, who did not miss, as she told Roger on 15 November, the fine irony of the situation: 'If this had happened 3 years ago when Clive was thinking only of Virginia, it might all have been easy! though I don't know it's wonderful how you did divert him to me again.'[22]

The countryside had now become Virginia's principal diversion. There she deepened some friendships. She visited Court Place, Iffley, Oxford, the home of the Pearsall Smiths, a Quaker family from the United States. Logan Pearsall Smith had already collaborated with his sister Mary Costelloe, who had married Bernhard Berenson in 1900, on the periodical *Golden Urn*. There was also the unpredictable and often raucous Gumbo – Marjorie Strachey, Lytton's sister – to whom she bore a strong resemblance. Gumbo aroused the comical, surreal side of Virginia, who, in January 1911, observed her seated at a piano, singing to her own accompaniment. She was dressed in a tight green jersey, which made her look like a lean cat: 'The accompaniment ends: she flings her hands up, and gives vent to a passionate shriek; crashes her hands down again and goes on. A dry yellow skin has formed round her lips, owing to her having a fried egg for breakfast.'

Gumbo's attitude to love seemed relatively uncomplicated: she would relinquish whatever talent she had if one person, preferably a man, would say she was lovely. Ka [Katherine] Cox held more complicated views. Ka was a Newnhamite, always a drawback for Virginia. She also bore 'a superficial resemblance to a far younger and prettier Sheepshanks'.[23] Despite these flaws, Virginia was immediately taken with her new acquaintance, especially when Ka admitted that she experienced very few emotions. Virginia was worried that she was similarly lacking.

At first glance, Ka, a hefty, robust Fabian, did not seem 'neo-pagan' – Bloomsbury's term for the poet Rupert Brooke and his circle. These young people were, for the most part, the children of Victorian intellectuals, but they had very different interests from their rival group: they were far less cerebral, much more hearty and athletic – they were inordinately fond of tents and canoes. For Virginia, this group was the embodiment of youth, sunshine, nature, cakes with sugar on top, bawdiness, primitive art, love, lust and paganism. In a letter to Virginia of 3 October 1910, Vanessa had made a crucial distinction: 'I find it odd, the way in which the minds of the rising generation seem to be almost perpetually & wholly engrossed in love . . . You & I in our young days paid it comparatively little attention.'[24]

In April 1911, Virginia was engrossed by the Ka Cox–Jacques Raverat–Gwen Darwin triangle. A year before, the French painter had proposed to Ka. She repeatedly said no. She even suggested he consider Gwen, who quickly fell in love with him. He proposed; she accepted. Jacques, who claimed to be in love with both women, suggested a compromise: he would marry Gwen, and Ka could become his mistress. In defence of his claims, Jacques preached against the uncharitableness of chastity, but both women were deeply uncertain about what they should do. For Virginia, Jacques was phallic man personified: 'red, quite unshaven, hatless, with only one book – Rabelais'.[25]

Virginia was set to go off to France with Ka in April, but her participation in that expedition was cancelled when she had to leave suddenly for Brusa. Four months later, Virginia accepted an invitation from Brooke, a friend from childhood (he had known the Stephens on holiday at St Ives), to stay with him at the Old Vicarage in Grantchester.

Rupert Brooke, the son of a master at Rugby School, was educated at Rugby and King's College, Cambridge, where he became a fellow in 1913. He was elected an Apostle in 1908 and in the following year president of the University Fabian Society. Even by 1911, Virginia's friend had become an icon, one who apparently combined love of the countryside, devotion to literature, political correctness and virility. Rupert, she later reflected, was a 'type of English young manhood at its healthiest and most vigorous . . . his feet were permanently bare; he disdained tobacco and butcher's meat; and he lived all day, and perhaps slept all night, in the open air'.[26] For Virginia, these were intriguing traits, worthy of firsthand inspection.

Just before she arrived, Rupert told Ka that the prospect of spending time with his St Ives chum intimidated him. As it turned out, though, there was nothing to worry about. Virginia occupied Ka's bed on the other side of the house; always self-conscious about her body, she was sufficiently unintimidated by Rupert one clear, moonlit night to follow his injunction, 'Let's go swimming quite naked.' Virginia even took it in her stride when Rupert performed his party piece: he jumped into the water and emerged with an erection.

One day they were sitting under the shade of chestnuts. Rupert was at a loss for a word to complete a poem.

'What's the brightest thing in Nature?'

'Sunlight on a leaf.'

'Thanks!'

In addition to helping him complete a poem, Virginia noticed that his habit of leaving spaces for 'unforthcoming words' made his manuscripts look like puzzles with missing pieces.

During this visit, Rupert persuaded Virginia to join him and his friends on a camping expedition to a meadow near Clifford

Bridge, on the banks of the River Teign, five miles from Drewsteignton in Devon. Ka met Virginia at the railway station and, during the arduous eight-mile walk to the camp, she assured Virginia, who had become testy, that a wonderful meal would be awaiting them. When they arrived, no one was there and the hungry women began to eat the remains of a blackberry summer pudding before noticing that it had gone off. Things went better after that: the group, which included James Strachey and John Maynard and Geoffrey Keynes, visited Lytton, who was in lodgings in nearby Manaton, took a long walk to Yestor and, on the way back, had a manhunt (Brynhild Olivier, the quarry, outwitted her pursuers) and even had play-readings. Virginia said little of this holiday, apart from writing to Roger Fry: 'From my observations shaving is unknown among the younger generation.'[27]

Rupert Brooke, who did not like the 'atmosphere' of Bloomsbury, was the type of man Lytton Strachey loved to hate. He found him sexually attractive but considered him a simple-minded romantic. In 1911, Virginia found it difficult to make such an easy judgement on an old friend. Like her, Brooke understood the power of the natural world, with which he wanted to dwell in peace. Like her, he was in pursuit of a literary career. He was the embodiment of *ideals* which attracted her. Since he was the preserve of Ka Cox, Virginia could take a close look at him without fear of any real involvement, and, since their friendship never progressed beyond the boundaries of childhood, she could, without apparent discomfort, bathe in the nude with him.

There was another aspect of Brooke which Virginia discerned in 1911: his great physical beauty had impoverished rather than enhanced his existence. In fact, there was an androgynous edge to Brooke's breathtakingly handsome face. He was aware of his prowess, but he was worried that his splendour might be only what it appeared to be: skin-deep. His sexuality tortured him: was he heterosexual or homosexual? He did not know. He was simply too attractive and, ironically, was wounded by the very traits which made him such a success. What Virginia saw that summer was a young man who, she later noted, was in large part 'jealous, moody, ill-balanced'.[28] She is most likely commenting on Brooke's excessive self-centredness, which left room for little more than extravagant emotions. In him, she saw a ravishing man-child, a person incapable of enduring life's tough battles.

Throughout 1911, Virginia's insecurities reigned triumphant: 'To be 29 and unmarried – to be a failure – childless – insane too, no writer'.[29] This inventory is nothing less than a series of self-inflicted indictments. Without doubt, she was much too harsh on herself. One barometer of pervasive, psychic strain was her continuing fascination with Miss Thomas's inmates. One of these leaped when she beheld Virginia, and Jean assured her that such excitements were the wine of life. In January 1911, Jean managed to visit her at Little Talland House, in an interval between discharging a woman who wanted to commit murder and taking in one who wanted to kill herself. 'Can you imagine living like that? – always watching the knives, and expecting to find bedroom doors locked, or a corpse in the bath?'[30] This question was directed at Violet, who, under similar circumstances, had been Virginia's vigilant caretaker at Welwyn.

In June 1911, Virginia's anxiety about her mental instability and her sexuality had reached such a peak that she told a startled Janet Case of George Duckworth's 'malefactions'. In turn, Janet confessed her intense dislike of him and how, years before, she had been scandalized when she observed him fondling his half-sister while she was attempting to study Greek. The teacher had said to herself: 'Whew – you nasty creature.' Janet was also shocked when, to pass the time on a rail trip, she innocently asked what Virginia was daydreaming about. Taken by surprise, Virginia told her the truth: 'Supposing next time we meet a baby leaps within me.'[31] Janet primly instructed Virginia that this was an unsuitable way to speak. Virginia was trying to see what the connection was between George's conduct in the past and her present fear of sexuality. She might have been linking her 'childless' condition with having been abused as a child, but she was also flirting with the idea of having a child.

One way of dealing with stasis was to change houses. By July 1911, Virginia and Adrian had determined to give up Fitzroy Square. At first they considered sharing a house in Bedford Square with friends. Then brother and sister pondered the possibility of augmenting their incomes by taking in lodgers at Fitzroy Square. Then they decided to move to 38 Brunswick Square, where there would be paying guests. Virginia was to live in rooms of her own on the second floor; Adrian was to have the first storey; Maynard Keynes would have a pied-à-terre on the ground floor which would double as Duncan Grant's studio. Only the vacant top storey was unaccounted for.

If Virginia was hoping to stir things up, she succeeded admirably. George was flabbergasted by this scheme: a young unmarried woman could not simply go off on her own with three unmarried men, even if one of them was her brother. Vanessa ribbed him by pointing out that Virginia's new home was near the Foundling Hospital, where she could presumably get rid of any babies. Violet also objected, stoutly maintaining that Julia Stephen would never have approved of her youngest daughter acting in such an unladylike manner. Eventually, Duncan painted, in what Vanessa called his leopard style, a London street scene in the ground-floor drawing room. He also did a mural for Adrian's room: a tennis game between male nudes in the manner of Matisse. Above them, Virginia's rooms remained undecorated – and messy.

An unexpected note of discord surfaced on 20 July 1911, when hesitant, bumbling Walter Lamb invited Virginia to go with him on an excursion to Richmond Park. Variously known as Wat, Wattie and The Corporal, he had read classics at Trinity and was often mocked for his short stature and obsequiousness. The essential paradox of his nature was well drawn by Lytton Strachey, when he observed that Lamb was 'like a fellow with one leg who's not only quite convinced that he's got two but boasts of his walking exploits'.[32] At the outset of their expedition, Lamb pompously lamented the general dearth of admirable human beings. Then they turned to the slightly less philosophical, potentially more gossipy topics of love and women.

Seizing the moment, he asked her: 'Will you tell me if you've ever been in love?'

Without replying to the question, Virginia asked if he knew about Lytton's proposal.

'Clive told me a good deal,' he assured her.

This angered Virginia, but she tried not to show it. She told Walter that she would confide in him if he was not inquiring out of mere curiosity. He avowed that he really wanted to know what she felt and would be glad to hear anything she might like to tell him. She proceeded to give him an 'abstract'.

Virginia apparently passed some sort of test, which allowed him to proceed to another level of intimacy: 'Do you want to have children and love in the normal way?'

The second part of the question might have seemed to pose some difficulties but nevertheless she answered yes.

This led to a declaration of sorts: 'I do care for you very much.'

'But you're quite happy?'

'There are such dreadful complications.'

'What?'

'You live in a hornet's nest. Besides marriage is so difficult. Will you let me wait? Don't hurry me.'

At this point Virginia, who had not been hurrying anyone, became rather touchy: 'There is no reason why we shouldn't be friends – or why we should change things and get agitated.'

He agreed: 'Of course, it's wonderful as it is.'

Then the conversation rambled on further. He could not let himself fall in love because he wasn't sure what Virginia felt. She puzzled him; she made spiders' webs out of emotional problems; she might turn against him. He asked if she would flirt if she were married. 'Not if I were in love with my husband,' she countered. However, Virginia owned up to being excessively self-centred, whereupon he assured her that Clive had told him horrific stories confirming this. Then Lamb shifted ground by praising Vanessa. Soon afterwards the conversation turned to a discussion of his gout.

There was an interval. They had tea and went to the opera. He walked her home and unfortunately Adrian was out when they arrived back at Fitzroy Square. His absence led to further ruminations on Walter's part. He might want to live near her in the autumn. Virginia, obviously wondering if he was suggesting some sort of trial engagement, became uneasy. She turned the conversation to the beauty of friendship, a fairly safe topic.

Finally, her long day with Walter was over. He made Virginia uncomfortable, even though she admired him for being honest. Nevertheless, the prospect of another long talk with him appalled her. He was, she realized, a rather pathetic character. 'He's desperately afraid of making a fool of himself, and yet conscious that his caution is a little absurd.'[33] He continued to express his passion – if it can be called that – in a series of watery letters, but his cause was hopeless.

Walter's indiscreet references to Clive's gossip about Virginia's character caused further trouble. Virginia vented her irritation with Clive by telling her sister in great detail about the day at Richmond Park. Clive, furious at having his confidences broken and jealous that Walter wanted to whisk Virginia away, never spoke to him again. On her part, if she was not going to fall in love with him, Virginia felt that she could not accept any further compliments from Walter Lamb. Yet again, Virginia was made to feel a dismal failure, a person of inordinate vanity who attempted to consume men with what she termed her 'vampire like suction'.[34]

As usual, her writing was a source of gnawing anxiety. In September 1911, Virginia told her friend Desmond MacCarthy how much she admired his professional attitude towards writing. In contrast, she remained a 'perfect amateur'.[35] Desmond, educated at Eton and Trinity College, Cambridge, where he had been an Apostle and a close friend of Thoby, had already established his reputation as a drama critic. In December 1906, he had married Molly (Mary) Warre-Cornish, a niece by marriage, like Virginia, of Anny Ritchie. In the long run, the life of a journalist took a heavy toll on Desmond's creativity but in 1911 Virginia could discern only the apparent ease with which he wrote.

Again, a measure of her restlessness can be seen by her search for yet another country retreat. If Little Talland House was a mean suburban villa which just happened to be in the country, Asheham (or Asham) House, at Beddingham, off the Lewes–Newhaven road, was splendidly dreamy. This small early-nineteenth-century house, which Virginia did not take possession of until early in 1912, set among tall elms under Itford Hill, looked across the Ouse valley to Rodmell. Its small central block and two single-storey wings were pierced by tall, thin french windows. This dwelling, of which Vanessa was again the co-tenant, never seemed quite of the real world. Under Virginia's influence, it took on the character of a pleasantly haunted house.

That November, Virginia, Adrian, Duncan and Maynard finally moved into Brunswick Square. For Virginia, this was a moment of triumph: 'We are going to try all kinds of experiments,' she assured Ottoline.[36] The same note of exhilaration can be seen in a letter to Violet of 20 November: 'I am now undertaking an entirely new branch of life.'[37] If she wished to, Violet could continue to offer advice, but this had to be on Virginia's terms: she had to be free to reject it.

By 2 December, a tenant had been found for the top floor. Leonard Woolf, a close Cambridge friend of Thoby, was to live there. On that day, the mistress of the house sent him a set of rules, which reads in part:

> Meals are:
>
> | | |
> |---|---|
> | Breakfast | 9 a.m. |
> | Lunch | 1. |
> | Tea | 4.30 p.m. |
> | Dinner | 8 p.m. |
>
> Trays will be placed in the hall punctually at these hours. Inmates are requested to carry up their own trays; and to put the dirty plates on them and carry them down again *as soon as the meal is finished.*
>
> . . .
>
> It is not possible as a general rule to cater for guests as well as

> inmates. If notice is given, exceptions can sometimes be made. Particular desires will be considered. A box will be placed in the hall in which it is requested that inmates shall place their requests or complaints.

Virginia's covering letter was not quite so brusque, although she did emphasize that their experiment in freedom had to be governed by punctuality: at all costs, Sophie and Maud, the maid, had to be kept in good spirits. In general, she was sanguine, although she wanted to ask her lodger 'about other small things: whether you like fish – but that can wait'.[38] Unknown to her, Leonard was in love with her. He was poignantly aware that by taking the room he was putting himself in a dangerous situation: 'I see it will be the beginning of hopelessness. To be in love with her – isn't that a danger? Isn't it always a danger which is never really worth the risk?'[39]

*

> Each soul is but a half circle, there is somewhere its complement & we are all striving, searching to find the other half. Sometimes we find one that is almost – but not quite – the complement, the soul of a man or woman alive or the soul of a dead man living in music or poem – & there is a flash of soul fire & for a moment we live. But the flame dies down for the circle was not complete & then the old wandering in the wilderness of Boredom begins again. If only one could really complete the circle! Poets, artists & musicians are the happiest – for they create another soul out of their own & these two half circles – the old & the self-created souls – join & there is a flash that never dies down & *they* always live.[40]

In 1901, twenty-year-old Leonard Woolf believed in the transforming power of love and art. Indeed, his language and symbols are robustly Wagnerian as well as Platonic. He also held strong convictions about how to do battle with the great pest, boredom. As the metaphor of fire suggests, he was – and remained – a deeply passionate man, one who was willing to fight, usually against the odds, to 'complete the circle'. However, his idealism was bought at a high price: estrangement from his family, his early environment and his Jewishness.

Leonard's Kensington childhood home at Lexham Gardens was ample and spacious. It had to be, since he was the fourth of ten children born to Sidney Woolf, a barrister, and his wife, Marie de Jongh, who came from a Dutch family which had settled in London in the mid-nineteenth century. Marie had a great deal of resourcefulness and common sense, but Leonard, who thought she loved him least of the children, was disturbed by the sugary mawkishness with which she confronted life. Leonard was his father's favourite. From him he inherited many of his physical traits, including the nervous tremor in his hands. Without doubt, the twelve-year-old was shattered by his forty-eight-year-old father's death from tuberculosis and heart failure in 1892. The family, forced to live in reduced circumstances, moved to Colinette Road, Putney.

The loss of his father and childhood were obviously traumatic, but even before, Leonard had often felt overwhelmed by a sense of cosmic disorder and evil. His melancholia was, he knew, constitutional and he dealt with it by coming to the (lifelong) conclusion that 'in the end, nothing matters'. Boy and man, he had a long, narrow face; sunken eyes were accompanied by high cheekbones. These two features gave his countenance a marked austerity, somewhat in the manner of an Old Testament prophet. Leonard's sadness was thus apparent to everyone who met him. Not so easily discernible were his strong feelings. He revealed that side of himself reluctantly. Such detachment was protective, insulating him from disappointment. This stance allowed the youngster to get on with his schooling. He went from Arlington House, Brighton, to St Paul's; in 1899 he gained entry as a classics scholar to Trinity College, Cambridge. There, the boy who had lived without hope became a man who saw a sliver of light.

In his autobiography, Leonard wrote at length of Cambridge without saying very much about his studies or his teachers. Instead, those pages are suffused with the enormous pleasure he took at being recognized for his considerable intellectual capacity, with his delight at becoming an Apostle and with the joy of knowing like-minded persons such as Maynard Keynes, Desmond MacCarthy, Clive Bell, E. M. Forster and Saxon Sydney-Turner. His closest friends were Lytton Strachey and Thoby Stephen. Above all these men towered the philosopher G. E. Moore, who provided Leonard with a scientific basis for affirming the primacy of friendship and art. It was this slightly older man who first offered Leonard a glimpse of a perfect circle. Through him, he learned to distinguish between the nice and the good, between the superficial appearance of conviviality and the rigorous pursuit of love and commitment.

These convictions were dearly bought. During his first year at university, Leonard suffered a nervous collapse, about which he wrote in July 1901:

> For soon Doubt came upon me black as Hell,
> And everything seemed slipping from my grasp
> And the whole world was vanity – I saw
> For the first time into the heart of things,
> Beneath the shining surface of this pool.[41]

Although he had once again confronted the desolating power of darkness, Cambridge proved the existence of a good, however insubstantial, worth pursuing.

Cambridge may have brought Leonard back to life, but in the process it made him deeply suspicious of his origins. In his *roman-à-clef*, *The Wise Virgins*, Leonard drew a harsh, satirical portrait of the snobbish, withdrawn, difficult side of himself in Harry Davis, the book's protagonist. Harry, a would-be painter, is the consummate outsider within his suburban family; he especially dislikes his Jewish family's easy acceptance of Anglo-Saxon standards of behaviour. Although he realizes that his Jewishness puts him into contact with an emotive, potentially liberating sphere of existence, he spurns that inheritance in the hope of being accepted by a semi-bohemian clique. Ultimately, Harry Davis is a shallow rebel, one very much without a cause.

Leonard's portrayal of Harry Davis shows his ability to look at himself with an exceedingly caustic eye, but he often found it difficult to translate his powers of self-analysis into action. In particular, the idealism he imbibed at Cambridge inhibited him. Ordinary life simply did not offer enough scope for the potential he had seen in himself. He did not know how to focus his considerable energy, yet he had to earn a living. He sat the Civil Service examination, came in fifty-sixth and had to settle for an Eastern Cadetship (an entry-level position in the Colonial Civil Service). In the autumn of 1904 he sailed for Ceylon.

Not surprisingly, Leonard was a brilliant, compassionate administrator, one who developed a deep affection for the Ceylonese and their land but considered the machinery of empire repulsive and disgusting. For six exceedingly long years, he was steadily promoted: Koddu superintendent at Pearl Fishery, acting assistant government agent in Mannar, office assistant in Kandy and, in August 1908, assistant government agent in Hambantota.

Behind his façade of impenetrable reserve, Leonard was a desperately unhappy man, cut off from what mattered most to him: his Cambridge friends. Over and over again, Leonard told Lytton of professional and emotional burnout. There is palpable despair in his letter of 21 March 1906:

> I sometimes wonder whether I shall commit suicide before the six years are up & I can see you again: at this moment I feel as near as I have ever been. Depression is becoming, I believe, a mania with me, it sweeps upon & over me every eight or ten days, deeper each time. If you hear that I have died of sunstroke, you may be the only person to know that I have chosen that method of annihilation . . . And then there are the flies – they are bred in the millions of rotting oysters that lie about the camp . . . They are crawling over one's face & hands all day long & owing to the putrid filth on which they feed every little scratch or spot on one becomes sore.
>
> Can I write to you about Duncan or the Society out of this?[42]

What possible relation, Leonard wondered, was there between his golden Cambridge past and his grim present as a colonial officer?

There were many other important differences between Leonard and Lytton. 'If,' Leonard assured Lytton, 'you live in tempests & crises, I live in a hell of lunatics.'[43] This acute piece of observation is more complex than it first appears. The 'tempests & crises' with which Lytton filled his letters were often centred on his homosexuality, whereas Leonard was very much a heterosexual. In a letter of 1904, Lytton commented on the 'curious masculinity' which separated Leonard from most of his Cambridge friends, including himself: 'Why are you a man? We are females, nous autres, but your mind is singularly male.'[44] Like Lytton, Leonard was tortured by a strong sex drive:

> Among other things I have been in love lately [May 1907] . . . The only thing is that I am mad enough to be able to go on as if I weren't, as if nothing happened or existed. In another week I shall, I think, be petrified completely. It is none the less unpleasant & filthy. I am beginning to think it is always degraded being in love: after all 99/100ths of it is always the desire to copulate, otherwise it is only the shadow of itself, & a particular desire to copulate seems to me no less degraded than a general. One day I shall fall in love with a prostitute.[45]

Despite the liberating influence of Moore, love and sex were difficult for Leonard and Lytton to conjoin. In contrast, both men perceived friendship as one of the highest goods and Thoby Stephen had been their ideal friend. For Leonard, Thoby was the anchor, one who was above everyone in his nobility, and for him Thoby's death was yet another instance of the darkness which threatened the fragile hold of the good on life.

When he first saw Vanessa and Virginia in Thoby's rooms at Trinity in the spring of 1903, Leonard declared that 'their beauty literally took one's breath away'.[46] In contrast, Virginia had been morbidly fascinated by the man 'who trembled perpetually all over' and asked her brother the cause of this:

> Thoby somehow made me feel that it was part of his nature – he was so violent, so savage; he so despised the human race . . . I

> was of course inspired with the deepest interest in that violent trembling misanthropic Jew who had already shaken his fist at civilization and was about to disappear into the tropics so that we should none of us ever see him again.[47]

Virginia may have been curious about Leonard, but before Thoby's death Leonard had fancied himself in love with Vanessa, not Virginia.* His feelings for the elder sister, he knew, were aroused by her kinship with Thoby, with whom she shared 'something monumental, monolithic, granitic'.[48] When he learned in July 1905 that Clive Bell was pursuing her, he was unnerved. He had always thought that Clive was in love with one of the Stephen sisters: 'though strangely I thought it was the other'. Then he asked Lytton:

> You think that Bell is really wildly in love with her? The curious part is that I was too after they came up that May term to Cambridge, & still more curious that there is a mirage of it still left. She is so superbly like the Goth. I often used to wonder whether he was in love with the Goth because he was in love with her & I was in love with her, because with the Goth.[49]

Leonard was trying to analyse extremely complicated emotional issues: he did not know how much of his sexual attraction to Vanessa, who looked like her brother, was tied to his devotion to Thoby. However, this is not a case of repressed homosexuality: by becoming Vanessa's lover he would have formed an alliance with the sister of a man who embodied the highest ideals of friendship. In this scheme of things, Eros took a back seat to Agape.

Any possibility of Leonard marrying Vanessa was dashed by Thoby's death and her marriage to Clive. Leonard had to endure

* In his *Autobiography* (II, 14), Leonard was brutally frank: 'Vanessa was, I think, usually more beautiful than Virginia. The form of her features was more perfect, her eyes bigger and better, her complexion more glowing . . . Vanessa in her thirties had something of the physical splendour which Adonis must have seen when the goddess suddenly stood before him.'

his exile's life for four more years and his existence continued to be a mix of physical misery and emotional deprivation. On 19 February 1909, Lytton told Leonard of his proposal to Virginia and of the disastrous consequences which would have ensued had they remained engaged. He had an idea: 'I think there's no doubt whatever that you ought to marry her. You *would* be great enough and you'll have the immense advantage of physical desire . . . If you came and proposed she'ld accept. She really would.'[50] Lytton's assurance may have been a bit breezy but, as time proved, he was an excellent matchmaker. And he was an indomitable one, as his letter to Leonard of 21 August 1909 makes clear:

> Your destiny is clearly marked out for you, but will you allow it to work? You must marry Virginia. She's sitting waiting for you, is there any objection? She's the only woman in the world with sufficient brains: it's a miracle that she should exist; but if you're not careful you'll lose the opportunity. At any moment she might go off with heaven knows who – Duncan? Quite possible. She's young, wild, inquisitive, discontented, and longing to be in love. If I were you I should telegraph. But at any rate come and see her before the end of 1910.[51]

Despite his adroit understanding of Virginia's character, Lytton had an extremely limited notion of how 'immense' an advantage sex would play in any love affair with Virginia Stephen.

Leonard did not send a telegram. In fact, he did not arrive back in England until June 1911, and even then he moved slowly, despite having only a year's leave. He later described the next six months as the most supremely happy of his life. He went to Cambridge and attended a meeting of the Apostles, travelled to Scandinavia and spent time in a Dartmoor cottage with Moore and Strachey. However, that August he confided to his brother Edgar that he intended to marry Virginia, who was becoming even more expert at rejecting unsavoury advances. When she visited the Ritchies in December 1911, she was so appalled by Richmond's lecherous overtures that she quickly left the house. She also dealt summarily with the just about to be divorced Sydney Waterlow when he proposed. The previous year, that suitor had confided to his diary his view of the two sisters: 'Vanessa icy, cynical, artistic, Virginia much more emotional, and interested in life rather than beauty'.[52] Almost everyone else had the opposite impression, but Waterlow caught a glimpse of the inner warmth beneath Virginia's sometimes frosty exterior.

When she renewed her acquaintance with Leonard in the summer of 1911, Virginia took to him. She invited him to Firle, told him to call her by her Christian name and, of course, asked him to take part in the Brunswick Square experiment. At the very same time, as she told Vanessa, she was again seriously thinking of marriage, despite its attendant drawbacks: 'I suppose though there is a kind of unity in marriage (barring children) which one doesn't get from liaisons . . . My quarrel with it is that the pace is so slow, when you are two people.'[53] Leonard, despite Lytton's imprecations, continued to move very slowly in his pursuit of Virginia, but as the negotiations regarding Brunswick Square brought him into closer contact, he found it increasingly difficult to restrain himself. Did he want to take the risk of falling in love and very possibly being rejected?

Risk or not, on 10 January he declared himself. He was staying in Frome, Somerset, and telegraphed Virginia, asking for an interview the next day. At that meeting, he told her that he had resolved not to propose unless he was certain that she loved him and would marry him. A bit earlier, when he discussed with her the possibility of his going back to Ceylon, he realized just how hopelessly infatuated he really was, even though he was uncertain as to whether she loved, could ever love or even like him. Since he could no longer act rationally, he had sent the telegram. Virginia stalled. In case he hadn't noticed, she assured him, she was very self-centred. Moreover, her position was diametrically opposed to his: she was very much outside the ring of fire. If she was not consumed with passion, should she take such a risk? Before she could say no to the proposal, she was interrupted by the unexpected arrival of Walter Lamb.

'Don't you think the entrance of Walter almost proves the existence of a deity?'[54] Leonard jokingly asked Virginia the next day. On 13 January, on her way to catch the train for Firle, she told him that she had, for the moment, nothing further to say. She hoped their friendship could continue as before and she wished to be free – and honest. However, Virginia's indecisiveness can be clearly seen in this sentence: 'I have decided to keep this completely secret, except for Vanessa; and I have made her promise not to tell Clive.'[55] Not surprisingly, Vanessa instructed Virginia that she should not marry unless she was in love. She did not want to unduly influence her sister in any way, but in the tortured logic of this sentence her real feelings can be seen: 'It's quite true that Leonard is the only person I have ever seen whom I can imagine as the right husband for you, but I also see that it's not the least necessary that you should marry at all & also it's quite possible that other people may arise as suddenly as he did.'[56]

Within a week, Virginia had taken to bed with what she called 'a touch of my usual disease'.[57] She was filled with conflicting feelings – something which had not happened when others had proposed. This is clearly reflected in her letter to Violet of 7 February: 'I'm now rampant, feeding on bullocks' blood, and henbane; or the heads of red poppies which make me dream wild dreams – about you, and alabaster pillars, and dogs defiling them.'[58] Virginia tried to go on as before. She went to Niton in the Isle of Wight to stay with Vanessa; in February she held a housewarming party at Asheham, which Leonard attended. By 16 February, she could no longer cope with her indecision and returned to Jean Thomas's nursing home. Soon after her release about three weeks later, she wrote to Leonard: 'I shall tell you wonderful stories of the lunatics. By the bye, they've elected me King. There can be no doubt about it. I summoned a conclave, and made a proclamation about Christianity . . . I now feel very clear, calm, and move slowly, like one of the great big animals at the zoo.'[59]

Despite her comicality, Virginia is indirectly telling Leonard just how shaken she has been by his proposal and is also being extraordinarily candid about her fragile condition. Although she did not confess this to Leonard, he had deeply altered her ideas about marriage. In the past, she told a friend, she had held tremendously idealized, and thus absurd, beliefs about matrimony. Then, her bird's-eye view of many marriages had disgusted her. 'Now I only ask for someone to make me vehement, and then I'll marry him!'[60]

Of course, Leonard was making Virginia more and more vehement, but she was also very unsure of her feelings, especially sexual ones. Although overwhelmed by passion, he assured her on 29 April that his love for her was 'not only physical . . . though it is that of course'. He also counted the physical side as 'the least part of it.'[61] In her reply of 1 May 1912, Virginia carried her principle of truthfulness to extraordinary lengths:

> is it the sexual side of it that comes between us? As I told you brutally the other day, I feel no physical attraction in you. There are moments – when you kissed me the other day was one – when I feel no more than a rock. And yet your caring for me as you do almost overwhelms me . . . I feel I must give you everything; and that if I can't, well, marriage would only be second-best for you as well as for me.

She attempted to define her ideal of marriage in even more precise terms: 'We both of us want a marriage that is a tremendous living thing, always alive, always hot, not dead and easy in parts as most marriages are.'[62] Here, she is telling Leonard that she is not sexually attracted to him but knows that they both want a complete marriage, one which is, in part, 'always hot'. There is a cruel paradox at work here, one which was never resolved.

There were certainly many affinities. In Leonard, Virginia could discern many character traits of Thoby and the ghost of her dead brother created a strong bond between them. Being a Jew, Leonard was an outsider; Virginia did not fit comfortably into any conventional definition of womanhood. Both placed a great reliance on work. In Leonard, Virginia saw a man very much like Roger Fry: strong but nurturing. For her, Leonard was a *deus ex machina*, a strong, silent man who had hunted tigers in Ceylon. Her very first impression had been of his magnificent savagery. Perhaps he could help to quell her inner demons. Virginia and Leonard were vulnerable in similar ways: both were constitutionally melancholic and, at approximately the same age, had been traumatized by the death of parents.

Virginia's lack of sexual feeling obviously went back to a fear of intrusion. Her father had been tyrannical, and George's and Gerald's conduct had been sexually overbearing. At some basic level, these men had threatened her femininity and yet for a long time she had wanted to do away with the virgin coldness which threatened her work and her sense of herself. She desired change and at the same time she was rigorously honest with Leonard, who, she intuitively knew, loved and would care for her. Still, a basic misunderstanding arose. Despite Virginia's ferocious honesty, Leonard thought that the power of their love would ultimately overcome the physically reserved side of her nature. On that score, he was to be bitterly disappointed.

At this time, in a series of character sketches (the Aspasia papers*) of Virginia, himself and other friends and acquaintances, Leonard portrayed his beloved as a beautiful Olympian with a fearless mind. Her voice was particularly enchanting. In addition, she confronted reality directly.

> She is one of possibly three women who know that dung is merely dung, death death & semen semen . . . She does not really know the feeling – which alone saves the brain & the body – that after all nothing matters. She asks too much from the earth & from the people who crawl about it. I am always frightened that with her eyes fixed on the great rocks she will stumble among the stones.

Sometimes, he wondered if she had a heart. But then, he assured

* Aspasia was Leonard's name for Virginia in his diary. The name comes from Plato: 'Menexenus: Truly Socrates, I marvel that Aspasia, who is only a woman, should be able to compose such a speech, she must be a rare one' (Benjamin Jowett, *The Dialogues of Plato*, II, 532).

himself, 'I swear this cannot be true, that the sun in her comes from a heart.' When she read this piece, Virginia was hurt: 'I don't think you have made me soft or loveable enough.' She also asked: 'Who is it says that I am vain & a liar? . . . Do you really think I haven't got a heart?'

In the Aspasia papers, Leonard was particularly hard on himself: 'He is lustful, a whorer, a gazer after women, vicious because he loves the refinement of vice . . . He is romantic, sentimental with himself . . . He is obsessed, languid, tortured by himself. This obsession cools his passions, his fire [cools] his affections . . . It makes him silly, vain, mean, jealous, a liar, a coward.' In his portraits of the other female characters (Sophia, Dorothea, Lady Mary Robinson), Leonard gazes with a very critical mind at women who are too devoted to virginity or who are prone to forget they possess bodies. Lady Mary 'has copulated, I suppose, because she has had eight children, yet the word copulation has never passed her lips & she would faint if she heard the word fuck'.[63]

Although Virginia may have become increasingly certain that she did not wish to remain a single woman, she never took any enjoyment in the sexual pleasures of the body. Leonard craved such enjoyment. The Aspasia papers may clearly demonstrate Leonard's devotion to Virginia, but they also reveal the discords which were to arise between them.

In the spring of 1912, Virginia and Leonard were drifting closer together, close enough for Leonard, who in February had asked the Colonial Office to extend his leave by four months, to resign on 2 May, the day he received Virginia's letter. They agreed to get on with their writing and Leonard suggested that Virginia complete *Melymbrosia* before deciding whether to marry. On 3 May, she and Leonard attended the inquiry into the sinking of the *Titanic* on 14–15 April. The fate of that liner fascinated Virginia. Perhaps the fact that the seemingly impregnable vessel had been struck on its maiden voyage by a submerged iceberg made her wonder if her own life was subject to similar, hidden forces.

On 22 May, Virginia pointed out to Violet somewhat facetiously that she was afraid lest Violet should tell her just how complete a failure she was as a woman and as a writer.* If that happened, 'I shall take a dive into the Serpentine which, I see, is 6 feet deep in malodorous mud.'[64] With Virginia, any joke about death by water has a strong resonance; here it indicates the acute discomfort which the prospect of marriage raised in her.

Exactly a week later, Virginia finally told Leonard she would marry him. Appropriately, one of the first people Leonard informed of his engagement was Lytton: 'I'm so happy that that's the only thing that I can say to you, simply that I am.'[65] Virginia was unwell and in bed throughout most of June, but her happiness can be clearly seen in her letter to Violet of 4 June:

> I've got a confession to make. I'm going to marry Leonard Wolf [*sic*]. He's a penniless Jew. I'm more happy than anyone ever said was possible – but I *insist* upon your liking him too . . . You have always been such a splendid and delightful creature, whom I've loved ever since I was a mere chit, that I couldn't bear it if you disapproved of my husband . . . My novel is just about finished. Leonard thinks my writing the best part of me. We're going to work very hard. Is this too incoherent? The one thing that must be made plain is my intense feeling of affection for you. How I've bothered you – and what a lot you've always given me.[66]

Virginia was attempting to blend her past and her present. Violet had been a generous caretaker. Here Virginia was thanking her, wanting her approval and obliquely suggesting that Leonard was to replace her. Virginia made similar announcements in letters to Madge and Janet, but she waited until Vanessa returned to London in early June before breaking the news to her. When Clive heard, he was distraught: 'whatever happens, I shall always cheat myself in to

* Violet's letter of 20 or 21 May (MS Sussex) had begun, 'Are you pregnant, or married?' Virginia was not amused when this letter was delivered opened. Violet had written 32 rather than 38 Brunswick Square and her letter was opened – and presumably read – by a Miss Stephen who lived at 32.

believing that I appreciate and love you better than your husband does'.[67]

That July Virginia felt revitalized. At long last she was able to envisage the completion of *Melymbrosia.* That saddened her, but she had some new ideas for fictional projects. However, her sense of renewal extended beyond her work. 'Next year,' she confided to Violet, 'I must have a child.'[68]

Chapter Eight

A WILD SWAN

(1912–15)

At first, Virginia's boldness in having agreed to marry Leonard confounded her, almost as if her engagement were a miracle – an answer to a prayer but certainly not an event in which she had actively participated. At long last, fate was on her side. Gradually she was filled with an extraordinary sense of well-being. The fairy-tale element in this romance led Virginia to describe her Prince Charming in exaggeratedly glowing terms: 'he has ruled India, hung black men, and shot tigers'.[1] What was more, he was also a would-be novelist.

There was trouble in paradise, however. That June Virginia confessed to Violet that love, work and Jews in Putney – the Woolf family – exhausted her. Virginia often spoke of Jews in extremely negative terms. Her anti-Semitism can be explained but not explained away. She embodied many of the anti-Semitic opinions of her class, although, it must be remembered, she also rebelled against her class. She disliked most members of Leonard's family, but rather than analysing her feelings, she often saw their bad behaviour in terms of their Jewishness. This is a comparatively easy way to deal with complex responses to individuals. When she became angry at Leonard's miserliness, she tended, in a similar manner, to attribute this to his Jewishness rather than to see it as a personal character trait. Although she did not like to admit it, Virginia was deeply attracted to Jews because she felt they were outsiders who were in touch with vital emotions from which members of her own class – herself included – were excluded.

Marie Woolf was excessively polite, reserved and self-assured during her initial encounter with Virginia, as can be seen from the following conversation at that tea party:

'A sandwich, Miss Stephen – or may I call you Virginia?'

'What? Ham sandwiches for tea?' Virginia often answered questions with questions, but Mrs Woolf was not amused. In fact, she felt insulted.

'Not *Ham*: potted meat. We don't eat Ham or bacon or Shellfish in this house.'

Virginia countered: 'Not Shellfish? Why not shellfish?'

Now Mrs Woolf felt that she was dealing with a rather tiresome child. 'Because it says in the Scriptures that they are unclean creatures.'[2]

Unfortunately, nothing more of this conversation survives. According to Virginia, who recorded this intriguing snippet, the encounter had been 'queer'. Of course, the two women were sparring with each other, and the prize was Leonard. However, Mrs Woolf was probably well aware that she would be the loser in any conflict of loyalties, and Virginia was simply seeking confirmation of this. In *The Wise Virgins*, Harry's mother, the tedious Mrs Davis, is based upon Marie Woolf:

> The big curved nose, the curling, full lips, the great brown eyes would have made a fine old woman of her, if she had been squatting under a palm-tree with a white linen cloth thrown over her head and drawn round her heavy oval face. The monotonous sing-song of her voice would have sounded all right if she had sung the song of Miriam which tells how the Egyptian horse and his rider were overwhelmed by Jehovah in the sea; it came incongruously through the large nose in her quiet, precise, voluble and thin-sounding English.[3]

When Camilla, the Virginia Stephen character, finally meets Mrs Davis, she beholds 'a very large, dark old woman in the middle of an immense number of rich and important clothes, with two pathetically big eyes, two strong, thick lips, two deep furrows in all that time had won from powder and puffs out of a sallow face under an enormous lop-sided festoon of purple ostrich feathers'. Mrs Davis is excessively conventional – she is from the suburbs and as such is to be despised. There is also a low-grade but pervasive air of anti-Semitism in the presentation of her. In his mind, Leonard drew a comparison between his real-life mother's limited intellectual capacities and Virginia's unbridled imagination.

United in their disdain for Marie Woolf, Leonard and Virginia also shared a dislike for priggish Will Vaughan, and Leonard, even more so than Virginia, found Madge's flightiness unbearable. However, Marny, Will's sister, soon became a favourite of Leonard. Intrigued by her enthusiasm about her work with the poor at the Care Committee in Hoxton, he accepted her invitation to visit her there. That meeting was an important event in his conversion to socialism. As to Violet Dickinson, for many years she had been a mother figure to Virginia and Leonard assured Virginia that he had never met anyone he liked so much as her.

So determined were the engaged couple in their antagonism towards Leonard's mother that, in order to accommodate Vanessa and Clive, they married on the Sabbath, the one day of the week Mrs Woolf would not attend a civil ceremony. In response, Marie, who rightly felt that she had been cut by Leonard and Virginia, sent her wayward son a stiff letter five days before the event. Virginia expressed surprise at Marie Woolf's reaction, almost as if the elder woman had no right to feel insulted. In fact, Virginia, in referring to her as 'poor old Mother Wolf',[4] reduced her to the status of a beast from a fairy-tale. A bit later, she claimed that her mother-in-law was amused by everything and yet understood nothing.

Virginia and Leonard's wedding took place on Saturday, 10 August, rather than the originally scheduled Monday, 12 August, at 12.15 at St Pancras Register Office in a room overlooking a cemetery. The registrar, who was half blind, may also have been a bit hard of hearing. The raging thunderstorm provided a further distraction. The fact that Vanessa and Virginia both had names beginning with V was too much for him and he confused the bride with her sister. Once this was straightened out, Vanessa made things even more muddled when she interrupted the proceedings to ask the now thoroughly dazed official what the procedure was for changing her son's name from Quentin to Christopher. The other guests were Saxon, Duncan, Aunt Mary Fisher, George and Gerald Duckworth and the exceedingly mangy-looking artist Frederick Etchells, a friend of Duncan, who mumbled something about the financial benefits accruing from pawning one's clothes. Certainly, the slovenly apparel of the two artists stood out in marked contrast to the frock coats in which the Duckworths were attired. Despite these obstacles, Virginia's love of humour prevailed; she enjoyed the ceremony very much. Now her surname was Woolf, but 'to shops I shall be the ordinary animal, because it's simpler'.[5]

The wedding luncheon was at 46 Gordon Square. After the couple left for Asheham, Clive penned a letter in which he declared: 'You must believe that, in spite of all my craziness, I love you very much, and that I love your lover too.'[6] Later that summer, he assured her that marriage gave a couple a profound, mystical sense of possessing and being possessed. A few days later, Virginia blandly assured him: 'Your letter made a great deal of difference to both of us.'[7] Well before the wedding, Leonard was deeply irritated by the remnants of the affair with Clive: he was jealous of his brother-in-law's hold over his wife and thought Virginia's attraction to Clive was a manifestation of bad taste on her part.*

The Woolfs spent two nights at Asheham, returned briefly to London and then spent a few days at the Plough Inn, Holford, Somerset, in the Quantocks. Earlier, the Woolfs had briefly considered the idea of journeying to Iceland, but that plan was jettisoned in favour of a honeymoon in Provence, Spain and Italy, for which they left on 18 August.

* Pompous, excessively stuffy Trevor Trevithick in *The Wise Virgins* is based on Clive: 'No passion, no feeling even to which weak humanity is subject had ever moved or vibrated through the sallow, parchment-like skin of his face' (London: The Hogarth Press, 1979, 48). In a nice turn, Camilla's father, the wry, arch Mr Lawrence, is not based on Leslie Stephen but on Lytton Strachey.

The newly-weds encountered bad food in Barcelona and overpowering heat in Madrid before going on to Toledo, Saragossa and Valencia. They quickly developed a routine of two days in one spot, then a day travelling to another. When not on trains, they walked in the morning, read in the afternoon, had tea, walked by the seashore and then sat near the local café after dinner. Their attempts to sleep were often disrupted by mosquitoes; by morning, they had bloodied the walls with the corpses of these pests. On 1 September, Leonard told Saxon: 'We stayed in an inn in a village under Montserrat – sleeping over a urinal, a pigsty & a washing tub which stank more than either.'[8] Virginia and Leonard talked incessantly during these seven weeks, becoming in the process, Virginia observed, 'chronically nomadic and monogamic'.[9] On the surface, this extended foray was splendidly haphazard and serendipitous. There was another, crucial dimension.

On 4 September, in a letter to Ka, Virginia broke her silence on the sexual aspects of married life: 'Why do you think people make such a fuss about marriage and copulation? Why do some of our friends change upon losing chastity? Possibly my great age makes it less of a catastrophe; but certainly I find the climax immensely exaggerated.'[10] Such nonchalance is in glaring contrast to Leonard's claim that when he tried to make love to Virginia, 'she had got into such a violent state of excitement that he had to stop, knowing as he did that these states were a prelude to her attacks of madness'.[11] He also observed that it was as pleasant to be with Virginia in the furnace of Spain as in the rain and biting wind of the Grand Canal in Venice. However, in April 1913, Virginia told Vanessa, who had just returned from Venice, that she thought the city detestable *both* times she had visited it: 'once it might be due to insanity but not twice'.[12] Virginia was obviously linking her first disastrous stay there in 1904 with the unsettling sides of married life.

Virginia had toyed with a new style of life when she moved to Brunswick Square and at the very same time she was testing the limits of the genre of fiction. In many ways, marriage for her was a similar exploration of uncharted territory, a journey which might save or destroy her. From the outset, Virginia declared that her marriage – her newest experiment – worked very well. Without doubt, this was true. It was true, however, only up to a point. Sexual intercourse was ultimately unacceptable to her. In part, such activity rekindled in her mind the invasive behaviour of the Duckworths – it was a basic intrusion into her sense of self. She could not reconcile herself to it, even though she was very much in love with Leonard.

In his turn, Leonard tended to be silent about his reaction to a wife who did not respond to him sexually, but the Woolfs consulted Vanessa about this difficult matter in December 1912, four months into their marriage. Vanessa was bemused, as she told Clive:

> [They] seemed very happy, but are evidently both a little exercised in their minds on the subject of the Goat's coldness. I think that I perhaps annoyed her but may have consoled him by saying that I thought she never had understood or sympathized with sexual passion in men. Apparently she still gets no pleasure at all from the act, which I think is curious. They were very anxious to know when I first had an orgasm.[13]

Here, Vanessa is extremely condescending to Virginia, who had not been pleased to learn on her honeymoon that her elder sister had, against her wishes, told Leonard some secrets that she did not wish divulged. According to Vanessa, Virginia could be 'annoyed' while, at the same time, Leonard 'consoled'. Sexual passion was supposed to be Vanessa's domain, from which she wanted to exclude her younger sister.

After 1912, it is unlikely that Leonard and Virginia slept together, even at those times when Virginia flirted with the idea of having children. Leonard's feelings about Virginia's sexual frigidity can be seen in *The Wise Virgins* in this Lawrentian confrontation between Harry and Camilla:

> His voice was dull and passionless. His dark view of life seemed to her to throw a gloom over the bright day. She fought in

> herself against that view. He had not said what those dried-up spinsters missed, what he was afraid for him and her missing. In his mind it had meant what the male wants, a certain fierceness of love, mentally and bodily; something which romance and civilization and all the generations which lie behind mankind have made, at least in our hopes and imaginations, a flame that shall join and weld together and isolate from the rest of the world. She knew vaguely, felt vaguely what he meant. But it was not in her, a woman and unmarried, to know the want. There was no gap yet in her life. She was too beautiful to have lacked or to lack admiration and the love of men, and too alive not to like and to be excited by it. And there her knowledge, her experience, and therefore her desires, ended. Among men, as among animals, it is the young male who is fierce and dangerous, and roars and bellows and makes all the noise.[14]

The egocentric, self-destructive Harry possesses a fierceness which is warm, passionate and dangerous. Camilla is excited only by the idea of desire. Here, the basic incompatibility of this fictional couple is chillingly delineated. This passage from *The Wise Virgins* is far more savage and direct in its treatment of repressed sexuality than anything in its dress-rehearsal, the Aspasia papers. In the novel, Harry's sexual desires eventually lead him to impregnate and later marry Gwen, who is portrayed as earnest and pedestrian. In mythology, Camilla's existence was consecrated to Diana, goddess of the moon and chastity. In his real life, Leonard married a Camilla, one who could not accept his sexual embraces.

Despite the barriers between them, Leonard and Virginia were devoted to each other and, rather reluctantly, returned on 3 October to London and Brunswick Square. Five days later, Leonard took up his post as secretary to the second Post-Impressionist Exhibition (i.e. Roger Fry's assistant) at the Grafton Galleries. Late that month, they moved to 13 Clifford's Inn, an old building in a small court sandwiched between Chancery and Fetter Lanes, just a few yards from Fleet Street. A move to such a bustling part of London, Virginia was sure, would lead to a week of intense misery, two weeks of profound discomfort and finally, at Christmas, a permanent state of bliss. These chambers, according to Leonard, were old, draughty and dirty. Virginia thought them delightful. They overlooked a sliver of grass and there was, in the manner of a Cambridge college, a porter and bedmaker. Virginia became so relaxed that she did not mind their maid seeing Leonard and her naked every morning. Her ever-observant eye was fascinated by the daily events in the lives of the other tenants.

In early October, just after the Woolfs arrived back in London, Violet sent them a cradle – a bold hint and a prosaic way of dealing with the facts of life. More than anyone else, Violet knew how important the idea of having a baby was to Virginia; after all, she had tried to find a baby for her in 1904. Virginia decided that her child would indeed sleep there and she thought the patch of green an ideal place 'for my brats to play in'.[15] When London threatened to overwhelm her, she could retire to Asheham.

Whether in the city or the country, husband and wife continued to write. They considered the possibility of starting a magazine but could not raise the requisite £2,000. There were some domestic tensions. Leonard and Adrian did not get along and there was even more friction when Vanessa took her brother's side. Throughout their marriage, Leonard remained bitterly convinced that Virginia preferred her family, particularly Vanessa, to himself.

In 1912, these were relatively minor matters. On 21 December, Virginia began rewriting the middle section of *Melymbrosia*, the chapters leading up to Rachel's death. At that time, the frequent headaches which had bothered her earlier in the month became overwhelming. In addition, Leonard was ill with malaria, a disease with some of the features of the mysterious illness which carries Rachel off.

In revising her first novel for publication, Virginia drained the narrative of elements which were directly autobiographical. Theresa, Rachel's mother, is much more prominent in *Melymbrosia*.

Lesbian desire becomes modified, although Virginia observed to Vanessa as late as October 1928 that she still held those sentiments in response to her: 'thank goodness your beauty is ruined, for my incestuous feeling may then be cooled'.[16] Rachel, who has decided opinions on literature in the earlier version, is not particularly well read in the final one. For example, in *Melymbrosia*, when Richard Dalloway says that Jane Austen is 'incomparably the greatest female writer we possess', Rachel responds by saying that perhaps 'the Brontës also qualify.'[17] These observations are removed from *The Voyage Out*. In the process of revision, Virginia transformed Rachel from proto-feminist into innocent victim. In the earlier narrative, Rachel is a woman fascinated with and repelled by her own sexuality. By making her more naïve and Helen less obviously malicious, by eliminating much of the erotic undertones in their relationship and by introducing stylistic changes which make the conflict between Rachel and Helen much more ambiguous, Virginia obscured much of the autobiographical elements around which *Melymbrosia* had been constructed.

In particular, Rachel's death scene was extensively and continuously revised. In *Melymbrosia*, the reader sees these events from Rachel's perspective, which surprisingly is objectified, detached and therefore unemotional. What is remarkably different in *The Voyage Out* is that Rachel's deathbed perception of life as a wasteland – and her resultant feeling of total exhaustion – emanates from the perspective of the seemingly more detached omniscient narrator: 'She did not wish to remember; it troubled her when people tried to disturb her loneliness; she wished to be alone. She wished for nothing else in the world.'[18] Ultimately, Rachel's death is much more movingly rendered in *The Voyage Out* than in *Melymbrosia* because its more impersonal description of her final days makes her plight more symbolic of the terrors facing women caught in the grips of a male-dominated culture.

The Voyage Out is about the dilemmas of young women in society. Should they marry? What does a single life offer them? Is sex a destructive force? All these issues are treated in a format not completely dissimilar to E. M. Forster's, but Virginia shies away from some of the comfortable conclusions in a novel like *A Room with a View*. Without doubt, she attempted to make the conflicts in *The Voyage Out* of more general appeal than they would have been if they were too tied to her own unhappy past. She lost some of the raw power of *Melymbrosia*, but she did gain a compensating expansiveness of vision. Moreover, she employed the form of polite fiction to undermine polite society.

At the very same time that she was removing the more personal elements from her narrative, Virginia was forced to confront her past. In particular, Virginia Woolf had to ask herself if she should have remained Virginia Stephen. In marrying Leonard, she had tried to avoid the pitfalls of maiden coldness and male intrusion. To a large extent, she had hit upon a workable compromise between these two seemingly irreconcilable extremes. However, she now had a new set of dilemmas: she wanted to have a baby, but she did not wish to endure sexual intercourse. She wanted to nurture a baby, but she herself had never been properly nurtured. In December 1912, the conflicts at the heart of Rachel's existence began to overtake Rachel's creator.

The headaches continued into January and, during that month, Leonard began to consult medical experts as to the wisdom of Virginia having a child. There is a strange causality at work here. Leonard did not seek medical advice on Virginia's health but rather on a matter indirectly related to it, although her anxieties might have been centred on the child issue, making it appropriate to take advice on what might have appeared to be a secondary concern. Leonard might also have wondered if Virginia's vulnerabilities would allow her to take proper care of a child. He might possibly have felt that her lack of interest in sex indicated ineptitude as a mother. At first glance, Leonard's explanation of his conduct seems straightforward:

> In the next few months, I became more and more uneasy about one thing. We both wanted to have children, but the more I saw the dangerous effect of any strain or stress upon her, the more I began to doubt whether she would be able to stand the

strain and stress of childbearing. I went and consulted Sir George Savage; he brushed my doubts aside.[19]

But Leonard already entertained serious reservations about Savage's *laissez-faire* approach. He certainly did not like Sir George's cavalier, condescending advice about the possibility of Virginia becoming pregnant: 'Do her a world of good, my dear fellow; do her a world of good!'[20] So Leonard consulted two other physicians, Maurice Craig and T. B. Hyslop, as well as Jean Thomas. He summarized their advice perfunctorily: 'They confirmed my fears and were strongly against [Virginia] having children. We followed their advice.'[21] At this point, Virginia had not met either Craig or Hyslop.

Savage had been Virginia's doctor since 1904. Like many physicians who dealt with psychiatric problems, he recommended rest and food as the best remedies against mental instability, which, according to him, occurred when the 'moral nature or the moral side of the character is affected greatly in excess of the intellectual side.'[22] Leonard may have felt that Savage, who turned seventy in 1912, was no longer in the vanguard of the treatment of mental illness. Craig and Hyslop were in their mid-forties.

Even more than Savage, Craig – who was Vanessa's doctor – believed that 'insanity' indicated a lack of harmony between the individual and society: 'Completely out of tune there, [such a patient] is a social discord of which nothing can be made.'[23]*

* Craig would have seen Virginia's flights of fancy in conversation as indicative of what he calls 'mania': 'These patients are frequently considered brilliant in their conversations. This is not actually the case, for when analysed this seeming brilliancy will be found in large measure to be due to the unconventional character of their chatter. They say quaint things which strike the hearer who is not used to home truths and personalities, as amusing. These patients are often more entertaining when ill than during health, for through loss of control they will in illness make remarks which they would in health perhaps think, but forbear to utter (*Psychological Medicine*. London: J. and A. Churchill, 1905, 94).

Like many other doctors who treated patients with mental disorders,

Hyslop maintained that 'the removal of woman from her natural sphere of domesticity to that of mental labour not only renders her less fit to maintain the virility of the race, but it renders her prone to degenerate and initiate a downward tendency which gathers impetus in her progeny'.[24]* Even more than the genial Savage, Craig and Hyslop were firm believers in conformity as the goal in psychiatric treatment.

If anything, these younger doctors were more threatened than Savage by the possibility of women departing from their prescribed roles. In any event, all three men were not really interested in exploring the aetiology of Virginia's headaches, refusals to eat and depressed feelings. They wanted to keep her quiet and, in the case of Craig and Hyslop, they felt that she should not 'initiate a downward tendency' in the race by having children. This was another way of keeping her silent – and invisible.

Moreover, there are further, curious discrepancies in Leonard's account. Vanessa's letters to her sister and brother-in-law demonstrate just how vexed and complicated the issue of children had become. In speaking to Leonard of Craig's opinion, she said: 'I have been coming to think that on the whole one does plunge into a new & unknown state of affairs when one starts a baby & once it's started there's no going back . . . I suppose he thinks the risk she runs is that of another nervous breakdown & I doubt if even a

---

Craig was a firm believer in 'stuffing' (the normal goal was a weight gain of 30 lb in two months). Rupert Brooke made this comment about the regimen Craig devised for him in 1912: 'My nerve specialist's treatment is successful and in a way pleasant . . . I have to eat as much as much as I can get down, with all sorts of extra patent foods and pills, milk and stout. I have to have breakfast in bed about 10 every day, go to bed early, never take any exercise, walk never more than two miles, and do no kind of brain-work' (to E. J. Dent, 11 March 1912, Rupert Brooke Archive, King's College, Cambridge).

* Hyslop's hostility to Virginia having children would derive from his conviction that 'the more our women aspire to exercising their nervous and mental functions so they become not only less virile, but also less capable of generating healthy stock' ('A Discussion of Occupation and Environment as Causative Factors of Insanity', *British Medical Journal*, 2, 1905, 942).

baby would be worth that.'[25] To her sister, she added this observation: 'I wouldn't run a really appreciable risk of another bad breakdown or even of getting your nerves into a permanent worse state for if you did you couldn't much enjoy the baby when it came.'[26] (She also mentioned that Jean Thomas was in favour of Virginia having a baby.) Then, as often happened, Vanessa – less than a week later – softened her stand:

> I shouldn't worry about the baby question. One can never really settle these matters beforehand. They always settle themselves eventually, at least they have for me so far generally, accidentally. However of course you must think about it but don't worry for anything may turn up. I wonder why Leonard has gradually come to think child bearing so dangerous?[27]

Soon after, she reported that she had discussed this matter with Craig: 'he seemed to think it possible that you could get into a state when the risk would be very much less'.[28]

Leonard's own attitude towards having children is captured in this passage from his autobiography: 'I can see and sympathize with the appeal of helplessness and vulnerability in a very young living creature – I have felt it myself in the case of an infant puppy, kitten, leopard, and even the much less attractive and more savage human baby.'[29] It could well be that Leonard's own sense of psychic weakness would have been unduly exacerbated by having to take care of a baby.

Leonard presented the pregnancy as a more or less closed issue: Savage had advised them to have a baby, whereas all the other experts had disagreed. But in the case of Jean Thomas, this was not so. Also, Vanessa, who had modified her original opinion, did not understand why Leonard had become so inflexible. In any event, Leonard may have used the wrong pronoun: he – not 'we' – followed professional advice. That April, Virginia did not feel that the issue of having a child was a closed book: 'We aren't going to have a baby, but we want to have one, and 6 months in the country or so is said to be necessary first.'[30] However, there would be no children.

This failure haunted Virginia, who told a friend, the American-born painter Ethel Sands, in February 1927: 'I'm always angry with myself for not having forced Leonard to take the risk in spite of the doctors.'[31] Virginia may have blamed Leonard for this turn of events because she realized that he did not wish to have children under *any* circumstances, but her anger was really turned against herself, as she reflected in September 1926: 'a little more self-control on my part, & we might have had a boy of 12, a girl of 10: This always makes me wretched in the early hours.'[32]

On 9 March 1913, in the midst of this crisis, the typescript of *The Voyage Out* was delivered by Leonard to Gerald Duckworth in Henrietta Street. Edward Garnett was the enthusiastic publisher's reader and the book was accepted for publication little more than a month later, on 12 April. On the surface, the selection of a publisher was straightforward. Gerald had recently set up his firm and was presumably in need of titles for his list. However, he was one of the half-brothers whose inappropriate behaviour had made Virginia afraid of men and such concerns are central to *The Voyage Out*. Her choice of publisher could only have added to her anxiety about the success of her first book.

That March and April, Virginia travelled with Leonard, who was studying the Co-operative Movement, to Liverpool, Manchester, York, Carlisle, Leicester and Glasgow. She was writing for the *Times Literary Supplement*, mainly, as she put it, 'reviews and articles and biographies of dead women'.[33]

Despite incessant rain, Asheham provided a glorious retreat in the spring of 1913, although Virginia and Leonard had to battle to keep the garden alive. On the surface, husband and wife had achieved the perfect balance, a genuine half-and-half existence: 'a taste of people, and then a drench of sleep and forgetfulness, and then another look at the world, and back again'.[34] Simmering beneath the surface were the unresolved issues of sex and children.

That June, the Woolfs visited Virginia's cousin Katherine Stephen, the Principal of Newnham College, and attended the Women's Co-operative Congress at Newcastle upon Tyne. At this event,

Virginia experienced a very limited sympathy for the working-class women whose lives were so very different from her own:

> One could not be Mrs Giles of Durham because one's body had never stood at the wash-tub; one's hands had never wrung and scrubbed and chopped up whatever the meat may be that makes a miner's supper . . . [Those women] did not sign a cheque to pay the weekly bills, or order, over the telephone, a cheap but quite adequate seat at the Opera. If they travelled it was on excursion day, with food in string bags and babies in their arms.[35]

She did not like the cheap gibes directed by members of the Congress at women of her own class, but she later realized that it might be possible to blend the worlds of women who attended the plays of Shakespeare and those whose phrases and gestures had a bravado Shakespeare would have enjoyed. However, in 1913 the barriers seemed insurmountable.

The Woolfs entertained Morgan Forster, Lytton Strachey and Molly MacCarthy, among others, at Asheham. On 1 July, Virginia was thrown from her horse, but she sustained no injuries. There was one minor irritation: Vanessa was annoyed because Virginia, without first informing her co-tenant, had announced her intention of letting Asheham for August. By mid-July, Virginia was feeling increasingly unwell and a week later, when she attended the Fabian Society Congress with Leonard at Keswick, she was very ill. Two days later, under instruction from George Savage, Virginia returned to Jean Thomas's nursing home at Twickenham.

Jean was certain that this depression was directly related to anxiety about *The Voyage Out*. Indeed, she felt, as she told Violet, that her family had completely mismanaged Virginia's illness. She was probably right about the direct cause of this breakdown: reading proofs* that July no doubt exacerbated Virginia's increas-

* *The Voyage Out* was in proof (presumably galleys) about three months after being accepted. Virginia was probably not well enough to attend to these until the summer or autumn of 1914. The delays in proofreading probably explain why the novel was not published until March 1915.

ing sense of fragility and her concern about having children. Symbolically, her books were her offspring and she was worried about how this first baby would be received.

Virginia's anger with Leonard – her principal symptom – was direct and sharp: he was her enemy and she did not want to be with him. There can be no doubt that the imposed decision regarding children made Virginia furious with her husband. Leonard could be distant and controlling and Virginia was in part reacting to that side of him. However, Leonard, who often wrote even to close friends in a style reminiscent of military dispatches, had exceedingly tender feelings for his wife. These emotions are plainly visible in the childlike tone of his Mongoose letters to his beloved Mandrill.

> If it weren't so late I should sing you a Mongoose song of joy which begins
> I do adore.
> I do adore.
> I feel so certain after seeing you today that it will be [a] much shorter time to our being together again. Never talk again, dearest, of causing me anything but the most perfect happiness, because literally & honestly that is what I get merely from sitting quietly reading by you. I shall think of you tomorrow as a brave beast lying quietly in its straw & cleaning its dear self from time to time by remembering that.[36]

Those words were penned on 27 July, and the Mandrill's corresponding feelings of warmth can be seen in this snippet from 3 August: 'I want you Mongoose, and I do love you, little beast, if only I weren't so appallingly stupid a mandril. Can you really love me – yes, I believe it, and we will make a happy life. You're so loveable. Tell me exactly *how* you are.'[37]

A mandrill is a large, fierce West African baboon, whereas a mongoose, a species of lemur common in India, is a small, carnivorous animal celebrated for its ability to attack and kill venomous snakes. In giving such nicknames to each other, Leonard and Virginia were fuelling their marriage with animal-like feelings which did not find a corresponding physical expression. There is also a certain amount of gender reversal at work: a mandrill is an exceedingly aggressive animal, whereas the tiny mongoose gets its way by conniving. In their relationship, Virginia felt free to take on some stereotypical male roles, while Leonard could at times take on a seemingly feminine role. If their love did not encompass sexual intercourse, the use of nicknames shows that their marriage was charged with some strong erotic feelings and indicates that this union gave both partners a lot of breathing space to explore the unconventional. There was also a wish on Virginia's part that her Mongoose would slay or disarm the venomous side of her nature, those 'vile imaginations'[38] which threatened to overwhelm her.*

During her stay at Twickenham, Leonard promised his wife a reward: as soon as she was well, they would go on holiday. The Woolfs returned to Asheham on 11 August, but Leonard was convinced that something was still desperately wrong with Virginia. Eleven days later, the couple went to London, where Leonard consulted Savage, who 'pooh-poohed' the possibility of not going on holiday. Leonard must fulfil his pledge. If he did not, Virginia would take this as a vote of no confidence and, as a result, might attempt suicide. When he visited Gordon Square, Leonard discussed this tricky situation with Vanessa and Roger. Fry suggested that Leonard obtain advice from Henry Head, who had treated his deranged wife. Leonard rang Head, who agreed to see him immediately.

* In 'Lappin and Lapinova' (published in 1938 but begun at Asheham in the 1910s), Ernest and Rosalind, a young married couple, in a manner similar to the mandrill and the mongoose, take on the identity of rabbits: 'He was King Lappin; she was Queen Lapinova. They were the very opposite of each other; he was bold and determined; she wary and undependable. He ruled over the busy world of rabbits; her world was a desolate, mysterious place, which she ranged mostly by moonlight' (*Complete Shorter Fiction*, 263). When Ernest no longer wishes to live in a make-believe world and the masquerade can no longer sustain itself, 'that was the end of that marriage' (p. 268). Some of Virginia's fears about the sexual incompatibility between herself and Leonard can be seen in this story.

Of all the neurologists who treated Virginia, Henry Head was the one who was most prepared to understand the aetiology of her depressions and resultant breakdowns. Unlike Savage, Craig and Hyslop, he did not see persons suffering from nervous disorders as nonconformists who must be made to toe society's line.* During that first meeting, Head, who had to rely solely on Leonard's description of Virginia's behaviour, concurred with Savage's opinion. He also suggested that Leonard keep a close watch on Virginia. If things got out of hand, they must immediately return to London, at which point Leonard, who had begun a secret diary in Sinhalese and Tamil characters recording his wife's fluctuating moods, would have to persuade Virginia to come to his consulting room.

With considerable trepidation on Leonard's part, the couple took the train to Bridgwater and then motored out to the Plough Inn at Holford. Soon after they arrived, Virginia's symptoms returned. She was certain that villagers and her fellow guests were mocking her; she became convinced that her body was monstrous; she endured sleepless nights. She imagined herself a huge belly demanding food. As usual in such a state, she wanted to starve her monstrous body and thus prevent it from getting larger and from excreting foul waste matter. It is likely that the Plough Inn had been the setting for one of Virginia and Leonard's disastrous attempts to have sex. On such grounds, it was a place best avoided. Virginia's fantasy about a swollen belly was probably a manifestation of her feelings of repugnance at the sexual act which would

* 'Abnormal mental experiences must be brought into the main stream of the individual personality, and, if possible, the patient must be induced to regard them from a more favourable point of view. A terrifying object, that can be logically examined, tends to lose its fearful aspect. We dread the unknown; and to drag these half-appreciated horrors into the light of day may discharge the greater part of their emotional energy. If possible, a sorrow must be sublimed; the loss of some dearly beloved person should not be repressed, but be brought up to form an integral part of the sacrifice at the altar' ('Observations on the Elements of the Psycho-Neuroses', *British Medical Journal*, 1, 1920, 392).

make her pregnant and an indication that her depression this time might have arisen in part from the fact that there was no child inside her womb.

For Leonard, his worst possible scenario was coming to life. He alerted Vanessa to what was happening. When she wrote to her sister on 28 August, she could scarcely conceal her desperation. To her it was perfectly clear that Virginia was in the same sort of 'badly nourished state' that she had been at Welwyn, although, she tried to assure Virginia, 'not nearly so bad as that for of course you aren't quite incapable now as you were then of using your brain at all'. The best hope for Virginia was to think back to those days and how she had pulled through. Then, the solution had been to stop starving her body. Despite her reluctance to do so, would Virginia eat?

> No one will tell you to eat if it's not necessary. Why should they? It *is* most necessary & is the only way of preventing you from getting really bad. Now Billy do be sensible & don't make things difficult for Leonard but realize that at this moment he is far more sensible than you are & trust him to know how to get things right . . . When you were bad before, you thought just as you do now, that we were all mistaken, that there was nothing the matter & that it was cruel to make you eat. But you know now we were right.[39]

Of course, Leonard and Vanessa were offering excellent counsel, but theirs was a dangerous logic as far as Virginia was concerned. She wanted to kill a body which did not allow her to enter fully into life. She was awash with guilt for not being a dutiful daughter, sister and wife. At the same time, she was filled with a poignant sense of loss – of her privacy, of her mother, of self-love – and unfortunately she took full responsibility for these deprivations.

Desperate and frightened, Leonard telegraphed Ka Cox, who joined the Woolfs at Holford on 2 September. Despite the quiet routine of walks and rest, Virginia remained unsettled and Leonard reached breaking point. He confronted Virginia, suggesting that they return to London, where they could consult a doctor of her choice. If that physician said she was not ill, Leonard would abide by the decision; if the consultant said she needed to eat or enter a nursing home, she must follow his instructions. At first Virginia objected, but then she agreed that this might be a good idea. She did not know that Leonard had seen Head, but she proposed him, probably because she had heard Roger speak highly of him. Leonard telegraphed for an appointment, which was made for the afternoon of 9 September. On the afternoon before, the party of three returned to London. During that trip, Virginia was in such a black state of melancholia that Ka and Leonard were frightened that she might throw herself from the train.

After a tense night at Brunswick Square (they were staying in Adrian's rooms), Virginia and Leonard went to two doctors: Maurice Wright in the morning, Head in the afternoon. Leonard had once seen Wright about his palsy; perhaps the consultation with him centred on the more medical aspects of Virginia's health. At the meeting with Head, Virginia and Leonard each had their say. Virginia insisted that there was nothing wrong and that she could overcome her problems without assistance. Head, who was not seeing Virginia in a genuinely therapeutic situation, informed her that she was incorrect in her assessment, but he deftly pointed out that she was suffering from an illness such as a cold or typhoid. He assured her that if she followed his advice – which was in substance what Savage had already prescribed – she would get better.

Later that day, back at Brunswick Square, Vanessa came to tea. Then Leonard went off to make peace with Savage, because he had consulted Head without informing him. While he was in Savage's consulting room, Ka called through to tell him that she had just found Virginia unconscious on her bed. Leonard took a cab back to Brunswick Square, where he discovered that Virginia had come upon the case where he stored drugs: it was unlocked and 100 grams of the sleeping draught veronal were missing. Leonard called Head, who agreed to come round at once, accompanied by a nurse. Meanwhile, Geoffrey Keynes, Maynard's doctor brother who had taken Leonard's room at Brunswick Square, happened to come by before Head and the nurse arrived. Realizing the seriousness of the situation, he told Leonard that the two of them must obtain a stomach pump from St Bartholomew's as soon as possible; they had to wash Virginia's stomach out and prevent her body from absorbing the drug. The two men hailed a cab, shouting 'Doctor, Doctor!' to wave aside the policemen who tried to stop the careering vehicle, fetched a long rubber tube and funnel and arrived back to find Head waiting for them. The two physicians then spent a good part of the evening washing out Virginia's stomach.

It was a close call. Thoroughly exhausted, Leonard went to bed at 12.30 and, according to Vanessa, Virginia almost died about an hour later. By six, she was out of danger. On the following day, she remained unconscious. Leonard now faced an agonizing decision. A person who had attempted suicide was usually institutionalized. Did he wish to persuade the attendant doctors to disregard this legal requirement? Yet another doctor, Sydney Henning Belfrage, the Bell family physician, was consulted. Belfrage, who was interested in the relationship between nutrition and nervous disorder, gave advice which was similar to that originally offered by Savage.

Leonard inspected some mental homes. To him they were 'dreadful, large gloomy buildings enclosed by high walls, dismal trees, and despair'.[40] Under these grim circumstances, Leonard was not willing to have his wife certified. Then the doctors involved (presumably Head, Savage and Belfrage) agreed to ignore the normal procedures, provided that Virginia was removed to a house in the country where she could be attended by her husband and two to four nurses. Leonard acquiesced, but Asheham was too small for such a number of people for any considerable length of time. At that point, George Duckworth volunteered his country house, Dalingridge Place, near East Grinstead in Sussex. According to Leonard, this retreat 'was in full working order with cook, parlourmaid, housemaids, and gardeners. So all we had to do was to go down there and settle in.' Just as Leonard had not thought it potentially disastrous to return to Holford the previous month, he never seemed to consider that using a house belonging to one of the Duckworth brothers might add to Virginia's torment.

On 20 September, Virginia, Leonard and a nurse motored down to Dalingridge Place, Ka and another nurse having preceded them earlier in the day. Ka remained there only a week, but her brief stay allowed Leonard to get away briefly to Asheham. During the next two months, Virginia gradually improved, although she was often resolute in her refusal to eat. However, more and more, she came to accept Head's observation that her breakdown was a manifestation of illness, not a condition to which moral judgements should be attached. On 18 December, she was considered well enough to be moved to Asheham, still under the care of two nurses.

Meanwhile, Leonard had to deal with some angry complaints. The first was from George Savage, who was furious that Leonard had continued to seek advice from other neurologists without consulting him. He assured Leonard that he was not jealous, but his feelings had been hurt. Marie Woolf was even more direct after reading the typescript of *The Wise Virgins*, threatening to break off contact with her son if the book was published without substantial revision: 'You have not convinced me one jot that the people at Rickstead [Putney] are one bit less valuable to the common working of the Universe, than the people at Bloomsbury.'[41] Marie Woolf was attacking Leonard where he was very vulnerable: his snobbery. In turn, as he told Lytton on 12 December, Leonard was inclined to be defiant: 'My family think it a rotten bad book & forbid me to publish it. Now if it is rotten or even poorly, it isn't worth while bringing all these people about my ears, obviously. But if it's otherwise worth publishing, I shouldn't mind, I think, telling the whole lot of them to go to Hell.'[42]*

* Ultimately, Leonard made thirty-six alterations to *The Wise Virgins*, but those changes were made at the suggestion of his publisher, Edward Arnold.

The acerbic side of Leonard can be glimpsed in the letter to Strachey; the tender part of his personality is clearly visible in one of his mongoose letters of a week earlier: 'You don't know & now – because of that terrible company of bees & nits & all manner of horrid winged things buzzing in your brain – you don't believe how I long to see you when I'm away.'[43] His affection was repaid by the mandrill, who responded:

> Would it make you very conceited if I told you that I love you more than I have ever done since I took you into service, and find you beautiful, and indispensable? I am afraid that is the truth.
>
> Goodbye Mongoose, and be a devoted animal, and never leave the great variegated creature. She wishes me to inform you delicately that her flanks and rump are now in finest plumage, and invites you to an exhibition. Kisses on your dear little pate. Darling Mongoose.[44]

Virginia's health continued to improve that December. However, Craig told Leonard not to expect a complete recovery until early spring.

By January, Virginia was able to see friends, walk on the downs and type Lytton's story 'Ermyntrude and Esmeralada'. A month later, Belfrage told Leonard that he was in full agreement with him: the time had come to rely on Virginia's self-control. Two weeks later, the last nurse left Asheham. From 7 to 18 March, Ka, Janet Case and Vanessa took turns staying with Virginia while Leonard, suffering from severe headaches, went on holiday to Lytton's. On Leonard's behalf, Virginia made notes on manuals about the Co-operative Movement; she also read Clive's *Art*, in which he articulated his theory of 'significant form'. When Leonard was away, the mandrill wanted 'her master so badly and last night his empty bed was so dismal, and she went and kissed the pillow'.[45] In turn, the mongoose was lonely – he cried when he received her letter. She replied: 'I love your little ribby body, my pet.'[46]

That spring was thankfully uneventful as far as Virginia was concerned. The only adventures at Asheham were those of the dogs and cats who felt spring in their bones and behaved accordingly. In April, the Woolfs travelled to London, where Maurice Craig pronounced Virginia well enough for a vacation. Unlike their outing to Holford, their three-week spring holiday in 1914 in Cornwall was a resounding success. Virginia's happiness is transparent in a letter to Violet: 'We crept into Talland House itself yesterday, and found it wonderfully done up and spick and span, and all the garden brimming with flowers and rock gardens – very unlike what it was in our day.'[47] Talland House was a proud, beautiful survivor of the happiest moments of Virginia's childhood. Although she was still given to bouts of despair, this encounter with her old haunt gave her the feeling that she too could prevail.

By the summer, Virginia's health had improved markedly. Even though he felt that his wife was too fixed on her aversion to food, Leonard was cautiously optimistic that the worst was behind them. Virginia gradually began to supervise the household and to look after the two dogs, Mike and Shot. That June, Leonard decided to attend the Women's Co-operative Guild meeting for two days and to leave Virginia by herself. He drew up a treaty between himself and his wife which contained a number of conditions: she was to rest on her back with her head on a cushion for a full half-hour after luncheon; she was to eat as much as if he were at home; she had to take breakfast in bed; she had to drink a glass of milk in the morning; she had to be in bed by 10.25 each night and to go to sleep at once. Virginia signed with a flourish and evidently obeyed the regulations. In early July, Leonard presented her with a bicycle. She was now well enough to range beyond the limited confines of Asheham.

On 4 August 1914, England declared war on Germany. For Virginia, this event was a throwback to Napoleonic times. Like most civilians, she expected an invasion. Soldiers dug trenches and the Asheham barn was converted into a hospital. All this reminded her that they were practically under martial law. In a subtle way, the war in Europe would gradually become for Virginia the outward metaphor for the inner war she continued to face – and fight.

Early that August, the Woolfs escaped to Northumberland, staying at Wooler and Coldstream until the middle of September. In the wake of her improved health, Virginia insisted that they should return to London, where they house-hunted in Hampstead, Highgate, Westminster, Holborn and Chelsea. Finally, they settled on Richmond – conveniently close to London and yet very rustic. From this base, Leonard could easily attend his political meetings, but the hurly-burly of a real urban existence would not unduly distract Virginia. That October, they took lodgings at 65 St Margaret's Road, Twickenham, and then moved to nearby Richmond on the 16th. Their landlady at 17 The Green was Mrs le Grys, a Belgian. The Woolfs, looking for a house in the same area of Richmond, had their furniture and books, which had been in storage since they had abandoned Clifford's Inn, sent to this temporary address.

Their new abode provided many memorable moments. There was Lizzy, the housemaid, who nearly set the house on fire and once made the empty boiler red-hot, in the process bringing it to the point of explosion. Her successor, Maud, claimed that she was a colonel's daughter and sought to impress Virginia with her genteel conversation and sophisticated views. One of the other lodgers, a refugee known as 'The Count', spat in his bath and thus irritated the hapless Mrs le Grys.

Despite these distractions, Virginia was well enough by mid-October for Leonard to discontinue his daily record-keeping of her condition. Although Mrs le Grys provided all their meals, Virginia determined that December to improve her domestic skills and so took cookery lessons in Victoria Street. Her fellow pupils included sailors and grey-haired ladies of great refinement. There were also specimens of young English womanhood: they had canine eyes, long plaits down their backs and were adorably stupid. Virginia felt a bit out of place in their midst. As she told Janet Case, 'I distinguished myself by cooking my wedding ring into a suet pudding!'[48]

Christmas 1914 was spent with Lytton near Marlborough. Just after this, the Woolfs came upon Hogarth House, a Georgian residence half-way up Paradise Road, only a short walk from the main square in Richmond. In 1720, Lord Suffield had built a large country house with an appropriately sized garden. In the nineteenth century, it had been divided into two: Suffield House and Hogarth House. The two halves shared a central porch and symmetrical sash windows. The garden of Hogarth was 100 feet long and each room but one, according to Leonard, was perfectly proportioned. Virginia, who was more concerned with cosiness, called the house 'nice, shabby, ancient, very solid'. The ensuing negotiations for the lease were lengthy and byzantine. Virginia also had serious qualms about life in any suburb, where only vile houses were usually for rent and the locals were unduly houseproud. There was, she observed, a 'great rivalry among neighbours', but in reality their rooms were draped in semi-darkness and were, she supposed, 'rank with the smell of meat & human beings'.[49]

While in the middle of negotiations for Hogarth House that January Virginia began another diary. She also completed '4 pages of poor Effie's story',[50] the originating point of *Night and Day*, her second novel.* Two weeks later, she was doing background reading for 'The Third Generation', then the novel's working title. To her diary, Virginia also confessed her deficiency in patriotic sentiments. If there was a lack of guile about the nitty-gritty (i.e. water-closets and copulation) in English life, then there might be a corresponding, shared honesty about universal emotions such as love of one's country: 'As it is, an appeal to feel together is hopelessly muddled by intervening greatcoats & fur coats. I begin to loathe my kind, principally from looking at their faces in the tube.'[51] Here Virginia is suggesting that some members of her class ignore the facts of life while, at the same time, embracing meaningless, empty sentiments. In an oblique way, she is attacking people like the excessively sentimental and secretive George Duckworth.

* At one point in the surviving manuscript (MS Berg) of *Night and Day*, the name 'Effie' appears by mistake for 'Katharine'.

However, Virginia was often unaware of her real feelings. On 9 January, when she came across a 'long line of imbeciles' on the towpath, she noted sharply in her diary: 'They should certainly be killed.'[52] Many years before, Virginia had been frightened by the boy in Kensington Gardens. She had also shunned her half-sister Laura. As child and woman, Virginia was threatened by people whose countenances betrayed, she felt, some sort of psychic deformity. Although she did not want to be like them, she feared that her inner self was damaged in a similar way.

That January, Virginia was unsure of the direction her life was taking. To her diary, she mused: 'I'd give a lot to turn over 30 pages or so, & find written down what happens to us.'[53] She was a fascinated witness to Marjorie Strachey's affair with the politician Josiah Wedgwood and Molly MacCarthy's with Clive Bell. When she dined with Maynard Keynes, she noticed that his good manners were blended with a metallic quality. For her, he was 'a little inhuman, but very kindly, as inhuman people are'.[54] She became a Fabian, although the idea that those 'frail webspinners'[55] could affect the destiny of nations seemed to her fantastical.

As a place to live, she felt Richmond did not deserve to be taken seriously. And yet she was suffused with a mellow sense of happiness which led her to have a joyous thirty-second birthday. Earlier, Virginia had made Leonard promise that he would not give her a present on 25 January, but on that day he crept into her bed and presented her with a green purse and a copy of Walter Scott's *The Abbot*. In the afternoon, they went up to London to a picture palace, then to Buzzard's Tea Room in Oxford Street, where they decided three things: to take Hogarth House if they could circumvent the tedious procedures blocking their way, to buy a bulldog to be called John and to purchase a printing press. On the way back to Richmond, Leonard gave his wife a packet of sweets. She told her diary: 'I don't think I've had a birthday treat for 10 years ... In fact, I don't know when I have enjoyed a birthday so much – not since I was a child anyhow.'[56]

The happiness Virginia experienced was short-lived. Less than a week later, she read *The Wise Virgins*, which had been published some three months earlier, on 9 October 1914. She had very little to *say* about the novel: 'a remarkable book; very bad in parts; first rate in others . . . I like the poetical side of L. & it gets a little smothered in Blue-books, & organizations.'[57] However, just before she began the book – perhaps in anticipation of what she would discover there – she and Leonard had a blazing row, the origins of which she was not sure of: 'O dear! We quarrelled almost all the morning! & it was a lovely morning, & now gone to Hades for ever, branded with the marks of our ill humour. Which began it? Which carried it on? God knows. This I will say: I explode: & Leonard smoulders.'[58]

For the next few days, the Woolfs seemed to go on as before. On 6 February, they went to Rye and stayed at the Old Flushing Inn; on the next day they walked to Playden and then Winchelsea. On 8 February, they were in Hastings. An increasing sense of Virginia's fragility can be glimpsed in her diary entry of 13 February: 'There was a great downpour this morning. I am sure however many years I keep this diary, I shall never find a winter to beat this. It seems to have lost all self control.'[59] Of course, Virginia was afraid that she was about to lose self-control once again. Two days later, she went up to London and rambled down to Charing Cross in the evening. She was making up phrases and incidents to write about in *Night and Day*. Such stumbling about in the dark in the city, she realized, was one of the ways 'one gets killed'.[60]

Once again she slept badly and endured awful headaches. On 22 February, she told Margaret Llewelyn Davies, General Secretary of the Women's Co-operative Guild, that she remained excited about the idea of purchasing a printing press. There is the distinct possibility that Virginia was jealous of this woman who shared so many of Leonard's professional interests. Virginia was also apprehensive about the critical reception that would be accorded to *The Voyage Out*.

For a variety of reasons, she became incoherent and distraught on 23 February. On that day she conversed with her mother: she was so upset that the boundary between reality and fantasy had been blurred. Three days later, she was a little better and could, in a letter to Lytton, plot against Clive: 'Let us all subscribe to buy a Parrot for Clive. It must be a bold primitive bird, trained of course to talk nothing but filth, and to indulge in obscene caresses – the brighter coloured the better.'[61]

Such bravado was soon stifled. On 4 March, Virginia became so violent that nurses had to be in constant attendance. Meanwhile, the Woolfs were scheduled to take possession of Hogarth House on 25 March, so Virginia had to be removed to a nursing home while the move took place. Financial difficulties added to the couple's distress. Although Virginia had capital of about £9,000, the annual return on this sum was approximately £400, much of which was quickly eaten up by medical and nursing fees. Leonard had little money of his own and felt overburdened by yet another aspect of his wife's mental distress. Reluctantly, he asked Jack Hills, who allowed Virginia £100 a year out of Stella's estate, to advance these funds at once.

Virginia's breakdown took most of its accustomed forms. She wanted to do away with herself and she was violently angry with the person closest to her. She was like an anguished child who is so desperately furious at a parent that she wants to kill them but, at the same time, is so guilt-ridden for harbouring such sentiments that she wants to destroy herself. Much of Virginia's anguish must have come from the realization that she had at long last gone public: she had written a book which would not only subject her to the whims of the reviewers but also describe – if in a muted form – many of the anxieties at the core of her being. In addition, she had recently endured the unpleasant experience of reading about herself in *The Wise Virgins*. In that book, Camilla may be extraordinarily intelligent, witty and beautiful, but she is also sexually cold. As we have seen, many of Leonard's reservations about his own marriage found their way into that book. More to the point, this narrative by a very disappointed man suggests that it is not possible to overcome the perils of frigidity. Virginia must have felt that this particular experimentation – her marriage – was a dismal failure.

She returned to Hogarth House on 1 April. At times, she would eat and put on a bit of weight. Then, she would be awake for long stretches of time – sixty hours or more. During those periods of intense anxiety, she would not follow any kind of instruction and would threaten violence against her keepers, Leonard in particular. In May, Leonard took Virginia to yet another consultant, whose surname was Mackenzie. Nothing is known about the meeting, except that Leonard was unsure of this person and decided to rely on Craig. On 27 May, Vanessa described the gloomy situation to Roger:

> I saw Woolf yesterday. He too was very dismal. Virginia seems to go up & down, at times being pretty reasonable & at others very violent & difficult. The only thing to do is to hang on as long as possible he thinks in the hope that she may get well enough to be able to go to some nursing home & not have to go to an asylum which he thinks might have a disastrous effect on her. The question is whether the nurses will stand it. Woolf himself seemed to have reached a stage when he didn't much care what happened, which was rather dreadful; & one couldn't say anything much.[62]

Two weeks later, Virginia's health began to show signs of improvement. By August, Leonard was able to take her out in a wheelchair or for drives in their car. However, Vanessa was not certain that Leonard's new-found optimism was justified:

> Ka had been to see Virginia & thinks she's really getting better slowly, but it sounds most depressing as she seems to have changed into a most unpleasant character. She won't see Leonard at all & has taken against all men. She says the most malicious & cutting things she can think of to everyone & they are so clever that they always hurt.

Vanessa was afraid that her sister had simply 'worn out her brains'.[63]

Gradually, Virginia's animation returned, as can be seen in this naughty observation on spinsterish Morgan Forster, who 'is timid as a mouse, but when he creeps out of his hole very charming. He spends his time in rowing old ladies upon the river, and is not able to get on with his novel.' Such remarks had to be confined to postcards, the only form of writing permitted Virginia, but she did add this wistful observation to her remarks on Forster: 'But . . . what's the use of my writing novels?'[64]

On 11 September, Virginia, Leonard, a nurse, a cook and a housemaid moved to Asheham. Virginia read Latin and French, found nothing but 'faintly tinged rose water' in Henry James and was swept away by Dostoevsky. A glimpse of the distress lingering below the surface – especially of her fear of sexual activity – can be seen in Virginia's cutting remarks about one of her former suitors, Sydney Waterlow, and his new wife, who had rented Asheham for part of 1914: 'I don't know why exactly, but no one I've ever met seems to me more palpably second rate and now the poor creature resigns himself to it and proposes to live next door to us at Richmond and there copulate day and night and produce 6 little Waterlows. This house for a long time stank to me of dried semen.'

By October, Virginia, who ordinarily weighed 9 stone, was 12 stone as the result of the regimen of Craig and associates. As a consequence, she could 'hardly toil uphill'.[65] However, her energy and good spirits were sufficient by 4 November to return to Richmond. A week later, her nurse left. Although she felt sheltered in Richmond, the ever-present Zeppelin threat to London was a source of anxiety. In particular, she was worried about the safety of Vanessa and Ka.

Virginia's increased sense of well-being would have been bolstered by some of the reviews of *The Voyage Out*, which Forster in the *Daily News and Leader* hailed as a 'book which attains unity as surely as *Wuthering Heights*, though by a different path'.[66] By linking a major experimental novel by a woman from the nineteenth century with Virginia's first novel, the mouse paid his friend a high compliment. However, he expressed a major reservation: 'there is one serious defect in her equipment; her chief characters are not vivid'. Allan Monkhouse in the *Manchester*

Guardian had an intuitive understanding of Virginia's 'penetration into certain modes of consciousness'. This was a book not merely of 'promise, but accomplishment'.[67] The reviewer in the *Observer* was not accustomed to use the word 'genius' but he discerned such in the talent of this unknown writer. He was taken with the book's honesty, originality and poignancy. This novel tried to 'say the real thing' and in the process it was a 'wild swan' among the good grey geese of contemporary fiction.[68]★

★ Negative criticism of *The Voyage Out* tended to emphasize the looseness of its plot construction. However, the anonymous reviewer in the *Times Literary Supplement* (1 April 1915), commenting on Rachel's illness and death, realized that this seeming weakness might conceal strength: 'And it *is* illogical, this sudden tragedy, but it is made almost to seem like the illogic of life; it is so intense that one is desolated by a sense of the futility of life and forgets the failure of design.'

Part Three

PHANTOMS

Chapter Nine

THE SHADOW OF THE UNDERWORLD

(1916–18)

On the eve of her thirty-fourth birthday in January 1916, Virginia was continuing to make a good recovery from the depressive anxiety which had overwhelmed her during the previous four years. She no longer felt completely invaded and, as her inner conflicts lessened, she became more attentive to the war, which invaded every aspect of English domestic life. Her anger at this outrage was direct and forceful: she saw the fighting as a 'preposterous masculine fiction'[1] which needed some vigorous young woman – a sort of Joan of Arc – to remedy.

As Virginia began to be more aware of the world around her and her own place in it, she realized how dependent she was on the domestics who assisted her and Leonard. On 1 February, two new servants, Nelly (or Nellie) Boxall and Lottie Hope, arrived, fresh from service with Roger Fry at Guildford. Lottie, the maid, was simple, generous and impulsive, whereas Nelly, the cook, was more steady but ultimately more passionate. They were to remain with the Woolfs for many years.

Virginia had mixed feelings about domestics. Like many members of the upper and professional classes, she had been born into a family which employed large numbers of servants. As a child, she had at various times adored and loathed Sophie Farrell, who was now employed by Adrian Stephen. As an adult who did not know how to do housework, much less supervise it, Virginia, who lived a far simpler life than her parents, relied on only one or two servants to cook, clean and in general give order to her outer existence.

In the late nineteenth century, many men and women of the lower classes had relied on getting jobs in service. During the war and in its aftermath, work in factories became more readily available and the salaries there were higher than those paid by the increasingly financially pressed upper classes. To a large extent, the old order had changed; the lifestyle of Julia Stephen and members of her set was a thing of the past. Now servants had to be cajoled to do their work properly and their salaries ate up a considerable amount of their employers' money (in 1916, the Woolfs' expenses amounted to £678, of which almost £200 was given over to the servants' wages and their food). In order for Virginia to write, she was totally dependent on the competence, energy and goodwill of Nelly and Lottie, but because of the slowly changing nature in the relationship between upstairs and downstairs, Virginia had to be pleasant to her two servants. She could not appear aloof or condescending; she may have been the mistress, but she also had to appear to be a friend. Virginia constantly felt that she was walking a particularly treacherous tightrope. Her irritation can be seen in a diary entry for 13 December 1917: 'I limited the reconciliation scene with Lottie to 15 minutes at eleven sharp . . . The poor have no chance; no manners or self control to protect themselves with; we have a monopoly of all the generous feelings.'[2]

Virginia might have been directing the irony against herself in her use of the adjective 'generous', but she was exasperated at having to expend so much energy to coax the 'poor' into doing their work. And to a large extent she felt guilty about manipulating women who did not have inner (or financial) resources upon which to fall back. Also, she frequently had to act as a referee between the sometimes bad-tempered Lottie and the frequently hot-tempered Leonard, who barked at each other.

The presence of Lottie and Nelly meant that Virginia could easily re-establish a routine in her life: she wrote in the morning, walked in the afternoon and read in the evening. Also, once or twice a week she accompanied Leonard to London, where she would borrow books from Mudie's and the London Library. She could also take lunch or tea with friends as varied as Nelly Cecil,

Saxon Sydney-Turner, the Waterlows and Bob Trevelyan, the poet and classical scholar. She was also free to plan her life as a writer and to conduct her adjunct existence as a diarist and letter-writer.

The search for a coherent pattern had now become an obsession. When Lytton told her that he felt that *The Voyage Out* failed in its overall conception, she admitted in her reply that he was correct. Somehow her aim of presenting the vast tumult of life had, she now felt, overwhelmed rather than enriched the book. As a writer, Virginia was torn between extremes: there were those such as Arnold Bennett who were too concerned with realism and those such as Viola Meynell who had abandoned realism. Was her place, she wondered, in the uncomfortable middle?

Such vexing questions were difficult to resolve, especially when the air was filled with terror. At Asheham in February, there was a huge crash on the terrace in the middle of the night. In the morning, the Woolfs discovered that two enormous trees had come down and had settled on the drawing-room roof, completely blocking the light at one end. The war brought another anxiety: would Leonard and their male friends be forced into military service or would they obtain exemptions?

Virginia also had to deal with the enormous alterations in her sister's life which had occurred while she was ill. In 1911, as we have seen, Vanessa had taken up with Roger Fry, an ardent lover who was eager to take care of his beloved. His devotion was intense, but ultimately his strong, nurturing feelings stifled her. Though Vanessa could give affection in a most generous way, she became deeply uncomfortable when this aroused reciprocal feelings in others. By 1913, Roger's devotion was grating on her. Almost as an escape, she fell in love with Duncan Grant, whose homosexuality she knew of firsthand: for three years, he had been Adrian's lover. In fact, Duncan's interest in Vanessa was aroused in part because he was losing Adrian to Karin Costelloe, a research fellow in philosophy at Cambridge. So Vanessa spurned the affection of a man who burned for her in order to pursue a man who could not love her sexually; at the same time, she must have realized that

Duncan saw her as a substitute for Adrian. Unlike Virginia, Vanessa had a strong sexual appetite, but she began a process by which she abandoned that side of herself to live in what was, for the most part, a celibate marriage with Grant. Like her younger sister, Vanessa's early life had been poisoned by her father and the Duckworth brothers, but different constitutional factors led the sisters to take different routes to similar sexual destinations.

In March 1916, a further complication to Vanessa's existence was added when she went to live in Wissett, Suffolk, with Duncan Grant and David Garnett, who took up fruit-farming there in order to strengthen their claims for exemption from military service. Vanessa agreed to keep house for Duncan that spring and summer. Her departure from London meant, Virginia lamented, that Bloomsbury had vanished like the morning mist. In Suffolk, the already complex became baroque: Duncan was deeply attracted to the superbly muscular, virile Garnett, who was only half-heartedly interested in homosexual love-making – indeed, Garnett, whose nickname was Bunny, found Vanessa attractive; in turn, Vanessa was repulsed by Bunny's childishness and his hold on Duncan, though Duncan urged Vanessa to accommodate herself to Bunny. And so, by the summer of 1916, Vanessa was existing in an increasingly fraught *ménage à trois*, while Virginia's life, in contrast, was positively tranquil.

When Leonard was away briefly that spring, she assured him: 'There's no doubt I'm terribly in love with you. I keep thinking what you're doing, and have to stop – it makes me want to kiss you so.'[3] Virginia was relieved at the end of May when her husband was granted an exemption from military service because of the tremor in his hands. As Leonard became more and more the still point in her life, she started to re-evaluate old friends such as Janet Case and Violet Dickinson. The stasis in the existences of these spinsters frightened Virginia, who discerned anew the positive side of her decision to marry.

In early April, Grant and Garnett appeared before a local tribunal in Suffolk, which awarded them non-combatant service, a decision upheld by the Appeal Tribunal at Ipswich. Under prodding from Vanessa, Virginia asked Nelly Cecil to intervene with her brother-in-law, James, the Marquess of Salisbury, who was chairman of the Central Tribunal. Nelly told Virginia that Jem was not the sort of person to be swayed by personal influence. In any event, the two men were exempted from all military service on condition they undertake farm work for the balance of the war. This victory allowed Virginia, in words which proved wonderfully prophetic, to press the claims of Charleston, a farm a mile from Firle and four miles from Asheham, on Vanessa and the other members of her entourage: 'It has a charming garden, with a pond, and fruit trees, and vegetables, all now rather run wild, but you could make it lovely.'[4] Virginia was sure the challenge of Charleston would appeal to Vanessa: all the rooms needed wall-papering, but it was obviously a house with tremendous possibilities for anyone with a flair for decorating and a penchant for a semi-bohemian mode of life.

While visiting Vanessa in Suffolk that July, Virginia used her best powers of persuasion on behalf of Charleston. She also scrutinized her sister carefully and decided to use her as the model for Katharine Hilbery, one of the central characters in *Night and Day*. Vanessa's life provided endless fascination for Virginia because, in part, she saw in her a version of herself. Vanessa explored opportunities closed to or rejected by her younger sister, who attempted in this new piece of long fiction to write about a woman with whom she shared many traits but who was also markedly different from herself. In a mock reprimand, Virginia told Vanessa, 'It's fatal staying with you – you start so many ideas.'[5]

That summer, Virginia ventured further afield. She and Leonard stayed with the Webbs, the social reformers, in Sussex, where Charlotte and Bernard Shaw were fellow guests. Sidney Webb pounced on Virginia, rather, she thought, in the manner of a moulting eagle; Beatrice was simply crude, whereas Charlotte Shaw, whom Virginia dubbed a fat, large, white Persian cat of a woman, retreated into the comforts of woolly Indian mysticism. Shaw told interminable stories – about himself. Then there was a short stay with Roger Fry, who could not stop bemoaning the passing of his youth. Virginia found him pathetic, but she was touched when Lady Strachey, a fellow guest at Fry's, read Pope aloud to a gathering at Guildford until her nose bled. This elderly woman showed magnificent spirit.

Meanwhile, Virginia was becoming quietly fascinated by Katherine Mansfield, who, she observed, 'has dogged my steps for three years – I'm always on the point of meeting her, or of reading her stories, and I have never managed to do either.'[6] Katherine was a friend of Ottoline Morrell, and the mistress of Garsington Manor in Oxfordshire was the conduit of information. However, Lytton Strachey may have arranged the first meeting between the two women, probably late in 1916.

Virginia constantly reminded herself that she had to avoid being overwhelmed. When a frightened Margaret Llewelyn Davies, ill with cancer, wanted to discuss her options, Virginia deliberately attacked her 'in every possible way, so as to keep things brisk. I believe it's the only way of keeping these ardent spirits from overwhelming one entirely.'[7] For Virginia, a good offence remained the best defence: she was not unsympathetic to Margaret's plight, but she was afraid of being hurled into a current of strong feelings which might drown her. A bit later, Virginia and Leonard visited Cornwall with Margaret and her friend Lilian Harris, assistant-secretary of the Women's Co-operative Guild. During that holiday, Virginia and Margaret argued about art and morality. Virginia hoped to puncture Margaret's piety, but, as she pointed out, her task was an impossible one: 'a life rooted in good works is hard to injure'.[8]

Despite her best efforts, some of Margaret's propensity for good works did rub off on Virginia, who organized, chaired and held the meetings of the Richmond branch of the Guild at Hogarth House for the next four years. Middle-aged women with advanced ideas remained a threat, but Virginia was more ill at ease with younger women such as Barbara Hiles and Dora Carrington, the Bloomsbury bunnies or copperheads. These women were not sure of their sexuality, but they were eager to experiment, anxious to taste the new freedom unleashed by the war.

Julia Jackson in 1867.
Photograph by Julia Margaret Cameron.

Leslie Stephen.
Photograph by Julia Margaret Cameron.

Above: Virginia as a young girl. *Left*: The Stephen Family in a photograph taken *circa* 1894. Back row: Gerald Duckworth, Virginia, Thoby and Vanessa Stephen, George Duckworth; front row: Adrian, Julia and Leslie Stephen. *Right*: Laura Stephen.

22 Hyde Park Gate.

Talland House.

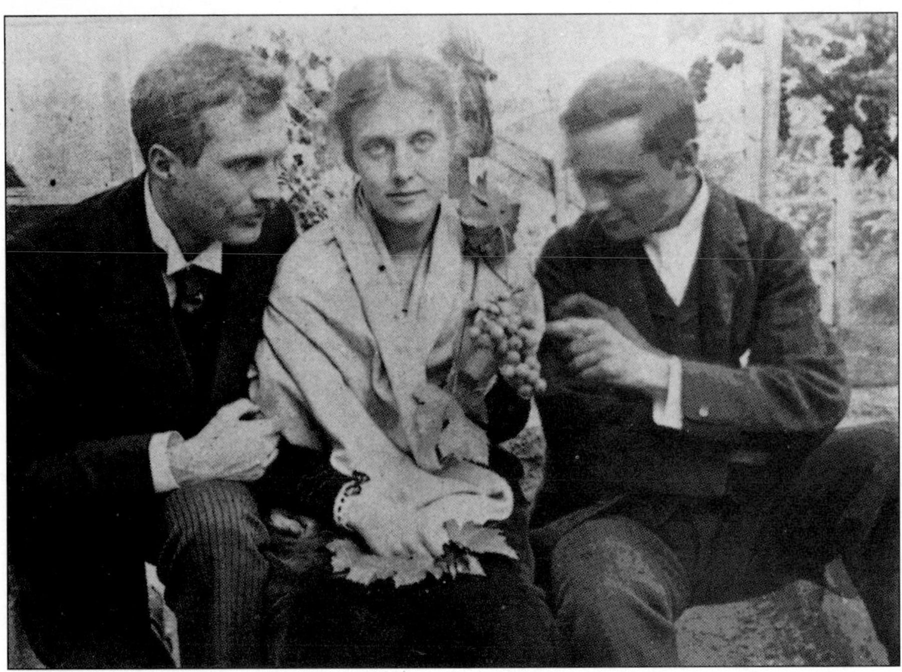

Above: Vanessa Stephen, Stella Duckworth, Virginia Stephen, *circa* 1896.
Below: George Duckworth, Stella Duckworth and Jack Hills.

Above left: Vanessa Bell, 1907.
Photograph by George Beresford.
Above right: Thoby Stephen, 1906.
Photograph by George Beresford.

Adrian Stephen.
Portrait by Duncan Grant.

Virginia with
Violet Dickinson, 1902.

Virginia in 1902.
Photograph by
George Beresford.

Above: Virginia with Clive Bell at Studland Bay, Dorset, 1910. *Below left*: Virginia with Rupert Brooke in Devon, 1908. *Below right*: Virginia, at about the time of her engagement.

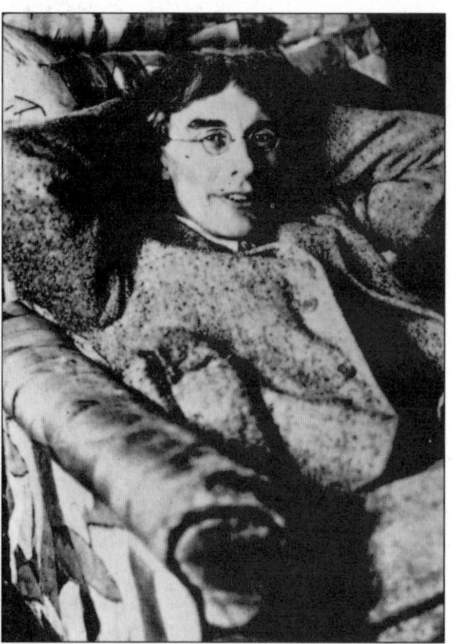

Above left: Duncan Grant and Maynard Keynes, 1912. *Above right*: Roger Fry.
Below: Dora Carrington, Ralph Partridge and Lytton Strachey in the garden at Ham Spray, Lytton's Wiltshire home.

Carrington had thick blonde hair, blue eyes and a charming stutter. She had trained at the Slade and in 1916 was working for Roger Fry on the restoration of the Mantegna frescos 'The Triumph of Caesar' at Hampton Court. That October, she and Barbara had accompanied David Garnett to Charleston, for his meeting with a farmer who was to employ him once he, as a member of Vanessa's entourage, had moved from Suffolk to Sussex. The interview took longer than expected and the trio had nowhere to sleep as darkness overcame them. With only a little trepidation, they decided to stay at Asheham, which was empty, the Woolfs being in Richmond. As they were departing that morning, the small group was observed by the caretaker, who gave a slightly exaggerated report of tables being overturned and beds stripped to her employers. Leonard and Virginia were angry at being taking advantage of, but Virginia put up a good front when David Garnett sent some poems in apology: 'As a matter of fact, we are not at all annoyed – it seems a very sensible thing to do.'[9]

Vanessa saw through her sister's air of nonchalance. As she told Roger Fry, Virginia, who had summoned Carrington to dine, would try with great subtlety to worm out the inconsistencies in Garnett's account: 'I don't believe Carrington will be a match for Mrs Woolf as one knows her powers if she wants to find out something.'[10] When Virginia had finished with her, Carrington cried out: 'What an examination!!!'[11] Inherent in Vanessa's response to this fracas was her growing sense that the Woolfs, particularly Leonard, disapproved of her: 'I think the Woolves have a morbid terror of us all – I can't think why. They seem to think we should contaminate the atmosphere & bring wicked gaieties into Virginia's life.'[12] If Leonard had developed what Lytton called a 'pollution theory', this was partly in response to what he considered Virginia's overwhelming fascination with her sister, to whom she confessed on 24 October 1916: 'How pleasant it would be to see you here, or to roll on the downs together, and the Ape would steal kisses from the most secluded parts!'[13]

The other side of Virginia's sexuality can be seen in her response to the Saxon Sydney Turner Barbara Hiles Nicholas Bagenal imbroglio. Small and vivacious, Barbara had an elfin face, red cheeks and bobbed hair. During the war, she wore trousers and rode a motorcycle; she was very much a new sort of woman. Without doubt, as Virginia perceived, she could be brittle and heartless. In his typically detached way, Saxon fell in love with her, but she then met and fell in love with Nick. At the same time that she resolved to marry Nick, Barbara decided to keep Saxon as a lover. Virginia, who sometimes played both ends against the middle, remembered Saxon's great devotion to Thoby and his low-key courting of herself. She was torn. First of all, she was a tiny bit jealous. Second, she did not like to see Saxon abused. Third, she knew what a bore Saxon could be. Despite conflicting feelings, she offered him some advice in November 1916: 'I think you can trust yourself because you have made a habit of honesty. And, dear me, one never regrets *feeling* things in this life; not even if mere disappointment follows, which I think utterly impossible in this particular case.'[14] However, Saxon soon afterwards became angry at Virginia when, at a dinner party, she told a story about his lack of real emotions.

When she got caught up in this romantic triangle, Virginia must have been recalling her own indecisiveness about whether or not to marry Leonard. Her passion for Leonard was real, but it was not sexually generated – or sustained. And there was her sister, who, once she had settled at Charleston, seemed 'to have slipped civilization off her back, and splashes about entirely nude, without shame, and enormous spirit'.[15] Although Virginia could be taken aback when the Richmond members of the Co-operative were outraged by a lecture which discussed venereal disease, her own sense of unease is best glimpsed in this snippet from a letter to Vanessa of February 1917: 'I have had a slight rapprochement with Katherine Mansfield; who seems to me an unpleasant but forcible and utterly unscrupulous character, in whom I think you might find a "companion".'[16]

Virginia's adjectives refer to aspects of Mansfield's sometimes abrasive personality, but they also have an erotic tinge to them, as if Mansfield's wantonness might find its equivalent in a similar licence in Vanessa. Katherine's first extant letter to Virginia (24 June 1917) has such an edge:

> My God, I love to think of you, Virginia, as my friend. Don't cry me an ardent creature or say, with your head a little on one side, smiling as though you knew some enchanting secret: 'Well, Katherine, we shall see' . . . But pray consider how rare it is to find some one with the same passion for writing that you have, who desires to be scrupulously truthful with you – and to give you the freedom of the city without any reserves at all.[17]

Katherine Mansfield, a writer obsessed by a childhood composed of an equal mixture of happy and unhappy moments, was, like Virginia, born to a mother who was emotionally aloof. Mansfield's lesbian impulses were in large part an attempt to gain from other women the emotional warmth her mother had deprived her of; in general, her erotic activities re-enacted an earlier, failed search for parental comfort and nourishment. Unlike Virginia, however, Mansfield had a strong sex drive.

At their first meetings, Virginia was offended by this gulf separating them: 'She seems to have gone every sort of hog since she was 17';[18] according to her, Katherine stank like a 'civet cat that had taken to street walking'.[19] These are extremely defensive statements, but they merely conceal another rift. From the very first, Virginia realized just how gifted a writer Mansfield was and, what is more, she recognized that they were both women writers who aimed to overthrow the masculine regime in fiction. Although they wanted to be confederates, they remained rivals.

From 1910 to 1915, the voice of Virginia Woolf the critic had been silenced (she published seventeen pieces of journalism in 1909, thirteen from 1910 to 1915). Once she decided to re-enter that arena, she did so with a new acumen and vigour, and she wrote frequently: ninety-three pieces in the last three years of the war. There was also a new imperative at work: a resolute and determined decision to question the way literature was written.

The war may have been a 'preposterous masculine fiction', but her own battle was to attack, and hopefully dismantle, the idea that only the male view mattered in writing.

In December 1904, Mrs Lyttelton had published Virginia's essay about her visit to Haworth parsonage, the home of the Brontës. In two pieces from 1916 and 1917, Virginia began to define her own goals as a professional writer by carefully scrutinizing Charlotte Brontë, who, Virginia observed, exerted such tremendous powers on her readers that they found it impossible to lift their eyes from her pages:

> She has you by the hand and forces you along her road, seeing the things she sees and as she sees them. She is never absent for a moment, nor does she attempt to conceal herself or to disguise her voice . . . There are two reasons for this astonishing closeness and sense of personality – that she is herself the heroine of her own novels, and (if we may divide people into those who think and those who feel) that she is primarily the recorder of feelings and not of thoughts.[20]

Virginia is suggesting that women are more interested than men in creating (or at the very least exploring) a language of feeling.

Hand in hand with a sense of herself as the literary daughter of Charlotte Brontë was Virginia's certainty that English fiction could renew itself if it were to take heed of the experiments undertaken in Russia by Chekhov and Dostoevsky, recently translated into English by Constance Garnett. Virginia certainly saw Dostoevsky as the most important innovator in the realm of fiction.

> Alone among writers Dostoevsky has the power of reconstructing those most swift and complicated states of mind, of rethinking the whole train of thought in all its speed, now as it flashes into light, now as it lapses into darkness; for he is able to follow not only the vivid streak of achieved thought, but to suggest the dim and populous underworld of the mind's consciousness where desires and impulses are moving blindly beneath the sod

> ... This is the exact opposite of the method adopted, perforce, by most of our novelists. They reproduce all the external appearances – tricks of manner, landscape, dress, and the effect of the hero upon his friends – but very rarely, and only for an instant, penetrate to the tumult of thought which rages within his own mind.[21]

In her critical writings from 1916 to 1918, Virginia was forging her own future as a writer. Her search for a new language and literary identity can be most clearly seen in the short stories from these years, particularly 'The Mark on the Wall', which is about the changing nature of perception. The sensibility of the narrator, intrigued by the mark, wanders in a variety of directions as she considers the identity of the mysterious object.

> In certain lights that mark on the wall seems actually to project from the wall. Nor is it entirely circular. I cannot be sure, but it seems to cast a perceptible shadow, suggesting that if I run my finger down that strip of the wall it would, at a certain point, mount and descend a small tumulus, a smooth tumulus like those barrows on the South Downs which are, they say, either tombs or camps ... No, no, nothing is proved, nothing is known. And if I were to get up at this very moment and ascertain that the mark on the wall is really – what shall I say? – the head of a gigantic old nail, driven in two hundred years ago, which has now, owing to the patient attrition of many generations of housemaids, revealed its head above the coat of paint, and is taking its first view of modern life in the sight of a white-walled fire-lit room, what should I gain?

'The Mark on the Wall' is more about process than product, although the reader is given the solution to the mystery in the story's last sentence: 'It was a snail.'[22]

Letter-writing and diary-keeping now became integral parts of Virginia's life as a writer. Rather tentatively, Virginia resumed her diary on 3 August 1917. Twenty years before, after Stella's death in July 1897, Virginia's journal entries had become sparse, as if the writer had been drained of the energy essential to record daily events in any extended, descriptive manner. A similar hesitation can be seen in the Asheham diary, but many of these entries, though terse, are extraordinary in their use of vivid metaphor.

> *Sunday 19 August*
> Sat in the hollow; & found the caterpillar, now becoming a Chrysalis, which I saw the other day. A horrid sight: head turning from side to side, tail paralysed; brown colour, purple spots just visible; like a snake in movement.[23]

From November 1917, the entries become more extended, but they never acquire the fullness of feeling which is so pronounced in Virginia's letters. This is a fascinating paradox – the reverse of what might ordinarily be expected. In fact, that November, Virginia opened her eyes wide in astonishment when Ottoline confided that she kept a diary devoted to her inner life. Shocked, Virginia reflected that she had no such existence.

The truth is that glimpses of Virginia's inner life are best seen by reading the diary in conjunction with her letters to close friends. In these, she reveals her secrets in a childlike way, in the expectation that the recipients will be touched by the truth. Of course, the gossipy, malicious and sometimes vindictive side of Virginia can also be seen there, but this means that the reader is able to see Virginia in all her complexity, whereas the diary, with significant exceptions, is a storehouse of information to which Virginia relegates anxiety, anger and conflict. The joyful, exuberant side of her personality is often absent from its pages, where the feelings of the heart are expressed but often in an unsifted way.

There was another new aspect to Virginia's career as a writer. Without doubt, she found it difficult to deal with her publisher, her half-brother Gerald Duckworth. In March 1918, she compared him to a pampered, overfed pug: 'There is hardly a gleam of life, let alone intelligence in his eye. The feebleness of his hold on life save through the stomach must be fearful . . . His commercial view of every possible subject depressed me, especially when I thought of my novel [*Night and Day*] destined to be pawed & snored over by him.'[24] Of course, Gerald had 'pawed' her six-year-old body, and she did not wish him to perform a similar act on her manuscripts. As early as June 1916, Leonard and Virginia had determined to use a promised income-tax refund to purchase a long-desired printing press, but the refund did not materialize and they did not order the press until March 1917.

Initially, the Woolfs applied for admission to the St Bride Foundation Institute in Bride Lane to learn the art of printing. Since they did not intend to become members of the printers' trade union, they were turned down. They finally purchased a printing press and instruction booklet in nearby Farringdon Road; for an additional nineteen shillings they also obtained some 'Old Face' type. When the machine arrived, husband and wife were soon absorbed: 'I see,' Virginia remarked to Vanessa, 'that real printing will devour one's entire life.'[25] She was able to say this even though the press arrived smashed in half and needed instant repairing. When the going proved difficult, Leonard lamented that he had ever purchased the thing but, to Virginia's extraordinary relief, he went on to say: 'Because I shall never do anything else.'[26] By July 1917, the couple, working at a frantic pace, produced the first publication of the Hogarth Press: *Two Stories* ('The Mark on the Wall' and Leonard's 'Three Jews'; these were accompanied by Dora Carrington's woodcuts).

At the outset, Leonard hoped that typesetting would prove a pleasant diversion for his wife. What he did not foresee was that their imprint would blossom into a major house. Eventually, Virginia would become her own publisher and, in the process, liberate herself from the likes of Gerald Duckworth. (From *Monday or Tuesday* (1921) onwards, all of Virginia's books carry the colophon of the Hogarth Press.) Such independence was to prove central to her quest to redefine – and alter fundamentally – the face of literature.

Virginia's recovery from mental illness was so complete that within a relatively short time she was able to both rededicate herself to her writing and expand the frontiers of what the life of writing meant to her. As she uncovered her nascent powers, she put herself in touch with a corresponding amount of ambition. When David Garnett complimented her on 'The Mark on the Wall', she gleefully replied: 'In a way it's easier to do a short thing, all in one flight than a novel. Novels are frightfully clumsy and overpowering of course; still if one could only get hold of them it would be superb. I daresay one ought to invent a completely new form.'[27] Such a transformation – like that of chrysalis into butterfly – would be arduous to accomplish, but Virginia was committed to the idea.

Although revitalized by her dedication to the profession of writing, Virginia experienced what she called the 'occasional swinge of the tail'[28] – moments of sadness in which she reflected on just how extremely insignificant her position was in the world. She sometimes responded to such awful moments by becoming snappish, but she also found great joy in friendship. In May 1917, she paid the insecure Ottoline Morrell a graceful tribute: 'My images, after leaving you, were all of the depths of the sea-mermaid Queens, shells, the bones of the shipwrecked. I was incapacitated for normal life for some time after seeing you. It was a great pleasure, and reassurement to find that my memory had not been nearly mythical or romantic enough.'[29] The other side of Virginia can be seen in her tendency to utter hurtful words of malice but to attribute them to others. On 29 July 1917 Virginia had Katherine Mansfield to supper. During the evening, she repeated to her rival some unkind remarks made about her the day before by Clive Bell and Maynard Keynes. On the surface, Virginia, who shared Clive and Maynard's hostility, was being merely indiscreet, but she had the pleasure of insulting Katherine without having to take responsibility for what she said and she also got her two male friends into trouble. As Vanessa maintained, Virginia could be very dangerous.

Her bantering side could be tart as well as comic, as when she drew, for Carrington's benefit, a pointed and somewhat insulting moral reflection from a small incident which took place at Asheham in the autumn of 1917: 'A swarm of bees conglobulated suddenly over our heads on the terrace – in an ecstasy of lust – drove us in – then made for the chimney, and all settled in the attic. Please tell us what to do. We want the honey; the males were all dead – But I forgot: you don't like the fact of copulation, only the theory – What an odd generation yours is!'[30] *Pace* Virginia, Carrington's generation was sexually adventurous in theory and practice.

Virginia was drawn to Mark Gertler, the tormented young painter whose unhappy love affair with Carrington was chronicled in Gilbert Cannan's *roman-à-clef, Mendel: A Story of Youth*, which Virginia read when it was published in 1916. There was a passionate intensity in Gertler's canvases which deeply attracted Virginia, who found the paintings of Duncan, Roger and even Vanessa timid in comparison.

Gertler may well have reminded Virginia of what she liked and disliked about Leonard. Her grudging admiration for the painter is evident in this aside from 1918: 'There is something condensed in all Jews . . . I felt about [Gertler], as about some women, that unnatural repressions have forced him into unnatural assertions.'[31] Of course, Virginia could also be viewing an alienated aspect of herself in Gertler, upon whom 'the shadow of the underworld' rested. In any event, she was attracted to men who felt strongly but whose feelings had been repressed; in consequence, they sought to express themselves artistically in ways which mirrored – and thus captured – the intense amount of feeling which had been driven underground.

Leonard's contribution to *Two Stories*, 'Three Jews', had been written some years before. The story is about the assimilation of Jews into English society and, as it concludes, the central character feels an irrational nostalgia for the old code which forbade intermarriage. What Virginia called the 'testy, dispiriting, & tepid'[32] side of Leonard is present in this narrative, but she was attracted to the honesty which accompanied his negative traits, by his refusal to conform to the rules. Although Vanessa continued to complain about Leonard's punctilious guardianship of his wife, Virginia welcomed his ministrations. When her weight began to go down to just under 10 stone in the summer of 1917, Leonard sounded an alarm, which Virginia was quick to heed: 'Leonard has been in rather a state again, and I've promised to be very quiet.'[33] Virginia saw herself not as a willing prisoner but as a beloved companion in need of nurturing.

For Virginia, excessive shyness and excessive sharpness sometimes went hand in hand. She could empathize with Saxon, but his indecisiveness deeply irritated her. He was, according to her, a man whose lack of virility led him to prettify and, in the process, belittle his own emotions. In contrast, Vanessa was a person who gave the impression 'of a whole nature in use'. Sometimes, Virginia saw her sister as being in perfect 'working order',[34] as if she were some kind of machine. In her relationship with her sister, the full range of Virginia's emotional life can be discerned, from uncontrollable rage to limitless passion. In 1916, Vanessa was simply not able to attend to her younger sister: even after she and her extended family had settled into Charleston, she had a multiplicity of tasks to attend to; she was also still peripherally involved with the Omega Workshops, which she had helped to found in 1913. Their aim was to combine the symmetrical patterns and bright colours of Post-Impressionism with interior design and they sold a wide variety of painted furniture, cloth, rugs, carpets and pottery; they also sought commissions for murals, mosaics and stained-glass windows. Vanessa's absence was hard to tolerate, as was Lytton's rise to fame.

In May 1918, Virginia had to cope with that new swinge of the tail: Lytton Strachey's extraordinary success with *Eminent Victorians*. From 1912 to 1918 – wasted years in her career as a writer as far as Virginia was concerned – he had worked on this book, about which she, in company with many others, had very mixed feelings. Before its publication, she had been frank with Lytton about the character of General Gordon, which did not seem quite believable. Later, after the book became both celebrated and controversial, she observed in a slightly unkind way that sudden fame had transformed her old friend into 'a newly wedded Bride'.[35] When Lytton became ill in October 1918, she tetchily reminded him that 'boils, blisters, rashes, green and blue vomits'[36] were all ordained by God for those whose books went into four editions within six months. Shingles was only the first instalment of the divine retribution. Yet behind the teasing was her sense of Lytton's brilliant mind. His sensibility was the

> softest to impressions, least starched by any formality or impediment. There is his great gift of expression of course . . . he is a figure not to be replaced by any other combination. Intimacy seems to me possible with him as with scarcely any one; for, besides tastes in common, I like & think I understand his feelings – even in their more capricious developments.[37]

Later, when Lytton asked her to review the book, she agreed, but she subsequently decided that there was something unethical about reviewing the work of friends.

Virginia was afraid that she lacked her friend's quickness. In November 1917, she saw herself, in comparison with some of the Bloomsbury bunnies, as a specimen of mature matronhood. For example, she peremptorily warned her sister, who was searching for a tutor for her boys, against selecting one who was excessively masculine. Virginia was certainly shocked by the Barbara–Nick–Saxon trio, by David Garnett's pursuit of Alix Sargant-Florence and by the complications of life at Charleston. In comparison, her own existence sometimes seemed to her sedate, but she could become distraught at the prospect of buying hats or, especially, clothes. The search for the latter was a dangerous and potentially embarrassing activity for a person who kept her underclothes pinned together by brooches. Sometimes, Virginia could conquer her horror by looking directly into the eyes of shopkeepers and declaring her wishes boldly.

Virginia's sense of life's unfairness remained constant. She felt little joy when the Suffrage Bill was passed by the Lords in January 1918. This law gave women over the age of thirty the right to vote. For Virginia, it was an exceedingly hollow victory: 'It's like a knighthood; might be useful to impress people one despises.'[38] A good barometer of how men really felt about women was contained, she felt, in a piece of gossip which came her way in June 1918. Leonard told her that the Germans used women pilots to carry out raids over England and this led to a grim reflection: 'Women's bodies were found in the wrecked aeroplanes. They are smaller & lighter, & thus leave more room for bombs. Perhaps it's sentimental, but the thought seems to me to add a particular touch of horror.'[39]

The competing sides of Virginia Woolf can be seen in the following two passages from about the same time. The first is a fantastical burlesque portrait of one Leonard Merrick, the author of two books she reviewed in 1918. On 25 February, she imagined his existence as

> a poor unappreciated second rate pot-boiling writer of stories about the stage, whom I deduce to be a negro, mulatto or quadroon; at any rate he has a grudge against the world, and might have done much better if he hadn't at the age of 20 married a chorus girl, had by her 15 coffee coloured brats and lived for the rest of the time in a villa in Brixton, where he ekes out his living by giving lessons in elocution to the natives.[40]

This cruel confection comes from Virginia's own sense that she might be turning into the same kind of hack. She is also describing a person led astray by his sexuality.

A very different Virginia Woolf can be seen in this diary entry from March 1918. In the lift at Holborn underground station, she had stood next to a boy of fourteen or fifteen:

> I noticed that it was an extremely interesting, sensitive, clever, observant head; rather sharp, but independent looking. One couldn't tell from his cap whether he was well off or not. I came to the conclusion that he was the son of an officer with whom he stood. When we got into the street I looked once at his legs. His trousers had holes in them. From that one could judge what a wretched affair his life will be.[41]

The boy's potential will never be exploited and this is one of Virginia's fears about herself. Here, in a quiet passage in which she shows the limitations of first impressions, she identifies with the lost boy, whose poverty will keep him from ever having a satisfactory existence.

Sometimes the divisions in Virginia can be seen in the way she reacts to the same person with very different emotions within a matter of minutes. Virginia intensely disliked her sister-in-law, Karin, who was fat, had terrible taste in clothes, talked too much and was in general a nuisance. In February 1918, Karin accepted an invitation from Virginia to lecture at a meeting of the Richmond Women's Co-operative Guild.

> Karin came to give her lecture. She arrived at tea time. I can't help being reminded by her of one of our lost dogs – Tinker most of all. She fairly races round a room, snuffs the corners of the chairs & tables, wags her tail as hard as she can, & snatches at any scrap of talk as if she were sharp set; & she eats a great deal of food too, like a dog . . . But I see that Adrian must find her energy, her not fastidious or critical but generous & warm blooded mind, her honesty & stability a great standby –[42]

In this diary entry, Virginia's first impulse is to carp, but then she backs down, sees the goodness in a woman who in truth was often, like herself, desperately sad and lonely. Virginia dismantles her own paper dart and ends her remarks on a note of empathy. Despite contrary impulses, she sought to embrace whole rather than partial truths. In August 1918, reflecting on her sister-in-law, Virginia declared: 'My stages [of emotion in response to Karin] are on the whole nearer to warmth & liking than to irritation.'[43]

Night and Day was a deliberate attempt to capture the complete truth. Virginia perceived her elder sister as a natural, a person whose body and spirit were in harmony. She insisted on seeing Vanessa in idealistic terms and from the outset she claimed the book was about her. Certainly, when it was almost complete, in April 1918, Virginia told Vanessa: 'I've been writing about you all the morning, and have made you wear a blue dress; you've got so immensely mysterious and romantic, which of course you are; yes, but it's the combination that's so enthralling.'[44]

Virginia's claims about the genesis of her new novel can be accepted without reservation, but they are not an accurate guide to the resulting book. Katharine Hilbery, the central character, is the daughter of a lawyer father and a mother whose father was one of the most distinguished poets of the nineteenth century. When the novel opens, Katharine is assisting her mother in the writing of his life, a task of endless fascination for Mrs Hilbery but one over which she continually procrastinates.* Mrs Hilbery lives in the past and Katharine, her dutiful daughter–companion, is stuck there as well. Unbeknown to her mother and father, Katharine harbours a secret passion for mathematics, a subject seemingly alien to literary pursuits.

At the beginning of the book, Katharine is being pursued by a literary dandy, William Rodney, to whom she is attracted in only a lukewarm way. Katharine's sheltered existence is interrupted by the arrival at her house of Ralph Denham, an outspoken, bumptious, hyper-critical lawyer, who looks at Katharine's privileged life with a very jaundiced eye. From the outset, sparks fly between the two: they disagree over important things and are willing, sometimes eager, to vent their feelings. Katharine and Ralph have a mutual friend, Mary Datchet, whose life is devoted to the suffragette cause, for which she is a badly paid organizer.

Quite soon, the narrative becomes a comic drama of purgation, a mixture of Shakespearean comedy of mistaken identity, Jane Austen comedy of manners and *The Magic Flute*: Mary falls in love with Ralph, who loves Katharine, who becomes engaged to William. The threads begin to wind together when William, who is intelligent but superficial, falls in love with Katharine's glamorous cousin, Cassandra. Mary, who realizes that she must live in the service of others, renounces Ralph, who ultimately comes to an understanding with Katharine: their love for each other may not

* Virginia would experience similar, inhibiting restraints when she wrote her biography of Roger Fry.

be perfect, but it is the best which can be hoped for in an imperfect world. Besides, they learn that it is 'life that matters, nothing but life – the process of discovering, the everlasting and perpetual process . . . not the discovery itself'.[45]*

William Rodney is a composite manufactured from some of Virginia's old beaux: Hilton Young and Lytton Strachey come to mind. Virginia herself said that he had more than a dash of Walter Headlam and George Duckworth in him. Mary's dedication to a cause is reminiscent of Janet Case and Margaret Llewelyn Davies's commitment to feminist issues. Mrs Hilbery's somewhat scatter-brained but wise character is obviously a re-creation of Anny Ritchie, Thackeray's daughter and Virginia's aunt. Ralph's ram-shackle way of dressing may be based on Duncan Grant, but his acerbic, fiery though generous character is obviously grounded in Leonard's personality; his mother is very much like the character of Marie Woolf drawn by Virginia in her letters and diaries.

If Ralph Denham is Leonard Woolf, can Katharine Hilbery be merely a portrait of Vanessa Bell? Obviously not. Although she did not wish to admit it, Katharine's forceful, argumentative character is based just as much on herself as it is on Vanessa. Katharine's interest in mathematics may have a real-life correspond-ence to Vanessa's interest in art in the literary household of Hyde Park Gate, but mathematics also symbolizes Virginia's interest in creating a separate literary space for herself apart from her father and his friends; the science of numbers may also represent the state of abstraction to which Virginia felt she had to push the conven-tions of literary representation.

In order to discover her true self. Katharine must reject or redefine the literary inheritance she has received from her mother. Virginia had to do the same with regard to her father or be stuck in the nineteenth-century past and its literature. Katharine also rejects the idea of becoming an angel of the house, a vision of womanhood espoused by William Rodney. Katharine's acceptance

* This passage is a paraphrase from Dostoevsky's *The Idiot*; E. M. Forster had cited it in his review of *The Voyage Out*.

of Rodney's proposal of marriage parallels Virginia's acceptance of Lytton Strachey. William Rodney is emotionally undemanding; marriage to him would be an alliance in name only, very much like the sexually undemanding relationship marriage to Lytton would have implied. Like Virginia, Katharine feels that marriage offers a change, not a solution, but does one want to swap realities for dreams and then find out that, in the process, one has sacrificed independence only in order to live a life of sacrifice?

In essence, *Night and Day* is a novel about compromise, about finding a half-way house between the realm of night, the kingdom of illusion, and day, the realm of dreary reality.* In this narrative, opposites attract, quarrel with each other and ultimately fuse. The vision of Virginia's second novel stands in complete contrast to the unwavering grimness with which *The Voyage Out* concludes. In the 1910s, Virginia was worried about her sexual unresponsiveness and early in *Night and Day* there are many comments on Katharine's lack of warmth, a condition of being which evaporates as she becomes more and more committed to Ralph.

If there is a great deal of Virginia in Katharine, there is also a lot of her in Mary Datchet, who decides to live a life of heroic renunciation. Although Virginia was never much interested in the practicality of politics, she was attracted to the idea of the single life, of discovering her destiny in isolation. In some ways, Mary is the most attractive – certainly the most valorous – of the characters in *Night and Day*. Her choice of life is the path not taken by Virginia and that gives a special poignancy to the depiction of this courageous, outspoken woman.

Night and Day is often said, correctly, to be the most conventional of Virginia Woolf's novels. Without doubt, she retreated

* The only surviving manuscript (MS Berg) of the novel is entitled 'Dreams and Realities' (it begins in the middle of Chapter XI with an entry dated 6 October 1916 and runs to half-way through Chapter XVII, the last recorded date being 5 January 1917). This working title suggests that the novel was intended to comment on two contradictory states, which do not necessarily follow each other as night follows day.

from the nihilist conclusions of *The Voyage Out*, but, as she recalled in 1930, there were other reasons for her use of a realism which is vastly different from that of Dostoevsky or her own short stories written during the same time span:

> I was so tremblingly afraid of my own insanity that I wrote Night and Day mainly to prove to my own satisfaction that I could keep entirely off that dangerous ground. I wrote it, lying in bed, allowed to write only for one half hour a day . . . Bad as the book is, it composed my mind, and I think taught me certain elements of composition which I should not have had the patience to learn had I been in full flush of health always.[46]

In this passage, Virginia states her aims in negative terms. However, during the writing of the book, she had become fascinated by the actual texture of life, by how things really look, by accuracy in description. This passion overwhelmed her. In October 1918, while finishing *Night and Day*, she told Roger Fry: 'I'm not sure that a perverted plastic sense doesn't somehow work itself out in words for me. I spent an hour looking at pots and carpets in the museums the other day, until the desire to describe them became like the desire for the lusts of the flesh.'[47]

If *Night and Day* is the most traditional, it is also the most romantic of Virginia's novels. The quarrels between Ralph and Katharine are certainly full of energy: these two people find each other very attractive, but they have to find a mutually acceptable way to live together. At one point, an exasperated Katharine tells Ralph that he is in love with a fantasy idea of her: 'you go home and invent a story about me, and now you can't separate me from the person you've imagined me to be. You call that, I suppose, being in love; as a matter of fact it's being in delusion.'[48] At another juncture, the two have an exchange which displays the open hostility and latent desire between them:

> 'I thought that you criticized me – perhaps disliked me. I thought of you as a person who judges.'
>
> 'No; I'm a person who feels,' he said, in a low voice.[49]

As he himself points out, Ralph has strong, pent-up feelings, whereas Katharine is more rational. Her tendency to be cold vanishes as she becomes angry with Ralph and engages in a series of lively exchanges with him. Gradually, Katharine exchanges a life of certainties for an existence in which the only truth will be found within herself. This can be only a frail beam, even though there will be many dark passages.

Eventually, the two lovers, each with great ideals and serious flaws, find one another enthralling. At the Orchid House in Kew Gardens, their sexuality is discreetly suggested by juxtaposing them with the luxuriantly beautiful blooms:

> when he saw Katharine among the orchids, her beauty strangely emphasized by the fantastic plants, which seemed to peer and gape at her from striped hoods and fleshy throats, [Ralph's] ardour for botany waned, and a more complex feeling replaced it. She fell silent. The orchids seemed to suggest absorbing reflections. In defiance of the rules she stretched her ungloved hand and touched one. The sight of the rubies upon her fingers affected him so disagreeably that he started and turned away. But the next moment he controlled himself; he looked at her taking in one strange shape after another with the contemplative, considering gaze of a person who sees not exactly what is before him, but gropes in regions that lie beyond it.[50]

The exotic, fierce loveliness of the orchids stirs Ralph's desire for Katharine, who touches one of the flowers. Although Katharine's gesture manifests in part a corresponding sexual attraction to Ralph, she touches a flower, not him. He is jealous and has to control himself. At the end, Katharine and Ralph realize that through the power of love they can tolerate each other's separateness.

In addition, they have no illusions about the darkness of the world. The power of love could not survive such knowledge in *The Voyage Out*, but the compact forged by Katharine and Ralph allows them to triumph over the forces which destroyed Rachel and Terence. *Night and Day* may seem a deliberate retreat into orthodoxy, but it displays Virginia's understanding of life's possibilities, possibilities which had been severely discounted in her first novel. Her second novel also shows an intuitive understanding of tradition. Here she demonstrates a genuine sympathy with the conventions she would once again, with renewed vigour, seek to overthrow. However, she avoids a happy ending: the frictions between Katharine and Ralph are simply too open-ended for the reader to feel that marriage is a 'happily ever after' solution to the dissensions dramatized in the narrative.

Virginia's declaration of independence from the established precepts of fiction is contained in 'Modern Novels', published in the *Times Literary Supplement* ten days after the typescript of *Night and Day* was submitted to Gerald Duckworth. This essay, which attacks the stolid, materialistic narratives of Wells, Bennett and Galsworthy, maintains that these three men adhere to a form of storytelling which replicates the outward forms of life while not paying sufficient attention to inner realities. In contrast, she provides a new recipe:

> The mind, exposed to the ordinary course of life, receives upon its surface a myriad impressions – trivial, fantastic, evanescent, or engraved with the sharpness of steel. From all sides they come, an incessant shower of innumerable atoms, composing in their sum what we might venture to call life itself; and to figure further as the semi-transparent envelope, or luminous halo, surrounding us from the beginning of consciousness to the end. Is it not perhaps the chief task of the novelist to convey this incessantly varying spirit with whatever stress or sudden deviation it may display, and as little admixture of the alien and external as possible?[51]

Of course, in *Night and Day* Virginia had attempted to beat her three male rivals at their own game. Having waged that battle successfully, she would try to discover a prose style which captured the 'incessantly varying spirit' of existence.

Virginia made great headway with *Night and Day* during the winter of 1918. She was spurred on by being 'rejected' by the

Times Literary Supplement, which was not asking her to review books at the frenetic pace established in previous months. Once upon a time, she had been thrilled when Leonard called her to the phone: 'You're wanted by the Major Journal!' Like a tradesman, she would run down to take her weekly orders.

There was another inducement to get on with the novel: her rivalry with Katherine Mansfield. During the writing of *Night and Day*, Virginia was very much aware of how Katherine Mansfield exploited the possibilities of traditional narrative form in her short stories. If Virginia was attempting to vanquish her, she did not succeed in *Night and Day*. In fact, in partial recognition of her rival's genius, she and Leonard asked Mansfield for a story in April 1917. This request spurred her to revise 'The Aloe', which became 'Prelude', the second publication of the Hogarth Press. 'Prelude' is particularly successful in its description of the sensitivity of the little girl Kezia and of her mother Linda's fear of sexual intimacy. Virginia would also have liked the way in which Mansfield linked various spots of time by concentrating on epiphanic moments and thus ignored some of the more usual ways of dealing with the passing of time. Although the story may have been watered down with some cheap effects, Virginia recognized a living power in 'Prelude', through which shone the 'detached existence of a work of art'.[52]

If Virginia could sympathize with the themes of 'Prelude' and its deft handling of time, she was dismissive of 'Bliss', which in August 1918 she threw to the floor, exclaiming, 'She's done for!'[53] According to Virginia, 'Bliss' was unutterably vulgar; she was probably offended by its overt depiction of lesbianism. For Virginia, Mansfield the woman and Mansfield the writer were too exhibitionistic. Virginia had had similar reservations about James Joyce, when his devoted admirer, the exceedingly conventional-looking Harriet Weaver, asked her and Leonard in April 1918 to publish *Ulysses*.

Virginia, recognizing the experimental nature of the Irish writer, realized that Joyce was trying to reform the novel very much along lines to which she was sympathetic: 'he leaves out the narrative, and tries to give the thoughts'.[54] However, she did not think he had anything interesting to impart. In reality she was put off by the vulgarity in the manuscript which Miss Weaver offered her: 'Possibly the poor woman was impeded by her sense that what she had in the brownpaper parcel was quite out of keeping with her own contents. Why does their filth seek exit from her mouth?'[55] In order to get out of a ticklish situation, Virginia told Miss Weaver a partial truth: the Hogarth Press did not have the facilities to typeset such a long book. However, Virginia's prudishness is evident in a letter to Nick Bagenal of 15 April:

> a compatriot of yours, called James Joyce, wants us to print his new novel. I should hesitate to put it into the hand of Barbara, even though she is a married woman. The directness of the language, and the choice of incidents, if there *is* any choice, but as far as I can see there's a certain sameness – have raised a blush even upon such a cheek as mine.[56]

Hand in hand with her dislike of Joyce and her admiration of Dostoevsky went Virginia's increasing sense that the male point of view was corrupting and thus destroying the English novel. The year before she had informed Saxon that she intended to reject his enthusiastic recommendation that she read Henry James's *The Sense of the Past*: 'my old image must still hold good . . . the laborious striking of whole boxfuls of damp matches'.[57] When Clive Bell, in his new book *Potboilers*, referred to her, Hardy and Conrad as the three best living novelists, she quickly discounted her old lover's praise. All in all, Virginia remained fascinated by Katherine Mansfield.

The war could not be disregarded. There were many nights in Richmond when Leonard, looking very much like a funerary statue, slept on the kitchen table, while Virginia hid beneath it. Nelly and Lottie had bunks nearby and Leonard would become angry if Virginia chatted at too great a length with them.

In the midst of surviving these bombings, Virginia had to

confront what she called the shadow of the underworld – a force which she associated with Mansfield and Gertler. In these two, Virginia beheld artists who directly confronted and thus exploited the darker sides of their natures. In so doing, they unleashed considerable energy, even though it was in large part self-destructive. Such an exploration – which is central to *The Voyage Out* – frightened Virginia. She had already paid a heavy price for honesty, but she began to realize that she would once again have to mine the demon side of herself. Good writing, she knew well, often exacted a high price.

A woman who would be a good writer belonged to a select band and Virginia constantly monitored the other women in her set, whether or not they were writers and artists. In so doing, she unearthed subject matter, but she also began, at the very same time, to learn about the status of women in society. When she finally visited Ottoline at Garsington in November 1917, Virginia did not fail to notice the languid, fetid air of this country manor to which writers and artists were summoned by their intellectual hostess. Aldous Huxley toyed with great round discs of ivory and green marble; the painter Dorothy Brett attempted to make some sort of statement about a new sense of freedom by always wearing trousers; Ottoline was encased in velvet and pearls, and her two pug dogs, who accompanied her everywhere, had the bearing of courtiers. Despite – or perhaps because of – so many things which put her off, Virginia saw the real vitality in Ottoline: 'in private talk her vapours give way to some quite clear bursts of shrewdness'.[58]

Virginia's own insecurities surfaced whenever she thought about the now-lost possibility of the single life. Large, warm Ka Cox was for Virginia a maternal figure whom she wished to keep to herself. When, in July 1918, Ka announced her engagement to William Arnold-Forster, Virginia was irritated: 'I am glad that [Ka] should marry, though she bade fair to be a marked spinster, but marriage with W.A.F. will be merely a decorous & sympathetic alliance, making her more of a servant of the state than ever.'[59] Virginia reserved her fury for the man Ka had selected: 'He looked unusually small, drawn & pallid, like a face seen under a gas lamp . . . He reminds me rather of one of those old ladies, who have yellow hair & very pink cheeks, but you can count their years in the way the flesh is drawn tight across the bone.'[60] Will's failings seemed to be linked to effeminacy, almost as if Ka had abandoned Virginia for another woman. His lack of real substance is listed as his great crime, even though he will be a modern husband in the best sense of that expression. Virginia is jealous, but she is also expressing some of her own regrets about marriage, her own included.

If Virginia was prone to be overly critical of her single friends, some of them were more than willing to manifest their sharp disapproval of the way Virginia conducted her professional life. For a long time, Virginia had been certain that Janet Case was the type of person who read for information and edification rather than pleasure and her worst fears were proved correct when her old teacher advised her in November 1918 to write biography rather than fiction. Miss Case pointed out that many novels were published and that none was immortal. Virginia was depressed on two scores: the musty morality hiding behind the statement and the implied criticism of *The Voyage Out*. Although discouraged, she reflected that writing was what she did best, that the quest for praise was one of the curses of a writer's existence and that she took great pleasure in the act of writing.

Her childlessness continued to haunt her. In September 1918, she confessed to the pregnant Barbara Bagenal that she had become so domestic that she now realized that nothing could be quite so important as childbearing: 'I'm so envious that I don't think I shall speak to you.'[61] Vanessa Bell was also pregnant again. Virginia admired Vanessa's fecundity, but she also reminded her: 'there's a good deal to be said for the firstborn'.[62] Virginia was, of course, referring to herself. Could a woman so resolutely determined to remain someone's child become a mother? This dilemma, never fully resolved, remained a deep hurt.

Relations between Asheham/Hogarth House and Charleston were not always cordial. The 'great Charleston affair', as Virginia called it, began in about April 1918. Charleston housed many people: at this time, there were Vanessa, Duncan, David Garnett, a governess and her lover, four children including the governess's daughter and nephew, a cook and a kitchen-maid. When the cook gave notice, Virginia attempted to engage a replacement in London while Vanessa scoured the villages near her in Sussex. All these inquiries came to nothing. Then Virginia had an idea: she and Leonard would lend Nelly and Lottie for two weeks. Perhaps, she thought, they might stay on. She and Leonard were hard up and they might consider jettisoning this responsibility. On the other hand, if Leonard got an editorship, they would have to entertain more, but then they would have the money to do so – and thus the two servants could come back to them.

During the complex negotiations between the sisters, Virginia did not tell Nelly and Lottie that they might be leaving for good, although they suspected as much. They were hurt, confused and resentful. In the midst of this, Vanessa became ill and sent Trissie, the cook who was leaving her, to Richmond to interview Nelly and Lottie. Trissie managed things so badly that the two refused to go to Charleston. This happened at precisely the moment when a vacillating Vanessa, who had delayed securing the services of a local girl, Miss Ford, saw her snatched away by someone else. Exasperated, Vanessa now became convinced that Leonard had been hostile to the entire scheme from the outset and had somehow undermined it.

This Charleston débâcle was soon followed by another. Virginia got into 'hot water'[63] this time because she supposedly told Mark Gertler that Vanessa did not like Mary Hutchinson, Clive's mistress and the wife of the lawyer, St John Hutchinson. Vanessa, who wanted to stay on good terms with the man who was her husband in name only, was distraught. If, as is likely, Virginia did use Gertler as the instrument of her wicked tongue, she managed to anger a lot of people. On 26 October, Clive told Vanessa: 'I just wanted to put you right on one point. It was not I who said that Virginia had been telling Gertler tales. I merely said that tales had been told and it was someone else – you I rather think – who suggested Virginia as the *fons et origo*. We all agreed that this was probable and I think so still.'[64] According to Virginia, Mary made a particular nuisance of herself by being 'conveyed about London in a fainting condition in taxicabs'.

This round of what Virginia called 'agonies & desperations'[65] occurred just as the war was coming to an end. The long-awaited peace was not only anticlimactic but also dispiriting. For four years, all strata of society had been united in a fight against a common enemy. Now, according to Virginia, the lower classes were bitter, impatient, powerful and unreasonable. Englishmen were no longer concentrated on a single point: 'We are once more a nation of individuals.'[66]

Even though Leonard reassured his wife that the new melancholia which was trying to establish itself in her would wane, she was deeply apprehensive. In a poignant aside in a letter to Vanessa of 13 November, Virginia reflected on her pervasive feeling of insubstantiality and on the corresponding poignant sadness which filled her when she thought about her childlessness.

> Do you ever feel that your entire life is useless – passed in a dream, into which now and then these brutal buffaloes come butting? or are you always certain that you matter, and matter more than other people? I believe having children must make a lot of difference; and yet perhaps it's no good making them responsible for one's own inefficiency – but I mean rather transparency – nonentity – unreality.[67]

Chapter Ten

THE SHADOW LINE

(1919–20)

On Christmas Day 1918, Vanessa gave birth to a girl, whose name, after much debate, became Angelica. During her confinement, Vanessa asked her sister to look after Julian and Quentin, a task about which Virginia had mixed feelings: 'Do they want a great deal? – Also, can they safely be left to amuse themselves with occasional visits most of the morning? Some mornings I have to write in order to get reviews finished.'[1] Virginia's feelings of nonentity might have been sharpened by her sense of having been deprived of the opportunity to have children, but she also became aware of how much looking after children would hinder her work. The boys stayed with Leonard and Virginia at Asheham and then travelled to Richmond on 1 January. On the following day, Virginia had a tooth extracted and remained in bed for a fortnight; a week later, the children were sent home.

Without doubt, Virginia had divided feelings about the arrival of Angelica, who was displacing her as Vanessa's daughter. Perhaps Virginia, as the lover of her sister, could supplant Duncan as the father?* 'I want to set on foot a scheme of mine which I may tell you is to confuse [Angelica's] mind from the first as to her maternity; she is going to think me something more than an Aunt – not quite a father perhaps, but with a hand (to put it delicately) in her birth. I warn you I shall drop hints at every opportunity.'[2] Vanessa, who had quarrelled bitterly with her sister during the great Charleston crisis, was wary of such banter.

* As she makes clear in *Deceived with Kindness*, Angelica was allowed for many years to believe that Clive Bell was her father.

One way Virginia had of evading the net of insubstantiality was to confide her musings to her diary and thus, in a sometimes haphazard and cumbersome way, to enshrine seemingly worthless pieces of information which, over the course of time, might turn out to be 'diamonds of the dustheap'.[3] She also categorized and labelled various portions of her life: Hyde Park Gate, Fitzroy days, 'the Cambridge stage of life',[4] Brunswick Square. How did these various parts add up to Virginia Woolf the woman and writer? What process of metamorphosis had been at work? Would she remain only a diamond in the rough?

That January, Virginia turned her observant eye towards Cambridge. For her, the university encapsulated a variety of suspect masculine attitudes. At that time, Alix Sargant-Florence confided in Virginia that Harry Norton, in order to rid himself of suppressed feelings, had suggested that they have sex every ten days. Virginia, in part shocked by the Trinity College mathematician's attempt to timetable the emotions, offered straightforward advice: 'I told her on no account to copulate from a sense of duty.' She also observed: 'Norton is the pure flower of Cambridge, isn't he?'[5]

Another side of male arrogance could be all too plainly discerned in Lytton Strachey. How, she asked herself, had he come to dominate his generation at Cambridge: 'How did he do it, how is he so distinct & unmistakable if he lacks originality & the rest?'[6] Virginia had become suspicious of other deficiencies in her friend's work, particularly the absence of warmth or generosity in his description of his subjects. The metallic side of Strachey upset her, but she admired his brilliant, lively style. Still, he lacked an essential quality in a great writer: vitality. And it was precisely that attribute for which she was searching.

Virginia also suspected that Tom Eliot lacked the warmth and energy with which she wished her writing to be suffused. When she first met him in November 1918, she was impressed by the strange, handsome young man's admiration for and eloquent defence of Pound, Joyce and Wyndham Lewis, but the steely, over-polished and intellectually arrogant edge of his personality grated on her. Like Strachey, he had a creed; Virginia was searching for one. She felt that these two men were easily content with the solutions they had found. In them, she did not discern any reflection of the struggle which consumed her.

Eliot the person remained an enigma and Virginia was not surprised when Clive told her that Eliot abhorred her. When Tom and Vivien Eliot dined at Hogarth House in April 1919, Virginia was delighted when another guest, Gumbo, insisted upon talking of purges, bottoms and water-closets in her typically outlandish manner. Virginia also amused herself by seeing how 'sharp, narrow & much of a stick Eliot has come to be, since he took to disliking me'. She was also pleased that Vivien Eliot turned out to be a 'washed out, elderly & worn out looking little woman'.[7] A few days later, Virginia's perceptions of Eliot had to be readjusted when she learned that Tom had praised her extravagantly to Katherine Mansfield and her husband, the critic Middleton Murry, whom she married in 1918. This was a difficult mystery to unravel. To discover the truth she would have to find a way to 'draw the rat from his hole'.[8]

Meanwhile, Virginia was sure, men who had not been able to construct strong systems of impregnable belief suffered in consequence. Morgan Forster had been transformed in Virginia's mind from a mouse to a blue butterfly, so transparent and light was his personality. Desmond MacCarthy, Virginia had been assured, would never produce a great work of literature: 'I'm told he wants power; that these fragments never combine into an argument.'[9] As she was uncomfortably self-aware, Virginia saw reality in a correspondingly fragmentary way. Were the sensibilities of Forster and MacCarthy essentially feminine and, because of that, blighted? Virginia did not believe this, but she was trying to find a new form of writing while, at the same time, not being absolutely sure that it was possible. She certainly lacked the easy assurance of an Eliot or a Strachey.

Shortly after Anny Ritchie died in late February 1919, Virginia published an obituary of her in the *Times Literary Supplement*. Virginia, who had a great deal of affection for the aunt upon whose exuberant character she had in large part drawn to create

Mrs Hilbery in *Night and Day*, knew that these strong feelings were at least 'half moonshine'.[10] However, she realized that the daughter of one of the truly great novelists of the previous century had created novels which contained 'an entirely personal vision of life, of which her books are the more or less complete embodiment'. What is more, 'every stroke proceeded directly from her own hand; a more natural gift than hers never existed. It came to her directly, and owed nothing to discipline or to the painstaking study of other writers.'[11]

Despite the fact that she was Thackeray's daughter and might have inherited her literary inclinations from him, Anny was an original, a person who had charted her own territory. For Virginia, also the daughter of a great man of letters, there were some obvious lessons in the career of her aunt: she too would have to cultivate her own talents, that entirely personal vision of life for which she sought. At the very same time she was writing so movingly of her aunt, Virginia was preparing an essay for the *Times Literary Supplement* to commemorate the centenary of George Eliot's birth.

In the unrealizable goals of Eliot's heroines, Virginia saw a reflection of the hazards with which she was grappling:

> They do not find what they seek, and we cannot wonder. The ancient consciousness of woman, charged with suffering and sensibility, and for so many ages dumb, seems in them to have brimmed and overflowed and uttered a demand for something – they scarcely know what – for something that is perhaps incompatible with the facts of human existence. George Eliot had far too strong an intelligence to tamper with those facts, and too broad a humour to mitigate the truth because it was a stern one.[12]

Of the work of her own contemporary Dorothy Richardson and of that writer's advocacy of what she called 'interior monologue', Virginia did not have the highest opinion. Nevertheless, she recognized in Richardson a writer who, like herself, perceived the chasm separating tradition from innovation: 'She is one of the rare novelists who believe that the novel is so much alive that it actually grows.'[13] As such, Richardson's failures were much more interesting than most novelists' successes.

Virginia was starting to write a different kind of literary history, one which included the many accomplishments of women. However, she remained fearful of the female hack, someone like her parents' old friend Mrs W. K. Clifford, whom in April 1920 she characterized as an Oriental turkey with a 'mouth opening like an old leather bag, or the private parts of a large cow'.[14] This elderly woman, dressed all in black, lurched about like a beetle that had lost a front leg. Virginia *wanted* to hate her but Mrs Clifford's courage moved her to tears.

Katherine Mansfield remained Virginia's ideal of the modern woman writer. However, the more Virginia glanced at the lives of Mansfield, Richardson or Ritchie, the more she became aware of another kind of shaping process, that imposed by experience. In Marjorie Strachey, seduced and then abandoned by Josiah Wedgwood, she saw a woman subjected to cruel disappointment. Virginia was not sure that she could evade such a snare, since she was well aware that she was dealing with 'an attitude of mind – the way one looks at life'.[15]

If Morgan Forster was a benign butterfly, Clive had become for Virginia the Yellow Cockatoo or Yellow Bird of Bloomsbury. Next to such resplendence, she felt colourless, no longer connected to the heartland of bohemia. In fact, she playfully informed Vanessa, it was her fate 'to be sucked under by the Bourgeois'.[16]

Gerald Duckworth, who was to publish *Night and Day*, held the professional clubman's view of literature. Virginia did not wish to write for such an audience. Yet she realized that *Night and Day*, although not as experimental as *The Voyage Out*, was more mature in outlook. This was not necessarily a bad thing and, besides, she told her diary: 'English fiction being what it is, I compare for originality & sincerity rather well with most of the moderns.'[17] When her cousin H. A. L. Fisher, now Minister for Education, visited, Virginia saw in him the epitome of the public man. He had long passed 'the shadow line': he looked at things not to see things but rather to collect 'objects for the good of his soul.'[18] Although she could not avoid the onslaught of age, she hoped to escape such complacency.

Katherine Mansfield, she knew, was incapable of being insufferably middle class or a hack. Virginia was not as confident about herself. When she read *Moll Flanders*, she was astounded how a truly great writer – very much a denizen of Grub Street – could still impose his voice after two hundred years. She now saw London through Defoe's eyes and in the process her sense of the power of writing was renewed. When she ran into Morgan Forster at the London Library and learned that he had never read a word of the eighteenth-century writer, she commanded him to do so. Still, her own search for form evaded her. Meanwhile, her diary gave her enormous pleasure; it was, she hoped, 'loose knit, & yet not slovenly, so elastic that it will embrace any thing'.[19]

While she was searching for a breakthrough in her fiction-writing, Virginia had to cope with the loss of Asheham, the quiet setting which had been so conducive to fuelling her imagination. Frank Gunn, the bailiff to Mrs Hoper the owner, informed the Woolfs in February that he and his mother were moving into the house that September. Virginia had mixed feelings: Asheham now became the embodiment of earthly perfection and yet, at the very same time, the search for a new house would be for her, she knew, great fun.

The Woolfs' first extended house-hunt near Asheham was in April. That proved unsuccessful and Virginia, in compensation, attempted to rent three connecting cottages at Tregerthen near Gurnard's Head, four miles from St Ives.* Despite anxiety about where she was to move to, Virginia was filled with a remarkable

* These cottages at Tregerthen had been rented in 1916–17 by D. H. and Frieda Lawrence. *Women in Love* had been written there. For a short period, Katherine Mansfield and John Middleton Murry had occupied one of them. Katherine suggested the cottages to Virginia, and there was an exchange of letters between Leonard and Lawrence.

sense of well-being. Her happiness was centred on the fact that she and Leonard were both working well. These strong positive feelings were unshaken even when she contemplated fat, smooth, stoat-like, unsmiling Gerald Duckworth smoking a cigar as he read the manuscript of *Night and Day*, which she had delivered to him on 1 April.

At the end of May, Virginia had the enormous pleasure of being toasted in the *Times Literary Supplement*, where Harold Child said *Kew Gardens* – the Hogarth Press's seventh publication – demonstrated how unimportant subject was next to style:

> And Mrs Woolf writes about Kew Gardens and a snail and some stupid people. But here is 'Kew Gardens' – a work of art, made, 'created', as we say, finished, four-square; a thing of original and therefore strange beauty, with its own 'atmosphere', its own vital force . . . the more one gloats over 'Kew Gardens' the more beauty shines out of it.[20]

The reviewer, who at first glance had been dismayed by Vanessa's illustrations, came to see how they accompanied Virginia's text perfectly. Up to this time, forty-nine copies of the hand-printed edition of 150 had been sold. Then, in the wake of the rave review, came an avalanche of orders, forcing the Woolfs to order 500 additional copies from Richard Madley, a commercial printer.*

However, despite Child's kind words, Vanessa had been very upset by what she considered the poor quality of both the type and the woodcuts. She refused, under the prevailing conditions, to do any more work for the Hogarth Press. An ordinary printer would do a much better job, she assured her sister. This stung Virginia, especially as Vanessa had justified cause for complaint. Of course, Vanessa's anger with Virginia on many

* This was the second time the Woolfs sent a book to another printer (Middleton Murry's *The Critic in Judgment*, 1919, was done by the Prompt Press). Of the 440 titles published by the Hogarth Press up to 1938, only thirty-four were hand-printed.

Vanessa Bell. Cover design and illustrated page 1 of Kew Gardens *(1927)*

other scores had found an outlet. On professional grounds, where she as artist could speak with considerable assurance, Vanessa voiced extreme displeasure. Subsequently, Vanessa designed the cover for *Monday or Tuesday* and the dust-jackets for *Jacob's Room* and all of Virginia's next books (plus many other Hogarth Press editions). She also devised the colophon of the wolf's head. In many ways, Vanessa's designs capture in visual terms the essence of her sister's words: her designs of tables, chairs, flowers are very recognizable as such, but they move in the direction of abstraction.

On the evening of 1 June, the sisters quarrelled. The next day, a very shaken Virginia tried to restore herself by house-hunting. Leonard had asked her to look at the White House, which stands on Cuilfail, the hill dominating Lewes on the east. She thought it too smug and refined. In a now doubly bad mood, Virginia trudged back into Lewes and asked the estate agent's wife, Mrs Wycherley, if anything else suitable was on offer. She mentioned several possibilities before thinking of one which was small, old and perhaps a bit humble in comparison to Asheham. Immediately, Virginia took off, up Pipes Passage and saw rising at the top of the sloping path a 'singular shaped roof, rising into a point, & spreading out in a circular petticoat all around it'.[21] This was the Round House, a converted windmill, standing on the western walls of

Lewes Castle; a small two-storey cottage was attached to the main structure. The tower was truncated and covered by an eight-sided pointed slate roof.

Virginia was immediately taken with the Round House's small rooms, wide sitting room, surrounding ancient walls and view. She also liked the way in which the town dropped from the garden, leaving the residents on a triangular island. In general, the oddness of the structure and its setting overwhelmed her. As she herself confessed, she quickly became an ardent lover who had to have full possession of the beloved. Mr Wycherley was a bit hesitant about consummating a purchase then and there; he mentioned that someone else was interested in the house. This only increased Virginia's determination to buy, which she did for £300. Ten days later, once the heat of passion was over now the cherished one had been secured, everything was blamed on Vanessa: 'Did you realize that it was your severity that plunged me into the recklessness of buying a house that day? Something I must do to redress the balance, to give myself value in my eyes . . . the blood will therefore be upon your head.'[22] Virginia was not quite honest about the heat of this particular obsession and the fact that her love of her sister had been transferred – momentarily – to a house.

Although he was polite, Leonard did not share Virginia's enthusiasm for the Round House when they inspected it on 26 June. Virginia, as she demurely put it, discovered that a 'slight shade of anti-climax had succeeded my rather excessive optimism; at any rate the Round House no longer seemed so radiant & unattainable when we examined it as owners'. Earlier, on the road from the railway station at Lewes, Leonard and Virginia had noticed a placard on the auctioneers' wall: 'Lot 1. Monks House, Rodmell. An old fashioned house standing in three quarters of an acre of land to be sold with possession.' Leonard had observed: 'That would have suited us exactly.' Taken aback, Virginia nevertheless reassured her husband of the merits of the house he was about to see for the first time. After that viewing, she decided to visit Rodmell, three miles south of Lewes, the next day.

This time, Virginia was determined to keep herself in check. Her initial impressions were a list of negatives: small rooms, bad kitchen, no grate, no hot water, no bath, no evidence of an earth closet. Next to Asheham, fifteenth- or sixteenth-century Monks House (it received its name from supposedly having once belonged to the monks of Lewes Priory, who used it as a retreat) was in every way 'unpretending': this weatherboard house was long, low, had many doors, eight or nine oak-beamed rooms and fronted on to the main village street. The origin of the village's name is also a matter of dispute: the mill on the road is one possible derivation, or it might derive from the reddish tinge of the soil in the area. In 1919 the street in front of the house was little more than a cart track running out to the flats of the water-meadows. However much she wanted to restrain herself, Virginia could not do so when she beheld the 'size & shape & fertility & wildness of the garden. There seemed an infinity of fruitbearing trees; the plums crowded so as to weigh the tip of the branch down; unexpected flowers sprouted among cabbages.'

When Leonard viewed the property the next day, he, like his wife, was pleased beyond expectation and became a 'fanatical lover of that garden'. Virginia's language is tinged with more than a hint of eroticism, almost as if she and Leonard perceived that the fecundity of the garden might become a substitute for the libidinousness totally absent in the physical side of their marriage. In any event, the beautiful prodigality of the landscape forced husband and wife to overlook the many disadvantages of the house itself and the huge array of subsidiary buildings with which the property was strewn: three large outhouses, a stable, a hen house, a shed full of beams of ancient oak, a shed filled with pea props and all the machinery of a granary.

Although Leonard and Virginia had been aroused by Monks House and quickly decided to sell the Round House, they determined that £800 was their limit at the auction on Tuesday, 1 July. Although Wycherley assured them they had a good chance of success, the five minutes which it took them to buy the house were as packed with sensation as any Virginia had previously experienced. Before the sale at the crowded White Hart began, she anxiously studied every face, in particular every coat and skirt, for any sign of opulence. She reassured herself when she found none. Then, she wondered, did Leonard look like a man who had £800 in his pocket? Someone started the bidding at £300, but the auctioneer sneered at this: it was a beginning, not a serious offer. Luckily, Wycherley, who was acting for the nervous couple, maintained a cool demeanour and obtained the house at £700, although Virginia's heart was beating fast when the 'auctioneer raised his hammer, very slowly; held it up a considerable time; urged & exhorted all the while it slowly sank towards the table'.[23] At the moment of victory, Virginia had turned purple whereas the normally phlegmatic Leonard was trembling like a reed.

The triumphant purchase of Monks House came in the midst of correcting the page proofs of *Night and Day*. Virginia completed this task on 17 August, two weeks before the move to Rodmell. Now that the possibility of taking the cottages in Cornwall had been abandoned, Virginia had a considerable amount of time free. That spring and summer, she turned her attention to verse. For the first time, she was genuinely impressed with Yeats when she read *The Wild Swans at Coole* (1917), but her most important poetic discovery was of the reclusive, posthumously published Gerard Manley Hopkins, in whom she recognized the urge to explore undiscovered, seemingly worthless terrain: 'he makes a very strange jumble; so that what is apparently pure nonsense is at the same time very beautiful, and not nonsense at all'.[24] Although Virginia discerned in Hopkins a kindred spirit, she did not share his ability to allow his considerable light to be hidden under a bushel. She confessed to her diary: 'the worst of writing is that one depends so much upon praise'. Nevertheless, she knew what was paramount: 'the fact of my own pleasure in the art'.[25]

Virginia was becoming increasingly aware of the seductive sweetness of fame and how it could draw interest from all quarters. Momentarily, when she stayed a weekend at Garsington that June, she could uncharacteristically be more worried about her appearance than the publication of *Night and Day* on 20 October: 'Why am I calm & indifferent as to what people say of Night & Day, & fretful for their good opinion of my blue dress?'[26] Virginia had certainly reached a new plateau in self-confidence, as can be seen in her sounding of a brusque warning to Lytton, who must, she told him, avoid becoming a 'superior dilettante'.[27]

Virginia was even sure that she had reached a 'kind of durable foundation'[28] in her friendship with Katherine Mansfield, with whom she shared a passion for writing which had an aura of religious devotion. Five months earlier, Virginia had not been so sure of the other writer:

> It is at this moment extremely doubtful whether I have the right to class her among my friends . . . The truth is, I suppose, that one of the conditions unexpressed but understood of our friendship has been precisely that it was almost entirely founded on quicksands . . . We have been intimate, intense perhaps rather than open; but to me at any rate our intercourse has been always interesting & mingled with quite enough of the agreeable personal element to make one fond – if that is the word – as well as curious . . . But meanwhile, for no reason given or to be guessed at with any certainty, she falls silent; I get no thanks, no answers, no enquiries.[29]

Where did the truth lie in this curious relationship? Were they indeed priestesses residing in the same temple? That autumn, Virginia was not certain.

As the publication day of *Night and Day* approached, Virginia experienced the occasional twinge of anxiety. She found it difficult to write even a letter: 'I can't bring myself to break the virginity of a sheet of paper.'[30] An additional worry was the move to Monks House in September. This proved traumatic on many scores: when the kitchen flooded on their first night there, Nelly and Lottie became hysterical and packed their cases; an outraged Leonard attempted to take the upper hand by dismissing them, whereupon Virginia pacified them, which led to a precarious peace.

Monks House possessed none of Asheham's flawless beauty and, in the judgement of her friends, Virginia did little to decorate it. The bilious green colour scheme was usually the focus of their sarcasm, although, they conceded, the oak beams did give the interior a pleasant antiquarian look. The Woolfs were interlopers, but the villagers welcomed them. Nearby were the Old Poor Cottages, Sweet Briar Cottage, the Park Cottages (purchased by the Woolfs in 1929 so that they could do without resident servants in Monks House itself: the cook, Annie Thomsett, lived in one, whereas the other was for the gardener, Percy Bartholomew), and Thatched Cottage, the home of Colonel Gardner and his family, Labour Party supporters.

The house's remoteness from the hurly-burly of London made it an ideal retreat on alternate weekends, at Christmas and Easter and for long stretches in the summer. Renovations were later made to Monks House itself, but Leonard's energy was immediately consumed by reclaiming and adding to the garden: by 1930, he had four vegetable gardens, a fruit pen, two lonicera hedges, two ponds, beehives, two greenhouses, a lawn for bowls and archery, an area for pampas grass, a hazelnut copse and an orchard.

Such consolation took a while to assert itself. Virginia missed Asheham terribly and, taking a page from Dora Carrington and David Garnett's book, she and Leonard broke into Asheham on Saturday, 27 September. There, when they discovered their former drawing room turned into a pink boudoir, they came to the horrendous realization that Asheham was being made over to look like a glossy, respectable member of the *haute bourgeoisie*. Although their old home managed to remain as dim and mysterious as ever, Monks House was gradually improving, 'after the fashion of a mongrel who wins your heart'.[31]

Virginia had other worries. The strike by the National Union of Railwaymen, which lasted from 27 September until 6 October, meant for the Woolfs that the working class was not as docile as they had once feared: 'They have held the country up for eleven days,' Virginia joyfully observed. And she was proud of her own small role: 'We did a little to support them too, & kept one man on strike who would have gone back without our pound.'[32] Her concern about houses and strikes receded as 20 October approached. On the 21st, she was calm: 'Am I nervous? Oddly little; more excited & pleased than nervous.'[33]

Ford Madox Hueffer in the *Piccadilly Review* dubbed *Night and Day* a skilfully written, moral-less and 'very entertaining book which is all ado about nothing'.[34] In the *Times Literary Supplement* of 30 October, Harold Child voiced his objection to a small mistake in detail: roses could not be cut in December in a rectory garden in Lincoln. This was a tiny point in a notice of considerable enthusiasm:

> We hesitate to use the word wisdom because it suggests something pompous and dull; but *Night and Day* is a book full of wisdom. And having said that, let us hurry on to talk of its brilliance – a quality that is much less obvious than it was in *The Voyage Out*, but underlies the whole book and is here and there allowed to come to the surface.

He was also overwhelmed by the ingenuity displayed in the book's construction.

Virginia had to wait three long weeks for Katherine Mansfield's review in the *Athenaeum*. She began with some reflections on the fate of the novel: was it dying or just about to be born? In words which Virginia Woolf could easily have written, she announced: 'But in all this division and confusion it would seem that opinion is united in declaring this to be an age of experiment. If the novel dies it will be to give way to some new form of expression; if it lives it must accept the fact of a new world.' Having uttered those bold words, the reviewer declared *Night and Day* a relic:

> To us who love to linger down at the harbour, as it were, watching the new ships being builded, the old ones returning, and the many putting out to sea, comes the strange sight of *Night and Day* sailing into port serene and resolute on a deliberate wind. The strangeness lies in her aloofness, her air of quiet

perfection, her lack of any sign that she has made a perilous voyage – the absence of any scars. There she lies among the strange shipping – a tribute to civilization for our admiration and wonder.

Mansfield managed to compliment many aspects of *Night and Day* – she compared Virginia to Jane Austen – but then decided that, unlike Austen, there was too much conflict between life and writing in this particular narrative. According to her, 'Mrs Woolf' had made the dream world of Katharine and Ralph too much of a 'deep secret from her readers'. In Mansfield's final sentence, her negative feelings about *Night and Day* emerged crystal-clear: 'In the midst of our admiration it makes us feel old and chill: we had never thought to look upon its like again!'[35] Leonard, in an extremely acute way, pointed out that Mansfield's wish for Virginia to fail had had its way with her pen: 'He could see her looking about for a loophole of escape. "I'm not going to call this success – or if I must, I'll call it the wrong kind of success."'[36] In particular, Virginia did not appreciate being labelled a 'decorous elderly dullard'.

Mansfield's review was nasty, inspired in part by envy. She was well aware of why Virginia, despite inclinations to the contrary, had retreated back to the 'aloofness' and 'quiet perfection' of *Night and Day*. The reviewer's language is nautical, almost as if she is using the symbolic language of *The Voyage Out* to wound its author and to taunt her for her failure to capitalize on the advances made there. The review is not so much inaccurate as insensitive, as if the writer were pleased by her friend's failure to experiment with 'the fact of a new world'.*

* Virginia's despondency about this review would have been compounded by her realization that Mansfield had five months earlier (on 13 June 1919) penned an enthusiastic notice of *Kew Gardens*: '. . . Mrs Virginia Woolf's story belongs to another age . . . The tiny rich minute life of a snail – how she describes it! the angular high-stepping green insect – how passionate is her concern for him! Fascinated and credulous – we believe these things are all her concern until suddenly with a gesture she shows us the flower-bed, growing, expanding in the heat and light, filling a whole world.' *Kew*

In contrast to Katherine, Morgan Forster took great pains – even though he liked *Night and Day* – to explain to Virginia why he preferred *The Voyage Out*: he felt that the classical formality of *Night and Day* required characters who were more lovable, characters with whom the reader could more easily empathize. When Forster offered this criticism, he spoke freely of the considerable difficulties he was facing with the writing of *A Passage to India*. For Virginia, this was not criticism to discourage. 'Perhaps intelligent criticism never is,' she reflected.[37]

Many of *Night and Day*'s first readers shared Forster's doubts. * For Vanessa, the portrayal of the Hilbery household brought back painful memories of prison days at Hyde Park Gate. Virginia was surprised at this reaction, but she told her sister that she could never have survived, much less have become a writer, without her: 'Where should I have been if it hadn't been for you, when Hyde Park Gate was at its worst?'[38] Janet Case found Katharine cold – a charge which Virginia did not deny: 'It's the conflict that turns the half of her so chilly.' To the same friend, she uttered her own strong criticism of the book:

> then there's the whole question, which interested me, again too much for the book's sake, I daresay, of the things one doesn't say; what effect does that have? and how far do our feelings take their colour from the dive underground? I mean, what is the reality of any feeling? – and all this is further complicated by the form, which must sit tight.

As Virginia herself recognized, she may have paid too much attention to form at the expense of 'the things one doesn't say'[39]

Gardens heralded a glorious future, whereas, according to Mansfield, *Night and Day* belonged to the dismal past.

* Leonard may have been expressing a similar objection when he pointed out to his wife that the book was essentially pessimistic, despite the commitment which Katharine and Ralph make to each other at the book's conclusion.

but which must somehow, in the novel of experiment, find expression.

A bit earlier that November, Margaret Llewelyn Davies, in her abrasive but acute way, remarked that she and Janet preferred Virginia's April 1916 piece on Charlotte Brontë to any of her novels, which, in their combined opinion, were too lacking in emotion. Virginia became furious and flew at her, accusing both of her friends of excessively conventional views of what it was to be human. 'But it's *you* that are narrow,' Margaret retaliated. Virginia asked her if she thought Janet excessively moralistic. Margaret agreed to this, but then in a flash realized that the same was true of herself. She was staggered to suddenly see herself as a forceful, powerful woman who routinely excluded 'the greater half of the human heart'. Virginia was victorious, but Margaret 'took the blow well. It was as if one had suddenly drawn some curtain.'[40]

If she had not known it before, Virginia was now very aware of just how varied readers could be in their reactions to the same text. Sir George Savage called *Night and Day* one of the great novels of the world, whereas Kitty Maxse thought it a thoroughly bad book (her opinion was largely based on the fact that she could see no resemblance between Katharine Hilbery and her old friend Vanessa Stephen). Roger Fry told Virginia that he liked her new book, but she was so sure he was lying that she could 'trace veins of irrational prejudice in him'.[41]* In the end, as Virginia reminded Margaret the day after their spat, it was a question of how one saw the human heart: 'and cutting out the rotten parts according to one's convictions. That's what I want to do, and that's where we differ, and that's why you dislike Night and Day, and I shan't mind much if you do; but I should mind quite enormously if you didn't like me.'[42] In response to a confusing multiplicity of views,

* In a diary entry of 21 January 1920, Virginia analysed what she perceived to be the petulant, unyielding side of Roger Fry: 'R.'s work never meeting with the right sort of appreciation, he suffers perpetually from an obscure irritation. The main form it takes is irritation against England.'

Virginia woefully reflected, 'So all critics split off, & the wretched author who tries to keep control of them is torn asunder.'[43]

Virginia suffered further adverse criticism when H. W. Massingham in the *Nation* of 29 November ridiculed what he perceived as Virginia's obsession with tea-drinking and taxis in *Night and Day*; he labelled her main characters 'Four Impassioned Snails'. Virginia was resilient in the face of such snide treatment: he was 'annoyed and abusive in a way that makes me feel I've done some good'.[44] Leonard's constant, unreserved support buoyed her up. Otherwise, she believed, she would have felt like an abandoned youngster: 'I'm almost alarmed to see how entirely my weight rests on his prop. And almost alarmed to find how intensely I'm specialised. My mind turned by anxiety, or other cause, from its scrutiny of blank paper, is like a lost child – wandering the house, sitting on the bottom step to cry.'[45]

When the New York publisher George Doran bought the American rights to her two novels, Virginia was elated. However, that emotion was quickly deflated when, during a conversation with her sister, she felt how puny her accomplishments were next to Vanessa's. Her self-esteem was restored only when she 'crept home a good deal abashed, and only managed, under the shelter of Leonard, to fan a subdued glow'.[46] If, Virginia realized with considerable trepidation, she had married Lytton, he would have imposed many ties on her and complained bitterly if she had attempted to free herself.

That December, she had to run the gamut of conflicting emotions. She was on the verge of becoming a 'small Lioness',[47] a celebrity. Virginia, who always retained her fascination with the aristocracy, delighted in taking lunch with Lord Cranbourne, Prince Antoine Bibesco and his wife, Elizabeth Asquith, the only daughter of the former prime minister. She enjoyed the dilemma of whether or not to wear pearls for the portrait photograph requested by George Doran. At the very same time, there was a downside to her emotions. When she went into London in early December, she became terribly frightened by the sight of a pregnant, drunken char. That woman became a symbol of what was wrong with London and with life in general, especially its sexual side: 'that's my feeling, something lewd about it, as well as indecent and detestable'.[48] For most of that month, Leonard was ill with malaria. Just as he was recovering, Virginia came down with influenza, 'prolonged, & sponging on the head as it always does'. Despite the setbacks they had both endured, Virginia's mood was upbeat: 'We think we deserve some good luck. Yet I daresay we're the happiest couple in England.'[49]

Virginia's alliance with Leonard bestowed upon her a comfortable mix of independence and dependence. In part, their unconventional, experimental marriage gave her the impetus to find a corresponding freedom in the art of writing. Her birthday, 25 January, was sometimes an unhappy day for Virginia, but on the following day she saw, in a visionary moment, all sorts of possible new turnings:

> I'm 38. Well, I've no doubt I'm a great deal happier than I was at 28; & happier today than I was yesterday having this afternoon arrived at some idea of a new form for a new novel. Suppose one thing should open out of another – . . . doesn't that give the looseness & lightness I want: doesn't that get closer & yet keep form & speed, & enclose everything, everything? My doubt is how far it will enclose the human heart.[50]

For a long time, Virginia had confined the experimental side of her writing to her short stories: what if she simply extended the size of her canvas from ten pages to 200 or so? Without being fully aware of it, she was also beginning to consider the loosely knit form of her own diary as a possible organizing principle of a long piece of fiction.

The loss of Asheham had reminded the Woolfs of their precarious status at Richmond. In an attempt to provide themselves with a more secure footing there, in January 1920 they purchased both Hogarth and Suffield Houses from Ida Lavinia Brewer for £1,950

(Suffield House continued to be let).* However, Monks House was Virginia and Leonard's real home, where they gardened, walked and attended auctions.

Despite the mixed reviews – written and spoken – which had greeted her second novel, Virginia was now someone to know. She wanted fame, but it had to be of the right kind. She remained aware that it was particularly difficult for a woman to make her mark.† She did not wish Leonard and herself to become a professional London couple in the mould of the loathsome Webbs, but they embarked on an arduous social round. For example, at a party at Ottoline's Bedford Square home on 13 February 1920 they mixed with the Eliots, Aldous Huxley, Morgan Forster and the critic J. C. Squire; there was a lunch the next day at the Webbs, and they entertained Adrian, C. P. Sanger, the Chancery Barrister and former Apostle, and Doris Hussey, the writer, that evening. Quite soon, this busy social life proved unnerving for Virginia: she grew weary of going out to tea, but she found it

* In 1921, the Woolfs sold Suffield House to C. G. Turner, a local solicitor. Three years later, when they moved to Tavistock Square, they leased Hogarth House to Saxon Sydney-Turner for three years. In 1927, Hogarth House was sold to Mrs F. E. Hazle.

† Virginia's pervasive sense that women writers were overlooked and thus denigrated can be seen in her response to the death of Mary Augusta Ward, better known as Mrs Humphry Ward, who died on 24 March 1920 in her seventieth year. Like Virginia, Mrs Ward had a distinguished pedigree: she was the granddaughter of Thomas Arnold of Rugby and the niece of Matthew Arnold. Although she opposed women's suffrage, she supported the movement for higher education for women. Her novels often deal with the struggle between religious belief and the values of intellectual and spiritual freedom.

On 10 April, Virginia wrote in her diary: 'Mrs Ward is dead . . . & it appears that she was merely a woman of straw after all – shovelled into the grave & already forgotten. The most perfunctory earth strewing even by the orthodox.' In fact, *The Times* gave her a two-column obituary, her coffin was preceded by a detachment of the Hertfordshire constabulary and the Dean of St Paul's proclaimed her as 'perhaps the greatest Englishwoman of our time'.

difficult to turn down invitations. There was another uncomfortable aspect to more formal events: 'dressing for gentlemen' – as for George Duckworth – 'induces some disease of the complexion when examined by pure feminine light'.[51]

There were more mundane worries that winter: who was spreading head lice – Leonard or Lottie? Virginia preferred to catch it from Leonard. Virginia's excursions in society led her to the rather strong conviction that some of the 'nice' people she encountered there were more gentle than her close friends in Bloomsbury. However, her group, she was certain, possessed passion.

On 4 March, Virginia was relieved to be attending a new gathering of those close friends, the first meeting of the Memoir Club, an offshoot of a previous group, the Novel Club. Both groups were devised by Molly MacCarthy in an attempt to provide a forum in which Desmond might write something other than journalism. The members dined together once a month; afterwards, they gathered in someone's home in order to read chapters from what were expected to become full-length autobiographies. That first evening was a very mixed bag: Sydney Waterlow explicated a dream, Clive was purely objective, Vanessa was overcome with emotion after a matter-of-fact opening, Duncan was 'tongue enchanted', and Roger was too detached. In sum, the gossipy side of Virginia was a bit disappointed: 'I doubt that anyone will *say* the interesting things but they can't prevent their coming out.'[52]

Virginia had reached a level of serene self-confidence, one which allowed her to re-read *The Voyage Out*, which she now saw as a sort of patchwork harlequinade that made her cheeks burn. Despite such feelings, she could, as a slightly older woman, look back with considerable affection at her younger self: 'On the whole I like the young woman's mind considerably. How gallantly she takes her fences – & my word, what a gift for pen & ink!'[53] Yet Virginia realized fully how precarious the place of the woman writer really was. She was afraid that her writing was too refined, too precious and too cordial; yet at the same time she knew that women were expected to write in this manner – would, in fact, be severely criticized if they abandoned such niceties.

Buoyed up by self-assurance, Virginia determined on 10 April to begin work the next week on her third novel, *Jacob's Room*, the one which would encapsulate 'new form'. However, she winced when she read a review of Katherine Mansfield in the *Athenaeum* in which she was favourably compared to Chekhov and Dostoevsky. Virginia quickly discounted the piece. Ten days later, just as she had made a start on that book, Virginia saw in *The Times* the announcement of the birth of Ka's son. For the remainder of that day she was bothered by twinges of jealousy. By 11 May Virginia was also experiencing considerable difficulty in writing *Jacob's Room*: the honeymoon period was over and the 'creative power which bubbles so pleasantly on beginning a new book quiets down after a time'.[54] Writing, she reminded herself, was always difficult.

Nine days later, Virginia was working well on *Jacob*, 'the most amusing novel writing I've done; . . . in the doing I mean'.[55] That 'doing' was going well enough for Virginia, after much trepidation, to pen an admiring postcard to Katherine Mansfield, who had returned from the Mediterranean in early May. Almost a week later, Katherine wrote a curt reply, thanking Virginia for her kind words about 'The Man Without a Temperament'. She would be delighted to see her but warned that she had grown '*very* dull'. Virginia was not sure what Katherine really meant: '*she* hurt with *me*?'[56] It was a good question. After all, it was Katherine who had inflicted pain upon her in the *Athenaeum* review of *Night and Day*. In any event, Virginia visited the invalid on Friday, 28 May.

When she arrived, Katherine was starchy. She certainly took no pleasure in seeing Virginia. Their conversation maintained itself in a perfunctory vein until they touched on the theme of solitude, whereupon Virginia heard Katherine 'expressing my feelings, as I never heard them expressed'. Then the two women began talking in earnest, as if the past eight months in which they had not seen each other were only minutes, before Middleton Murry interrupted them. At that point, Aldous Huxley's *Leda and Other Poems* became the object of their combined displeasure.

After her husband left, Katherine spoke of having made a new turning in 'The Man Without a Temperament'. Virginia noticed how thoroughly self-absorbed and hard her friend became. Virginia pretended that she did not know how to write. This surprised Katherine: 'What else is there to do? We have got to do it? Life –' Then she asked Virginia to write short fiction for the *Athenaeum*. All too aware of the painful review to which she had been subjected in that journal, Virginia replied: 'But I don't know that I can write stories.' Katherine turned on her, reminding her of how much she had accomplished in 'Kew Gardens'.

'Well but *Night and Day*?' Virginia rejoined, although she had not meant to touch on that tricky subject.

'An amazing achievement. Why, we've not had such a thing since I don't know when –'

'But I thought you didn't like it?'[57]

Rather than answering the question, Katherine observed that she could pass an examination on that book. Deftly, she switched topics by asking Virginia to lunch with her on 2 June. At that meeting, Katherine assured her that *Night and Day* was a first-rate novel, although she felt it suppressed a great deal. Puzzled, Virginia observed: 'You've changed. Got through something.'[58] At that moment, Virginia was sure that Katherine had so completely taken command of herself that she no longer needed to resort to subterfuges.

With Katherine, Virginia once again experienced a common understanding, 'a queer sense of being "like" – not only about literature – & I think it's independent of gratified vanity. I can talk straight out to her'.[59] Virginia was able to have such feelings, even though Katherine had less than a year before subjected her to a double humiliation: she had publicly shamed her and, what was more important, she had betrayed their friendship.

Katherine was definitely, although obliquely, telling her that her new novel had to go in the direction of stories such as 'Kew Gardens' and 'The Mark on the Wall'. In a flash, Virginia realized that Katherine – even though she might have been jealous of her – had, in the *Athenaeum* review, given vent to another side of her feelings – a sense of profound dismay that Virginia had betrayed herself and their friendship in *Night and Day* by not moving away from the established confines of fiction!

As she continued to work on *Jacob's Room*, Virginia became understandably more and more in touch with just how much her own generation had been scourged by the war. In *Night and Day*, Katharine Hilbery had been based, in part, on Vanessa; in her new novel Virginia's memories of her dead brother were used to construct the personality of Jacob Flanders. However, Jacob dies at war and Virginia's conflation of an event from 1906 (Thoby's death) with the Great War is an attempt to link her own personal sense of loss to the pervasive feeling of loss and disintegration which impinged on everyone in England in the early 1920s.

Even seemingly peripheral events touched Virginia deeply when she was writing *Jacob*. When Vanessa returned to London from Italy on 14 May, she learned that her housemaid, Mary, had been confined to an infirmary, having been driven mad by the sudden deaths, all within a fortnight, of her mother, father and lover. The dire news of these tragedies had been conveyed in a series of phone calls from a district nurse in Bedfordshire to Blanche, Vanessa's cook. Mary recovered and returned to work on 18 May. Then the district nurse wrote asking that Mary be sent to her to recuperate. Vanessa agreed to this, and Blanche and Mary set out by train. Before they reached their destination, Mary vanished.

In order to get to the bottom of these mysterious events, an obviously agitated Vanessa set out for Bedfordshire. There, she discovered that Mary had fabricated everything: she had made the phone calls and forged the letter from the district nurse. Subsequently, Mary began wandering aimlessly in Bloomsbury, was decoyed back to Vanessa's, captured, certified and carried away in a van. Virginia saw Mary as a storyteller whose imagination had got the better of her: her motive had arisen from a wish 'to act a day dream, & then, poor creature, stepping too far & believing it'.[60] Creativity can touch the deepest parts of the self and, as such, can be dangerous. Virginia also saw Mary as a victim of a cruel society. The incident must also have reminded her of her own previous bouts of mental illness, when she had been dependent on her sister.

On her way home after hearing Mary's story, Virginia saw an old beggar woman sitting against a stone wall in Kingsway, clasping a brown mongrel. The woman sang in a shrill voice, but for her own amusement. Her defiant bravery – and artistry – deeply moved Virginia: like her, the woman created from an inward sense of purpose.* At the very same time that Virginia was touched by the woman and the vitality of London, she thought of the dead who had once walked its streets.

A third incident intruded itself. At a dance given at 50 Gordon Square by Alys Russell, Bertrand's estranged wife, on 26 June, some people had been sitting on the roof. A young man named Wright stepped near the edge, perhaps to light a cigarette, and fell 30 feet on to the flagstones. Adrian, who was the only person to witness the incident, summoned a doctor. However, there was no hope for the young man, who died in the ambulance that came to fetch him. Virginia was warily fascinated: 'A strange event – to come to a dance among strangers & die – to come dressed in evening clothes, & then for it all to be over, instantly, so senselessly.'[61] She might have been recalling Thoby's sudden, senseless death, but in any event the callousness of the other partygoers – who, once their dance was disrupted, telephoned to find news of other festivities in progress that night – deeply disturbed her, making

* This incident found its way into Part V of *Jacob's Room*: 'Long past sunset an old blind woman sat on a camp-stool with her back to the stone wall of the Union of London and Smith's Bank, clasping a brown mongrel tight in her arms and singing out loud, not for coppers, no, from the depths of her gay wild heart – her sinful, tanned heart – for the child who fetches her is the fruit of sin, and should have been in bed, curtained, asleep, instead of hearing in the lamplight her mother's wild song . . .' (56).

her poignantly aware of how her generation no longer wanted to feel deeply, if at all.*

If her generation had been anaesthetized, this was largely due to the masculine point of view, which she saw as pervasive and deadly. Even Roger Fry and G. E. Moore did not escape her wrath. According to Virginia, Fry's June 1920 exhibition filled three rooms 'garishly, as with coloured sheets of tin'.[62] She also continued to wonder why Moore had been so important to many young men at Cambridge. These were private reflections, but she was quite willing to do battle publicly. In August 1920, she relished taking up her vendetta against H. W. Massingham, who had made a cutting remark about *Night and Day* in the *Nation.*

In the 10 July issue, writing as 'Wayfarer', Massingham had ascribed the recent defeat in Parliament of the Plumage Bill to the vanity of women. This controversial bill sought to restrict the importation into England of exotic birds and feathers. Like Massingham, Virginia supported this piece of legislation (which was ultimately passed in July 1921), but she rightly resented his claim that women were responsible for the difficult time the bill had received in Parliament. What about male greed? After all, they were the ones who killed, starved and tortured the birds. Also, she implied, was not the custom of women adorning themselves with such feathers more attributable to male desire than to female choice? Virginia ended with an arrow launched directly against Massingham: 'But the interesting point is that in my ardour to confute "Wayfarer", a journalist of admitted humanity, I have said more about his injustice to women than about the sufferings of birds. Can it be that it is a graver sin to be unjust to women than to torture birds?'[63]

Virginia's next skirmish was with her close friend Desmond

* The circumstances of Wright's death – although he did not commit suicide – and the fact that he was a stranger at the party may have been in Virginia's mind when she wrote in *Mrs Dalloway* of Septimus Smith's suicide by throwing himself from a window, the news of which reaches Clarissa during her party.

MacCarthy. In September 1920 Arnold Bennett published *Our Women*, a collection of essays which asserted that men were intellectually superior to women. Virginia was outraged and considered writing a counterblast. In the *New Statesman*, Desmond, in his guise of 'Affable Hawk', reviewed Bennett, agreeing in the main with his denigrating comments on women. This was too much for Virginia, who wrote a letter to the *New Statesman* which was published on 9 October under the heading 'The Intellectual Status of Women':

> I cannot swallow the teaspoonful administered in your columns last week by Affable Hawk. The fact that women are inferior to men in intellectual power, he says, 'stares him in the face' . . . How, then, does Affable Hawk account for the fact which stares me, and I should have thought any impartial observer, in the face, that the seventeenth century produced more remarkable women than the sixteenth, the eighteenth than the seventeenth, and the nineteenth than all three put together? . . . the advance in intellectual power seems to me not only sensible but immense; the comparison with men not in the least one that inclines me to suicide.

Having established a strong female pedigree, Virginia turns her contempt on the so-called advances made by men: 'Thus, though women have every reason to hope that the intellect of the male sex is steadily diminishing, it would be unwise, until they have more evidence than the great war and the great peace supply, to announce it as a fact.' In his rejoinder, Desmond remained unconvinced: women did not show any real aptitude in pursuits requiring pure intellect; the conditions of men had never been remarkably superior to those of women; the highest achievements in literature belonged to men. In a strong reply, Virginia denied these claims and added:

> But it is not education only that [women need]. It is that women should have liberty of experience; that they should differ from men without fear and express their differences

openly (for I do not agree with Affable Hawk that men and women are alike); that all activity of the mind should be so encouraged that there will always be in existence a nucleus of women who think, invent, imagine, and create as freely as men do, and with as little fear of ridicule and condescension.

This is a vivid, sharp declaration of independence, defining in precise terms the struggle to which Virginia would continue to dedicate herself. In the face of these strong words, 'Affable Hawk' withdrew but with a slight sneer: 'If the freedom and education of women is impeded by the expression of my views, I shall argue no more.'

Virginia did not fear public battle against male dominion, but she could not help being stifled by it. When Tom Eliot visited the Woolfs at Rodmell in September, Virginia noticed that his eyes, in contrast to his dour upper lip, were lively and youthful. He even managed a joke or two, but Eliot, who talked about the verse dramas he was about to embark on, ignored Virginia's claim to be taken seriously as a fellow writer. She probably agreed with his own assessment of his conduct at Garsington: 'I behaved like a priggish pompous little ass.'[64] She certainly observed a great deal of concealed vanity and self-doubt in Eliot's mask-like countenance, but immediately after his visit she could not work on *Jacob*. Perhaps, she reflected, what she was trying to do as a writer was being better done by James Joyce, the fiction writer so much admired by Eliot. Briefly, the Woolfs again considered the possibility of publishing *Ulysses*.

Another measure of the enormous discomfort Virginia felt in the presence of men can be seen in her reaction to powerfully built, virile, heterosexual Ralph Partridge, who from August 1918 was emotionally involved with Lytton and Carrington, whom he eventually married. By August 1920 the demands of running the Hogarth Press were proving too much for Leonard and Virginia to handle on their own. They needed help in managing their accounts, setting type and selling their wares. That month, the Woolfs invited Partridge to join the Press at a salary of £100 a year plus 50 per cent of the profits; he took up his post on 6 October.

Ralph was well aware of his beautiful physique, which had attracted Strachey's attention. However, he was in love with Carrington, who showed little interest in any aspect of her would-be lover. As far as she was concerned, he was at Lytton's home, the Mill House in Tidmarsh, Berkshire, only because of Lytton's unrequited passion for him. In order to break the bonds of this unsatisfying *ménage à trois*, Ralph would sometimes appear before Carrington stark-naked and strike provocative poses. In conversation with the Woolfs, Ralph could be similarly exhibitionistic, as when he described a visit to a brothel where girls paraded before him so that he could make a choice. In her diary, Virginia expressed her dismay: 'that was what pleased him – the sense of power.'[65] In politics, literature and sex, men sought to dominate, and such reflections made her poignantly aware, once again, of her Duckworth half-brothers.

That November, Virginia was fascinated to hear that Gerald Duckworth was to marry a Miss Chad. She asked Violet: 'why is Gerald marrying her, and is she an heiress, and elderly; or the daughter of a stockbroker, and virginal?'[66] Was Gerald marrying an older woman in order to obtain money or was he marrying a younger, sexually inexperienced woman for the same purpose? Virginia's contempt for Duckworth motives is clearly evident. Gerald's engagement and Virginia's contemporaneous dealings with male arrogance may have provided the spur for her presentation to the Memoir Club on 17 November 1920: this was '22 Hyde Park Gate', the piece in which she first publicly exposed George's deeds.* Virginia triumphantly recalled: 'The Memoir Club was fearfully brilliant – I mean I was.'[67]

London frays could be momentarily ignored in Sussex. There in particular, Leonard embodied for Virginia a very different kind of

* Neither of the Duckworths would have been privy to information revealed at Memoir Club meetings.

man from the Duckworths, Bennetts and Partridges. Sometimes, in flashes, Virginia felt envious of Leonard, particularly of his rigorous analytical mind. At other times, she was certain that she was forcing him to sacrifice his career in favour of hers. She felt especially guilty when she thought of throwing over review work in favour of fiction-writing. However, the tranquillity of Monks House allowed both of them to renew themselves, giving them a strong sense of community in their marriage and neighbourhood, where everyone did the same things at the same times.

On occasion, Virginia's fears followed her to Monks House, as when Nelly Cecil announced her intention of staying with them. All of a sudden Virginia viewed her home with what she considered to be Nelly's penetrating and haughty aristocratic eye. As she soon rediscovered, the almost totally deaf Nelly did not really like women of her own elevated station. Indeed, she hankered after the company of literary people. Nelly's face, Virginia now saw, showed the enormous solitude her noble station had given her: 'Her body incredibly little & shrunk; eyes slightly fading; cheeks sunk in'.[68]

Aristocrats in Sussex were comparatively easy to deal with. Back in London, Virginia continued to be obsessed with – and loathe – Mary Hutchinson. The dislike seemed mutual. In an unguarded moment in a letter to Roger Fry of 1 August 1920, Virginia gave voice to the other side of her emotions for this glamorous, silent woman. These feelings were unleashed at a party, the sort of event which sometimes had the effect of making Virginia do what she would not have contemplated in more ordinary circumstances. On this evening, Virginia caught 'Mary Hutch by the neck, and embrace[d] her passionately'.[69] To her diary, she put it this way: 'my chief pirouetting was with Mary whose hand I took, held, & kissed, on the sofa with Clive on the other side of me. She said she hated & feared me. I wooed her like a wayward child. Does one speak the truth on these occasions, reach it on tiptoe from where it hangs inaccessible in less exalted moments?'[70] Her answer was yes. One side of Virginia claimed to hate aristocratic women, but she was intrigued by them. By the same token, she was fascinated with the splendid beauty of Mary, who possessed a magnificent physical sense of self, one which bypassed intellect and art.

Virginia's conflicting feelings about other women remained centred on Katherine Mansfield. In December 1920, she was glad to hear someone abuse her friend's work. She asked herself: 'Now why? Partly some obscure feeling that she advertises herself; or Murry does it for her; & then how bad the Athenaeum stories are; yet in my heart I must think her good, since I'm glad to hear her abused.'[71] That was a truthful answer to a perplexing question. Earlier, on 26 July and 2 and 23 August, Virginia had made a series of goodbye calls on Katherine, who was leaving for the Continent. At the first farewell, Katherine asked Virginia to review her new book. She refused, on the grounds that reading a book for review spoiled the pleasure. Katherine was quick to take her point. After Katherine had finally left, Virginia felt a listless depression, leading her to further queries about what Katherine meant to her: 'Do I feel this as much as I ought? Am I heartless? Will she mind my going either?' Despite mixed feelings, Virginia realized that she and Katherine were shadow selves. They were the 'only women . . . with gift enough to make talk of writing interesting'.[72]

This numb desolation was augmented on 11 November, when Virginia and Molly MacCarthy attended the ceremony at which the King unveiled the Cenotaph at Whitehall, after which followed the interment of the Unknown Warrior at Westminster Abbey. For her, this was like a scene from Dante's *Inferno*. The crowd resembled an army of sleepwalkers, their faces bright and lurid in the cold and windless air. Women cried out, 'Remember the Glorious Dead' and held out chrysanthemums. In moments such as this, Virginia assailed herself for not being a success even to herself. She had no children, frequently lived away from close friends, failed to write well, spent too much on food and grew old. Work was her only refuge from despair – and it provided only momentary respite.

Hers, she was also certain, was a doomed generation, in which every newspaper placard shrieked forth some new affliction. In part, Virginia's acute sense of agony was derived from her exploration in *Jacob's Room* of the roots of societal despair. Why, she asked, was life tragic, so like a little insignificant 'strip of pavement over an abyss', into which, when she looked down into it, she felt giddy? Her answer was clear and precise: 'It's a feeling of impotence: of cutting no ice.'[73] Such awful sensations invaded her, but she now had considerable strength in vanquishing them. In her diary entry of 19 December, as the year came to an end, she looked, with considerable gratitude, at a host of blessings:

> I ought to say how happy I am, since one of these pages said how unhappy I was. I can't see any reason in it. My only guess is that it has something to do with working steadily; writing things out of my head; & never having a compartment empty . . . I can't help suspecting that both Mr & Mrs Woolf slowly increase in fame . . . My book seems to me rather good.[74]

Chapter Eleven

A PROCESSION OF SHADOWS

(1921–3)

'I'm not in the least jealous of Katherine, though every review praises her,'[1] Virginia a bit too peremptorily assured her sister on 7 January 1921. If Virginia's acquisition of fame was slow but steady, her rival's new book, *Bliss*, was an immediate success. With considerable malice, Virginia hoped that Romer Wilson's novel *The Death of Society* would beat Mansfield for the Hawthornden Prize. If, as Virginia rightly predicted, that honour was stolen from her friend's grasp, she would have cause for celebration.

A measure of the other side of Virginia's feelings can be discerned in her reaction to the 'Bibesco Scandal' – Middleton Murry's philandering with Princess Elizabeth Bibesco while his wife was sick and lonely at Menton. A very guilty Murry told Virginia on 11 February that, despite good reviews, Katherine was tortured with self-doubt. He pleaded with Virginia to write her, which she did two days later:

> I'm wondering what you think about your book, and what people have said about it. The reviews are enthusiastic, but then the reviews are stupid. Shall I write you a criticism of it one of these days? I sometimes think that though we're so different we have some of the same difficulties. I'm in the middle of my novel now . . . I don't know that it's readable though. What I admire in you so much is your transparent quality. My stuff gets muddy; and then in a novel one must have continuity, but in this one I'm always chopping and changing from one level to another. I think what I'm at is to change the consciousness, and so to break up the awful stodge. Does this convey anything to

> you? And you seem to me to go so straight and directly, – all clear as glass – refined, spiritual.[2]

Just over a year later, on 20 March 1922, Virginia, who had previously undergone severe criticism at the hands of Janet Case, offered her Greek teacher another point of view: 'I read Bliss; and it was so brilliant, – so hard, and so shallow, and so sentimental that I had to rush to the bookcase for something to drink . . . But she takes in all the reviewers.'[3] Where, in the midst of apparent contradiction, can the truth be found?

Somewhere in the middle – side by side – can be discovered Virginia's deep admiration for and deep hatred of Mansfield: she was jealous of her 'transparent quality', an effect which evaded Virginia in her own work. At times, she could respond to a writer who seemed to achieve easily what she was approaching only with the utmost difficulty. At other times, Katherine's talent was reduced, in Virginia's mind, to a rubble heap of cheap tricks. If Mansfield the writer troubled Virginia, she loved Mansfield the woman. Her letter of February 1921 concludes with a plea: 'Please Katherine, let us try to write to each other.'[4]

In Virginia Woolf, love and hatred for the same person were often closely linked. Sydney Waterlow, her old suitor, was a frequent butt of Virginia's wit. She made many cutting observations about his sex life, slovenliness, poor taste in literature and complacency. In August 1922, when he was staying at Monks House, she peered at him while he was bathing, very much against his expressed wish: 'My God! What a sight he looked bathing! like Neptune, if Neptune was a Eunuch! – without any hairs, and sky pink – fresh, virginal, soft – I sat on the bank and peered through the rushes.'[5] This mischievous sally, in which a man whom Virginia felt was too sexually active is castrated, has to be juxtaposed with some candid observations of 19 January 1921 in which she countered complaints against her made by Sydney:

> You say people drop you, and don't want to see you. I don't agree. Of course I understand that when one feels, as you feel,

> without a core – it used to be a very familiar feeling to me – then all one's external relations become febrile and unreal . . . If I treat you as a joke (and my manners are far too haphazard) that's only a method. Of course, one of the things about you that I like, admire, and find interesting is this sensibility – this introspection – this sense of the importance of things.[6]

This letter contains a great deal of empathy, but Virginia does not take back any of her negative opinions about Sydney. She merely observes that those emotions coexist with many positive sentiments. Mixed feelings, she implies, cannot be reconciled: the really important question to be resolved is which side of things predominates in a relationship.

Another person about whom Virginia had complicated feelings was Lytton Strachey. She was delighted when he asked permission to dedicate *Queen Victoria* to her, but she stipulated that her name appear in full: the book was for Virginia Woolf, not Virginia. Curious as to why the book was not inscribed to Carrington, she confronted him with this seemingly difficult question. He shrugged: 'Oh dear no – we're not on those terms at all.'[7] In other words, his relationship with Carrington was domestic, whereas Virginia was a fellow writer whom he took seriously.

That winter, in the midst of anticipating the reaction to her collection of short stories *Monday or Tuesday*, which was published on 7 April, and completing *Jacob's Room*, Virginia participated in the negotiations for the sale of Suffield House to C. G. Turner, a local solicitor, and accompanied Leonard, a Labour candidate for the Combined English Universities,* on a speaking engagement to Manchester. There were many emotional claims. When twenty-year-old Richard Hughes's longish short story 'Martha' was under consideration at the Press, Virginia found the young man, who had a stammer, irresistible. On the very same day, she kissed Ralph Partridge on the neck. As she pointed out to Vanessa, such

* This constituency consisted of the seven universities other than Oxford and Cambridge.

'elderly passions'[8] could be dangerous. (The Woolfs turned down Hughes's story.) Four months later, Virginia found the muscular thighs of a young aristocrat enticing: '. . . if I had passions anymore, I should have seized [him] by the neck.'[9]

At the very same time, Virginia began to see Tom Eliot in a new light on the March evening they failed to catch a train. Even worse than the sensation of loss experienced when one missed a train was, he told her, the feeling of humiliation. Rather than taking him up directly on that observation, Virginia demanded: 'Are you as full of vices as I am?'

'Full. Riddled with them,' he assured her.

Again, seeming to change subjects, she observed: 'We're not as good as Keats.'

If this claim was intended to rattle Eliot, it worked perfectly. He swiftly countered her: 'Yes we are . . . We're trying something harder.' However, he gave in slightly: 'Anyhow our work is streaked with badness.'

Virginia was unbudging, but turned the arrow of guilt against herself: 'Compared with theirs [the great nineteenth-century writers], mine is futile. Negligible. One goes on because of an illusion.'

Eliot assured her that she didn't really mean what she was saying. Virginia had been sincere, but in that moment knew that she 'could probably become very intimate with Eliot because of our damned self conscious susceptibility'.[10] But, she was certain, she was more of a risk-taker than he was. In any event, she realized that he had a fine laugh, and a shared sense of humour became another building block in their increasingly complicated relationship.

Virginia also had to reassess her fraught dealings with Mary Hutchinson, who, in January 1921, was no longer Clive's mistress (that position had been taken by the fiercely beautiful but, according to Virginia, incredibly stupid Juana Gandarillas). As soon as Mary had 'fallen off her perch',[11] Virginia could see her old enemy as a worthy opponent, not merely as a disreputable rival for the favours of an old beau.

One woman Virginia found it impossible to look at in a new

way was Violet Dickinson. Their friendship had been renewed in 1919, at which time Virginia sent her a copy of *Night and Day* as a token of affection and gratitude. Despite the claims of the past, Violet irritated Virginia, as she candidly told her diary: 'Then Violet Dickinson came to tea here – grown half a foot taller, but otherwise unchanged; wrists a little coarse & even dirty; pearls & emeralds round her neck; asking questions, never listening, rapid, intuitive, humorous in her slap dash way . . . One of the lay sisters who go about doing good, & talking gossip.'[12] Virginia did not wish to be tied to the past, especially one which reminded her of angels of the house.

An aspect of her past Virginia treasured was her memory of the luxuriant, turbulent beauty of Cornwall, about which she remained incurably romantic. While on holiday there from 23 to 30 March, the Woolfs stayed at Zennor, near Ka and Will Arnold-Forster. They had June weather and walked among mounds of bright yellow, nutty-smelling gorse, basking on cliffs below which the sea turned various shades of green and grey. Seals bobbed up out of the water, looking first like logs and then like 'naked old men, with tridents for tails'.[13] During this visit, to her own surprise the half-transparent granite colour of the landscape impressed itself upon Virginia more than the sea did.

A week after her return from Cornwall, Virginia had to worry about the reviews of *Monday or Tuesday*. In many ways, she should not have been totally surprised by the polite disdain which greeted the book. The eight stories in the collection ('The Mark on the Wall', 'Kew Gardens', 'An Unwritten Novel', 'A Haunted House', 'A Society', 'Monday or Tuesday', 'The String Quartet' and 'Blue & Green') are bold experiments in the use of form. Even the *Times Literary Supplement*'s exceedingly sympathetic Harold Child could not judge the collection a success.

> The piece which gives its title to the new volume, *Monday or Tuesday*, is an example of the 'unrepresentational' art which is creeping across from painting to see what it can make of words.

> It sounds beautiful; it suggests beautiful, or at least life-full things – the heron flying, the busy street, the fire-lit room, and others. The trouble with it is that even this sort of art cannot empty itself altogether of intellectual content. One sentence seems to 'mean' – that is, to represent – something; the intrusion of this representation makes the next sentence, or the other portions of the same sentence, 'mean' nothing. We complain of *Monday or Tuesday*, not that it means too little that is intelligible to the plain mind, but that it cannot help meaning too much for its purpose. Prose may 'aspire to the condition of music': it cannot reach it.[14]

According to Child, since this collection of short stories aspired to a condition never intended for prose, it was a failure from the outset.

The narratives vary widely in style and content. The traditional form of 'A Society', which incorporates in part the events of the '*Dreadnought* Hoax' concerns a group of young women who investigate what centuries of male domination have produced. In the end, the women learn that men cannot be trusted, that male aggressiveness is at the heart of the world's problems and that until men bear children and thus learn something about true veneration for life, this state of affairs will continue.

The lyrical 'Kew Gardens' (published on its own two years earlier) is the finest and perhaps the boldest of the stories. It concerns a flowerbed, its resident snail and four couples who move past it. In one sense – that of traditional story-telling, with its dependence on causality – nothing happens. In another – that of life as a shimmering 'semi-transparent envelope' – everything happens.

> Thus one couple after another with much the same irregular and aimless movement passed the flower-bed and were enveloped in layer after layer of green-blue vapour, in which at first their bodies had substance and a dash of colour, but later both substance and colour dissolved in the green-blue atmosphere.

Vanessa Bell. Cover design for Monday or Tuesday *(1921)*

> How hot it was! So hot that even the thrush chose to hop, like a mechanical bird, in the shadow of the flowers, with long pauses between one movement and the next; instead of rambling vaguely the white butterflies danced once above another, making with their white shifting flakes the outline of a shattered marble column above the tallest flowers.[15]

In this passage, a thrush becomes – in a Yeatsian moment – a mechanical bird and the butterflies take on the form of a marble column: the worlds of art and nature are interchangeable and mutually enhancing. In its bold originality, *Monday or Tuesday* bears comparison with another collection of stories, Joyce's *Dubliners* (1914). Virginia publicly disdained Joyce, but her agenda in these short narratives is similar to the Irishman's: both search for the epiphanic moment, that miraculous instant in which truth is conveyed intuitively and mystically.

Monday or Tuesday was so revolutionary that Virginia was perhaps wrong to be stung by the fact that not many readers were interested in what she was doing. After all, innovators often have to pay a bitter price for their efforts. Virginia was aware of this, but she was also deeply hurt: 'What depresses me is the thought that I have ceased to interest people – at the very moment when, by the help of the press, I thought I was becoming more myself.'[16] Her vanity was further wounded by the fact that her book received a comparatively short notice in the *Times Literary Supplement*, whereas Lytton was given almost three columns of unqualified adulation in the same journal. Her suspicion that Lytton had taken a far easier path to literary fame was underscored by the fact that *Queen Victoria* sold 5,000 copies in its first week of publication, whereas *Monday or Tuesday* sold only 300. Insult was added to injury when, at a party held to celebrate the appearance of *Queen Victoria*, Lytton did not refer to the existence of her new book. A few days later, she assured him his biography was magnificent; nevertheless, she was too conscious while reading it of being entertained. Virginia, sure that her own book was nothing more than a 'damp firework',[17] found it impossible to work on *Jacob's Room*, the eleventh chapter of which had been completed the previous month.

Gradually, good news trickled in. 'Affable Hawk', with whom she had fought the previous year, was generous in his review in both understanding and praise. However, remembering their quarrel, he did not like the feminist bias he could discern in 'A Society'. When she 'writes from contempt, her work is not her best'.[18] Lytton thought 'The String Quartet' strong and Roger Fry, who understood the difficulties Virginia was encountering in attempting to introduce pictorial techniques into language, assured her that she was on the track of important discoveries. Leonard's support was constant, but Virginia was upset when the *Daily Mail* hailed as a masterpiece one of the stories ('Pearls and Swine') in her husband's new book, *Stories of the East*. Wistfully, she told Vanessa: 'My feelings as an artist were ravaged.'[19]

That May, Virginia soldiered on with *Jacob's Room*. She also tried to help Desmond MacCarthy to come into his own as a writer. For years his friends had been of the opinion that his true brilliance was reflected in his witty and incisive conversation. If those reflections could be captured on paper, perhaps there would be a new turning in his career. In May, Virginia gave a dinner party for Roger and the MacCarthys. Minna Green, Leonard's secretary, surreptitiously recorded Desmond's words, but when she transcribed her efforts, she informed Leonard and Virginia that it was a dull read. Desmond's effervescence could not be reduced to plain words – the magic had vanished.

When she took tea with Lady Cromer, Virginia was put in touch with her old, tortured feelings about the aristocracy and their splendid possessions, such as beautiful chintzes, large rooms, family portraits by Watts and Sargent, parquet floors, green-stained wood. In such a setting, her old friend, Katherine Thynne, was a true English countess, a veritable goddess. Time was, she remembered, 'when I thought this breeding & personality so distinguished & somehow celestial that it carried everything off'.[20] That 'somehow celestial' glow remained a source of fascination, but such glamour was tinged with uneasy memories of Hyde Park Gate.

The horror of that world was underscored by Madge Vaughan's recent cutting of Vanessa. Madge acted thus upon the orders of her husband Will, who was shocked by his cousin's bohemian lifestyle. As a child, Virginia had been devoted to Madge; later, she had seen her cousin as a kindred spirit, but they had drifted apart. That May, Madge was decidedly ordinary, a person whom life had thickened and stunted. 'And,' Virginia sadly reflected, 'this was the woman I adored!'[21]

Other memories of the past were stirred up by the death of one of her Fisher cousins, Hervey. Although afflicted since childhood with spinal tuberculosis and accompanying mental derangement, he had published one book, *A Romantic Man and Other Tales*, in 1920. As Virginia was well aware, a family legend claimed that his malady had been caused by being dropped on his head as an infant by his nurse. Whatever the origins of his disease, Virginia the child had regarded Hervey, nine years her senior, as a budding literary genius. When he died, 'the only fruit [of his life was] a volume of stories which are neither better nor worse than what one reads on a journey in a Red Magazine.' He had been 'mad' and 'never done anything he liked.'[22] In mourning Hervey, Virginia was anxious lest she meet a similar ignominious fate. Later that year, the Stephen and Duckworth children had to be concerned about Laura, whose annual expenses at her asylum had reached £100 above her income.

In her search for a new form of expression, Virginia was, in large part, rejecting the literary and personal legacy of her own Victorian childhood. Virginia Woolf the critic also wanted to revise the notion of literary history – an enterprise in which her father had taken an active hand. On 23 May, she told her diary: 'Now I think's the time to read like an expert. Then I'm wondering how to shape my Reading book; the more I read of other people's criticism the more I trifle; can't decide; nor need I just yet.'[23] Virginia's notion of expertise was vastly different from Leslie Stephen's, Desmond MacCarthy's or Arnold Bennett's. This is the first reference to what became the *Common Readers*, two book-length attempts to redefine literature according to the prescription outlined in 'Modern Novels'.

On 21 May, Ralph Partridge and Dora Carrington married. Virginia, who had given the couple what she called motherly advice, thought this alliance was more risky than most. A day later, in a self-congratulatory way, she told her sister that on this occasion she had been particularly well behaved: although she had known that the ceremony was about to take place, she had told no one. Virginia's diary and letters do not even begin to suggest the anger vented on her at this time by Ralph, Lytton and Carrington.

That May, things had reached boiling point between Ralph and Carrington. If she refused to marry him, he threatened, he would take himself off to Bolivia, where he would become a sheep farmer. In the midst of these imprecations, Lytton went to Italy. Shortly after this, on 15 May, Virginia broached this difficult subject with an obviously distraught Ralph, who insisted that his beloved was selfish and untruthful. Although she was sympathetic, Virginia informed Ralph that he was 'a bit of an ogre & tyrant'.[24]

According to Ralph, Leonard and Virginia urged him to marry Carrington at once or, if she were unwilling, to leave Tidmarsh for ever. Again according to Ralph, Virginia added some other points of information: after he returned from Italy, Lytton did not plan to spend much time at Tidmarsh; he was doing this because he was convinced that Carrington was staking a claim on him, a claim which arose from the intimacy engendered by living in daily contact with each other. In the midst of his confrontation with Carrington, Ralph repeated the gossip supplied by Virginia. Although she had earlier in the conversation agreed to marry Ralph, Carrington was shocked and affronted by this news. She wrote a long, touching letter to Lytton: 'All along,' she lamented, 'I have known that my life with you was limited.'[25] That letter reached Lytton in Florence on 20 May. In his agitated response, he branded Virginia a malevolent liar.

Within her circle, Virginia had the reputation of being a mischief-maker. In addition, she found Ralph Partridge's aggressive behaviour outlandish, although she did find him physically attractive. Virginia was envious of Lytton's recent success with *Queen Victoria* and, at this time, she did not find Carrington simpatico. Did she inject poison into her advice in a manner which a wounded Ralph would repeat and thus allow herself to strike a three-way blow? It is Ralph Partridge's word against hers, but Virginia did make a fairly detailed diary entry – which by implication contradicts Ralph – on the complications ensuing from this imbroglio. It is possible, but not certain, that Ralph, a man very much caught in the middle, put into Virginia's mouth some of his own worst suspicions about Lytton's detachment from Carrington and her obsession with him. Neither Lytton nor the Woolfs were present when Ralph and Carrington married at the Register Office in St Pancras.

That June, Virginia had to deal with another set of complaints, issued by the Ritchies, who were indignant at the use she had made of Aunt Anny in *Night and Day*. One way Virginia tried to escape such worries was by learning Russian under the tutelage of the Ukrainian-born translator and writer 'Kot' (Samuel Solomonovitch Koteliansky), so that she could assist him in rendering Chekhov into English. Despite Virginia's best efforts to live a secluded existence, she became ill on 10 June, her initial symptom being insomnia. This was followed by frequent headaches, a jumping pulse, backache, frets and fidgets; in the wake of these she had recourse to sleeping draughts, sedatives and digitalis. On 17 June, she went to Rodmell, but when she returned to Richmond on 1 July, she still could not sleep without medication. The Woolfs returned to Sussex on 18 July, where Virginia remained until 6 October. There was a new consolation at Monks House: one of the tool sheds had been transformed into a garden room with a large window overlooking the downs.

By late July, Virginia had improved considerably, although Leonard insisted on a regimen of only one visitor per day. Dr Vallence, one of the Sussex doctors who attended her, asked if she 'did anything'. She was sure that he considered her a hypochondriac and perfunctorily told him that she was a writer. To her intense displeasure, he could not conceal his surprise: 'What, novels? – light things?'[26] Despite such treatment, she was, by 29 August, much better, the proof of which was, according to the accepted medical wisdom of the day, the fact that she had put on 6 pounds.

Three weeks earlier, she made the first entry in her diary since 7 June. The dark underworld of sickness terrified her, but it offered the compensation of leisureliness, especially for a writer who spent every waking moment in some form or other of writing. Her inactivity eventually tortured her, especially as she realized full well that there was 'an infinite capacity of enjoyment horded [*sic*] in'[27] her, which could not find release.

During the two months which were rubbed out, Virginia began to reassess her friendship with Lytton, who, she knew, had become disillusioned by the attainment of fame. He now realized, in contrast to the 'thin, shining'[28] lionizing offered by lords and ladies, how important his old friends were to him. As she got better, Virginia once again dabbled in Katherine Mansfield's stories and then had to rinse her mind. Henry James also remained suspect: she was impressed by *The Wings of the Dove* (1902) but was 'vaguely annoyed by the feeling that – well, that I am in a museum'.[29] When Tom Eliot visited, she – to her great surprise – was no longer afraid of him. Such activities distracted her from completing a draft of *Jacob's Room*, a task which was finally completed only on 4 November.

If Virginia was less afraid of Tom Eliot, she nevertheless railed internally at his claim that *Ulysses* was the greatest work of literature of its age. In a desultory way, Virginia's friendship with Clive, another taste-maker, picked up that autumn. She felt that she had a God-given responsibility to wean him from his excessive interest in fine food, expensive wine and *haute couture*. He visited Richmond in order to confess his sins to Virginia, who suspected that he afterwards sinned the worse. Mary, who, with the ascent of Juana, remained out of favour with Clive, wanted to establish diplomatic relations with Virginia, who decided to play a delicate, teasing game. She would plan to be friendly, make arrangements to see her and then never let those plans come to fruition. Relations with Ralph Partridge, another difficult person, remained stormy, even though their helper was putting his back to the wheel. The compensation was that he had 'a very solid obdurate back'.[30] Work at Hogarth was made a bit easier by the acquisition for £70 10s. of a second-hand Minerva platen machine, worked by treadle.

Late that autumn Virginia had to deal with the extremely moralistic Dorothea Stephen, on leave from her post as a teacher of religion in India. She had taken a stand against Vanessa similar to that of Will and Madge Vaughan. Virginia minced no words with her: 'You, for example, accept a religion which I and my servants, who are both agnostics, think wrong and indeed pernicious. Am I therefore to forbid you to come here for my servants' sake?' If, after reading this letter, Dorothea still wanted to visit Virginia, she was free to do so. 'And,' Virginia concluded her letter, 'I will risk not only my own morals but my cook's.'[31]

There were further domestic emergencies when Nelly and Lottie came down with German measles, so for three days Leonard and Virginia became servants instead of masters. A week before Christmas, Bruce Richmond, the editor of the *Times Literary Supplement*, objected to Virginia's use of the word 'lewd' in a review of Henry James's ghost stories; he wanted her to substitute 'obscene'. This led to a New Year's resolution to give up reviewing 'now that Richmond rewrites my sentences to suit the mealy mouths of Belgravia'.[32]

That January, Virginia came down with influenza, seemed better by the middle of the month and then had a severe relapse which lasted throughout February. At that time, she experienced pain over her heart and wondered if this illness might suddenly wring her out like a dishcloth and leave her dead. This led to a new round of doctors. The following month, Harrington Sainsbury, a heart specialist of Wimpole Street to whom she was referred by D. J. Fergusson, her Richmond doctor, advised her against taking a planned trip to Italy in the spring. In early May, she was bedridden for several days and then late in the month had three teeth extracted. The plan, she told Violet, was 'to catch the escaping microbes which harbour at the roots, and vaccinate me with them afresh'.[33]

A month later, a Harley Street specialist, Philip Hamill, thought her right lung 'suspicious' (i.e. tubercular). Fergusson disagreed with this diagnosis. On 9 August, Virginia saw both Sainsbury and Fergusson. With the former, she was witness to a semi-legal discussion of her health which ended up with quinine pills, lozenges and a brush with which to varnish her throat. Sainsbury's diagnosis was relatively straightforward: influenza and pneumonia germs; she found his manner insufferable: 'Equanimity – practise equanimity, Mrs Woolf'.[34]

Virginia, who was understandably confused by the conflicting diagnoses, was certain that she also had heart disease and consumption, a condition brought about, she imagined, by germs copulating too vigorously. Although she was relatively well that autumn, she was bedridden again in mid-January 1923 with pneumonia and was eventually inoculated in February with her own pneumonia germs. Another procedure amused rather than frightened her: 'They vaccinated a guinea pig with my spittle. It died, but no one knows what of – anyhow not tuberculosis which one idiot of a doctor discovered.'[35] The series of ineffectual doctors Virginia saw in 1922 and 1923 must have reminded her of the assortment of neurologists to whom she had been subjected in 1913. Her hatred of the medical profession, which she saw as a bastion of male privilege and stupidity, soon found its way into *Mrs Dalloway*.

Virginia's relatively secluded existence in 1922 inadvertently led to a series of remarkable changes in some close relationships. Although Vanessa visited her regularly, those meetings were deeply painful for each woman. Both had come to realize that they could indeed live separately from each other, but strangely enough Vanessa did not feel liberated. On the contrary, she thought she was now the unstable one, complaining to her sister that there was nothing binding in her relationship with Duncan. And Vanessa manifested her jealousy and insecurity by implying that Virginia was too dependent upon creature comforts. When she took her leave, Virginia felt depressed, resentful and discontented.

Another frequent visitor was Clive Bell, who, in a moment of whimsy, she imagined suspended above her 'like a Cherub, all bottom and a little flaxen wig'.[36] However, his intent may not have been entirely angelic, as Virginia reflected on 12 March: he was, after all, 'enough of my old friend, & enough of my old lover, to make the afternoons hum'.[37] Clive, an apostle of hedonism, preached his doctrine to a very amused mother-confessor. However, Vanessa could not have been entirely pleased to be told by Clive that he had 'as usual' fallen slightly in love with Virginia. On 1 March, he elaborated: 'I hope I shan't fall more deeply in love.'[38] Vanessa was thus an uneasy witness to a reprise of the events which had led so very decisively to the break-up of her marriage.

The person who aroused Virginia's erotic interest that winter was Elena Richmond, Bruce's wife. Elena was large, stolid and maternal. When she had first known her, Virginia had reacted negatively to what she perceived as the other woman's impenetrability. That February, she even condescendingly referred to Elena as a cultivated woman who represented the top layer of the general public, those who subscribed to Mudie's Library. Moreover, she was the type of woman to whom Leslie Stephen was attracted: 'She is a handsome . . . matron, with a double chin, settled complexion; & she dresses in a pepper & salt tailor made, wears spats, & has something of the American bust.'[39]

This does not seem a description which indicates sexual attractiveness, but Virginia, perhaps in an attempt to provoke her sister, told her: 'I think she is quite the nicest human being I have ever met – solid – splendid – sedate – with the body of a matron and the mind of a child and the tastes of a schoolboy; so maternal to me that I fell in love with her at once.' So overcome was Virginia that she told Elena of George's misdeeds. In turn, Elena mentioned that she and Bruce had never much liked her half-brother. Indeed, if she had known what Virginia had just told her, she would have hated him long before.

Virginia could not tell what Elena took in. After expressing shock, Elena blandly observed that 'much more goes on than one realizes'. Virginia's hope (a very improbable one) was that Bruce would spit in George's face when he next saw him at his club. Then George might be driven to 'shoot himself one day when he's shooting rabbits'.[40] Virginia's attraction to a woman whom she was certain her father would have found alluring indicates that Virginia saw traces of Julia in Elena; years before, Violet Dickinson had been such a maternal love object. In 1922, as she and Vanessa drifted apart, she needed a new woman to whom she could be emotionally attached. To this new mother, Virginia revealed one of the sexual crimes that had damaged and inhibited her.

That March, Virginia began work again on *Jacob's Room*. Her temperature was not normal, but her work habits were. However, thoughts of sexuality were always linked for Virginia with the idea of death. She tried to rid herself of such musings by considering her career as a writer, but she felt blocked there as well. She had to face the fact that she might never become a popular author – her own lot might be an unpleasant mixture of disregard and abuse. So, she decided, she would write what she wanted and take the consequences: 'My only interest as a writer lies, I begin to see, in some queer individuality: not in strength, or passion, or anything startling; but then I say to myself, is not "some queer individuality" precisely the quality I respect?'[41] On such terms, she could go on. In a way, she was relieved when thoughts of life interrupted her ruminations on death, but, she realized, 'I have taken it into my head that I shan't live till 70.'[42]

'Some queer individuality' in story-telling had once been a bond shared with Katherine Mansfield. When her friend's third collection of short stories, *The Garden Party*, appeared in March, Virginia was irritated: 'The more she is praised, the more I am convinced she is bad.'[43] That month, in a letter to Clive, she even interpolated a malicious parody of Mansfieldian prose style.

One writer to whom Virginia was able to give unqualified praise was Proust, whose sensuousness was very different from Joyce's: it was not so much a matter of sexual orientation as a fundamental difference in outlook. According to Virginia, Joyce was simply sordid; for her, Proust's language captured the actual processes of thought, perception and, most importantly, feeling:

> 'Oh if I could write like that!' I cry. And at the moment such is the astonishing vibration and saturation and intensification that he procures – there's something sexual in it – that I feel I *can* write like that, and seize my pen and then I *can't* write like that. Scarcely anyone so stimulates the nerves of language in me: it becomes an obsession.[44]

In many ways, Proust opened a new world to Virginia's eyes. In contrast, Tom Eliot's *The Waste Land*, which he read to her and Leonard, his publishers, on 18 June, impressed with its force of phrase, symmetry and tension: 'He sang it & chanted it, rhythmed it. It has great beauty & force . . . What connects it together, I'm not so sure.'[45] Although the strong emotions of that poem moved her, she did not see Tom as a writer from whom she could learn.

Virginia discovered Proust at Roger Fry's insistence and their mutual enthusiasm for the French writer was the prelude to a new direction in their friendship. For years, Virginia had been suspicious of Roger, whose puritan work ethic and sparse words of praise put her off. In April 1921, Roger stayed at Hogarth House while completing his restoration of the Mantegna frescos at Hampton Court. At that time, she noticed how sunny and open a person he really was. His kind words about *Monday or Tuesday* touched her, but it was Virginia's realization that they shared a common obsession that led her to see him in a different light. Like her, he lived for his work:

> we are grown rather intimate, & sit talking at our ease – practically of everything. This was not so a year ago . . . Roger grudges every minute now that he doesn't paint. So we reflected upon these strange, on the whole merciful, dispensations, by which Roger always sees masterpieces ahead of him & I see great novels – We have our atmosphere of illusion, without which life would be so much duller than it is.[46]

Virginia's heightened awareness of Roger was attenuated by being forced to live in close quarters at Richmond with Ralph Partridge: 'We have had a mad bull in the house – a normal Englishman in love . . . His stupidity, blindness, callousness, struck me more powerfully than the magic virtues of passion.' There was something truly 'maniacal in masculine vanity' and Virginia realized more and more that Roger Fry showed no inclination to be a 'male bully'.[47]

Although Virginia placed Tom Eliot's temperament in a precarious middle ground between a Roger Fry and a Ralph Partridge, she was anxious to help him when she learned of Ottoline's plan – complementary to a scheme (the Bel Esprit fund) initiated by Ezra Pound – to provide Tom with an assured income of £300 a year so that he could leave his job in the Colonial and Foreign Department of Lloyds. Virginia actively solicited contributions from

Bloomsbury, but the stratagem eventually came to an abrupt halt in September, when Tom told her that he needed a solid guarantee of £500 a year. A month earlier, Virginia had struck her name from the committee. 'I think it is a mistake,' she told Ottoline, 'to have two out of the three names feminine. It gives an impression that poor Tom is our lap dog.'[48]

She also had considerable trouble with an animal of a different sort. According to Virginia, Sybil Colefax was a black fox and thus perfectly entitled to her surname. She also nicknamed her 'The Coalbox'. This indefatigable hostess and exhaustive collector of rich and talented people, who on one occasion reminded Virginia of hard red cherries on a cheap black hat, could be very exhausting and rapacious. In this relationship, Virginia saw herself as Chanticleer: Sybil seemed to admire her as a word-maker but really, Virginia fantasized, she wanted to consume her. She also knew that Sybil's admiration for writers and intellectuals was tinged with an envious anger at those very accomplishments.

Another difficult woman who aspired to high society was Kitty Maxse, with whom Virginia had never felt at ease. When she encountered her at a funeral in May 1916, Virginia cut her. Nevertheless, Virginia admired her white hair, pink cheeks, ear-rings, gaiety and aura of smartness; behind this façade she could just manage to discern melancholia and to catch a glimpse of the occasional tear which betrayed inner torment. In one sense, Kitty was the woman, Virginia felt, Julia had wanted her to be. Since she could not live up to such expectations and was indeed hostile to them, Kitty became an enemy. In turn, Kitty, who through her husband was connected to the literary world but rejected intellectual interests in favour of the demands of society, saw Virginia as a kind of bohemian outcast.

Kitty died suddenly and mysteriously on 4 October after falling down some stairs in her London home. Before she died, she asked her husband: 'Shall I ever walk again?' Always the polite lady, she apologized to the doctor who attended her: 'I shall never forgive myself for my carelessness.'[49] What really happened?, Virginia wondered. She was certain Kitty had committed suicide.

Next to Lady Colefax and Kitty Maxse, Mary Hutchinson was much easier to deal with. Virginia was dumbfounded, pleasantly so, when Mary kissed her at a meeting of the Memoir Club in June 1922. Mary, who now had a large purr in Virginia's company, finally managed to pin Virginia to a dinner date. That evening, Mary's face was painted white, her dress made of black satin, her shawl orange and her shoes laced. She was the epitome of fashion, but Virginia saw behind the veneer: 'She is an impulsive generous woman, whose generosity still exists; but subterraneously I think, floored over by her society varnish.'[50] Mary was in trouble: she needed Virginia's help in maintaining her place in Bloomsbury and in Clive's affections. An additional incentive for Virginia to be sympathetic was the fact that Vanessa was no longer guarded in her hatred of Clive's former mistress. The balance of power in the sisterly dealings of Vanessa and Virginia had shifted considerably.

Rodmell in 1922 was also a hotbed of sexual intrigue. While on heat, Grizzle, the Woolfs' dog, escaped their custody and was, as Virginia put it, 'lined in the churchyard by the Vicar's pomeranian, Jimmy'.[51] For ten years, he had lived a chaste life. Now, the Vicar's wife told Nelly, he was a lost soul, running wild in the brooks. This event took place, appropriately enough, during Passion week.

There was further evidence of passion. The year before, Edward Shanks, the poet and journalist, and his wife had taken Charnes Cottage, separated from Monks House garden only by the church path. That August, Mrs Shanks ran away with a German, Mr Shanks took up with a prostitute with whom he flirted in the village, but, what was far worse for Virginia, some noisy Boy Scouts camped in the field bordering Monks House. Virginia, who now wrote in the garden house near the churchyard wall, was disturbed by their noise.

Despite such intrusions, Virginia resumed work on *The Common Reader*, began a short story, 'Mrs Dalloway in Bond Street', and revised *Jacob's Room*. She quipped to Ottoline that she would write a Garsington novel, an early reference to *Mrs Dalloway*; that novel, set in London, also had Kitty Maxse's death as a starting point. In any event, Virginia had come up with a new way to spend her writing time: she would work on a project, leave it for a while and go on to something else, take up perhaps another venture and so rotate her crops. That May, she and Leonard celebrated the fifth anniversary of the Hogarth Press. When Ka complained to Virginia about the negligible quality of some of the twenty-one titles they had published, she retorted: 'Consider the stuff we *don't* print.'[52] Ralph continued to be a nuisance. The next time they needed an assistant, she vowed, 'we must stipulate for eunuchs'.[53]

Virginia continued to be haunted by *Ulysses*, a book which puzzled, bored, irritated and disillusioned her. Reading that novel was like watching a 'queasy undergraduate scratching his pimples'.[54] How dare Tom Eliot praise it! And yet it exerted a considerable influence on the form of the book which became *Mrs Dalloway*. At this time she was 'laboriously dredging' her mind for that novel but was only 'bringing up light buckets'.[55]

By September, when she was correcting the proofs of *Jacob's Room*, Virginia was certain that it was thin and pointless. What, after all, she asked Roger, remained to be written after Proust? There were some compensations. 'Everyone' from her old Gordon Square set was now famous, especially Maynard Keynes, who had just taken up with the ballerina Lydia Lopokova. So despite her fears about the reception which would greet her new novel, Virginia remained cautiously optimistic: 'At forty I am beginning to learn the mechanism of my own brain – how to get the greatest amount of pleasure & work out of it. The secret is, I think, always so to contrive that work is pleasant.'[56]

Just before the publication of *Jacob's Room*, a clear-sighted Virginia saw the book as a 'necessary step, for me, in working free'.[57] She was afraid that the experimental nature of the book overwhelmed its content. Superficially, *Jacob's Room* bears some resemblance to a *Bildungsroman*, a novel which traces a hero's advancement from childhood to maturity. The reader first meets Jacob as a child studying a tidal pool on a Cornish beach; from the outset, Jacob's surname – Flanders – foreshadows his death twenty-six years later on a foreign battlefield during the Great War. Jacob lives in Scarborough with his widowed mother and his two brothers, Archer and John. He grows up there, studies Latin with the Reverend Floyd and goes to Cambridge when he is nineteen, where he makes friends with Richard Bonamy and Timothy Durrant. One long vacation, he travels to Timothy's home in Cornwall, where he meets Timothy's sister, Clara. After he goes down from Cambridge at the age of twenty-two, he lives in rooms in Lamb's Conduit Street. In London, he attends parties, has affairs, works, visits prostitutes, writes essays, goes to the opera. At the age of twenty-five, he goes abroad to France, Italy and Greece, where he falls in love with Sandra Williams, a married woman. He returns to England, the war begins and he is killed.

The narrative moves chronologically, but its fourteen chapters – varying enormously in length – concentrate on very specific moments in Jacob's life: two are devoted to his childhood, two to his Cambridge years, the ten remaining show him working in London and travelling abroad. Few connectives between the episodes are given; in fact, in revising the novel, Virginia tended to excise material which paid too much attention to plot development.*

'Conceive "Mark on the Wall", "Kew Gardens" and "An Unwritten Novel" taking hands & dancing in unity.'[58] This is

* In MS 1, 23 (Berg), the Reverend Floyd asks Jacob's mother to marry him. His proposal upsets her, and her misgivings are clearly stated: '"How could I think of marriage!" she thought to herself almost bitterly as she fastened the latch with a piece of wire. It was, probably, that the idea of copulation had now become infinitely remote from her. She did not use the word; & yet as she sat darning the boys' clothes that night it annoyed her to find that it was so. "And I dislike red headed men" she said; pushing away her work basket.' In the published version (15), the reader is given far less information and must, as it were, infer the cause of her agitation by making a connection between virility and red hair. '"How could I think of marriage!" she said to herself bitterly, as she fastened the gate with a piece of wire. She had always disliked red hair in men, she thought, thinking of Mr Floyd's appearance, that night when the boys had gone to bed.'

Virginia's extremely accurate description of her methodology in *Jacob's Room*. At the outset of her work on it, she saw her new novel as a conglomeration of the various experimental strands which eventually became *Monday or Tuesday*. Without being fully aware of it, she was also responding to a very different series of influences, particularly the writings of James Joyce, Tom Eliot and especially Lytton Strachey. At first glance, the literary form that *Jacob's Room* most closely resembles is biography, but at every possible turn this narrative avoids what Strachey defined in the Preface to *Eminent Victorians* as the task of biography: 'Human beings are too important to be treated as mere symptoms of the past. They have a value which is independent of any temporal processes – which is eternal, and must be felt for its own sake.'[59]

The emphasis in *Jacob's Room* is on the *room*, not *Jacob*; on symptoms, not persons. This is one of the reasons why, in the process of revision, Virginia removed pieces of information which could be considered psychological or biographical. The reader is asked to look at Jacob from the outside (although, strangely enough, the reader is not really told what he looks like). It is as if Virginia had turned Lytton's biographical principles inside out: she avoids the person and turns to his things. She also questions the notion that change and progress are synonymous: Jacob may have grown to adulthood, but did he really become an acceptable person? The book queries many other things about Jacob. Did he not see women only as creatures to be used for his personal whims? Did he perhaps have an inflated male point of view about the role of sex in human life? The reader is asked to ponder these questions.

> Then consider the effect of sex – how between man and woman it hangs wavy, tremulous, so that here's a valley, there's a peak, when in truth, perhaps, all's as flat as my hand. Even the exact words get the wrong accent on them. But something is always impelling one to hum vibrating, like the hawk moth, at the mouth of the cavern of mystery, endowing Jacob Flanders with all sorts of qualities he had not at all . . . what remains is mostly

a matter of guess work. Yet over him we hang vibrating.[60]

If the male idea of sexuality is wrong, this passage implies, perhaps Jacob is not as interesting as he at first seems. But he is a man and therefore will be invested with qualities he does not possess; it is in the nature of things that an audience will 'vibrate' over him.

In its refusal to go inside the mind of Jacob, *Jacob's Room* resembles more an avant-garde film scenario than a modernist novel: the reader is given plenty to look at, overhears many interesting conversations and has to piece together many seemingly unrelated pieces of information. Superficially, this superbly visual narrative seems to be based on the life of Thoby Stephen, about whose shadowy existence Virginia had attempted – unsuccessfully – to gain information from his friends. Although she had greatly loved Thoby, Virginia felt she had never really known him and the book is more a memorial to that poignantly sad fact than it is to Thoby himself. *Jacob's Room* is not a prose version of *In Memoriam* and Thoby is no Hallam: the book is concerned more with the sense of loss than the lost object.

Jacob's Room is very much a Cambridge novel, concerned as it is with the kind of epistemological and ontological questions which fascinated G. E. Moore and the Apostles: as such, it is a narrative about the limits of knowledge and the nature of being. Much more than that, *Jacob's Room* examines male attitudes towards life and pushes them to the extreme, at which point they break. Since intuition and transparency are not valued by most men, none of the delicacy of stories such as 'Kew Gardens' can be seen here.

This is also an outsider's book, written from the perspective of one who looks intently at men, their dealings with women, their institutions, their wars and their misuse of power. The latter is obliquely referred to in this novel as the 'unseizable force', which stands in marked opposition to 'the Greek spirit', the order produced by art. Thoby had shared his great love of Greek civilization with his youngest sister – and that mutual devotion is certainly enshrined in this novel – but, the book asks, would Thoby's ideals have survived had he lived? The book implies, but does not state, that the spirit of Greece must be rekindled by employing a different kind of writing, the kind of narrative envisioned in 'Modern Novels'.

Ultimately, *Jacob's Room* is an innovative novel which pushes the masculine aesthetic of Eliot and Joyce as far as it can go: its male protagonist is killed by the 'unseizable force' which governs his own rules of conduct. The book's weakness derives in large part from the fact that it is written in opposition: it does not really provide a counter-vision to the one being dismantled. Virginia attacks the linear, masculine point of view by describing it in a deliberately disjointed narrative technique that flows, flies and darts.*

The narrative's fragmentary style is its great strength and its great weakness: it is a difficult, erratic narrative written by someone who is interested in – but not allowed to participate in – the affairs of men.† When Leonard read Virginia's new novel, he told her that it was a work of genius. That was not necessarily a compliment. He also observed that it was peopled with ghosts, that it had

* In an important letter to Gerald Brenan of 25 December 1922, Virginia provided one of the finest justifications of what she had tried to accomplish in *Jacob's Room*: 'The human soul, it seems to me, orientates itself afresh every now and then. It is doing so now. No one can see it whole, therefore. The best of us catch a glimpse of a nose, a shoulder, something turning away, always in movement. Still, it seems better to me to catch this glimpse, than to sit down with Hugh Walpole, Wells, etc. etc. and make large oil paintings of fabulous fleshy monsters complete from toe to toe.'

If the human soul does indeed orientate itself afresh from time to time, then the achievements of the past must, to a large degree, be renounced. The beauty which comes from completeness must be rejected in favour of the possibility of writing something which captures the human soul of one's own generation: this is, of course, the agenda of modernism as seen – from varying directions – by Joyce, Eliot and Virginia Woolf.

† In the holograph, there was a woman character who was deleted from the published text (MS, I, 85–91, originally Chapter X; the section was labelled 'A Woman's College from Outside'). Angela Williams is a student at Newnham being educated 'for the purpose of earning her living' (190). Virginia's original intent had been to use Angela as a foil to Jacob, and to

no philosophy and that the characters were puppets, moved hither and thither by fate. He suggested that the next time she use her method on one or two characters. Nevertheless, he found the book interesting and beautiful.

Jacob's Room is a book in which one too readily feels its author's genius. A. S. McDowall, in the *Times Literary Supplement*, realized that Virginia was attempting to extend the methodology of her short stories to the novel, but the result was too 'limpid and definite'. Nevertheless, the story of a half-savage, self-absorbed young man worked, if taken on its own terms: 'This stream of incidents, persons and their momentary thoughts and feelings, which would be intolerable if it were just allowed to flow, is arrested and decanted, as it were, into little phials of crystal vividness.' Yet this reviewer was left with a nagging doubt: 'we should have to say that [the book] does not create persons and characters as we secretly desire to know them'.[61] In a notice of several books in the *Daily News* headed 'Middle Aged Sensualists', Lewis Bettany claimed that he found 'most of the book very pretentious and very cheap; but some of the observations and impressions seemed to me quite happy'.[62] The reviewer in the *Pall Mall Gazette* admired the book's technical adroitness, but felt it sterile. Rebecca West, in a long piece in the *New Statesman*, claimed that *Jacob's Room* had to be judged as a portfolio, not a novel: 'She can write supremely well only of what can be painted; best of all, perhaps, of what has been painted.'[63] In the *Daily Telegraph*, W. L. Courtney detected the influence of Impressionism: 'She does not describe; she merely indicates.'[64]

Perhaps unawares, Vanessa and Roger had indeed influenced the form of *Jacob's Room*. Roger was unstinting in his praise, but he told Virginia that he wished that a 'bronze body might somehow solidify beneath the gleams & lights'.[65] Lytton Strachey also had no doubts of the book's merits:

---

introduce into the novel a modern, professional woman with a room of her own and with a desire to forge her own destiny. See Appendix II, *Jacob's Room* (189–92).

a most wonderful achievement – more like poetry, it seems to me, than anything else, and as such I prophesy immortal. The technique of the narrative is astonishing – how you manage to leave out everything that's dreary, and yet retain enough string for your pearls I can hardly understand. I occasionally almost screamed with joy at the writing. Of course you're very romantic.[66]

Virginia thought her friend's praise too generous – and perhaps insincere: 'I can't believe you really like a work so utterly devoid of so many virtues . . . Of course you put your infallible finger upon the spot – romanticism. How do I catch it? Not from my father. I think it must have been my Great Aunts. But some of it, I think, comes from the effort of breaking with complete representation.' As a result, 'One flies into the air.'[67] Virginia's reference to the Pattle sisters is not entirely facetious; she is indicating that her pursuit of a new form owed more to her mother than to her father. In this context, to be 'romantic' is to soar free from established conventions.

Although Virginia was annoyed at being labelled an 'elderly sensualist' in the *Daily News*, she remained equitable about her new book's reception. When she congratulated David Garnett on his novel, *Lady into Fox*, she placed herself in a different category of writer, one who did not have to be jealous of someone else's accomplishment in an arena where she *seemed* to fail: 'All we battered old novelists find nothing so hard as perpetual story telling, and there you are doing it as a fountain bubbles.'[68] When an old friend, Bob Trevelyan, complained of the book's failings, she agreed with him: 'It is true, I expect, that the characters remain shadowy for the most part; but the method was not so much at fault as my ignorance of how to use it psychologically.'[69] Somewhat philosophically, she reflected: 'Either I am a great writer or a nincompoop.'[70] No one was perfect – a fact further drummed into her that November when she read the Book of Job: 'I don't think God comes well out of it.'[71] Overall, she was sure, her third novel was more an experiment than an achievement. However, it remained her own favourite of all her books.

★

Although Virginia had been deeply touched by Lytton's generous words about *Jacob's Room*, she had long been furious with him over his interference in Hogarth Press matters. Earlier, that September, he had visited and the conversation touched on Edward Gibbon, James Boswell, Mrs Thrale and the English prison system, but Lytton returned again and again to his obsession with Carrington and Ralph – especially Ralph – who, spurned by his wife, was in the midst of an affair with Valentine Dobrée. Lytton, whose sentiments towards Ralph commingled parental worries with suppressed sexual desire, saw events in Richmond entirely from Ralph's perspective.

For his part, Ralph felt the Woolfs disliked him, were using him and not giving sufficient time to the Press. Lytton wanted to discuss a host of possibilities: perhaps he should buy Suffield House back from the person to whom the Woolfs had sold it (presumably the *ménage* from Tidmarsh would then have a London base from which Ralph could give his full attention to Hogarth matters); perhaps the Woolfs should move back to 38 Brunswick Square, leaving the Tidmarsh trio to live in Hogarth House; perhaps Ralph should be set up on a farm. Later, there would be yet more, supposedly tempting alternatives: perhaps the Hogarth Press could become Lytton's publisher, if Ralph's position with Leonard and Virginia was solidified; perhaps there could be a joint imprint, Hogarth and Tidmarsh.

Two months later, things came to a head during a stormy weekend at Tidmarsh. For the Woolfs, the Hogarth Press, which had begun as a hobby, was now an integral part of their lives as professional writers. Virginia was convinced that Ralph was a rank amateur, an unstable person who would always act according to whim rather than reason. She also felt that he used his virile beauty as a way of keeping Lytton on a string. Ralph was Lytton's baby and that baby wanted a toy, the Hogarth Press, which was not his. Virginia and Leonard were caught in the middle and were understandably resentful. After a further display of Ralph's boorish conduct that November, Virginia concluded that he had to go.

That was no easy task, especially when almost immediately afterwards Constable made an offer to purchase the Hogarth Press. On Friday, 10 November, Ralph asked Virginia to be certain that Leonard did not sell the Press that weekend. During the same conversation, he implied that husband and wife were prepared to sell out to the highest bidder. Virginia was dumbfounded by Ralph's behaviour, but realized almost immediately that she had perhaps given him the impression that she was in favour of amalgamation with some big firm in order to increase profitability and her own public image. She vented her fury in a letter to him:

> What did make my blood boil was your assumption that Leonard and I are quite ready to be bamboozled with a bargain which would destroy the character of the press for the sake of money or pride or convenience; and that you must protect its rights. After all we have given the press whatever character it may have, and if you're going to tell me that you care more about it than I do, or know better what's good for it, I must reply that you're a donkey.[72]

The Woolfs no sooner said no to Constable than Heinemann made an unacceptable bid. Then Leonard and Virginia had to veto Ralph's new scheme whereby the Hogarth Press would remain in Richmond but Noel Carrington, Dora's brother, would become London manager.

The manipulative schemes of Ralph and Lytton were constant and intrusive. The Woolfs took their first steps towards liberation when, in the midst of considering the Heinemann offer, they overheard this snippet at their Club – the 1917 in Gerrard Street, Soho* – by a young, shabby, small-faced crophead: 'They say there's never been a woman printer; but I mean to be one. No, I know nothing whatever about it.' A once shy Virginia leaped in at

* It was called such after the February Revolution in Russia. Leonard was one of the founders of the club, which was started in the autumn of 1917 to provide a meeting place for those interested in peace and democracy.

this point, followed the young woman into an adjoining room and revealed herself as the proprietor of the Hogarth Press. Marjorie Thomson, who was in her early twenties, had been a student at the London School of Economics and taught at a private girls' school; she lived with Cyril Joad, then a civil servant in the Ministry of Labour. The lovers soon came to tea and the Woolfs hired the intrepid young woman. Virginia was very optimistic: 'Since heaven dropped the seed into her naturally, she will want no urging, & will cleave to it as to her own flesh & bone.'[73] Marjorie was no Virgin Mary and Virginia no Archangel Gabriel, but – except for her drawl – Virginia was pleased by her new helper. She stayed three years and Ralph – who seduced her – departed the press in March 1923.

That November, Virginia, who needed no further complications or obligations, was delighted when Leonard was not elected to Parliament. She was working on an edition of Aeschylus, finishing 'Modern Essays', busily engaged with *Mrs Dalloway* and thinking about *The Common Reader*. Gradually, her life had begun to take on some semblance of order. She once told Jacques Raverat: 'I find that unless I weigh 9½ stones, I hear voices and see visions and can neither write nor sleep.'[74]

But she often felt listless. If she could not be at 'full stretch',[75] she would ponder and loiter. At such times, depressed feelings invaded her. Shouldn't she have had children? Shouldn't she have chosen Vanessa's manner of life? Shouldn't she have opted for a less ordered style of existence? These shards would pierce her, but they would vanish when her work once again took over.

Virginia found it more difficult than usual to rid herself of such awful feelings when she learned of Katherine Mansfield's death on 9 January. Her first reaction – on 16 January – was that she had lost the spur to write. Twelve days later, her melancholia persisted as strong as ever. What was she to do? She knew the answer: 'Go on writing of course; but into emptiness. There's no competitor.'[76] She tried to follow Katherine's injunction of long ago: 'do not quite forget Katherine'.[77]

In some ways, *Jacob's Room* must have been an answer to

Katherine's review of *Night and Day* and now she could never be consulted about the incredible new direction which she had, to a large extent, helped foster. There was no other woman writer Virginia wanted to compete with, with whom she could vie for mastery. The truth was that Katherine Mansfield was the shadow self of Virginia Woolf, the woman writer who – in love and hatred – goaded her to do her best.

In August 1922, Virginia learned that the aristocratic, popular novelist Vita Sackville-West considered her to be the best woman writer, but she did not meet her until 14 December at Clive Bell's. At the outset, Virginia had mixed feelings, as she told her diary, about the mixture of male and female qualities she discerned in 'handsome, manly' Mrs Harold Nicolson: 'Not much to my severer taste – florid, moustached, parakeet coloured, with all the supple ease of the aristocracy, but not the wit of the artist.' She made Virginia feel 'virgin, shy, & schoolgirlish. Yet after dinner I rapped out opinions.' In sum, Vita may have been the aristocrat, but it was Virginia who took the upper hand that evening. Fascinated by the exotic concoction of persons dwelling within the same breast, she soon allowed Vita to begin a leisurely exploration of her vestal state. But Virginia was deeply uncertain: 'could I ever know her?' she asked herself.[78]

However, even before Katherine died, Virginia Woolf the writer knew that she had to go on alone and damn the consequences. When Gerald Brenan, whose love affair with Dora Carrington had begun less than a month after her marriage, wrote from Spain to tell Virginia how discouraged he sometimes was in his literary career, she urged him to press on, however difficult the effort. Really, there was no other choice: 'though I try sometimes to limit myself to the thing I do well, I am always drawn on and on, by human beings, I think, out of the little circle of safety, on and on, to the whirlpools; when I go under'.[79]

Part Four

THE REAL THING

Chapter Twelve

THE FORCE FLOWING FULLEST

(1923–5)

Virginia's safety net was largely provided by her husband. In comparison to many of her acquaintances and friends, 'dear old Leo' remained the still point in a fast-turning wheel. Sometimes, he seemed cold or unenthusiastic, but when he did kindle the glow was of 'the purest fiery red'.[1] In March 1923, Leonard's career was in turmoil. When he understandably became agitated, Virginia felt that the delicate balance she had established between her life and her work had been violated, perhaps permanently so.

For a number of years, the Woolfs had lived a precarious financial existence, one which demanded that each partner take on a number of obligations. Virginia's book-reviewing was the most sustained monetary contribution she made to keep their two residences running smoothly: of course, she also acted as printer, publisher's reader and bookbinder. She was also writing novels which, she hoped, would eventually make a substantial contribution to their finances. Leonard's career also had many facets. In December 1918, he had been appointed editor of *International Review*. When that journal closed a year later, he became an editor at *Contemporary Review* and six months later he became acting political editor of the *Nation*. In December 1921, he resigned from *Contemporary Review* and the following September became political editor of the *Nation*. Leonard's magazine work obviously provided the financial anchor for his other activities as publisher and author.

In 1922, Virginia made almost £70 from her book-reviewing and £33 from royalties. Leonard earned approximately £600 a year: £250 from freelance journalism, £250 from his editorships and £100 from royalties. Although they had income from investments, the Woolfs' expenses were well over £900 a year. If any piece in their complicated jigsaw of earned income failed them, they were in trouble. Leonard took a cut of £250 a year when he left *Contemporary Review* late in 1921. That year, he had also earned approximately £120 from the *Nation*: £80 for his post as political editor and £40 for book-reviewing. Suddenly, at the beginning of 1923, those wages were in jeopardy. H. W. Massingham, the 'Wayfarer' with whom Virginia had previously crossed swords, had edited the *Nation* since its founding in 1907 by the Rowntrees, who were Liberals. Sixteen years later, the *Nation* had become for all intents and purposes Labour and the Rowntrees wanted to pull out. Massingham was given first refusal to buy, but he could not obtain financial backing. Finally, Maynard Keynes and some other Liberals came forward and purchased the paper, the Rowntrees retaining a small interest. Since he was political editor, this solution was obviously not to Leonard's liking.

Virginia was fairly certain that Maynard Keynes could be relied on to continue Leonard's involvement – in some capacity – with the *Nation*, but she and Leonard were nevertheless faced with the possible loss of £370 in income. The *Nation* débâcle was resolved when Tom Eliot, staunchly backed by Virginia and Leonard, was offered but refused the literary editorship of that journal; at that point, Maynard turned to Leonard, who promptly accepted the post. On 6 March, Virginia reflected: 'But that is only £120 p.a. & we shall have to scrape up the rest rather dismally, doing journalism.'[2]

When Leonard became anxious, his gloom was pervasive and long-lasting, whereas his wife's was – as she claimed – like a mist that goes as quickly as it comes. The couple also differed in their attitude towards respectability: Leonard did not value form for form's sake, whereas Virginia was fascinated by the protocols and mystique governing social events such as parties. Leonard was quick to refuse invitations; Virginia was anxious to snap them up. Then there were conflicts about running the Press, which was so draining of her energy that Virginia facetiously likened it to six unruly children nursing at her breast simultaneously. At busy moments Leonard and Virginia spent long periods of each day apart: 'he in the basement, I in the printing room. We meet only at meals, often so cross that we can't speak, and generally dirty. His triumphs always coincide with my disasters.'[3]

Leonard's forbidding countenance disturbed Virginia, but she knew that she could look beyond the exterior to the kindly person who dwelt behind the mask. At times this was exceedingly difficult. One wet, windy night in September 1923 Virginia set out to meet Leonard's London train at Richmond station. A sense of foreboding took over as the horrible weather became symbolic for her of her life as an outcast. She could feel her body become rigid; there was little in the way of light and finally, at the station, the last likely train arrived without her husband. Filled with a nameless and numbing sense of terror, she decided to travel into London, bought a ticket and then, before she could board a train, spied Leonard walking briskly down a set of stairs. His response to his wife's agitation was cold anger. She went to the ticket office to retrieve her fare, more to set herself right with Leonard than because she wanted her money back. On their walk back home, they talked about a fight concerning reviewers which had erupted at the *Nation*. During this exchange, Virginia was relieved that her ordeal was over: 'Really, it was a physical thing, of lightness & relief & safety. & yet there was too something terrible behind it – the fact of this pain.'[4]

After more than ten years of marriage, Virginia was certain that there was a basic difference between her and Leonard: 'isn't he too much of a Puritan, of a disciplinarian, doesn't he through birth & training accept a drastic discipline too tamely, or rather, with too Spartan a self control?' Virginia knew that she possessed many of these traits, but she was aware that she also had 'a piece of jewellery I inherit from my mother – a joy in laughter'.[5] This social side was becoming increasingly crucial to her.

Some of the pain of isolation could be relieved, Virginia was certain, if she could travel to the Continent and there experience warmth, sunshine and a more relaxed style of life. Three of

Virginia's previous trips there had left her with a mixture of painful memories: of a breakdown in 1904, of the death of Thoby in 1906 and of fraught sexual relations with Leonard in 1912. In fact, she had not been physically or mentally well enough to travel to Europe for eleven years. So the decision to visit Spain and France in the spring of 1923 was symbolic of a strong sense that her life now contained far more lightness and safety than danger.

Leonard and Virginia took the Newhaven–Dieppe route and managed to avoid speaking to their fellow passengers, the Aldous Huxleys, who looked, to Virginia's disgust, as if they had stepped out of the pages of *Vogue*. The Woolfs then made their way to Paris, where, as years before, 'the spirits of the damned'[6] still inhabited hotel rooms. Then, by way of the south of France, they travelled to Madrid, where that Lent they tramped around after the figure of Christ dressed in what Virginia referred to as a purple dressing gown. From there they proceeded to Granada, where they were met by Gerald Brenan. The three stayed two nights with Brenan's friends Charles Lindsay Temple, a former Governor of Nigeria, and his wife, Olive, before travelling southwards by mule and bus to Brenan's cottage at Yegen in the Sierra Madre. The Woolfs remained there for two weeks with the young corduroy-clad Don Giraldo, who, according to Virginia, did nothing but read French and eat grapes. Life at Yegen was a delightful mixture of the local brasserie, begging children, young men playing dominoes and old men selling lottery tickets. Virginia's sense of well-being was so elevated by the mountains, which were always covered by snow, that she made herself a promise: 'I am determined never to live long in England again. The rapture of getting into warmth and colour and good sense and general congeniality of temper is so great.'[7] She was especially pleased to have escaped the ultra-respectable suburban existence of Richmond.

Gerald Brenan, lovesick for Carrington, spent his days reading and writing, but, as Virginia recalled, he tore everything up and then ran out to commune with the spirit of the mountains. There were long (twelve-hour) discussions about literature and a frankly puzzled Virginia subjected the young writer to endless, sometimes bantering, questions. Why did he live in this remote part of Spain? What were his real feelings about a writing life? She was trying to size him up, and in the process defended Scott, Thackeray and Conrad, attacked his high opinion of *Ulysses* and was even eager to hear his criticism of her novels. She also told him that she despised Lytton's *Queen Victoria*, but she had in fact never finished it. He was struck by her remarkable beauty and made a splendid pen portrait of her at mid-life, settled one evening in his cottage under the hooded chimney, a fire blazing and her hands outstretched to catch the warmth: 'Although her face was too long for symmetry, its bones were thin and delicately made and her eyes were large, grey or greyish blue, and as clear as a hawk's. In conversation they would light up a little coldly while her mouth took an ironic and challenging fold, but in repose her expression was pensive and almost girlish.'[8] This is Virginia Woolf the poetic novelist, but Brenan also saw, while they were scrambling one day on the hillside among fig and olive trees, a very different person. 'An English lady, country-bred and thin, her wide-open eyes scanning the distance, who has completely forgotten herself in her delight at the beauty of the landscape and at the novelty of finding herself in such a remote and Arcadian spot. She seemed, though quiet, as excited as a school-girl on holiday.'[9] In this moment, Brenan captured just how foreign Spain was for Virginia and how delighted she was by the penetrating warmth of this particular earthly paradise. He also discerned something of Virginia's sexual frigidity, a subject upon which Leonard indirectly commented when he told Brenan that the lush beauty of both the landscape and the local women was so overwhelming that he had had a wet dream every night of his stay with him.

The insecure side of Virginia was underscored for Brenan when she confessed to him how incomplete she felt next to Vanessa's fecundity. In a letter to her sister, Virginia, in an attempt to dramatize her love for the beauty of Spain, teasingly advised her to bring up her children Catholic: 'I think it induces to warmth of heart.'[10] Virginia's fragility can be seen in the same letter when she imagines that Vanessa and Duncan, who were staying at Monks

House, would comment on how stuffy the interior décor was. She had also become painfully aware how elderly everyone in Bloomsbury was becoming, even though they were looked up to. Had success been purchased at too high a price?

Such melancholic reflections were thankfully transitory. From Yegen, Brenan accompanied the Woolfs to Almeria, Murcia and Alicante, where they parted. Leonard and Virginia then proceeded to Valencia, Perpignan, Montauban and thence back to Paris. If Virginia saw Spain in a completely different light, the same was true of her rapturous response to France. On the way to Spain, she had been so overwhelmed by the Riviera that she wanted to purchase a seascape by Matisse, a painting which obviously captured jollity, sunshine and colour in a beautiful harmonious whole.

'I look forward to Paris with the excitement of a girl of 16,'[11] Virginia informed Roger, but as they approached the city of lights she was uncertain of her feelings about a place so much associated with glamorous femininity. She became decidedly uncomfortable: 'the train is crowded with these exquisite French ladies – all unapproachable, elegant and composed, while I feel like a farmyard boy who has lately rolled in the gorse bush'.[12] Leonard, anxious about the *Nation*, returned to London on 24 April, but Virginia stayed on three further days. While in Paris, Virginia wrote two short pieces, visited the Louvre (where she liked only the Poussins) and Notre-Dame, and dropped in on the writer Hope Mirrlees and her elderly companion, the classical scholar Jane Harrison.

Left alone, Virginia missed her dearest Mongoose, away from whom everything seemed pointless and second-rate. Although despondent in a city which was bitterly cold that spring, her recent travels had buoyed her up. In a matter-of-fact way, she told Leonard of a catastrophe, the aftermath of which she had witnessed: 'Just before I came to the Boulevard St Germain a drunk taxi driver drove straight onto the pavement into a tree and knocked five people down and bent the tree right over. But I was too late to see it.'[13] Just maybe, she was beginning to evade the horrible accidentalness of life.

*

When Virginia resumed work on *Mrs Dalloway* in the winter of 1923, she wondered if the influence of Proust would be visible. That spring, after her return from Spain and France, she intended to shelve it and *The Common Reader* in order to make way for 'paying' journalism. A visit in June to Garsington, where the artistry of the hostess was such that the sky was done up in pale-yellow silk and the cabbages were scented, made her resolve to capture the slippery soul in fiction of people such as Ottoline and later that month, while setting type for *The Waste Land*, she was working on Septimus Smith, the character who was to be the foil for Clarissa Dalloway. The following month, she wrote *Freshwater*, her comic play devoted to Julia Margaret Cameron. If only, she wished, she could write her novel as freely as she had galloped along with her farcical depiction of her aunt.

Despite herself, Virginia gave a great deal of time and thought to both *The Common Reader* and *Mrs Dalloway*. That August, she wondered about the possibility of using a conversational frame to unify the seemingly disparate essays in *The Common Reader*. Two weeks later, she had discovered a new fictional technique which would allow her to explore the psyches of her characters in her new novel. She would dig out 'caves' behind them: 'The idea is that the caves shall connect, & each comes to daylight at the present moment.'[14] Very much aware that she was on the verge of an important breakthrough in her work, thoughts of the sea, of St Ives and of the poetry of existence were 'fiercely close'[15] to Virginia. In the midst of this important breakthrough, she was easily shaken. One day, for example, she was badly frightened when she came upon two coffins in an Underground luggage office.

She was certainly hard on herself. Did she write from deep feelings or merely use words as some sort of elaborate fabrication? Did she really have the gift to write fiction? She did not know the answers to these vexing questions, but she felt, now that her new novel was well under way, her 'force flow[ing] straight . . . at its fullest'.[16] Nevertheless, she was fearful that she had too many ideas for her new book, which was to be about life and death, sanity and insanity and the social system.

Not surprisingly, in the midst of this painful struggle, Virginia compared her strengths and weaknesses to Katherine Mansfield's.

> My theory is that while she possessed the most amazing *senses* of her generation so that she could actually reproduce this room for instance, with its fly, clock, dog, tortoise if need be, to the life, she was as weak as water, as insipid, and a great deal more commonplace, when she had to use her mind. That is, she can't put thoughts, or feelings, or subtleties of any kind into her characters, without at once becoming, where she's serious, hard, and where she's sympathetic, sentimental.[17]

Katherine Mansfield had not had the necessary qualities of mind, in comparison to herself, to become a great writer. However, Virginia was worried, as she often was, that her work lacked fidelity to the texture of life. She became aware that using her mother's inheritance – the 'piece of jewellery' – might allow her to redress the balance. In a new way, she sought to merge the career of writing – her father's profession – with her awareness of her mother's femininity.

Virginia's heightened sense of what she called the 'party consciousness'[18] – the desire to commemorate publicly family, friendship and joy in life – became part of the fabric of *Mrs Dalloway*. It also led to increased dissatisfaction with Richmond as a place to live. She simply felt cut off from the vigour of London. During her stay in Spain, she had compared her staid Richmond neighbourhood with the vitality of Yegen, and her desire to leave the suburbs was heightened by the wanderlust brought on by travel. In the autumn of 1923, she had been deeply anxious when Leonard had not arrived on the London train. For a variety of reasons, she was determined – despite Leonard's objections – to be rid of Richmond. She yearned for the excitement of a sprawling, energy-filled city. The new vitality which filled Virginia was fuelled in part by her friendships with Vita Sackville-West and Jacques Raverat.

Two months after meeting Vita, Virginia remained suspicious but intrigued about this aristocrat who, she had heard, was a 'pronounced Sapphist' and who, she was also told, wanted to seduce her. Although Virginia felt the ravages of time, she was more than a little flattered that Vita found her beautiful: 'Snob as I am, I trace her passions 500 years back, & they become romantic to me.'[19] However, Virginia also felt that Vita was stupid, a quality of mind which she could never attach to the name of Katherine Mansfield. Nevertheless, Vita did have, she informed Clive in January 1924, the body and brain of a Greek god. Virginia does not specify the sex of the god, but it was undoubtedly a he-god of the civilization she adored. For Virginia, Vita's androgynous state was the starting point of obsession.

Vita (christened Victoria), ten years younger than Virginia, was born at Knole near Sevenoaks, Kent, on 9 March 1892, the only child of Lionel Sackville-West (later 3rd Baron Sackville-West) and his wife, also his cousin, Victoria Sackville. In 1913, Vita, who, like Virginia, was educated at home, married Harold Nicolson. They lived for a short time in Constantinople, where he was Third Secretary at the Embassy. On their return to England, they settled at Long Barn, a short distance from Knole. The couple had two sons, Benedict (b. 1914) and Nigel (b. 1917). From 1918 to 1921, Vita was engaged in a tempestuous on-again off-again love affair with Violet Trefusis. Harold Nicolson, who had strong homosexual drives, was largely understanding of his wife's pursuit of women, although he and Denys Trefusis pursued their wayward spouses when they tried to elope together to France in 1920. Virginia provided her own slightly far-fetched and facetious account of this episode: Vita and Violet 'contracted such a passion [for each other] that they fled to the Tyrol, or some mountainous retreat together, to be followed in an aeroplane by a brace of husbands'.[20]

During her affair with Violet, Vita on occasion masqueraded as a young man by the name of Julian. She delighted in the ruse, particularly when her disguise fooled policemen. She also took great pleasure when, on the streets of Monte Carlo, some parents eyed Julian as a suitable prospect for their daughter: 'I never appreciated anything so much as living like that with my tongue perpetually in my cheek.'[21] Vita's disguise was assisted in part by her dark, swarthy complexion, inherited from her grandmother, Josefa Durán, an internationally famous Spanish dancer better known as Pepita, who lived with but never married Lionel Sackville-West, the 2nd Lord Sackville.

From early childhood, Vita was poignantly aware that she could not inherit Knole, one of the grandest and most imposing of English country houses, because she was a woman. If she had been born male, everything would have been different: the enchanted house and its magnificent gardens would have been hers. There was another, more significant deprivation. According to Vita, her mother loved her as a baby but hated the child she became. Vita did not blame her. On more than one occasion, the sensitive little girl was informed that she was ugly. Vita certainly had no way of competing with the elderly, exceedingly imposing Sir John Murray Scott (6 feet 4 inches tall and weighing over 25 stone), who became her mother's lover in about 1900.

Vita was not an ugly duckling, but she was made to think she was. In the realm of her imagination, she eventually transformed herself into an imposing man who could vie for her mother's love and who, moreover, could reclaim lost territory. But she remained one of the dispossessed: despite her aristocratic birth, her enormous beauty and her imposing presence, she was a stranger within her own body, which had deprived her of the love and the land she craved. When Virginia first met her, Vita had published half a dozen books. Unlike Virginia, she had a conventional imagination, but, within those limits she was a dextrous writer, one perfectly attuned to the reading public.

Her lesbian impulses were also vastly different from Virginia's: Vita wanted to become a male lover who could compete for and win her mother's embraces, whereas Virginia's desire was to be hugged and cared for by a maternal woman. In the first years of their friendship, Virginia found it difficult to discern the motherly side of Vita. At the very same time that she was getting to know Vita, Virginia was rediscovered by an old friend and antagonist, Jacques Raverat, one of the neo-pagans.

Jacques's father, Georges, an intellectual who had made his fortune as head of the Le Havre docks, had been deeply impressed by reading of the spartan, character-building regimen at Bedales school and so sent his son there. Subsequently, Jacques took a degree in mathematics at the Sorbonne and then, a bit haphazardly, continued his studies at Emmanuel College, Cambridge, where he became a close friend of Rupert Brooke. In his early twenties, Jacques suffered an attack of acute hysteria which actually signalled the onset of multiple sclerosis, the diagnosis of which was not made until seven years later. When he seemed to recover from what seemed a mental breakdown, Jacques returned to England in 1909, settling in Chelsea that November. At first, he became an apprentice at the Ashendene Press and a student at the Central School of Art. Soon afterwards, he transferred to the Slade, where he came into daily contact with his future wife, Gwen Darwin.

Like Rupert Brooke, Jacques was a curious mixture. Upon his return to England, he became convinced that he had for far too long lived an existence of sexual repression. He wanted to eradicate his streak of puritanism, a significant portion of which had been instilled into him at Bedales. He was also deeply anti-Semitic, holding the view, for instance, that Jews were ruthless, plundering nomads. Jacques was, above all, a disciple of Hilaire Belloc and G. K. Chesterton: he promoted 'Distributism', a neo-medieval return to the idea of a Merrie Old England, where every man's home was indeed his castle. Jacques, strongly influenced by neo-paganism, returned in 1910 to France, where he became an active participant at Pontigny, the Cistercian abbey which became a stronghold for a European culture opposed to Americans, utilitarians, materialists and, of course, Jews.

The object of Jacques's sexual attention in 1910 was Ka Cox, who was in love with Rupert Brooke. Ka suggested that Jacques approach Gwen Darwin, to whom he became engaged early in 1911. However, the once-repressed Jacques wanted to marry Gwen and keep Ka as a mistress, a proposal which, as we have seen, shocked Virginia, who had ruminated on this state of affairs to Vanessa. However, Virginia had concealed from her sister some of her real feelings about Jacques, in particular how moved she was by his sexual ardour while at the very same time being repulsed by many of his beliefs. She certainly saw the love affair of Jacques and Gwen as the embodiment of passion between a man and a woman, although she had not been sure she herself wanted to participate in such activities. 'Perhaps,' Virginia told Gwen in 1925, 'I was frightfully jealous of you both, [having been fourteen years before] at war with the whole world.'[22]

After their marriage, the Raverats were united in their new-found religiosity, political conservatism, anti-Semitism and their scorn for feminisim. They were distressed to hear that Virginia had taken up with and married a Jew. By 1914, Jacques's previously mysterious symptoms were diagnosed. Two years later, he could barely walk. He also had to cope with the fact that his father, through a series of unwise investments, had lost most of the family fortune. Another blow to Jacques was his lack of success as an artist, whereas Gwen's woodcuts were in demand. In 1920, the Raverats and their two daughters settled in Vence in the Midi.

When he wrote to Virginia in the summer of 1922 to tell her how much he admired *Monday or Tuesday*, Jacques was a very different man from the person Virginia had loved and hated ten years earlier. 'What matters,' he was now convinced, 'is [a person's] reactions, sensations, actions, passions and pleasures. That's the sort of things that seem real to me.' He elaborated on what he now considered a misspent neo-pagan youth: 'Well, I can easily believe that I must have been, shall we say, a very difficult young man. Very proud and obstinate and umbrageous. But what you call condescension and flippancy was very often only a mask to hide extreme diffidence and fear of seeming ridiculous to you. You never realized, my dear Virginia, how much I admired you.' Jacques's painterly eye had instantly seen what Virginia was trying to accomplish in *Monday or Tuesday* and she was touched by the misfortunes of a man who told her very plainly: 'I have not the advantages of either death or life; not of life, because I have lost almost every pleasure in the world. Not of death because I am still damnably capable of feeling pain.'[23]

In the next three years, Virginia's letters to Jacques were among the most intimate she ever wrote: 'I believe,' she declared, 'I told him more than anyone, except Leonard.'[24] As he neared death, Jacques became poignantly aware of the mystical underpinning of life. Virginia shared this propensity. His horrible physical affliction had made him an outsider, giving this once phallically aggressive man the capacity to empathize with Virginia's feminine point of view. There was little likelihood that Jacques and Virginia would ever again spend much – or any – time in each other's company, thus their intimacy would not have the barrier of daily contact. Most importantly, in their letters to each other, Virginia and Jacques delved into their past and, in a sense, reinvented it. Old barriers were removed and in the process a new clarity emerged. They did not have to be bound by what had occurred if they came to a new understanding of their younger selves. For Virginia reinterpretation of personal and literary history remained *the* central task.

As 1923 drew to a close, Virginia became deeply aware of the burdens of her past when she reflected on Adrian's recent, severe depression, accentuated by the process of psychoanalysis. Virginia remembered that an old family friend had once observed that the *Dictionary of National Biography* had crushed Adrian's life before he was born. She knew that she too had been a victim of an obsessive father who had single-mindedly dedicated himself to that monument to himself: 'It gave me a twist of the head too. I shouldn't have been so clever, but I should have been more stable.'[25]

Stability was a prized commodity for Virginia, but there was always the possibility of having too much of a good thing and thus becoming stale. She saw many of her contemporaries getting stodgy. For her, real youthfulness essentially consisted of forging ahead, making things happen. And perforce moving house made things happen. She was determined to leave Richmond. By

3 November 1923, she had decided on 35 Woburn Square, but that house did not work out. In addition, Leonard was not enthusiastic about leaving Richmond, fearing that Virginia's mental health would be adversely affected by 'the mental fatigue produced by society'. He finally gave way that autumn, when he had 'to count the cost both of Virginia's growing feeling of being cabined and confined and, as our engagements in London increased, the increasing strain and fatigue of catching crowded trains or buses in order to keep them'.[26]

By January 1924, excited at the prospect of abandoning Richmond, Virginia devised an entirely new recipe for their lives. In this new order, Nelly and Lottie were to be dismissed and their domestic establishment would be entirely controlled by 'one woman, a vacuum cleaner, & electric stoves'.[27] Virginia acted quickly and decisively, when, less than a week later, on Monday, 7 January, her knack of finding houses worked once again. A secretary at her estate agent asked if she was still looking for a house. 'That's what I'm here for,' Virginia assured her. 'But I'd begun to think I'd better take a flat.' 'Oh well,' the young lady replied, '52 Tavistock Square might suit you. It has a large studio.'[28]

One of the estate agents gave Virginia inaccurate directions, she briefly lost her way and chanced upon Adrian, who accompanied her to 52 Tavistock Square, part of an early nineteenth-century terrace with four floors and a basement. It was surrounded by the customary iron railings but, unlike Gordon Square, its brickwork was unrendered. Brother and sister entered through the great green-baize doors of Dollman and Pritchard, Solicitors, who occupied the first and ground floors. They went up the stairs to look at the flat, cloaked in semi-darkness; then they scooted down to the basement, where Virginia rapidly lost count of the rooms; finally, they came upon a billiard room built under the garden and lit by a skylight. The eerie underwater look of that room convinced Virginia that she had indeed found her new home. Two days later, the Woolfs purchased a ten-year lease from the owners, the Duke of Bedford Estates. Dollman and Pritchard retained their space, the

Woolfs lived on the second and third floors, and the Hogarth Press was assigned to the basement.

Situated on the south side of the square, number 52 looked out upon not only the large garden in the centre but also St Pancras church and the Imperial Hotel in Russell Square. Gordon Square, the centre of the lives of so many of her friends, was only a few hundred yards to the west: Clive had a flat in Adrian's house at number 50; Vanessa rented number 37, which she shared with Duncan. For some years, Virginia had wanted to visit but live apart from her friends; her new party consciousness – a keen fascination with festive events – dismissed such caution and she apostrophized the city to which she would soon be returning: 'London thou art a jewel of jewels, & jasper of jocunditie – music, talk, friendship, city views, books, publishing, something central & inexplicable.'[29]

However, her new-found boldness also frightened Virginia, since she realized how much had been accomplished at Richmond. After all, her 'strange offspring,'[30] the Hogarth Press, had been born there. She was also acutely conscious that she had left London in August 1913 in circumstances which had almost led to the end of her life. Now she was brought face to face with the fact that she had first lived in Bloomsbury after her severe breakdown following her father's death: 'I feel as if I were going on with a story which I began in the year 1904.'[31] Would she be strong enough to survive this new development in the plot line of her life?

A month later, Virginia, in the midst of harnessing 'all the resources of civilization'[32] – telephone, gas, electricity – was determined to force Leonard into what he would consider the outrageous extravagance of spending £25 on interior decorations by Vanessa and Duncan. For the dining room, Vanessa designed a painted table and the accompanying pink, black and cream china. This room had a lighter look than the drawing-room with its vast panels of moonrises and bouquets, as one visitor, Stephen Spender, recalled:

Their drawing room was large, tall, pleasant, square-shaped,

> with rather large and simple furniture, giving . . . an impression of greys and greens. Painted panels by Duncan Grant and Vanessa Bell represented mandolins, fruit, and perhaps a view of the Mediterranean through an open window or a curtain drawn aside. These were painted thickly and opaquely in browns and terracottas, reds and pale blue, with a hatch work effect in the foreground with shadows of the folds of a curtain.[33]

Another visitor, May Sarton, thought the upstairs drawing room had so many bright patterns in it that it was like being inside a kaleidoscope: 'flowered prints on the chairs, a wall of French books in many-colored paper covers, and two hassocks by the fire'.[34]

Virginia's intellectual domain was the billiard room, which became a combination storage room for the Hogarth Press and her writing space. She did not mind that this area of the house was cold, draughty and incredibly ramshackle. Often the room would be piled high with dusty packets of books and old files, but Virginia's decoration – cheap matting, a rug, a table, a bed, a bookcase, an old armchair, some artificial flowers and some pictures provided by Vanessa – made the room undeniably hers.

The front room in the basement – once the kitchen – was the main administrative office of the Press. Here the secretaries had their desks. Behind them was a small, windowless room; piles of current titles were kept there. Down the corridor on the right was the scullery, where the treadle machine and stacks of type were stored. There was also a lavatory, in which old galley proofs served as toilet paper.

The Woolfs moved on 15 March. From the first, Virginia remained enthusiastic. Central London had a stony-hearted, callous side, but it was teeming with life and everything – especially shops and theatres – was so close. Even the moon was different, Virginia claimed. On her first night there she looked at it through the skylight in the billiard room: 'with drifting clouds, & it was a terrifying & new London moon; dreadful & exciting; as if the Richmond moon had been veiled'.[35] In contrast to his wife,

Leonard was downcast. He complained that he did not get a stroke of work done during the three weeks after leaving Richmond.

Virginia's London past caught up with her that April when Angelica and her nurse, Louie Dunnet, were knocked down by a car and rushed to the Middlesex Hospital in Mortimer Street. Virginia accompanied Vanessa and Duncan in the cab that took them to the hospital, where Louie's foot was bandaged but a very still Angelica lay behind a screen, her face turned away from them. Only when the child moved did her parents know that she was alive. A young doctor informed them that Angelica's case was hopeless: her stomach had been run over: there would have to be an operation as soon as the surgeon arrived. Virginia was sent off to fetch Clive and thus did not have to endure the long wait in the busy ward.

> What I felt was, not sorrow or pity for Angelica, but that now Nessa would be an old woman; & this would be an indelible mark; & that death & tragedy had once more put down his paw, after letting us run a few paces. People never get over their early impressions of death I think. I always feel pursued.[36]

Luckily, the young doctor was wrong: there was nothing wrong with Angelica. This time, fate had played only a cruel, harmless joke, but the accident must have reminded Virginia of how terrified she had been as a child of the very same London streets. But the sheer joy of having moved there, together with the excitement generated by the new paths she was taking in her writing career, was bracing. She had stepped on to 'a tawny coloured magic carpet'.[37]

Quite soon, Virginia settled into a comfortable routine: she would write for three hours in the morning and then, after lunch, would attend to Hogarth Press matters. She would, for instance, assist golden-haired George 'Dadie' Rylands in setting type; after taking his degree at Cambridge, he had joined the Press in July 1924. Often Virginia would be clad in some sort of housecoat. This young man made frequent appearances at the dinner tables of London's most celebrated hostesses and she would always ask him about these remarkable women. What did they wear? What kind of jewellery? What kind of make-up? What did they talk about? What was the latest gossip? Virginia could not get enough of such information. One celebrated partygoer who fascinated Virginia was the glamorous actress Diana Cooper. However, in a letter of 22 November 1924 to the overweight Molly MacCarthy, she told her friend not to compare herself to 'pert misses' of the Diana Cooper variety, who 'have shaved themselves to resemble nothing so much as tubes of piping'.[38]

Sometimes, Virginia herself was to be seen at parties. When she dined at Ethel Sands's in January 1924, her fellow guests included Roger Fry, Logan Pearsall Smith and Prince and Princess Bibesco, but the real treat was encountering one of her chief literary foes, Arnold Bennett. In person, he was a 'lovable sea lion, with chocolate eyes, drooping lids, & a protruding tusk'.[39] Such occasions could be tedious, though, as when she was forced to battle Middleton Murry: these were painful encounters, the two of them 'stuck together,' she recalled, 'like two copulating dogs'.[40] In July 1924, Virginia and Leonard were at Maynard's, where a transvestite ballet (*Don't Be Frightened* or *Pippington Park*) was performed. That evening at 41 Gordon Square was made memorable, however, by Berta Ruck's ruminations.

Two years earlier, Berta Ruck – the pen-name of Sally Onions, the popular novelist – had been killed off by Virginia in *Jacob's Room*. She had transformed Berta into Bertha and placed the name on a tombstone. The lady, very much alive, complained of her unseemly death through her husband's solicitor. Virginia, who had obviously seen the name Berta Ruck at Hatchard's or on an advertisement on a bus, apologized for her unseemly but unconscious murder. And so the two became friends. The party at Maynard's was agog to see the two women novelists embrace. Immediately, Mrs Onions lamented that she did not have the talent of a Virginia Woolf. Virginia, who knew full well that her fellow novelist made a lot of money from her books, asked her secret. This led to a torrent of reflections:

> Would you believe me, Mrs Woolf? I abominate my own books more than I can say? And they only bring me in £400 a piece, and I have to write two every year so long as I and my husband and our boys do live, and it's almost impossible to find another plot . . . since the war we don't make what we used to make; and do believe me, Mrs Woolf, I'm a cultivated woman. I read the classics, I know French; and if only I could write a paragraph – one paragraph – like Mr Lytton Strachey, I'd retire tomorrow.[41]

Virginia thought that there was more than a dash of crocodile tears in all this; she herself would have liked to be a victim of such success.

The unintentional slaying of Berta Ruck betrays Virginia's distrust of popular writers, among whom Vita Sackville-West must be numbered. A distinction can be drawn, however, between Virginia Woolf the writer and Virginia Woolf the publisher. The latter wanted Vita's books, as she made clear in January 1924: 'I was hoping to see you here, partly for your own sake, partly for the sake of the Hogarth Press, which is very anxious to know if there is any serious chance that you will let it have a book.'[42] Eight months later, Virginia was rewarded with the short novel, *Seducers in Ecuador*. And that beautiful book went a long way to change Virginia's mind. As she confessed to Vita, *Seducers* was the kind of book she herself would like to write.

Virginia the publisher could change her mind about Vita the novelist, but Vita the aristocrat remained a source of morbid fascination. Earlier, when Nelly Cecil had spent time with her in Sussex, Virginia had seen Monks House through her friend's eyes and found it shabby and tawdry. The same process repeated itself when Vita visited Rodmell. When Virginia and Vita took lunch with Lord Sackville at Knole in July 1924, Virginia noticed – her reverse snobbery in full operation – that half the house was roped off and that all sense of life had vanished from the place.

If she could, with comparative ease, dismiss Knole, Virginia found it much more difficult to push Vita aside. After the lunch, she told her diary: 'All these ancestors & centuries, & silver & gold, have bred a perfect body. She is stag like, or race horse like, save for the face, which pouts, & has no very sharp brain. But as a body hers is perfection.'[43] She was also fascinated by Vita's lack of inhibition; she had no false reserve. Yet Virginia felt that Vita's mind was indiscriminate and unduly common. The truth was that Vita herself was so contradictory that Virginia could not really make up her mind about her:

> her real claim to consideration is, if I may be so coarse, her legs. Oh they are exquisite – running like slender pillars up into her trunk, which is that of a breastless cuirassier (yet she has 2 children) but all about her is virginal, savage, patrician; and why she writes, which she does with complete competency, and a pen of brass, is a puzzle to me. If I were she, I should merely stride, with 11 Elk hounds, behind me, through my ancestral woods.[44]

Virginia did not yet grasp what Vita meant to her. She simply did not know if her heart was at all engaged.

In contrast to the black, stagnant opening of 1923, 1924 promised to be comparatively unruffled. Virginia was certain that, in *Mrs Dalloway*, she might at long last have uncovered her gold mine as a writer of fiction. The trick was to get all the gold out, that precious metal lying 'so deep, in such bent channels'.[45] By 5 April, she had finished 'the Dr chapter', the one devoted to Bradshaw, the nerve specialist who treats Septimus callously. At the same time, she worked on *The Common Reader*, with no evident policy except to follow her 'whimsical brain'.[46] By May, she had devised a work schedule which allowed her to follow the principle of rotating her crops. She would work on *Mrs Dalloway* throughout September, shift to *The Common Reader* until January, at which point she would spend four months revising the novel.

For the most part, Virginia kept to her plan, although work on *Mrs Dalloway* continued until early October and she returned to

The Common Reader for what seemed like the eightieth time in August. To avoid brooding, she fell back on the wide assortment of tasks awaiting her at the Press. Sometimes, she could not avoid the awful thought that she was only of value because of her writing: 'Were it not for my flash of imagination, & this turn for books, I should be a very ordinary woman. No faculty of mine is really very strong.'[47] Nevertheless, her work on both books reinforced an important insight: life consisted of 'splinters & mosaics; not, as they used to hold, immaculate, monolithic, consistent wholes'.[48] One splinter from the past was a surprise encounter in August 1924 with the brothers Duckworth at the funeral of her cousin Katherine Stephen, Principal of Newnham from 1911 to 1920. With a bit of malice, Virginia told Violet, 'I had the shock of my life last week running in to George and Gerald . . . George can't speak, and totters like an aspen: What has happened? He has no teeth? And he seems already far gone in senile decay of every sort.'[49] In comparison, Gerald seemed spry.

Virginia's persistent low self-esteem was due in part to the Duckworths and she seems to have taken some pleasure in telling Violet of the physical and mental collapse of George. The Duckworths were linked in Virginia's mind to the male-dominated literary establishment, which sought to impose its views on all humankind. This was the sham world of *apparently* consistent wholes. In her mosaic-like diary, she had learned the craft of a new kind of fiction; in it can also be discerned a new view of life: 'in this book I *practise* writing; do my scales; yes & work at certain effects. I daresay I practised Jacob here, – & Mrs D. & shall invent my next book here; for here I write merely in the spirit.'[50] If the form of Virginia's diary became the style of her fiction, the themes of that diary – her daily struggle to encapsulate 'the spirit' – were similarly transformed into the autobiographical content at the heart of her writings, whether novels or literary criticism.

Although Virginia could refer facetiously to her whimsical mind, her defence of writing as essentially non-linear – and to a great degree, whimsical – comes from strongly held convictions that the male point of view had confined verbal expression to a 'formal railway line of sentence'.[51] One of Virginia's most important revolutionary declarations was uttered, as we have seen, in 'Modern Novels'. From 1919 to 1924, she wrote a series of important theoretical pieces – 'Reading' (1919), 'Byron and Mr Briggs' (1922–5), 'On Re-reading Novels' (1922), 'How It Strikes a Contemporary' (1923), 'Mr Bennett and Mrs Brown' (1923), 'Character in Fiction'* (1924) – which supplement that essay.

Mrs Brown is the elusive personality who has evaded all fictional attempts to capture her and Mr Briggs is the common reader. In Virginia's short story 'An Unwritten Novel', the narrator, during a rail journey, studies the countenance and mannerisms of the woman seated opposite her. She gradually reconstructs this person's life, about which she speaks with great poise and conviction. At the conclusion of the trip – when she is proved drastically wrong – the narrator is filled with wonder rather than irritation: 'If I fall on my knees, if I go through the ritual, the ancient antics, it's you, unknown figures, you I adore; if I open my arms, it's you I embrace, you I draw to me – adorable world!'[52]

Arnold Bennett, John Galsworthy and their ilk were certain they knew how to apprehend 'unknown figures'. According to Virginia Woolf, their neo-realistic techniques may capture externals, but the essence of character escapes these essentially materialist writers, who ignore the existence of Dostoevsky and Constance Garnett's translations of him into English. The hunt for Mrs Brown was, according to Virginia, the essential quest for a modern writer.

> With all his powers of observation, which are marvellous, with all his sympathy and humanity, which are great, Mr Bennett has never once looked at Mrs Brown in her corner. [Bennett and writers of his persuasion] have looked very powerfully, search-

* 'Mr Bennett and Mrs Brown' first appeared in the *Nation and Athenaeum* of 1 December 1923; it was rewritten and expanded as a lecture delivered on 18 May 1924. This latter version was published in the *Criterion* in July 1924 as 'Character in Fiction' and, with relatively few changes, by the Hogarth Press as a pamphlet entitled 'Mr Bennett and Mrs Brown' in October 1924.

> ingly, and sympathetically out of the window; at factories, at Utopias, even at the decoration and upholstery of the carriage; but never at her, never at life, never at human nature.[53]
>
> The capture of Mrs Brown is the title of the next chapter in the history of literature; and, let us prophesy again, that chapter will be one of the most important, the most illustrious, the most epoch-making of them all.[54]

To a degree, as we shall see, Virginia is commenting on her own agenda in *Mrs Dalloway*. Of almost equal importance to her, however, was the elusive Mr Briggs, the subject of the other book she was writing.

Mr Briggs, spectacle-maker of Cornhill, is an avid reader in touch with the great literary tradition of England. In her portrayal of him, Virginia Woolf fleshes out Samuel Johnson's notion of the common reader. When such a person reads Byron, his

> mind is trying to make a whole. It is trying to sort out and sharpen its perceptions. It is trying to stop itself from thinking irrelevantly. It is trying to refer its impressions as accurately as possible to the poem itself . . . It is trying to grasp the poet's conceptions entire. According to conditions and to education it is trying to grade this 'shock of emotion' by comparing it with emotions received from other poems.[55]

Although Mr Briggs reads for enjoyment, he tries to read accurately, realizing that such pleasurable activity can improve his intellect. He is distinctly aware of a literary tradition into which he fits what he reads. As such, his pleasure is communal in that it is shared by many others – this is what Johnson and Woolf mean by the word 'common'. Moreover, Mr Briggs is moved by the act of reading; he is on the lookout for 'shocks of emotion' which are delineated in a coherent, ordered form. Neither scholar nor professional man of letters, he is the kind of person who allows great literature to be produced. After all, he is the consumer all authors strive to please since his love of reading matches their love of writing. For novelists such as Arnold Bennett, Mr Briggs is as elusive as Mrs Brown: if Mrs Brown is not captured in works of literature, how can works of literature touch deeply at the reading life of Mr Briggs?

The Common Reader is a series of essays on various aspects of literary history arranged in chronological order. They are, for the most part, vastly different from Virginia's theoretical pieces. In reality, they are examples of applied criticism in which Virginia – as the common reader – responds to, among others, Defoe, Addison, George Eliot, Austen and Conrad. She does not seek to dismiss the literary tradition; she tries to expand it. There might not be a distinctly feminist aesthetic at work, but there is – as in her theoretical writings – an implied one: her whimsical mode of perception, one which attacks prevailing notions of how reality should be depicted, is in full swing and, by implication, seeks to displace prevailing critical notions. Like Tom Eliot in *The Sacred Wood* (1920) – a book she much admired – Virginia wanted to define the living tradition of England's literature, but she wanted that tradition to be reanimated with a genuine feminine sensibility.

By late December 1924, Virginia was putting the finishing touches to both *Mrs Dalloway* and *The Common Reader.* Her optimistic forecast had come true: she and Leonard had moved to London with only one servant, Nelly (Lottie was now working nearby for Karin and Adrian). Not only did Virginia now live in London; she also had the sense of having moved into the inner circle of its society: 'To know everyone worth knowing . . . just imagine,' she told herself, 'being in that position – if women can be.'[56] That was a big 'if', but her self-confidence bounded forward: She wrote more stories about the party consciousness* and she was witnessing the first stirrings of her next novel, *To the Lighthouse.*

One discordant note was struck by Bloomsbury's response to Vita. If Virginia remained puzzled by the glamorous aristocrat, her friends were united in their combined dislike. On 19 December, Vita and Roger dined at Tavistock Square. The critic-painter

* These eight stories, all set at Mrs Dalloway's party, are collected together in *Mrs Dalloway's Party: A Short Story Sequence.*

could usually be counted on to be courtly. However, Vita's breezy patrician manner made Roger's Quaker blood boil. Roger's grumpiness rattled Vita, who started to talk in a rather haphazard but opinionated way about art, which made a tension-filled situation even worse. When Morgan Forster, who had assured Virginia he wanted to meet Vita, was presented with that opportunity in May 1925, he ignored her, preferring instead the company of Edith Sitwell. So Vita sat 'hurt, modest, silent, like a snubbed schoolboy'.[57]

Another friendship was in the process of revision in the mid-1920s. Maynard Keynes may have become a world-famous economist, but for Virginia and Vanessa he remained a close friend of Thoby and an early denizen of Bloomsbury. Virginia always found Maynard a bit frosty, but Vanessa saw herself as his 'Bloomsbury mother'. For several years, Maynard had been involved in a number of fleeting, low-key homosexual affairs. His life was transformed when he became involved with Lydia Lopokova, the Russian-born ballerina. Vanessa was appalled by this alliance. Virginia followed suit, as can be seen in this snippet from a letter of 8 June 1924 in which Lydia is seen as a vamp who is carrying a somewhat reluctant Maynard off to her lair: 'Maynard is passionately and pathetically in love, because he sees very well that he's dished if he marries her, and she has him by the snout . . . Lydia's pranks put us all on edge.'[58] Lydia was resplendently glamorous, a woman who cultivated her own femininity – and the limelight. As such, Virginia was understandably suspicious and envious. Like Virginia, Lydia sometimes affected a somewhat dishevelled, scatterbrained demeanour, but she was very much a hard-nosed, dedicated professional. In time, Virginia came to see Lydia as a person of *natural* grace and beauty, as someone filled with 'glorified instinct'. She never completely trusted Lydia, but she did see both sides of her.*

* Rezia, Septimus Smith's wife in *Mrs Dalloway*, is based in part on Lydia, who on 16 May 1924 told Maynard that she had just completed reading that book: 'it is very rapid, interesting, and yet I feel in that book all the human beings only puppets. Virginia's brain is so quick that sometimes her pen

At the time of their marriage, the Keyneses purchased a life interest in Tilton, a plain early-nineteenth-century farmhouse – which they soon modernized – only a few hundred yards along a track from Charleston. The economist, who housed his splendid collection of paintings at this country residence, eventually became an enthusiastic fruit and vegetable gardener and a breeder of pigs. Leonard, Virginia, the Bells and Duncan Grant visited Tilton regularly, as did friends of Lydia such as Vivien Leigh and the dancer Robert Helpmann. Maynard was a person whom others envied. Virginia was certainly bothered by his possessions. For example, he had a Degas in the lavatory at Tilton and a Cézanne in his bedroom.

In contrast to Vita, Maynard and Lydia was Lytton, whose nature was an 'exquisite symphony'[59] when all his 'violins get playing'. However, when she visited France in March 1925, Virginia did not like the various 'Bugger-Bloomsbury'[60] young men, friends of Lytton, she encountered at Cassis. She did not allow them to spoil her holiday. In general, she felt more resilient. When a bit later, in Paris, she witnessed an accident in which a woman was pinned against the railings with a car on top of her, Virginia could, with comparative ease, no 'longer feel inclined to doff the cap to death'.[61]

Virginia could turn away from death with such considerable aplomb because her whole existence had been infused with a new sense of purpose and energy, both of which are readily visible in *Mrs Dalloway* and *The Common Reader*. Her first book of criticism was an attempt to redefine – and stake her own claim on – a domain in which her father had found his niche. She was following in his footsteps, but she was also trying to alter substantially the critical tradition he had helped to form. That enterprise was joined to an even more important and personal one: an attempt, in her

---

cannot catch it, or it is I who is slow. However I shall pursue the book to the end in a short time, and be established in the criticism' (*Lydia and Maynard: Letters between Lydia Lopokova and John Maynard Keynes*, edited by Polly Hill and Richard Keynes. London: Papermac, 1992, 323).

fourth novel, to understand her inheritance from her mother, the mysterious 'piece of jewellery'.

Despite the incredible vigour which filled Virginia at the outset of the project, the writing of *Mrs Dalloway* was arduous. The major stumbling block was the character of Clarissa, who appeared to her creator a 'tinsely'[62] figure. At times, Virginia had to stick herself with a sharp spur to make herself jump. In October 1924 she was relieved to be 'quit of [the book], for it has been a strain the last weeks'. Yet, she was certain that she had, with considerable trepidation, won this particular battle: she had less of the 'usual feeling that I've shaved through, & just kept my feet on the tight rope'.[63]

Clarissa Dalloway is the second great Clarissa in the history of the English novel. Richardson's Clarissa Harlowe, fearful of and yet deeply attracted to Lovelace, ultimately chooses chastity and death. This was a side of Virginia Woolf, but in *Mrs Dalloway*, although the heroine, a married woman with a grown daughter, is sexually frigid and fascinated by death, she decides to hold a party, which brings together a group of people. In her, Virginia Woolf combines portions of her own character with that of her mother. She had become more and more convinced that her talents as a writer came in large part from the French side of her maternal ancestry. Thus the character of Clarissa explores a possible meeting ground: she is an inventive, creative hostess who shows an artist's sensibility. Like Julia, Clarissa may be wife and mother, but, like Virginia, she is sexually dormant. That paradox is central to the book.

In March 1923, Lytton Strachey, looking at a photograph of Julia, remarked that he did not like her character. According to him she had a complaining mouth. At that moment, a 'shaft of white light' fell across Virginia's 'dusky rich red'[64] past, as if her friend had positioned his critical finger precisely at the spot where Virginia knew her mother was culpable. Virginia was herself vulnerable to enchanter figures, those mysterious people who 'never quite come out of the wood, and carry on such intrigues in the gloom [so as to be] always the pursued and desired'.[65] For Virginia, her mother continued to exert a considerable influence and the daughter wanted to examine the mother in the light of day. Virginia may have been digging out caves behind her characters, but she was also trying to construct a tunnel which would link her to her mother.

Like Joyce's *Ulysses*, the action of *Mrs Dalloway* takes place on a single day. On this particular June day, Clarissa Dalloway, the wife of Richard Dalloway, MP, sets off to buy flowers for a party to take place that evening. She has important encounters with Peter Walsh, an old suitor whom she rejected; her husband, Richard; her daughter, Elizabeth, and her spinster tutor, the appropriately named Miss Kilman; the political hostess, Lady Bruton; and an old childhood friend, Sally Seton. However, the shell-shocked Septimus Warren Smith, who hears the sparrows sing in Greek in Regent's Park and who, at the end of the day, commits suicide by hurling himself out of a window, is the real foil to Clarissa in this novel. The two never meet, but the abrasive Harley Street nerve specialist Sir William Bradshaw, who treats Septimus cold-heartedly, tells Clarissa, in the midst of her party, of Septimus's death.

If Julia and Virginia are merged in the character of Clarissa, two portions of Virginia's personality are analysed in the twin characterizations of Clarissa and Septimus. In one of her notebooks, Virginia made this distinction:

> Suppose it to be connected in this way:
> Sanity & insanity.
> Mrs D. seeing the truth. S. S. seeing the insane truth . . .
> The pace is to be given by the gradual increase of S's insanity on the one side; by the
> approach of the party on the other . . .[66]

Clarissa represents the side of Virginia Woolf which, despite impulses to the contrary, chooses life over death; Septimus is a dramatization of Virginia Woolf's sense of despair when she experienced a psychotic breakdown.* Clarissa's party is an offering to life, whereas Septimus offers his death in the service of humanity.

* In her introduction to the Modern Library edition of *Mrs Dalloway*, Virginia wrote that 'in the first version Septimus, who later is intended to be

Septimus is the living dead, whereas Clarissa is not certain that life is worth living.

Virginia deeply feared intrusion and invasion, but she bravely tried to conquer those fears: her embracing of London in 1923 demonstrates how much she wanted to choose life. However, she lived in fear of another possible breakdown; in such a state, death seemed her only choice. There are many other autobiographical strands in the narrative. Superficially, Clarissa bears a more than passing resemblance to Kitty Maxse, the society hostess who, Virginia felt, might have committed suicide. Virginia's sexless marriage may be the source for the similar relationship between the Dalloways.* The manipulative Lady Bruton is based on Sybil Colefax. Virginia's childhood crush on Madge Vaughan is reanimated in Clarissa's obsession with Sally Seton, but Virginia's fear of lesbian love is captured in her chilling depiction of the religious fanatic Doris Kilman. Virginia's own malleable early womanhood is portrayed in Elizabeth, Clarissa's daughter. The author's fear of sexually aggressive men is seen in Peter Walsh, who, in an extremely exhibitionistic way, continually opens and closes his penknife. Details of Virginia's own experience of mental breakdown are drawn upon to re-create Septimus's precarious mental state and the harsh characterization of Septimus's two doctors – Dr Holmes is stupid, whereas Sir William is indifferent to his patients' needs – is a composite portrayal of all the medical men who had treated the author. There may be another link between Virginia and Septimus: victims of shell-shock were frequently – very much like female patients – subjected to bad treatment from so-called experts in mental health.

The working title of Virginia's fourth novel had been *The*

---

her [Mrs Dalloway's] double had no existence; and . . . Mrs Dalloway was originally to kill herself, or perhaps merely to die at the end of the party' (vi).

* The personalities of Clarissa and Richard Dalloway from *The Voyage Out* have little or nothing in common with the same characters in *Mrs Dalloway*.

Hours. This gave way gradually to *Mrs Dalloway*, which displays a shift in emphasis from technique to character. However, it is a curious title, one which ties the central character to the world of men. Perhaps this was intentional, making the telling point that society often sees women only in relation to men. As the early notebook draft of *Mrs Dalloway* at the Berg Collection in New York makes clear, Virginia, in an elaborate comparison of Clarissa and the prime minister, had originally intended her criticism of the social order to be much more extensive. This plan was considerably modified, although the published book contains sharp barbs against the medical and political establishments. Septimus is the victim of poor medical treatment and he is also the dupe of the war machine: unlike Jacob Flanders, he has survived the war but, like many of his generation, his life has been irrevocably and tragically altered by that conflict.

The origins of Clarissa's tragic existence are obliquely hinted at, but from the outset she is associated with 'a virginity preserved through childbirth which clung to her like a sheet.'[67] Clarissa feels that she lacks an essential something in her character: 'She could see what she lacked. It was not beauty; it was not mind. It was something central which permeated; something warm which broke up surfaces and rippled the cold contact of man and woman, or of women together.'[68] The contact of women, however, is something that she can dimly perceive: 'she could not resist sometimes yielding to the charm of a woman . . . she did undoubtedly then feel what men felt. Only for a moment; but it was enough.'[69] Indeed, the most exquisite moment in Clarissa's life was when, as a young woman, she had been kissed on the lips by Sally Seton: 'The whole world might have turned upside down! The others disappeared; there she was alone with Sally.'[70] This is the emotional history of Virginia Stephen masking itself as the fiction of Clarissa Dalloway.

However, although the novel tends to avoid any discussion of the aetiology of Clarissa's inner life, she fights coldness and isolation by holding a party, which is celebratory and communal. If Virginia chose not to discuss the origins of her or Clarissa's sense of being emotionally chill, she dealt indirectly with that issue by having Clarissa embrace Julia Stephen's 'party consciousness'. The most dramatic and fully realized re-enactment of the blended sensibilities of Virginia and Julia takes place when, after hearing from the Bradshaws about Septimus's demise, Clarissa retires from the party and, in bold, fierce language, imagines his death: 'Up had flashed the ground; through him, blundering, bruising, went the rusty spikes. There he lay with a thud, thud, thud in his brain, and then a suffocation of blackness. So she saw it.'[71] Here, Clarissa as society hostess and Clarissa as artist merge.

Septimus's death was also, Clarissa realizes, a defiance. She is aware of the possibility of making such a choice, sees it as no disgrace, although she has held back from that solution. She looks out of the window and sees her neighbour, the old lady, preparing to go to bed alone.

> The clock began striking. The young man had killed himself; but she did not pity him; with the clock striking the hour, one, two, three, she did not pity him, with all this going on. There! the old lady had put out her light! the whole house was dark now with this going on, she repeated, and the words came to her, Fear no more the heat of the sun. She must go back to them. But what an extraordinary night! She felt somehow very like him – the young man who had killed himself. She felt glad that he had done it; thrown it away while they went on living. The clock was striking. The leaden circles dissolved in the air. But she must go back.[72]

In *Mrs Dalloway*, a very fine line is drawn between sanity and insanity, life and death. The old lady is isolated but faces her existence stoically; presumably, she will die in the near future at a time determined by her body. Like Clarissa, the old lady is aware of the persuasive force of death, but she chooses life. And this is precisely what Clarissa does at the conclusion of the novel, when she rejoins the party: 'For there she was.'[73]

As a tribute from the living to the dying, in February Virginia sent proofs of *Mrs Dalloway* to Jacques Raverat, who responded with glowing praise: 'Almost it's enough to make me want to live a little longer, to continue to receive such letters and such books.'[74] The other reader of the proofs was Leonard, who told her *Mrs Dalloway* was her best book. He maintained that it had more continuity than *Jacob's Room* but was a difficult read because of the apparent lack of connection, at times, between Clarissa and Septimus. Leonard must have realized that his wife's success this time round might have come in part because she had taken his advice to concentrate on one or two characters.

When Jacques died that March, Virginia told Gwen that since she had not seen him for so many years, she had no trouble keeping him alive. She also told the widow that she liked the uncompromising reality and lack of sentimentality of her husband. Of course, Virginia had incorporated those very qualities into the twin stories of Clarissa and Septimus. As she awaited the publication of *The Common Reader* on 23 April and *Mrs Dalloway* on 14 May, she was only a shade nervous about the novel. Why was this so? she asked herself: 'Really I am a little bored, for the first time, at thinking how much I shall have to talk about it this summer. The truth is that writing is the profound pleasure & being read the superficial.'[75]

Virginia felt fully alive when writing fiction and she is seizing upon this crucial fact. She also observed: 'My love of clothes interests me profoundly; only it is not love; & what it is I must discover.'[76] She certainly saw a link between 'frock consciousness'[77] and party consciousness. Of course, in *Mrs Dalloway*, Virginia had re-established some crucial links with her long-dead mother, links which would be examined even more fully in *To the Lighthouse*, the book upon which she was eager to embark.

If she was only a bit nervous, a thin-skinned Virginia nevertheless had the ability to distort words of commendation. She claimed that the 7 May review of *The Common Reader* in the *Times Literary Supplement* contained 'sober & sensible'[78] praise, one distinctly lacking in fervour. On the contrary, the review is enthusiastic:

A lively zest for human beings runs through these volumes . . . It was not Mrs Woolf's ambition to evoke principles, and it can hardly be said that she does, although she lets fall sentences which illuminate a great deal. But we find a standard which we never distrust, and this is possibly something rarer. It has the breadth which only a real possession of the past can give, and the vitality of a fresh imaginativeness.

Before that review appeared, Goldie Dickinson and John Hayward bestowed unqualified praise on the author. Virginia's grumbling about the *TLS* piece was only diminished when she read Hugh I'Anson Fausset's notice in the *Manchester Guardian*: 'Certainly we have seldom read a volume of essays which, by their sufficiency and freshness, insight and accomplishment, so captivate and satisfy the mind.'[79]

In comparison to *The Common Reader, Mrs Dalloway* had a decidedly rough critical ride. The anonymous reviewer in the *Times Literary Supplement* was cavilling but praised the author's imagination, one steeped in an 'emotion and irony . . . which enhance the consciousness and the zest of the living'.[80] P. C. Kennedy in the *New Statesman* took little care to hide his disdain for an author, he suggested, who, despite her claim of originality, was decidedly old-fashioned: 'Mrs Woolf has really imposed on several quite different stories a purely artificial unity . . . she never makes me feel that the person credited with [an emotion] is other than an object of the keenest and most skilful study.'[81] The *Western Mail* and the *Scotsman* condemned the book, whereas in his favourable notice in the New York *Saturday Review of Literature* Richard Hughes declared the prose style Cézannesque.

If Virginia found the reviewers divided on the merits of *Mrs Dalloway*, she discovered the same was true of her friends. Vita told her that she much preferred her book of criticism to her 'will-of-the-wisp'[82] of a novel. Lytton Strachey disliked *Mrs Dalloway*: he claimed that there was a discrepancy between the ornament (the beautiful prose style) and the events, which he considered humdrum. He also pointed a finger at what Virginia herself had called the 'tinsely' aspects of Clarissa's character. Roger Fry and Morgan Forster were sympathetic. In the midst of such conflicting opinions, Virginia was deeply touched by a letter from a young man in Earls Court: 'This time you have done it – you have caught life & put it in a book.'[83]

A strong, overriding sense of purpose now filled Virginia, who liked Lytton all the better for being so open about his dislike of the book. It was as if Virginia had told the truth so well in *Mrs Dalloway* that she had nothing to fear from negative reactions to it. In the midst of the myriad of responses to both her new books, Virginia encountered on a bus a mother, her seven-year-old daughter and three-year-old son. The girl asked her mother how many inches there were in a mile. The mother turned to Virginia, who told the girl that she must go to school and find out for herself. The mother assured Virginia that her daughter did attend school: 'So I gave them two biscuits left over, & the little girl (see my egotism) with her bright excitable eyes, & eagerness to grasp the whole universe reminded me of myself, asking questions of my mother.'[84] Virginia had been inclined to be a bit standoffish with the girl – to act like her own mother would have – but then her heart warmed to the child and in that moment she caught a glimpse of her younger self, the person who had so much wanted – despite so many obstacles – to love and be loved by her mother. In part, *Mrs Dalloway* was, for its author, about the possibility of turning the clock back, of finding renewal and nourishment in the embers of the past.

Chapter Thirteen

WHITE FIRE

(1925–7)

As she was putting the finishing touches to *Mrs Dalloway* in October 1924, Virginia caught an unexpected, imaginary glimpse of a person she called 'the Old Man'.[1] This was the moment of inspiration which led to *To the Lighthouse*. By July 1925, that sighting of her father had metamorphosed into a plan for a book to be divided into three parts, each with a specific focus: One, 'The Window', the view from the drawing room of the summer home occupied by a family called Ramsay; Two, 'Time Passes', in which seven years go by; and Three, 'The Lighthouse', the voyage (postponed from Part One) to the lighthouse. In writing a book based upon her childhood memories of St Ives (although the narrative is ostensibly set in the Hebrides), Virginia was anxious to avoid sentimentality, but she obviously intended to write a book which would deal openly with her positive as well as negative feelings about her parents.

The tunnelling process used in *Mrs Dalloway* was to be displaced by a new technique: she would tell in a relatively straightforward fashion the story of her childhood but would enrich it by giving it 'branches & roots', which, she confided to her diary, she did not yet perceive. Yet again, she had to surrender to the mystery of a new adventure. The advantage was clear: 'A new problem like that breaks fresh ground in one's mind; prevents the regular ruts.'[2]

Her new book, she realized, might even be more of an elegy than a novel – it would be a direct confrontation with the past. She was anxious about such a step and the urge to experiment in fiction by writing about her childhood was accompanied by an acute anxiety which manifested itself in a concern about her appearance. In the aftermath of Gerald Duckworth's molestation, six-year-old Virginia had been afraid to look at herself in a mirror.

Although she did not really wish to behold herself in a looking glass, the process of writing her new novel brought into sharp focus the joys and sorrows of the past and the present, particularly the sharp memory of being somehow guilty of a crime she had no memory of ever having committed. Certainly no other fictional writing of Virginia's examines her past so acutely and remorselessly as does *To the Lighthouse*. The dead, she learned again, can exert considerable power over the living.

Time, she was also poignantly aware, had begun to take its toll. At forty-three, the asymmetry of her long, slender, beautiful face had become more noticeable, often giving her a careworn look. Her countenance was now criss-crossed with lines. Her insecurities were reinforced when Clive Bell, commenting on a photograph of her taken the year before, observed: 'That is charming – but must be taken very long ago, I suppose.'[3]

There were moments of elation when she could evade the past and the future. Virginia feasted on these, but they were short-lived. At times, she wanted to relinquish the experimentation which had become the hallmark of her reputation. She candidly informed Roger Fry: 'For my own part I wish we could skip a generation – skip Edith [Sitwell] and Gertrude [Stein] and Tom and Joyce and Virginia and come out in the open again, when everything has been restarted, and runs full tilt, instead of trickling and teasing in this irritating way.'[4]

Once again, Janet Case proved a relentless critic. In her aloof manner, she accused her former student of preferring form to content. Virginia shot back: 'What is form? What is character? What is a novel? Think them out for me. The truth is of course that no one for 100 years has given a thought to novels, as they have done to poetry: and now we wake up, suffocated, to find ourselves completely in the dark.'[5] This an excellent defence by Virginia Woolf of herself as a modernist, but she was well aware that her father had given considerable thought to the place of the novel in English literature. By expanding the frontiers of the novel, she was following in his footsteps. This was an act of filial homage, but in basing a central character in another of her major experiments on Leslie, she relentlessly catalogued his failings. Another project was also making her more than usually aware that she was Leslie Stephen's daughter: she was struggling with a theoretical book ('Phases of Fiction'*) on the novel.

The conflicts which arose during the writing of *To the Lighthouse* display how suffocatingly intertwined her life and her work had become. She experienced what she labelled a great deal of 'rat-gnawing'[6] at the back of her head. She was not even sure what form she was using: 'Thinking it over, I see I cannot, never could, never shall, write a novel. What, then, to call it?'[7] Death, she became convinced, was hurrying near: 'how many more books?' she asked herself.[8] Such troubling questions often found answers when she realized that she was 'the only woman in England free to write what I like'.[9] The other side of desperation was anger. When Vita upbraided her for accepting commissions from short, fat Dorothy Todd, the editor of *Vogue*, she heatedly countered: 'And what's the objection to whoring after Todd? Better whore, I think, than honestly and timidly and coolly and respectably copulate with the Times Literary Supplement.'[10]

At the time she was struggling with *To the Lighthouse*, Virginia's passion for Vita heightened. A glimpse of these strong feelings is contained in a letter of 24 August: 'I have a perfectly romantic and no doubt untrue vision of you in my mind – stamping out the hops in a great vat in Kent – stark naked, brown as a satyr, and very beautiful.'[11] Poignancy was added to passion when Virginia learned of Madge Vaughan's death that November. She could not manage even a solitary tear and, searching her emotions, she discovered

* This title was announced as a Hogarth Press publication (part of the Hogarth Lectures on Literature Series); it was first published serially in the *Bookman* in April, May and June 1929. Later, it was included in *Granite and Rainbow*.

only dead leaves. Yet, as she told Janet Case, Madge had been an important part of her childhood. In those days, she had worshipped her.

Although the vision of 'the Old Man' had been the inspiration for *To the Lighthouse*, that novel is also concerned with the Ramsay family before and after the death of Mrs Ramsay. How does the death of a parent influence the subsequent life of a child? Virginia was writing about that crucial issue at the time of Madge's passing. Another loss asserted itself when Virginia went to Hampstead and felt the presence of Katherine Mansfield's ghost. Then Virginia had to deal with another, unforeseen loss. In the spring, Vita was 'doomed'[12] to accompany Harold to Tehran, where he had been appointed Counsellor to the British Legation. Who was doomed, Vita or Virginia? Certainly, Virginia's passion for Vita was triggered when she was about to be separated from her.

Before the autumn of 1925, Vita and Virginia had conducted a love affair but not a sexual liaison. Virginia's sexuality was one which found expression in words and in flirting. Without doubt, she had stronger sexual feelings for women than for men, but she did not seek to use her body – which as a child she had been made ashamed of and which she did not wish to behold in a mirror – to express sexual feelings. Vita was different: sexual acts gave her enormous pleasure. Virginia's anxieties were so enormous by December 1925 that she wanted to express her love for Vita physically, perhaps in an attempt to retain Vita's affection. For her part, Vita had mixed feelings. She wanted to sleep with Virginia, but she was afraid that her high-strung friend might be overwhelmed by having sex.

At Long Barn in December 1925, Virginia and Vita finally slept together. The most straightforward account of what happened was provided by Vita nine months later in a letter to Harold:

> You mention Virginia: it is simply laughable. I love Virginia – as who wouldn't? but really, my sweet, one's love for Virginia is a very different thing: a mental thing; a spiritual thing, if you like, an intellectual thing . . . Virginia is *not* the sort of person

one thinks of in that way; there is something incongruous and almost indecent in the idea . . . I *have* gone to bed with her (twice), but that's all . . . Now you know all about it, and I hope I haven't shocked you.[13]

Shortly after she returned to London, Virginia politely but firmly distanced herself from this physical expression of love in a diary entry: 'These Sapphists *love* women; friendship is never untinged with amorosity . . . What is the effect of all this on me? Very mixed. There is her maturity & full breastedness: her being so much in full sail on the high tides, where I am coasting down backwaters.' Virginia is defining herself in opposition to Vita, who is a 'Sapphist': the clear implication is that Virginia is not assigning such a label to herself. In fact, she goes on to state that what she really wants from Vita is a mother's love: Vita 'lavishes on me the maternal protection which, for some reason, is what I have always most wished from everyone. What Leonard gives me, & Nessa gives me, & Vita, in her more clumsy external way, tries to give me.' In addition, Virginia envied Vita for being 'in short (what I have never been) a real woman.'[14] Vita was at home in society, comfortable in her dealings with servants and adept in all the ways of the world.

Virginia had never fully recovered from her mother's death and that was the 'reason' she placed her greatest confidence in those who could act in a maternal way towards her. The paradox was that Virginia had never received much attention from her mother and had, from her earliest days, been drawn to her father. Without doubt, her notion of herself as a woman had been badly damaged. She certainly was not a 'real woman' in Julia's sense of that expression. Vita's 'clumsy external way' was sexual, the love for which Virginia hankered was very different. Nevertheless, she hoped that Vita, very much a woman of the world, could provide a consoling substitute. This desire led to sexual activity but then, in a manner reminiscent of her reaction to Leonard's lovemaking on their honeymoon, Virginia drew back.

Unlike Harold Nicolson, Leonard was probably not kept

informed of his wife's sexual activities, but there can be little doubt that he was fully aware of what was happening. Much earlier, he had been badly disappointed by Virginia's sexual unresponsiveness. Now he had to confront the fact that Virginia was in love with Vita. He remained silent, but his fury was manifested in two ways. Muted, residual anger can be glimpsed when, in his autobiography, he introduces Vita as a person of apparently attractive contradictions: in the prime of life, she was both 'an animal at the height of its powers' and 'a beautiful flower in full bloom'. She was born to rule, to live in a castle, whereas, he pointed out, 'a castle is almost the only place in which I could not under any circumstances be comfortable'. In the best and worst senses, Vita was for Leonard 'a very simple person'.[15] Although Leonard held his tongue to Virginia and Vita, he later displaced his fury on to the poet Dorothy Wellesley, who was also a lover of Vita.

Virginia did not admit it to herself, but her relationship with Vita erected barriers between herself and both Leonard and Vanessa. That January, she was ill again. Elinor Rendel, Lytton's Newnham-educated physician niece and Virginia's doctor since 1924, diagnosed German measles, a condition which may have been exacerbated by Virginia's anxious state. If Vita wanted to retain Virginia's love, Virginia commanded her to break out into spots as well, but she was certain that Vita would not be compliant: 'for if ever a woman was a lighted candlestick, a glow, an illumination, which will cross the desert [to Persia] and leave me – it was Vita'.[16]

In the midst of Vita's imminent departure and a persistent flu, the world became spectral to Virginia. When Vita took leave of her on 19 January, Virginia strolled the London streets, which that evening were enveloped in a dim fog, the lights dull and hard to discern. As she walked towards the sound of a barrel organ in Marchmont Street, she interrogated herself: what are my real feelings about Vita? She could not provide herself with a satisfactory answer. 'She is not clever; but abundant & fruitful; truthful too.'[17] For Virginia, Vita was a cornucopia, a person whose fecundity – the energy she gave to every aspect of her life – made her bewitching. Virginia, who felt drained of her femininity, sought refuge in the company of a woman of abundant generosity.

Even Vita had her limits, as she informed Virginia in a letter written on the train to Dover:

> I am reduced to a thing that wants Virginia. I composed a beautiful letter to you in the sleepless nightmare hours of the night, and it has all gone: I just miss you, in a quite simple desperate human way. You, with all your un-dumb letters, would never write so elementary a phrase as that; perhaps you wouldn't even feel it. And yet I believe you'll be sensible of a little gap. But you'd clothe it in so exquisite a phrase that it would lose a little of its reality. Whereas with me it is quite stark: I miss you even more than I could have believed; and I was prepared to miss you a good deal.[18]

Virginia was stung: 'why do you think I don't feel, or that I make phrases? "Lovely phrases" you say which rob things of reality. Just the opposite. Always, always, always I try to say what I feel.' Although Virginia did not wish to admit it, Vita had put her finger precisely where she differed from Virginia. Vita acted instinctively, whereas Virginia often had to try to feel. This difference tantalized Virginia, but it also irritated her. She replied in the most elementary language she could summon: 'I have missed you. I do miss you. I shall miss you. And if you don't believe it, you're a longeared owl and ass.'[19]

Earlier, in the autumn, Virginia entertained Doris Daglish, a would-be novelist who, detecting a 'human heart'[20] in Virginia, had sought her advice about creating a heroine who could titillate an audience and thus launch her creator as a writer of fiction. Doris proved to be a poor, shifty, shabby, shuffling housemaid who, in the midst of consuming a huge chunk of cake, asked Virginia, who had seen a sample of her work, if she had sufficient talent to devote her entire life to literature. Virginia was polite, but Leonard settled the issue by counselling Miss Daglish to become a cook.

★

That autumn, Virginia had written 'On Being Ill' for Tom Eliot's *New Criterion*. In this essay, she had remarked on the paucity of literature dealing with illness; with the exception of a Proust,

> Literature does its best to maintain that its concern is with the mind; that the body is a sheet of plain glass through which the soul looks straight and clear . . . Those great wars which [the body] wages by itself, with the mind a slave to it in the solitude of the bedroom against the assault of fever or the oncome of melancholia, are neglected.

Illness isolates the sufferer from the healthy: 'we cease to be soldiers in the army of the upright; we become deserters. They march to battle. We float with the sticks on the stream.'

The 'we' is important because Virginia is discussing the isolation in which she spent so much of her life. She paid a heavy price for her withdrawals from the world, but there were compensations too:

> In illness words seem to possess a mystic quality. We grasp what is beyond their surface meaning, gather instinctively this, that, and the other, – a sound, a colour . . . In health, meaning has encroached upon sound. Our intelligence domineers over our senses. But in illness, with the police off duty, we creep beneath some obscure poem by Mallarmé or Donne, some phrase in Latin or Greek, and the words give out their scent, and ripple like leaves, and chequer us with light and shadow.

In her response to the frequent mix of influenza and depression which overwhelmed her, Virginia made a virtue of necessity. During illness, one might, for instance, consider living one's life over in a different way, 'now as man, now as woman, as sea captain, court lady, Emperor, farmer's wife, in splendid cities and remote moors, in Teheran and Tunbridge Wells'.[21] In this musing is the embryo of *Orlando*.

That winter, Virginia made a rapid recovery, despite a number of setbacks. In the *Adelphi*, John Middleton Murry condemned *Mrs Dalloway*, together with *The Waste Land*, to an early death:

they would not be read in fifty years' time. There were the usual fractious exchanges between Nelly and her employers. Through all this, Virginia worked, mindful of the fact that she missed Vita but, she realized, not very intensely. In fact, to her own surprise, Virginia was writing with great speed and assurance: 'as fast & freely as I have written in the whole of my life'. Somehow or other, she had taken the right path, the one which would lead to the tree where all the 'fruit hang[ing] in [her] soul' was to be reached.[22] Now she would pluck that fruit.

Why, she asked herself, was she all of a sudden enveloped in such self-confidence? Was it in part because she was a fanatical enthusiast like her father? In any event, she had touched a self-healing reservoir. 'I don't think I'm ever bored . . . but I have a power of recovery.' Once again, she was in contact with the 'restless searcher' within herself, but wondered if she would ever really find the 'it' for which she hankered? She sensed a break-through: 'I have a great & astonishing sense of something there . . . It is not exactly beauty that I mean . . . Who am I, what am I, & so on: these questions are always floating about in me.'[23]

The 'it' was close at hand because she was, in writing *To the Lighthouse*, re-creating her childhood, the who and what of her earliest existence. When Gwen Raverat and the novelist Rose Macaulay dined with the Woolfs on 23 February, the conversation turned to Julia and Leslie. Virginia was proud that Rose had been informed of Julia's radiant loveliness but felt 'rather queer' to think that when people read her new book they would 'recognize poor Leslie Stephen & beautiful Mrs Stephen'.[24]

As she informed Vita, Virginia had discovered yet another new organizing principle, one especially appropriate for her work in progress: rhythm. This was a stylistic device which infused itself into the text and thus went deeper than words: 'A sight, an emotion, creates this wave . . . and then, as it breaks and tumbles in the mind, it makes words to fit it.'[25] The crescendo of the wave gives the resulting piece of prose a poetical texture and allows meaning to be derived not only from traditional narrative exposition but also from the intricate juxtaposition of patterns.

Meanwhile, there were other, more mundane causes for celebration: the Woolfs were constructing two water-closets at Monks House, one paid for by *Mrs Dalloway*, the other by *The Common Reader*. Both, she assured Vita, were dedicated to her. There were moments of comedy, even though of an embarrassing kind. While at dinner at Rose Macaulay's on 24 March, Leonard, reaching under the table to retrieve what he thought was the journalist Barbara Gould's napkin, grabbed her petticoat (when Virginia told the story to Vita, she claimed that he retrieved a sanitary napkin). That evening, Virginia was also not at her best. She heard Rose's lover, the former Catholic priest Gerald O'Donovan, mention the Holy Ghost. He had in fact referred to the 'whole coast'.

'Where is the Holy Ghost?' Virginia asked.

'Where ever the sea is,' the startled speaker rejoined. At this point, Virginia suspected something had gone badly wrong. 'Am I mad,' she asked herself, 'or is this wit?'

She tried again: 'The Holy Ghost?'

'The whole coast!' O'Donovan, who now suspected she was mocking him, angrily retorted.[26]

These interludes occurred amidst great tribulations. What would happen to her diaries, Virginia wondered, if she died suddenly? Accompanying that fear was resolute courage. When Leonard announced that he intended to resign as literary editor of the *Nation and Athenaeum*, his wife, despite the possible financial set-back, was jubilant; in fact, she felt eighteen years younger and fancy-free:

> The situation appears to be that L. shall make £300; I £200 – & really I don't suppose we shall find it hard; & then the mercy of having no ties, no proofs, no articles to procure, & all that, is worth a little more exertion elsewhere . . . To upset everything every 3 or 4 years is my notion of a happy life . . . But with £400 assured & no children, why imitate a limpet in order to enjoy a limpet's safety? The next question will be, I see, the Press. Shall we give that up too, & so be quit of everything? . . . For, speaking selfishly, it has served my turn: given me a chance

> of writing off my own bat, & now I doubt if Heinemann or Cape would much intimidate me. But then there's the fun – which is considerable.[27]

In subsequent years, another crucial aspect in the life – and the financial resources – of the Woolfs was to be the growth of the Hogarth Press: fourteen titles in 1923 and 1924, twenty-eight in 1925, thirty-one in 1926, forty-two in 1927, thirty in 1928, thirty-one in 1929 and 1930. The profits from this increased activity were especially significant from 1929 until the middle of the 1930s.

From the mid-1920s, the Hogarth Press needed more of Leonard's time, even though the number of staff was correspondingly increased. As their imprint became better known, husband and wife maintained a strict control over quality: books were published because the Woolfs considered them intellectually or aesthetically respectable. In particular, Leonard wanted to publish works which would stir up controversy and he also felt that his Press should issue books dealing with psychoanalysis, one of the great intellectual innovations of the twentieth century. In the case of Vita Sackville-West, the Woolfs landed themselves a best-selling author and their financial basis became more secure once Virginia got to be established.

Virginia's renewed feeling of power was accompanied by the realization that her work often gave her 'intense' happiness, but the writing of *To the Lighthouse* led to the corresponding awareness that she had never experienced 'natural'[28] happiness, that derived from family love and closeness. In a sense, she saw herself as the author of one kind of happiness, one constructed by the self in the absence of the other. The distinction is a crucial one because intense happiness is forged by the self and is much more precarious than the natural variety. Moreover, if intense happiness should founder, Virginia was afraid that she would have nothing to put in its place.

The consequence of this insight was Virginia's increased awareness of just how much she differed from her mother – a wound that she had attempted to heal in *Mrs Dalloway*. This separation is dramatized in the gulfs separating Mrs Ramsay from her artist friend Lily Briscoe. Lily adores Mrs Ramsay, but she knows that Mrs Ramsay has a prejudice against unmarried women, particularly those who are artistically inclined: 'Could loving, as people called it, make her and Mrs Ramsay one? for it was not knowledge but unity that she desired, not inscriptions on tablets, nothing that could be written in any language known to men, but intimacy itself.'[29] It takes a desperate courage to go on without such intimacy and this had been the desperate task of Virginia's life.

Mrs Ramsay is also a person filled with great sorrow, one who knows there is 'no treachery too base for the world to commit'.[30] As a result, she exerts an excessive amount of control, a trait which irritates her friend Mrs Doyle: 'Wishing to dominate, wishing to interfere, making people do what she wished – that was the charge against her, and she thought it most unjust.'[31] The accusation is harsh but true. Mrs Ramsay's desire for dominion – arising from her own sense of privation – does not bring her great pleasure. As she takes her place at the head of the dining table, she asks herself: 'what have I done with my life?' And she is consumed with failure: 'Nothing seemed to have merged. They all sat separate. And the whole of the effort of merging and flowing and creating rested on her.'[32] The dinner party is, like Lily's painting, an act of creativity, but it is one stemming from an uncertain notion of self. However, Mrs Ramsay does have a genuine sense of triumph when she realizes that her careful ordering has led to a moment of profound togetherness, of having conquered chaotic forces: 'There it was, all round them. It partook, she felt . . . of eternity; as she had already felt about something different once before that afternoon; there is a coherence in things, a stability; something, she meant, is immune from change, and shines out . . . in the face of the flowing, the fleeting, the spectral, like a ruby.'[33] A good dinner party and a good painting may share the ruby's immortality, but the activities of a hostess and an artist seem vastly different: once again, Virginia asked herself, could she reconcile seeming opposites?

★

As she completed the writing of Part One of *To the Lighthouse*, Virginia felt that, once more, she had wrapped herself too tightly in her own personality. Unlike Beatrice Webb, whose career as a social reformer was coherent and ordered, Virginia envisioned herself as the pioneer of a kind of literary incoherence. In comparison to the older woman, Virginia was a tattered mongrel. In fact, she was now frightened that *To the Lighthouse* had had too easy a gestation.

> I cannot make it out – here is the most difficult abstract piece of writing – I have to give [in Part Two] an empty house, no people's characters, the passage of time, all eyeless & featureless with nothing to cling to: well, I rush at it, & at once scatter out two pages. Is it nonsense, is it brilliance? Why am I so flown with words, & apparently free to do exactly what I like?[34]

Was she taking too many liberties or had she discovered yet another rich goldmine?

Part One of *To the Lighthouse* is centred on the Ramsays: oversensitive – and, as a result, overbearing – Mr Ramsay and the seemingly placid Mrs Ramsay, whose attention to others is universal but, as a result, diffuse and ineffective. Mr Ramsay may be childish and inordinately self-centred, but a large portion of his anxiety is, like Leslie Stephen's, centred on the fact that his wife never openly declares her affection: 'A heartless woman he called her; she never told him that she loved him. But it was not so – it was not so. It was only that she never could say what she felt.'[35]

Marital tensions centre on the desire of the youngest child, James, to visit the lighthouse and on the determination of Mr Ramsay, who is obviously jealous of his son's hold over his wife, to thwart him. The power struggle of this couple is one between a man who is openly irritable and vexatious and a woman who has learned to maintain control through silent manipulation. 'The Window' ends on such a note. Mr Ramsay's pessimism about the weather proves to be correct (there can be no journey to the lighthouse), but he has once again shown himself to be unduly petulant.

In the chilly conclusion to Part One of *To the Lighthouse*,

Virginia enshrined many of the dynamics of her parents' marriage: Leslie's testy demands had never been openly rebuffed by Julia, but she resented them and sought to minister to a wide assortment of friends and relatives. In such a household, the needs of the children were obviously overlooked and thus neglected. Having written with great eloquence about her childhood, Virginia now turned her attention to the lyrical Part Two, 'Time Passes', during which Mrs Ramsay dies. The house stands empty, visited occasionally by the housekeeper, Mrs MacNab.

> But slumber and sleep though it might there came later in the summer ominous sounds like the measured blows of hammers dulled on felt, which, with their repeated shocks still further loosened the shawl and cracked the tea-cups. Now and again some glass tinkled in the cupboard as if a giant voice had shrieked so loud in its agony that tumblers stood inside a cupboard vibrated too. Then again silence fell; and then, night after night, and sometimes in plain mid-day when the roses were bright and light turned on the wall its shape clearly there seemed to drop into this silence this indifference, this integrity, the thud of something falling.[36]

If Virginia needed any reassurance concerning her experimental blending of poetry and prose in 'Time Passes', the General Strike of 1926 provided her with yet another example of how old, established systems were a failure.

To the Lighthouse is in large part about domestic politics, whereas the workers in 1926 challenged the existence of England's entire socio-economic system. Although Virginia Woolf seems at first glance not to be a political writer in the tradition of an Elizabeth Gaskell or a George Eliot, her novels are infused with a strong conviction that traditional, patriarchal power – whether in Parliament or in literary criticism – is corrupt and must be subdued, modified or replaced. Virginia's sympathies were with the economic outsiders; their desolation became hers. And she found the presence of the military jarring: 'I saw this morning 5 or 6 armoured cars slowly going along Oxford Street; on each two soldiers sat in tin helmets, & one stood with his hand at the gun which was pointed straight ahead ready to fire.'[37] Violence had become an everyday occurrence, a fact underscored for Virginia when the lovers Ralph Partridge and Frances Marshall* were among those injured on 10 May in a railway accident at Bishop's Stortford in which one person was killed. Virginia's politics are evident, if muted, in Part Two's haunting lament for the young killed in the Great War, those lives stolen from her generation.

In the midst of social upheaval, Virginia had another attack of what she called her 'clothes complex',[38] a problem she attempted to solve by shopping with Dorothy Todd, whose expert eye, she hoped, would be of assistance. 'I tremble & shiver all over at the appalling magnitude of the task I have undertaken – to go to a dressmaker recommended by Todd . . . Perhaps this excites me more feverishly than the Strike.'[39] The compromise was that Todd gave Virginia the address of the shop, whereupon Virginia refused to have lunch with her. Virginia realized that her feelings about shopping were both confused and confusing. However, this side of herself, Virginia reflected, was 'very instinctive',[40] a quality of mind ultimately indicative of a powerful person.

In Virginia's mind, there was an obvious conflict between supporting the proletariat and shopping with Todd. Virginia resolved this clothes crisis by returning to Miss Brooke, who had long served as her dressmaker. Instinctively, Virginia desired social revolution; at the same time, her sociable side wanted her – justifiably – to look her best. The battle between these opposing forces was one between a wish to tear down the patriarchy and an ambition to pursue her femininity. These are not irreconcilable aspirations, but they often seemed so to Virginia. She questioned the ways in which men impose their will on women, but she

* They lived together during the week at 41 Gordon Square, Ralph returning at weekends to Ham Spray near Hungerford, the house to which Lytton, Dora and Ralph had moved in 1924. Frances and Ralph married after Carrington's death in 1932.

also had a badly damaged vision of herself as a woman; at such times, she worried when she gave too much thought to her appearance.

She was certainly giving a great deal of thought to Vita, who arrived back in England that May. Virginia, who was to lunch with her on 21 May, was not certain what she felt: 'I am amused at my relations with her: left so ardent in January – & now what?'[41] The reality proved a very poor second to the fantasy:

> how shy one is; how disillusioned by the actual body; how sensitive to new shades of tone – something 'womanly' I detected, more mature; & she was shabbier, come straight off in her travelling clothes; & not so beautiful, as sometimes perhaps . . . I chattering, partly to divert her attention from me; & to prevent her thinking 'Well, is this all?' as she was bound to think, having declared herself so openly in writing.[42]

Once again, as in the early days of their friendship, Vita was an enigma. Despite her attempt to reconcile 'disillusionment' of the body with 'solidity' of the soul, Virginia poignantly realized that her relationship with Vita would never be as strong as it had been in the previous two years.

While she was confused about the direction her friendship with Vita was taking, she was deeply uncertain about the form *To the Lighthouse* was assuming. She confessed to her diary: I 'cannot conceive what The Lighthouse is all about'.[43] The heat of that summer left her indolent. She was filled with 'disagreeable memories of parties, & George Duckworth; a fear haunts me even now, as I drive past Park Lane on top of a bus'.[44] George's intrusive behaviour had occurred after their mother's death and Part Three of *To the Lighthouse* is devoted to that time period. By writing about the past, she had summoned up its demons.

For a long time, Virginia had paid scant attention to Vanessa. On 31 May, she attended an exhibition of her sister's and in a letter to her of 2 June offered frank criticism. The small paintings were amazingly good, but 'still I think the problems of design on a large scale slightly baffle you'. (Of course, Virginia was grappling with similar dilemmas in writing *To the Lighthouse*.) That letter shows Virginia in a prickly mood. She sniggers at Leonard's ability to charm the acerbic Gertrude Stein – 'Leonard, being a Jew himself, got on very well with her' – and she asked her sister for an honest opinion: did she have a bad temper? Then, Virginia returns to the thorny subject of herself and Vanessa as creative people: 'your genius as a painter, though rather greater than I like, does still shed a ray on mine. I mean, people will say, "What a gifted couple!" Well: it would have been nicer had they said: "Virginia had all the gifts; dear old Nessa was a domestic character:" – Alas, alas, they'll never say that now'.[45]

By touching on their rivalry and expressing her feelings of jealousy, Virginia was attempting to get a strong reaction from Vanessa and thus revive, even in a tumultuous fashion, their friendship. Eleven days later, Virginia again tried to inflame:

> Vita is now arriving to spend 2 nights alone with me – L. is going back. I say no more; as you are bored by Vita, bored by love, bored by me, and everything to do with me, except Quentin and Angelica . . . Still, the June nights are long and warm; the roses flowering; and the garden full of lust and bees, mingling in the asparagus beds.[46]

The complaint is clear enough: Virginia is the neglected child who seeks to divert the mother's attention back to herself. The truth was that Virginia was bored by Vita and wanted her sister restored to her. Vanessa, supremely aware of exactly what Virginia was attempting to do, wrote her on 16 June: 'Give my humble respects to Vita, who treats me as an Arab steed looking from the corner of its eye on some long-eared mule – But then you do your best to stir up jealousy between us, so what can one expect?'[47]

Virginia, as she admitted to herself, had become subject to a weathercock of a sensibility which veered in all sorts of contrary directions. Understandably, she was deeply hurt when Clive and Duncan criticized her new hat: 'I came away deeply chagrined, as unhappy as I have been these ten years.'[48] This had been a direct and cruel hit on her fragile sense of herself as a woman.

There was trouble with Leonard, who in his wife's opinion had become a sort of butcher-judge, one who formed harsh opinions about others, including her. During the strike, their opinions differed enormously: both were pro-worker, but Leonard wanted a socialist victory, whereas Virginia was willing to settle for peace. This quarrel allowed Leonard to displace his strong feelings about sexual fidelity on to the safer, more impersonal topic of politics. In the midst of these bad, hurt and angry feelings, *To the Lighthouse* had become for Virginia a python with which she had to struggle. And there was the pervading fear that she was not using her life properly: 'This is human life: this is the infinitely precious stuff issued in a narrow roll to us now, & then withdrawn for ever; & we spend it thus.'[49]

On 23 July, Virginia, accompanied by Leonard, paid a long-postponed trip to Thomas and Florence Hardy at their home, Max Gate, near Dorchester. Although she had facetiously informed Vita that this was to be a visit to the 'immortal fount' in order to touch the 'sacred hand',[50] her reverence for Hardy was almost unbounded. As editor of the *Cornhill Magazine*, Leslie Stephen had been the supportive publisher of young Thomas Hardy, although he broke the connection in 1877 when he found portions of *The Return of the Native* too dangerous for a family magazine. Therefore, Virginia's visit had a threefold purpose: she wanted to speak with a living legend, to inspect the existence of a person who had devoted himself to the literary life, and to pay a social call on a writer whose early career – like her own – had been fostered by her father.

At the door to Max Gate, there was a case of mistaken identity when Virginia thought the small, thin parlourmaid who answered the door was Hardy himself. Florence Hardy talked nervously about her dog and in her countenance Virginia saw the 'sad lack lustre eyes of a childless woman'. Hardy, who was not at all interested in discussing literary matters, was nevertheless completely at ease. As far as Virginia could discern, he was remarkably different from her in that he was completely detached from all the trials and tribulations of a writer's life. He had sympathy, even pity, for those plying such a trade, but he was pleasantly aloof.

'Do you think one can't write poetry if one sees people?' the would-be recluse asked him.

'One might be able to – I don't see why not. It's a question of physical strength.'

Hardy was very much aware that Virginia was Leslie's daughter: 'Your father took my novel – *Far from the Madding Crowd*. We stood shoulder to shoulder against the British public about certain matters dealt with in that novel.' When he inscribed a book for her, Hardy was less certain how to spell Virginia's married surname, which he rendered Wolff.[51]

Hardy's ordinariness was both upsetting and comforting. He took greatness in his stride, but it did not seem to matter very much to him, whereas the pursuit of a literary career was a central focus of Virginia's existence. A few days later, she experienced a 'nervous breakdown in miniature',[52] one in which the power to make images deserted her. A week later, safely ensconced at Rodmell, she was able to work again on *To the Lighthouse*.

That summer was dominated by a feeling of 'washing in boundless warm fresh air'.[53] There had not been, she rejoiced, such a magnificent August in years. She took great joy in Pinker (sometimes called Pinka), a spaniel puppy given to her by Vita. By 8 August, Virginia was sufficiently recovered to tease the gift-giver: 'Thinking about copulation, I now remember a whole chapter of my past that I forgot, I think, to tell you.'[54]

As August gave way to September, Virginia was concerned with how to link Mr Ramsay with Lily Briscoe in the concluding pages of *To the Lighthouse*. This was a major worry, one she was now positive she could solve. Nevertheless, she feared that the book was a bit thin, though she thought it a more subtle and human book in comparison to *Jacob's Room* or *Mrs Dalloway*. She was now convinced that 'Time Passes' worked and did not interfere with the remainder of the narrative. Contentment began to reign, but then her mind wandered to Vanessa's children and Maynard's possessions: 'My own gifts & shares seemed so moderate in comparison; my own fault too – a little more self control on my part & we might have had a boy of 12, a girl of 10: This always rakes me wretched in the early hours.'[55]

Great sadness accompanied the completion of Virginia's new novel, leading to the memory of Morgan Forster telling her how certain he was that *A Passage to India*, as he completed it, was a failure. She also continued to be bothered by Janet Case's strictures. Did her new book have real substance and had it evaded the trap of sentimentality? She remained uncertain. On 15 September she endured a horrible night.

> Woke up perhaps at 3. Oh it's beginning, it's coming – the horror – physically like a painful wave swelling about the heart – tossing me up. I'm unhappy, unhappy! Down – God, I wish I were dead. Pause. But why am I feeling this? Let me watch the wave rise. I watch. Vanessa. Children. Failure. Yes; I detect that. Failure, failure. (The wave rises).

An acute sense of horror eventually gave way to one that was diffuse. This allowed Virginia to pull herself together for the next round of invading blackness.

> No more of this. I reason. I take a census of happy people & unhappy. I brace myself to shove, to throw, to batter down. I begin to march blindly forward. I feel obstacles go down. I say it doesn't matter. Nothing matters. I become rigid & straight, & sleep again, & half wake & feel the wave beginning & watch the light whitening & wonder how, this time, breakfast & daylight will overcome it.[56]

No other passage in Virginia's letters or diaries gives such a dramatic sense of her see-sawing inner demons. On the morning of 16 September she was relieved to hear Leonard in the passage and was comforted by his cheerfulness. Drained by her restless night, she asked herself: 'Does everyone go through this state? Why have I so little control?'[57] She felt cheerful by the time breakfast was over, but the invasive forces were always there, ready to pounce, and at times she wondered if she would become their victim.

There was, she recognized, a mystical side to these black episodes: 'it is not oneself but something in the universe that one's left with'. She even glimpsed a 'fin passing far out' and thus saw a glimmer of the book which eventually became *The Waves*. Nevertheless, her own existence remained a puzzle. As a child, she had once been unable to step across a puddle without asking herself: who am I? The same question still haunted her. Meanwhile, she had to take things in hand. She was going to sort out her clothes complex by buying some cheap day frocks and a good dress from Brooke: 'No longer shall I let a coat for £3 floor me in the middle of the night, or be afraid to lunch out because "I've no clothes." A broader & bolder grasp is what is wanted.'[58]

Despite the melancholia which invaded Virginia as she completed *To the Lighthouse*, that book ends on a note of triumph. Mr Ramsay and two of his children, James and Cam (Camilla), finally reach the lighthouse; although filled with self-doubt, Lily Briscoe captures on canvas the revelation of shape-in-chaos imparted to her by Mrs Ramsay. These parallel activities are not completed without great torment.

As usual, Mr Ramsay is both hopeless and hapless. He declaims passages from William Cowper's 'The Castaway', which reads in part:

> No voice divine the storm allay'd,
> No light propitious shone;
> When, snatch'd from all effectual aid,
> We perished, each alone:
> But I beneath a rougher sea,
> And whelm'd in deeper gulfs than he.

Virginia was well aware of her father's devotion to the late eighteenth-century writer, but at first glance Mr Ramsay's use of Cowper seems to indicate yet another aspect of his overly active self-centredness. In his final poem, Cowper describes the horrible death of a seaman and, only after having evoked the horror of that event, informs the reader that his despair is 'deeper' than that of the wretched sailor. In choosing to have Mr Ramsay bellow out lines from 'The Castaway', Virginia may be suggesting that his morbidity is genuinely Cowperian: the despondency may be impossible to elucidate fully but is very real.

During the trip, James is consumed with his murderous hatred of his father. If, as was likely, his father once again acted unreasonably, he would at long last take action: 'I shall take a knife and strike him to the heart.'[59] Although she is well aware of her father's failings, Cam is divided in her loyalties between father and brother. Potential tragedy is averted when James handles the skiff dextrously in the difficult water and receives his father's unqualified praise. 'There! Cam thought, addressing herself silently to James. You've got it at last.'[60] They reach the lighthouse, the attainment of which gives James a genuine sense of achievement.

Back on shore, Lily is struggling with her canvas. In Part One, Mrs Ramsay posed for her; now her ghost sits for her. Lily's approach to the task at hand resembles Virginia's during the writing of *Mrs Dalloway*: 'She went on tunnelling her way into her picture, into the past.'[61] Lily is obviously haunted by the dead, especially the ghost of Mrs Ramsay: 'Oh Mrs Ramsay! she called out silently, to that essence which sat by the boat, that abstract one made of her, that woman in grey, as if to abuse her for having gone, and then having gone, come back again.'[62] Part of Lily's difficulty is that she is uncertain what the problem is:

> She must try to get hold of something that evaded her. It evaded her when she thought of Mrs Ramsay; it evaded her now when she thought of her picture. Phrases came. Visions came. Beautiful pictures. Beautiful phrases. But what she wished to get hold of was that very jar on the nerves, the thing itself before it has been made anything . . . It was a miserable machine, an inefficient machine . . . the human apparatus for painting or for feeling; it always broke down at the critical moment; heroically, one must force it on.[63]

The vision eludes Lily until the moment when she takes pleasure in the realization that Mr Ramsay must have reached the lighthouse. From that moment of empathy is born true inspiration:

> Quickly, as if she were recalled by something over there, she turned to her canvas. There it was – her picture. Yes, with all its greens and blues, its lines running up and across, its attempt at something. It would be hung in the attic, she thought; it would be destroyed. But what did that matter? she asked herself, taking up her brush, again. She looked at the steps; they were empty; she looked at her canvas; it was blurred. With a sudden intensity, as if she saw it clear for a second, she drew a line there, in the centre. It was done; it was finished. Yes, she thought, laying down her brush in extreme fatigue, I have had my vision.[64]

The 'line' is the lighthouse (now triumphantly associated with Mr Ramsay) and at long last she is able to find a place for it in the background of the portrait of Mrs Ramsay. In a moment of artistic ecstasy, Lily blends the two Ramsays – background and foreground of the canvas – together in perfect unity, something that never happened in their married lives. Through the power of her art, she has remade their tragic past. The canvas might be destroyed or forgotten. That is of no importance because she has found, at long last, the very 'thing itself'. Virginia had long been searching for the elusive 'it' of creativity and Lily undertakes a similar quest. Like her creator, she is dedicated to experimentation, to a new form of artistic expression.

In a manner reminiscent of Virginia's love for Vita Sackville-West, Lily longs for physical closeness with Mrs Ramsay:

> Sitting on the floor with her arms round Mrs Ramsay's knees, close as she could get, smiling to think that Mrs Ramsay would never know the reason of that pressure, she imagined how in the chambers of the mind and heart of the woman who was, physically, touching her, were stood, like the treasures in the tombs of kings, tablets bearing sacred inscriptions, which if one could spell them out would teach one everything, but they would never be offered openly, never made public.[65]

Lily wants to unearth sacred tablets which contain the secret of life, but ultimately the priestess, Mrs Ramsay, remains remote. Lily despairs because she is shut off from Mrs Ramsay and, later, her ghost. Her way of transcending the limitations of that relationship is by putting the finishing touches on a coherent piece of art. This is her ruby, her method of creating something 'immune from change'. In Part One, Mrs Ramsay the hostess triumphs in the creation of the dinner party; in Part Three, Lily performs a parallel act during her moment of vision. Mrs Ramsay and Lily are artists, but of very different kinds.

When speaking of her origins as a writer, Virginia Woolf always stressed her French blood, derived from her mother. The recipe with which Mrs Ramsay ultimately succeeds is Boeuf en Daube. Virginia had long suffered from her suspicion that her creativity – the focal point of her life – had little or nothing to do with her mother, despite her certainty that it was derived from her. In this book, as in *Mrs Dalloway*, she conjoins the world of the society hostess with that of the artist, but here she finds a more direct and personal way back to her long-dead mother and the lost language of childhood.

Although *To the Lighthouse* speaks eloquently of the bleak side of existence, it is a book in which the tragic past is redefined and changed. Part One is Paradise, but a paradise filled with unresolved tensions; in Part Two, that Paradise is lost through death and war; Paradise is regained in Part Three when Mr Ramsay is able to bestow praise and Lily is able to complete her canvas. *To the Lighthouse* is also a book in which there is great generosity of spirit: although Mr and Mrs Ramsay's failings are catalogued, they both have strong redeeming characteristics.

If Mr and Mrs Ramsay are fictional re-creations of Leslie and Julia, Virginia depicts herself in the form of several characters: her venomous hatred of Leslie can be seen in James; the side of Virginia which admired Leslie and understood his dilemmas is depicted in Cam; but the most sustained self-portrait can be seen in Lily, who, like Virginia, struggles mightily with the process of creativity.

In February 1927, while commenting on Cowper's *The Task*, Virginia told Vita: 'Now there's a man with a dash of white fire in him . . . what I call central transparency.'[66] Virginia was a woman with more than a dash of white fire in her. The fire has become translucent because it has reached its moment of highest intensity and purity. In *To the Lighthouse* Virginia found a way to resolve some of the paradoxes at the heart of her own existence. The moment of 'central transparency' is one wherein the fullness of life – the tragic and the comic – stands revealed. For her, this was the 'real thing' to which her art aspired.

Virginia's triumph in manufacturing 'intense' happiness in *To the Lighthouse* made her even more aware than before of the gulfs separating her from Vita. A 'natural' writer like Vita – with her strong sense of tradition – tended to write too easily of emotions or ideas: 'I don't mean that one ought to strain, to write showily, expressively, or so on: only that one ought to stand outside with one's hands folded, until the thing has made itself visible.'[67] Virginia sounded this note of caution because she did not see enough evidence of struggle in Vita's books.

Meanwhile, Virginia was haunted by the idea for a new project, a semi-mystical life of a woman contained in a single incident in which time would be obliterated. Her concern with time led her to think anew of death, 'the one experience I shall never describe'.[68] But she thought the event would be one of great excitement – 'something positive; active?' At the very same time, thoughts about Vita began to displace the book about the nameless woman, or, rather, those ideas were subsumed into a narrative about her. Although Vita had 'broken down more ramparts than anyone',[69] there were many barriers between them. In fact, Virginia now writes dispassionately of their friendship: 'we go on – a spirited, creditable affair, I think, innocent (spiritually) & all gain, I think; rather a bore for Leonard, but not enough to worry him'.[70]

Vita had long feared becoming copy for Virginia. This would happen, she must have intuited, once their friendship was in decline. In late January at Knole, Virginia beheld 'Vita stalking in her Turkish dress, attended by small boys, down the gallery, wafting them on like some tall sailing ship – a sort of covey of noble English life'.[71] Seven weeks later, she had determined to write a fantasy:

> Sapphism is to be suggested. Satire is to be the main note – satire & wildness . . . For the truth is I feel the need of an escapade after these serious poetic experimental books whose form is always so closely considered. I want to kick up my heels & be off . . . I think this will be great fun to write; & it will rest my head before starting the very serious, mystical poetical work which I want to come next.[72]

A good indication of Virginia's aloofness from Vita can be seen in a letter to her of 31 January:

> D'you know it's a great thing being a eunuch as I am: that is not knowing what's the right side of a skirt: women confide in one. One pulls a shade over the fury of sex; and then all the veins and marbling, which, between women, are so fascinating, show out. Here in my cave, I see lots of things you blazing beauties make invisible by the light of your own glory.[73]

A year before, Virginia had immediately distanced herself from her lovemaking with Vita, who was a 'Sapphist'; she was not. A similar kind of separation takes place here. She might hint at lesbianism in her proposed book, but she was writing from the subject position of someone who lived outside the sexual domains of both men and women. *Orlando*, written after the heights of Virginia's emotional involvement with Vita were over, allowed Vita to be fodder for her pen.

Virginia's eunuch state found dramatic expression when she allowed her friend Bobo Mayor to shingle her hair. This was, she observed facetiously in her diary, the most important event in her life since marriage. Unlike Pope's Belinda, Virginia claimed to be delighted with the loss of her locks, even though she looked from behind like the rump of a partridge. She mockingly implored Vita: 'You won't go and leave poor Virginia again will you, even if she does have her hair cut and looks a fright?'[74] When Vanessa blamed Vita for her sister's remarkable change in appearance – for what she considered an act of self-mutilation – Virginia told her sister that Vita had sworn her not to undertake such a rash act since it would ruin her appearance: 'All the same, though it loses me the love of sister, lover, and niece, I don't regret it . . . But then I was always a second rate work, and am now much the worse for wear, so it don't matter.'[75] In fact, Virginia was uncomfortable with any battle between the sexes. As a declared non-participant, she would write a new book which would look at phenomena by which she was fascinated but not directly engaged. *Orlando* is very much the work of a voyeur.

If gossip is voyeuristic and thus a modified form of sexual activity, Virginia had an active sex life. Her status as eunuch meant that she could be very actively involved in both intrigue and flirtation. At this time, she was asked to mediate yet another quarrel between Clive and Mary. As usual, Mary, somewhat illogically, put all the blame for Clive's philandering on Virginia's shoulders. This was a charge to which Virginia rightly refused to plead guilty and the two women were set to fly at each other when a male friend unexpectedly presented himself at Tavistock Square.

Virginia's reputation as a provocateur was still in the ascendant. In addition, Philip Ritchie, now the apple of Lytton Strachey's eye, told Virginia that she had the reputation of being the chief coquette in London. The news of this led Virginia to – supposedly – let her stockings down. She asked Vita: 'why didn't you tell me one must fasten one's suspenders properly?'[76] Accompanying the flirtation, however, was a real sense of herself as a sexual failure.

She had other worries. When the Woolfs took refuge at Monks House that winter, one of the water-closets had flooded and Rose, the local girl who cooked for them, at first declined taking up her post because an absent-minded Virginia had forgotten to advise her of the date of their arrival. In London, the Hogarth Press was showing a slight profit, but Leonard and Virginia were becoming more and more convinced that their manager, Angus Davidson, who had joined the Press in December 1924, was unsatisfactory: they needed a dedicated fanatic, not an easygoing gentleman. There was the possibility that the Press would acquire Francis Birrell's bookshop, but this idea was soon dropped.

Virginia's sadness was low-key but persistent. She was particularly concerned that her friends would dislike *To the Lighthouse*. If that happened, she might have to turn her back on fiction and write memoirs or lives of the obscure. She was certain that a holiday would prove the perfect antidote to such depressed feelings. After that, she would be bubbling again, feeling the extraordinary exhilaration writing gave her. She would experience anew the 'lust of creation',[77] the only lust with which she was genuinely comfortable.

Her doubts about the new book were considerably modified that winter when Leonard read *To the Lighthouse*. He informed her that it was not only her best book but a masterpiece: an entirely new kind of psychological poem. Virginia's suspicion that Leonard's judgement was correct led to a corresponding generosity towards her sister, whose new exhibition she visited in early March: 'The point about you is that you are now mistress of the phrase. All your pictures are built up of flying phrases . . . They have an air of complete spontaneity.' Vanessa's discovery of the 'flying phrase' was the pictorial equivalent of the 'rhythm' her younger sister had recently unearthed. In any event, both of them were, Virginia told her sister, 'mistresses of our medium as never before; both therefore confronted with entirely new problems of structure'. Virginia warned Vanessa that she had 'to buttress up this lyricism with solidity,'[78] but this was also a concern Virginia had about her own work. Virginia's renewed bond of love with her sister – a bond built upon their shared artistic impulses – came in the midst of a feeling of self-loathing: 'I went to buy clothes today & was struck by my own ugliness.'[79]

Vita was again away in Persia and this meant that Virginia's passionate feelings for her were once more on the ascent. When Lytton asked Virginia whether one should go all out for love, 'over the precipice, or stop short at the top', she could only think of Vita and cried out, 'Stop, stop!' She asked her: 'Now what would happen if I let myself go over? Answer me that.'[80] Virginia was willing – eager – to go 'over the precipice' in pursuit of the perfect piece of fiction, but she could not allow herself similar freedom in matters of the flesh or of the heart.

The Woolfs' annual, month-long sojourn on the Continent began on 30 March 1927. For months, Virginia had dreamed of escape from England, of being transported to the sunshine of France and Italy. She was not disappointed. They went first to Paris and then on to Cassis, where they stayed at the Hôtel Cendrillon while visiting Vanessa, Duncan and Clive at the Villa Corsica. On 6 April, they left Toulon by train for Rome, where they remained overnight, having time only to see the Colosseum and consume a huge dish of macaroni. They arrived in Palermo on 9 April. At the railway station there, Virginia caught a glimpse of D. H. Lawrence, the closest they ever came to meeting. The Woolfs were at Palermo for five days. On the return journey they spent three nights in Naples and a week in Rome.

Of Cassis, Virginia remembered rolls of bread, oranges and wine bottles. So intoxicated was Leonard with this part of France that he thought of buying a farmhouse and living there six months of the year. Virginia was an enthusiastic supporter of such a scheme. 'Live near me in Provence,' Virginia commanded Vita; 'we will sit under the cypresses and drink wine'.[81] In contrast to peaceful France, Italy was abuzz with the kind of activity Virginia adored. Once again, she was intrigued with Catholicism: 'I like the Roman Catholic religion. I say it is an attempt at art; Leonard is outraged – We burst into a service of little girls in white veils this morning which touched me greatly.' On the crossing from the mainland to Sicily, Virginia shared a cabin with a Swedish lady, who complained that there was no lock on the door, whereupon

Virginia poked her head through the curtains and said in her best French, 'Madame, we have neither of us any cause for fear.'[82]

At Syracuse, they bumped into the wealthy aesthete Osbert Sitwell, who, in contrast to the Woolfs' cheap inn, was staying in a grand hotel. There, they chanced upon a rehearsal in the ruins of the Greek amphitheatre, where they saw a Medea in a sulphur-coloured wig and an Alcestis in a bowler and overcoat. Moonlight in Syracuse captivated Virginia, especially the way the light bathed the bay, the schooners and the white pillars. She fell in love with the local girls, who looked, she said, like Millais drawings.

Pompeii was profoundly depressing. At first, the ruins merely reminded Virginia of a deserted mining town, but then she was touched by the hills, the colour of the bricks and 'one or two skeletons, people dead on the top of their treasure chests'. Rome was a completely different experience. The Judas trees, cypresses, lawns, statues and great azalea bushes made her put aside any attempt to read Proust. She was like a fish undulating 'in and out of leaves and flowers and swimming round a vast earthenware jar which changes from orange red to leaf green'.[83] On the outskirts of Rome she found an idyllic landscape:

> Figure us sitting in hot sunshine on the doorstep of a Roman ruin in a field with hawk coloured archways against a clear green grape coloured sky, silvery with mountains in the background. Then on the other side nothing but the Campagna, blue and green, with an almond coloured farm, with oxen and sheep, and more ruined arches, and blocks of marble fallen on the grass, and immense sword-like aloes, and lovers curled up among the broken pots.[84]

Imagine, she told Vanessa, having to abandon this paradise in favour of a basement in Bloomsbury!

During Virginia's stay in Italy, the two sisters had an exchange of views about motherhood. On 16 April, Vanessa wrote: 'I wonder how you'd really like the problem of children added to your existence. I don't feel at all equal to dealing with it myself.'[85] Vanessa is making a crucial distinction between a desire to have children and the ability to mother them properly. Virginia, who conceded that her sister had made a good point, was now sure that she would have been a vile mother and she confessed that she had grown to distrust the maternal instinct. Vanessa expressed serious reservations about marriage as an institution, whereas Virginia had come to distrust parenthood: 'In fact what you feel about marriage I feel about motherhood, except that of the two relations motherhood seems to me the more destructive and limiting.' In any event, she did not like profound feelings – 'not in human relationships'.[86]

After her arrival back from Italy, Virginia had to wait a week for the publication of *To the Lighthouse*. She suffered from intermittent headaches. Persistent, low-lying depression was replaced by anger when she learned that Clive had been made privy by Vanessa to her recent letters. Clive acted the buffoon by laughing at her rhapsodic accounts of Italy and by claiming that the letters were complete fabrications. Virginia, he claimed, had in fact been bored by Italy. Virginia told her sister: 'Clive must have a genius for invention . . . I should be much interested to know why he does this. There must be some obscure jealousy at work I think. He grudges, not your affection for me, which doesn't exist, but mine for you.'[87] Clive was paying Virginia back for her flirtation with him from years before. Once again, Vanessa was drawn into the middle when she had to endure Virginia's ridiculous claim that she had no genuine fondness for her.

On 5 May, *To the Lighthouse* was published. The timid review in the *Times Literary Supplement* depressed her, but the advance sales (1,690) were so good the Woolfs could buy a car. Soon afterwards came a rapturous review in the *Spectator* by Rachel A. Taylor, the Scottish poet:

> Nothing happens, and everything happens. To the lighthouse the child James desires to go; and, sitting by his mother's feet, is tauntingly denied by his despotic, myriad-mooded father. To the lighthouse, long years after, he does go, dragged there

> reluctantly by that despotic myriad-minded father, and is suddenly, mysteriously reconciled with him in his heart . . . In this book there are secret flames in flowers and inanimate things, waking in response to the fixed gaze of the unconscious symbolists who are weaving them into the tapestry of their dreams. Subtle sensations are caught here that are elusive as a fragrance or a flavour. Psychical processes are laid bare by burning piercing images.[88]

A good review came from an unexpected source. The previous autumn the Woolfs had again encountered Arnold Bennett, this time at the home of H. G. Wells. He found the couple gloomy but 'liked both of them in spite of their naughty treatment'[89] of him in the press. Less than a month later, on 2 December, Bennett had attacked Virginia's writing in the *Evening Standard*:

> She has written a small book about me, which through a culpable neglect I have not read. I do, however, remember an article of hers in which she asserted that I and my kind could not create character. This was in answer to an article of mine in which I said that the sound drawing of character was the foundation of good fiction, and in which incidentally I gave my opinion that Mrs Woolf and her kind could not create character.

According to Bennett, Virginia's school of fiction displayed three major defects: their characters did not live, logical construction was absent and form was non-existent. There was an absence of 'vital inspiration'. Bennett concluded with a bit of half-hearted praise: 'In the novels of Mrs Woolf some brief passages are so exquisitely done that nothing could be done better. But to be fine for a few minutes is not enough. The chief proof of first-rateness is sustained power.'[90]

The next day, 3 December, Virginia attended a party at Argyll House, the home of Arthur and Sybil Colefax, where Bennett was a fellow guest. Although stung by Bennett's attack, Virginia claimed that she was that night more concerned with her appearance than his cutting words. When Sybil led her up to Bennett, she did admit to feeling like a lamb being taken to the slaughter.

'I am sorry, Mrs Woolf,' he stammered out, 'that I slanged your book last night.'

'If I choose to publish books, that's my own look out. I must take the consequences.'

Bennett remained embarrassed: 'Right, right. I didn't like your book. I thought it a very bad book.'

'You can't hate my books more than I hate yours, Mr Bennett,' she assured him.[91] Differences having been put aside, the two novelists had a cosy chat. This was Virginia's recollection ten years after the event – she may not have been quite as brave as she asserted.*

However, the December 1926 encounter with Bennett might have worked a certain charm, for in his review of *To the Lighthouse*, in the *Evening Standard* of 23 June, he offered grudging praise:

> I have read a bunch of novels. I must say, despite my notorious grave reservations concerning Virginia Woolf, that the most original of the bunch is *To the Lighthouse*. It is the best book of hers that I know. Her character drawing has improved. Mrs Ramsay almost amounts to a complete person. Unfortunately she goes and dies, and her decease cuts the book in two . . . The middle part, entitled 'Time Passes', shows a novel device to give the reader the impression of the passing of time – a sort of cataloguing of intermediate events. In my opinion it does not succeed. It is a short cut, but a short cut that does not get you anywhere . . . I have heard a good deal about the wonders of Mrs Woolf's style. She sometimes discovers a truly brilliant simile. She often chooses her adjectives and adverbs with beautiful felicity. But there is more in style than this. The form of her sentences is rather tryingly monotonous, and the distance

* In 'Am I a Snob?', where this story is related, Virginia incorrectly speculates that the encounter with Bennett took place in 1928, just after the publication of *Orlando* (a book Bennett viciously attacked).

between her nominatives and her verbs is steadily increasing. Still, *To the Lighthouse* has stuff in it strong enough to withstand quite a lot of adverse criticism.

Vita was not completely comfortable with Virginia's new book: 'It's as though you juggled with the coloured stars of a rocket, and kept them all alight, all flying.' She also told her: 'if I had read it without knowing you, I should be frightened of you.'[92] The most important review Virginia received was from Vanessa:

> it seemed to me that in the first part of the book you have given a portrait of mother which is more like her to me than anything I could ever have conceived of as possible. It is almost painful to have her so raised from the dead . . . It was like meeting her again with oneself grown up and on equal terms and it seems to me the most astonishing feat of creation to have been able to see her in such a way. You have given father too I think as clearly but perhaps, I may be wrong, that isn't quite so difficult . . . In fact for the last two days I have hardly been able to attend to daily life.[93]

Virginia responded ecstatically to Vanessa's praise: 'I was so pleased and excited by your letter that I trotted about all day like a puppy with a bone.'[94]

And Virginia reacted to Vita's many positive comments with considerable candour. She had been afraid that Part Two, written during the General Strike, was impossible as prose. She then commented on Vita's observation that Virginia was very much like Mrs Ramsay. This was indeed a great compliment: 'I don't know if I'm like Mrs Ramsay: as my mother died when I was 13, probably it is a child's view of her: but I have some sentimental delight in thinking that you like her. She has haunted me: but then so did that old wretch my father: Do you think it sentimental?'[95]

From the moment of *To the Lighthouse*'s conception, Virginia had been worried about excessive sentimentality. Now she realized that she had found an ideal balance. Before, she had been so convinced that Roger Fry would disapprove of the book that she did not follow her impulse to inscribe it to him. She was frank with him: 'the non-dedication is a greater compliment than the dedication would have been' because he had kept her 'on the right path, so far as writing goes, more than anyone'.[96]

The entire creative process still remained shrouded in mystery, but Virginia could now joke about her fifth novel; she pointed out to Vita that the Seafarers' Educational Society had bought two copies: 'It's an awful thought that the merchant service will be taught navigation by me: or the proper use of foghorns and cylinders.'[97] She remained unsure of what – if any – symbolism should be attached to the lighthouse itself: 'One has to have a central line down the middle of the book to hold the design together.'[98]

Although uncertain about her next project, Virginia had been fascinated by a letter from Vanessa in which she described how her maternal instinct had led her to allow an enormous moth into the villa at Cassis.

> We let it in, kept it, gave it a whole bottle of ether bought from the chemist, all in vain, took it to the chemist who dosed it with chloroform for a day – also in vain. Finally it did die rather the worse for wear, & I set it, & now, here is another! a better specimen. But though incredibly beautiful I suspect they're common – perhaps Emperor moths. Still I know how one would have blamed one's elders for not capturing such things at all costs so I suppose I must go through it all again. Then I remembered – didn't Fabre try experiments with this same creature & attract all the males in the neighbourhood by shutting up one female in a room? – just what we have now done. So probably soon the house will be full of them.[99]

Virginia did not know what kind of fiction she could make of the moths, but her imagination, as she told both Vita and Vanessa, had been fired up.

Having finally become an established writer, Virginia had to face the consequences: 'They don't laugh at me any longer. Soon they will take me for granted'.[100] Perhaps, she mused, she might become really famous. Virginia Woolf the celebrity was fundamentally a different person from Virginia Woolf the writer. The persona she adopted was labelled by the novelist Rosamond Lehmann as 'Gothic madonna'[101] and the critic David Cecil as 'mocking madonna'.[102] Both were struck by how her quiet, refined, angular beauty was offset by her bouts of frenzy, maliciousness and overbearing inquisitiveness. This side, as Lehmann recalled, could be extremely creative: 'She delighted to draw people out, plying them with questions, riotously embroidering upon what they told her, and generally suggesting to them a conception of themselves as leading lives of superlative interest and originality.'[103] In her public encounters, Virginia was a superb actress, who believed that attack was the best form of defence. Her discomfort could be gauged by her movements: she was a tall, elegant woman whose gait and gestures were laboured, often ungraceful.

For many years, Vita had seen behind Virginia's façade. In the wake of Vita's intuitive understanding of her new book, Virginia was drawn to her again. Aristocratic women like Vita, she told Vanessa, were an endless source of fascination. Such a woman might purchase an expensive silk dress and then carelessly pitch custard on to it at lunch. Virginia certainly became bolder in her advances: 'Look here Vita – throw over your man, and we'll go to Hampton Court and dine on the river together and walk in the garden in the moonlight and come home late and have a bottle of wine and get tipsy.'[104]

The most important event of the summer was a train trip to north Yorkshire. Virginia, Leonard, Vita, Harold and Eddy Sackville-West, the writer who was Vita's cousin and the heir to Knole, travelled there to observe a total eclipse of the sun.

> Then, for a moment we saw the sun, sweeping – it seemed to be sailing at a great pace & clear in a gap; we had out our smoked glasses; we saw it crescent, burning red; next moment it had sailed fast into the cloud again; only the red streamers came

> from it; then only a golden haze, such as one has often seen. The moments were passing . . . I thought how we were like very old people, in the birth of the world – druids on Stonehenge: . . . The clouds were turning pale; a reddish black colour . . . Then one looked back again at the blue: & rapidly, very very quickly, all the colours faded; it became darker & darker as at the beginning of a violent storm; the light sank & sank: we kept saying this is the shadow; & we thought now it is over – this is the shadow when suddenly the light went out. We had fallen. It was extinct. There was no colour. The earth was dead. That was the astonishing moment: & the next when as if a ball had rebounded, the cloud took colour on itself again, only a sparky aetherial colour & so the light came back . . . We had seen the world dead. This was within the power of nature . . . How can I express the darkness?[105]

At the time of her mother's death, Virginia had beheld a similar, mystical conjunction of red and black. In *To the Lighthouse*, the book in which she attempted to come to grips with her lifelong obsession with her mother, she both found and expressed the darkness – and, what is more, she triumphed over it.

Chapter Fourteen

A THIN SILVER EDGE

(1927–8)

In the summer of 1927, Virginia could still not make up her mind about Vita. On 4 July, after spending the weekend at Long Barn, she sent a sexually charged letter in which she warned her friend about the consequences of going to bed with someone else: 'You only be a careful dolphin in your gambolling, or you'll find Virginia's soft crevices lined with hooks.'[1] Virginia's bestowal of one of her nicknames for Vanessa on Vita shows how much she valued her. Nevertheless, there were real limits to this intimacy, limits imposed by nature – Vita's and her own. On the very same day, Virginia candidly informed her diary of Vita's circumscribed intelligence: 'She never breaks fresh ground. She picks up what the tide rolls to her feet.' Vita lacked a 'cutting edge',[2] a capacity for experimentation which was native to Virginia. Vita may be the great lover but Virginia is, she reminds herself, the genius.

Virginia's feelings about her own sexuality are captured in the short story 'Moments of Being: "Slater's Pins Have No Points"', the genesis of which can be traced back to September 1926. As often happened, 'side stories' were by-products of a just-completed novel. This time, 'the whole string' was pulled out from a sentence of Clara Pater's, '"Don't you find that Barker's pins have no points to them?"'[3] On 8 July 1927, she told Vita: 'I've just written, or re-written, a nice little story about Sapphism, for the Americans.'[4] When she received £60 from the editor at *Forum*, she saucily informed her friend that the point of the story had evaded him.

The editor may have been dense, but the Sapphic element in the narrative is obliquely treated. More crucial to an understanding of this important story is Virginia's desire, dating from the year before, to capture the essence of a woman's life by concentrating on a single incident. The young and tender Fanny Wilmot is at the home of her piano teacher, Julia Craye, who is playing a Bach fugue. A pin falls from Fanny's dress; while pupil and teacher search for it, Fanny's thoughts stray to and become an extended meditation on the life of the spinster. Although she has a tendency to see Julia Craye's life as unfulfilled, Fanny's vision expands considerably. She realizes that Julia may have served others, but she has also evaded a number of pitfalls: most importantly, she has lived an independent life. For the first time, she truly beholds her.

> She saw Julia open her arms; saw her blaze; saw her kindle. Out of the night she burnt like a dead white star. Julia kissed her. Julia possessed her.
>
> 'Slater's pins have no points,' Miss Craye said, laughing queerly and relaxing her arms, as Fanny Wilmot pinned the flower to her breast with trembling fingers.[5]

Immediately after Fanny imagines her bestowing the passionate kiss, Julia – the choice of name is significant – becomes Miss Craye once again. Fanny is shaken because she has been undeniably inflamed by her vision.

This short story is a remembrance of things past, a retelling of Virginia's conflicts from the early 1910s. Should she follow the example of women such as Janet Case and the Pater sisters and lead the life of a spinster, or should she marry? Earlier, Virginia had been frightened by the consequences inherent in leading a single life. At the end of this story, Fanny trembles but does not reject the life of a Miss Craye; the emotional centre of the story, though, belongs to the warm kiss. In the warmth of that 'possession' lies Virginia's lesbianism.

From the outset of her affair with Vita, Virginia distanced herself from genital sexuality ('These Sapphists'); in essence, she drew a line between her sexuality and Vita's. Her needs were real, but, as she increasingly realized, they were different from Vita's.

Perhaps when she was Fanny Wilmot's age she had seen the world divided into two sharply defined camps. In this story a richer, more provocative description of the life Virginia had chosen not to embrace emerges. In a work of art, Virginia could envision the totality of her experience, but, as she told Vanessa on 23 July, real life often seemed very different: 'poor Billy isn't one thing or the other, not a man nor a woman, so what's he to do?'[6]

One thing Virginia and Leonard did was to purchase on 15 July a long-wished luxury item: a motor car – a second-hand Singer – for £275. The pursuit of freedom rather than financial prosperity influenced this decision, although Virginia's growing sureness of her stature as an important and marketable writer allowed her to throw caution to the wind. In its first year of publication, *To the Lighthouse* sold almost 4,000 copies in England and 7,600 in the United States. (Although these sales were markedly superior to *Mrs Dalloway*'s total sales of 7,336 in 1925, the Woolfs' combined income – because of a decline of overall sales at the Press – dropped from £1,658 in 1926 to £1,496 in 1927.)

Virginia soon became absorbed by the car. Frederick Pape, the husband of Angelica's nurse Louie, was a professional chauffeur and had earlier taught Vanessa to drive. Leonard took six lessons from him and was able to drive by himself two weeks later. Virginia also received instruction from Pape but Fred Harris, a professional driving instructor, was her real teacher. Immediately after acquiring the dark-blue automobile with its pale-blue line of trim, much of her time was spent behind the wheel. Harris assured her that she was much above average, although he warned her about a tendency to keep too much to the left. Within eight days of acquiring the Singer, Virginia could motor alone in the country, although she soon abandoned driving and let Leonard take over. She may justifiably have been annoyed with her confidence in her husband when he bumped the back of the car on the gatepost at Rodmell a few months later. In any event, in giving her the car for writing *To the Lighthouse*, 'the world' made Sussex and the Continent far more accessible. Above all, she loved the serendipity of the road: 'What I like, or one of the things I like, about motoring is the sense it gives one of lighting accidentally, like a voyager who touches another planet with the tip of his toe, upon scenes which would have gone on, have always gone on, will go on, unrecorded, save for this chance glimpse.'[7]

The Singer may have consumed much of Virginia's agitated energy, but her concerns about her sexual identity became even more problematic when she had to deal with Clive Bell's increasing sense of despair. As far as he was concerned, life – particularly a sex life – after forty-five was not worth living. 'I admire you for having tried to kill yourself,' he assured Virginia. When he visited her, he told her how he had bedded a new mistress and proclaimed himself – despite his gloomy air – the Don Juan of Bloomsbury. On both Vanessa's and her own account, Virginia was offended by this confession: in part, she felt guilt because she had helped to unravel the Bell marriage, but she was also hurt because she, as a much younger woman, had been the object of Clive's desire. 'Why does he always wish to hurt me?' she asked her diary.[8] Obviously, Clive still felt diminished by his affair with Virginia and wanted to pay her back.

Then there was a new would-be lover. For years, Virginia had been aware that Philip Morrell was smitten with her. On 26 July, he declared himself. She may have found him as 'coarse as an old ram' but she was touched. However, the excitement which she felt was an uneasy one, 'that is of physical desire making someone . . . too restless & emotional.'[9] This interview was broken up by the arrival of Leonard and Pinker the cocker spaniel bitch given to the Woolfs by Vita in the summer of 1926. Soon afterwards, Morrell poured his feelings into a letter, but Virginia was really interested only in the possible effect of such a suitor on Vita, who had picked up that something was wrong in Virginia's letter of 3 August. Virginia waited a few days and then coyly responded.

> What do you mean? It was the nicest, lovingest, tenderest letter in the world, a little rasped at not seeing you perhaps, but after all that's to your taste isn't it? Or did you, with the marvellous

> intuition of the poet, discover what I have tried to keep concealed from you? that I am loved, by a man; a man with an aquiline nose, a nice property, a wife of title and furniture to suit . . . What do you wish me to do? I was so overcome that I blushed like a girl of 15.[10]

Virginia admits to a blush, but hers is a cool, teasing letter which allows her to put Morrell's advance to good use. She may have been angry with Clive for tormenting her, but she was quite capable of wielding power in a similar way. Here, she tried to wound Vita. Virginia, who distrusted all sexual expressions of feeling, almost completely masks her agitation in this letter. She wanted something from Vita which was not essentially sexual, but, since she was not sure what she wanted, she conceals – from Vita and from herself – her real object of desire: a warm, possessing embrace from another woman.

Virginia was afraid of being stuck in the past, a complaint she voiced about Ka Arnold-Forster: 'Why can't she ever wake up from the year 1911? There she sticks with Rupert copulating in Berlin.'[11] She had once again formed a low opinion of her own writing, especially in contrast to Katherine Mansfield's. Even her bedroom at Rodmell offered no sufficient retreat; it was so damp that 'dark sweats break out on the walls and ooze up underneath one's feet'.[12] In late July there was a brief respite when Virginia briefly visited her American friends Ethel Sands and Nan Hudson, who had restored their Normandy home, the Château d'Auppegard, to its seventeenth-century splendour. The château itself, only one room deep, received light from the north and the south and as a result the house possessed an aura of delicate insubstantiality, an effect to which Virginia responded warmly. In addition to the vases of carefully arranged flowers, rugs from Samarkand and magnificent antiques, there was the consoling presence of Vanessa, who, together with Duncan, had arrived three days before, having been commissioned to paint decorations on the loggia.

Some of Virginia's dissatisfaction with herself and her own writing soon spilled over into a quarrel with Morgan Forster, who had complimented her in June on *To the Lighthouse*: 'It's awfully sad, very beautiful both in (non-radiant) colour and shape; it stirs me much more to questions whether & why than any thing else you have written. The uneasiness of life seems to well up between all the words, the excitement of life on the other hand to be observed.'[13] In his extremely tactful way, Forster may have been hinting that there was some sort of discrepancy between 'uneasiness' and 'excitement' in that book. According to Virginia, there was certainly such a conflict at the very heart of Forster's work: he could not make up his mind to which camp he belonged. Was he a preacher or an artist? From this lack of certainty followed major flaws: 'The poet is twitched away by the satirist; the comedian is tapped on the shoulder by the moralist; he never loses himself or forgets himself for long in sheer delight in the beauty or the interest of things as they are.'[14] The clear implication is that Forster, who saw a draft of the article on him which appeared in the *Atlantic Monthly* that November, is very much a compromised writer. He objected strenuously: 'I don't believe my method's wrong! The trouble is I can't work it.'[15]

That autumn, Virginia renewed her attack in a review of his critical book *Aspects of the Novel*, which had been given earlier in the year as the Clark Lectures. According to her, Forster was too tied to the actual fabric of life in his narratives and thus bound to some sort of compact to describe, say, a tea-table in minute detail. In the process, the real essence of life evaded him. Forster was simply not bold enough.

> If the English critic were less domestic, less assiduous to protect the rights of what it pleases him to call life, the novelist might be bolder too. He might cut adrift from the eternal tea table and the plausible and preposterous formulas which are supposed to represent the whole of our human adventure. But then the story might wobble; the plot might crumble; ruin might seize upon the characters. The novel in short might become a work of art.[16]

Stung, Forster accused Virginia of envisioning a kind of literature in which each sentence 'leads to an exquisitely fashioned casket of which the key has unfortunately been mislaid'.[17] Until Virginia could find her set of keys, he did not intend to search for his own.

Virginia is defending principles which she had held for some time. Here, rather than attacking someone like Bennett or Galsworthy, she turns a sharp critical eye on a fellow denizen of Bloomsbury. Her willingness to quarrel with Forster – who understood and had defended her position publicly – shows how much on edge she was that summer. She made this diary entry on 10 August: 'An odd incident, psychologically . . . has been Morgan's serious concern about my article on him. Did I care a straw what he said about me? Was it more laudatory? Yet here is this self possessed, aloof man taking every word to heart, cast down to the depths, apparently, because I do not give him superlative rank, & writing again & again to ask about it.'[18] Virginia is being a bit obtuse here: she would have been deeply offended by a similar piece about her by Forster. All she offered him was a muted apology; her article had been official and thus impersonal: 'Unofficially & personally I'm afraid I've hurt or annoyed you . . . I didn't mean to. The article was cut down to fit The Nation, and the weight all fell in the same place.'[19]

That summer, Virginia had begun work on a very different piece of prose fiction from anything Morgan Forster would have undertaken. Whereas Forster had written but was unwilling (and unable) to publish *Maurice*, a novel dealing openly with homosexual love, Virginia's nebulous sexual interest in Vita spurred her to write *Orlando*. Forster was certain about his homosexuality and had penned a book which dealt openly with the love that dared not speak its name; Virginia was very uncertain about her sexuality and her new book is about a person who starts life as a man and then becomes a woman. Orlando inhabits two gender worlds and this was precisely Virginia's dilemma. Her new book is about a person who 'isn't one thing or the other, not a man nor a woman'.[20]

Orlando may be a lavish, beautiful tribute to Vita Sackville-West and thus a celebration of the ways in which she incorporated male and female qualities. However, Virginia's new book is also about herself, about her attempt to understand, for example, how she could be touched by Philip Morrell's overtures and yet, almost immediately, use that declaration as a weapon with which to goad Vita. She was looking at even more basic issues. Could she be a woman in her mother's mould and yet have followed in her father's footsteps by becoming a writer? Why was she sexually attracted to women and yet married? Did she possess a sort of composite gender, one which was neither female nor male? To answer these questions she wrote a truly fantastic biography, one which traces the history of the aristocratic, androgynous Orlando through four centuries of male and female manifestations.

Virginia also wanted to capture Vita's attention, which had wandered – she had recently begun an affair with Mary Campbell, the wife of the poet Roy Campbell. She also wanted to hurt her. She reduced Vita to tears when she told her that she was utterly bored by hearing about this relationship. In fact, she suggested, if it were not for Mary Campbell's presence in Vita's life, she might write her a letter of 'lovemaking unbelievable: indiscretions incredible'. Instead of which, Vita would have to settle for a chaste missive. *Orlando* itself is an exquisite book in which sexuality is dealt with in a restrained way. Once again, Virginia's lovemaking is confined to paper.

By describing her hero/heroine's adventures through four centuries, Virginia found a way to write a brilliant parodic history of English literature. Although the form of the book may be picaresque, the style changes as the centuries advance. Perhaps, it suggests, society's notion of sexuality has to be modified just as the English language itself has undergone a metamorphosis. On 9 October, Virginia announced the project to Vita: 'suppose Orlando turns out to be Vita; and it's all about you and the lusts of your flesh and the lure of your mind . . . Shall you mind? Say yes, or No.'[21] That was a hard question to answer, especially when the would-be writer promised a confection which would revolutionize the genre of biography. The subject proved a very willing victim:

> My God, Virginia, if ever I was thrilled and terrified it is at the prospect of being projected into the shape of Orlando. What fun for you; what fun for me. You see, any vengeance that you ever want to take will lie ready to your hand. Yes, go ahead, toss up your pancake, brown it nicely on both sides, pour brandy over it, and serve hot.[22]

Vita's cooperation extended to posing for or providing three photographs (Orlando on Her Return to England, Orlando About the Year 1840, Orlando at the Present Time); in addition, she furnished Virginia with reproductions of four paintings from Knole; two of these (Orlando as a Boy and Orlando as Ambassador) provide the visual evidence of Orlando/Vita's masculinity. (Angelica Bell posed for the remaining photograph of Orlando's Russian love, Sasha.)

Clive Bell proved a harder nut to crack. When Virginia expressed sincere admiration for his new book, *Civilization*, he was convinced that her praise was so excessive that she must be lying. She was furious: 'I am enough of a prig and conceited enough to attach some value to my judgements of books and don't like it to be assumed that though I may lie about everything else, I lie about them.'[23] Duplicity regarding her life was a strong possibility, but it was an option which did not extend to literary matters.

Both Leonard and Dadie Rylands exhorted her to complete her book on the nature of fiction. Although she had ridden roughshod over Forster about his book on this troubled subject, it was not a task to which she responded warmly. She could not 'screw'[24] the necessary words out of herself. Dadie possessed a rigorous critical sensibility, one he was not averse to aiming in Virginia's direction when he observed that she had a tendency in her fiction to allow her style 'to get on top of her'. He also pointed out that she lacked logical power and lived and wrote in a sort of opium dream. 'And,' Virginia agreed, 'the dream is too often about myself.' She feared that she was little more than a self-centred humbug, a writer whose style in writing and conversation was merely flashy.[25]

Just as she was becoming increasingly worried about the worth of her writing, Virginia's previous concern about having children diminished considerably. When she attended Angelica's birthday party in December, she saw the beautiful little girl as the 'epitome of all womanliness; & such an unopened bud of sense & sensibility'. And yet, she realized, a long-held desire had simply vanished: 'And yet oddly enough I scarcely want children of my own now. This insatiable desire to write something before I die, this ravaging sense of the shortness & feverishness of life, make me cling, like a man on a rock, to my one anchor. I don't like the physicalness of having children of one's own.' Her books were her real children. Previously, she had been able to 'dramatize' herself as a parent. And perhaps, she was sadly aware, she had killed the desire to have children 'instinctively; as perhaps nature does'.[26]

These reflections were uttered at about the same time that Virginia experienced the onset of what she called 't. of l.'[27] Although menopause had not yet begun, she awaited, with trepidation, its onset. Her concern with the forces of mutability was underscored by Thomas Hardy's death in January 1928: each writer, she was reminded afresh, was allotted only a limited span of time in which to make his or her mark.

Orlando was conceived as and reads like a high-spirited romp, but Virginia remained listless during its writing. Self-criticism expanded to an overly critical view of her friends. She was certainly justified in being irritated with Ka, who disliked Virginia's dallying with women such as Lady Colefax and Vita: 'I suppose,' she taunted Virginia, 'you're entirely taken up with great people now.'[28] Although Helen Anrep, Roger Fry's companion, was given the benefit of being intelligent, she was a 'sharp tongued harlot'. And Roger's liaison with Helen allowed Virginia to torment her sister. Roger made the mistake of telling Virginia that Helen was even more in love with Vanessa than he was. This casual observation led Virginia to ask Vanessa: 'Do you have

Helen one way and Roger t'other? Well, well, I never suspected you of that.'[29]

This volley has much more to do with Virginia's sexuality than her sister's. And Virginia continually and gleefully reminded Vanessa of Clive's quarrels with Mary Hutchinson – and of their sexual escapades, present and past. Clive acted 'crazed' when he met or was about to meet a virgin he might seduce; Virginia elicited from Mary 'an account of copulating with Clive on a hard bed on a cold night at Asheham' many years before.[30] The tone may be jocular, but Vanessa did not like to have the past dredged up so relentlessly.

When Vanessa told Virginia that January of her delight in La Bergère, the small ramshackle cottage near Cassis which she and Duncan rented from a Colonel Teed, this gave Virginia pain rather than pleasure. The simple truth was that she did not want the *real* Dolphin to escape. When she was planning to visit her sister in France that spring, Virginia confessed delight and dismay:

> I am very excited, partly at the thought of seeing you again. I am like a sea anemone which has had to keep all its tentacles curled up, and when it's put in water (i.e. Dolphin) they come out and wave and tumble and are of an exquisite and incredible beauty: but Lord! Dolphin bites: or she squirts acid: Dolphin can't be depended on for more than 2 seconds – Dolphin's a heartless brute, but nothing to Duncan, whose heart is made of purest emerald.[31]

In the final observation is a nice piece of back-stabbing: Duncan's homosexuality made Vanessa 'nothing' to him, whereas Vanessa had a tendency to bite the person who truly loved her best.

Although Vita does not escape Virginia's criticism in *Orlando*, she emerges triumphant. In this book, she is mythologized into a Janus-like figure, a person who incorporates male and female qualities:

> For it was this mixture in her of man and woman, one being

> uppermost and then the other, that often gave her conduct an unexpected turn . . . She is excessively tender-hearted. She could not endure to see a donkey beaten or a kitten drowned. Yet again, they noted, she detested household matters, was up at dawn and out among the fields in summer before the sun had risen.[32]

The duality of Orlando is a reflection of Vita's real personality and, despite gently mocking the genre, Virginia accomplishes one of the most important tasks of any biographer: she brings her subject – in all her complexity – to life.

In *Jacob's Room*, Jacob is an elusive figure and the book attacks the very notion of biography. In *Orlando*, the subject is almost always present, but his/her life is presented in two distinct ways. There is a great deal of satire directed at the pretensions of the aristocracy, at some of the more ludicrous aspects of English history and society (the comic venom is directed mainly against the Victorians) and at the ways men have debarred women from power. More central is the lyrical strain. Virginia had long been convinced that women had been excluded from the poetic tradition and, although she had not yet written any poetry, she had long been attempting to make the language of prose attain the condition of verse. Despite its elegant comic tone, *Orlando* is filled with sharp, intense passages which reflect some of the great poetical genres, particularly the elegy, the seduction poem and the topographical poem.

Orlando blends biography with fiction, satire with poetry. This is particularly appropriate for a book which is about a woman who wished that she had been born a man and who often acted a masculine role. After all, *Orlando* was written to console Vita for being born a woman and – because of that single fact – for being deprived of Knole. Vita was a person who was deeply proud of her distinguished ancestry and the entire conception of the book turns on that central fact. By having Orlando be a man in the first portion of the book, his claims on the male-dominated aspects of English culture are firmly established. Since Orlando becomes a woman only after she has been a man, her pedigree (and right to inherit) have been deftly established. The fact that Orlando changes sex but her/his personality remains constant in the book is also a way of justifying Vita's supposedly male characteristics, particularly her aggressive pursuit of other women.

Although Virginia later felt that she did not attain complete control of her material, the serious concerns which underscore the book are always present, despite its seeming lightness and frivolity. There are many moments of incredible beauty, as when Orlando and Sasha skate on the Thames: 'hence, they had the river to themselves. Hot with skating and with love they would throw themselves down in some solitary reach, where the yellow osiers fringed the bank, and wrapped in a great fur cloak Orlando would take her in his arms, and know, for the first time, he murmured, the delights of love.'[33] The passage is strong in its own right, particularly from a writer who is not often celebrated for her ability to portray physical affection. The description of this thwarted Renaissance romance is Virginia's attempt to retell the bittersweet romance between Vita and Violet Trefusis.

Vita's marriage – which had nearly been broken up by her liaison with Violet – is evoked towards the end of the book, when Orlando falls in love with and marries Marmaduke Bonthrop Shelmerdine, Esquire.

> 'Oh! Shel, don't leave me!' she cried. 'I'm passionately in love with you,' she said. No sooner had the words left her mouth than an awful suspicion rushed into both their minds simultaneously.
>
> 'You're a woman, Shel!' she cried.
>
> 'You're a man, Orlando!' he cried.[34]

Harold Nicolson's pet name for Vita was 'Mar', but in *Orlando* Shel is so dubbed by Orlando. Can a marriage between two homosexuals work? In *Orlando* such a marriage – in most ways a very successful one – prevails.

The descriptions of 'Snowdon', Orlando's ancestral home, are lifted from Vita's book of 1922, *Knole and the Sackvilles*, but

Virginia often puffs and embroiders them. The effect is both comical and satirical. Parody, however, extends to herself, when she pokes fun at the 'Time Passes' sequence from *To the Lighthouse*.

> Here he came then, day after day, week after week, month after month, year after year. He saw the beech trees turn golden and the young ferns unfurl; he saw the moon sickle and then circular; he saw – but probably the reader can imagine the passage which should follow and how every tree and plant in the neighbourhood is described first green, then golden; how moons rise and suns set; how spring follows winter and autumn summer; how night succeeds day and day night; how there is first a storm and then fine weather; how things remain much as they are for two or three hundred years or so, except for a little dust and a few cobwebs which one old woman can sweep up in half an hour; a conclusion which, one cannot help feeling, might have been reached more quickly by the simple statement that 'Time passed' (here the exact amount could be indicated in brackets) and nothing whatever happened.[35]

Vita is a writer: the reader's attention is constantly directed to this central fact. Although Vita may have lost Knole, she re-created it on paper and thus staked her own claim to imaginative ownership. Orlando – man and woman – writes a poem, 'The Oak Tree', over the course of three centuries. The poem is finally published in the twentieth. Of course, Virginia is paying tribute to Vita's best-selling book-length poem of 1926, *The Land*. Vita may not, in Virginia's judgement, have written a great poem, but she was paving the way for other women to undertake similar, necessary tasks.

By introducing fanciful elements into her mock-biography, Virginia, like Lytton Strachey, was attempting to revolutionize the art of biography. She is suggesting that it is a form of fiction, not of history. And, if the essence of character is re-created, should one question the method? Although written in a seemingly more orthodox fashion than, say, *Jacob's Room*, *Orlando* is another revolutionary work of art which undercuts society's view of male and female roles.

In addition to bestowing manhood and Knole on Vita in *Orlando*, Virginia attempted to give her another present. At the end of the book, Orlando is awaiting the arrival of Shel, who leaps to the ground from an aeroplane. At that very moment, 'there sprang up over his head a single wild bird. "It is the goose!" Orlando cried. "The wild goose . . ."'[36] Orlando herself, as she told Harold, was puzzled by this incident. Had Virginia's imagination simply gone over the top? The goose represents something which Virginia did not really feel Vita deserved: lasting literary reputation. Vita's pursuit of such fame may have been a wild-goose chase, but the book in its final moment presents her with that gift.

Virginia could not make Vita a major writer. The irony is that Virginia achieved that distinction, *Orlando* being one of the brightest jewels in her crown. If *Orlando* is an undisguised, deliberately grandiose fictional biography of Vita, it also contains strands of disguised autobiography, albeit of a muted sort. In the late 1920s, Virginia saw conflicting strands of male and female qualities in her own make-up. This led her to think of herself as an 'it'. In this book, she redefines her own psychic terrain as one in which the male and female can exist comfortably side by side. Moreover, as a woman, Orlando forms a very low opinion of the sex to which she once belonged. Perhaps all the best human beings are, after all, bisexual composites? *Orlando* is very much about the glory of androgyny. For a time, this doctrine provided Virginia with answers to many elusive questions.

When she completed *Orlando*, on 22 March 1928, Virginia felt that the joke had gone too far for her liking. For the previous six weeks, she had felt too involved in the lives of others: 'rather a bucket than a fountain; sitting to be shot into by one person after another. A rabbit that passes across a shooting gallery, & one's friends go pop-pop.'[37] She was no longer going to be an easy prey to the whims of others. One way to escape such a fate was a holiday on the Continent.

Four days later, the Woolfs made the Newhaven–Dieppe Channel crossing. They drove through Beauvais, Troyes, Beaune, Vienne, Orange and Aix. Leonard and Virginia would have a leisurely one- or two-hour lunch, visit a church or two and then motor on. Their destination was Cassis, where Vanessa now spent part of each year. The Woolfs stayed in rooms at the Château de Fontcreuse, which belonged to Colonel Teed, although they took most of their meals with Vanessa and Duncan at La Bergère. Life *en famille* was delightfully eccentric: Duncan danced solo to the gramophone, Angelica and her friends collected frogs, Julian's manner replicated the manners and mores of a German professor, Vanessa cut the heads off the moths which, of an evening, battered on the window in her studio and Clive ostentatiously presented a young woman with a pair of sky-blue pyjamas. Leonard assisted Angelica by collecting spiders for her imprisoned frogs.

The return journey, begun on 9 April, was not congenial. They stopped overnight at Tarascon, Florac, Aurillac, Guéret, Blois and Dreux on their way to Dieppe. On 11 April, they journeyed 130 miles through the mountains in a bad snowstorm. That day, their tyres were punctured three times and on several occasions they came dangerously close to the edges of precipices. Five days later, their crossing from Dieppe was very rough.

From Orange on 31 March, Virginia had written to Vita: 'I think of [you] at Long Barn: all fire and legs and beautiful plunging ways like a young horse.'[38] Immediately upon arriving back – and without any new information about Vita's liaison with Mary Campbell – she told her: 'And ain't it wretched you care for me no longer: I always said you were a promiscuous brute – Is it a Mary again; or a Jenny this time or a Polly? Eh?'[39] The second letter may be deliberately jocular, but it is calculated to wound Vita – something which Virginia would not attempt to do when she was separated from her. She may not have wanted to sleep with Vita, but she wanted her to herself.

Waiting Virginia's return was a letter of apology from Clive for some sharp words he had thrown her way at Cassis, but he then reminded her that he had once again been informed that she had been making fun of him behind his back. In turn, Virginia was convinced that Vanessa was repeating confidences. In her reply to Clive, Virginia wondered aloud 'what itch' this smacking was gratifying. Why was she always the victim? Meanwhile, she passed on a nice piece of gossip to him: 'Vita has had a terrific, culminating and final scene with [her mother] in a solicitor's office.'[40] Even for Virginia gossip had its limits. She was dismayed a few weeks later to learn that Lady Sackville was publicly stating that 'Harold's a bugger, and Vita a sapphist'.[41]

Soon, Virginia found herself back in the whirlwind of a London existence: supper with Maynard and Lydia, tea with the critic Raymond Mortimer, dinner with Vita. That April was wet and windy. In vain, Virginia searched the park in the Square for spring colour and found none. There was a corresponding despondency in her own work. As far as she was concerned, *Orlando* was simply a freak book, one needing a great deal of polish which she was not going to be able to bestow on it. Despite the struggles which beset her, she nevertheless remained convinced that the 'only exciting life'[42] was the imaginary one.

A fascinating outsider's view of Virginia and Leonard that spring can be found in the young Richard Kennedy's diary. For a long time, the Woolfs had been dissatisfied with Angus Davidson's laissez-faire attitude towards publishing. When he finally left the Press that winter, his spot was taken by Kennedy. The sixteen-year-old, who had done badly at Marlborough, was placed at the Hogarth Press by his architect uncle, who had learned from Leonard, on meeting him at the Cranium Club, that he was on the lookout for an apprentice publisher. This is what Leonard told Richard's uncle. In fact, Kennedy became a glorified office boy.

Kennedy was a strange choice to replace Davidson, but Leonard's decision was inspired in part by a desire to have a young man around to whom he could act as a father figure. He invited Richard to walk Pinker with him and he was quite frank with him about his views on politics and sex. But, of course, shop business intervened. Richard often saw a whining, exasperated Leonard, who would fly at him or the other help, Mrs Cartwright and Miss

Richard Kennedy. Pencil sketch of Virginia Woolf

Belcher. The young man's primary interest was his budding love life, not the affairs of the Hogarth Press.

For Virginia, Kennedy was very much a peripheral figure. He was certainly very curious about Virginia Woolf. One night when he took supper with them and Dadie Rylands, Virginia was in a particularly exuberant mood: 'She said she had been to a nightclub the night before and how marvellous it was inventing new foxtrot steps. I thought LW's back looked a bit disapproving as he was dishing out the strawberries . . . George Rylands egged Mrs W on to talk about how much she enjoyed kicking up her heels. I couldn't help feeling a little shocked.'[43] Kennedy may have been a bit prudish, but he left a fascinating account of the informal Virginia rolling her shag cigarettes, working with demon speed to wrap parcels of books, setting type with considerable dexterity, knitting (a hobby taken up at this time) and, clad in her nightgown, staring through the glass window in the workroom door to be certain she would not encounter any visitor if she entered the room. The young man had an excellent eye, as can be seen in this pen portrait of a slightly dishevelled Virginia in her studio-stock-room: 'She looks at us over the top of her steel-rimmed spectacles, her grey hair hanging over her forehead and a shag cigarette hanging from her lips. She wears a hatchet-blue overall and sits hunched in a wicker arm-chair with her pad on her knees and a small typewriter beside her.'[44] Kennedy was also a careful listener. One night, he heard Virginia observe how the outsider position of working-class writers bore a striking resemblance to the similar status of women in society.

Kennedy's most penetrating – if perhaps too strong – observation was to see Virginia as Olympia. For him, Leonard was the demonic magician who kept everything going through sheer force of will: 'Mrs W is a beautiful magical doll, very precious, but sometimes rather uncontrollable. Perhaps, like the doll, she hasn't got a soul. But when she feels inclined, she can create fantasy and we all fall over ourselves, or are disapproving.'[45]

Virginia was certainly in touch with the contradictory strain in others. When she met the writer Rebecca West that May, she admired her vitality and intelligence, although she felt that she had exceedingly bad taste. Earlier that month, the popular novelist Hugh Walpole had presented Virginia with the Femina-Vie Heureuse Prize for *To the Lighthouse*. His great sorrow, unlike Virginia's, was that he could never sell less than 20,000 copies of a book but had to endure ridicule from the highbrow critics. When his chauffeur praised a book of his, Hugh, although a homosexual attracted to working-class men, was cut to the heart. Despite their appeals to very different sections of the reading public, Hugh and Virginia became fast friends.

Some opposites could simply not be reconciled. One such was Rose Macaulay in whom Virginia (unconsciously) may have seen aspects of herself:

> Some houses have gone too far to be repaired – she is one. If we had rescued her before she was 30 – but she is now 45 – has

> lived with the riff raff of South Kensington culture for 15 years; become a successful lady novelist, and is rather jealous, spiteful, and uneasy about Bloomsbury; can talk of nothing but reviews . . . she is a spindle shanked, withered virgin: I never felt anyone so utterly devoid of the sexual parts.[46]

Although she was pleased that Hyde Park Gate was sold for £4,925 that spring, Virginia was much more concerned with Rodmell, which was threatened with development. In order to shore up their own boundaries, that August the Woolfs purchased a field which gave them a view of the Asheham cement works. The landscape at Rodmell nevertheless offered the prospect of adventure, as when she went out alone on the river and encountered twenty-three swans, wings outstretched, circling her.

Rather than being relieved, Virginia was more than a bit disappointed that summer when Leonard told her that *Orlando* was in some ways better than *To the Lighthouse*: more interesting and more attached to life. For Virginia, this was a dubious compliment. She wanted to lie low for a while, 'to keep the hatch down', but she was already thinking about something 'abstract poetic'.[47] Before she could turn her hand to any new major project, though, she had to spend five to seven hours a day correcting the proofs of *Orlando* and signing 800 copies of the limited (American) edition of the book. Virginia's inner turbulence was dissipated when Vanessa arrived back in England in the third week of June: 'She is a necessity to me – as I am not to her. I run to her as the wallaby runs to the old kangaroo.'[48]

Since Vita was no longer a necessity, Virginia was determined to gnaw down the various strata in their friendship. This resolve was made at the time she had a strong, vivid dream of Katherine Mansfield. For Virginia, Katherine – far more than Vanessa or Vita – was the external embodiment of her own unique creative forces, almost as if the spirit of the dead woman had passed into her. This is the handing on of the feminist tradition in literature – Katherine had died; Virginia was alive and must carry on the struggle.

A curious sense of insubstantiality had certainly taken over

Virginia. When an acquaintance, the writer Eddy Sackville-West, visited her, she felt there was no real communication between them. He left her with 'the usual feeling: why is not human intercourse more definite, tangible: why aren't I left holding a small round substance, say of the size of a pea . . . I am so important to myself: yet of no importance to other people: like the shadow passing over the downs.'[49] A good indicator of Virginia's vulnerability was an encounter with Mrs Woolf in early September. In most of her references to her mother-in-law, Virginia is castigating or condescending. Mrs Woolf is a Jewess – that makes her different from Virginia and allows her to be slotted into some unimportant pigeonhole.

What deeply annoyed Virginia was that the usually dense Mrs Woolf observed, 'You must often think of your writing when you are not writing, Virginia.' This remark smacks of empathy. As soon as the remark was uttered, Virginia was repulsed at the possibility of intimacy that was opened up. Why, she asked herself, was she so upset? 'I felt the horror of family life, & the terrible threat to one's liberty that I used to feel with father, Aunt Mary or George.' She imagined that she was being scratched with horrible, menacing claws.

> How strangely she made everything commonplace, ugly, suburban, notwithstanding a charm too: something fresh & vital such as old women have, & not, I think, old men. But to be attached to her as daughter would be so cruel a fate that I can think of nothing worse; & thousands of women might be dying of it in England today: this tyranny of mother over daughter, or father; their right to the due being as powerful as anything in the world. And then, they ask, why women don't write poetry. Short of killing Mrs W. nothing could be done.[50]

Guilt at not being able to respond with kindness towards Mrs Woolf transformed itself into a sense that the old woman was a predator who must be destroyed lest she destroy. These powerful feelings arose because Virginia, in a flash, was put in touch with just how much she had been deprived of by her family, particularly by Leslie's selfishness and George's intrusiveness. A part of Virginia wanted to respond warmly to Mrs Woolf's kindness, but her early hopes had been so badly dashed that she could see her mother-in-law's inquiry only as a selfish, devouring act.

Of course, much of Marie Woolf's conversation was tedious and repetitious, but at this troubled encounter she raised Virginia's hackles when she expressed her grave reservations about Radclyffe Hall's lesbian novel, *The Well of Loneliness*, which had just been banned. Her daughter Bella had been at school with the author, and this had led Mrs Woolf to acquire the book at Harrods: 'Of course I cannot say all that I would like to say if we were alone together. I may be foolish, but I cannot speak to you and Len as if Len were not there. But I would like very much to talk to you alone about it.' Leonard and Virginia encouraged her to continue:

> It is a dreadful pity I think that such a book should have been published. I do not mean for the ordinary reasons. What I mean is that there are many unmarried women living alone. And now it is very hard on them that such a book should have been written . . . And you may think me very foolish – I am seventy six – but until I read this book I did not know that such things . . . went on at all. When I was at school there was nothing like that.

Now it was Leonard's turn to become impatient: 'We did at my boarding school. It was the most corrupt place I have ever been in. And you let me go there when I was twelve years old.' Mrs Woolf countered by saying that she had given her son good principles. The son fervently denied this: 'You had given me no principles at all.'[51] In referring to lesbianism, Mrs Woolf claimed a lack of knowledge, whereas Virginia was reluctant to embrace such knowledge.

That September, Virginia was in what she called a 'state of violent excitement' about a trip she and Vita were taking to Burgundy: 'we might go to moonlight ruins, cafés, dances, plays, junketings: converse for ever; sleep only while the moon covers herself for an instant with a thin veil'[52] This jaunt infuriated

Leonard, who displaced his fury on to Dorothy Wellesley, the wealthy poet and intimate friend of Vita, when he and Virginia visited her at her new home, Penn in the Rocks. Her husband's anger troubled Virginia, whose pleasure in the excursion was now diminished. As she told Vita, she was poignantly aware of what Leonard meant to her: 'You see, I would not have married Leonard had I not preferred living with him to saying good bye to him.'[53] What Virginia did not confess to Vita was that there was another dimension to the trip which frightened her; she was afraid that Vita might 'find me out, I her out'.[54]

The two women left for Burgundy in September. On this trip, Virginia evoked Vita's maternal side: she was, according to Virginia, a 'perfect old hen, always running about with hot water bottles'.[55] As she told her husband, Vita felt very protective of Virginia: 'The combination of that brilliant brain and fragile body is very lovable. She has a sweet and childlike nature, from which her intellect is completely separate.'[56] Vita's comment is astute: the sweet, confiding side of Virginia's personality was often at odds with her acute powers of observation and reflection.

Immediately upon being separated from Leonard, Virginia was in touch with her tender feelings for him:

> I don't think I could stand more than a week away from you, as there are so many things to say to you, which I can't say to Vita – though she is most sympathetic and more intelligent than you think . . . Poor Mandril does adore your every hair of your little body and hereby puts in a claim for an hour of antelope kissing the moment she gets back.[57]

As soon as the pursuit of the exotic was under way, the mandrill was desperately lonely for the mongoose, whose claims on his beloved's loyalty were upheld. Once again, there had been a sharp discrepancy between reality and fantasy. The trip to Burgundy, it turned out, was merely a pleasant domestic interlude.

During their brief trip, Virginia and Vita decided not to talk about *Orlando*, which was published on 11 October. J. C. Squire in the

Observer dismissed it as a 'pleasant trifle',[58] but most reviewers agreed with Rebecca West's pronouncement in the *New York Herald Tribune*: the book was a 'poetic masterpiece'. Not surprisingly, Arnold Bennett in the *Evening Standard* of 8 November expressed disappointment, obviously tinged with envy.

> You cannot keep your end up at a London dinner-party in these weeks unless you have read Mrs Virginia Woolf's *Orlando*. For about a fortnight I succeeded in not reading it – partly from obstinacy and partly from a natural desire for altercation at table about what ought and ought not to be read. Then I saw that Hugh Walpole had described it as 'another masterpiece', and that Desmond MacCarthy had given it very high praise.
>
> I have a great opinion of the literary opinions of these two critics. So I bought the book and read it. I now know exactly what I think of it, and I can predict the most formidable rumpuses at future parties.
>
> It is a very odd volume. It has a preface, in which Mrs Woolf names the names of 53 people who have helped her with it. It has, too, an index . . . Further, the novel, which is a play of fancy, a wild fantasia, a romance, a high-brow lark, is illustrated with ordinary realistic photographs . . . This is the oddest of all the book's oddities.

After these opening sallies, Bennett homes in on some very basic objections to Virginia's new book:

> The theme is a great one. But it is a theme for a Victor Hugo, not for Mrs Woolf, who, while sometimes excelling in fancy and in delicate realistic observation, has never yet shown the mighty imaginative power which the theme clearly demands. Her best novel, *To the Lighthouse*, raised my hopes of her. *Orlando* has dashed them and they lie in iridescent fragments at my feet.[59]

Bennett is hoisting Virginia on her own petard. She had vehemently attacked him as the proponent of the realistic novel. If she ventured into the terrain that he had made his own, he would show just how far short she fell in her exploitation of it.

For vastly different reasons, Vita's mother hated the book. On 14 October she wrote to Virginia: 'You have written some beautiful phrases in Orlando, but probably you do not realize how *cruel* you have been. And the person who inspired the Book, has been crueller still.' Lady Sackville pasted a photograph of Virginia in her copy and wrote alongside it: 'The awful face of a mad woman whose successful mad desire is to separate people who care for each other. I loathe this woman for having changed my Vita and taken her away from me.'[60] Eddy objected to a character whose initials were 'S. W.' and his father was furious because photographs of portraits at Knole were reproduced without his permission. Vita had in fact sought her uncle's permission but had concealed from him the nature of the book in which his family portraits would appear.

On 21 November, a disgruntled Virginia told Eddy: 'All right. I have written a humble letter of apology to your father and sent him a copy of the Edition de luxe. Mr S. W. was (if anybody) Sydney Waterlow. How could it have been you? Lord, Lord, why does one write books!'[61] One reason was to receive the letter Vita wrote her on 11 October:

> I am completely dazzled, bewitched, enchanted, under a spell. It seems to me the loveliest, wisest, *richest* book that I have ever read, – excelling even your own Lighthouse . . . It is like being alone in a dark room with a treasure chest full of rubies and nuggets and brocades. Darling, I don't know and scarcely even like to write, so overwhelmed am I, how you could have hung so splendid a garment on so poor a peg . . . It is your fault, for having moved me so and dazzled me completely, so that all my faculties have dropped from me and left me stark . . . Also, you have invented a new form of Narcissism, – I confess, – I am in love with Orlando – this is a complication I had not foreseen.[62]

The writer, awed by such wonderful words of praise, telegraphed: 'Your biographer is infinitely relieved and happy.'[63]

The book brought other rewards, including an invitation to take tea at the table of that most redoubtable of society hostesses Emerald Cunard, whose daughter's *Parallax* Virginia had recently set in type. Earlier, the pre-publication sales of *Orlando* had been dismal, partly because the booksellers had been confused as to where to shelve it. Travellers for the Hogarth Press assured customers that the book was a work of fiction, but many of the booksellers insisted that the book's subtitle clearly indicated it had to be treated as non-fiction. But *Orlando* proved to be a rocket, a verbal firework display which intrigued the book-buying public. This notoriety, fuelled in part by *The Well of Loneliness* controversy and the obvious fact that it was a *roman-à-clef*, led to unprecedented sales for Virginia's work: 8,104 copies sold in England and 13,301 in the United States during the first six months.

Virginia's enhanced status as a celebrity led to a meeting with dapper, elegant Noël Coward at Sybil Colefax's. Before she even met him, Virginia felt slightly in love with him. But, she assured Vanessa, he was only a passing fancy: 'with you I am deeply, passionately, unrequitedly in love – and thank goodness your beauty is ruined, for my incestuous feeling may then be cooled'.[64]

That October, Virginia, together with Leonard and Morgan, agreed to testify in defence of Radclyffe Hall. Virginia's passionate feelings about her sister and her less than enthusiastic response to the literary qualities of *The Well of Loneliness* were at the forefront of her mind when she travelled to Cambridge on Saturday, 20 October. She was accompanied by Leonard, Vanessa and Angelica. Virginia had been invited to read a paper at Newnham nearly a year before and had planned to speak there in May. Although the paper had been ready that spring, illness and the pressure of completing *Orlando* had led her to postpone her visit to Newnham and Girton, where she had also been asked to speak.

The Woolfs, who were staying with Pernel Strachey, the Principal of Newnham, arrived nearly an hour late for the college dinner at which Virginia was to speak. She made a difficult situation worse because she was accompanied by Leonard, whose unexpected appearance at high table disrupted the seating arrangements. Elsie Phare, the President of the Newnham Arts Society, has left the only account of Virginia's talk that evening.

> The reasons why women novelists were for so long so few were largely a question of domestic architecture: it was not, and it is not easy to compose in a parlour. Now that women are writing (and Mrs Woolf exhorted her audience to write novels and send them to be considered by the Hogarth Press) they should not try to adapt themselves to the prevailing literary standards, which are likely to be masculine, but make others of their own; they should remake the language, so that it becomes a more fluid thing and capable of delicate usage.[65]

Another member of the audience, U. K. N. Carter, was surprised by a compliment that Virginia paid her on her dress, but she was struck by the variety of emotions she saw on Virginia's face: her 'look held a hint of a smile, a hint of compassion, but it was above all an absolutely ruthless look; my pretty frock was no proof against it'.[66]

Next day, on the Sunday, Dadie gave a luncheon party for Virginia and Leonard in his spacious rooms at King's, rooms which had been decorated by Carrington and overlooked the Backs by the Cam. The other guests were Lytton Strachey and Maynard Keynes. The following Friday, Virginia, accompanied this time by Vita, returned to Cambridge. That afternoon, she visited Julian in his rooms at King's. In the evening, she and Vita had dinner with two students from the Girton ODTAA (One Damn Thing After Another) Society, a group modelled on both the Apostles and the Cambridge Heretics Society. To the relief of the impoverished students, the two guests paid for their own meals. The four then went to Girton, where Virginia noticed the stark difference between the luxury of King's and the penury of Girton. She told them, as she put it, 'to drink wine & have a room of their own'.[67] The poet and critic Kathleen Raine was one of the undergraduates in attendance:

> With Virginia Woolf had come her friend Victoria Sackville-West: the two most beautiful women I had ever seen. I saw their beauty and their fame entirely removed from the context of what is usually called 'real' life, as if they had descended like goddesses from Olympus, to reascend when at the end of the evening they vanished from our sight.[68]

What did Virginia Woolf say to the women of Newnham and Girton? Both her talks were probably based on 'Women and Fiction', which was published in the American magazine *Forum* in March 1929. This piece is a curious hybrid: while working on the troublesome 'Phases of Fiction' at the end of 1928, she wrote this essay and sent it off to America. It indirectly addresses many of the contentious issues which had arisen between her and Forster, but it also reflects her thinking about women late in 1928. In the best tradition of academic debate, the writer at the outset reminds the reader that the title is ambivalent.

> The title of this article can be read in two ways: it may allude to women and the fiction that they write, or to women and the fiction that is written about them. The ambiguity is intentional, for, in dealing with women as writers, as much elasticity as possible is desirable; it is necessary to leave oneself room to deal with other things beside their work, so much has that work been influenced by conditions that have nothing whatever to do with art.[69]

Woman as subject has been a more than acceptable tradition in Western literature, but women have been impeded at every step in their desire to produce literature. Only in the nineteenth century did major female writers appear: Jane Austen, Emily and Charlotte Brontë and George Eliot. The novel, as 'the least concentrated form of art', became their domain.[70] Nevertheless,

> it is still true that before a woman can write exactly as she wishes to write, she has many difficulties to face. To begin with, there is the technical difficulty – so simple, apparently; in

reality, so baffling – that the very form of the sentence does not fit her. It is a sentence made by men; it is too loose, too heavy, too pompous for a woman's use. Yet in a novel, which covers so wide a stretch of ground, an ordinary and usual type of sentence has to be found to carry the reader on easily and naturally from one end of the book to the other. And this a woman must make for herself, altering and adapting the current sentence until she writes one that takes the natural shape of her thought without crushing or distorting it.[71]

It is probable, however, that both in life and in art the values of a woman are not the values of a man. Thus, when a woman comes to write a novel, she will find that she is perpetually wishing to alter the established values – to make serious what appears insignificant to a man, and trivial what is to him important. And for that, of course, she will be criticized; for the critic of the opposite sex will be genuinely puzzled and surprised by an attempt to alter the current scale of values, and will see in it not merely a difference of view, but a view that is weak, or trivial, or sentimental, because it differs from his own.[72]

In these crucial passages, Virginia provides a prescription for change: she prophesies that women will continue to add to the literary tradition by writing not only fiction but also in all the other major genres. She then looks forward to a golden age when women will have what 'has so long been denied them – leisure, and money, and a room to themselves'.[73]

This essay may be a battlecry, but it is also a description of Virginia's own literary career: although she saw herself as the descendant of the four great women novelists of the nineteenth century, she was also attempting to infuse the poetic spirit into the novel, change the form of the sentence and, in so doing, alter the established values. This is both literary and social revolution. That November, Virginia wanted, as we have seen, to put theory into practice by agreeing to testify at Radclyffe Hall's trial. Although Virginia felt *The Well of Loneliness* was so sweet, pure and sentimental as to be unreadable, she recognized that it was an attempt to describe a realm of experience which is part of her own agenda in *Orlando* and which society does not wish to hear lest it be in some way changed.

Morgan Forster warned Leonard that it would be dangerous for Virginia to offer testimony. In turn, Leonard and Vanessa told her that she 'mustn't go into the box, because [she] should cast a shadow over Bloomsbury.'[74] On 1 November she attended a meeting at the home of the architect Clough Williams-Ellis, where Vita, Bernard Shaw and Rose Macaulay were also present. Virginia was determined to testify and attended the trial on 9 November, at which Sir Chartres Biron, the magistrate, very much in the manner of a Harley Street specialist, ruled that only experts in obscenity could offer testimony. Afterwards, in the hallway, Virginia renewed her acquaintanceship with Hall's companion, Una Troubridge, whom she had last met when they were children at a tea party in Montpelier Square. Virginia found Hall – who was usually called 'John' – 'lemon yellow, tough, stringy, exacerbated'.[75]

A week later, Biron ordered the book seized and destroyed. On 14 December, an appeal against the decision was denied. Virginia did not attend on this day, which provoked Vita. Virginia told her: 'I was very much upset to think you had been angry (as you said) that I didn't go to the bloody woman's trial – (and yet I rather like you to be angry).'[76]

Desmond MacCarthy certainly had the capacity to make Virginia angry, as when he called on her and sat in her armchair for three and a half hours without seeming to be aware that she might be busy or might want to do something else with her time. Virginia and Desmond had very different ideas about the status of women and had publicly quarrelled. In contrast to Desmond was Vita, who had all the 'sanity & strength of a well made body'.[77] Vita had inspired *Orlando*, which had taught Virginia about certain male virtues, such as the direct sentence and narrative continuity. Yet she had to turn in a new direction: her new novel would be an 'abstract mystical eyeless book: a playpoem'. She wanted to explore the full implications of what she had said at Newnham and Girton. This led to an interest in writing a history 'say of Newnham or the woman's movement, in the same vein' as *Orlando*.[78] Above all was a strong sense of what really mattered to her in her career as a writer: 'it's the writing, not the being read'.[79]

Virginia's renewed sense of herself as a writer was augmented when she read Lytton's new book, *Elizabeth and Essex*, which she found superficial. She was secretly pleased, especially since a significant portion of *Orlando* is given over to a stunning evocation of Renaissance England. On the other hand, if Lytton's book had been a masterpiece, she could have taken pleasure in that. Her feelings were very mixed: 'that Lytton whom I loved & love should write like that. It is a reflection on my own taste.' Without meaning to, in *Orlando* Virginia had invaded Lytton's very male terrain of biography and bested him. On 28 November, her father's birthday, thoughts about Lytton led her to think about Leslie Stephen and his influence on her career. He had actively encouraged his daughter to follow in his own footsteps. But what if he had lived? If he were alive, he would have been ninety-six,

> but mercifully was not. His life would have entirely ended mine. What would have happened? No writing, no books; – inconceivable. I used to think of him & mother daily; but writing The Lighthouse, laid them in my mind. And now he comes back sometimes, but differently . . . He comes back now more as a contemporary. I must read him some day.

Virginia's feelings about her father were jumbled. He had inspired her to write, but she had paid a great price for being so enabled. She adored and resented him and, she knew full well, his life would have taken hers. Her feelings about Lytton and Leslie were very similar: both men had fostered her writing but saw her career as a kind of addendum to their own. For a long time, Virginia had known that women must break the satellite mould, must produce a literature of their own. She must practise what she preached. If Lytton could be judged by her own standards and fail, Virginia would have to undertake a similar evaluation of her father, measure him as a contemporary. This was a necessary step in breaking away from the past.

This sense of loosening the ties of the past supported her as she waited for her new project to unfold, to impregnate her: 'I am going to hold myself from writing till I have it impending in me: grown heavy in my mind like a ripe pear; pendant, gravid, asking to be cut or it will fall. The Moths still haunt me, coming, as they always do, unbidden, between tea & dinner.' One thing she was sure of: her new book must be filled with poetry, that element of creativity often absent in the writing of women. On that score, she intended to be ruthlessly professional – she did not have time to be a 'dreamy amateur'.[80]

Filled with a dramatic new sense of self, her mind ventured back to the black despair which had invaded her two years before, on 15 September 1926. After that horrible night, Virginia had made an important resolution. She must have more direct control over finances. Leonard had been adamant: they must pool everything. Virginia hardly ever burst into tears, but she did on that occasion. Finally, they reached an agreement to share money after their communal expenses had been paid. Only then did Virginia open her own bank account and begin keeping a 'hoard'. The extraordinary success of *Orlando* also gave her the impetus to disburse money freely. So 18 December 1928 became a red-letter day: 'For the first time since I married 1912–1928 – 16 years – I have been spending money.'[81]*

* Virginia's account differs from Leonard's: 'At the end of the 1914 war I invented a system with regard to our finances which we found both useful and amusing and which we kept until Virginia's death. At the end of each year I worked out in detail an estimate of expenditure for the coming year. This was to provide for only the bare joint expenses of our common life together; it therefore covered rents, rates, upkeep of houses, fuel and lighting, food, servants, garden, upkeep of car (when we got one), doctors and medicine, an allowance to each for clothes. At the end of the year I worked out what the actual expenditure had been and also the total actual combined income, and then the excess of income over expenditure was divided equally between us and became a personal "hoard", as we called it, which we could

Virginia also felt a measure of affectionate distance from Vita, who gave Virginia a string of amber beads that Christmas. 'Potto' rolled himself round in them to the extent that his front paws could not be dislodged. This reminded him of the night three years before when Vita herself had been ensnared, but now the nature of their friendship had changed: 'You never write to me,' Virginia complained, 'and your image has receded till it is like the thinnest shadow of the old moon.' Just as Vita was about to disappear, 'a thin silver edge appeared, and you now hang like a sickle over my life'.[82] *Orlando* is the 'thin silver edge' of the moon in which Vita and female friendship are immortalized.

---

spend in any way we liked. For instance, when we decided to have a car, I bought it out of my "hoard", and if Virginia wanted a new dress which she could not pay for out of her allowance, she paid for it out of her hoard' (*Autobiography*, II. 291–2). The topic of heated discussion in 1928 probably was about the threshold regarding 'excess of income over expenditure', Virginia wanting the ceiling to be lowered so that she could actually obtain money.

Chapter Fifteen

WRITING FOR WRITING'S SAKE

(1929–30)

Virginia could tolerate the idea of losing Vita to another woman, but she could not be separated from her. This anxiety was triggered anew when Vita went to Berlin to spend the Christmas of 1928 with Harold, who had been posted there the year before. Vita, who found the life of a diplomat's wife unbearable, hated the German capital, although its decadence was sometimes faintly amusing, as when she attended the 'sodomites' ball': 'A lot of them were dressed as women, but I fancy I was the only genuine article in the room.' Orlando went on to tell her creator: 'There are certainly very queer things to be seen in Berlin, and I think Potto will enjoy himself.'[1]

Potto was not so sure but resolved to make the trip, although he/she would be not as gloriously costumed as Vita's current lover, Hilda Matheson, director of radio talks at the BBC: 'We are coming in our shabbiest clothes; my mother in law has given me a coat like the pelt a sheep wears when it's been on a high mountain alone for weeks.'[2] Although Vita was never quite the vamp Virginia imagined, she had a fantasy about her dressed in 'black and scarlet under a lamp'.[3]

'We' was not only Leonard but also Vanessa, Duncan and Clive, who were making a tour of galleries in Germany and Austria. On 17 January, one day after the Woolfs had settled in at the Prinz Albrecht Hotel, the other three joined them there. Eddy Sackville-West was also in Berlin and, to complicate things even more, Harold, who had his own circle of friends, was put out when the Woolfs and their ménage refused to attend two luncheon parties he had arranged for them. Vanessa did not see why she should be expected to spend any time at all with the Nicolsons. For Virginia, it was a 'rackety' experience.[4] This is not surprising: Vanessa was openly jealous of Vita's hold on her sister and did not mind expressing her disdain. Although Virginia enjoyed her trip to Sans Souci, Frederick the Great's palace at Potsdam, the Wellenbad, a huge indoor swimming pool equipped with a wave-making machine, and an evening visit to the top of the Funktrum, Berlin's Eiffel Tower, feelings of desperation began to overtake her. As the searchlight went round and round the tower, she became, to her friend's surprise, more and more indiscreet. Vita's diagnosis was simple: 'SUPPRESSED RANDINESS.'[5]

Virginia paid a heavy price for a holiday which lasted less than a week. Just before beginning the return crossing from the Hook of Holland to Harwich, she took a seasick draught. When the ship docked, she felt intoxicated and had to be carried off the boat by Leonard. She slept on the train to London and then had to be dragged into a taxi. She took to her bed, where she shivered, ached and slept. For the next six weeks she was once again an invalid, one most grateful for a husband who, like a judge, passed sentence on her illness. 'He brings home huge pineapples; he moves the gramophone into my room and plays until he thinks I'm excited. In short, I should have shot myself long ago in one of these illnesses if it hadn't been for him.'[6]

Leonard was convinced that Virginia needed serenity – she must not get wound up. The necessary balance between these two states was hard to establish, given Virginia's very real need for stimulation. It was also exceedingly difficult to rest in London: the noise of a pump in the basement of the Royal Hotel next door shook her studio at regular intervals: twenty-five minutes on, twenty-five off. That winter was desperately cold. Since all manner of pipes became frozen, there were no baths, water-closets or gas fires. The basement flooded, destroying many books. The drawing-room door became stuck one day, leaving Virginia imprisoned inside and unable to attend to the call of nature.

Then there was the perpetual quarrelling between Clive and

Mary. At the time, Virginia had been playing mediator in their spats but that January and February she had, upon the insistence of her doctor, Elinor Rendel, to close her door to them and all other visitors. However, she did write teasing letters to Vita, to whom she announced: 'I shall have Mary.' But then, in a volte-face, she continued: '. . . as I shall be in my nightgown – But no. I am very faithful. It's odd how I want you when I'm ill.'[7] And she told Vita that she was responsible for the rise in the number of lesbians in America. Once again, she tried to distance herself from such women, who were, according to her, Vita's 'race', but sometimes she was forced to count herself among their number. Early that spring, in the midst of purchasing some pills in a chemist's shop, the sisters were discussing Virginia's passion for Vita. 'But do you really like going to bed with women?' a disingenuous Vanessa asked. Then, in the midst of taking her change, she added – as if she had no knowledge of such matters – in a loud voice: 'And how d'you do it?'[8]

Virginia may have been suffering from 'suppressed randiness' but she was certainly enduring a 'suppressed imagination',[9] a condition which she attempted to remedy by working on 'The Moths' and 'Women and Fiction', the full-length manuscript of which became *A Room of One's Own*. In such periods of hibernation – forced to retreat from the everyday realities of life – the passivity of her body stood in sharp contrast to the creative activity of her mind. She began to plan her next novel and decided to cast her two recent visits to Cambridge into fictional format.

While Virginia was working on *A Room of One's Own*, she was also devising an extension to the back of Monks House which would allow her two rooms: a bedroom opening on to the garden and above it a sitting room. There was no door from this addition into the other part of the house, so Virginia in the evening could walk outside at the kitchen door and then enter her bedroom sanctuary, which faced the orchard. A window at the side opened out on to a large field. One night, a cow poked its head through the window, sending a startled Virginia into peals of laughter. In the morning, she would walk to her garden study, where she continued to do most of her writing.

Like the main living room, Virginia's new bedroom was painted the dull eggshell green which her friends often mocked. A narrow single bed, a chest of drawers, a table and a chair were the furnishings; two large, low windows and Vanessa's surround in the fireplace of a boat sailing towards a lighthouse are the principal ornaments of this chaste, cloister-like retreat. The bed was by the window, so that she could welcome the morning. There was a tender pathos in this arrangement, as if the occupant were a child yearning for the light which would release her from the tyranny of the night. Although Virginia could return to the house and Leonard whenever she wanted, her bedroom, sitting room and study gave her much-needed and valued space and time to be alone.

Orlando's success paid for these improvements (that year the Hogarth Press made a £400 profit); the book also gave the Woolfs the necessary financial security to exchange their old car for a new one – a coffee-and-chocolate-coloured Sun Singer convertible. Despite the money which it earned, Virginia continued to see *Orlando* as a mere joke. When the painter Dorothy Brett, who now lived in Taos, New Mexico, got in touch with her that winter, Virginia rejoiced that her old friend liked *To the Lighthouse*. Then she added: 'Would Katherine? I wonder.'[10]

Her new novel would continue the line of experimentation valued by Katherine but interrupted by *Orlando*. However, such a probing of the possibilities of fiction could be unnerving. Would she be able to stand another round of such daring? Although Virginia saw herself as 'withering', she knew that within herself bubbled an impetuous torrent. She might look in the mirror and see ugliness but 'inwardly I am more full of shape & colour than ever'. She was also bolder than before: 'I feel on the verge of some strenuous adventure . . . So when I wake early, I brace myself out of my terrors by saying that I shall need great courage.'[11] Inner strength was not the same as outer strength. Virginia was certainly taken aback when her oculist observed that she needed stronger glasses and added: 'Perhaps you're not as young as you were.'

Virginia was reminded anew of the anguish ageing can bring when she visited Marie Woolf. The seventy-eight-year-old was ill, but she demanded more and more of life. Virginia was moved. Perhaps there was a very basic – healthy – instinct which kept people alive. 'One will not perhaps go to the writing table & write that simple & profound paper upon suicide which I see myself leaving for my friends.'[12] For Virginia, writing was *the* way of staying alive. 'What a born melancholiac I am!' she told herself. 'The only way I keep afloat is by working.'[13]

For years, Virginia had wanted to keep her friendship with Lytton alive, but that had become an increasingly difficult task, especially because, as we have seen, she hated *Elizabeth and Essex* (published the year before), which she considered utterly beneath her friend's normal standards. Should she hold her tongue or take the considerable risks honesty would entail? That June, she chose truth. The conversation began badly, but she soon discovered that Lytton had been more hurt that nothing had been said. This allowed Virginia to tell him what bothered her: the book had no irony, was too confined to telling a story and was unimaginatively rendered. In short, Lytton was getting a bit sentimental; he was also, she felt, surrounded by a coterie either unwilling or unable to be honest with him. In part, Virginia felt that she had gained the upper hand in her rivalry with Lytton – she no longer had anything to envy him for. In fact, with *Orlando* she had beaten him at his own game. Rivalry aside, this conversation restored something vital to the two participants: a sense that honesty and openness were the essential ingredients in any real friendship.

That winter and spring, Virginia had many other worries: Nelly was being more difficult than usual and Vita was becoming more attached to Hilda Matheson. Her own writing, Virginia felt, was too loose. She needed an escape and was delighted to spend ten days with Vanessa at Cassis, where 'all is heat and vineyards; people swim about naked in the air'.[14] The weather may have been glorious, but there was a heated exchange between the sisters when Virginia became exasperated by Vanessa's boasting:

'My elder son is coming tomorrow; yes, & he is the most promising young man in King's; & has been speaking at the Apostles' dinner.'

Virginia countered: 'I made £2,000 out of *Orlando* & can bring Leonard here & buy a house if I want.'

Vanessa was taken aback: 'I am a failure as a painter compared with you, & can't do more than pay for my models.'[15]

Despite the sisterly bickering, Leonard and Virginia went as far as negotiating the lease of La Boudard, a three-room peasant hut near Vanessa's villa. They even had windows fitted and sent furniture over by sea, but the negotiations were stopped before the Woolfs ever occupied the place. Upon their return to England, they settled in at Rodmell for the remainder of the summer, where Virginia saw 'the Moths rather too clearly, or at least strenuously'[16] for her comfort. She also had to correct 'that much corrected book, Women & Fiction'.[17]

As soon as she had made a substantial recovery from her bout of illness following the Berlin trip, Virginia began to mould her Cambridge talks and *Forum* article into a book, 'half talk, half soliloquy'.[18] Her first draft, 'Women & Fiction', written in March 1929, is a transitional document and shows the links between earlier thoughts and *A Room of One's Own*. Here, for the first time, are most of the well-known sequences: the walk on the forbidden grass, the visit to the British Museum, the discussion of androgyny, Judith Shakespeare (called Mary Arden), the comparison of the wealth of the men's colleges at Cambridge to the poverty of Newnham and Girton. In this draft, the reader can see Virginia Woolf conjoining her reflections on women and fiction and her visits to Cambridge into a narrative which gives her considerable fictional licence. For example, the circumstances of her own stays at Cambridge are considerably expanded and embroidered.

That spring and summer Virginia vigorously tightened her manuscript. The decision to move away from the *Forum* article's focus is best demonstrated in her choice of a new, declarative title:

women must have £500 a year and rooms of their own. Despite the change in name, *A Room* is a very open-ended book in which the author asks a number of questions, sometimes scathingly, sometimes satirically, usually with great equanimity. In particular, sections 1 through 3 are very interrogative. Why is the wealth at Cambridge concentrated in the hands of men? Why is the professor at the British Museum angry at women? Why are women legitimate subjects but authors by stealth? Why have men cornered the poetic impulse? (An answer to this difficult question can be attempted, Virginia suggests, only when women realize that poetry is the most self-reflexive of the major genres and that to employ it the poet must have a strong sense of self to express.) Why has the novel been the only genre in which women have excelled?

Embedded in the questions are a series of brilliant examples of just how badly things have gone for women, who for too long have been content to be the second sex. The fictitious Judith Shakespeare may have been as naturally gifted as her brother, but whereas he was able to use his wildness to his own advantage, all the constraints of society acted against her.

> She was as adventurous, as imaginative, as agog to see the world as he was. But she was not sent to school . . . Perhaps she scribbled some pages up in an apple loft on the sly, but was careful to hide them or set fire to them. Soon, however, before she was out of her teens, she was to be betrothed to the son of a neighbouring wool-stapler. She cried out that marriage was hateful to her, and for that she was severely beaten by her father. Then he ceased to scold her. He begged her instead not to hurt him, not to shame him in this matter of her marriage.[19]

Caught like young Virginia Stephen between two kinds of male power (George Duckworth's brutality and Leslie Stephen's excessive sentimentality), Judith escaped to London, where she wanted to act. Warned off a profession seen as closely linked to prostitution, she tried to find some way to express her creativity. Once again, she was victimized.

> at last Nick Greene the actor-manager took pity on her; she found herself with child by that gentleman and so – who shall measure the heat and violence of the poet's heart when caught and tangled in a woman's body? – killed herself one winter's night and lies buried at some cross-roads where the omnibuses now stop outside the Elephant and Castle.[20]

One way out of the tangle created by the discrepancy between a 'poet's heart' and 'a woman's body' was for women to stake their claim to write poetry and to recognize that there did not have to be a sharply held distinction between male and female: 'Coleridge perhaps meant this when he said that a great mind is androgynous. It is when this fusion takes place that the mind is fully fertilized and uses all its faculties. Perhaps a mind that is purely masculine cannot create, any more than a mind that is purely feminine.'[21] The section on androgyny is the final one in the book. It is conciliatory, certainly conciliatory to a point which Virginia would later find totally unacceptable: 'It is fatal to be a man or woman pure and simple; one must be woman-manly or man-womanly.'[22]*

In fact, A *Room of One's Own* is decidedly uncomfortable with anger, especially when Virginia suggests that this emotion destroyed both Charlotte Brontë's life and her art: 'She will write in a rage where she should write calmly. She will write foolishly where she should write wisely. She will write of herself where she should write of her characters. She is at war with her lot. How could she help but die young, cramped and thwarted?'[23] Virginia analyses in some detail the resentment men direct towards women, but she shies away from the uncomfortable feelings aroused in her when she touches upon her own rage at the many ways in which men – mainly because they do not wish their own inadequacies to be challenged – have marginalized women. Anger was a very vexed issue for Virginia, probably because she had the fantasy that

* Androgyny ultimately became suspect to Virginia because she felt that it eradicated and thus denigrated femininity.

this emotion could lead to the uncontrolled expression of feelings – and thus to 'madness'. At this time, she was still careful to curtain off anger from the justifiable resentment she harboured against male-dominated institutions. In April 1930, she declared: 'Much though I hate Cambridge, and bitterly though I've suffered from it, I still respect it.'[24]

If Virginia curbed herself in *A Room of One's Own*, she also managed to insert a great deal of disguised autobiography into it, particularly when discussing the fictitious novelist Mary Carmichael and her two creations, Chloe and Olivia. This gave Virginia the opportunity for an oblique commentary on the *Well of Loneliness* case and its presiding magistrate.

> Are there no men present? Do you promise me that behind that red curtain over there the figure of Sir Chartres Biron is not concealed? We are all women you assure me? Then I may tell you that the very next words I read were these – 'Chloe liked Olivia . . .' Do not start. Do not blush. Let us admit in the privacy of our own society that these things sometimes happen. Sometimes women do like women.[25]

If women are allowed such things as private incomes and rooms of their own, there will be some necessary consequences. They might be able to create psychic space for themselves, discover a poetic language suited to their own sensibilities and even write fiction about their friendships with each other; they might even write polemics which, like Carlyle's *Sartor Resartus*, blend fiction with philosophy. Virginia is also commenting on the possibility of lesbian fiction, a genre which would – by her definition – embrace both *The Well of Loneliness* and *Orlando*.

In many other ways, *Orlando* and *A Room* are closely linked. In this particular instance, however, practice came before theory: *A Room* sets out prescriptions for a new social order based on the androgyny brilliantly exploited in *Orlando*. In literary terms, *A Room* provides a fascinating commentary on the literary career of Virginia Woolf, whose career as a novelist was dedicated in large part to infusing prose fiction with poetry's lyric strain. This was certainly to be her agenda in *The Waves*.

As 24 October – the publication date of *A Room* – approached, Virginia became more and more apprehensive. She had to wait a week for the *Times Literary Supplement's* praise and almost a month for Arnold Bennett's piece in the *Evening Standard*. He began by referring to the supposed existence of a feud between 'the queen of the high-brows' and himself, a 'low-brow'. Although Bennett discounted this quarrel (he claimed that he had not bothered to read the essay about himself and Mrs Brown), he disputed the central argument of Virginia's treatise:

> And I beg to state that I have myself written long and formidable novels in bedrooms whose doors certainly had no locks, and in the full dreadful knowledge that I had not five hundred a year of my own – nor fifty. And I beg to state further that from the moment when I obtained possession of both money and a lockable door all the high-brows in London conspired together to assert that I could no longer write.

The low-brow chip on his shoulder is brilliantly exploited by Bennett, who goes on to accuse Virginia of 'wholesale padding' and unnecessary 'floral enticement'.[26] Earlier, on 31 October, Vita spoke on 'New Novels' for the BBC but began with *A Room*, because it was written by a distinguished novelist and was concerned in part with women and fiction. Vita, Virginia's living proof of the triumph of androgyny, proclaimed her friend as the embodiment of the very same principle: 'She enjoys the feminine qualities of, let us say, fantasy and irresponsibility, allied to all the masculine qualities that go with a strong, authoritative brain.'[27] Such praise, penned by Orlando, must have deeply pleased the recipient. And she was gratified by the book's strong sales. Yet the writing of *The Waves* was proving to be a traumatic experience, one leading Virginia, who always had a racing pulse, to dream on the night of 1 November that she would die of heart disease within six months.

★

In *The Waves*, Virginia traces the lives and, more importantly, the sensibilities of a group of six friends – Bernard, Susan, Rhoda, Neville, Jinny and Louis – from childhood to late middle age. Although Virginia bears a superficial resemblance to Rhoda, elements of her personality are present in each member of the group. In *Orlando*, the central character had – like both Vita and Virginia – male and female existences, while in her new book the 'woman-manly' and 'man-womanly' parts of Virginia are diffused among six characters. This helps to explain the considerable anguish she experienced during the book's writing, almost as if she had separated herself into six parts and then had to reconstitute herself. Later she would say: 'The six characters were supposed to be one.' She especially felt how 'difficult it is to collect oneself into one Virginia; even though the special Virginia in whose body I live for the moment is violently susceptible to all sorts of separate feelings'.[28]

'Separate feelings' are articulated in the six childhood friends. Rhoda, who eventually commits suicide, is a dreamer, always feeling alienated from her environment. Early on, Louis observes that Rhoda seems completely unaware that she has a body; at school she avoids seeing her reflection in the glass: 'I have no face.'[29] In a grim piece of irony, Jinny (one of Leslie's pet names for Virginia) desires to look at her body in the mirror and obtains great pleasure from lovemaking. Susan, a much more elemental person than the other two women, revels in having children. Neville, the aesthete, pursues the bodies of other men, whereas Louis, who has an affair with Rhoda, is the most detached of the six. Bernard, the professional man of letters, is uncomfortable with separateness. He embraces life in its great and shapeless variety.

Of course, Vanessa can be discerned in Susan, Vita in Jinny, Lytton in Neville, Leonard in Louis and Desmond MacCarthy in Bernard. Such identifications – valid though they are – are not of much use in interpreting the book, because all the biographical evidence upon which Virginia drew was collected in order to highlight sides of herself: for example, her desire to have children is articulated in Susan's conflicting feelings about maternity and her wish to be a creature of her own body is reflected in Jinny.

One historical event is perhaps paramount: Virginia's continuing, poignant sense of her loss of Thoby. Her new book certainly deals much more openly than *Jacob's Room* with Thoby's premature death. In *The Waves* Thoby is vividly rendered as Percival, an enchanter figure: he is the still point to which the six other characters constantly return. Put another way, he is the flame to which the moths are drawn. His premature, accidental death in his mid-twenties in India occurs half-way through the book and allows its focus to shift from a concern with the meaning of life to a meditation on the fact of death.

The speech patterns of the six friends are not remarkably different, but each is associated with a distinct cluster of images. In addition, the sensibility of each is rendered in an opera-like manner, almost as if the reader is listening to individual recitatives which are part of an enormous sextet. The musical analogy is an apt one, since the main choral portion of the text is punctuated by sections of lyrical prose that describe the rising and setting of the sun over a seascape of waves and shore: nine crucial episodes in the lives of the six characters are counterpointed to the impersonal interludes, which are confined to a single day.

The Waves is in every way a bold book, one in which the author pulled out all the stops in her pursuit of a new aesthetic. However, majestic freedom of expression could be purchased at too high a price and this was Virginia's new worry. In attempting to write a novel which would not tell a story in any conventional way, she knew that she would have to impose a strong sense of unity on the narrative. The proper method to accomplish this eluded and deeply troubled her. That October, as she candidly informed Gerald Brenan, she still had no idea, despite years of experience, of 'how to go on: one never sees more than a page ahead; why then does one make any pretensions to be a writer? Why not pin together one's scattered sheets?'[30] She could not write with any sense of pleasure. Her design was elaborate, her writing suffused with vagueness. She felt enclosed in a world of silence in which she recalled her anguish when Thoby died.

Despite the sorrow which filled her, though, she knew that she had to experience a dark night of the soul if she were to have any hope of writing what she wanted: 'If I never felt these extraordinarily pervasive strains – of unrest, or rest, or happiness, or discomfort – I should float down into acquiescence. Here is something to fight: & when I wake early I say to myself, Fight, fight. If I could catch the feeling, I would: the feeling of the singing of the real world.'[31]

For Virginia, vacillation became a necessary condition. Ten days later, uncertainty was to a limited extent banished: her new book would be called *The Waves*, not, as she had once thought, *The Moths*. Although it would be about a set of characters whose lives revolve around a mysterious, aloof figure, it would be more concerned with the ebb and flow in the lives of the six friends. More importantly, as Virginia made clear in her essay 'The Death of the Moth', these insects accept death as an entity far stronger than they are. In her new book, death may be an inevitable fact of life, but it is a force to be battled with.

The Waves is both a continuation and a repudiation of *To the Lighthouse*. In the earlier book, Virginia had drawn upon childhood memories in order to recast her parents and herself into fictional form. As such, it is a deeply personal book, but in the late 1920s she had begun to feel, like Tom Eliot, that the finest literature was an 'escape from personality' and that 'the more perfect the artist, the more completely separate in him will be the man who suffers and the mind which creates'. Virginia was not blindly following Eliot. She had long been convinced that women had to discover their own poetic language and, moreover, write novels which ceased to be mere dumping grounds for personal emotions. The agenda was difficult: women had to look beyond personal and political relationships to the wider questions which the poet tries to solve – destiny and the meaning of life. But the purpose of existence seemed both crystal clear and darkly elusive. Was life solid or shifting, Virginia asked herself on 4 January 1929: 'I am haunted by the two contradictions.'[32]

Like *To the Lighthouse*, *The Waves* attempts to answer the unanswerable by looking closely at the landscape of childhood, but it is also about the contrary strands in a single person which give utterance in six voices. As a child at St Ives, Virginia had witnessed the tranquil beauty of the ocean world, but she had also seen the sea in its monstrous incarnations; as an adult in 1926, she beheld a fin passing far out beyond the waters. 'What image can I reach to convey what I mean? Really there is none I think.'[33] Three years later, she sought that elusive image.

Thoughts of childhood brought back some happy memories – of making autumn plans with Vanessa as they took long, leisurely promenades at the end of summer, of the incredible, wild pleasure she had taken in the volumes of Elizabethan prose writers which her father had lugged home from the London Library. She also recalled her atheistic childhood when she heard the church bells at Rodmell. Although she hated the arrogance of Christianity, she remembered that she had always been fond of its ceremonies.

Monks House was a much-treasured respite from London, where noises from the Royal's pump and from the jazz band in its ballroom continually intruded. In rural Sussex, everything was much more peaceful. There Virginia's day began with a leisurely breakfast at which she read the post; then she bathed. After she dressed, she would write or correct for three hours. Lunch was always simple – sometimes a rissole and a custard. Then she read and smoked cigarettes for two hours. This was followed by a walk with Pinker, perhaps as far as Asheham. Tea was usually at four, after which Virginia wrote letters and looked at the second post. After dinner, Leonard and Virginia would listen to music on the gramophone. Virginia now allowed herself a cheroot and, of course, more reading. And so to bed.

That summer was glorious, the garden alive with vivid colours: reds, pinks, purples and mauves. As autumn approached, Virginia shut down her work on *The Waves*. She also became touchy with Vita, although she told her on 13 November that she wanted her to be in a warm comfortable room with a fire: 'I don't mind if it's a room with a double bed and someone else in it, as long as you

Above left: Leonard and Virginia Woolf at Asheham. *Above right*: Virginia hiking in Cornwall, 1916. *Below*: Asheham.

Portrait of Virginia by Vanessa Bell, *circa* 1912.

Snapshot by Ottoline Morrell of Virginia at Garsington, June 1923.

Above left: Katherine Mansfield.
Above right: Ottoline Morrell.
Photograph by Cecil Beaton.

Jacques Raverat.
Painting by Gwen Raverat.

Virginia in 1925.

Virginia at Monks House,
June 1926.
Photograph by Vita
Sackville-West.

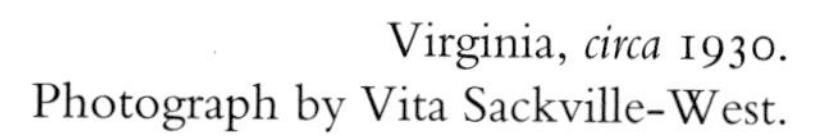

Virginia, *circa* 1930.
Photograph by Vita Sackville-West.

Above: Monks House.
Below: The garden at Monks House, 1938. Photograph by John Lehmann.

Clockwise from top left: E. M. Forster and T. S. Eliot at Monks House; Vita Sackville-West, 1924; Virginia with Angelica Bell, *circa* 1932; Ethel Smyth.

Above: Virginia in 1935. Photograph by Man Ray. *Below left*: Virginia at Monks House, *circa* 1937. Photograph by Leonard Woolf. *Below right*: Virginia in 1939. Photograph by Gisèle Freund.

are warm.'[34] However, a little more than ten days later, some of her jealousy of Hilda Matheson's hold over Vita vented itself when she became furious with Hilda's insistence that cuts be made to her radio talk on Beau Brummell. Virginia then poured 'rage as hot as lava'[35] over Vita, who was accused of existing in a second-rate schoolgirl atmosphere.

Her recent attempt to find new common ground with Lytton had not been really successful, Virginia reminded herself. How could she have ever contemplated marrying him? 'Had I married Lytton, I should never have written anything.' Like her father, Lytton checked and thus inhibited her. Although Leonard could be severe, he was always stimulating. 'Anything is possible with him,' she told herself.[36] Clive was another old friend who proved to be a hindrance rather than a help when he pointed out to her that her books were devoid of that most essential of ingredients, sex.

Although her new book also lacked that staple, it was certainly filled with death. At this time, Virginia became even more vividly aware of Thoby's form looming behind her. He was the 'queer ghost' whose presence is central to *The Waves*, but the memory of his death brought her painfully back to her younger self: 'I think of death sometimes as the end of an excursion which I went on when he died.'[37] In forcing herself to confront that past, she wondered if she really wanted to experience anew that horrible inward journey.

When the Woolfs arrived back in London that autumn, they returned to relative tranquillity: they had won their civil suit against the Royal Hotel. The round of parties nevertheless proved grating, particularly since Virginia did not like being lionized by either visiting Americans or society hostesses.

In January 1930, she attended the celebration of Angelica's twelfth birthday, a costume party devoted to the theme of Alice in Wonderland. Virginia, clad in an appropriate pair of ears and paws, was the March Hare. Leonard, wearing a green-baize apron with a pair of chisels, was the Carpenter. The real star turn, however, was Roger Fry as the White Knight. He was the Pied Piper to whom all the children were immediately drawn.

On their way home, still in costume, the Woolfs encountered a drunken prostitute who, having been insulted by three inebriated men, answered them back in their own foul language. The resulting brouhaha attracted a policeman, who was inclined to blame the woman. Leonard, his rather undignified get-up notwithstanding, pointed out to him that the woman was not to blame – she had merely met insult with insult. This helped diffuse the situation and husband and wife made their way home.

London life may have been tedious, but 1930 brought some very bright spots. After seven years, Leonard was delighted to hand over the literary editorship of the *Nation* to the poet and critic Edmund Blunden. He was able to do this because the Hogarth Press – due in large part to the sales of Virginia's books – was doing very well. Later that year, the Woolfs published Vita's new novel, *The Edwardians*, a best-seller. Virginia's income in 1929 totalled £3,020, a remarkable sum for a writer who had been content to make £200 for many years.

Her self-confidence, however, was not boosted when she wrestled with *The Waves*: 'But how to pull it together, how to compost it – press it into one – I do not know.'[38] She might end up with a gigantic conversation rather than a readable novel. She followed her customary pattern of writing in the morning and typing what she had written in the afternoon, but by 10 February – the day after the death of her old friend and supporter, Charlie Sanger – she was ill again, this time with influenza. Once more, she used the situation creatively: 'I believe these illnesses are in my case – how shall I express it? – partly mystical. Something happens in my mind. It refuses to go on registering impressions. It shuts itself up. It becomes chrysalis.'[39] As she retreated from the everyday world, she touched the poetic forces about which she wanted to write, almost as if she entered the domain of the waves and the mysterious fin.

This illness delayed Virginia's first meeting with Dame Ethel Smyth, who had written to her that January to express fervent admiration for *A Room of One's Own*. Smyth, who turned seventy-two in 1930, had been born in Sidcup, Kent, to Emma (Struth) and Major-General John Hall Smyth, an artillery officer, who was opposed to his daughter's ambition to become a writer or musician. From early childhood, Ethel had been a precocious reader and writer; forbidden to keep diaries, she had covered up her disobedience by burying them. At the age of nineteen, she enrolled at the Leipzig Conservatorium. There she met Brahms and Grieg and also developed a passion for mountaineering. Her early chamber works, very much in the Romantic style, were performed in Germany. She first attracted attention in England with her *Mass in D*, performed at the Albert Hall in 1893. Her operas, *Fantasio*, *Der Wald* and *Der Strandrecht*, were premièred in Germany between 1898 and 1906. In 1909, *Der Strandrecht* was performed in English as *The Wreckers*, conducted by Thomas Beecham.

From the age of twenty-five, Ethel carried on a long professional and personal relationship with Henry Brewster, who wrote the libretto for *The Wreckers*. Although passionate, Ethel's relationship with Brewster, a married man, filled her with trepidation and guilt. She did not wish to betray another woman.

In 1908, deeming the suffragette battle incompatible with her own struggle to become a composer, Ethel left England. Three years later, she changed her mind, having come to the conclusion that the aims of the Women's Social and Political Union were identical with her own as a woman and an artist: the refusal to give women the vote was symptomatic of 'the Machine's' attempt to exclude women from any form of creativity. Ethel devoted two years to the 'cause'. She was even imprisoned in Holloway. When Beecham visited her there, he saw her leaning out of her cell, toothbrush serving as baton, conducting her fellow prisoners in the yard below; they were singing her composition 'The March of the Women'.

Although she was created a Dame Commander of the Order of the British Empire in 1922 and four years later became one of the first women to receive an honourary doctorate from Oxford, Ethel felt that these honours were mere trifles which did not make up for the privations she had to endure because of her sex. As she grew older, she became more and more angry at the injustices and condescensions which all women, but particularly those who were writers, artists and musicians, suffered. She had obtained recognition, but she was perfectly aware that she would have achieved a great deal more if she had been born male. She also had the uncomfortable feeling that hers was a token success, bestowed upon her condescendingly. When she read Virginia's polemic, she was certain she discerned a kindred spirit.

Ethel, who had a cottage of her own at Woking and was always costumed in three-cornered hats and suits, had the look, George Rylands recalled, of a larger-than-life Victorian cook, one who was boisterous, opinionated, bossy, pertinacious and ultimately overwhelming. Although her appearance was a bit comical, no one who met her could doubt her extraordinary intelligence, which manifested itself in speech as well as in writing. As she later confessed, Virginia had *seen* Ethel in November 1919, 'coming bustling down the gangway at the Wigmore Hall, in tweed and spats, a little cock's feather in your felt, and a general look of angry energy, "So that," I said, "that's Ethel Smyth!" – and felt, being then a mere chit, she belongs to the great achieved public world, where I'm a nonentity'.[40] Two years later, Virginia had penned an unsigned review of one of her volumes of autobiography, *Streaks of Life*, in which she called Ethel impressionable but discriminating, strident but never sentimental: 'she possesses the combination of enthusiasm and shrewdness which fitted her for . . . the great pursuit of her life – the pursuit of friendship'.[41] Now Virginia would discover just how accurate that evaluation was.

When she responded to Ethel's letter, Virginia recalled what pleasure she had taken in another of Ethel's books, *Impressions That Remain* (1919), in particular the account of her great-grandfather James Pattle's uncorked body exploding into the air before his distraught widow's eyes. Virginia was delighted that Ethel liked *A Room*, her own 'wild venture', and warmly responded when Ethel invited herself to Tavistock Square: 'There is nothing I should like better than to see you – and you might like me. Who knows?'[42]

Without doubt, Virginia would never be completely sure of the answer to her own question. On the surface, they were remarkably different women. Virginia, who was often reserved in company, allowed her high spirits full expression only with close friends. Ethel was explosive. Often Virginia dressed cheaply, her femininity not extending itself to her outward appearance. Ethel was always in uniform, her professionalism evident. On occasion, Virginia's penchant for gossip and ensuing indiscretions could be kept under strict control. Ethel had no such filter. With her, plain-speaking sometimes seemed a vice. When someone condescendingly referred to a 'poor hermaphrodite', Ethel shot back: '*Poor* hermaphrodite indeed?? Why, she has two ways of amusing herself.'[43] When Ethel played the piano, she attacked it as if it were a hapless critic who had dared to offer anything less than an adulatory assessment of her music.

Quite soon after they met, Ethel made a declaration of 'violent but platonic love'[44] to Virginia. This is not a paradox. Ethel adored Virginia, but it was not a love of the body. Although, like Virginia, Ethel had a divided sexuality, she hankered, like Virginia, after a love which was strong but chaste. On 2 May 1930, Ethel wrote Virginia a moving letter which shows the close emotional affinity between the two. The composer gives a vivid description of her attitude towards the relationship between love and sexuality: 'Do you know in this happening [her friendship with Virginia] I have found confirmation of a theory I have always had – that with me and I think many women the root of love is in the imaginative part of me – its violence, its lewdness, its hunger.' This hunger and violence Ethel traced back to her love of her mother: 'She died 38 years ago & I never can think of her without a stab of real passion; amusement, tenderness, pity, admiration are in it & pain that I can't tell her how I love her . . . Now you can imagine how much sexual feeling has to do with such an emotion for one's mother!!'[45] Very much like Virginia, this was the 'chord' Ethel sought in all close relationships.

The strongest emotional commitment made by each woman was to a man and there were other strong bonds between them. In

The Waves, Virginia was attempting to merge musical form with prose fiction: in large part, that novel aspires to the condition of opera. Thus from the outset Virginia recognized that her struggles as a writer mirrored Ethel's as a composer.

There was a major incongruity in this friendship. Quite soon after they began to see each other regularly, Virginia suspected that Ethel did not really like or appreciate her novels. However, rather than destroying the friendship, this realization may even have strengthened it. This is strange but perhaps not surprising. Although Ethel could harshly criticize Virginia's work and was often rude to her, she bestowed upon her unconditional love, such as some mothers are able to give their children. It was as if Ethel said to Virginia: I love you for who you are, not for what you can accomplish. This is the kind of love for which the inner girl in Virginia yearned, as she frankly told Ethel in July 1930: 'you are, I believe, one of the kindest of women, one of the best balanced, with that maternal quality which of all others I need and adore'.[46]

Ethel may have been kind and maternal, but she also could be exasperating, as was apparent when the two women finally met on 20 February. Virginia's invitation to tea had shown her worried but comical side.

> I am *not* infectious.
> You won't mind if I wear an old dressing gown.
> You will excuse my stupidity and put it down to influenza.
> If you don't come then, we may go away, and never meet for years.
> Also, I can telephone on Thursday a.m. if anything terrible happens.
> So I shall expect you on Thursday 4.30. Is this explicit?[47]

The invitation may have been explicit, but Ethel arrived at four when Virginia was still napping. Ethel burst into Virginia's sitting room. 'Let me look at you,' she commanded her hostess. That formality aside, Ethel got down to business: 'First, I want to make out the genealogy of your mother's family.' Within fifteen minutes, they called each other by first names and, as Virginia somewhat sarcastically observed, 'the basis of an undying friendship' was established. The conversation, eagerly orchestrated and conducted by Ethel, who rested her feet in Pinker's basket, was helter-skelter, but Virginia saw beyond the rant: 'There is something fine & tried & experienced about her.'[48] Virginia was intrigued by Ethel's claim that writing music was like writing novels, but she was not completely sure of her new friend's pedigree.

Saxon Sydney-Turner knew a great deal about music, so Virginia asked him: 'What is your opinion of Ethel Smyth? – her music, I mean? She has descended upon me like a wolf on the fold in purple and gold, terrifically strident and enthusiastic – I like her – she is as shabby as a washerwoman and shouts and sings – but the question of her music crops up.'[49] As a writer, Virginia observed, 'she . . . takes every fence'. Of course, Virginia the writer took every possible risk, and this was another important bond between the two women.

Virginia was not loath to poke fun at Ethel. On 14 May she told her nephew Quentin: 'An old woman of seventy one has fallen in love with me. It is at once hideous and horrid and melancholy – sad. It is like being caught by a giant crab.'[50] But Virginia did see Ethel's passionate energy as very different from the complacent socialism of elderly unmarried women such as Margaret Llewelyn Davies or Lilian Harris. Virginia allowed Ethel to be brutally frank and, in so doing, found succour and freedom: 'Good God, Ethel, I daresay you're perfectly right. I daresay I'm a d—d intellectual.'[51]

Perhaps more than she ever did to anyone else, Virginia bared herself to Ethel. At times, she could be sarcastic and cruel to Leonard, Vanessa and Vita, but she found it difficult to detach herself from them. Virginia, aware of how outlandishly eccentric and bombastic Ethel could be, never had trouble keeping her distance from her and in the process found someone who could act as a repository for her most intimate feelings.

The day after Ethel's first visit, Sir George Duckworth called on his half-sister. The encounter was disturbing but in a subtle way. This incredibly complacent man found in her some 'shadowy likeness'[52] and in him, she realized, were preserved elements of her past. He was no longer in a position to do her harm, but just as she was attempting in *The Waves* to deal once again with the loss of Thoby she was reminded anew of the cruelty of her half-brothers.

On 29 April, Virginia finished the first draft of *The Waves*. The writing had been arduous, but suddenly she was eager to polish the book, to make the 'good phrases shine'.[53] Shortly thereafter, Leonard and Virginia toured south-western England, acting as travelling salesmen for the Hogarth Press. Some of the booksellers were rude and as a result Leonard was often on the verge of losing his temper, but they did visit St Ives, where, Virginia poignantly recalled, 'I saw my Lighthouse, and the gate of my home, through tears – thinking how my mother died at my age.'[54]

Before resuming work on *The Waves* on 13 June, Virginia visited Long Barn on 23 May and was driven by Vita to inspect Sissinghurst, the ruined castle to which she, Harold and the children were soon to move. In early June, the Woolfs spent a week at Rodmell, returning to London on 11 June to see Paul Robeson, Sybil Thorndike and Peggy Ashcroft in *Othello* at the Savoy Theatre. There were more servant problems. Lottie, who was still working for Adrian and Karin, was caught stealing and dismissed. She had nowhere to go and stayed one night at Tavistock Square. In early June, her friend Nelly Boxall became violently ill and had to be taken to hospital with Virginia in attendance in the ambulance. Virginia was not pleased when an obviously ill Nelly was sent back to them for a day on 16 June.

Through a complicated series of stratagems on Vanessa's part, the Woolfs were briefly landed with Mrs Taupin, an incompetent Frenchwoman who, in quick succession, lost Virginia's keys and broke tumblers. She was followed by an American, Mrs Karl Walter, who had a son at King's; she stayed for the six weeks before the Woolfs went to Rodmell for the summer. Despite their good fortune in securing the services of Mrs Walter, Virginia wanted to be rid of servants; having them bred conflicting emotions: trust and suspicion, benevolence and condescension, philanthropy and exploitation.

Ethel was proving to be a trial and in particular a great cause for complaint on Leonard's part. One June morning, Virginia looked out the window at Tavistock Square and saw an elderly char in a white alpaca coat. This turned out to be Ethel, who was so costumed for a lunch with Beecham. Although she claimed that she was only popping in, she did manage to deliver one speech which lasted twenty minutes, the large vein in her temple swelling all the while. To her diary, Virginia confided: 'I daresay the old fires of Sapphism are blazing for the last time.'[55] Perhaps this remark was meant to distance herself from Ethel, but soon after Virginia wrote her a series of letters which, taken together, form an intimate, miniature autobiography. At the very same time, Virginia was not above provoking Ethel, as in her letter of 26 July: 'Well, here I am lying in Vita's adulterous sheets.'[56]

Rodmell remained a refuge from Ethel and all other would-be intruders. Here Virginia's life assumed an entirely different shape. In London, she was an anonymous person who took great pleasure in exploring all the fascinating byways of a great city; in Rodmell, she was a local, one who played a prominent role in village life. That June, she took part in the village festival by attending a performance of *A Midsummer Night's Dream* and guessing the weight of a cake. Rodmell also bestowed its own special privacy, for as well as the two-room addition, there was also the pleasure of the large, communal sitting-cum-dining room, where Leonard and Virginia sat, ate, played the gramophone, propped up their feet by the fire and avidly read countless books.

Within two months of meeting, Virginia needed to take flight from the overly sensitive Ethel. To this continually complaining person, she was unfailingly honest: 'How I hated marrying a Jew – how I hated their nasal voices, and their oriental jewellery, and their noses and their wattles – what a snob I was: for they have immense vitality, and I think I like that quality best of all.'[57] Ethel was also passionate. Virginia, sometimes alienated from the creative juices within herself, treasured Ethel, who in turn exhausted her.

About sex, she was very frank with Ethel. On 15 August, she told her: 'Perversion. Yes, I am afraid I do agree with you in thinking it silly.' Early in their relationship, Virginia confided to Ethel that she had only once felt a strong physical feeling for a man, who had not reciprocated. After thinking the matter over, she offered her new friend an expanded, revised version of this aspect of her past: '. . . when 2 or 3 times in all, I felt physically for a man, then he was so obtuse, gallant, foxhunting and dull that I – diverse as I am – could only wheel round and gallop the other way. Perhaps this shows why Clive, who had his reasons, always called me a fish.'[58]

That summer at Rodmell, Virginia breathed easily: 'I walk; I read; I write, without terrors & constrictions. I make bread. I cook mushrooms.'[59] Gradually, she had come to realize that some of the critical principles she was trying to establish in her fiction had become part of her daily existence: 'I am more & more attracted by looseness, freedom, & eating one's dinner off a table anywhere, having cooked it previously.'[60] Her life had a rhythm rather than a plot – and the rhythm of *The Waves* was the essential rhythm of her own existence. Her rustic retreat was an elemental, perfect landscape: marsh, down, church and pear tree. Virginia's extremely candid letters to Ethel were complemented by the pleasure she took in writing her new novel.

Then, on a very hot and sunny 29 August, while she and Leonard were strolling in their garden with Maynard and Lydia, Virginia suddenly fainted. Leonard carried her into the house, where she promptly fainted again. A few days later, she felt much better, although her heart jumped 'like a mulish pony'. She had experienced a heatstroke, one in which she slipped in and out of consciousness. To Ethel and Vita, she dismissed the entire episode, but in her diary she wrote: 'this brush with death was instructive & odd. Had I woken in the divine presence it would have been with fists clenched & fury on my lips. "I don't want to come here at all."' The sometimes caustic Leonard acted like an 'angel', fetching chamber-pots and running about with trays of food and medicine.[61] Immediately afterwards, Virginia re-evaluated some of her old friendships. She and Lytton no longer fitted into each other's existences. She kept up with Morgan in only a spasmodic way.

On 8 September, still traumatized by her fainting spells, Virginia recalled that Thoby would have turned fifty on that day. She resumed work very slowly, acutely conscious that she had to reconstruct her world before she could write about it. She was aware that she was often 'at sea' with other people's feelings. Such uncertainty often made her 'appear egotistical and unsympathetic because I'm afraid to discharge my sympathy when it is out of place and therefore offensive'.[62]

Virginia remained distanced from Forster, who spent a Sunday with the Woolfs in mid-September. The three of them passed part of the day skulking behind the churchyard wall in order to watch the bishop bless the new spire. Forster, now transformed into a moth by Virginia, had renounced fiction and gave off the stale, chilly atmosphere of Cambridge. She could see the considerable merit of his work, but it was 'impeded, shrivelled and immature'.[63] In part, she felt this way because she saw herself as working in opposition to the inherited traditions of fiction-writing which Forster had defended in *Aspects of the Novel.* Virginia had become almost fiercely critical of Cambridge. When Julian published a volume of verse that autumn, she did not feel his poems hit the mark: 'Common sense & Cambridge are not enough.'[64] Although Carrington assured Virginia that Lytton preferred his old friends to his new ones, Virginia was not sure that she believed her.

When she returned to London that autumn, Virginia had further servant problems, was faced with the possibility of having her lease on 52 Tavistock Square terminated by the Bedford Estates and had to contend with Ethel, who wanted Virginia to become her literary executor and possibly her biographer. On 12 November, she finally agreed to allow Nelly back for three months from 1 January, but she was appalled at how easily she had caved in: 'How am I ever to apologize to myself sufficiently?'[65]

The Woolfs, increasingly harassed by the drain of time and effort the Press represented, seriously considered selling up. Virginia was also worried about her appearance. She decided to grow her hair in response to Angelica's claim that her aunt was

Cecil Beaton. Pencil sketches of Virginia Woolf from The Book of Beauty *(1930)*

repulsive-looking. She was also restless. On 28 October, in the secret hope that Ethel would act outrageously, Virginia accompanied her to a concert at the Austrian embassy. True to form, during a slow passage Ethel remarked in a loud voice: 'This is like the movement of one's bowels.'[66] Virginia also had to contend with the Woolfs and the air of conformity which pervaded all encounters with them. After telling Ethel about Marie Woolf's birthday party, she asked her: 'By the way, what are the arguments against suicide?'[67]

Virginia also had to battle Cecil Beaton, who had in 1927 asked to photograph her for *The Book of Beauty*, which included Margot Asquith, the society beauties Teresa and Zita Jungmann, and the actress Tilly Losch. Denied this right, Beaton drew two pencil sketches and added a brilliant verbal portrait which blends a sense of her austere Victorianism with her modernism.

> Although she would look like a terrified ghost in an assembly of the accepted raving beauties, she would make each one separately appear vulgar and tawdry in comparison with her. She has all the chaste and sombre beauty of village schoolmistresses, housekeepers, and nuns, and one cannot imagine her being powdered and painted: the mere knowledge that *maquillage* exists is disturbing in connection with her, for when one sees her so sensitively

nervous and with the poignant beauty of the lady in the faded photograph in the oval frame . . . one realizes that a face can be a reverend and sacred thing. Her fine skin is parchment-coloured, she has timid startled eyes, set deep, a sharp bird-like nose and firm pursed lips. Her lank hair and aristocratic wrists are of supreme delicacy, and one imagines her spending eternities of dreamy leisure sewing and gazing out of the window. She wears cameo brooches and cotton gloves, and hatpins, and exudes an atmosphere of musk and old lace and the rustle and scratch of stiff ivy-coloured taffeta, but her old-fashioned dowdinesses are but a conscious and literary game of pretence, for she is alertly contemporary, even a little ahead of her time. Many of her confrères see her as a Juno, awe-inspiring and gaunt, but she herself is frightened, a bundle of tentative gestures, and quick nervous glances, as frail and crisp as a dead leaf; and like a sea-anemone she curls up at contact with the outer world.[68]

Virginia was aghast: 'I was never asked [for permission to have the sketches included in the book] – never sat – never saw the horrid worm – and there I am seized for ever.'[69] She was sufficiently irritated to send two letters expressing her outrage to the editor of the *Nation and Athenaeum*.

Another unpleasant experience was being a fellow dinner guest with Arnold Bennett at Ethel Sands's. Virginia was convinced that Bennett had engineered the encounter in order to get on good terms with her. She was wary but responded to his immense charm. At last, Virginia drew David Cecil, then a fellow of Wadham, into the conversation and they joined forces to taunt Bennett about his disdain for the often remote stance from life taken by Bloomsbury. Finally, Bennett rose to depart, saying: 'I don't think I possess more life than you do. Now I must go home. I have to write one thousand words tomorrow morning.'[70] Virginia found it difficult to work the next day.

In contrast to her reaction on meeting Bennett, almost against her will, Virginia was deeply moved when she encountered Yeats at

Ottoline Morrell's on 7 November. She had not seen him for more than twenty years: 'He is very broad; very thick; like a solid wedge of oak. His face is too fat; but it has its hatchet forehead in profile, under a tangle of grey & brown hair; the eyes are luminous, direct, but obscured under glasses; they have however seen close, the vigilant & yet wondering look of his early portraits.'[71] That 'wondering look' was the essence of a man who had committed himself to his writing. This deeply moved her, for she too had given over her life for what often seemed the insubstantiality of art. She was also aware of the importance Yeats attached to dreams. Although the meaning of her own often evaded her, she realized that her life was 'almost entirely founded on' them. In particular, she was deeply frightened that she would encounter the 'suicide dream one of these days'.[72] That might mean that fantasy would become reality. When they parted that evening, Virginia pressed the great poet's hands, almost as if she were trying to obtain his benediction.

Next to Yeats, Tom Eliot, who had come to tea the day before, seemed very insubstantial. He was 'all suspicion, hesitation & reserve'. Vivien was paranoid: 'Tell me, Mrs Woolf, why do we move so often? Is it accident?' Virginia, who had no wish to be drawn into the Eliots' marital problems, did not venture an opinion and attempted to change the subject: 'Have some honey, made by our bees.' This was not a wise move. Vivien now became convinced that Virginia kept hornets under her bed. She even suspected that Virginia and Tom might be romantically attached.[73] This was not true, but the estranged wife was perhaps correct in picking up on some sexual feeling between the two writers. Six years later, Virginia told Vanessa: 'I had a visit, long long ago from Tom Eliot, whom I love, or could have loved, had we both been in the prime and not in the sere; how necessary do you think copulation is to friendship? At what point does "love" become sexual?'[74] Tom was handsome, in a very delicate way. She found that mixture of masculinity and femininity deeply attractive, but she also realized that his sexuality was, very much like hers, not one which was unduly concerned with physical expression.

At the end of 1930, Virginia was more directly concerned with playing Ethel and Vita off against each other. As she well knew, the arousal of the green-eyed monster could be a very useful bargaining chip. On 6 November, she told Vita how much she and Potto were pleased to have dined with her the night before: 'And of course I'm rather glad that you can be jealous, even of that old seamonster encrusted with barnacles.'[75]

An extremely morose Roger Fry dined with the Woolfs just before Christmas. He railed against Vita, Ethel, his sense of poverty and the neglect of his art. Virginia argued vehemently with him but to no avail. She herself endured an unpleasant experience when buying Christmas presents at Marshall & Snelgrove. She put her purse down when trying on a coat and, while her back was turned, a thief snatched it. Stranded there without money, keys or spectacles, she could not prevail upon the department store to lend her any money: she did not have an account with them and therefore did not exist. She made her way home with the ten shillings one of the store detectives had lent her.

The autumn and early winter in London had been particularly trying, but Virginia managed to forge ahead with her revisions to *The Waves*. On 21 December, while listening to a Beethoven quartet, she saw a way of bringing the book to a satisfactory conclusion. The stark, almost disjointed sounds of the four instruments emerged, combined and blended. She was touched and decided to make Bernard's final speech end with the words, 'O Solitude'.* In the darkly beautiful melodies of Beethoven she had finally discovered the musical equivalent of her long quest to fuse poetry and prose, of her desire to write a book in which individual voices could have their say and yet be merged into a single entity.

*The novel concludes: 'Against you, I will fling myself, unvanquished and unyielding, O Death!'

Chapter Sixteen

THE SINGING OF THE REAL WORLD

(1931–3)

Virginia's new confidence in her ability to surmount the technical difficulties presented by *The Waves* led her to consider the possibility of writing a sequel ('Opening the Door') to *A Room of One's Own*, devoted to the sexual life of women. Her new ideas, outlined in a speech given to the National Society for Women's Service on 21 January, were based on the possibility of a new world order brought about by the entry of women into the workforce, by the renunciation of the notion of women as angels of the house and by the recognition that women's experience was – and must remain – distinct from men's. Her preoccupation with these beliefs temporarily impeded her ability to work on her novel, since didactic prose was so different from the dramatic tone of fiction. Also, concerned that her work was too detached from reality, the previous autumn she had begun to collect newspaper headlines for insertion into her diary. By 26 January, the day after her forty-ninth birthday, she had shaken off the obsession with both headlines and sequel and returned to *The Waves*: I have 'this instant,' she told her diary, 'seen the entire book whole.'

On her birthday the day before, under an almost unnatural and unexpectedly hot sun, Virginia and Leonard took a walk at Rodmell, where she saw men dash from a car and run across a field. Then she beheld a silver and blue aeroplane, apparently unharmed, resting with the cows in the middle of the field. They had continued on their walk. Only the next day did she learn that three men had been killed as the plane crashed. 'But,' she reflected, 'we went on, reminding me of that epitaph in the Greek anthology:

when I sank, the other ships sailed on.'[1] In contrast, *The Waves* is concerned with how people are connected to each other, how seeming obliviousness can be surmounted.

By hook or by crook, Virginia was convinced that she had succeeded in the difficult task of reining in the disparate forces which make up *The Waves*. But she was afraid that the 'hookedness may be so great that it will be a failure from a reader's point of view'.[2] Despite the high temperature accompanying a bout of influenza, she went on with the book. As she finished the draft, she was overcome with raw feeling, with the strong conviction that she had triumphed over the nihilism of death.

> I wrote the words 'O Death' fifteen minutes ago, having reeled across the last ten pages with some moments of such intensity & intoxication that I seemed only to stumble after my own voice, or almost, after some sort of speaker (as when I was mad). I was almost afraid, remembering the voices that used to fly ahead. Anyhow it is done; & I have been sitting these 15 minutes in a state of glory, & calm, & some tears, thinking of Thoby . . . Whether good or bad, it's done . . . how hastily, how fragmentarily I know; but I mean that I have netted that fin in the waste of waters which appeared to me over the marshes out of my window at Rodmell when I was coming to an end of To the Lighthouse.[3]

Once again, illness had assisted the writing of the book, almost as if Virginia's body needed to be blazing hot in order for her to capture the necessary intensity of artistic vision. This time, her temperature broke just as she completed the second draft of the book in February 1931.

Later that month, Virginia told Clive Bell that her new book was a failure. It was simply too jerky and inchoate. Yet, she reminded her old friend-enemy, 'what's the point of writing if one doesn't make a fool of oneself?'[4] She was also aware that Arnold Bennett was dying. He had been a harsh and often dismissive critic of her work, but Virginia had enjoyed wrangling with him, such creative fighting being the very essence of life. When he died on

27 March, she characterized him as a lovable man, although one with a shopkeeper's view of literature: 'he abused me; & I yet rather wished him to go on abusing me; & me abusing him'.[5]

Although her alliances with Vita and Ethel were central to her at this time, Virginia revitalized her friendship with the sometimes irascible Roger Fry. After attending an exhibition of his paintings, she was unreservedly complimentary: 'What intrigued me and moved me to deep admiration was the perpetual adventure of your mind.'[6] For her, this was the necessary condition for real art. If writers or painters did not take risks, they might as well resign themselves to failure. And, of course, one could be a wise fool in the service of art.

There were also the demands of ordinary life. Leonard and Virginia attempted to relieve some of the burdens of running the Hogarth Press by hiring a trainee manager, John Lehmann, a young poet who had become a close friend of Julian Bell at King's. That winter, John was 'panning out well, in his doghole behind the W.C.'.[7] Virginia had decided that she could step up the clothing allowance she gave to Angelica to £30 a year.

There was nothing ordinary about Ethel Smyth. On 24 February, Virginia attended a performance of Ethel's *The Prison* and then went on to a party in the composer's honour at the Countess of Rosebery's. There Ethel behaved in an outrageously vain way and Virginia was offended. In addition, the party reminded her of her appearance at the Countess of Carnarvon's many years before. In fact, the bullying side of Ethel was reminiscent of the Duckworths. Virginia did not mince words:

> I don't know when I have suffered more; and yet why did I suffer? and what did I suffer? Humiliation: that I had been dragged to that awful Exhibition of insincerity and inanity against my will (I used to be dragged by my half-brothers against my will – hence perhaps some latent sense of outrage). Then, that you liked the party – you who are uncompromising, truthful, vehement. 'Ethel likes this sort of thing' I said, disillu-

> sion filled me: all belief fell off me. 'And she has planned this, and worse still, subjected me to it.' . . . It seemed to me that you wantonly inflicted this indignity upon me for no reason, and that I was pinioned there and betrayed and made to smile at our damnation.

Then, in a metaphor similar to one she used to describe the dying Rachel in *The Voyage Out*, Virginia compares the sense of impending madness which she experienced at the party to the 'end of a drainpipe with a gibbering old man'.[8] Virginia was warning Ethel: don't go too far or be excessively demanding.

She did, however, have strong positive feelings about Ethel, who often acted like a guardian angel:

> what you give me is protection, so far as I am capable of it. I look at you and (being blind to most things except violent impressions) think if Ethel can be so downright and plainspoken and on the spot, I need not fear instant dismemberment by wild horses. It's the child crying for the nurse's hand in the dark. You do it by being so uninhibited: so magnificently unselfconscious.[9]

Their friendship needed balance, Virginia was telling Ethel. Otherwise, it would have to be dissolved.

That Easter, in the midst of a pleasant stay at Rodmell, Virginia also took the opportunity to remind Ethel that she had a husband who looked after her: 'poor Leonard, whose breast I pierce daily with hot steel, is divinely happy here; we giggle and joke, and go and poke at roots and plan beds of nasturtium'.[10] Four days later, she told her diary: '[after] nineteen years [of marriage], how moving to find this warmth, curiosity, attachment in being alone with L.'. There were, though, certain feelings about Leonard and her marriage that she did not explore: 'If I dared, I would investigate my own sensations with regard to him, but out of laziness, humility, pride, I don't know what reticence – refrain. I who am not reticent.'[11] The reticence might have been the result of a basic distrust of men, a distrust with which, in the case of the Duckworths, she was very much in touch.

Virginia was certainly expert in manipulative behaviour. Quite soon after Vanessa and Ethel met, Ethel told Virginia that she preferred her sister. At the same time, Vanessa realized that she had much in common with Ethel. Virginia, refusing to be baited by either, shrugged her shoulders. This little contretemps occurred a week before Leonard and she set out on a two-week tour of western France, travelling by way of La Rochelle, south of Périgueux; they visited the château at St Michel-de-Montaigne, the home of the essayist, and the Château du Milieu at Chinon, where Joan of Arc stood trial before Charles VII. In between changing flat tyres, Virginia read D. H. Lawrence for what she claimed (inaccurately) was the first time;* *Sons and Lovers* was indeed a work of genius and Virginia was upset that Middleton Murry's attacks on Lawrence had prevented her from reading him when he was alive. Nevertheless, Lawrence's genius was, she felt, an obscured and distorted one.

The weather in France that spring was a mixture of thunder, lightning and hail. In addition to punctures, the steering wheel of the Woolfs' car was always on the point of breaking. Such setbacks aside, the landscape was an amazing, heightened arrangement of green, blue and purple, and husband and wife greedily consumed pâtés 'absolutely mellow and yellow with liver. It's a disgusting taste which I expect we share with the dogs, but for once I like to feel wholly and rabidly canine.'[12] On the road, having left behind the curtained-off portions of her life, Virginia was always more open to animal pleasures. She had no wish to return to London to be 'jerked daily by the telephone'.[13]

Back in England, Virginia realized that D. H. Lawrence's short

* On 10 May 1930, Virginia told Dorothy Brett: 'I have never read any of [Lawrence's] books, or more than half of two of them.' In fact, she had reviewed *The Lost Girl* in the *Times Literary Supplement* of 2 December 1920. Virginia's letter to Desmond MacCarthy of 27 January 1930 makes it clear that Mr A, the novelist in *A Room* who protests against the equality of women by asserting his own superiority, may be based in part on Lawrence. She also read *Women in Love* when it was published in 1921.

life had given her a great deal to think about, particularly 'about writing for writing's sake'. His example – although his ideas about the novel were diametrically opposed to hers – helped her to refocus her ambitions, to recommit herself to her own writing. Like Lawrence, she was a true original, an artist with a mission. Visitors were to be 'regulated' so that her time was not consumed in spendthrift fashion. She also realized that her abilities as a critic were moving in a new direction: she was becoming more fearless. She wondered why, and soon came up with the answer: '"Because of a R. of one's Own," I said suddenly to myself last night.'[14]

Virginia had to remain alert in dealing with Ethel, who sensed that Virginia might try to regulate her. This was simply an impossibility, since Ethel was like a white, tailless, uncastrated cat which had once belonged to the Stephen family at Hyde Park Gate: 'This superb brute used to spend his nights fighting; and at last got so many wounds that they wouldn't heal; and he had to be put out of life by a vet. And I respected him; and I respect you. Only I think you don't altogether realize how, to the casual onlooker, you seem exaggerated – how it strikes an outsider.'[15] When Ethel railed for three hours about how terribly the conductor Adrian Boult had treated her, Virginia could stand it no longer. Finally, 'I had to shout that I had such a headache that unless she stopped talking I should burst into flames and be combusted.'[16] Of course, a deranged Ethel did little to give Virginia time and space in which to write. And Ethel could be offensive as well as excessively demanding. When Virginia casually mentioned that her period was a week late, Ethel – rather than observing that this might be a sign of menopause – asked Virginia if she was pregnant.

The truth was that Ethel, who claimed to be tender-hearted, was frequently callous in her dealings with others. Her claims upon Virginia reminded the younger woman of Leslie's excessive demands – demands made by a father who confused obligation with love and, in the process, lost the affection of his children. On 4 July, Virginia once again attempted to set limits: 'I confess that your letter with its multitudinous embroidery of a personal grievance seemed ... to make a huge and at the moment unwarrantable demand on my sympathy.'[17] At the same time that she was drawing much-needed boundaries between herself and Ethel, Virginia told Vita: 'I can't help liking her, in her wild idiocy, and her frankness.'[18] Ethel had put Virginia in touch with some vibrant feelings – and for that reason she could not put this particular feline to sleep.

Briefly, her friendship with Vita remained on a relatively even keel. Virginia bestowed grudging praise on Lytton's new book, *Portraits in Miniature and Other Essays*, a work more appropriate to his talents than *Elizabeth and Essex*; its smallness, she observed, 'suits him far better, I think, than the larger scale, needing boldness, originality, sweep'.[19] Another friendship to be redefined was that with Katherine Mansfield. In June 1931, Virginia dreamed of an encounter beyond death in which they simply shook hands. Two months later, she told Vita about the troubled history of that friendship: 'she had a quality I adored, and needed; I think her sharpness and reality – her having knocked about with prostitutes and so on, whereas I had always been respectable – was the thing I wanted then.'[20] Through Ethel, Virginia had been forced to become less priggish about expressing strong feelings and in this way drew closer to Katherine.

Without intending to do so, Ethel Smyth continually gave Virginia valuable lessons about the expression of emotions. On this topic, Virginia made an incredible confession to her in December 1931:

> I don't think you're right about my caring for 'so few' ... But then, for months on first knowing you, I said to myself, here's one of these talkers. They don't know what feeling is, happily for them. Because everyone I most honour is silent – Nessa, Lytton, Leonard, Maynard: all silent; and so I have trained myself to silence; induced to it also by the terror I have of my own unlimited capacity for feeling ... But to my surprise, as time went on, I found that you are perhaps the only person I know who shows feeling and feels.[21]

At the very outset of her career, Virginia had perhaps confused the pursuit of fame with the maintenance of respectability. She had abandoned any such notion when she started to experiment with form and to proclaim the rights of women writers. Nevertheless, she perceived a certain fettered quality in her own work. She began to discover that the sensuous feelings captured in Katherine Mansfield's stories were not after all cheap – or out of her reach. On a more personal level, she had been taught to repress her feelings. She was no longer sure she wanted to be 'trained' to silence.

Without doubt, *The Waves* is the most sensuous of all of Virginia's books. The second draft, begun in June 1930 but not completed until February 1931, shows the writer taking full command of her material. In the first draft, a 'Lonely Mind' or solitary woman* reflects on the lives of the six main characters; this figure began to disappear as work on the second draft advanced. Only in the final typescript, prepared for the printer, was this character completely eliminated. In the second draft, Bernard emerges more clearly than before as the main speaker of the six. The assignment of this role to a male character might seem strange, but Virginia was still championing androgyny as an ideal.

The final form of *The Waves* proved elusive. For example, Virginia decided to print the interludes in italics in July 1931, just as the book was sent to press. She had a good idea of what she wanted to accomplish, but the precise means of encasing her vision was hard to establish. Her ability to dismiss an exterior, controlling voice might have been assisted by her realization that D. H. Lawrence's great weakness as a writer was his inability to allow his strong, vibrant images to stand by themselves. A truly poetic novelist might have to hazard the risk of seeming looseness of construction, but in so doing the colour of language – as in Lawrence's lyric poems – might be unleashed. This was a particularly

* Since 1926, Virginia had wanted to devote an entire novel to the life of such a person.

hazardous gamble for a prose writer: unbridled emotions versus controlled form. That summer, when Leonard read the book, he was impressed with how skilfully the two modes intersected. He pronounced *The Waves* a masterpiece but sounded a note of caution: he was uncertain if the common reader would be able to understand it.

That August, Virginia could work only intermittently on correcting the proofs of *The Waves*. There were the pleasures of Rodmell, but she was startled one afternoon when, boating quickly downtide, she came upon a group of twenty-two swans who, surprised themselves, stretched out their necks menacingly and hissed loudly. She and Leonard quarrelled on their perennial sore spot: her disdain for his family. Sybil Colefax, for whom Virginia never harboured overly warm sentiments, complained loudly about severe financial setbacks and then showed up at Monks House with her Rolls-Royce and attendant chauffeur. Virginia was irritated with Vita, who had taken up with the journalist Evelyn Irons: 'But,' as she ironically informed the mistress of Sissinghurst, 'you'll never find anyone you like as much as me; because I'm so clever, so good, so pure'.[22]

Virginia felt overwhelmed and this reminded her of how difficult people were to capture – in life or in fiction. The human condition was one in which 'we sit in dark tunnels, tapping on the wall – That's friendship – that's communication.' Letters were a way of 'penetrating for those who are, like me, blind into the dark damp deeps' of the soul.[23] The sexual implications of this metaphor are obvious, but beyond that was a pervasive feeling that she, like Rhoda, was completely shut off from others. In Rhoda's grim, silent address to her five companions some of her creator's deepest fears can be discerned.

> Inwardly I am not taught; I fear, I hate, I love, I envy and despise you, but I never join you happily. Coming up from the station, refusing to accept the shadow of the trees and the pillar-boxes, I perceived, from your coats and umbrellas, even at a distance, how you stand embedded in a substance made of repeated

> moments run together; are committed, have an attitude, with children, authority, fame, love, society; where I have nothing. I have no face.[24]

To Bernard, the professional man of letters, is assigned the summing up, a long brilliant monologue in which he weaves everything together. Although he accepts differences, he proclaims communality. And he defies the extinguishing force of death.

> And in me too the wave rises. It swells; it arches its back. I am aware once more of a new desire, something rising beneath me like the proud horse whose rider first spurs and then pulls him back. What enemy do we now perceive advancing against us, you whom I ride now, as we stand pawing this stretch of pavement? It is death. Death is the enemy. It is death against whom I ride with my spear couched and my hair flying back like a young man's, like Percival's, when he galloped in India. I strike spurs into my horse. Against you I will fling myself, unvanquished and unyielding, O Death![25]

Percival, like Thoby, is long dead. Rhoda has already succumbed to death's charms while Bernard intends to fight that inevitable extinguishing force. In 1931, Virginia was being pulled in two directions.

That September, while awaiting the publication of *The Waves*, Virginia was apprehensive on many other counts. She was deeply annoyed by Desmond MacCarthy's snide comment on modern novels such as *Mrs Dalloway*; he claimed that 'events have become merely interruptions in a long wool-gathering process'.[26] She told Ethel to 'ignore' the whole subject of her health: 'As for your brilliant medical diagnosis – that headache is caused by inspiration – why then did I have two fairly complete attacks earlier in the month [August] when inspiration was miles away?'[27] When Winifred Holtby, who was completing a sensitive study of her work, told her that *The Waves* was the most poetic and subtle of her books, Virginia perversely observed: 'What I want is to be told that this is solid & means something.'[28] She was, she herself knew,

Vanessa Bell. Cover design for The Waves *(1931)*

acutely depressed, but, very much in the manner of Bernard, she could feel rising within herself the 'hard & horny back of my old friend, Fight, fight.'[29]

Three weeks before publication, Virginia provided John Lehmann with a trenchant review of her book's strengths and limitations.

> it was, I think, a difficult attempt – I wanted to eliminate all detail; all fact; and analysis; and myself; and yet not be frigid and rhetorical; and not monotonous (which I am) and to keep the swiftest of prose and yet strike one or two sparks, and not write poetical, but purebred prose, and keep the elements of character; and yet that there should be many characters, and only one; and also an infinity, a background behind – well, I admit I was biting off too much.[30]

Having decided that the 'stunt'[31] book was in the main a failure, Virginia was not quite prepared for the enthusiastic but careful notice in the *Times Literary Supplement* on 8 October, publication day.

> What kind of a book does one write after *Orlando*? That was an exception and a prodigy in more ways than one. Here, in *The Waves*, is something visibly in the line of Mrs Woolf's novels, and a return to the life we live, yet so singularly unconventional in its texture and form that one might fancy *Orlando*'s vivid flashes of the past were the real, and this the dream and the prodigy.
>
> For the book is, at it were, a piece of subtle, penetrating magic. The substance of life, as we are accustomed to see it in fiction, is transposed and the form of the novel is transmuted to match it . . . A poetic novel, as it certainly is, it is still – however peculiarly – a novel. The six people all have their idiosyncrasy of nature . . . Alive as the novel is with the vividness of things, one feels in more than one sense that its spirits roam through empty places. Yet it is simpler, after all, to be grateful for a book that achieves its own aim and that no one else could have written.

The anonymous reviewer obviously admired *The Waves* enormously but shared some of its creator's reservations. Virginia saw the notice as a mixture of moonshine and condescension; she also seemed disheartened that her handling of the characters was praised. After all, she had meant to have none.

The truth was that the book had so deeply stirred its author that she could not bear to hear it praised or condemned. 'How odd,' she observed, 'that people can read that difficult grinding stuff!'[32] Momentarily, she had forgotten that the common reader can respond with great enthusiasm to new experiences in literature. Despite her own sense of its limitations, Virginia felt that she had at last created a book in her own unique style. Since there was so much more of herself in this work, she was especially sensitive to the responses of her friends.

Virginia had disliked *Elizabeth and Essex* but had been relieved that she could respond with some enthusiasm to *Portraits in Miniature*. She was certain that Lytton, ill with a gastric disorder, disliked the book. In fact, he was repulsed by a book in which he only dabbled. On 4 November he told a friend: 'It's perfectly fearful . . . I shudder and shiver – and cannot take the plunge. *Any* book lying about I seize up as an excuse for putting it off.'[33] Hugh Walpole labelled the book unreal; Vita found the first 100 pages extremely dull; Dorothy Wellesley could not get through it. Deeply moved by a book which could have as its epitaph 'Only connect', Morgan Forster, with whom Virginia had quarrelled about form in fiction, told her: 'It's difficult to express oneself about a work which one feels to be so very important but I've the sort of excitement over it which comes from believing that one's encountered a classic.'[34]

Ethel's report came in stages, the first in a telegram: 'Book astounding so far. Agitatingly increases value of life.'[35] Ultimately, however, the novel was for her a failure because its sadness was unrelieved; no moral principle was at work. Virginia was furious. Summarily, she informed Ethel that she had not really thought her capable of appreciating it and then informed her that Lowes Dickinson had discerned the morality at its centre. In his letter of 23 October to the embattled author, he observed: 'Your book is a poem, and as I think a great poem. Nothing that I know of has ever been written like it . . . For there is throbbing under it the mystery which all the poets and philosophers worth mentioning have felt and had their little shot at.'[36] Both Forster and Dickinson, ardent disciples of G. E. Moore, had been deeply touched by the book's strong mystical undertones, by how it suggests that the pursuit of the good, the reasonable and the beautiful are life's real goals.

Vanessa was touched in another way. In part, she responded to the moving tribute paid to Thoby, who for both sisters had remained an enigmatic person very much in the mould of Hamlet: 'if you wouldn't think me foolish I should say you have found the "lullaby capable of singing him to rest"'.[37] Beyond the personal, she assured her sister, was another dimension: the sheer impersonal force of a great piece of writing.

The notices in the *Evening News*, *New Statesman and Nation*, *Week-end Review* and *Fortnightly Review* were divided as to the book's effectiveness as a reading experience, although most reviewers conceded that *The Waves* was an important experiment. In a long piece in the *Bookman*, Edwin Muir described how Virginia's interest in the creative and destructive powers of the sea, especially evident in *The Voyage Out* and *To the Lighthouse*, had now found the perfect verbal expression: 'In *The Waves* this prose has put away all hesitation, and cuts out images and thoughts in one sweep. It is impatiently, almost violently immediate.'[38] If some reviewers found the book too difficult, this was not a judgement seconded by the market-place: by the end of 1931, over 10,000 copies were sold in Britain (the American sales were slightly better). The common reader had delivered a strong message.

Virginia's morbid sensitivity now had to give way, very reluctantly, to Leonard's. His new book, *After the Deluge*, was not getting much attention in the press; the notice given to it in the *Times Literary Supplement* was short and unenthusiastic. At breakfast on 23 October, Virginia mentioned that she was reviewed in the *Manchester Guardian*. Leonard asked: 'Is it a long review?' Feeling 'like a mother to a hurt & miserable little boy', she had to tell him yes.[39]

One way Virginia discovered to relieve her anxiety about *The Waves* was to begin work on a new biography, a life of Flush, the cocker spaniel given by Mary Russell Mitford to Elizabeth Barrett to cheer her solitary, invalid days. Like *Orlando*, *Flush* was conceived as a joke (it was originally intended to be published as a booklet for the Christmas trade). One day, tired of working on *The Waves*, Virginia rested in the garden at Rodmell and read the Browning love letters; Flush made her laugh. There was a very mischievous side to the fun: she wanted to 'play a joke on Lytton . . . to parody him'.[40] But the book grew into a serious piece of humour, one in which the observant spaniel is a sympathetic witness to his owner's reclusive life, her love affair with Robert Browning, her elopement and subsequent life in Italy. Flush is an outsider who, despite his doggy ways, understands the fluctuations of the human heart and, of course, Virginia often felt herself an outsider in a similar way. One of the book's finest conceits is the frontispiece, a photograph in which the male, red cocker subject of the book is represented by Pinker (or possibly her mother), the blond cocker spaniel bitch given by Vita to the Woolfs. As in *Orlando*, a male subject's sexual identity is transmuted.

Since literary London was nothing more than a 'parrot house',[41] it was good to escape to Rodmell, where there were vexations of a different order. The society she longed for, Virginia sarcastically observed, was that of someone like Miss Dixey, who bred lemon-coloured cockers. One day she said: 'Mrs Woolf, I've planted this bed with yellow and white roses, because my yellow and white bitch is buried there; and that one with red and orange roses, because that's the grave of the red bitch. It's a mistake to have so much sentiment, ain't it?'[42] The ironical side of Virginia would have answered yes, but there was a considerable portion of her being which sympathized deeply with the breeder.

Rodmell life as the Woolfs knew it was continually threatened by extinction at the hands of developers, but there was the sheer relief in Sussex of fresh air, their garden and the downs. However, it could provide no escape from death. For many years, Virginia and Lytton had preserved an amiable distance from each other. She had many reservations about his work, and she was certain he held mixed feelings about hers. Virginia did not like Roger Senhouse, the new man in Lytton's life, or Dora Carrington. The two women were jealous of each other. Dora was envious of the adoration Lytton had once paid Virginia and Virginia saw Dora as a sharp-eyed girl who had intruded into her cosy friendship with Lytton.

In early December, Clive told Virginia that Lytton was leaving soon for Spain. This news prompted a letter – the first (surviving) one to Lytton in almost three years: 'I have just woken from a dream in which I was at a play, in the pit and suddenly you, who were sitting across a gangway in a row in front, turned and looked at me, and we both went into fits of laughter.'[43] While the mood was still upon her, she could not resist writing to the 'bearded serpent'. The fear of separation always aroused deep-seated but often concealed (even from herself) feelings in Virginia. Only five days later did she learn that her friend was dying of what was diagnosed as paratyphoid or ulcerative colitis (in fact, he had stomach cancer).

Suddenly the past, which hovered very much on the edges of *The Waves*, had caught up with Virginia once again. Her new book was in part an elegy to her strong, silent brother and to her own youth. Now Lytton was in danger. 'After all,' she told Ethel, 'I don't suppose I care for anyone more than for Lytton (after my Jew). He's in all my past – my youth.'[44] If Lytton were to die, so could she or Leonard. More importantly, the world as she had known it was about to dissolve. She thought of things she wanted to say to the old friendly snake, moments they could still share. She was in touch with 'the desire for life – the triumph of life'.[45]

On Christmas Eve, both Leonard and Virginia burst into tears as they contemplated the possible death of their friend. Two days later, the news from Ham Spray was encouraging. Virginia could envisage a future in which she would laugh with and abuse Lytton. She could also fantasize about the next twenty, productive years of her life: 'Can we count on another 20 years? I shall be fifty on [the] 25th, Monday week that is; & sometimes feel that I have lived 250 years already, & sometimes that I am still the youngest person in the omnibus . . . And I want to write another 4 novels.'[46] The other side of literary ambition was personal despair. If Lytton died, Virginia told Vita, she would mind it to the end of her days.

The Woolfs remained in Sussex until 10 January. Four days later, they drove to Ham Spray, which they had last visited in October 1924. Virginia was immediately envious of the house's tranquil, picture-book setting of flat lawn, carefully arranged trees and rising downland. In comparison, endangered Rodmell was a mess. Lytton was not well enough to see the Woolfs, but they were told that he was pleased that they had visited. Virginia's recollection of her brief stay at Ham Spray was of the frail, beautiful house, of nurses popping in and out, of a light emanating from Lytton's room and of the shadow of a screen. The aloof, mysterious world of death must have brought back to her memories of the nurses and sickrooms when Julia, Leslie and Thoby died.

On 20 January, assured by phone that Lytton was much better, Leonard and Virginia attended a fancy-dress party in Angelica's honour at Vanessa's studio in Fitzroy Street. At one point, the sisters' feelings about Lytton got the better of them: they burst into tears. The next morning, Virginia learned that much better had in fact been much worse: Lytton had died the previous day. Now, she could see Lytton 'coming along the street, muffled up with his beard resting on his tie: how we should stop: his eyes glow'. Next to that vivid recollection was the effacing presence of death. Vanessa told her sister: 'He is the first of the people one has known since one was grown up to die.'[47] They had reached a grim milestone.

Lytton simply disappeared. There was no public funeral, no communal way in which to commemorate his passing. Even his letters could not be published for fifty years. One way to celebrate his life was to revisit Ham Spray and offer condolences to Carrington. In the past Virginia had been afraid of being absorbed by Lytton and in a very real sense this is exactly what had happened to Carrington. In the younger woman Virginia saw a reflection of the kind of person she could have become. She was both intrigued and repulsed. Carrington, whose physical beauty was reminiscent of Jinny in *The Waves*, also had a very Rhoda-like side to her.

When the Woolfs arrived at Ham Spray on 11 March, Carrington was very much in retreat: she was like a small, pale, suffering animal, one who will soon steal away into a quiet corner to die quietly. The lunch was succulent, but Virginia thought that Carrington might resent the visit, feel that she was being spied on. The three of them visited Lytton's study and then, at Leonard's suggestion, took a walk. Carrington left them – she had letters to write. Leonard tinkered with the car. Virginia wandered by herself in the garden, then returned to the sitting room, where Carrington came upon her.

The two women walked upstairs to get a view from a window.

Carrington began talking of maintaining Lytton's rooms as they were, as a kind of shrine. Then they went back to Lytton's sitting room, where the stale air of death was palpable. Carrington burst into tears. When Virginia took her in her arms, Carrington spoke in a disjointed, darting way of what Lytton had meant to her: 'People say he was very selfish to me. But he gave me everything. I was devoted to my father. I hated my mother. Lytton was like a father to me.' Those telegram-like sentences contained the emotional truth of her life. Also clearly evident in her words was the despair that now invaded her: nothing could ever be right again.

Virginia knew that Carrington could not go on much longer. Leonard returned and the three took tea in a room which seemed, despite the roaring fire, cold. As the Woolfs were leaving, Carrington – contrary to the wishes of the Stracheys, who did not want Lytton's things given away – presented Virginia with a little French box and said, 'I gave this to Lytton. Take it.' Virginia accepted the present, observing how frightened Carrington was, like a child who had been reprimanded. At the front of the house, she kissed Virginia several times and, in response to Virginia's 'Then you will come & see us next week – or not – just as you like?', she said, 'Yes, I will come, or not.'[48]

Carrington killed herself the following day. That night Leonard and Virginia walked the silent, dark-blue streets of London, morbidly aware that the scaffolding on some of the buildings could easily tumble to the ground and kill them. The streets seemed quiet, but Virginia discerned an air of menace which might suddenly manifest itself, leaving violence and destruction in its wake. Could such terror be contained or would it suddenly burst its boundaries?

Her sense of grief at losing Lytton was compounded by the tragic conviction that their friendship had been on the verge of being restored: 'we were about to meet again, much more often – and then he died'.[49] That April, the Woolfs advised James Strachey, Lytton's executor, to have his brother's letters typed and circulated among his friends. These documents could stand as a memorial. When James pointed out that Lytton had said very unpleasant things about her and all his other friends, Virginia shrugged her shoulders. As she remarked to Vanessa: 'as we all do that, I don't see that it matters'.[50]

In March 1932, Virginia was 'glad to be alive & sorry for the dead'.[51] She was also afraid of being buried alive by the full-length studies of her which were beginning to appear. As she observed, 'It's difficult to see one self as a mummy in a museum.'[52] Once again, she had been incensed, this time by H. G. Wells's claim that women must be ancillary and decorative in the world of the future. She disdained such chauvinistic crystal-ball gazing and thought of reviving work on 'Opening the Door' (now called 'A Knock on the Door'), which she had placed aside in favour of *The Waves*. A new title suggested itself, 'Men are Like That', but she rejected it as 'too patently feminist'.[53] Nevertheless, she felt that she had collected enough powder to blow up St Paul's and planned to include four photographs as visual support for the claims she was going to make in her new polemic.

Virginia was also repulsed by the Potocki case. In February 1932, Count Geoffrey Wladislaw Vaile Potocki de Montalk, who was descended from a Polish aristocratic family but claimed to have been born in New Zealand, was sentenced to six months in prison for attempting to commission a printer to print his poems, one of which was dedicated to 'John Penis in the Mount of Venus'. Leonard, who did not like lavatory humour but felt that pornography had a place in a free society, contributed £20 towards his bail. Virginia was sympathetic in principle to the issue of freedom of speech, but she felt that Potocki, who wandered the streets of London in a red cassock, was yet another example of the reckless stupidity of men. She could, however, be reckless herself. When she and Ethel took tea in Rottingdean at Maurice Baring's, the novelist's disreputable-looking footmen handed out anchovy sandwiches which she loathed and soon secreted in her purse. When, a little later, Baring asked her for a light, she handed him one of his own discarded sandwiches.

Men such as Wells and Potocki vividly reminded Virginia of

how women remained outsiders. So it was not surprising that she rejected an invitation from the Master of Trinity to deliver the Clark Lectures. She was gratified, however, especially when she realized that her father would have blushed with pleasure that his daughter had been asked to succeed him in such a distinguished venture. The proposed honour made her aware of just how far she had come from the time she had been 'the uneducated child reading books in my room at 22 H. P. G.'. She did not wish to give up her time to prepare these talks and, much more importantly, felt that acceptance of the invitation would make her a 'functionary' within the male-dominated hierarchy; it would, in addition, seal her lips 'when it comes to tilting at Universities'.[54] To Clive Bell, she made a joke of it: 'Indeed, as Desmond was once a Clark lecturer, the honour is not overwhelming, even to a vain woman like myself.'[55]

For many reasons, Virginia was delighted to escape England for a month on 15 April. The Woolfs' destination was Greece, which Virginia had last visited in 1906. In view of the aftermath of that early trip, Virginia was apprehensive – and doubly so because she and Leonard were making the trip with Roger and his sister, Margery. Virginia had offered to pay Helen Anrep's way, but Roger's companion refused this offer of assistance. Virginia was afraid that the expedition would end in bugs, quarrels and endless games of chess. The train trip from London to Venice was uneventful and Virginia, who always remained a great admirer of the aesthetics of Roman Catholicism, responded rapturously to a Tiepolo church, where the thick yellow air of incense weaved an enchanted web. 'This is the magic we want: & magic there must be,' she reminded herself, 'so long as magic keeps its place.'[56]

The Woolfs travelled first class aboard the SS *Tevere*, which sailed from Brindisi to Athens on Sunday, 17 April. Virginia was glad to be segregated from the Frys, who were in second. The truth was that Virginia was a bit afraid of Margery, a feminist very much of the Margaret Llewelyn Davies type. Although she had served as Principal of Somerville College from 1926 to 1931, Margery had dedicated her life to penal reform. Virginia felt that

Roger's sister considered her a would-be, fly-by-night feminist, although, as it turned out, Margery had an inferiority complex of her own when in the company of writers and artists. When Virginia observed that Margery knew all about politics, the older woman was surprised: 'My dear Virginia, when will you get that silly illusion out of your head? I'm merely good at bluff. That's how I take people in.'[57]

Such direct honesty helped to dismantle some of Virginia's negative feelings about Margery and her 'suppressed, half Quaker, half virgin attitude'[58] towards the world. While visiting the Parthenon, Virginia had a moving encounter with an even stranger woman: her own ghost, 'the girl of 23, with all her life to come'.[59] At the hotel in Athens, Virginia proudly inscribed her age as fifty. Although grey-haired, she was much more in touch than ever before with the 'vital, the flourish in the face of death'.[60] She responded eagerly to the colours of Greece, to the deep-red poppies which carpeted the hills and to the peasant girls. On 2 May, she wrote to Vanessa: 'if ever I had a turn towards Sapphism it would be revived by the carts of young peasant women in lemon, red and blue handkerchiefs, and the donkeys and the kids and the general fecundity and bareness: and the sea; and the cypresses'.[61]

Virginia was also deeply touched by Roger's fantastic curiosity, very much that of a young man. Although he was warned about the difficulties inherent in travelling to the monastery Hosios Loukas, with its famous mosaics, he refused to be put off. On the day of that expedition, they did not arrive back in Athens until 8.30 in the evening, having broken a spring, punctured a tyre and run over a snake. Roger claimed that only by such experiences could a traveller get a real insight into the Greek soul.

So remote was Greece from her ordinary life that Virginia felt she was wandering in the fields of the moon. Such was her reaction to Athens, Sounion, Aegina, Corinth, Delphi, Nauplia and Mycenae. Once again, she responded to the monumental remains of Greece's classical past, but she was much more alive to the natural world. When she visited Agamemnon's tomb, she noticed how the bees had taken it over, making the stones hollow like a vast hive. The nightingales, scarlet anemones and liquid-jelly blue water were the real delights of this visit. In her diary, she paid Greece the highest possible compliment: she could love this country as 'I once loved Cornwall, as a child'.[62]

Towards the end of this expedition, Virginia wrote to John Lehmann, who had been left in charge of the Hogarth Press: 'I've often thought of you with sympathy when one wheel of the car has been trembling over a precipice 2,000 feet deep, and vultures wheeling round our heads as if settling which to begin on.'[63] Lehmann also felt on edge and he voiced his discontent to Leonard and Virginia soon after his holiday, which he took after the Woolfs returned to England on 12 May. Lehmann certainly took no pleasure in the manager's office, which he suspected had once been a housekeeper's or butler's room: cupboards were built against one wall and the only window looked out on to an external corridor. One day, in desperate need of fresh air, Lehmann tried to open the window. He succeeded only in breaking one of the panes and covering his hands with blood.

Lehmann found Leonard a tiresome person to work for, someone who could be counted on to be edgy and bad-tempered over trivial matters. In a major crisis, his conduct was markedly better: on such occasions, he would simply throw up his arms and shrug his shoulders. John also learned that for Leonard and Virginia the Press was the child their marriage had never produced and that they were jealous of anyone else's involvement with that offspring. When he joined the Press, Lehmann was to have the option of becoming a full partner within a year or two. By the autumn of 1932, certain that he would never be given any real power to choose books, Lehmann did not want to be tied down to a job which involved a great deal of attention to relatively inconsequential matters. He also wanted to be free to travel. Although Leonard and John negotiated a rather complex scheme by which John would work an average of two hours daily, he ultimately decided to make a complete break with the Press and the Woolfs. Leonard was furious, and Virginia – to John's dismay – followed suit.

Within two weeks of her return to England, Virginia was in a complete daze. She was worried about the Press, 'The Knock on the Door', a new novel, Rodmell, buying clothes, the contempt men felt for women and 'terror at night of things generally wrong in the universe'.[64] Her thoughts were chaotic. She simply did not know what was wrong. On 26 May she told Ethel: 'I can't tell you how down in the mud and brambles I've been – nearer one of those climaxes of despair that I used to have than any time these 6 years – Lord knows why . . . and was incapable of any vision of hope.'[65] The past haunted her. For example, she asked herself why was Clive always so horrible to her. 'What did I steal 20 years ago that he should never feel the debt paid?'[66]

When she dined with Shaw, she was impressed with how vigorous the seventy-four-year-old man of letters was and wanted to be infused with similar creative juices. And at Rodmell that June the air was alive with the buzzing of the bees: 'like arrows of desire: fierce, sexual . . . the whole air full of vibration: of beauty, of this burning arrowy desire'.[67]

Virginia was frightened that life had passed her by. On 29 June she dined with Katharine Furse, a childhood friend* whose 'dashing youth' had been replaced by the 'scraped bare look' of middle age.[68] Had the same thing happened to her, Virginia asked herself. That evening, when Leonard came in, he looked sunburnt and remarkably vigorous. Perhaps they were still young. And so, when they parted that evening, Virginia could imagine Katharine as an old woman upon whom she condescendingly bestowed a kiss.

Now that her books were making a relatively large sum of money, she and Leonard were generous to their relatives and friends. Nevertheless, Virginia felt overcome by obligations. She had many friends who had been kind to her since the time she had been, as she characterized herself, 'a gawky, tongue tied, impossible girl'.[69] How could she tell them that her career as a writer and publisher prevented her from seeing them? On 6 July, she fainted at a restaurant, the Ivy, and had to be led away by Clive.

* Nine years older than Virginia, she was the daughter of John Addington Symonds and the sister of Madge Vaughan.

When Virginia explain to Ethel how oppressed she felt, the composer was certain that Virginia intended to deprive her of visiting time and insulted her by characterizing her as a magpie who, poor health or not, had to be the centre of attention. Virginia countered by asking Ethel if she remembered the name of the last person who had begged for an interview: 'Ethel Smyth. Do you know that lady?'[70] What Virginia now desired was immunity, 'to exist apart from rubs, shocks, suffering; to be beyond the range of darts'.[71]

Of one thing Virginia was very certain. She had come to hate Ethel's scene-making propensities. On that score, she confronted her on 28 July:

> And as you never quarrel with your friends, and as I certainly never quarrel with mine, the fact does seem to point to some incompatibility between us . . . What I do find harassing and unnerving and odious to an extent that I don't think you realize is the resulting 'scene'. I think I told you last summer how I loathed it . . . And to me the memory of that discussion [the previous week] is one of such horror – it makes me feel so degraded – so humiliated – . . . well, I don't see how I'm to see anyone easily, or write, or speak freely to anyone who may insist upon a scene like that again.[72]

Ethel, frightened now that the tables had been completely turned on her, was conciliatory. In her reply, she referred to Virginia's letter as fair, temperate and generous. Having gained the upper hand, Virginia, who claimed that such outbursts provided the composer with a mild continuous orgasm, was relentless:

> though I quite accept what you say – that you can control yourself, that there'll be no more scenes – still I'm left doubting – isn't it rather a cribbed and confined sort of friendship when one has to be controlled and on one's best behaviour? Doesn't the need point, as I said, to some queer, no, not queer, natural, – incompatibility between us? . . . We are both extreme in character . . . I don't know your friends nor you mine, so that the

> natural background is missing. But what is important is that I suspect that your violences are part of your virtues – and so are my exaggerations and obtusenesses part of mine . . . Obtuse and variable as I am, I still think, seriously nothing more important than relationships – that they should be sound, free from hypocrisies, fluencies, palaver.[73]

But Virginia found it impossible to live without some kind of internal 'palaver'. On 4 August, she was deeply saddened to learn that Goldie Dickinson, who had been generous in his praise of *The Waves*, had died. His death led to several reflections. She had the feeling that her life might be part of some vast, mystical operation. Or she might be like a worm crushed by a car: 'what does the worm know of the car – how it is made?'[74]

Leonard pointed out that for the remainder of their lives now they would have to face the fact that their friends would be dying off. One of the best ways to fight the extinguishing force was to make little efforts, like inviting old friends such as Saxon down for the weekend, or to spend the day with Leonard's mother, who gave Virginia a pair of pearl earrings on Thursday, 11 August.

That day had been incredibly hot, but the heat dissipated as darkness approached. In the evening, Virginia and Leonard sat out on the terrace. Virginia noticed a white owl flying out to catch mice from the marsh. Suddenly, her heart

> leapt; & stopped; & leapt again; & I tasted that queer bitterness at the back of my throat; & the pulse leapt into my head & beat & beat, more savagely, more quickly. 'I am going to faint' I said & slipped off my chair & lay on the grass . . . Then pain, as of childbirth; & then that too slowly faded; & I lay presiding, like a flickering light, like a most solicitous mother, over the shattered splintered fragments of my body. A very acute & unpleasant experience.[75]*

* In a document among the Monks House Papers (MS), Leonard Woolf left a detailed account of this incident. According to him, Virginia was particularly vulnerable to such attacks at the beginning of a period: 'She then had

Virginia felt birth pangs, but what was she giving birth to? She was on the threshold of some new direction, but would she survive the anguish of such a pregnancy? Then she became the mother who looked after her own body, a body very much in need of tender nursing. One of the most tragic aspects of Virginia's life was that she felt, rightly, that she had never been sufficiently cared for by her own mother. As an adult, she sought out people who could or would act towards her in a maternal way, but the inadequacy of her childhood nurturing simply could not be made up. She had to care for herself, but this remained a dubious enterprise: why should she look after herself when her own mother had obviously not thought her worthy of such attention? This kind of conflict became especially oppressive to Virginia when she had finished a book or was uncertain about a new direction in her career. At such times, when her attention could not be sufficiently diverted by her work, she felt the lonely anguish of childhood. While recovering from this new bout of depressive illness, she dreamed that Angelica had died. Of course, she was really worried that her own inner girl had perished long ago.

★

---

acute menstrual pains similar to those when the period is coming on. She had a considerable motion of the bowels, diarrhoeic. The heart and head symptoms were now much less, but she felt very cold and was trembling all over. After the motion the menstrual pains lessened gradually and were over about 10.15 . . .

'The attack was almost precisely similar to that which she had two years ago on a very hot day. All the symptoms were the same in the previous attack but all of them were I think more severe. Two years ago it began with the same pounding of her heart and head and the bitter taste in the mouth. She was however much more flushed and scarlet in the face. She actually fainted and lost consciousness for 3 or 4 minutes. The diarrhoea was much more violent. The only symptom which was less violent was the menstrual pain. The attack lasted at least an hour longer than that of yesterday.

'She also had a fainting attack on July 6th this year. This occurred at dinner in a very hot restaurant. It was much more like an ordinary fainting attack, i.e., it began with a feeling of faintness and giddiness and for a short time she lost consciousness.'

Leonard insisted on treating Virginia 'like the Princess who feels a pea through 6 mattresses'.[76] Within two weeks of this wonderful regime, she felt much better, but she had a convenient excuse if she wanted to put off callers. The writing of *Flush* proved a happy, diverting 'freak',[79] one interrupted by a request from *The Times* to write a piece on the centenary of her father's birth. She was inclined to say no but prepared the essay, in which her father's great charm is elucidated.

During the summer of 1932, Virginia was at a crossroads in her career. Should she continue in the experimental vein of *The Waves* or should she pursue a different kind of reality, one more in accord with the everyday realities which confronted ordinary women? She was not sure and that uncertainty helped to breed a great deal of psychic conflict. Torn in many, varying directions, she could not find a clear way forward.

When Virginia wrote to Ottoline Morrell on 6 September, she reflected on letters as potentially publishable documents. 'I'm as vain as a cockatoo myself; but I don't think I do that. Because when one is writing a letter, the whole point is to rush ahead; and anything may come out of the spout of the tea pot.'[78] Unsure of what she wanted to 'come out', in 1932 Virginia tried her hand at a number of pieces: a touching portrait of old Mrs Grey, a Rodmell neighbour; 'A Letter to a Young Poet' (addressed to Lehmann), in which she mixed encouragement and caution; a new series of essays in which she examined the plight of the female writer. Virginia, who had been somewhat unsympathetic to Charlotte Brontë's anger in *A Room of One's Own*, had now come to realize that she would give all that Jane Austen had written for just half of what the Brontë sisters had produced.

In *A Room*, Virginia had commented about the obscure lives led by most women – and the fact that those lives had to be commemorated. She had assigned such a task to the imaginary novelist, Mary Carmichael. That concern, evident in the first *Common Reader*, is much stronger in the second one, published that autumn.

At this time, Virginia herself felt compelled to take up the agenda once consigned to Mary Carmichael: she decided to write a novel-essay called *The Pargiters.** The starting point for this project was the paper she had read to the National Society for Women's Service the year before. She saw this new piece of writing as a continuation of *A Room*, but the form, one which would ground her in the realities of the world, would obviously be a mixture of the traditional and experimental. In the holograph of *The Pargiters*, she redrafted her earlier speech: this book would examine the Victorian past of today's women, beginning with the lives of their grandmothers. The book might have a radical agenda, but it would use traditional methodology: 'What has happened of course is that after abstaining from the novel of fact all these years – since 1919 – & Night & Day. Indeed, I find myself infinitely delighting in facts for a change, & in possession of quantities beyond counting: though I feel now & then the tug to vision, but resist it. This is the true line, I am sure, after The Waves.'[79] In the years ahead, certainty would give way to grave doubts.

The manuscript of *The Pargiters* comprises seven and a quarter manuscript volumes; of those, almost two volumes (the principal scenes from the 1880s) are written in the novel-essay format. Generally speaking, fiction precedes essay: the fictional sequences provide examples of the points to be discussed in the essays. Like Virginia's own family, the Pargiters are a comfortably situated upper-middle-class family which educates its sons and ignores its daughters. The verb 'parget' can mean to plaster inside a chimney and Virginia may have chosen this surname to suggest how strong feelings in this family are hidden away or papered over. All the Pargiters repress their emotions, but women are especially subject to such a regime.

This is very much the subject matter of *A Room*, but the pieces of fiction embedded into her new text give a dramatic focus to the

* The novel portion of *The Pargiters* eventually became, after extensive changes, *The Years*; the soon-abandoned essay portion of this narrative was reworked into *Three Guineas*.

polemic. Although the early sections of *The Pargiters* do not have the sexual focus Virginia first envisaged, the story of the child Rose brilliantly elucidates how women are used sexually by men. A curious, assertive child, she escapes the house to buy a rubber duck, but she is made to pay a terrible price for her desire for independence. Outside by herself as darkness falls, the child comes upon a sinister man from whom she attempts to escape.

> When she reached the pillar box there was the man again. He was leaning against it, as if he were ill, Rose thought, filled with the same terror again; [but] he was lit up by the lamp. There was nobody else anywhere in sight. As she ran past him, he gibbered some nonsense at her, sucking his lips in & out; & began to undo his clothes.[80]

In the essay following this incident, the narrator remarks that such an assault is common enough in the London streets; she then goes on to talk of the psychological consequences for Rose.

> She felt that what had happened was not merely 'naughty' but somehow wrong. But in what sense did she feel it to be wrong? The grey face that hung on a string in front of her eyes somehow suggested to her a range of emotion in herself, of which she was instinctively afraid; as if, without being told a word about it, she knew that she was able to feel what it was wrong to feel.[81]

Rose assumes the guilt for the action performed by the man in much the same way a very young Virginia Stephen had felt shame for her body after she was assaulted by Gerald Duckworth. The Pargiter family not only closes the doors of education to its female members but also forces them to live in a condition of intellectual and emotional servitude which does not allow any open vista. In this family, women are by definition guilty if they experience any sexual feeling, whatever its origin.

The brightest spot in the essay-fiction portion of the holograph is the attention devoted to a man who held positive views on the role of women in society: Joseph Wright (1855–1930), who had been Professor of Comparative Philology at Oxford and the editor of the six-volume *English Dialect Dictionary*. In July 1932, Virginia read the recently published biography of him by his wife, Elizabeth. There she learned about a man who held some strong, unorthodox opinions. A workhouse boy whose mother had served as a char to put him through school, Wright in turn had devoted himself to the education of working women. At the end of this section of the holograph, the narrator speculates that Kitty Malone, daughter of an Oxford don and cousin of the Pargiters, might have learned a great deal from Wright's existence:

> he certainly held a view of life which might have puzzled Kitty, accustomed as she was to the views held by men who had had every advantage that education can bestow . . . 'In the first place,' Joseph Wright remarked, 'the world may talk of the "weaker sex" as much as it likes, the whole idea is based upon the body and not upon the mind, soul, and heart. I have always held woman far higher than man in God's creation.' . . . his conception of marriage was revolutionary. His wife was not to darn his socks; she was not to do housework. 'It is my greatest ambition that you shall *live*, not merely exist; and live too in a way that not many women have lived before, if unlimited devotion and self-sacrifice on my part can do anything towards attaining that end.'[82]

The introduction of Wright, whose views were shared by Leonard Woolf, allowed Virginia to cite the history of a successful man who held – and lived out – an unbounded admiration for women. Wright provides an object lesson: relations between the sexes can be improved.

Although the novel-essay portion of *The Pargiters* shows Virginia Woolf attempting to both extend *A Room of One's Own* and invent a kind of non-fiction novel, the two kinds of narrative sit uneasily side by side and do not interact sufficiently. Also, the treatment of socio-economic and feminist issues in this draft do not really advance beyond *A Room*.

★

That September, Virginia's precarious self-esteem suffered a blow when she learned that a snapshot of her by Leonard would serve as the frontispiece to Winifred Holtby's book: 'my legs show; & I am revealed to the world . . . as a plain dowdy old woman'.[83]* For the next three months, she worked steadily on *The Pargiters*. She also had a built-in excuse for not attending parties and avoiding unwanted visitors: Elinor Rendel's stethoscope revealed that the systolic action of her heart was too wild. She advised Virginia to take digitalis and rest.

So Virginia remained bloody but very unbowed, possessed by the strong conviction that she was only now poised to find her true mark as a writer. On 2 October, she reminded herself: 'I don't believe in ageing. I believe in forever altering one's aspect to the sun.'[84] The Woolfs' financial prospects were excellent, magnificently assisted by Vita's new novel *Family History*, which sold more than 6,000 copies before publication.

Later that autumn, the Woolfs purchased their third car, a Lanchester, 'shaped like a fish, green on bottom, silver on top'.[85] When it was delivered in January, it led Virginia (in a letter to Vita) to produce what she called her first and last attempt at advertising copy: 'It glides with the smoothness of eel, with the speed of a swift, and the . . . power of a tigress when that tigress has just been reft of her young, in and out, up and down Piccadilly, Bond Street.' 'Isn't this a good blurb?' she asked her friend.[86] The resulting problem was that Virginia, in order to be worthy of the car, had to purchase the requisite, sleek clothing.

The Woolf marriage had never been better: 'I don't think we've ever been so happy, what with one thing & another. And so intimate, & so completely entire, I mean L. & I. If it could only last like this another 50 years – life like this is wholly satisfactory.'[87]

There were some minor set-backs, such as Virginia's dispute with Logan Pearsall Smith about the reasons behind the constant fighting between his forces (Chelsea) and hers (Bloomsbury). Winifred Holtby's book – a good one – made Virginia roar with uneasy

* The photograph was cropped so that Virginia's legs were not on display.

laughter.* Towards the end of the year, she became dissatisfied with *Flush* and uncertain of what she was doing with *The Pargiters.* In that book, she resolved to keep her sarcasm under control and to find the correct balance between freedom and reserve. Compared to *The Waves*, the writing was easy and unforced. All in all, she reflected on the last day of 1932, the autumn had been a time of tremendous revelation and a great season of liberation. She did not intend for the usual black despair to follow this 'intoxicating exhilaration'.[88]

A month later, she decided to leave out the 'interchapters' (essays) and work them into the fictional text. Her new novel would in fact blend the technique of *Night and Day* with that of *The Waves*. Of one thing she was very certain: when, that March, the University of Manchester offered her an honorary doctorate, she refused it. She would take nothing from a corrupt society. She recoiled 'at all that humbug'.[89]

Although she often wrote to complain of Ethel's excesses, Virginia's friendship with Vita had been low-key for several years. Suddenly, in the autumn of 1932, Virginia was filled with jealousy as she thought back to the summer of 1929, when Vita had gone off to the Alps with Hilda Matheson. These buried feelings were

* On 15 January 1933, she wrote a polite but reserved letter to Holtby: 'I have finished Virginia Woolf. I enjoyed it very much. Of course I suspect a good many things happened to her, by way of life, that she concealed successfully, but it seems to me, speaking as an outsider, that you have made an extremely interesting story out of her books, and I only wish, for all our sakes, that they had as much virtue in them as you make out. She was always full of excitement, I think, when she was writing them, but as she never read them after they were written, she can't say much about them now. What an idiotic thing – to give Mrs Dalloway one father in The Voyage Out, and another in Mrs Dalloway! That comes of working from memory.

'But though I was ashamed of her carelessness, I felt that you suggested so many extremely interesting points of view that I long to write a book on V.W. myself; still more to write another novel by V.W. herself. Not a word offended me: though had I known that my random remarks about my mother's family were to appear in print, I should have been more careful – not that I mind being rather sketchy about relations – but they do.'

very likely unleashed because of Vita's forthcoming lecture tour of the United States, for which the Nicolsons left on board the *Bremen* on 29 December 1932. A month later, Virginia's imagination cooked up a particularly vivid fantasy, similar to the wild flights of fancy she was capable of in conversation, about Vita's experiences in the new world: 'Oh my God - how I envy you, slipping off your skin and adventuring through fields where the flamingoes rise in flocks and the old black women stand at the doors, a baby at each breast!'[90]

Despite her racing heart and rigorous work schedule, 1933 was the normal social round. Between 17 February and 25 March, the Woolfs visited Hampstead, Ivinghoe Beacon and the Royal Horticultural Society Flower show; they saw a René Clair film and attended the Sadler's Wells ballet and at least five concerts; Elizabeth Bowen and Rose Macaulay were among the visitors received at Tavistock Square. However, the pleasure taken in such events was tempered yet again by death – in this case the death of Gwendolen Cecil, whom Virginia had known since childhood. Virginia regretted that she had refused a luncheon invitation from this old friend and once again felt incredibly old: 'I feel I've been living ever since there was a crocodile in the Nile.'[91]

On 28 April, Virginia met Bruno Walter, the former director of the Städtische Oper in his native Berlin and of the Gewandhaus Concerts in Leipzig. Early in 1933, the Jewish conductor had been forced to leave Germany in the wake of Hitler's rise to power. This encounter, arranged by Ethel, brought little pleasure to Virginia, who dismissed Walter as swarthy and fattish. He was, she thought, obsessed with the Nazi poison. During their brief encounter, the conductor urged the Woolfs to speak out against Hitler. 'We,' a sceptical Virginia recorded, 'must band together. We must refuse to meet any German. We must say that they are uncivilized. We will not trade with them or play with them – we must make them feel themselves outcast – not by fighting them; by ignoring them.'[92] Virginia did not want to gaze at this early piece of writing on the wall.

In the spring of 1933, Virginia's attention was focused on her annual trip to the Continent, this time to France and Italy. The Woolfs left London in their new car on 5 May and made the Newhaven–Dieppe crossing that night. They drove through France and via the Grande Corniche to Siena, which they reached on 13 May. They did not care for the redolence of either the French or the Italian rivieras ('pink pyjama country',[93] Virginia labelled them), but they admired Rapallo: 'its bay stretched with gold silk ... humming scented villas; all orange blossom'.[94] Virginia bestowed even more approval on Shelley's villa, the Casa Magni, on the shore between San Terenzo and Lerici. In fact, she imagined his death by drowning: 'Shelley's house waiting by the sea, & Shelley not coming, & Mary & Mrs Williams watching from the balcony & then Trelawney coming from Pisa, & burning the body on the shore'.[95]

At Pisa, which they reached on 12 May, Virginia remembered that she and Leonard had, while there on honeymoon, encountered some family friends from whom she had tried to hide. The couple travelled to Siena on 13 May and spent four nights there. The deeply green landscape of little pointed hills adorned with poplars and cypresses was particularly appealing. Leonard and Virginia also visited Lucca, San Gimignano and Piacenza. Throughout their stay in Italy, they were keenly aware of the omnipresent Blackshirts – another sign that Europe was slowly but surely being taken over by hostile forces. Virginia was glad to return to England and to resume work on *The Pargiters*. Her holiday had worked a certain amount of magic: on the last day of May, while driving through Richmond, a rested Virginia came to an important realization about the 'synthesis' of her being, of 'how only writing composes it: how nothing makes a whole unless I am writing'.[96]

While abroad, she had written a mock abusive letter to Ethel inquiring what she was up to: 'inducing a large penis into a small hole?'[97] Back in England, Virginia was more reserved. She hated the indulgent and intrusive figure Ethel cut in her new volume of autobiography, *Female Pipings in Eden*, the manuscript of which she was reading with an eye to suggesting revisions. In particular, Virginia wanted one character removed from the book: herself. 'I think you weaken your case by bringing in VW. I have ventured to put [in] a couple of brackets to show how she could be omitted with advantage.'[98] That August, when Virginia was bedridden with headache, an outraged Ethel, who came to Rodmell from Rottingdean, was forbidden entry to Monks House by a resolute Leonard. He would not allow the composer even two minutes with his wife.

Even when her work was going well, Virginia found it difficult to eradicate other concerns. That autumn, she responded in a heightened way to any kind of stimuli. When she visited the reptile house at London Zoo with Mary Hutchinson and Leonard, Mary twined around herself one of the bright electric-blue pythons. When she touched one, Virginia experienced the eerie sensation of feeling 'muscles moving under a shiny plated skin'.[99] An exhibition of Burne-Jones's work brought back sad memories of her youth: 'The suavity, the sinuosity, the way the private parts are merely clouded – it's all a romantic dream, which makes me think of tea at Hyde Park Gate.'[100]

Animal metaphors began to enter Virginia's language at a faster rate than usual. On 31 July, she had told Ethel: 'You see you're a great lioness and I'm only a dun coloured mouldy mouse. You know how chameleon I am in my changes – leopard one day, all violet spots; mouse today.'[101] A few weeks later, she changed animals: 'If I hadn't a heart of gold under the skin of a shark I should never write to you again.'[102] Metaphor became reality when a wild Alsatian ran into the Lanchester: 'we gave him a great bang – he lay squirming – dead, I thought, then reeled up & went galloping over the field'.[103]

That autumn, *The Pargiters* was assuming the shape of a family chronicle – a form made popular by John Galsworthy, Hugh Walpole and, of course, Vita. In order to distance herself from all such competitors, Virginia thought of calling the book 'Here and Now'. She was trying to put more flesh on the bone of the novel, to make this new book more objective and realistic, in the manner of Jane Austen. Slowly but surely, however, *The Pargiters* returned

Virginia to the world of Hyde Park Gate. If that book had remained an essay-novel, she might have been able to keep her distance from the unhappy childhood and adolescence so graphically re-created there, but in this case re-creating eventually meant reliving.

All of Virginia Woolf's novels are autobiographical, but in the writer Elvira Pargiter she created the most sustained – and realistic – self-portrait of her dark side. Elvira and her sister Maggie (Magdalena) were introduced into *The Pargiters* only after the 1880 section of the novel-essay was completed and that format abandoned. The sisters, the daughters of Abel Pargiter's younger brother, Sir Digby, enter the book when Abel calls upon his sister-in-law, the exotic half-Spanish Eugénie, in 1891. The widower is in love with her and deeply fond of the conventionally beautiful Maggie. Like her elder sister, Elvira is a lively child, but she is a bit shy, because of a slight deformity: when she was a baby, she had been dropped and as a result one shoulder is higher than the other.

Sixteen years intervene. In the 1907 sequence, Elvira is alone in her bedroom on a hot summer evening. She has stayed at home to rest her back. Through her window, she looks out on a neighbour's party. Her sister and eventually her mother visit her. Her deformity has helped to make her an outsider, a person who asks many questions about life but considers herself apart from it. In fact, Elvira feels that she must learn subtler methods of interrogation in order to elicit the truth.

Three years later, Maggie and Elvira live together in a shabby section of London. Their parents have died and the two sisters have not been well provided for. Maggie has invited Rose Pargiter, now a middle-aged suffragette, to visit them. During this encounter, Elvira is outspoken in her hatred of her father. Rose is upset by this and feels that the sisters are too sheltered from the social and political oppression which women endure. Rose's protest is political; Elvira's much more personal. Elvira expresses shock when Maggie later suggests that Rose is a lesbian: 'My feeling was this: when you said Rose flung herself into the arms of Mildred in a greenhouse, a shock; horror; terror . . . Something that lights up the whole of the dim past of the human race.'[104] Virginia was sympathetic to political protest but was never really politically active; in a similar way, she was drawn to lesbianism but distanced herself from the lesbian aspects of herself. Rose, whose sexuality has been linked to the incident with the man who exposes himself, obviously shares some traits with her creator, but Elvira, the outsider, is the person with whom Virginia most identified.

This woman does not participate in the life of her time. When we next meet her, in 1914, she has become decidedly eccentric. Her sister, who now has a baby, cannot spend as much time with her and Elvira seeks the consolation of religion. On the steps of St Paul's, she encounters her cousin Bobby, who takes her to a chophouse for lunch. During their extended conversation, his materialism and her disdain for his values emerge clearly, but she is presented as an essentially negative and difficult person.

In the 1910 and 1914 sections, an additional important contrast is developed between Elvira and her older cousin, Eleanor, Rose's sister. Eleanor has never openly rebelled against her society; instead, she attempts to alleviate the sufferings of others. Although she has some pretensions to being a writer, Elvira exists in a position of detached marginality: she hates society, sees its flaws, but does nothing to change things. As *The Pargiters* moves back and forth between the visionary and the ordinary in its examination of the lives of these two unmarried women, Virginia was obviously looking at various sides of herself, but she became distraught by her resemblance to Elvira. On 25 March 1933, she reflected: 'I hardly know which I am, or where: Virginia or Elvira.'[105]

Elvira is a very unflattering self-portrait, in turn dismissive, haughty, acutely self-centred and selfish. This is a depiction of the parts of herself of which Virginia was – and remained – deeply ashamed. Her foil, Eleanor, is a troubled person but a complacent do-gooder. There are many other portrayals of women, ranging from the kindly but ineffectual society woman Kitty (later Lady Lasswade) to the largely sympathetic portrait of Maggie, who chooses to have children and thus abandons her sister. A great deal of Vanessa Bell can be found in her and Rose, with her outrageous behaviour, has a direct counterpart in Ethel Smyth. In one scene, Rose buys flowers for Elvira and then, while calling her a liar, knocks her against a wall.

Although their personalities are vastly different, neither Elvira nor Eleanor does anything to change the sordid fabric of contemporary life. Up to the 1914 sequences, Elvira and Eleanor are parallel characters who never meet. When, in December 1933, Virginia was forced to have these two characters confront each other in the raid sequence (set in 1917), she became deeply anguished, almost as if the Elvira part of herself was encountering in Eleanor a character who bore an uncanny resemblance to Julia Stephen.

While struggling with *The Pargiters*, Virginia read another kind of family book, Vera Brittain's haunting *Testament of Youth*, an account of the author's loss of her brother and lover during the Great War. Although she thought that Brittain had a hard-boiled sensibility, Virginia was touched by the book, perhaps by the fact that it deals in large part with the death of a much-loved brother.

Tom Eliot, recently returned from America, now looked much younger. According to Virginia, he resembled a 'glorified boy scout in shorts & yellow shirt'.[106] His return meant that his estranged wife was even more fierce in circulating stories which linked her husband to a huge assortment of mistresses, of whom Virginia was reputed to be one. She also had to put up with abusive letters from Vivien. Ethel was another source of continual irritation. Her table manners were atrocious: she oozed, chortled and then blew her nose on her table napkin. Then she poured the cream into her beer. 'I had rather dine with a dog,'[107] Virginia confided to her nephew Quentin, to whom she also related the consequences of Hugh Walpole's mistake, on his way to visit the Woolfs, in knocking on the wrong door: 'a lady with purple hair and carmine lips answered him. "No, I am not Mrs Woolf," she said – indeed it was obvious what her trade was – not mine; and when Hugh said he must go; "Oh no," she said, "just come in all the same." This was very upsetting, Hugh said; his tastes being what they are.'[108]

Virginia, who felt that she had prostituted herself in writing *Flush*, was sure that book would be labelled charming, delicate and ladylike. Although the spaniel took a good 'first fence'[109] in the *Times Literary Supplement*, Rebecca West abused her soundly in the *Daily Telegraph*: 'It sometimes produces the effect . . . of a family joke that has been too hardy in leaving the four walls of its origin, and facing the rude airs of the great world.'[110] Those sentiments were seconded by Geoffrey Grigson in the *Morning Post*: 'Its continual mock-heroic tone, its bantering pedantry, its agile verbosity make it the most tiresome book which Mrs Woolf has yet written.'[111] David Garnett and Desmond MacCarthy wrote appreciative notices, but Virginia had from the outset been bothered by the whimsicality of this venture. Those doubts were reinforced by an anonymous review in *Granta*: 'the deadly facility of [*Flush*] combined with its popular success mean . . . the end of Mrs Woolf as a live force. We mourn the passing of a potentially great writer who perished for lack of an intelligent audience.'[112] The writer of this notice also lambasted *Orlando* and *The Waves*. Virginia immediately distanced herself from this attack, which she likened to a snub from a 'little pimpled undergraduate'[113] who might put a frog in someone's bed, but stung she was.

She wanted to rid herself of vanity, a word she equated with the name Virginia. If she lived an entirely private life, she might be able to cut the string that tied her 'to that quivering bag of nerves – all its gratifications & acute despair'.[114] This was an impossible task: she was a celebrity and an important publisher. Again, she briefly thought of discarding the latter role entirely.

In early December, while walking through Leicester Square, Virginia was startled to come upon this notice on a newspaper poster: 'Death of Noted Novelist'. At first, Virginia thought Hugh Walpole had died suddenly, but the reference was to Stella Benson, aged forty-one, who had just died in China. At once, Virginia mourned an acquaintanceship which might have blossomed into friendship. She remembered that she had once stopped Stella at the door at Rodmell and asked her to call her by her first name. There was a reproach in that death, which reminded her of Katherine

Mansfield's: 'I go on; & they cease. Why?'[115] She felt diminished and guilty. Had she really made the best use of her talents, taken them to their limit? She was overwhelmed with a sense of the transitoriness of life. Ten days later, she burst into tears when she read her diary entries made during the early days of her marriage: 'The sense of all that floating away for ever down the stream, unknown for ever.'[116]

Part Five

THE OUTSIDER

Chapter Seventeen

BETWEEN TWO WORLDS

(1934–5)

The intrusion of the past into the present continued to haunt Virginia, who also found it difficult to combine her writing life with her social life. At the beginning of 1934, she had an additional burden. She had reached that part of *The Pargiters* which deals with the Great War – for her and all other members of her generation the cataclysmic event which had irrevocably altered everything. While she was attempting to re-create that trauma, she was aware that Europe might be thrown once again into a similar upheaval. On 15 February, she told Quentin: 'We are to have Mosley within five years. I suppose you and Julian will be in for it. What Angelica will live to see boggles me.'[1]*

To make things worse, there were domestic wars. The Bedford Estates, the owners of Tavistock Square, insisted that the Woolfs contribute £270 towards the redecoration of number 52. While this work was carried out, Leonard and Virginia had to move briefly to 51 Gordon Square, where Philippa Strachey, the Secretary to the National Society for Women's Service, and some other sisters of Lytton lived. There were also servant problems. Nelly Boxall's cow-like refusal to use an electric stove brought Virginia to breaking point. For three years, she had been angry with herself for allowing Nelly to return after her operation; the cook's doctor had pleaded on her behalf and Virginia's heart had temporarily melted. But the daily strifes had continued: Nelly would be

* Sir Oswald Ernald, 6th Baronet Mosley, founded the British Union of Fascists in 1932 after the rout of his New Party in the general election of 1931.

obstinate and then, when Leonard or Virginia exploded, back off.

Part of the problem was that Nelly had been with the Woolfs for eighteen years and, during that time, familiarity with them had bred a curious mixture of contempt and friendship. Finally, feeling like executioner and executioner's victim in one, on 27 March Virginia summoned Nelly, who, sensing what was afoot, had attempted in the preceding days to apologize and cajole. This time Virginia was resolute: she could stand the strain no longer – Nelly must go immediately. 'Why does this scene, this long drawn out struggle with a poor drudge,' Virginia asked, 'demoralize one more than any love or anger scene with one's own kind?' She obviously experienced pangs of guilt for dismissing another woman, one who had little or no financial wherewithal. In any event, this particular 'aching tooth [was] removed for ever!'[2] Nelly, who was gone when the Woolfs returned from the Easter weekend on 10 April, was replaced by a daily, Mabel, who proved to be silent and trustworthy. No longer did Virginia have to worry about ingesting dust when she drank a cup of tea.

From August 1934, Louie Everest replaced Annie Thomsett at Rodmell. She quickly learned her new employers' routine. Only Leonard was allowed to make coffee and Virginia, who considered herself an expert in the art of making bread, gave her lessons in that skill. Meals were to be simple, although the Woolfs did have a liking for game, elaborate sauces and light puddings. Virginia, she noted, made her own cigarettes from a mild, sweet-smelling tobacco called My Mixture. She also observed that Virginia had the habit of leaving bits of paper everywhere, especially on the floor of her bedroom – these scraps would sometimes contain variants of the same sentence. Pencils and paper were placed by Virginia's bed so that she could write if inspiration struck in the night. At the outset, the 'cook-general' found one habit of Virginia's particularly strange:

> The floors in Monks House were very thin, the bathroom was directly above the kitchen and when Mrs Woolf was having her bath before breakfast I could hear her talking to herself. On and

> on she went, talk, talk, talk: asking questions and giving herself the answers. I thought there must be two or three people up there with her. When Mr Woolf saw that I looked startled he told me that Mrs Woolf always said the sentences out loud that she had written during the night. She needed to know if they sounded right and the bath was a good, resonant place for trying them out.[3]

This 'merry little brown eyed mongrel',[4] as Virginia called her, did not mind playing the occasional joke. One April Fool's Day, she told her employer that the head of the local Women's Institute had paid a surprise visit. Virginia, who could not abide that particular woman's harsh, domineering voice or manner, rushed from her study to her bedroom, hastily combed her hair, made herself tidy and then burst into gales of laughter when she discovered the truth of the situation.

Some people – such as Ethel Smyth – were not as easily dismissed as Nelly Boxall. Virginia accused the composer of being 'an attitudinizing unreal woman', one 'living in a mid Victorian dentist's waiting room of emotional falsity'.[5] Why, she asked her, should she 'kowtow to the bragging of a Brigadier General's daughter?' Virginia was unsure of the answer. And she was also deeply troubled by the questions about the past raised by her new novel. In December, while trying to summon up the courage to write of the Great War, she was reduced to tears. The new year provided no respite. By the end of January, she was longing to be rid of this part of the book.

The 1907, 1910 and 1914 sequences are centred on Elvira, whereas the two sections of *The Pargiters* dealing with 1917 focus on Eleanor, who gradually becomes aware of her complicity in a society which condones war as an instrument of imperial power. Up to 1917, Eleanor had attempted to alleviate the plight of the poor and the oppressed. What if she were one of the oppressors? This thought dawns on her when she reads in the newspaper of the death by drowning of a young seaman who had held the door open for her at her brother's home.

> For a second the scene appeared quite clearly: The calm swaying waves; For all she could do to stop it she could not help seeing his face, politely smiling up at the moon; & then she looked & realized it was a dead face, quite helpless, drifting away, something like anger, guilt, terror rose in her. [But] I didn't ask it [of you] she said, as if she had been telling him not to hold the door open for her.[6]

In the second sequence from 1917, on a cold winter night during the blackout Eleanor goes to dinner at the home of Maggie and her husband, Renny. There, she meets Nicholas, a Pole. Elvira arrives late. She mentions that she has just upbraided George, 'Eleanor's nephew', who is going off to fight. Nicholas supports Elvira but points out that George's behaviour is understandable, given his education, profession and class. Eleanor defends her nephew; Elvira and Maggie argue with her. In fact, Elvira counters Eleanor by pointing out that war is an attempt to defend territory and that Christ had maintained the only freedom was not to own anything. Nicholas then observes that the two sisters are genuine outsiders, 'who are absolutely uneducated; they have received nothing from their country; they cannot practise professions, they are kept purely as slaves for the breeding of children: & that system it seems [has] abolished all feelings of patriotism'.[7]

As the guests sit down to dinner, they hear a siren announcing an air raid and remove themselves to the cellar, where they continue their meal and discussion. In the flickering candlelight Nicholas, who now resembles a priest addressing a small congregation huddled together in a catacomb, argues that the war is a mere interruption in human history. He is more concerned with the overall direction in which society is moving; for him the war is the principal symptom of a pervasive, wasting disease. At first, Eleanor is shocked by his assertions, but she then begins to rethink her own experiences as an angel of the house. She realizes that war has replaced religion as the opiate of the exceedingly poor masses. Nicholas, who agrees that war provides a distraction, goes on to speak at great length of the enormous corruption engendered by the prevailing forces running society and an obvious link is being made between a microcosm (the corrupt family system of the Pargiters described at the beginning of the book) and a macrocosm (a rigidly controlled political-social system which has led to the institutionalized murder of war).

In particular, Nicholas attacks the Victorian propensity for specialization which has propped up all manner of corruption and offers a solution: 'The men were educated in one way; to make money; the women in another, to bear children. The result is war . . . [I'll] tell you what matters; It is to develop not this faculty which makes money, not that faculty which breeds children; – it is to develop the whole soul, the whole being.'[8] Nicholas then reveals to Eleanor his own outsider status: in addition to being a foreigner, he is a homosexual. At first Eleanor, who had thought Elvira and Nicholas were lovers, shrinks from the truth when she learns that their relationship is one – like Vanessa's with Duncan Grant – which strays beyond rigid definitions. 'I must annihilate,' she tells herself, 'little, timid, defensive, self-protective warding off – hoarding up.'[9] Like Elvira, Eleanor has never succumbed to worldly values, but hers has been a cloistered, nun-like existence which has never seriously questioned the *status quo*. Nicholas suggests that she learn to enjoy cigars, love, wine and knowledge.

Re-creating the fabric of the Great War was in itself distressing to Virginia, but in the 1917 passages she was examining two conflicting views of women and attempting to integrate them into a radically new image of society. Part of the distress was that in Eleanor Virginia was dealing with aspects of her own mother and in the process changing and redefining that part of the past. In mid-February, she told her diary: 'The difficulty is the usual one – how to adjust the two worlds. It is no good getting violently excited: one must combine.' She also added: 'All last week they were fighting in Vienna: this somehow comes closer than usual to our safe London life: the people shot down. Why?'[10] Her new novel was dealing with that 'why', but in attempting to see the interconnections between private and public worlds she had begun to uncover the sources of her own unhappiness.

In a series of episodes set in 1921, Eleanor's transformed sensibility is dramatized. In a conversation with her cousin Kitty she tells her just how marked a change she has undergone: 'I can say to Nicholas things I never dreamed of saying to my own brother. Why I was never in love; for instance . . . And his feelings are so interesting; he's always loved men, not women; how Rose loves women & not men.'[11] Eleanor's post-war sensibility is not reflected in her society, which is rushing towards self-destruction.

> One of the big shops was being pulled down, a line of scaffolding zigzagged across the sky. There was something violent and crazy in the crooked lines. It seemed to her as she looked up, that there was something violent and crazy in the world tonight. It was tumbling and falling, pitching forward to disaster. The crazy lines of the scaffolding, the jagged outline of the broken wall, the bestial shouts of the young men, made her feel there was no order, no purpose in the world, but all was hurtling to ruin beneath a perfectly indifferent moon.[12]

At the end of April, Virginia was glad to leave for a fortnight's holiday in Ireland, a necessary respite before she went on with the 'Present Day', the final section of *The Pargiters*. Virginia's interest in Ireland had been aroused in part by Elizabeth Bowen, whom she met at Ottoline Morrell's in December 1931, on which occasion Virginia was guilty, as she admitted, of 'dreadful boasting'.[13] At first she saw in the younger woman a pale imitation of herself and, when they met again in March 1932, she mistook appearance ('stammering, shy, conventional'[14]) for reality. In fact, Elizabeth might be a sort of sleeping beauty, as Virginia slyly hinted to Vita the following October.

> Anyhow my Elizabeth comes to see me, alone, tomorrow. I rather think, as I told you, that her emotions sway in a certain way . . . I'm reading her novel to find out. What's so interesting is when one uncovers an emotion that the person themselves, I should say herself, doesn't suspect. And it's a sort of duty don't you think – revealing people's true selves to themselves?[15]

By November 1933, the enigmatic Elizabeth was improving. In April 1934, Virginia was not impressed with the thirty-four-year-old woman's zebra-like outfit but saw some common point of identification: 'Had also been brought up to repress, by moral ancestors'.[16]

As Virginia suspected, there was a lesbian streak in Elizabeth, but it was a very subdued one which did not surface often. More to the point in their relationship was a common obsession with a childhood landscape which dominated their subsequent lives and writings. Although born in Dublin, Bowen's Court, Kildorrey, her family's eighteenth-century County Cork home, which she inherited in 1930, was the place which loomed large in Elizabeth's imagination, one infused with a mixture of nostalgia, mystery and futility. Like Virginia, she wanted to create fiction which aimed at the non-poetic statement of a poetic truth. Both women shared a common emotional history: Elizabeth's mother had died in 1912, when she was only thirteen.

The Irish-born writer had a vivid recollection of her first encounter with Virginia, clad in a soft lavender muslin dress, at Ottoline's and the subsequent, somewhat formal tea party at Tavistock Square, which lightened considerably when Virginia talked about making green gooseberry ice-cream. And Elizabeth remembered the naughty side of Virginia: 'She was fiendish. She could say things about people, all in a flash, which remained with one. Fleetingly malicious, rather than outright cruel.' She also recalled her inquisitiveness which searched relentlessly for material: 'I never knew her to probe *deeply* into anything, and I don't know whether she really took much interest in people's affairs of the heart or not. She never tried, as far as I was concerned, to discover anything deep down about me, or about anybody we knew in common. Past a point, her imagination took over.' Virginia's quest for information obviously went far deeper than Elizabeth ever realized. She thought that Virginia's fantasies about her were merely superficial, as when she inquired: 'when are you going back to your ancient Irish castle?'[17]

On 25 April, the Woolfs set out from Rodmell, spending that

night at Salisbury and the next at Abergavenny. Then they went to Fishguard, whence they sailed for the Irish Free State. After taking lunch at Lismore, they drove to Bowen's Court, where they stayed the night with Elizabeth and her husband, Alan Cameron. According to Virginia, the house was all it should be: 'pompous & pretentious & imitative & ruined – a great barrack of grey stone, 4 storeys & basements, like a town house, high empty rooms, & a scattering of Italian plaster-work, marble mantelpieces'. The lingering desolation and ghostly silences of the house provided their own kind of pleasure, but Virginia's attempts at romanticization were interrupted by the other two house guests, the critic Cyril Connolly and his American wife, Jean. The 'baboon' and his 'gollywog slug wife'[18] injected too much of sharp and smart London into what was meant to be an exploration of the past. Nevertheless, Ireland was for Virginia a mixture of Greece, Italy and Cornwall. She was particularly aware of contrasts: loneliness, poverty and isolation were offset by great stretches of virgin seashore and the sense that this landscape had retained, like Cornwall, its ancient look. On 29 April, the Woolfs made their way to Glengariff on Bantry Bay, spending two nights in Eccles Hotel.

While staying at Waterville on 1 May, Virginia read in *The Times* of George Duckworth's death on 27 April. She recalled how he had once played an important part in her life as a child – 'the batting, the laughter, the treats, the presents'[19] – and that when she had seen him the previous year she had experienced a genuine glow of pleasure. Her tendency to idealize George was only overcome when Vanessa wrote her a (now lost) letter in which she mentioned that the dying George had wanted Virginia and Vanessa to telegraph. 'What was in his mind?' Virginia wondered, 'some old memory? some regret?'[20] In her missive, Vanessa spoke of the horror their half-brother had imposed upon them. Only then did Virginia recall his 'half insane quality'.[21] Virginia's questions and her own inability to recall George's old misdeeds – about which he may have felt very guilty – demonstrate her sometimes remarkable ability to dissociate herself from some of the pains of the past.

From Waterville, the Woolfs went to Glenbeigh, Adare, Galway and Dublin. Of her visit to the National Gallery, she decided to say nothing, only that the pictures were highly cleaned. Two impressions were paramount: of Ireland as a nation living in the shadow of English culture and of a cold, indifferent sarcasm lingering in the melodic, fluent speech of the Irish themselves. As soon as she arrived home, Virginia was ill with flu and glad to have an excuse not to work on *The Pargiters*.

Elinor Rendel took a throat swab, submitting it to a specialist who claimed it was swarming with a bacillus called viridans and advised inoculation. But, Virginia asked her, had she ever known influenza or any other disease cured that way? Elinor said no. The truth, Virginia reflected, was that doctors knew absolutely nothing. She seemed unaware of the psychic distress which may have weakened her frail constitution, but she told Vita that she and Elizabeth had clasped hands over the wishing well in the garden at Bowen's Court. She teased Vita, asking what she thought they had wished. Then she told her the truth: 'plainly and frankly, my one wish is to make you jealous'.[22]

For Virginia, the summer of 1934, a hot and dry one, felt more fragmentary than usual. Aldous Huxley, to whom Virginia had written to express her pleasure in *Beyond the Mexique Bay*, came to tea. He was rather antiseptic, although he was too inclined to use words like 'penis' and 'fuck'. Nevertheless, she found him appealing. Marie Woolf 'carried on' a flirtation with an old man called Legge, who gave her Burgundy and took her on strolls. Virginia began French lessons and, much as usual, Desmond MacCarthy outlasted his welcome. She was disappointed by Tom Eliot's pageant play, *The Rock*, but her reaction was mild when compared to Roger Fry's rage. As publishers, the Woolfs were worried about sado-masochistic elements (a woman being flagellated in a cave) in Vita's new book, *The Dark Island*. Vita herself, who had recently taken up with Gwen St Aubyn, Harold's younger sister, had grown opulent, bold and tomato-coloured.

On 25 July, to the household of the mongoose and mandrill

Leonard added a marmoset called Mitz, his constant companion for the next four years. The animal, acquired from a London junkshop by the zoologist Victor Rothschild for his wife Barbara, had not been a success. When the Woolfs visited the Rothschilds at Cambridge one evening, the poor little rickety animal took to Leonard. Soon afterwards, Victor wrote Leonard to ask if he would look after the animal while they were abroad. Later, much to the relief of the Rothschilds, Leonard refused to part with Mitz.

Although Leonard could be harsh to his pets, his deep-seated affection for them was encompassing, almost as if they supplied him with a physical warmth he did not find in his marriage. Once, when Mitz climbed into a tree, as was her wont, and would not come down, Leonard devised a method of trapping her. He and Virginia stood beneath the tree and Leonard kissed Virginia. Mitz, chattering with rage, climbed down as fast as she could and perched on her master's shoulder. A bit later, after they had purchased a dog, Virginia told Ethel that the animal had immediately fallen 'passionately in love with Leonard. It's a curious case of hopeless erotic mania – precisely like a human passion.'[23] This remark was not uttered in a completely ironic manner.

At about this time, Virginia's menopause began. She did not say anything about it in her diary and letters from 1934 but two years later – on 25 July 1936 – she told Ethel that this event, about which she had been nervous, 'came and passed, as gently and imperceptibly as a lamb, 2 years ago'.[24]

The daily patchwork of contrasting events gave both pain and pleasure to Virginia, but she felt that her life had to be seen in a broader context. In early June, she and Leonard took his brother Phillip, his wife, Babs, and their three children to London Zoo, always a place of extraordinary fascination for Virginia. On that day, she thought of the chilling events occurring in Hitler's Germany: 'Meanwhile these brutal bullies go about in hoods & masks, like little boys dressed up, acting this idiotic, meaningless, brutal, bloody, pandemonium . . . It is like watching the baboon at the

Zoo; only he sucks a paper in which ice has been wrapped, & they fire with revolvers.'[25]

Work on *The Pargiters* continued in a desultory way during early July; Virginia also decided to attack her old bugbear, 'Phases of Fiction'. A month later, she felt fully energized by her own novel and its conclusion: 'I want a Chorus. A general statement. A song for 4 voices. How am I to get it? I am almost within sight of the end.'[26] Although Virginia's desire to end with a final Chorus may have been inspired in part by Eliot's interest in poetic drama, she was also attempting to impose a form similar to that used throughout *The Waves* to the final section of *The Pargiters*.

Bernard does the final summing up on behalf of six characters in the earlier novel; in the opening section of 'The Present Day', Virginia wanted to employ four voices: Eleanor, Elvira, George and the exceedingly conventional Peggy, George's sister and a physician. The flats of Eleanor and Elvira provide the settings, and each of the women discusses her adaptation to the modern world. Elvira keeps her commercial writing separate from her creative work; George sees in Elvira a woman psychologically crippled by a physical defect which has segregated her from others. He wonders if her work prevents her from having to bear too much reality: 'Probably people who have been bullied when they are young, find ways of protecting themselves. Is that the origin of art he asked himself: (phrase making, singing) making yourself immune by making an image?'[27] This is obviously a question Virginia often asked herself.

In the ensuing years since 1921, Eleanor has become much more like Elvira, especially in contrast to Peggy, who later becomes angry when her brother shows an interest in an attractive young woman. Peggy may have become a professional, but, very much like her creator, she is deeply worried about any kind of sexual activity.

> I so suppressed I can feel practically nothing: George all sex. So we go on; breeding – producing . . . But perhaps it was better to produce [children] than to be, as she was, so sexless, so

> inhibited, so aware of all the things she mustn't be, so abused from childhood for any breach of the conventions that she could never let herself go in any relation without a sense of guilt.[28]

When she wrote this passage, Virginia's cheeks burned and her hands trembled, almost as if she had touched yet another inaccessible part of herself.

The final section of 'The Present Day' is devoted to a family reunion, hosted by Delia. All the characters from the book gather and the form of the book changes from quartet to symphony. Although hampered, Eleanor and Elvira have made a good run at life. Their efforts are compared to the more halting efforts of some other members of the family, but a spirit of generosity reigns. Towards the end of the book, Eleanor goes to the window.

> She looked at the square. She thought how she had walked round it, all those years ago. How she had explored the back streets: how she had felt rather afraid. How the people had seemed to her alien and hostile; And then she must have been young, almost a girl; the sleeping street seemed for a moment the grave; & the pigeons were crooning a requiem for her past; for one of the selves that had been; for one of the many million human beings who had walked, who had suffered, who had thought so intensely . . . And now a new moment was coming into being . . . made of the dust of generation upon generation . . . 'I have enjoyed myself,' she said to Delia.[29]

The lives of Eleanor and Elvira have been touched by adversity and Peggy, the independent, professional woman, does not escape the familial repressions with which the book began: the sins of the fathers are still visited upon their daughters. *The Pargiters* ends on a note of tragic inevitability. In May 1934, Virginia had hoped that the final portions of the book would enrich and stabilize the earlier ones and 'give the other side, the submerged side'.[30] By the end of September, despite considerable trepidation, Virginia felt that her plan had been accomplished. 'Anyhow,' she told herself, 'if I die tomorrow, the line is there.'[31]

Virginia's work on *The Pargiters* was halted by Roger Fry's death on 9 September. Virginia, who was visiting Vanessa and Clive at Charleston when the news arrived, was dazed. She felt wooden. Suddenly, a thin, blackish veil seemed to cover everything. Virginia recalled her mother's death and the fact that she had simply not known how to respond to it: 'I . . . was afraid I was not feeling enough. So now.'[32] As a child, she had laughed. In this recollection, she makes the further, unlikely suggestion that Stella had conspired with her to laugh at the nurse, who was pretending to cry. Once again, death made Virginia deeply uncomfortable. Was she feeling the right things? How should one feel? As child and adult, she felt passionately – perhaps too much – but she also had to protect herself from being drawn too deeply into a vortex from which she would not be able to escape.

Roger's funeral was at Golders Green Crematorium on the afternoon of 13 September. The service was simple, dignified and wordless, the silence broken only by some music by Bach. The body was placed under an old red brocade with two bunches of brightly coloured flowers on each side. The mourners sat before open doors leading into a garden. Various words came to Virginia as she thought about her dead friend: dignity, honesty, largeness, variety, generosity, curiosity. She felt the power of death, 'the vanquisher, this outer force'. In comparison to this alien force, the living were small, fine and delicate. 'A fear then came to me, of death. Of course I shall lie there too before that gate, & slide in; & it frightened me. But why? I mean, I felt the vainness of this perpetual fight.'[33] Then the coffin moved slowly away. After the ceremony, Desmond asked Virginia to take a walk in the garden. Uncharacteristically, she laid her hand on his shoulder. 'Don't die yet!' she said, and he replied, 'Nor you either.'

A bit later, Pamela Diamand, Roger's daughter, wrote to assure Virginia how much her father had treasured her. In her reply, she paid her dead friend a generous compliment: 'I don't think I ever realized that I could mean much to Roger – perhaps that was because he meant so much to himself.'[34] Virginia had not been as close to Roger as Vanessa had been. Surprisingly, his death mattered more to Virginia than Lytton's: 'Why I wonder? Such a blank wall. Such a silence. Such a poverty. How he reverberated!'[35] Roger Fry had never lost his joy in living and in experimenting. In this way, he and Virginia had been kindred spirits. Lytton had been a close friend whom Virginia felt she had surpassed; Roger was the same kind of artist as herself. To the end, he had remained childlike in his openness to the mysterious beauty of the world.

One week after the funeral, Virginia was in an exalted frame of mind, one which was accompanied by an awareness of being above time and death. Of course, Roger Fry had often experienced such flashes: this had been a shared bond. One of the reasons Virginia decided that autumn to accept Helen Anrep and Margery Fry's invitation to write Roger's biography was that his life would provide a wonderful but challenging opportunity to write about the creative process so central to both their existences.

Meanwhile, as she resumed work on *The Pargiters*, Virginia remained steadily critical of Ethel Smyth, who had rhapsodized about her friend Maurice Baring's *The Lonely Lady of Dulwich*, comparing it favourably to Mérimée's *Carmen*. Virginia was brutally frank: 'Why Carmen, which I read 2 weeks ago by chance, is like an oak tree; this is a piece of chewed string. Every word in Carmen has the thickness of a giant's thigh: this is thin as a blade of green that a butterfly makes wobble.'[36] According to Virginia, Baring's book was 'brash' (her word for babies' diarrhoea) and Ethel needed a purge. Virginia was being deliberately nasty because Ethel, a close friend of Baring, was wont to praise his books to Virginia and in the process compare her work unfavourably to his. Virginia was also honest with Vita about her dislike of *The Dark Island*; she made what was for her a crucial point: 'You give me the impression of writing too much in the personal zone, as if you couldn't get far enough off to convey the outside aspect.'[37] Virginia could be so direct with Vita because she herself was becoming increasingly worried about this facet of *The Pargiters*.

The insecure side of Virginia took a knock when she noticed in the *Times Literary Supplement* of 11 October an advertisement for Wyndham Lewis's *Men without Art*, which contained chapters on Eliot, Faulkner, Hemingway and Virginia Woolf. She wondered whether she would be among *the* English novelists after her death. Although she claimed not to think too much about this possibility, why did she immediately shrink from reading Lewis's book? 'Why am I sensitive?' she asked. 'I think vanity. I dislike the thought of being laughed at.' She would wait a year, then read this new slur. Having made this resolution, she could feel the calm that sometimes came when her back was against the wall. There was also the 'queer disreputable pleasure' in being famous enough to be attacked and in being a martyr.[38]

Virginia waited three days – not a year – before taking the 'arrow' of Wyndham Lewis into her heart. In his typically aggressive but trenchant way, Lewis attacked 'Mr Bennett and Mrs Brown' and labelled Virginia an outsider at the portals of fiction, 'a peeper, not a looker, a fundamental prude' (her summary). Virginia admitted to herself that the charges might be true, but she had resolved two years before to 'adventure & discover, & allow no rigid poses: to be supple & naked to the truth'.[39]

She was certainly not going to rearrange *The Pargiters* to suit Wyndham Lewis. But she could not respond publicly to him and she found it difficult to get on with her work in the face of such intrusive hostility. On the next day, she asked herself some questions:

1) What is the sensible attitude to criticism?
   Not to read it.
2) What should I do now of a morning – creation flagging?
   Read.[40]

The Woolfs resolved to save up for foreign travel. Perhaps they would fly to America or go as far as China or India. But the only complete escape from depression was her work, hostile criticism of which tended to depress her.

That autumn, Virginia had to face the fact that she usually became terribly despondent when she completed a book.

> I looked up past diaries – a reason for keeping them – & found the same misery after Waves. After Lighthouse I was I remember nearer suicide, seriously, than since 1913 ... Well, so there's nothing to be done the next 2 or 3 or even 4 weeks but dandle oneself: refuse to face it: refuse to think about it. This time Roger makes it harder than usual.

In the wake of his death, Virginia felt ugly and old. As she strolled through London, she would imagine the lives of other people. She found it difficult to work or read. 'I feel so drowsy, as if my brain were dilated: can't contract: then I suddenly lapse into sleep.'[41]

During this difficult time, Leonard's support was unwavering, but Virginia felt some of her friendships were in a bad state of repair. On 30 October, she told Vita that she had taken Potto to the vet, who had been concerned about that animal's mangy tail: '"Has this animal suffered in his affections, ma'am?" Whereupon such a wail went up; and the name Nick, Mrs Nick resounded: and all the dogs barked and cats wailed.'[42]

An unexpected boost came when Virginia and Leonard were taking a walk at Rodmell over the downs one Sunday morning and came upon an enormous yellow-green ape that had escaped from the zoo at Peacehaven. All of a sudden, in response to this sighting, Virginia could feel her brain rising out of the mist. In a moment, she realized that the vitality of her imagination had found – and would continue to find – release. In a flash, she felt young and vigorous. By the middle of November, she began to tackle the monumental task of revising the eight volumes of manuscript notebooks which comprised *The Pargiters*.

On 27 November, Virginia was sufficiently revitalized to sit for Man Ray's camera. In his portrait photographs, the American artist captured the likeness of an aloof, alluring and confident person. Two days earlier, Man Ray had proffered his invitation at his exhibition at Lund Humphries in Bedford Square. There Virginia met the wealthy, glamorous and passionate Argentinian Victoria Ocampo, the publisher of the magazine *Sur*. Victoria was there because her friend Aldous Huxley had told her that there was a good chance that Virginia would be at the opening.

Virginia was smitten: 'she was very ripe & rich; with pearls at her ears, as if a large moth had laid clusters of eggs; the colour of an apricot under glass'.[43] As was her custom, she barraged her fellow publisher with questions about her childhood, life in Argentina, her travels and her favourite books. Victoria enjoyed the onslaught and even told her inquisitor of her interview in Rome with Mussolini: 'Il Duce' had been so simple and kind that she had forgotten to call him Excellency. In her turn, Virginia, who took pleasure in being lionized by this charming younger woman, let her guard down.

A pleasant but very unequal friendship soon developed, one in which the younger woman was allowed the occasional visit into Virginia's temple at Tavistock Square.

> Often, after the foggy cold of the street, I entered the comfort of that room, and above all, of that presence. As soon as Virginia was there, all else disappeared. Virginia, tall and slender, wearing a silk blouse whose blues and grays . . . harmonized admirably with the silver of her hair. Virginia, made even more slender by a very long, black velvet skirt. Virginia, sitting in an armchair, her dog asleep on the floor.[44]

These verbal portraits complement the Man Ray photographs: in each, the strong, resilient, public side of Virginia is on display. At this time, Virginia was also excited by the work being done to her outdoor study at Monks House: 'My Lodge is demolished; the new house in process of building in the orchard. There will be open doors in front; & a view right over to Caburn. I think I shall sleep there on summer nights.'[45]

That autumn, Leonard and Virginia had to be resolute in their dealings with Vanessa. Virginia had read some of Julian's poems, returned the manuscript to him and made no suggestion that the Hogarth Press should publish them.* Although Virginia sometimes felt that her nephew's caustic wit was, like his father's, at her expense, her strong feelings of affection for him were complicated by her jealousy of his hold on her sister.

> I was always critical of his writing [she wrote in 1937], partly I suspect from the usual generation jealousy; partly from my own enviousness of anyone who can do in writing what I can't do: & again (for I can't analyse out the other strains in a very complex feeling, roused partly by L.; for we envied Nessa I suspect for such a son; and there was L.'s family complex which made him eager, no, on the alert, to criticize her children because he thought I admired them more than his family).[46]

Ultimately, Virginia thought Julian a careless writer. When it came to any criticism of her children, Vanessa was understandably not the easiest of persons to deal with. For some time, she had been concerned with Julian's mode of life: he had failed the year before to obtain a fellowship at Cambridge and she was not pleased with the young women with whom he had affairs. Her lack of ease with her eldest son made her even more sensitive to any complaints about him. When, at dinner, the Woolfs broached the topic of Julian's poems, his mother immediately ruffled like a 'formidable hen'. This angered Virginia: 'This is the religion & superstition of motherhood.'[47] In his calm, logical manner, Leonard attempted to smooth things over; in turn, Vanessa was reasonable but grew exceedingly cold and reserved. Virginia felt guilty and what should have been a pleasant evening ended with exacerbation rather than consolation.

Virginia was further saddened by the realization that a good friend, the biographer and bookseller Francis Birrell, was dying of a malignant brain tumour. 'What would it be like to lie there,

* In 1930, Chatto had published Julian's first book of verse, *Winter Movement*; the Hogarth Press published *Work for Winter and Other Poems* in March 1936.

expecting death?' she asked herself.[48] Some comic relief was provided by reworking *Freshwater* (first written in 1923) for a presentation that Christmas (the performance actually took place on 18 January 1935 in Vanessa's Fitzroy Street studio). And there were amusing complexities generated by Virginia's lingering affection for Hugh Walpole, whose novels were the very opposite of hers. The previous June, he had gone off to Hollywood to write the screenplay for an adaptation of *David Copperfield* for Metro-Goldwyn-Mayer, who had in addition engaged him to play the Vicar of Blunderstone.

In the midst of her own uncertainty, Virginia had become more and more aware of how often the rights of women were downplayed or ignored, often by women themselves. When Elizabeth Bibesco requested her support for a proposed anti-Fascist exhibition, Virginia asked why the 'woman question' was omitted from the description of the event. Princess Bibesco replied that there would be such a section, but then added: 'I am afraid that it had not occurred to me that in matters of ultimate importance even feminists could wish to segregate & label the sexes.'[49] Such high-handedness did not sit well with Virginia, who would not have minded 'giving that woman a toss in the air'.[50] Virginia's conviction that Rebecca West dealt openly and brilliantly in *The Harsh Voice* with the economic servitude of women led Virginia to write her a letter of praise, even though West had publicly savaged *Flush* two years before.

Virginia's long-held conviction that women were perceived as outcasts was reinforced when she encountered Morgan Forster at the London Library on 8 April. After polite greetings, he reminded her that he was on the Committee: 'And we've been discussing whether to allow ladies –.' Virginia interrupted him: 'Oh but they do. There was Mrs Greene.' At this point, Morgan told her the rest of the story. His colleagues had observed: '"Yes, yes – there was Mrs Greene. And Sir Leslie Stephen said, 'never again. She was so troublesome.'"' Morgan had responded: 'Haven't ladies improved?' But his fellow committee members were all quite determined, as he informed Virginia: '"No, no, no, ladies are quite impossible." They wouldn't hear of it.'

In her own words, Virginia 'flew into a passion' which made her tremble. Morgan had obviously intended to propose Virginia's name for the Committee and been turned down. There was a particularly cutting irony here: Virginia's father had encouraged her to follow him in his profession, but he had been largely responsible for the absence of women on the Committee. So once again she was reminded that even professional women are outsiders. Virginia did not wish to be the exception to male rules. If she became the exception, she would betray other women. 'You can't bribe me now,' she inscribed in her diary.[51] Fired up by her encounter with Forster, she wanted to begin work on her new polemic, now titled 'On Being Despised', but decided to postpone this project until *The Pargiters* was finished. When, later that spring, Ramsay MacDonald offered to submit her name for inclusion in the King's Birthday Honours as a member of the Order of Companions of Honour, she refused.

That winter and spring were very troubling in many other ways. Virginia quarrelled with Sybil Colefax, who remained annoyed because Virginia had refused to attend a dinner party the previous summer at which she was to meet Noël Coward for the second time. Virginia accused Sybil of being unjustly rude and insulting to her. Not used to such honesty, Sybil's defences crumpled. That disagreement was mild compared to Virginia's conviction that her friendship with Vita, which had diminished considerably in intensity over the years, was quietly over: 'And there is no bitterness, & no disillusion, only a certain emptiness.'[52]

She was not very honest with herself about this particular sadness; very much in need of Vita's attention, she was upset by her affair with Gwen St Aubyn. On 27 March, Virginia dextrously encouraged Ethel Smyth to goad Vita. Ethel, outraged on behalf of Christopher St John (Christabel Marshall), who had been thrown over by Vita, proposed to mount an attack, about which she sought Virginia's advice. Virginia goaded her:

> Of course I don't altogether see eye to eye with you, as I said. I mean, love seems to me to queer all pitches. But given your

> relations with Vita – and the St John complication – I daresay you're right to shoot this sad and severe dart. Whether it'll do any good to the person herself [Gwen St Aubyn], I doubt; whether any writing or speaking can; but I daresay it will clear the air between you, which is in itself a good, of course. I shall be much interested to hear if she answers, and what. You won't . . . say or write anything to bring me in: because I wouldn't like Vita to hear a word about my feelings except through me.[53]

When Vita, stung by Ethel's letter, complained to Virginia, she pretended to know very little. In fact, she claimed to be an exceedingly innocent bystander:

> Lord what a nuisance about old Ethel!
>
> I'm afraid I can't throw much light on it because I don't understand it myself . . . As far as I could make out, she had come to the conclusion that her relations with you were on a false footing . . . I did my best to persuade her not to write, but of course she wouldn't listen.[54]

Virginia also fought with Leonard. The Woolfs were planning another holiday on the Continent and, as usual, Leonard had carefully worked out their itinerary. Then, in order to have more time with Vanessa, who had already left for Italy, Virginia suggested that they spend ten days instead of a week in Rome. Leonard 'turned stony' and 'cut up rusty'.[55] Once again, his anger and irritation with Virginia about her preference for her family over him surfaced. She was also concerned that her husband was becoming 'more & more addicted to solitude & astute – the old wretch – at finding good reasons for it'.[56] She had similar tendencies but expected Leonard to counter them. Meanwhile, they had decided on a dangerous venture for any Jew in 1935: they would travel through Hitler's Germany *en route* to Italy.

Ten days before they were to set off, the Woolfs invited Ralph and Ava Wigram, who lived at Southease, the village next to Rodmell, to tea at Monks House. Wigram, who worked at the

Foreign Office, had the previous month accompanied the Foreign Secretary, Sir John Simon, and his successor, Anthony Eden, then Lord Privy Seal, to Berlin, where he had witnessed firsthand a very frightening Hitler. Wigram told the Woolfs that Hitler had ranted and raved about the injustices which had been heaped on Germany in the wake of the Great War; he saw himself as 'the regenerator, the completely equipped & powerful machine'.

Wigram, who was a 'cripple, with iron rods down one leg', seemed to Virginia a particularly vulnerable, thin, rigid Englishman. So she became doubly frightened – by the power of a demonic Hitler and by the weakness of the men who were supposed to defend England from his all-consuming desire for supremacy: 'there is some reason . . . to expect that Oxford Street will be flooded with poison gas one of these days. And what then?'[57] England would be reduced to a German colony.

When Leonard asked Wigram if it was true that the Foreign Office advised Jews not to go to Germany, he admitted that was official policy. 'But,' Leonard recalled, 'privately as a friend, he could say that he thought it nonsense, and that I should not hesitate to go to Germany.'[58] Just in case there was trouble, Wigram arranged for Prince Bismarck, the Counsellor at the German Embassy, to provide the Woolfs with a letter which would guarantee them a safe passage.

On Wednesday, 1 May, Leonard, Virginia and Mitz crossed by the night boat from Harwich to the Hook of Holland. The cosy prosperity of the Netherlands impressed Virginia, although the narrow roads and innumerable cyclists proved a hazard: 'no accidents, except killing one hen, but it was the hen's fault'.[59] She felt, as she told Ethel, that she had been thrown back to Elizabethan times: 'figure to yourself Shakespeare's England still lived in, with Canals and whole banks of red tulips, yellow laburnum'.[60]

In contrast, Nazi Germany was a harsh reminder of the pervasive ails of the twentieth century. When they crossed the frontier from Roermond into Germany, near Jülich, Mitz immediately attracted the attention of the German officials and, in the process, distracted them from the Woolfs and their dubious racial status. A few moments later, when he entered the Customs shed, Leonard was appalled by the treatment of a peasant who had forgotten to remove his hat. The official brutally castigated the man as he informed him that any office of the Reich was to be treated as if it were a church.

Leonard and Virginia drove to Cologne and then on to Bonn. As they approached its outskirts, they noticed that theirs was the only car on the autobahn and that at intervals of twenty yards stood soldiers with rifles. When they reached the centre of the city, they were confronted with an excited policeman who told them that the road was closed because Herr Präsident, Hermann Goering, was on his way there. Leonard asked if there was any road open which would take them to Mainz, but the man was too overwhelmed to give him an answer. The Woolfs parked their car and made their way to Beethoven's house. Then they found a tearoom and pondered their next step. Leaving the shop, Leonard asked directions from a passer-by, who kindly got into the car to help guide them across the river. However, both sides of the road were lined with soldiers and schoolchildren, and Leonard and Virginia felt hemmed in, as if something horrible was about to happen. The day was swelteringly hot and the roof of the car was open.

The mood suddenly changed. The crowd cheered Mitz and shouted '*Heil Hitler*' to her and the Woolfs. Virginia returned the salutes, although she was later furious with herself for doing so: 'People gathering in the sunshine – rather forced like school sports. Banners stretched across the street "The Jew is our enemy": "There is no place for Jews in –". So we whizzed along until we got out of range of the docile hysterical crowd. Our obsequiousness gradually turning to anger.'[61] That day, the Woolfs made their way to a hotel at Unkel; subsequently they drove through Mainz, Darmstadt, Heidelberg, Stuttgart, Ulm, Augsburg and Munich on their way to the Austrian frontier and snow-covered Innsbruch, which they reached on 12 May.

All along the way, Mitz remained a sensation, a *liebe, kleine Ding*. Leonard bitterly observed: 'It was obvious to the most anti-Semitic stormtrooper that no one who had on his shoulder such a "dear little thing" could be a Jew.'[62] Later that summer, when Virginia saw a snake eating a toad, she was reminded anew that Germany was attempting to devour the European civilization she treasured: 'it had half the toad in, half out; gave a suck now & then. The toad slowly disappearing. Leonard poked its tail; the snake was sick of the crushed toad, & I dreamt of men committing suicide & could see the body shooting through the water.'[63]*

On 13 May, the Woolfs crossed the Brenner Pass into Italy and three days later reached Rome, where they joined Vanessa, Angelica and Quentin, who were living in a rented studio. Despite the presence of the Blackshirts, the beauty of Italy was not dimmed. They were happy to have escaped Germany and Austria. From Siena, Virginia sent Clive a postcard: 'It was on the spot now marked by a cross that Clive Bell quarrelled with his sister in law in Sept. 1908. I dropped memory's tear there today under the orange blossom.'[64]

Italy aroused other bittersweet memories: of Violet Dickinson thirty years before, of Roger Fry, of her honeymoon. The Woolfs left Italy at Ventimiglia on 24 May and drove through France, arriving at Monks House on 31 May. That journey had a sad postscript. Just as they arrived home and were contemplating the joy of seeing Pinker, they encountered the gardener, Percy, carrying her body in her basket. The spaniel had become ill two weeks before, had had three fits, grown weaker and finally died of meningitis the previous day. Leonard was very sad, as was Virginia: '8 years of a dog certainly mean something. I suppose – is it part of our life that's buried in the orchard?'[65]

The Woolfs returned to London on 2 June. The 'usual depressions come', Virginia said. 'And I wish for death.'[66] At such times, 'the heart of an oak in which a toad sits imprisoned has more sap and green than my heart'.[67] A few days later, Virginia took a walk in the hopes of curing her violent mood swings. When she reached Regent's Park, she was flooded with ecstasy: 'There is no doubt

* This incident is worked into *Between the Acts*, where the same thing happens to Giles.

that the greatest happiness in the world is walking through Regents Park on a green, but wet – green but red, pink & blue evening – the flower beds . . . emerging from the general misty rain.'[68] In such moments, she saw two parts of the totality of life: the cavernous recesses of death and broken friendships and the stunning, consoling beauty of the natural world.

Virginia had plenty of books to worry about: she wanted to complete *The Pargiters*, to renew work on the sequel to *A Room of One's Own* and to begin her biography of Roger Fry. His sister Margery had now made it clear that she wanted Virginia to write this book, and the impetus to undertake the task was fuelled when Helen Anrep informed her that the Stracheys had been offended when she did not offer to write Lytton's biography. 'I am so oppressed by the thought of all the books I have to write,' Virginia observed, 'that my head is like a bursting boiler.'[69]

Leonard's bad temper also brought Virginia to the boil. Although he had in theory a great sympathy for the working classes, Leonard did not always practise what he preached. He could be surly, overdemanding and rigid when dealing with servants. Virginia thought her husband was uncertain of his own place in the class system: he was not sure that he was really a gentleman and so could never be genial 'in the presence of the lower classes' whom he had to dominate. Virginia, who was never completely comfortable with servants, had a natural sympathy with the women who worked for them and at times defended their rights. When this happened, she would be the recipient of Leonard's severity, although she could give as good as she got: 'I get up & curse him.'[70]

On 29 June, the Woolfs went to Ickenham, where they purchased Sally, a thirteen-month-old black and white cocker spaniel, for £18. Virginia resented paying so much, but the breeder told them that if Sally's nose had been an eighteenth of an inch longer she would have been champion material and have fetched, like her sister, a price of £200 or £300. This new animal was not so sure of herself as Pinker had been, but she fell in love with Leonard at first sight. Virginia's distance from Vita can be in part measured by the fact that Virginia did not accept Vita's invitation to present her and Leonard with another dog.

That summer, Virginia renewed her childhood friendship with Susan Buchan (née Grosvenor), who had recently become Lady Tweedsmuir when her husband, John, was created the 1st Baron Tweedsmuir on being appointed Governor-General of Canada that May. Susan was a good friend of Elizabeth Bowen, and the three women arranged a visit to Charles Wade, a necromancer who lived at Snowshill Manor in the Cotswolds, forty miles from the Buchans' house Elsfield Manor, near Headington. The drive, through villages of yellow stone, to the austerely beautiful medieval house was pleasant, and the party felt that they had come upon an enchanted castle when they reached the remote house and its grounds, which sloped down into the wide valley.

The necromancer looked like he had stepped from the pages of Thomas Shadwell's *The Virtuoso*. He wore his hair long and was clad in a moleskin waistcoat. The three women visited the 'laboratory', where Virginia's eyes gleamed as she beheld alchemical bowls and stuffed crocodiles. The party felt that they had stepped out of time when Mr Wade showed them the bedrooms, full of dark corners and strange curios. Susan had certainly stepped out of time sufficiently to forget that Virginia had to catch a train back to London. They rushed to Oxford station and caught the train with only moments to spare. That was Susan's account. As for Virginia, if she had been impressed by Mr Wade, she did not convey as much to Vanessa when she told her of a house 'filled with old clothes, bicycles, mummies, alligators, Italian altars – not, I thought, very interesting, and [Mr Wade] I think rather a fraud, as he pretended to have no watch, and so I lost my train, and only got back at 8:30'.[71]

Just over a week later, Virginia travelled to Bristol to deliver the opening address for the Roger Fry memorial exhibition. That was definitely not a pleasant experience: '200 stout burgesses, crammed and dripping, and having to talk about art after losing my way in the most hideous of all towns'.[72] Virginia was certain that both Margery and Pamela had been disappointed by her performance.

Virginia's own anxieties were focused on *The Pargiters*. For a short time, she considered changing the title to 'Ordinary People', before settling that September on *The Years*. That autumn and early winter, she was unremitting in the changes she made to her large typescript of 740 pages. On 17 July she told herself: 'I think I can shorten: all the last part is still rudimentary & wants shaping; but I'm too tired in the head to do it seriously this moment.'[73] A month later, she was attempting to type 100 pages a week of the revised manuscript. On 16 October, she had come to the realization that 'there must be contrast: one strata [sic], or layer can't be developed intensively',[74] and ten days later she decided not to hurry the book: 'I'm going to let every scene shape fully & easily in my hands, before sending it to be typed, even if it has to wait another year.'[75] She wondered why she allowed time to hurry her along, but a month later she had resolved to finish by Christmas 'this incredibly tough old serpent – a serpent without any of the charm of the Nile, only with all the toughness of what is evil and perennial'.[76] All in all, she observed that autumn, as a reminder to herself, 'I never think, seriously, of dying.'[77] By New Year's Eve, the book was seen as an inaccessible rocky island, one which she obviously could not reach, much less explore.

For a considerable period of time, Vita had also become inaccessible and Ethel a nuisance. Virginia's strong feelings for her sister were rekindled, although Angelica, a ravishing sylph, became a sort of surrogate for her mother, who cannot have been too pleased by this snippet in Virginia's letter to her: 'twice I dreamt I was kissing Angelica passionately, across a hedge, from which I can only deduce that incest and sapphism embrace in one breast'.[78] She knew that her sister would have mixed feelings about it, but Virginia reacted enthusiastically and supportively to Julian's announcement that he had obtained a professorship in China, even though this meant that his recently undertaken role as the fact-gatherer for her Fry biography would have to be abandoned. To Ethel she joked: 'why don't they make me Professor of English – I'd teach 'em'.[79]

The long, dry, hot summer of 1935 supplied diversions: Virginia, sometimes an obsessive and competitive sportswoman – as a child she had been nicknamed 'the demon bowler' – had many chances to hone her skills. On 10 August, she revelled in the roasting heat and the parched land: 'orange fields, yellow grasses, and a green running river'.[80] A month later, she thrilled to the sighting on the river of a kingfisher, with its bright orange and chocolate underside.

Monks House could provide a much-needed respite from *The Years*, but no control could be exerted over the worsening political situation. That summer, Mussolini rejected Anthony Eden's concessions over Abyssinia and invaded. The Council of the League of Nations declared Italy an aggressor and imposed sanctions. Virginia was confused and frightened, as her diary entry of 4 September makes clear: 'The most critical day since Aug 4th 1914. So the papers say. In London yesterday. Writings chalked up all over the walls. "Don't fight for foreigners." "Britain should mind her own business."'[81] The threat of war seemed more real after Virginia attended the Labour Party conference in Brighton, where on 1 October she was moved to tears by George Lansbury's pacifist stand, even though she thought him a bit of a poseur.

Unable to decide what was the best approach, she washed her hands of the matter. As a woman, she was not responsible for the wretched state of society. However, she felt compelled to dash off a chapter of 'On Being Despised'. This portion of the book ('The Next War') soon became 'absolutely wild, like being harnessed to a shark'.[82] As soon as she had finished that task, she was convinced that she had found the perfect division of labour. Once again, she would allow her projects to spell each other off: 'some book or work for a book that's quite the other side of the brain'.[83] Such was the path towards refreshment and, she hoped, improvement.

Although she had experienced considerable trouble with her own writing, she remained convinced that Tom Eliot's recent forays into verse drama were disastrous. On 13 November, she told Ethel about her reaction to *Murder in the Cathedral*: 'I went to his play last night, and came away as if I'd been rolling in the ash bin; and somehow filled my mouth with the bones of a decaying cat thrown there by a workhouse drab.'[84] She might have labelled Tom a green, sick, American eunuch, but she was probably jealous of Emily Hale, her friend's 'dull impeccable Bostonian lady',[85] when she took tea with them. In her turn, Miss Hale was astonished by Mitz: 'this tiny furry ball has a long tail which hangs down from [her] master's neck like a short queue, slightly confusing at first'. As was her custom, Virginia assailed Emily with questions, and the American woman showed a sensitive, deft understanding of Virginia's methodology: 'She addressed several questions directly to me, suddenly but very carefully, so to speak, as if it really mattered what you answered her . . . The impression of cool half-mocking detachment began to lessen.'[86]

A bit later that afternoon, Vita arrived. She had gained a great deal of weight and Virginia could not forgive her for that, nor for her 'tomato cheeks and thick black moustache'. As if Vita could have helped growing older, she catalogued the inventory of faults in a letter to an enthusiastic, receptive Ethel: 'Surely [these changes were not] necessary: and the devil is that it shuts up her eyes that were the beaming beauty I first loved her for, and altogether reduces her (to look at) to the semblance of any fox hunting, turnip stalking country lady.'[87]

That November provided a wide spectrum of public events: the Duke of Gloucester's wedding, a general election in which Stanley Baldwin and the Conservatives won a majority and war in Abyssinia. Virginia kept busy by working on *The Years*, sorting through Roger Fry's papers and attending Labour Party meetings at Rodmell. On 14 November, the day of the general election, the Woolfs were in Brighton, where Leonard drove voters to the poll. Four days before, Virginia teased Vita: 'I think I shall call on Lady Sackville and ask for a cup of tea. Then I should drop dead, foaming at the mouth, poisoned.' The newspaper placards would carry the legend: 'Lady Novelist poisoned by Peeress'.[88]

An exhausted Virginia had just about reached the much-desired end of *The Years*: 'the no man's land that I'm after; & can pass from outer to inner, & inhabit eternity. A queer very happy free feeling, such as I've not had at the finish of any other book'.[89] A short while later, she consented to have her palm read by a friend of the Huxleys, Dr Charlotte Wolff, a psychologist and Jewish refugee from Germany. Virginia resented paying two guineas for a reading which 'got [some things] hopelessly wrong; others she guessed amazingly right'.[90]

> To Virginia Woolf language is something more than a poetical problem. By means of words alone she establishes a contact between the visible and imaginative world; they enable her to bridge the gap which divides her from reality and to unite all contradictory elements. To Virginia Woolf poetry is a constitutional necessity . . . The most striking peculiarity of this hand is the shape and position of the fingers, which are straight, pointed and introverted. They combine all the symptoms of unusual susceptibility to outside impressions and generally occur in extrovert types. I have often found it in the hands of actors. Virginia Woolf has a natural talent for acting which is turned inward upon her own imagination. She is able to identify herself to such an extent with the situations and figures of her imagination that her ego no longer exists. It is as though it has vanished.[91]

This is a brilliant account for two reasons. Dr Wolff understood the mediating, consoling power of words for Virginia, of how they existed for her in a state between the physical and the spiritual; she also recognized the dramatic side of Virginia's personality, particularly the way in which she was sometimes able to give utterance to deep-seated emotions by allowing a physical, energetic life in conversation.

About three weeks before she met Dr Wolff, Virginia had decided that human life existed in four dimensions: the I and the not-I; the inner and the outer. In a work of fiction or biography, the writer's task was to unite these elements. In Virginia's own life, as the German psychologist recognized, the act of writing gave her the opportunity to bring the warring factions within herself together. The consolations of writing and reading are captured in

Virginia's last diary entry for 1935: 'A wild wet night – floods out: rain as I go to bed: dogs barking: wind battering. Now I shall slink indoors, I think, & read some remote book.'[92]

Chapter Eighteen

UNDER THE SHADOW

(1936–7)

Although all Virginia's fiction contains strong autobiographical elements, *The Years* is a fundamentally different kind of book. Here, she shows how the gruesome events of childhood stalk her characters for the remainder of their lives. There is no breaking of the circle of the past, as in *Mrs Dalloway* or *To the Lighthouse*, and the fighting spirit with which *The Waves* concludes is largely absent. The past has exceedingly long tentacles in this book and the seemingly neutral title has ominous connotations: time marches on and carries many victims with it. This is a book about ageing, about how the years are running out.

After she abandoned her plan to have the narrative alternate between fiction and history/polemic, Virginia was left with a form very similar to the family chronicles used by many writers, including, for example, Thackeray and Galsworthy. Her alternative vision remained largely intact because *The Years* focuses on the lives of women, but she paid a high price. In *The Waves* she avoided a close description of her own Victorian childhood, whereas *The Years* begins with a brilliant re-creation of a tension-filled family waiting for the death of the mother, Mrs Pargiter. In her career, Virginia had, for excellent reasons, avoided the realist tradition, but when she returned to it in *The Years* she began to feel the pull of a past filled with overwhelming sorrow.

During 1935 and during the proofing of *The Years*, Virginia made many changes to the narrative. For example, Elvira became Sara. This may seem trivial, but Elvira is a far more exotic and specific name than Sara. Overall, the changes to the book diluted it of much of its intensity, almost as if the author felt that she had loaded the narrative with too many specifics, especially regarding sex and politics. In *The Pargiters*, much attention is devoted to Nicholas's criticisms of the social order; his remarks on such subjects are sketchily hinted at in *The Years* (this material was now being diverted to 'On Being Despised'). Although Nicholas's homosexuality is still mentioned, Rose's lesbianism has been airbrushed out of *The Years*; in *The Pargiters* a direct link is made between the incident where the man exposes himself and Rose's later sexuality. Virginia, who was well aware of a similar causality in the development of her own sexuality, retains the event but discards the commentary on it.

Although, for many years, Virginia had not flinched from introducing elements of her own life into her work, she had utilized alternative, poetical forms of storytelling in which her own personal history had been used as a vantage point from which to view more general truths about human experience. Much earlier, Virginia had transformed *Melymbrosia* into *The Voyage Out*, stripping it of its autobiographical content. *The Pargiters* underwent a similar process in 1935–6. Yet it seems unlikely that Virginia was performing an act of self-censorship, almost as if she felt that fiction with strong personal elements, especially those of a sexual nature, would or could not be accepted. She held the strong conviction that a work of art must go beyond the personal and singular. Like Tom Eliot, she felt that the best confessional writing had to transcend the personal circumstances of its creation. In revising her books, she always made artistic judgements about form and content. It can be argued that some of her decisions were bad ones, but she felt that *Melymbrosia* and *The Pargiters* were too tied to the facts of her own life to be good art. In *To the Lighthouse* and *The Waves* Virginia reinvented the past, whereas in *Melymbrosia* and *The Pargiters* she had merely re-created it.

Years earlier she had, with a considerable struggle, given birth to *The Voyage Out*. As she worked on *The Pargiters* she was painfully aware that she simply could not summon up either the energy or the inspiration to transform it into the type of narrative which was acceptable to her. By 16 March 1936, defeated, humiliated and trapped, she was certain that she had unleashed a monster:

> For my own guidance: I have never suffered, since The Voyage Out, such acute despair on re-reading, as this time. On Saturday for instance: there I was, faced with complete failure: & yet the book is being printed. Then I set to: in despair: thought of throwing it away . . . Yesterday I read it again; & I think it may be my best book. However . . .'[1]

That was an enormous 'however'. Even after she had made substantial changes to *The Years*, Virginia remained deeply unsure of the final form of her new novel. Her insecurity can be gauged by two important decisions: she did not ask Leonard to read the book before sending the first instalment of her typescript to the printers, R. & R. Clark of Edinburgh, on 10 March, and she instructed the compositors to set the book in galley form rather than page proofs (her customary practice was to have a book go directly into page proofs). Virginia took the opportunity to insert major changes while reading galleys: she cancelled two large sections centred on Eleanor and she introduced transitional and 'echoing' passages. The former, which anchor the book in time and place, situate the Pargiters within history and give much-needed texture; the latter, by the repetition of keywords, connect portions of the narrative which might otherwise seem to have nothing to do with each other.

No wonder the process of writing *The Years* was so arduous. Virginia was certain that her narrative was badly disjointed and needed to be patched together, that it had to be more anchored in time and place, and she wanted the book to have a universal significance. She was trying to do all this with material which rekindled painful memories. And the very form of the book – a family chronicle – reminded her that Hyde Park Gate had left a permanent mark on her psyche. Although *The Years* works on the terms Virginia finally established for it, the book, like its creator, was left with many scars: for example, Sara often seems a wilful, self-centred eccentric, and Eleanor's transformation is not effectively dramatized.* In removing bits of autobiography, Virginia destroyed much of the book's continuity. In January 1936, while struggling with a work which had assumed a life of its own, her opinion of it veered wildly. On the evening of 15 January the book was 'feeble twaddle',[2] whereas the next morning it seemed full, bustling and alive. That month, Virginia read Hardy's *The Trumpet Major*. Although she denounced the book as flat and tedious, she realized that Hardy possessed something she did not: a gift for 'minute obstinately individual observations'. Also, 'he had genius & no talent. And the English love genius.'[3] She doubted that she possessed either.

If Virginia was fearful that her new novel had taken on a life of its own, she was certain that the world as she knew it was equally out of control. When George V died, on 20 January, she saw the passing of this 'commonplace man' as the end of an era. The King might have been a patriarch, one who embodied for her the male privileges assiduously withheld from women, but rumours abounded that his successor, Edward VIII, was merely a 'cheap second rate little bounder'.[4] Feelings of instability in England were later heightened by Hitler's invasion on 7 March of the demilitarized zone of the Rhineland.

Everything was coming unstuck. The Woolfs were poignantly reminded of this one night when Virginia answered a tap on the door of the Press. She was surprised to find a young woman who was just about to faint. 'Can I have a drop of water?' she pleaded. Virginia asked her to come in, summoned Leonard, and the couple gave her some hot soup. The stranger, who lived by herself in a room in Bethnal Green, could no longer work as a seamstress

* In *The Pargiters*, young Delia Pargiter, denied the opportunity to become a professional musician, becomes very distant from her family and enamoured of the Irish revolutionary Charles Stewart Parnell. Thwarted in her desire to pursue a profession, she is impatient for her life to begin and for her sick mother to die. Her wish to become a musician is not mentioned in *The Years* and, as a result, her attitude towards her dying mother seems heartless.

because she suffered from neuritis. Her small hands were badly swollen. That day, after a breakfast which had consisted of a cup of tea, she had wandered the streets. Once the soup enlivened her, she noticed that Leonard and Virginia looked like brother and sister: both had long noses, she added. Then she confessed that she was a Jew. 'So's he,' Virginia said. The girl asked if she could take a bun home; the Woolfs also gave her some tongue, two eggs and five shillings. In the depressing spectacle of this twenty-year-old outcast's life, Virginia saw horror becoming visible 'but in human form'. And, she reflected, the young woman might have to endure twenty years or more of such an existence.[5]

The Woolfs had their own financial problems. The Press had had a bad year. When Leonard reminded his wife that she had not made enough in 1935 to pay her share of their expenses, she decided to take £70 out of her 'hoard'. Rodmell provided some consolation. One day in early January, the sky, after a rainstorm, was the colour of a tropical bird's wing. The lake reflected this deep, impure purple and scores of black and white plovers flew overhead. The dreamy, vibrantly coloured landscape brought only a momentary respite, however.

Increasingly frightened, Virginia felt alone. She could no longer count on Vita, whose friendship with Gwen had deepened. On 11 January, Virginia told Ethel: 'I don't think [Vita] will ever come back, wholly; I think G. answers to something deeper in her than I ever did.'[6] A few meetings with the glamorous, sensual writer Marchesa Iris Origo (née Cutting), who obviously reminded Virginia of Vita, provided only a passing distraction.

Virginia also felt estranged from her sister, who appeared immune from life's tribulations: 'Nessa seems more than usually cheerful. She's taken her own line in London life; refuses to be a celebrated painter; buys no clothes; sees whom she likes as she likes; and altogether leads an indomitable, sensible and very sublime existence.'[7] This portrait of Vanessa the maternal goddess displays the extent to which Virginia could idealize her sister and, in the process, distort reality. According to Virginia, Vanessa could abandon her career as an artist because her children were splendid examples of her fecundity. What about a woman – like herself – whose books were her offspring? What would happen to her if she could no longer write? Two years before, Virginia had felt that her menopause had passed 'gently and imperceptibly'.[8] Now she was no longer certain. Were the violent mood shifts she was experiencing evidence of the menopause? Were her creative talents waning at the very same time that her body reminded her that she could no longer bear a child?*

These upsetting thoughts were accompanied by the conviction that, since the biological portion of her life associated with sex and childbearing had ended, she was now placed outside the dominion of time. This led to a sense of freedom – and of anger. For example, Virginia became less concerned than before about her appearance and clothes; strangers in the street would sometimes comment loudly – and insultingly – on her dishevelled look. Often she was reduced to tears. At other times, she walked the busy streets of London as if she were in a day-dream; she seemed to have no idea that other people were near her. Rebecca West wrote candidly on this topic:

> Virginia was not well turned out. But she was certainly very beautiful in a Leonardo way. Both her face and her body could not have belonged to a person not of rare gifts. In the Crush Bar at Covent Garden I once heard a man say to his wife, 'Look at that funny-looking woman.' His wife peered through her glasses and objected, 'Ssh, you shouldn't say that about her. I'm sure

* Virginia was probably quite aware that contemporary medical opinion often linked the menopause with mental disease. In her valuable introduction to the Penguin edition (1992) of *Mrs Dalloway*, Elaine Showalter makes this crucial point (p. xxxiii): 'From the mid-nineteenth century on, menopause had been increasingly medicalized, and linked with depression, madness, and even suicide. Doctors warned that a menopausal woman's melancholia could lead her to kill herself. In a particularly grim description published in 1924, Helene Deutsch described menopause as a hopeless process of decline: "Everything she acquired in puberty is now lost piece by piece; with the lapse of the reproductive service, her beauty vanishes, and usually the warm, vital flow of feminine emotional life as well."'

she's . . .' and her voice died away in vague respect, almost awe.[9]

Unlike many other women, Virginia realized that she had exerted some degree of control over her body. That control had been purchased at a very high price, however. Her long-standing anger at a male-dominated culture which attempted to make women angels of the house deepened considerably – and she felt that anger in a much stronger, more vehement way than ever before. This can be put slightly differently: although her menopause made Virginia aware that a part of her life was over, it also placed her in touch with a strong sense of just how governed women's lives were by men's demands. Now that she had evaded one of time's nets, she had a corresponding sense of timelessness which allowed her to become an even more impassioned defender of the rights of women. So Virginia became increasingly indifferent to her appearance, clothes and displays of anger.

That winter, one bright spot was provided by Ethel's outspoken, affectionate inscription of *As Time Went On*, her new volume of autobiography, to Virginia:

> To dedicate your book to an author in token of admiration is an impertinence. To do it from affection is better. But what if the book turns out badly? That dedication may cost you a valued friendship. Therefore, avoiding seductive quagmires that begin with an 'a', such as affection and admiration, I step on to safe ground and declare that solely because this book was written at her suggestion do I venture to offer it to VIRGINIA WOOLF.[10]

Since the beginning of their friendship, Ethel had also had the capacity to make Virginia very angry. In her fights with the composer, Virginia unleashed the full force of her feelings. She remained loath to allow personal emotions into her fiction, but in a very real sense Ethel was the muse of 'On Being Despised', which was to become *Three Guineas*. Once she told Virginia: 'I feel very passionately two things about women 1) that they are the underdog 2) that, once they know of their susceptibility to male notions, something new in the way of light & heat will be diffused in the world.'[11] She also reminded Virginia that silence was not necessarily a good thing. Virginia removed the polemic from *The Years* in order to divert it into a literary form – the essay – in which passions could be given full, uncensored expression. However, in *A Room of One's Own*, her previous full-length essay, Virginia had pulled her punches; in contrast, *Three Guineas* takes direct aim at the corrupt male hierarchy.

Even before Virginia dispatched the typescript of *The Years* to Edinburgh, she became immersed in 'On Being Despised', which she briefly thought of calling 'Letter to a Gentleman'. On April Fool's Day, Virginia took tea with a man whose conduct towards her had helped to make the word 'gentleman' synonymous with 'villain' in her vocabulary: Gerald Duckworth. It was 'like visiting an alligator in a tank, an obese & obsolete alligator, lying like our tortoises [at Rodmell], half in & half out of water'.[12] The two talked publishing, and Gerald listed his various diseases. On the surface, the meeting of half-brother and half-sister was amiable, but Virginia, who saw the occasion as an excellent opportunity to do fieldwork on a particularly nasty specimen of male depravity, studied Gerald intently. Her time could have been more profitably spent, she decided, in attending Prime Minister Baldwin's speech on behalf of the Newnham College building fund.

Unfortunately, Virginia could not allow herself to become too absorbed in her tract. She had to worry about the proofs of *The Years* – and Leonard's reaction to them. By early April, Clark had begun to send her galleys. Although Virginia posted the last pages of typescript to Edinburgh on 8 April, she was delighted to learn shortly afterwards that Harcourt Brace could not publish *The Years* in the United States before October. So relieved was she by this news that she ignored the proofs. Leonard was silent about his reaction to the book, but Virginia was certain she could see a certain tepidity in his countenance.

Elinor Rendel, worried about her patient's constant headaches and low spirits, advised a holiday. Leonard and Virginia were happy to comply and on 8 May embarked on a motor tour of Dorset, Somerset and Cornwall. The weather they encountered in Dorset was overcast and depressingly sepulchral until they arrived in Lyme Regis. Virginia, who considered Weymouth the most beautiful seaside town in England, was disappointed not to visit it in ideal conditions. As usual, though, Cornwall exceeded expectations when the Woolfs arrived there a few days later: 'My word – what a country! Why do we ever spend any part of our short lives in Sussex, Kent or London? We dribble from bay to bay, and have discovered an entirely lonely virgin country . . . Here and there a castle, and an old man fishing in his river with the sea breaking behind ilex groves, and a rim of green hill.'[13] The rugged, remote landscape worked its customary magic momentarily, but the happy scene of childhood sharply reminded Virginia of just how miserable her young adulthood had been. Before returning to London, she wrote a letter to Julian, who had been in Wunan for almost six months, in which she told him how much she envied his carefree existence:

> I wish I had spent three years in China at your age – the difference was, though, that at your age, what with all the family deaths and extreme intensities – father, mother, Stella, Thoby, George, Jack – I felt I had lived through all emotions and only wanted peace and loneliness. All the horrors of life had been pressed in to our eyes so very crude and raw.[14]

Soon after her return on 22 May to Tavistock Square and to the proofs of *The Years*, all the benefits of Virginia's holiday were quickly erased. Elinor allowed her to spend only forty-five minutes a day on the galleys, a task resumed on 26 May. Within three days, Virginia had to take refuge at Rodmell, but she returned to London on 10 June. The following day, she made this entry – the first since 9 April – in her diary: 'I can only . . . say at last after 2 months dismal & worse, almost catastrophic illness – never been so near the precipice to my own feeling since 1913 – I'm again on top. I have to re-write, I mean interpolate & rub out most of The Years in proof.'[15]

However, Virginia was not in control of the situation. Her book refused to fall into place and the unfortunate author led a constrained, haphazard existence. She would work for half an hour, get up from her desk with a feeling of acute despair, lie down, get dressed, walk in the square and return to do another ten lines of proof. She took some consolation from reading Flaubert's letters and immediately identified with his search for the right word, the perfect phrase. Nevertheless, she realized that few people could be so tortured by writing as she was. She hoped that she would have the necessary courage and patience to bring this book off. Whatever the outcome, she was determined that *The Years* should be her last work of fiction.

Although remorseless in self-criticism, Virginia attempted to give Julian some diplomatic but frank advice about his own writing. Before he had left for China the year before, she had encouraged her nephew to write down his reflections on Roger Fry. He had done so in 'A Letter to A' and had sent it to his aunt in March, thinking that it would appear in the Hogarth Letters series. Virginia's struggle with *The Years* meant that she did not read Julian's essay until June, after she had sent it out to be typed. Although she was tactful, she expressed her reservations directly.

> I think it's full of ideas; full of sharp insights; and there are a mass of things I would like to pilfer if I write, as I hope next autumn. My criticism is; first that you've not mastered the colloquial style, which is the hardest, so that it seemed to me (but my mind was weak) to be discursive, loose knit, and uneasy in its familiarities and conventions. However you could easily pull it together. Prose has to be so tight, if it's not to smear one with mist . . . I wished there were more 'personality' but there's enough to give a hint of his relations with the younger generation.[16]

Like his aunt, Julian was thin-skinned, as can be seen in his letter to his mother of 20 September: 'I do think Virginia is exceedingly tiresome. She wrote me a letter saying she thought my Roger work needed rewriting etc. I really don't believe it. I don't think I could say it any better.'[17]

There were other revelations and revaluations that autumn. While working on his biography, Virginia discovered that Roger had good cause to be convinced that Clive had stolen some key ideas from him: 'and as Roger was half persecution mad – only he was far too sweet and sane to let the disease rip – he minded being pilfered far more than was reasonable'.[18] Although she praised Vita's new biography of Joan of Arc to the author, Virginia found the book both verbose and pious. Her opinion of Lytton rose higher the more she read other people's attempts at biography.

Virginia's sexual identity also seems to have taken a twist that summer when she confessed to her sister, as we have seen, how aroused she had been by a recent visit from Tom Eliot, whom she could have loved, she said, had she met him when they were both young.

Ethel could always be counted on to provide a diversion. In August 1936, she informed the 'Queen of Bloomsbury' that she hated everything Bloomsbury stood for. In countering this blast, Virginia was not entirely regal: 'What would interest me though would be to know how that word, has crystallized in your aloof and independent mind into the symbol of all you despise . . . you, on the contrary accept me, and don't fritter and fuss me. And then how I adore your broad human bottom.'[19] At this time, if she could get away with it, Virginia would use almost any excuse to avoid a meeting with Ethel. Sybil Colefax was placed in the same category. When she invited herself for a weekend at Rodmell in early September, Virginia lied her way out. To Ottoline Morrell she provided a fairly complete picture of the awful physical state to which *The Years* had reduced her. Once again, her headaches were like 'enraged rats gnawing'[20] at the nape of her neck.

On 1 November, Virginia sat down to work on the proofs. By the time she had reached the end of the first section of the book, she was reduced to 'stony but convinced' despair. On the next day, she read as far as 'The Present Time' and said to herself: 'This is happily so bad that there can be no question about it. I must carry the proofs, like a dead cat, to Leonard & tell him to burn them unread.'[21] The proofs would cost between £200 and £300 and, gladly, she would pay that out of her hoard, even though her savings would be reduced to £400. She made this resolution, felt an enormous relief and went out for a walk, during which she told herself that she was no longer Virginia the genius but Virginia the insignificant. When she returned, a very concerned Leonard – who had maintained a silence of many months on the book – told her that she might be wrong about it. A short time later, as he put the proofs down (he had read up to and including the 1908 section), he informed her that the book was 'extraordinarily good – as good as any of them'.[22] By the following day Leonard had read to the end of the 1914 section and pronounced it very strange, very interesting and very sad.

Virginia was not sure how sincere her husband's favourable reaction to *The Years* was. Perhaps she was exaggerating its defects while he was overemphasizing its merits? Perhaps they should seek Morgan's advice? On the night of 4 November, in part perhaps to avoid bringing Forster into the discussion, Leonard assured his wife that he was completely convinced of the book's merits. For Virginia, this was a miracle. Indeed, her husband had been reduced to tears as he put down the last sheet of the galleys at midnight. It was, he assured her, 'a most remarkable book',[23] better than *The Waves*. Four days later, when her doubts reasserted themselves, she clung to Leonard's verdict, a judgement which she rightly suspected was feigned. (Years later, in the volume of autobiography entitled *Downhill All the Way*, he simply stated: 'To Virginia I praised the book more than I should have done if she had been well.'[24]) However, he informed her that the book was far too long. Virginia was so sick of it that she could no longer be objective. She decided to publish and face damnation. Once the book appeared, she vowed never to look at it again.

Later that month, while returning to London from Rodmell, Leonard and Virginia encountered a particularly thick fog. In order to guide Leonard, Virginia got out of the car and walked along beside him. The car crashed into a wall, but the only damage was to one of the bumpers. At one point a little boy, a street ruffian, seemed to emerge miraculously out of the fog. Later, bystanders lined the pavement in order to see what would happen to the traffic and two men assisted them to navigate. Just as the Woolfs were about to head for a garage and then look for a station, a bus driver told them that 200 yards ahead the road was clear.

Leonard's reassurances and the dispersal of the fog strengthened Virginia considerably. Later that autumn, although she experienced some menopausal symptoms – 'swollen veins – the tingling; the odd falling; feeling of despair . . . Hot & cold' – she came to the comforting conclusion: 'Whatever happens I don't think I can now be destroyed.'[25] With a renewed sense of vigour, she returned to 'On Being Despised', certain she would not lose her way. A renewed and peppery Virginia Woolf started to look at things differently. She even thought of writing an article on the glorious coarseness to be found in the novels of Jane Austen.

Not many words were minced when Virginia spoke to the Memoir Club on 1 December. Her talk, 'Am I a Snob?', centred on her troubled friendship with Sybil Colefax. In a fine piece of reverse snobbery, Virginia admitted to being unduly interested in the lives of women who had a veneer of glamour; unlike them, though, she said she could at least lay claim to the ownership of an inner self. Virginia recalled her origins within an intellectual family on the fringes of the world of fashion. George Duckworth had tried to introduce her into society, but she was repulsed. 'My temptation,' she recalled, 'reached me in subtler ways – through Kitty Maxse originally, I think – a lady of the most delicate charm, of the most ethereal grace so that the great, whom she introduced, were sprayed and disinfected and robbed of their grossness.'[26]

Virginia may have remained inordinately curious about society women, who were for her a combination of the beautiful and the grotesque, but she was barred from becoming one of them, as she pointed out in a flippant but touching aside: 'I hate being badly dressed; but I hate buying clothes. In particular I hate buying suspenders. It is partly, I think, that in order to buy suspenders you must visit the most private room in the heart of a shop; you must stand in your chemise. Shiny black satin women pry and snigger.'[27]

Sybil Colefax was a relentless collector of famous people and as such was a very different kind of snob from Virginia. In October 1936, the recently widowed Lady Colefax, who years earlier had suffered a series of financial setbacks and started a business as an interior decorator, was on the verge of leaving Argyll House, the scene of her famous parties. On Tuesday, 27 October, Virginia took tea there for the last time. The house was filled with strangers who were inspecting or making an inventory of various pieces of furniture. Sybil, although deeply upset, clung to her own relentless cataloguing of the great and near-great she had entertained. As 'Am I a Snob?' concludes, Virginia, who is being given a lift in Sybil's chauffeur-driven Rolls, has to listen to Sybil 'trying to impress me with the fact that she had known Henry James'.[28]

Although Sybil was not a member of the Memoir Club, it was extraordinarily cheeky for Virginia to make her the prime illustration of vulgar snobbery. Virginia's paper is a guarded, measured assessment of a friend-enemy, but it never attempts to get below the surface. To her diary, Virginia confided the same facts, but she showed an extraordinary empathy with the unhappiness lurking at every corner of Sybil's life.

> She talked in a scattered nervous way, like a hen fluttering over the edge of an abyss. A brave hen. Her eyes were bright. And they say now that she has cancer in her breast. Nor could I always distinguish between the pose – I am going to show myself poetic & unworldly to Virginia – & the genuine gallantry . . . She is blinded by darkness; I mean when she is alone, without the stimulus & direction of other people's views she is uncertain. Flounders . . . But whether I imagined it or not, I felt something genuinely rising from the depths in her: a desire to fight her adversity, a momentary desire to break down; but then she was up again & off again.[29]

In her paper, Virginia accused Sybil of not being in touch with her real feelings. The irony is that Virginia erased many of her own feelings about Sybil from her talk. Virginia may have been a different kind of snob from Sybil but they shared an inability to display genuine emotions in public.

As 1936 drew to a close, Virginia charted the progress of the 'Simpson Affair', the constitutional crisis brought on by Edward VIII's determination to marry the twice-divorced Wallis Simpson. While taking a stroll on the evening of 10 December, Virginia chanced upon Ottoline, who assured her: 'We don't want a woman that's already had 2 husbands & an American when there [are] so many good English girls.'[30] Suddenly a newspaper car drove by with the word ABDICATION on a large placard. The car stopped and Virginia and Ottoline bought the first two copies in the bale. To Virginia, it seemed that 'this one little insignificant man'[31] had dislodged a pebble which started an avalanche.

A week earlier, Violet Dickinson, with whom Virginia now corresponded sporadically, had suddenly returned her early letters to her. This gust from her own tragic past hit Virginia hard. She asked Violet: 'Do you like that girl? I'm not sure that I do, though I think she had some spirit in her, and certainly was rather ground down harshly by fate.'[32]

After Boxing Day, Virginia spent the day with Ethel at Woking. The composer had replaced her recently deceased dog with a puppy, who had the effrontery to die. 'The truth is,' Virginia a bit heartlessly informed Vita, 'no dog can stand the strain of living with Ethel. I went down one day and found it on the verge of nervous collapse, simply from listening to her conversation.' Ethel, ever a fruitful source of gossip which Virginia could pass on to Vita, discoursed on the amorous pursuits of the Princesse de Polignac – née Winnie Singer – whose mellow exterior concealed the fact that she had supposedly ravished half the virgins in Paris. Virginia herself wanted to be petted by Vita: 'Excuse poor Potto's drool: I have just caught him a cuff on his tail and sent him back [to his reading].'[33]

Despite the tribulations of the year, Virginia felt possessed of a divine relief. For the first time in ten months, her mind had 'sprung up like a tree shaking off a load'. She knew that work for her was an absolute necessity. She always had to be pursuing something. Then she added ominously: 'Perhaps I'm now again on one of those peaks where I shall write 2 or 3 little books quickly: & then have another break.'[34]

1937 began with some ominous events. The sculptor Stephen Tomlin died on 8 January. Virginia had known him since 1924 and in the summer of 1931 had reluctantly sat for him. His portrait bust shows an excessively strife-ridden Virginia. In her view this was more a self-portrait than a rendition of herself. 'My own intercourse with him,' she recalled, 'broke over that bust, when I took a shudder at the impact of his neurotic clinging persistency, & perhaps behaved, though I didn't think so at the time, unreasonably, perversely'.[35] Perhaps the similarities between Tomlin and Virginia had been the real cause of her revulsion. Another blow was the sudden death of Margaret West, the Press's manager, which meant that Leonard and Virginia had to be even more involved in aspects of the operation they loathed: '[any] boy and girl who can buy a fountain pen and a ream of paper instantly writes a novel, ties it up and sends it to us'.[36]

Virginia was aware that the penetrating, damp cold of winter made the plight of the homeless even more unbearable. On the evening of 8 March, she and Leonard noticed a family of three on the street. The woman had a fire burning, the man was sitting up, amongst a heap of old clothes and bits of dirty paper, and there was a baby in a nearby perambulator. Their evening meal consisted of slices of dry bread.

Earlier, during January and February, while continuing work on her tract, Virginia had formed friendships with Elizabeth Robins, an acquaintance of her mother, and her companion, Octavia Wilberforce, a physician who lived in Brighton. Now in her mid-seventies, Robins, an American from Kentucky who had moved to England in 1899, had been one of the most successful Ibsen actresses of her generation. She was also a prolific playwright and novelist, relentlessly examining one of the greatest evils of her time, the so-called helplessness of women. Mercy-killing, sexual passion and pacifism were among her other themes. The much younger Wilberforce, who was almost forty in 1937, was the great-granddaughter of William Wilberforce and thus a distant relative of Virginia. In December 1936, Elizabeth had sent a typescript – perhaps her autobiography – to the Hogarth Press. The Woolfs, who had met her before, were interested in a book which required extensive changes and perhaps intrigued by the life history of this fascinating woman. They took advantage of the proximity of Rodmell to Brighton and called on her.

Although Elizabeth appeared old, gnarled and grizzled, she had intense faun eyes which were electrifying. Very much the professional actress, her movements were angular. However, Virginia felt that the old woman was rather mannered and was delighted when, just as Robins was about to launch into a stylized panegyric, a rosy-cheeked, healthy-looking Octavia arrived home. Immediately, Virginia was taken with her candid smile, which was accompanied by perfect teeth. She was also moved when the younger woman described the struggle she had had to become a doctor. Virginia was touched when it became clear that Octavia was a fan of hers. She positively glowed. Just the day before, she had been stung by a piece in which she was accused of lyrical emptiness.

Miss Robins may have been formidable, but she was easygoing next to an enraged Vanessa. On the evening of 21 January, Virginia introduced a difficult topic. Three weeks before, on 30 December, six months after her letter of 28 June, she had heard back from her nephew. In his letter, Julian was frank about his furious reaction to her criticisms. She immediately sent him an extremely apologetic letter in which she directed anger against herself for having badly expressed her reservations about the Fry piece: 'I certainly didn't mean to say anything that could possibly hurt you.'[37] As soon as the topic was broached, Vanessa turned to steel, 'a most curious transformation', a startled and hurt Virginia observed. Her sister behaved like a tigress 'in a cave, growling'.[38] In a particularly painful way, Virginia was reminded that Julian came much higher in his mother's estimation than she did.

Early that winter, Leonard's health provided some anxious moments. In mid-February, when he consulted a Harley Street specialist, Virginia paced the street for an hour, bought a newspaper, dropped her handkerchief and returned time and again to the swing doors of Number 149, anxious for a glimpse of her husband. After what seemed an eternity, Leonard emerged with a broad smile on his face. Nothing much was wrong with him, but he would have to reduce his intake of sugar.

In the midst of pre-publication jitters about *The Years*, which was to appear on 11 March, Virginia cultivated her friendship with Stephen Spender, of whom she provided a short, brilliant pen sketch: 'Rather a beautiful if too conventionally poetic young man: sunk cheeks, large blue eyes, skin always burning.'[39] Virginia was not shy about firing direct questions at him. Why did he bother to get married if he was in large part homosexual? He told her that he wanted to stabilize himself; in particular, he dreaded the lonely, prowling existence of someone like the South African-born novelist William Plomer, then in his early thirties. An old friend, Desmond MacCarthy, even though he habitually outstayed his welcome, was a foil to the younger generation. The paunchy, nearly bald Desmond had an odd, clubby, eighteenth-century look, as if he had just arrived from dining with Johnson or Boswell. 'And,' Virginia observed, 'as full of human kindness as a ripe grape with juice'.[40] Unlike herself, Desmond seemed content *not* to have written the great book.

Her usual worry about how a new novel would be received was coupled with unpleasant bodily sensations. Was this the menopause? she asked herself.

> A physical feeling as if I were drumming slightly in the veins: very cold: impotent: & terrified. As if I were exposed on a high ledge in full light . . . Very apprehensive. As if something cold

> & horrible – a roar of laughter at my expense were about to happen. And I am powerless to ward it off: I have no protection. And this anxiety & nothingness surround me with a vacuum. It affects the thighs chiefly. And I want to burst into tears, but have nothing to cry for. Then a great restlessness seizes me.

She felt like a Sisyphus, one who 'must go on doing this dance on hot bricks till I die'.[41] Of one thing she was very sure: her spiritual temperature had reached fever pitch.

Virginia did not feel like a lamb being dragged to the slaughter. Rather, she imagined herself a poor little rabbit, startled by the headlamp of a fast-approaching car, about to be run over. Then there was always the possibility that she would suffer the worst ignominy of all: her book would be damned by faint praise. Despite this, she felt that she had at long last established her own point of view as a writer and was 'fitted out' for two more books: her biography of Roger Fry and *Three Guineas*, the title on which she had at last settled for her tract. If her reputation as a celebrity declined, so be it. This would give her the chance to become an even more acute observer of her life and times. 'I am in a position to hold myself aloof,' she assured herself. 'I need never seek out anyone.'[42]

If she was afraid of being misunderstood, Virginia could not have found a much more sympathetic reviewer than Theodora Bosanquet* in the 13 March issue of *Time and Tide*:

> Is it, can it be, possible that Mrs Woolf, having considered with attention and some astonishment a few of the family chronicles now in fashion, caught the echo of a challenge? Did she, putting her ear to an acoustically curved shell, hear a voice, the assembled voice of the other English novelists, murmuring: 'Now it's your turn. You who have tossed about like a shuttlecock, disdained

* In November 1924, the Hogarth Press had published Bosanquet's *Henry James at Work* in the Hogarth Essays Series (First Series, No. 3).

> and defied the tolling of the hours, come off that lofty cloud. Let the years pass in the order of their chronological procession. Bridge your abysses in something more like the ordinary manner'?

This is a deft piece of criticism, one which was obviously attuned to the writer's intent. According to Bosanquet, Virginia had 'brought off the trick'. In the *Observer*, Basil de Selincourt showed the depth of his understanding of the process of composition: 'Being a much easier book to read, [*The Years*] may well, for that very reason, have been even more difficult to write.'[43]

There were many other tributes, including the anonymous reviewer in the *Times Literary Supplement*, Howard Spring in the *Evening Standard*, Richard Church in *John O'London's Weekly* and David Garnett in *New Statesman and Nation*. Edwin Muir, a long-time admirer, was appalled by the book, which he found discontinuous and thus disappointing. In his review in the *Listener*, he was blunt. The author, who had taken on the kind of task – a historical novel encompassing all strata of society – for which Tolstoy was justly renowned, had failed. In particular, the characters lacked motivation:

> Almost everything has been abstracted from these characters except the fact that at certain dates they are certain ages. To make them feel and think in accordance with their ages (they hardly act at all) required a fine and discriminating imagination. But they do not become real, they only become old. One has the feeling that Mrs Woolf has almost left them out.[44]

The good notices lifted Virginia's spirits only a little. She remained convinced that her book was feeble. However, she was furious at Muir, whose piece did not appear until the end of the month. He had 'smacked' her on the cheek and found her out. As she had feared all along, 'that odious rice pudding of a book is what I thought it – a dank failure'.[45]

Ultimately, favourable reviews were dismissed, while the bad ones had the power to wake her at four in the morning. She suffered other set-backs. An acquaintance, John Sparrow, then a Fellow of All Souls, reviewed her book unfavourably in the *Spectator* and then had the nerve to ask her not to read his piece.

On Saturday, 27 March, a reporter on assignment in London for the *New York Times* telephoned the Woolfs, who were spending the Easter at Rodmell. He was told that he could look at the outside of 52 Tavistock Square, if he so wished, but that Mrs Woolf declined to be interviewed. He did not take no for an answer, as Virginia found out the following day:

> At 4.30 as I was boiling the kettle a huge black Daimler drew up. Then a dapper little man in a tweed coat appeared in the garden. I reached the sitting room – saw him standing there looking round. L. ignored him. L. in the orchard with Percy [Bartholomew, gardener]. Then I guessed. He had a green note book & stood looking about, jotting things down. I ducked my head – he almost caught me. At last L. turned & fronted him. No, Mrs W. didn't want that kind of publicity. I raged. A bug walking over one's skin – couldn't crush him. The bug taking note. L. politely led him back to his Daimler & his wife. But they'd had a nice run from London – bugs, to come & steal in & take notes.[46]

Despite her own considerable reservations, the new book was by far her most successful, due to the enthusiastic response given by readers in the United States. By 1 June, *The Years* reached the top of the best-seller list in the *New York Herald Tribune*, where it remained for several weeks. Almost a month after the book's publication, Virginia was able, in a letter to Stephen Spender, to talk of the enormous risks she had taken in a book which attempted both to strike the death-knell of the middle classes and to offer constructive suggestions for the rebuilding of society.

> But what I meant I think was to give a picture of society as a whole; give characters from every side; turn them towards society, not private life; exhibit the effect of ceremonies; Keep one toe on the ground by means of dates, facts: envelop the

> whole in a changing temporal atmosphere; Compose into one vast many-sided group at the end; and then shift the stress from present to future; and show the old fabric insensibly changing without death or violence into the future – suggesting that there is no break, but a continuous development, possibly a recurrence of some pattern; of which of course we actors are ignorant. And the future was gradually to dawn.[47]

Perhaps, she realized, her ambitious reach had in this instance exceeded what could be grasped in one narrative. 'I am doubtful,' she told herself, 'if I shall ever write another novel – Certainly not unless under great compulsion such as The Years imposed on me.'[48]

That April, Virginia reached a level of bliss which had previously eluded her. She had waged a difficult battle, although she was not certain whether she was the victor or the vanquished. The most important thing was that she had fought a good fight: 'I lay awake so calm, so content, as if I'd stepped off the whirling world into a deep blue quiet space, & there open eyed existed, beyond harm; armed against all that can happen. I have never had this feeling before in all my life; but I have had it several times since last summer.'[49] This happiness tended to be ruffled during the day, but underneath everything resided a new peace beyond understanding.

A day after the publication of *The Years* Julian arrived back in England. He had resigned his professorship in China and sailed for Marseilles at the end of January. Although he asked Vanessa to meet him in France, he did not tell her that he planned to go on directly from there to Spain to drive ambulances for the International Brigade. Vanessa, shocked by this news when it was broken to her by the critic Charles Mauron, implored her son to return to England for a full discussion of the matter. Julian did this. Almost immediately after his return, he claimed that he was seriously thinking of remaining in England if he could find a suitable job.

When the Woolfs dined at Charleston with mother and son,

Virginia saw an embittered, depressed but vigorous young man who, for this occasion, was dressed in Chinese robes: 'I felt him changed: taut, tense, on the defensive: yet affectionate: but no longer spontaneous.'[50] If Virginia was trying to see both sides of her nephew, Leonard could not. He could neither forgive nor ignore the extreme self-centredness of Vanessa and Julian. Virginia was a bit impatient with Leonard's usual litany of grievances against her family, but she saw some truth in his complaints.

A month later, Virginia was certain Julian had something up his sleeve. His behaviour had become stranger. He laughed excessively, made outlandish faces and would quickly fly into a rage. He was now set on going to Spain; as far as he was concerned, the door was closed on that topic. When Virginia saw him three weeks later, he fulminated against the 'Bloomsbury habit of education. He had been taught no job; only a vague literary smattering.' He was clearly furious at his mother for the bohemian manner in which she had raised him. Virginia interjected: 'But I wanted you to go to the Bar.'

'Yes,' he shot back at her, 'but you didn't insist upon it to my mother.'

So there was Julian without a profession, claiming that the fault was partly hers. She was very upset; in her opinion, he was 'rather on the crazy edge of life'.[51]

As Virginia realized, Julian had some strange power over his mother, as if he were her lover as well as her son. He had told Vanessa that he could never care for another woman as he did for her. As a child, Julian had been hardy and vigorous, but he had also been emotionally defenceless, someone very much in need of special protection. As he got older, he was less well adapted to the world than either Quentin or Angelica. Virginia knew firsthand about such vulnerability and, of course, Vanessa had been a surrogate mother to her. She may have been a bit jealous of Julian, but she understood just how fragile he was. On the day Julian bemoaned his lack of proper education, Virginia, filled with a nebulous sense of foreboding, recalled her mother's death forty-two years before.

In the spring, Virginia became aware that Janet Case was dying of cancer. Relations between teacher and pupil had cooled considerably over the years, due in large part to Janet's disapproval of Virginia's career as a novelist. When she renewed her friendship with the Case sisters in 1937, Virginia remembered both the strong homoerotic urges and the childlike devotion she had felt for a much younger Janet. Although Virginia and Janet had later clashed on the 'visionary', Virginia nevertheless retained fond memories of her many visits to the small house in Hampstead and of a woman with beautiful veiled eyes which, like Julia Stephen's, could open suddenly with a quick flash of sympathy and laughter.

In an attempt to get away from the brouhaha surrounding the coronation of George VI, the Woolfs decided to holiday in western France. They crossed to Dieppe from Newhaven on Friday, 7 May, and travelled as far south as Albi. The weather, warm and mellow, was ideal. The supreme attraction of rural France for Virginia was very much in evidence: she could watch a lifestyle which had remained unchanged for over 200 years. The Woolfs went a long way back in time when they visited the caves at Les Eyzies and saw the brownish-red tracings of prehistoric animals half erased by the schoolchildren who had previously been allowed to play there. Their holiday would have been an unqualified success if Virginia had not been worried about Julian's approaching departure for Spain. They recrossed the Channel on Sunday night, 23 May, and successfully evaded detection by Customs of the cigars they were smuggling.

Sally jumped for joy when she saw Leonard. The previous month, she had been 'surgically mated',[52] her 'after marriage' lasting between twenty and twenty-five minutes. Three persons – Leonard, the breeder and a kennel man – assisted the spaniels, while Virginia 'prudently, & chastely sat in the car' and showed Mitz to some curious children. Virginia was disappointed – but not unduly so – when Sally did not become pregnant. Sharing some of her husband's strong sentiments about pets, she was quite happy to search the woods for the birds' eggs which Mitz greedily devoured, although she was a bit embarrassed when one of the eggs leaked on to the new carpet Vanessa had recently made for her. She was also quite willing to be sent up the road at Rodmell to fetch back the curious male tortoise who strayed beyond the pond at Monks House.

A shared fascination with animals was one bond between Virginia and the American poet and novelist May Sarton, who was twenty-five in 1937. Early that spring, a very timid Sarton purchased a bunch of primroses and presented the bouquet and a copy of her first book of poems to the servant who answered the door at 52 Tavistock Square. Sarton left hastily. She told a very sympathetic Elizabeth Bowen about her escapade and soon afterwards Elizabeth arranged a small dinner party at her London home in Clarence Terrace where the two women could meet. Virginia in the flesh, dressed in a long green *robe-de-style*, was much more impressive than any photograph. When Sarton confessed to having been the person who had left the flowers and verse, Virginia, in between puffs on her cigar, revealed that on that very day someone had given her a small Chinese vase and how delightfully startled she had been that flowers had appeared out of thin air. She immediately invited Sarton to tea, the date of which was hard to settle and became a source of anxiety to the young woman: 'But why,' Virginia later asked her, 'should you have been frightened, considering that I am as tame and mild as a very old giraffe?'[53]

At this meeting, Virginia's insatiable curiosity was much in evidence. She looked to the young American like 'some slightly unreal goddess, transparent to every current of air or wave, the eyes set in the sculptured bone in such a way that their beauty was perfectly defined'. The conversation was anything but ethereal. In fact, it was bawdy. Virginia teased her new friend, insisting that poetry was so much easier to write than prose, and then Sarton confessed that she was working on a novel.

Virginia was startled: 'You are writing a novel? Ah, then all this must seem totally unreal to you.' By 'this', Virginia meant the recently published *The Years*. The conversation suddenly took a new turn. Virginia told her that she had written that book in order to break the mould of *The Waves*. She had, she revealed to Sarton, 'worked at it in a curious way, many scenes at a time, picking out first one and then another like the pieces of a mosaic. So that the horror in this case, as she explained, had been the transitions, the linking passages.' Their talk was interrupted by Leonard's arrival, precisely at six. Sarton felt that this was the signal to leave, but she could not break away gracefully and began to launch into a glowing description of the zoo at Whipsnade, near where she was staying. Before she knew what she had done, she had invited the Woolfs out to see it.

Everything went wrong on 30 June, the day of the Woolfs' thirty-mile excursion. The sky was overcast, Leonard and Virginia arrived late and the promised wallaby with a baby in her pouch did not make an appearance. The lions and tigers had been shut in their boxlike cages – only their growly, mourning cries could be heard. There were a few saving graces: a baby giraffe gambolled about, and the restaurant selected by Sarton had excellent filet mignon. All in all, Sarton felt that she had persuaded the Woolfs 'to a long journey only to find some poor miserable tigers mewing in their boxes: a fiasco'.[54]

Virginia had experienced a débâcle of a different sort the previous month when the chocolate from the cake she had bought for Tom Eliot's tea melted down her legs in the tube during the rush hour. There was also a meal at which Ann Stephen, Adrian's daughter, served fried asparagus. Virginia, ever a dutiful aunt – and not a particularly good cook herself – was understanding, forgiving and amused. Most days that spring and early summer, she worked on *Three Guineas*, but she remained deeply worried about Julian, who had left for Spain on 7 June. His absence was brought even more forcibly to mind when she saw a long file of Spanish refugees from Bilbao walking through Tavistock Square. In early July, not wishing for any more distractions, she refused an invitation to a party where Matisse, of whom she was a great admirer, was the guest of honour.

By July 1937, after a number of difficult years, Virginia had just re-established a calm routine. This was rocked by Janet Case's death on 15 July and shattered by the news five days later that Julian had been killed in Spain on 18 July. He had been twenty-nine years old. At first, information was scanty: Julian had apparently been hit by a shell fragment while driving his ambulance. On the evening that Vanessa heard the news, the Woolfs went round to her studio in Fitzroy Street. Nessa, Duncan, Quentin, Angelica, Leonard and Virginia were consumed with grief. Vanessa suffered a complete physical breakdown, and for the next four weeks Virginia was in constant attendance on her elder sister, who seemed to derive comfort only from her sibling.

Virginia was crushed by the heavy toll Julian's death exerted on her sister, who now looked like an old woman. Vanessa reminded her of her father at the end of his life, when he took Thoby's arm for support. 'How,' Virginia pondered, 'can she ever right herself through?'[55] Virginia felt deeply guilty about the criticism she had made of Julian's work. At the time she had not felt that she was acting in a spiteful or jealous way, but now she was not so sure. Virginia also had to deal with her own deep, warm feelings for the young man. To one friend, she said: 'He was a great joy to us; [Vanessa's] children are like my own. But it had become necessary for him to go; and there is a kind of grandeur in that which somehow now and then consoles me.'[56] To Vita, she made the poignant statement: 'He was the first of Nessa babies, and I can't describe how close and real and always alive our relation was.'[57]

When Thoby had died, Virginia had lost a beloved companion. Now she felt like an old woman, one who is certain that she will never behold the young again. On 29 July, Leonard and Virginia drove Vanessa to Charleston and installed her on a day-bed overlooking the garden. Virginia was strong and resolute, but her sister's emotional bleeding made her doubt that anything in life was worth such piercing agony. In August Vanessa began to drift away from her sister into mute solitude. In order to recover from the death of her son, she had to re-establish her independence. Always a giver, she did not like to be dependent on others. She even found it impossible to thank Virginia for her considerable help, so she asked Vita to do so. Virginia became confused and was not sure how to respond. She wanted to take over the role of the responsible, nurturing elder sister, but Vanessa rejected this.

Not surprisingly, Virginia told her sister how vitally important she was to her and attempted to reforge the relationship they had enjoyed as children: 'I wish dolphin were by my side, in a bath, bright blue, with her tail curled,' she told her on 5 August. 'But then I've been always in love with her since I was a green eyed brat under the nursery table, and so shall remain in my extreme senility.'[58] She wrote love letters: 'How I adore you! How astonishingly beautiful you are!'[59] And she admitted to her that the green goddess jealousy had shot a bitter shaft through her heart when she thought Vanessa might prefer Helen Anrep to herself.

By 11 August, Virginia knew that she and her sister had reached the worst time in their attempt to deal with her nephew's death: 'We don't talk so freely of Julian. We want to make things go on.'[60] All this was very unreal and dispiriting. The tension was so great that when Leonard and Virginia were alone, they quarrelled more than usual.

Julian's death brought the sisters together, but it also drove them apart. Vanessa, who had just lost a child, did not want to mother Virginia. Although she probably agreed with it, she could not take any comfort in Virginia's claim of 17 August: 'I rather think I'm more nearly attached to you than sisters should be.'[61] For her part, Virginia was reminded of just how much her sister meant to her, but she also came to realize that Vanessa found some of her feelings excessive and inappropriate. One way in which Vanessa displayed enmity was by being spiteful or querulous about Virginia's great success as a writer: she was visibly relieved to hear that the actual number of copies of *The Years* sold (40,000) was much less than the figure reported to her.*

* Another measure of hostility can be glimpsed in Vanessa's initial desire to have Faber or, a bit later, Chatto & Windus, rather than the Hogarth Press, publish a collection of Julian's writings, even though Leonard and Virginia offered to do the book. T. S. Eliot refused the book on behalf of Faber. The Hogarth Press published *Julian Bell: Essays, Poems and Letters*, edited by Quentin Bell, in 1938.

The loss of Julian was harrowing and Virginia's relationship with her sister diminished. She was tempted to give up, to give way to death's vacant inanity. But her combative side soon reasserted itself. Very much in the manner of Bernard from *The Waves*, she was ready to fight: 'I will not yield an inch or a fraction of an inch to nothingness, so long as something remains.' She had her work, but what if that 'something' was taken from her? She knew the answer: 'Directly I am not working, or see the end in sight, then nothingness begins.'[62] Virginia was also desperately afraid of losing either Leonard or Vanessa. Could she take a narcotic successfully if they died? Or could she simply trust to life to run its course? She was far from certain.

Virginia was filled with affection for Leonard, the person who had been most steadfast in his devotion to her. However, when she proposed that they go to Paris for a weekend, he said he would rather not. Surprisingly, Virginia was overcome with happiness. 'Then we walked round the square love making – after 25 years can't bear to be separate . . . it is an enormous pleasure, being wanted: a wife. And our marriage so complete.'[63] Virginia's sense was that Leonard, who could be tetchy about trivial things, loved her unconditionally, very much in the manner of an indulgent parent.

If Julian had not died, Virginia was convinced that the summer of 1937 at Rodmell would have offered her profound happiness. As it was, she had to shut her mind to anything but work and her new passion, bowls. There was a crisis when Mitz escaped the house and was feared lost, but she soon turned up on the kitchen table, calmly nibbling a head of lettuce.

When she returned to London in the autumn, Virginia – if she needed any reminding – could see firsthand the worsening economic outlook. One Saturday, she came upon a man lying on the grass in Hyde Park, newspapers spread round him to keep the damp and cold at bay. Nearby were a cheap attaché case and half a roll of bread. Virginia was moved. The man was so uncomplaining and yet his life had been spoiled.

The nearest Virginia got to Paris was a trip to Seaford on the coast, where there was a gale: 'The waves broke over the car. Vast spouts of white water all along the coast. Why does a smash of water satisfy all one's religious aspirations? And it's all I can do not to throw myself in.'[64]

That October, Virginia's mind galloped through the last pages of *Three Guineas*: 'It has pressed & spurted out of me . . . like a physical volcano.'[65] She also had to confront the new information which had come to light about Julian. Five days before his death, his ambulance had been damaged by a bomb. Immediately, he had volunteered as a stretcher-bearer and been placed at the head of thirty men on one of the most dangerous parts of the front. Then, when a lorry was provided to evacuate the wounded, Julian was put in charge of it. The morning of his death had begun quietly and he had taken the opportunity to fill in shell-holes that pitted his route to the front line. While he was at work, aeroplanes flew overhead. Julian took cover but was hit by a side splash from a shell. A few minutes after being hit, he attempted to write his mother a note but got no further than two or three words. He was taken to hospital, remained fully conscious and apparently did not consider himself seriously wounded. The surgeon told him a lie: he had an 80 per cent chance of recovery. After the operation, Julian fell into a coma, spoke in French and died six hours later.

Surrounded by tragedy but nevertheless able to write at a furious rate, Virginia now began to suspect that the old rapture of novel-writing might be revivified: 'Will another novel ever swim up? If so, how? The only hint I have towards it is that it's to be dialogue: & poetry: & prose; all quite distinct. No more long, closely written books. But I have no impulse; & shall wait; shan't mind if the impulse never formulates.'[66] That was on 6 August. Two months later, the hint had become a glimpse of a new novel, one which, like *The Waves*, would be musical in its composition: 'singling out this & then that: until the central idea is stated'.[67]

Despite her optimism, she saw 1937 as a huge cat which had caught her in its claws. Leonard was ill again, and they went to

Rodmell for Christmas with that worry hanging over them. Nevertheless, life went on.

> How much do I mind death? . . . & concluded that there is a sense in which the end could be accepted calmly. That's odd, considering that few people are more immensely interested by life: & happy. It's Julian's death that makes one sceptical of life I suppose. Not that I ever think of him as dead: which is queer. Rather as if he were jerked abruptly out of sight, without rhyme or reason: so violent & absurd that one can't fit his death into any scheme. But here we are, on a fine cold day, going to mate Sally at Ickenham: a saner proceeding than to analyse here.[68]

Chapter Nineteen

FRESH ADVENTURES, VIOLENT FEELINGS

(1938–9)

Although Virginia was no longer certain that another novel was beyond her reach, she was sure that the Hogarth Press was too much of a burden for her and Leonard. Many times before, they had considered abandoning their child but had resisted the temptation. The advent of war made it even more necessary to do something. Then, early in 1937, the winds of gossip blew into John Lehmann's ear the information that if he made 'renewed advances'[1] to the Woolfs, they would be welcomed.

The lie of the land soon became clear. For £6,000 Leonard was willing to give up 'all business control',[2] but Lehmann did not have that kind of money. Even before Julian's death, any hope of a deal was deadlocked. Lehmann waited. He was shocked to learn in October 1937 that the Woolfs were on the verge of allowing the Press to die: they would maintain their backlist, refuse new titles and publish only their own books. Although Leonard later maintained that he had not intended to sell the Hogarth Press *as a whole* to Lehmann or anyone else, Virginia's diary entry of 22 October 1937 contradicts this claim:

> Leonard developed the idea of making the young Brainies take the Press as a Cooperative company (John; Isherwood; Auden; Stephen). All are bubbling with discontent & ideas. All want a focus; a manager; a mouth-piece: a common voice. Would like L. to manage it. Couldn't we sell, & creep out? That's the idea – & yet keep the soul.[3]

The price was still £6,000, but Auden, Isherwood and Spender could not find the money. Lehmann went back to the Woolfs: he himself could raise £3,000 but no more. Leonard and Virginia reconsidered the matter and came back with a counter-proposal. They would sell Lehmann a half-share in the Press for that amount. In a letter of 2 January 1938 to his new partner, Leonard attempted to make things crystal clear:

> Virginia would withdraw so that the other share would be owned by me alone, and the ownership would be a partnership between you and me . . . You would be managing director with a salary of £500 payable to you before profits are divided in which case I would have a salary of £200 payable before profits are divided . . . Each of us would have an absolute veto against the publication of any book.[4]

Unfortunately, clarity almost immediately gave way to confusion. One of Lehmann's prime motivations in going back to the Hogarth Press was to protect the existence of *New Writing*, a twice-yearly miscellany which he had started in 1936. Lehmann had a clear editorial policy: he was committed to an international roster of writers (Silone, Pasternak, Lorca, Brecht), the long short story or novella and the work of his fellow 'Brainies', which was often devoted to critical evaluation of the existing social and political order. In its brief life, the magazine-book had already gone through two publishers: Bodley Head issued three numbers before giving way to Lawrence & Wishart, who also did three. Lehmann's anticipated stability for *New Writing* soon foundered.

Obviously Leonard and Virginia were committed to new writing, but they both had serious doubts about Lehmann's periodical and earlier, in *A Letter to a Young Poet*, Virginia had expressed grave reservations about the impetuosity of the Auden generation. In May 1938 Virginia refused to contribute a short story to *New Writing*. In a letter that July, she framed her objections. The foreword put her off completely. If the magazine existed to further the careers of new and young authors, she had to admit to being neither. What really galled her was the claim that it sought out only those writers whose views were in sympathy with its manifesto: 'You may have sent some declaration which I've missed. If so, let me have it, and I'll consider it. But my instinct is to fight shy of magazines which have a declared character. Why lay down laws about imaginative writing?'[5] This was a clash of two modernisms, each with a different axe to grind. According to Virginia, Lehmann had a relentless tendency to be trendy. Although both Leonard and Virginia had strong left-wing convictions, neither was enamoured of literature which dealt in a traditionally realist manner with political and social issues.

If Leonard had intended to take a back seat to Lehmann in the affairs of the Hogarth Press, he simply could not do it. He disliked *New Writing* and voiced his objection by pointing out that, despite good reviews, it never made any money. Lehmann, painfully aware of this, maintained that the whole point of an enterprise like the Hogarth Press was to give house room to deserving causes. Lehmann may have been difficult, but Leonard and Virginia, whatever their intentions, were unwilling to give effective control of the soul of the Press to anyone. So a difficult situation soon worsened: the Woolfs had to protect the Press from the man to whom they had turned for assistance. In turn, Lehmann felt betrayed.

Virginia remained worried about Vanessa. On 3 February, the day before what would have been Julian's thirtieth birthday, she told her sister how helpless she felt to assist her in any meaningful way. That confession allowed Vanessa to be honest about her feelings: 'You do know . . . how much you help me. I can't show it. I feel so stupid and such a wet blanket often but I couldn't get on at all if it weren't for you – so you mustn't mind my being or seeming so grumpy.'[6] Although she did not say anything about this to her sister, Virginia's work on *Three Guineas* had led her to question further Julian's motives in going to Spain. Perhaps, she speculated, he had been blinded by some male instincts – self-assertion, an inordinate desire to be a public figure – which she criticized severely in her new book.

Almost immediately, Virginia was presented with the example

of a man acting in an extremely opportunistic manner. Eleven years before, Philip Morrell had made overtures to her. In February, he renewed his declaration when he wrote to tell Virginia how much he liked *Jacob's Room*, her own favourite among her books. As before, Virginia immediately retailed the news of Philip's conduct to Vita: 'The husband of a lady in high life. Wishes to meet me clandestinely. I put this in to see if I can rouse jealousy.'[7]

Thin, ascetic-looking David Cecil, who reminded Virginia of the 'stalk of a bluebell',[8] lacked any of the juice of life and, at thirty-six, told Virginia he was completely dried up. In contrast to Lehmann, Morrell and Cecil was Leonard, a man who could be trusted to provide a sympathetic response to *Three Guineas*. On 4 February, he told his much-gratified wife that the book provided an extremely clear analysis of the prevailing social order.

That winter, Virginia worked five hours a day to complete the notes to *Three Guineas* and to correct the proofs of the text. On 24 February, she was still in the process of completing her research. A fortnight later, Leonard issued a stern warning: unless the proofs and notes were dispatched by 16 March, the book's publication would have to be postponed until the autumn. She worked in haste to meet this deadline, but she was recasting the final page of the book on 22 March. She was completing these final touches at the same time that the Hogarth Press published Rose Macaulay's book on Morgan Forster. When Morgan called upon her, he handed her a cutting which referred to Macaulay's assertion that he was the best living novelist. Virginia felt consumed with jealousy and resentment.*

* Later, in September 1938, Virginia was convinced that Forster's 'credo', the essay 'What I Believe', which appeared in the *London Mercury* before being issued as a Hogarth Pamphlet in May 1939, was unjustly praised in comparison with *Three Guineas*. Her point was that Forster's essay – which contains the famous pronouncement: '. . . if I had to choose between betraying my country and betraying my friends, I hope I should have the guts to betray my country' – does not take the considerable risks of her polemic, which attempts not simply to redefine the patriarchy but to subvert it. By that time, Virginia might have been aware that Forster loathed *Three*

In addition, Virginia was worried about the fate of Europe. She was certain that as soon as the 'tiger, i.e. Hitler, has digested his dinner he will pounce again'.[9] She was extremely interested in a sensational murder, one dubbed 'The Torso Case' by the yellow press. That February, the headless and limbless body of a man had been found in the River Severn at Haw Bridge in Gloucestershire. Virginia saw this event as an example of how 'private English disputes come to the surface'.[10] In English families such as her own or the Pargiters, there was an inordinate amount of sexual repression. Passions were not vented and as a result sometimes came boiling to the surface in violent ways.

Having finished a book which is an indictment of the cruelties of men, Virginia was now free to work on her biography of Roger Fry, a man whose life had been devoted to attacking the philistinism of the English and, by implication, the corrupt social regime which fostered it. Moreover, like Joseph Wright, he was a man who had encouraged the professional aspirations of women. Without knowing fully why, she nevertheless found work on the biography unnerving and unsettling. She did not like being bound to the facts which are the spine of any such book. Her other biographies, *Orlando* and *Flush*, had been infused with heavy doses of irony – these are books which mock the form they gleefully imitate. The playful side of Virginia could not be unleashed this time. 'How can one cut loose from facts,' she asked herself on 3 May, 'when there they are, contradicting my theories?'[11] In order to escape the confinement of biographical writing, she had to find another outlet. And so she started to write *Pointz Hall*.* At first, she did not know if this new venture would be a play, a novel or a combination of both. Soon afterwards, she had become so absorbed in her new book that she had no time for Roger Fry.

Guineas: 'In my judgment there is something old-fashioned about this extreme feminism; it dates back to her suffragette youth of the 1910's . . . By the 1930's she had much less to complain of, and seems to keep on grumbling from habit.' (The Rede Lecture (1941), in *Two Cheers for Democracy*, New York: Harcourt, Brace & World, 1942, 242–58)

* The title was changed to *Between the Acts* only on 26 February 1941.

Without being precisely sure of the direction she was taking, Virginia envisaged Pointz Hall, a scenic old house, as the setting for a book which would be centred on 'we' rather than 'I'.[12] The coming of war had a great deal to do with this shift towards an emphasis on community. So did *Three Guineas*. According to that book, English civilization had been corrupted because there had been too much emphasis on the needs of the individual as opposed to the common good, which must be pursued by all the citizens of a nation. War made such a doctrine a necessity: if England was to survive Hitler, it would have to do so with a concentrated collective effort.

A further sense of the fragility of life hit Virginia that spring when on 21 April Ottoline Morrell and then, on 22 May, Ka died. The irony of Ottoline's death, as far as Virginia was concerned, was that it came about as a result of a stroke after being told that the would-be philanderer Philip had a heart condition which could prove fatal. Virginia was harsh on herself when she could not feel much about either death, particularly Ka's.

For Virginia, Ka's life was an example of arrested development: 'After Rupert's death, [Ka] was playing a part.' She had been devoted to her son, loved Cornwall and served as a justice of the peace. Earlier, she had acted as a devoted friend during Virginia's breakdown of 1913, but for ever after Virginia was self-conscious in Ka's presence. She also hated the 'Quack Quack' in her voice. After listing all the things she disliked about Ka, though, Virginia found her way back to the bedrock of affection which had existed between them: 'For there was a trustiness in her; a stable goodness; a tenderness . . . a good deal of fortitude, patience; a determination to oar her way.' The deep silence that had grown between them 'was threaded with something that could vibrate'.[13] Years earlier, Ka had supplied her friend with the maternal affection for which she craved.

Meanwhile, there was the spectre of Hitler 'chewing his little bristling moustache'.[14] Aeroplanes resembling sharks prowled the sky. In this climate of unrest, *Three Guineas* was published on 2 June. It asserts, in part, that society's insistence on placing a premium on the rational at the expense of the emotional has had a devastating effect on men, themselves the architects of the crippling system. The book makes many other key points: war, a long-accepted form of letting off steam, is a public forum for male aggression; murder and mutilation may be more private than war, but they are manifestations of the same terrible corruption; repressed feelings, when they are unleashed, tend to be brutal and vicious; those forces are often turned against women, who, in the end, pay the real price of repression. The rise of Hitler and the 'Torso Case' were public events – reported in the press – but Virginia, as we shall see, had recently become even more acutely aware that she had been the victim of such a system at the hands of Gerald Duckworth.

The voice of the female speaker in *Three Guineas* has the strong, forceful manner of an Old Testament prophet or a latter-day William Blake.* She castigates a society which has acted in a sinful way and admonishes the governing forces to repent. Early on, she makes a crucial point: although men and women may look at the same things, they see them differently. And it is the male gates of perception that have to be cleansed and then opened.

The book is cast in the form of a long letter. This female 'I' responds to a man who has written to ask her how war can be prevented. He is a decent sort, certainly a person of good intentions. However, he has unquestioningly accepted the privileges conferred on him because he was born male and he is extremely naïve about the oppressions endured by women.

> You, then, who ask the question, are a little grey on the temples; the hair is no longer thick on the top of your head. You have reached the middle years of life not without effort, at the Bar; but on the whole your journey has been prosperous. There is nothing parched, mean or dissatisfied in your expression. And without wishing to flatter you, your prosperity – wife,

* In her books, Virginia's aunt, Caroline Emelia Stephen, employed a similar rhetorical stance.

> children, house – has been deserved. You have never sunk into the contented apathy of middle life . . .[15]

This man never responds directly to the observations made by the speaker, but she is deeply sceptical of his complacency. She addresses him in various ways: in turn, she cajoles, scolds, lectures and threatens.

The guineas in the title refer to the payment to be exacted on behalf of women if any genuine change in the social order is to be effected: women must be educated, must enter the professions and must, once they have sufficient education and status, be allowed to remain outsiders at the very same time that they gain power and responsibility: 'we, daughters of educated men, are between the devil and the deep sea. Behind us lies the patriarchal system; the private house, with its nullity, its immorality, its hypocrisy, its servility. Before us lies the public world, the professional system, with its possessiveness, its jealousy, its pugnacity, its greed.'[16]

Constantly, Virginia refers to herself and other women of her class as 'daughters of educated men', but there is a fierce irony at work: would truly 'educated' men have allowed their daughters to exist in a society which excluded them? Moreover, women must be certain that education and professional status do not lead them to become like men. Women must always remain outside the confining values of the patriarchal system.

The anger unleashed in *Three Guineas* is global and personal. On the day before publication, Virginia characterized it as a 'piece of donkey-drudgery'[17] which only repeated in far more sober prose the themes of *The Years*. Since both books had begun life 'lumped' together, it was natural that Virginia would see them as essentially one book. She was quite prepared to have Vita and Ethel loathe *Three Guineas*, but she was relieved when Pippa Strachey, upon receipt of an advance copy, wrote enthusiastically to tell the insecure author that the book was exactly what the women's movement needed. Virginia was glad that the poison was at long last drawn.

In a review which aptly compared Virginia to Lysistrata, the anonymous reviewer in the *Times Literary Supplement* of 4 June

1938 claimed that although the author was renowned for her poetic prose, she had another side: 'It is in her criticism, whether of books or institutions, that the keen edge of her other tool becomes apparent; and that other tool is precision itself, consequence, logic, directed by an irony that is sharp but never inhuman. Mrs Woolf seldom writes a pamphlet, but she is the most brilliant pamphleteer in England.' In *Time and Tide*, Theodora Bosanquet, a great admirer of Virginia, characterized *Three Guineas* as a 'revolutionary bomb of a book, delicately aimed at the heart of our mad, armament ridden world'. This was a book about 'the dark womb of the unconscious . . . where various undesirable eggs hatch into monsters which thrust their way to the surface in fears and oppressions, dictators and mass murders'. There was the possibility that Virginia was merely a Cassandra, but Bosanquet saw her as an Antigone who understood that the real freedom women should pursue was not to break the law 'but to discover the Law, the true pattern of life'.[18]

The *Observer*'s Basil de Selincourt compared Virginia Woolf to Matthew Arnold and spoke of her 'deep wisdom';[19] in the *Spectator* Graham Greene called the book 'a brilliant essay',[20] although he felt that it became shrill when dealing with moral or religious issues. Excellent notices ushered in the 'mildest childbirth'[21] Virginia had ever experienced. She was jubilant, especially when she thought back to the horrible parturition which had accompanied *The Years*. In *Three Guineas* Virginia voiced in unequivocal language her disdain for the system which controlled England, had helped to kill her nephew and was about to lead her nation into another world war. There is nothing playful about the irony in *Three Guineas*: it is an indictment – often a deliberately heavy-handed one – in which Virginia spoke without restraint.

Three Guineas is a book which seeks to educate men and women about the underlying contradictions between them. Only when this issue has been aired and resolved can there be any peace. Dictators at home must be defeated before there is to be any possibility of overcoming dictators abroad. The endnotes are packed with all kinds of information which substantiate the argument, but the most chilling addition to the text is contained in the

Cartoon in Time and Tide, *25 June 1938. The accompanying editorial observed: 'Mrs Woolf's best-seller,* Three Guineas, *descending on the peaceful fold of reviewers, has thrown them into that dreadful kind of internal conflict that leads to nervous breakdown. On the one hand there is Mrs Woolf's position in literature: not to praise her work would be a solecism no reviewer could possibly afford to make. On the other hand there is her theme, which is not merely disturbing to nine out of ten reviewers, but revolting.'*

five photographs which Virginia collected to illustrate it: a general, heralds, a university procession, a judge and an archbishop. In each of these, men are dressed in ceremonial robes or military uniforms.

> [Such clothing] not only covers nakedness, gratifies vanity, and creates pleasure for the eye, but it serves to advertise the social, professional, or intellectual standing of the wearer . . . And still the tradition, or belief, lingers among us that to express worth of any kind, whether intellectual or moral, by wearing pieces of metal, or ribbon, coloured hoods or gowns, is a barbarity which deserves the ridicule which we bestow upon the rites of savages. A woman who advertised her motherhood by a tuft of horsehair on the left shoulder would scarcely, you will agree, be a venerable object.[22]

The photographs in the book are contrasted by Virginia with some others which any reader in the late 1930s could have seen virtually every day in any newspaper.

> Photographs, of course, are not arguments addressed to the reason; they are simply statements of fact addressed to the eye. But in that very simplicity there may be some help. Let us see then whether when we look at the same photographs we feel the same things. Here then on the table before us are photographs. The Spanish Government sends them with patient pertinacity about twice a week. They are not pleasant photographs to look upon. They are photographs of dead bodies for the most part. This morning's collection contains the photograph of what might be a man's body, or a woman's; it is so mutilated that it might, on the other hand, be the body of a pig. But those certainly are dead children, and that undoubtedly is the section of a house.[23]

Virginia is quite clear about the relationship between the five photographs in her book and the absent ones: 'Obviously the connection between dress and war is not far to seek; your finest clothes are those that you wear as soldiers.'[24] If men truly enfranchise women and, in the process, allow them to remain outsiders, there is the possibility that society will be truly changed and, in the process, war prevented. *Three Guineas* is a necessary first step in social revolution: if men learn to look anew, their eyes might finally be opened to the reality endured by all of society's outcasts.

As Virginia expected, her new treatise was not welcomed by some of her friends. Vita, who had responded enthusiastically to *A Room of One's Own* and its defence of androgyny, did not like the strict segregation between male and female in *Three Guineas*; she felt the book was a tissue of misleading arguments. Not unexpectedly, Ethel's response was even gruffer. She accused Virginia of being unpatriotic. Virginia understood the composer's feelings and assured her: 'of course I'm "patriotic" . . . only we must enlarge the imaginative, and take stock of the emotion[al]. And I'm sure I can; because I'm an outsider partly; and can get outside the vested interest better than Leonard even – tho' a Jew.'[25] When Margaret Llewelyn Davies wrote to congratulate her on her courageous book, Virginia told her that she had reacted to the obvious horror in their midst, a tyranny so awful that it 'finally made my blood boil into the usual ink-spray'.[26]

One way of making her blood boil less was to take a holiday. On 16 June, Leonard and Virginia set off on a motor tour of Scotland and the Western Isles. In Midlothian, they stopped at Dryburgh to see Scott's grave. From there they went, by way of Loch Ness, to the Isle of Skye. They stayed three days at Portree before going to Spean Bridge and Ben Nevis, but the torrential rains they encountered at Oban finally forced them to abandon Scotland. On 30 June, they reached Ambleside and then visited Dove Cottage the next morning. They spent the night at Newark and the following afternoon, after taking lunch in Cambridge, they arrived home.

As Virginia had hoped, this journey proved a 'lark'. One day, while Leonard cleaned spark plugs, she read *The Oxford Book of Greek Verse in Translation.* At Portree, the Woolfs met a couple who were fervent believers in the Loch Ness monster: 'They had seen him. He is like several broken telegraph posts and swims at immense speed. He has no head. He is constantly seen.' All this news was conveyed by an amused but sceptical Virginia to her sister, who, before Virginia had set out, had speculated on the fate of Winifred Hambro, the wife of the banker Ronald Hambro. She had been drowned in Loch Ness in August 1932 when her speedboat exploded. This led Virginia to even more hilarious speculations about the legendary creature.

> Well, after Mrs Hambro was drowned, the Insurance Company sent divers after her, as she was wearing 30,000 pounds of pearls on her head. They dived and came to the mouth of a vast cavern, from which hot water poured; and the current was so strong, and the horror they felt so great, they refused to go

> further, being convinced The Monster lived there, in a hollow under the hill, In short, Mrs Hambro was swallowed.[27]

In between moments of composing wonderful pieces of mock reportage, Virginia was taken with the rugged beauty of Scotland, particularly the lavender-coloured hills and mountains. In the Highlands, they came upon a lake in which the trees were perfectly reflected. This sight carried beauty to 'the extreme point'.[28] Virginia broke off this moment of euphoria to ask her correspondent, Ethel: 'Do you like descriptions of nature? or do you skip?'

This trip was a welcome mixture of the comic and the sublime. Virginia was certainly enthusiastic about the Isle of Skye, where, she claimed, the only two industries were sheep and terriers. Even gales of rain did not diminish her pleasure. There was even a happy fairy-tale ending to a horrible day:

> We had a terrific drive yesterday in one of the worst known gales, over the wildest passes. Trees were hurtling; rivers simply cataractuous, but very beautiful, if the rain had stopped; but it didn't. Our petrol gave out; and the oil clogged the engine. But miracles happen, and suddenly an Inn [the Park Hotel, Oban] appeared, in a black gorge; and on opening the door, there were 20 tables with cloths laid diamond shape, maids in white aprons, and 7 different cakes; including the best shortbread I've ever eaten.[29]

Virginia, feeling very much like a child who has survived a potentially disastrous adventure, took great pleasure in the nourishing food awaiting her at this enchanted hotel.

Upon their return, Virginia had to settle back to a very adult task, 'the appalling grind of getting back to Roger'. Again, she was overcome by the plethora of facts which confronted her. She became especially downcast when Marjorie Strachey unsparingly delivered her opinion: Roger Fry did not have a life worthy of biography. She meant that his had not been an existence filled with romantic adventures. Virginia felt that Gumbo might well be right, but she could do nothing to alter Roger's life. In fact, this was the problem; she hated having to lay her mind out in pigeon-holes. Finally, she came to a decision: 'I think I will go on doggedly till I meet him myself – 1909 [1910] – & then attempt something more fictitious. But must plod on through all these letters till then.'[30]

There was a cruel paradox at work. Virginia did not feel that she could give fictional touches to Roger's life until she reached that point in time when she had met him; before that, she was blocked. Her imaginative powers would simply not allow her to take charge of events up to 1909. Her ability as a writer allowed her to transform facts into fiction, but she found it extremely difficult to create from a script prepared by someone else – in this case, the facts of Roger Fry's life.*

Other constraints intervened. Her book had to be reticent about many aspects of her subject's life, especially the mental illness of his wife and his affairs, including the one with Vanessa. Virginia was trapped by this book that forced her to enter an arena in which her father had been a master.† On 29 August, she told Ethel: 'All the

* While completing *Roger Fry*, Virginia wrote 'The Art of Biography' (published in the *Atlantic Monthly* in April 1939), where she spoke of her personal dislike of the genre: '[Biography] imposes conditions, and those conditions are that it must be based upon fact. And by fact in biography we mean facts that can be verified by other people besides the artist.' She goes on to make a crucial distinction between the artist (writer of fiction) and the biographer: 'The artist's imagination at its most intense fires out what is perishable in fact; he builds with what is durable; but the biographer must accept the perishable, build with it, imbed it in the very fabric of his work.' For her the biographer's working terms were ultimately unacceptable.

† During the writing of *The Pargiters* and *The Years*, Virginia had been very concerned with just how much truth could or could not be revealed in a work of fiction. At the time the same issue surfaced in the writing of *Roger Fry*, Virginia was in touch with Katharine Furse, John Addington Symonds's daughter, who felt that the fact of her father's homosexuality had been unceremoniously airbrushed out of the surviving accounts of him. In preparing her account of her family, Furse was anxious to deal frankly with this controversial topic. In a letter of 9 November 1939, Virginia encouraged Furse to follow her inclination to deal 'openly' with this issue: 'I don't think

morning I work my brain into a screw over Roger – what did he do in 1904 – when did his wife go mad, and how on earth does one explain madness and love in sober prose, with dates attached?'[31] Then there was the fact that writing Roger's life made her poignantly aware of his death. In September 1938 she had two gruesome dreams. In the first Julian appeared. The aunt implored her nephew not to go to Spain. He promised to obey but then she beheld his wounds. A bit later, she dreamt that Roger had not died: 'Exactly the old relationship.'[32] Then she awoke to bitter reality.

Roger Fry was a book which tested its author severely. At times, she blessed Roger for giving himself to her to think about. In such a way, she could escape the welter of other unpleasant realities, particularly the fast-approaching war. This project might pose considerable difficulties, but it was a child's sandcastle. However, Hitler and Mussolini were preparing to destroy the real castle of Western civilization with gunpowder and dynamite. 'Much better,' Virginia reflected, 'to play bowls & pick dahlias.'[33]

To spite the masters of destruction, the Woolfs added a library to Monks House. And Virginia was quite capable of fun, as can be seen in her letters to Sybil Colefax, who persisted in inviting Virginia to parties. 'I'm a bat and you're a butterfly. And battishness grows on me. I shall nest in your hair. And aren't bats covered with fleas?'[34] A letter of 5 September to Sybil, who had invited herself to Sussex, is even merrier.

Dearest Sybil,

Yes delighted *Thursday 8th*, but:

(1) View is ruined

(2) No room for chauffeur in house

(3) The smallest possible doghole for you

(4) Village char is cook

Let me know if you are daunted. If not, whether we shall

---

for a moment it would damage your character – rather the other way.' This is excellent advice, but it was a kind of openness which Virginia found difficult to emulate.

meet a train: if so, which.

Yours in haste (not hate) Virginia

No clothes but nightgowns worn here.[35]

The approaching conflict made any attempt at comic bravado difficult. In fact, when she witnessed tank manoeuvres that August, Virginia saw just how much the world of *Three Guineas* was a reality: 'Small boys playing idiotic games for which I pay'.[36] Gas masks had become a necessity in London, where the streets were lined with sandbags. War and art came together when she went to the London Library on 28 September to research Roger's first Post-Impressionist exhibition. An elderly cleaner came by and interrupted her: 'They're telling us to try on our masks.'

'Have you got yours?' she asked him.

'No, not yet.'

'And shall we have war?' she added.

'I fear so, but I still hope not. I live out in Putney. Oh they've sandbags [in the Library]; the books will be moved; but if a bomb strikes the house?' He stopped – and then asked Virginia if he could dust under her chair.[37]

That summer, Virginia was touched by the plight of another elderly person. An old woman who lived near Rodmell had drowned herself: 'The body was found near Piddinghoe – my usual walk. Her son died; she turned queer.'[38] The death of a child or a friend could easily, Virginia was aware, lead to suicide, especially in an atmosphere reeking of the potential collapse of civilization. Virginia would question the point of going on, but then a new project would beckon.

In September 1938, all eyes in England were riveted on Germany, where Neville Chamberlain had gone to meet Hitler and von Ribbentrop. The Munich Pact seemed to purchase peace, but at what price? What if war broke out and the Woolfs evaded death, what then? 'For we, even if we escaped, should have had our noses rubbed in death; ruin; perhaps the end finally of all order.'[39] All their struggles would come to nothing in the wake of mass destruction. The new urban landscape of London was particularly frightening: 'There were heaps of sandbags in the streets, also men digging trenches, lorries delivering planks, loud speakers slowly driving and solemnly exhorting the citizens of Westminster, "Go and fit your gas masks."' Such was peace in our time.

When they were thrown together for long stretches of time in the country and the distractions of London were absent, Leonard and Virginia often quarrelled bitterly. This did not happen that summer or early autumn. Soon after they had settled in at Rodmell, they had a day when the weather was splendid. Virginia was looking forward to her lunch of grilled ham and mushrooms, a game of bowls and then, in the evening, Mozart on the gramophone. She told her husband that she could settle nicely into this 'immortal rhythm'. Leonard rejoined: 'You're not such a fool as you seem.' Usually, such a remark would have enraged her, but on this day she saw it as an affirmation of a shared wish. A bit later, Virginia made tea and was about to call Leonard in when she was stunned with how 'beautiful' he was: 'my heart stood still with pride that he ever married me'.[40]

Virginia was very much afraid that Leonard might die before her. The following spring, they had a discussion about which would mind the other's death most. Leonard claimed that he depended more upon their life together than she did. According to him, Virginia lived in a world of her own, going, for example, on long walks alone. They argued. She was happy to think that she was so much needed. A shared life may have been an immense responsibility, but it often gave great pleasure. If Virginia felt at times that she depended too much on Leonard, he was often fearful that she did not really feel that she needed him. He was also prone to accuse his wife of caring more for her sister than she did for him. Leonard could certainly be a harsh taskmaster. In November 1938, he sent a very reluctant Virginia out shopping in Regent Street to buy suspenders for her stockings, which had come down while they were taking a walk in Tavistock Square. On that day, the horror of shops, 'especially intimate underwear'[41] ones, had been too much and she had returned home empty-handed.

The greatest strength in the Woolf marriage ultimately resided in the understanding that each was the most important person in the other's life. They were also passionately committed to the same causes. Leonard, Virginia knew, was a man very much in the Joseph Wright mould. Priorities sometimes became confused or tangled, but such conflicts were aired. If Leonard was overly bossy, Virginia straightened him out. If Virginia became too obsessional about her work, Leonard warned her of the consequences. For this couple, life in common was not only a buffer but a consolation.

Their Christmas at Rodmell proved dispiriting when Jack Hills and then, two days later, Mitz died. Mitz's lifeless corpse was found dead on Boxing Day: 'her white old woman's face puckered; eyes shut; tail wrapped round her neck. Leonard buried her in the snow under the wall.' Of much more central importance was Jack's death on Christmas Eve. Although Virginia hardly ever saw Stella's husband, she remembered him as the one man in her youth who had been honest about sex. 'Of all our youthful directors,' she told her diary, 'he was the most open minded, least repressive, could best have fitted in with later developments, had we not gone our ways.'[42] Virginia remembered asking him if strong sexual feelings on the part of men could be honourable? Jack had been amused by Virginia's question but not in a nasty or underhand way. He was frank about his strong sexual impulses and that alone made him different from any other man Virginia had known in her youth. What is more, Virginia remembered the love which had enveloped Jack and Stella.

Throughout her life, Virginia had remained deeply troubled by any sort of strong sexual feeling. In December 1939, when she read Freud's *The Future of an Illusion* and *Civilization and Its Discontents*, she became very upset: 'If we're all instinct, the unconscious, what's all this about civilization, the whole man, freedom &c?'[43] Although she did not like to think about it, she had from childhood been deeply troubled by the difference between 'instinct' (which she associated with molestation on the part of Gerald Duckworth) and 'feeling' (the expression of emotions, including those of the body). Sexually speaking, were they not the same thing? They are not and do not have to be, but she found it extremely difficult to separate them. The man who abuses Rose in *The Years* and the general in *Three Guineas* remained for her identical in their aims. In her marriage, Virginia had needed a breathing space from sex because she ultimately saw intercourse with a man as intimidating and invasive. If she could keep this particular manifestation of the instinctual male at bay, she had a good chance of creating her own civilization and a good marriage.

Earlier, at the end of January 1939, when Barcelona fell, Virginia met Freud, for whom the Hogarth Press had long acted as English publisher, at his Hampstead mansion, where he had recently settled. The elderly, dying refugee presented her with a narcissus and assured her that the situation in Germany would have been even worse had England not won the First World War. The Woolfs and Freud, accompanied by two of his children, Anna and Martin, sat in the house's large library. Freud was behind a huge, shiny, scrupulously clean desk, while the others were 'like patients on chairs'.

Anna told the Woolfs that she and her father did not like the house as much as their flat in Vienna. They had been dispossessed. Virginia beheld a powerful man but one who was now shrunken: 'with a monkey's light eyes, paralysed spasmodic movements, inarticulate but alert'. When the Woolfs rose to take their leave, Freud came back to life. What was going to happen? What response would the English make to Hitler?[44]

On the same day, 28 January, Yeats died. Death was everywhere. Virginia asked Ethel: 'What's to be done; Oh dear Ethel, why did our parents conceive us so that we saw this particular stretch of time? I have such an immense capacity for sheer pleasure up my sleeve; and shan't use it this side of the grave.'[45] One 'sheer pleasure' was *Pointz Hall*, a medley to which she turned for relief from the welter of 'Fry facts'. She now saw a 'whole' conceived out of what had once been a 'thread'.[46] One of this book's pleasures was that she did not know what was coming next. Since she was not certain where she was going, it was a glorious adventure. Previously, Virginia would have become upset if she could not discern the precise direction a book was taking. Now, all of a sudden, the unknown proved exhilarating.

Another unknown which Virginia seized upon as relief from 'Fry facts' was the writing of further autobiography, 'A Sketch of the Past', which she began on 18 April. Much longer and more sustained than the earlier 'Reminiscences', '22 Hyde Park Gate' or 'Old Bloomsbury', 'A Sketch' is a vivid re-creation of her Victorian childhood and adolescence. Gerald's incestuous behaviour (divulged for the first time*) and Jack Hills's frank sexuality are described in detail, but the portraits of two women – Julia and Stella – are full, moving and sad. Theirs were thwarted, doomed lives, overshadowed by the insatiable demands of men.

After re-creating Roger's early life, which she found so difficult to imagine, Virginia was drawn back to her own early experiences, the strong memories of which filled her with sorrow, bitterness and now anger. The author of 'A Sketch', who had recently written *Three Guineas*, shows just how much the women of her family were mistreated by its men. In a very real sense, 'A Sketch' was everything that *The Years* had failed to become. One remarkable thing about 'A Sketch' (which was not published until 1976) is that its 'diary-autobiography' form closely resembles the abandoned 'novel-essay' form of *The Pargiters*. The past is always being interrupted by the present.

> 19th July 1939. I was forced to break off again, and rather suspect that these breaks will be the end of this memoir.
>
> I was thinking about Stella as we crossed the Channel a month ago. I have not given her a thought since. The past only comes back when the present runs so smoothly that it is like the sliding surface of a deep river. Then one sees through the surface to the depths.[47]

* George's incestuous conduct had been revealed in the two Memoir Club presentations: '22 Hyde Park Gate' (1921) and 'Old Bloomsbury' (1921–2).

There is a naked, unguarded side to this piece. It proclaims a freedom which the writer had never allowed herself in her published fiction. Seeing through the surface can bring a new sense of liberation, but it can also dredge up too much sewage. Then, it is possible to drown.

Virginia's continuing sense of malaise was also deepened by Hugh Walpole, who confessed to her that he was attracted only to men who were heterosexual. Not only did he suffer terribly from this inclination but he obviously could not use it in his fiction. Walpole lacked the courage to write about his real life, whereas Virginia was finding the courage to do exactly that. But, she discovered, opening up the past in this way can be a hazardous enterprise.

In late winter 1939, Virginia was both disturbed and pleased when Tom Eliot sent her a copy of his verse drama *The Family Reunion*, which is set in a country house, Wishwood. Although there were obvious similarities between it and *Pointz Hall*, Virginia was gratified when she read the play, which she considered an unsuccessful 'experiment with stylised chatter'. Eliot, she told herself, was lyric rather than dramatic. She was 'selfishly relieved' and asked herself: 'Had it been a success would it have somehow sealed – my ideas? does this failure confirm a new idea of mine? . . . Or is it jealousy?'[48]

One consolation among such uncertainties was provided by London and its ripe, tumultuous diversity. One day that winter, Virginia took the bus to Southwark and walked along Thames Street until she came to some stairs which went down to the river. She descended. Then the real adventure began: 'Very slippery; warehouse walls crusted, weedy, worn. The river must cover them at high tide. It was now low. People on the Bridge stared. Difficult walking. A rat haunted, riverine place, great chains, wooden pillars, green slime, bricks corroded, a button hook thrown up by the tide.' She wandered in Fenchurch alleys, through Billingsgate and Leadenhall Markets.[49] The sheer spectacle of the capital, of its mingling of the awful and the beautiful, was simply entrancing.

Before, Virginia's view of community had been largely confined to rural Sussex but now she saw the infinite variety of London as part of the same 'feeling: all England thinking the same thing – this horror of war – at the same moment. Never felt it so strong before'. The trouble was that such feelings of togetherness – which had been at their height during the Great War – could quickly evaporate, leaving behind only a sense of 'private separation'.[50] Even the safety of the countryside could be threatened. One March evening, just as she returned from dining at Charleston, Virginia heard a burglar laughing as he slammed the door to Monks House: he escaped with £6 from the Woolfs' cashbox.

In June 1939, it was still possible to escape to the Continent, this time to Normandy and Brittany. On 5 June, the Woolfs crossed the Channel to Dieppe. They visited Les Rochers, Mme de Sévigné's château near Vitré and continued to Vannes and round the Brittany peninsula to Dinan and Bayeux, where they could forget the coming war and retreat into a world of dancing gypsies and medieval doublets.

When Leonard and Virginia returned to Tavistock Square on 22 June, they had to prepare to move and find a new tenant for their London home. Although their lease at Tavistock Square ran until 1941, the noise caused by nearby demolition work was now overpowering. On 9 May they had viewed and resolved to take 37 Mecklenburgh Square. Mr Pritchard, their solicitor-tenant, moved with them, but he had been unsuccessful in persuading the Bedford Estates to accept an early surrender of the lease.

The house in Mecklenburgh Square, slightly to the east of Brunswick Square, was five storeys high, with cast-iron railings and an ornate entrance. The rent was steep (£250 a year) and there was the worry of finding someone to take on Tavistock Square. The arrangements at their new London home – the Hogarth Press in the basement, Dollman and Pritchard on the ground and first floors and the Woolfs' flat above them – were much as before, but the ground area of the new flat was substantially larger. Soon after they moved there that August, the Woolfs found their new quarters a disappointment: the kitchen was too small and the other rooms much too large.

Worries about two London residences were compounded by an invasion of 52 Tavistock Square by Victoria Ocampo and Gisèle Freund on 23 June. Virginia did not like to sit for photographers, especially as she got older, and she had already refused the twenty-six-year-old Freund, a Parisian of German-Jewish background who specialized in portraits of writers and artists. Without telling Virginia that she would be accompanied by anyone, Victoria had invited herself to Tavistock Square. Virginia was appalled, especially when the usually xenophobic Leonard was charmed by examples of Freund's work. So Virginia was photographed many times that afternoon (or the next day). Knowing that three against one was a difficult situation, she had succumbed, but she was furious, as she informed Victoria in a letter three days later.

> I was annoyed. Over and over again I've refused to be photographed. Twice I had made excuses so as not to sit to Madame Freund. And then you bring her without telling me, and that convinced me that you knew that I didn't want to sit, and were forcing my hand. As indeed you did. It's difficult to be rude to people in one's own house. So I was photographed against my will about 40 times over, which annoyed me. But what particularly annoyed me was that I lost all chance of talking to you. That you will agree is a proof that I did want to see you. And there won't be another chance till Heaven knows when. And Heaven knows too what is the point of these photographs. I can't see it. And I hate it.[51]

Virginia and Victoria never met again.

The surviving photographs from that sitting show an anxious Virginia Woolf, one who languishes under the intrusion of the camera. She looks extraordinarily tired and trapped, and seems to be pleading with the camera to leave her in peace. The day after their visit, Virginia learned of Mark Gertler's suicide. On 14 May, before their holiday in France, Virginia had invited Gertler to dinner in order to learn how the younger generation of artists responded to Roger. That evening, Gertler was in a strident mood and denounced the vulgarity of literature as compared to the integrity of painting. He had also been quite candid about previous attempts at suicide, to which he had been led by 'hitches' in his work. Recently, he had had a successful show. So why did he kill himself? Why did he turn on the gas? This was the closest Virginia could get to an answer: 'A most resolute serious man: intellectual; fanatical about painting, even if a fanatical egoist. And he seemed established . . . Poor of course, & forced to teach; & fundamentally perhaps too rigid, too self centred, too honest & narrow . . . to be content or happy. But with his intellect & interest, why did the personal life become too painful?'[52]

Virginia knew the answer to her query, but she did not want to face it. There is the possibility that one can be too 'fanatical' about work, wrapped up in it to the extent that it becomes the only way of validating the self. Whether an artist's work is actually in decline is irrelevant: if the artist sees the work as finished, he or she might not have anything to live for.

Less than two weeks later, Marie Woolf died. Although Virginia claimed to find Leonard's mother tiresome, she had a deep affection for her. Just as Leonard and Virginia arrived to visit her, she would always ask 'And Virginia?' This joke referred to Marie's supposed disappointment at seeing her non-Jewish daughter-in-law. Then they would laugh. The next question always was: 'And tell me what you have been doing?' Virginia always had a story prepared. However, Virginia did not like it whenever Marie evoked 'the daughter emotion' from her. In the end, Virginia realized that age had taken everything away from her mother-in-law, leaving behind the 'pathetic animal, which was very real; the body that wanted to live'. This passing also made Virginia uncomfortably aware that she had now become a member of the 'elder generation'. Marie's death was followed a few days later by further news of encroaching global strife: the Nazi militarization of the so-called Free City of Gdańsk (Danzig) in northern Poland.

Virginia wanted to be alone and yet not alone. She referred to this as the usual fight between solitude and society. That July she took pleasure in her two tasks: completing her biography of Fry and working on 'A Sketch of the Past'. Yet death had invaded her. When, in preparation for moving there, she visited 37 Mecklenburgh Square on 13 July, she asked herself: 'which of these rooms shall I die in?'[53] Three weeks later, she had become more sure of the interesting possibilities which such a topic presented a writer:

> how interesting it would be to describe the approach of age, & the gradual coming of death. As people describe love. To note every symptom of failure: but why failure? To treat age as an experience that is different from the others; & to detect every one of the gradual stages towards death, which is a tremendous experience, & not as unconscious, at least in its approaches, as birth is.[54]

Chapter Twenty

TRANSFORMATIONS

(1939–41)

The summer of 1939 at Rodmell was not the pleasant retreat to which Virginia had looked forward. She and Leonard fought bitterly about *his* new greenhouse. The proposed location would be a blot on the landscape, she informed him. A very upset Leonard told her that he would, at her insistence, abandon this project, but, at the point of winning this battle, Virginia was aware of his adroitness in 'fathering' the resulting guilt on her. So she felt badly about asserting her rights. A compromise was reached when the site of the greenhouse was relocated to a spot more acceptable to Virginia. Although this quarrel drained her, she was happy when they were reconciled. 'Do you ever think me beautiful now?' she asked. 'The most beautiful of women,' he assured her.[1]

A bit earlier, husband and wife had agreed to disagree about Virginia's essay 'Reviewing', published as a Hogarth Pamphlet on 2 November. In that piece, Virginia, whose own career as a reviewer was now winding down, attacked the profession, asserting it might be a duty to abolish it. Many conflicting judgements of books were continuously inflicted on the public. Might it not be better to take a Gutter and Stamp approach?

> The reviewer is already a distracted tag on the tail of the political kite. Soon he will be conditioned out of existence altogether. His work will be done – in many newspapers it is already done – by a competent official armed with scissors and paste who will be called (it may be) The Gutter. The Gutter will write out a short statement of the book; extract the plot (if

> it is a novel); choose a few verses (if it is a poem); quote a few anecdotes (if it is a biography). To this . . . the reviewer – perhaps he will come to be known as the Taster – will fix a stamp – an asterisk to signify approval, a dagger to signify disapproval.[2]

This was a 'modest proposal', a piece of mischief-making in which Virginia attacked some of the writers who had attempted to invalidate her. Leonard, who understood the droll side of his wife, nevertheless felt compelled to add a 'Note' in which he argued that many of the essay's 'conclusions seem to me doubtful because the meaning of certain facts has been ignored or their weight under-estimated'.[3] Historically, he argued, the reviewer came into existence when the reading public grew to such an extent that the role of the patron was eliminated. Although some reviewers abused their calling, they played, Leonard pointed out, a crucial role in providing readers with opinions on the merits of books they might wish to read or purchase.

A more serious disagreement surfaced early in 1940, when Leonard did not attempt to conceal his disdain for the Roger Fry biography. He gave his wife 'a very severe lecture' on the first half of the book, that portion of the narrative which Virginia herself felt was awful. The book's method, according to Leonard, was plainly wrong: she had chosen to write analysis rather than history. In addition, the book was dull and larded with quotations: 'His theme was that you can't treat a life like that: must be seen from the writer's angle, unless the liver is himself a seer, which R. wasn't. It was a curious example of L. at his most rational & impersonal: rather impressive; yet so definite, so emphatic, that I felt convinced: I mean of failure.'[4]

Leonard's criticisms were, in large part, valid, but why did he choose to be so brutally frank in March 1940? He later admitted that he had reacted 'too emphatically',[5] but this is odd, considering the pains to which he usually went in order to mollify his wife's anxieties. Leonard wanted to be sympathetic, but in 1939–40 he was overwhelmed: by worries about the physical and psychic survival of the Hogarth Press, by his mother's death, by his own recent bad health and by the war. Without doubt, he faltered in his attention to Virginia.

Virginia felt that the quality of life was dissipating, slipping irrevocably away. At Rodmell, there was another suicide – a man in a canoe who shot himself – and sightings of two escaped prisoners. On 28 August 1939, Virginia wondered if the nine o'clock broadcast would bring news of a declaration of war and thus an end to life as they had known it. That day, she walked the downs, lay under a cornstalk and looked at the empty land and pink clouds in front of her. Was all this threatened? Would she still be able to spend her afternoons attempting to beat Leonard at bowls? A few days later, Hitler invaded Poland, which led to England's declaration of war against Germany on 3 September. On that day, while sewing her blackout curtains, Virginia felt that her work as a writer was far more important than any war. At that time she told Vita: 'Of course I'm not in the least patriotic, which may be a help, and not afraid, I mean for my own body. But that's an old body. And all the same I should like another ten years.'[6]

What would another ten years be like? Virginia was concerned about money: would she have to sacrifice her 'old age of independence'[7] and begin writing journalism once again? In London, people ran in and out of each other's houses with torches and gas masks. Huge contraptions dug trenches in the squares. Many windows remained black all day. People scurried in the street, anxious not to be out for too long. There was a preponderance of ambulances but no buses. 'Rats in caves live as we do,' Virginia told Angelica.[8] As her fifty-eighth birthday approached that January, she also wondered whether English society – after the war – could reconstruct itself in such a way that men's 'disabilities' (their inability to relate to women) could be removed, or were 'sex characteristics' indelible? 'How,' she asked the activist Shena, Lady Simon, 'can we alter the crest and the spur of the fighting cock?'[9]

In early 1940, Virginia continued to work on the Fry biography. In addition to worrying about the two uneven parts of the book, which were badly sewn together, she became increasingly aware of how much it was a kind of memorial to Bloomsbury, its ideal of friendship and its special view of the world. Old Bloomsbury had long disappeared but in 1940 its values were threatened with obliteration. If Virginia's book was in part a history and defence of Bloomsbury, it was also an extraordinarily self-reflexive work, in which Virginia inscribed her own intellectual autobiography. She had been much closer to Vanessa, Clive and Lytton than she ever was to the dead painter, but Roger Fry, like herself, had been an innovator, an artist who welcomed the new. His boldness and wide-ranging curiosity were very much like her own. On 26 January, Virginia attempted to define the nature of this remarkable man. After a considerable struggle, she wrested from herself a statement (based in part on Kenneth Clark's assessment of Fry) about her friend which holds equally true for her: 'Although he was remarkably consistent in the main outlines of his beliefs, his mind was invincibly experimental & ready for any adventure, however far it might lead him beyond the boundaries of academic tradition.'[10] He was a person of transformations, a relentless, ruthless and restless voyager.

That January, the Woolfs were snowbound at Rodmell. The car wouldn't start and, even if it had, the roads were covered with ice. She used this 'frozen pause' to complete the long, last 'grind' of Roger.[11] The result was, she told Ethel, a piece of cabinet-making rather than a book. On 9 February, two weeks before sending her typescript to Margery for vetting, Virginia was able to take some pleasure in the book: 'I can't help thinking,' she assured herself, 'I've caught a good deal of that iridescent man in my oh so laborious butterfly net.'[12] Virginia's self-assurance took a knocking that March when Leonard voiced his dislike of the book, but Vanessa and Margery were unstinting in their praise. On 15 March, in a letter of thanks to her sister, Virginia told her that she had been 'haunted by the fear' that she wouldn't like it.[13]

Virginia's confidence suffered another severe blow when Hugh Walpole wrote her a curious letter.

> You are the supreme example of the aesthetic-conscience – there has never been such another in English fiction. But you *don't* write novels. What you write needs a new name. I am the *true* novelist – a minor one but a true one. I know a lot about the novel & a lot about life seen from my very twisted child-haunted angle. Had I been normal I might have been a major novelist.[14]

A week earlier, Hugh had been deeply hurt by Virginia's breezy criticism of his most recent book, *Roman Fountain*, as containing equal parts of good and bad writing. Stung, he decided to make her aware of just how much she and he were the 'opposite ends of the bloody stick'.[15]

Another set-back that winter was an encounter with an outspoken sales assistant at John Lewis. Virginia, who was battling with her 'complex', bought two new sets of clothes. In order to be let off the hook for a further purchase, Virginia told the saleswoman that, since she lived in the country, she did not have to worry about looking London-fashionable. Undaunted, the woman told her that she must have a blue striped coat: 'I don't want you, just because you're in the country, to fling on anything. You've got to think of others.' A demoralized, humiliated Virginia allowed herself to be bullied. It was an awful experience, as if the assistant had seen into her soul. 'Of course,' she reflected, 'I looked a shaggy dowdy old woman.'[16]

Virginia was also upset about her twenty-one-year-old niece Angelica's affair with forty-eight-year-old Bunny Garnett, a person for whom she had little respect, although she did admire his ability to write novels which enjoyed great commercial success. Her diary entry of 6 May is sharply to the point: 'Pray God she may tire of that rusty surly slow old dog with his amorous ways & his primitive mind.'[17] Virginia may have seen Garnett's involvement with her niece as tinged with incestuous feelings. If so, his conduct would have been reminiscent of the Duckworth brothers' towards herself.

★

Although she remained rather suspicious of him, Virginia's friendship with John Lehmann had been renewed. Her essay, 'The Leaning Tower',* demonstrates her growing awareness that the political poetry of the Auden generation could make an important contribution to England's renewal. Previously she had characterized their writings as self-indulgent navel-gazing, but perhaps they were correct to examine their psyches.

> I think there's something in the psycho-analysis idea: that the Leaning Tower writer couldn't describe society; had therefore to describe himself, as the product, or victim: a necessary step towards freeing the next generation of repressions. A new conception of the writer needed: & they have demolished the romance of 'genius' of the great man, by diminishing themselves. They haven't explored . . . the individual: they haven't deepened; they've cut the outline sharper.[18]

Cutting the outline sharper also meant getting more and more in touch with the underlying causes of one's victimhood, a process with which Virginia had now become intimately acquainted. Her mother, she realized, had had two characters, as did her father. 'How I see father from the 2 angles. As a child condemning; as a woman of 58 understanding – I should say tolerating. Both views true?'[19]† She was certainly trying to integrate these two perspectives, but it was proving an unnerving task. When she read *What Happened Next*, the last volume of Ethel's nine-volume autobiography, she told the author: 'you can confess so openly, what I should

* 'This essay was read to the Workers' Educational Association, Brighton, on 27 April 1940 and published in *Folios of New Writing* in the autumn of 1940.

† In 'A Sketch of the Past' (*Moments*, 108) she dated the following citation as of 19 June 1940, but she began reading Freud on 2 December 1939: 'It was only the other day when I read Freud for the first time, that I discovered that this violently disturbing conflict of love and hate is a common feeling; and is called ambivalence.' Her reading of Freud convinced her that it was thus natural (and not shameful) for her to have conflicting feelings about her parents.

have hidden so carefully'.[20] At times, as Virginia confided to her diary on 7 August 1939, she felt surrounded by 'invisible censors'.[21]

If Virginia looked at her parents with a child's eye, they – especially her mother – usually seemed beautiful, kind, ethereal creatures; to look at them in any other way – as she was doing in 'A Sketch' – was a deeply disturbing, and potentially self-destructive, experience. It was possible to paste over the traumas of the past, but there was a heavy price to pay: the truth had to be sacrificed. But genuine introspection could also exert an intolerably high price: it is easy to remember too much.

While Virginia was trying to sort out these two conflicting strands, she became more active in the Women's Institute at Rodmell, of which she later became Treasurer. On 6 April 1940, she told Margaret Llewelyn Davies that this group had just asked her to write a play for the villagers to act. Sometimes life has a curious way of imitating art: in *Pointz Hall*, Miss La Trobe writes and produces the village pageant. Virginia did not write a play for Rodmell, but she acted in village plays written by the gardener's wife and the chauffeur's wife. If England was to survive, she was convinced, individuals had to allow their identities to be subsumed into collective projects, such as pageants.

Virginia also had the curious feeling that her own 'writing "I"' had vanished and that an audience for her work was fast disappearing. These feelings were deepened by the mass evacuation at Dunkirk and by her sighting on 30 May of a hospital train laden with the wounded. She was also afraid of what a German victory would mean to her personally, as the wife of a Jew. She and Leonard had decided not to face death in a concentration camp; they would asphyxiate themselves in their garage. That spring and summer, Rodmell burnt with rumours that invasion was imminent. Some of the villagers were convinced that German spies had infiltrated the area. On 25 May, the tongue-wagging concerned the nun on the bus who paid her fare with a hand that looked suspiciously like a man's. Meanwhile, life went on. The Woolfs played bowls most days and shuddered during the nights that aeroplanes flew overhead.

She did not want a 'garage to see the end of me'.[22] That summer, even though she endured her usual 'after book' depression, she renewed her wish for ten more years in which to write. This time, the twinges were not too bad, but she was left with conflicting emotions. She was glad to have given Roger a 'kind of shape' after death. She even felt sexually joined to her subject, 'as if we together had given birth to this vision of him: a child born of us'.[23] These were very consoling thoughts, in part because the biography contains so many deeply personal elements.

And yet, she asked herself, why did she bother to write? Each of her books accumulated a 'little of the fictitious V.W. whom I carry like a mask about the world'.[24] To what extent, she wondered, had her books removed her from life? The irony is that the writing life was the only existence she knew – or had ever really wanted. What if that pursuit had been a false one? What if she could no longer do it?

In the *Spectator*, Herbert Read praised Virginia's skills as a biographer, strengths markedly different from those demonstrated in her fiction and essays: 'Some of Mrs Woolf's readers, accustomed to the very personal quality of her imaginative writing, will perhaps be surprised at the cool and level stretch of this narrative; and if they have found her critical essays sometimes too oblique and coy, they will be pleased with a new firmness and directness.' According to him, the book's limitations were obvious: it was an insider's point of view. At this juncture in his review, Read castigated both Fry's life of privilege and Bloomsbury. Ultimately, all of Fry's efforts 'did not bring him into any very vital sympathetic relationship to his own age'.[25] This was a very questionable judgement, one which infuriated Virginia. If Fry's life had been worthless, so, Virginia could reasonably draw the conclusion, was hers. Read's view of Fry was seconded by D. S. MacColl in the *Observer*.

What would Bloomsbury, which had disdained *Three Guineas*, think of the book? As Virginia expected, Desmond MacCarthy was laudatory in the *Sunday Times*, but she had been worried that Morgan Forster would refuse to write on it. She was thus deeply pleased by his notice in the *New Statesman and Nation*, in which he mentioned that everything Fry stood for was being destroyed:

> Good sense has gone, so have the pursuit of truth, peacefulness, and France. In their places stand pernicious idealism, propaganda, violence, Hitler . . . the book, besides being good and sad, is sustaining. Directly and indirectly, it counsels endurance. Directly, because Fry had a great deal of private sorrow to bear and surmounted it successfully and even gaily. Indirectly, because we see functioning through him one of the finer sorts of human activity . . . Like most of us, Mrs Woolf preaches best when she does not preach, and her accurate account of her friend's life, her careful analysis of his opinions, have as their overtone a noble and convincing defence of civilization.[26]

Morgan understood that, in addition to being a defence of Bloomsbury, her new book was an apologia for friendship, the quest for truth and the pursuit of the good. When Ethel read the book she detected an 'invisible' and 'submerged'[27] Virginia at every turning and thus discerned the book's autobiographical content. Violet Dickinson enjoyed the Fry biography enormously. The grateful author told her that she was pleased that the long labour was over: 'I'm so old I could write a life of myself.' Significantly, she added: 'But I remember too much.'[28]

A serious objection to the Fry biography came from the edge of Bloomsbury. In 1938, Benedict, Vita's elder son, assisted Virginia by annotating, from his perspective as an art historian, some of Roger's essays. Virginia was thus a bit surprised when Ben, who was serving in an anti-aircraft battery, wrote that August to voice complaints about *Roger Fry* which were similar to Herbert Read's: 'I am so struck by the fool's paradise in which he and his friends lived. He shut himself out from all disagreeable actualities and allowed the spirit of Nazism to grow without taking any steps to check it.'[29] Virginia thought her book proved the opposite, as she angrily informed the young man on 13 August:

> Lord, I thought to myself, Roger shut himself out from disagreeable actualities, did he? Roger who faced insanity, death and every sort of disagreeable – what can Ben mean? Are Ben and I facing actualities because we're listening to bombs dropping on other people? And I went on with Ben Nicolson's biography. After returning from a delightful tour in Italy, for which his expensive education at Eton and Oxford had well fitted him, he got a job as keeper of the King's pictures. Well, I thought, Ben was a good deal luckier than Roger. Roger's people were the very devil; when he was Ben's age he was earning his living by extension lecturing and odd jobs of reviewing . . . Who on earth, I thought, did that job [of making people aware of the transforming power of art] more incessantly and successfully than Roger Fry? Didn't he spend half his life, not in a tower, but travelling about England addressing masses of people, who'd never looked at a picture and making them see what he saw? And wasn't that the best way of checking Nazism?[30]

Ben wrote back to say his quarrel was really with Bloomsbury, not Roger Fry.* In a draft response (not posted), she reiterated her point that Bloomsbury had served useful social purposes and she used her own life as a woman – not an existence as privileged as Roger's or Ben's – to prove this:

> But in fact I am not responsible for anything Roger did or said. My own education and my own point of view were entirely different from his. I never went to school or college. My father spent perhaps £100 on my education. When I was a young woman I tried to share the fruits of that very imperfect education with the working classes by teaching literature at Morley College; by holding a Women's Cooperative Guild meeting weekly; and, politically, by working for the vote. It is true I wrote

* Benedict Nicolson to Virginia Woolf, 19 August 1940 (Monks House Papers, MS Sussex): 'Bloomsbury despairing of educating the masses, ignored the stupidity and ignorance surrounding it, to cultivate the exquisite sensibilities which it alone understood and valued.'

books and some of those books, like the Common Reader, A Room of One's Own and Three Guineas . . . have sold many thousand copies. That is, I did my best to make them reach a far wider circle than a little private circle of exquisite and cultivated people.

. . .

My puzzle is, ought artists now to become politicians? My instinct says no; but I'm not sure that I can justify my instinct. I take refuge in the fact that I've received so little from society that I owe it very little. But that's not altogether satisfactory; and anyhow it doesn't apply to you. I suppose I'm obtuse, but I can't find your answer in your letter, how it is that you are going to change the attitudes of the mass of people by remaining an art critic?[31]

The letter which Virginia finally sent may have been more pacific, but her fury was very real. She had become even more aware of two classes of people: outsiders and insiders. The women and the poor were outsiders, whereas most men of her class were insiders: 'I like outsiders better. Insiders write a colourless English. They are turned out by the University machine. I respect them. Father was one variety. I don't love them. I don't savour them. Insiders are the glory of the 19th century.'[32] Virginia was of the twentieth century, the one which had promised – but failed – to take the privations of the outsiders into account.

The Battle of Britain began on 10 July when RAF fighter-command airbases in south-east England became the targets of the Germans. Until the London Blitz began two months later, rural Sussex was thus one of the prime targets of the German offensive. In the first flush of success, Hitler even invited England to capitulate on 19 July. The nightmare had become reality.

On 28 August Virginia saw a large two-decker plane circle slowly over the marsh. Then it dipped into the fir trees in the direction of Lewes. Presently, she heard a droning sound as two planes flew high overhead. The first plane – 'a Jerry' – had been hit and was looking for a safe place to land. The other two were RAF in pursuit. Two days later, while bombs were being dropped over Sissinghurst, Vita telephoned Virginia, who a few minutes later penned a letter to her friend: 'I've just stopped talking to you. It seems so strange. It's perfectly peaceful here – they're playing bowls – I'd just put flowers in your room.'[33] Sometimes, life still seemed so ordinary, but this was only a veneer. Later that afternoon, Virginia played bowls and enjoyed the hot summer weather. In the night the sound of the planes was deafening. That noise was followed by explosions as bombs found targets.

There was a brief, uneasy lull before the Blitz began. On 10 September, a bomb dropped on 37 Mecklenburgh Square but did not detonate. John Lehmann and the Woolfs had made contingency plans to move the Press and on the next day Leonard and Virginia went up to London to assist John in making some sort of arrangements. When they reached the square, they discovered that their new London residence was sealed off because of the unexploded bomb. Virginia and Leonard pushed their way through the assembled crowd and saw the smoking remains of the house opposite theirs. Then they walked to Holborn: 'All heaps of glass, water running, a great gap at top of Chancery Lane; my typist's office demolished.'

Back in Rodmell the next day, Virginia conceived the idea for a new book while picking blackberries. Some of Churchill's defiant courage had penetrated her. She could have another creative decade 'if Hitler doesn't drop a splinter into my machine'. But her heart was filled with sadness at the fate of London, of its alleys and little courts. The day before she had walked to the Tower in order to feel anew her love for the city and its history. She was especially touched by the tough resilience of the cockneys. On that day, she had seen a grimy old woman, badly shaken by the raid, preparing herself for yet another. That was real courage. 'Dear me,' she told Ethel, 'I'm turning democrat.'[34]

The bomb at number 37 finally went off a few days later. Most of the books in the flat remained unhurt on their shelves, but in the basement books, files, paper, cases of type and the printing machine were reduced to a sodden mess. On 24 September, Leonard and Virginia cleared out what they could from their former living quarters and plans were finalized to move the Hogarth Press to the Garden City Press at Letchworth, an hour's train-ride north-east of London. That autumn, the Woolfs moved house to Rodmell. Virginia was selfishly glad to be going to the country, but she felt guilty about leaving Lehmann and the other staff at the Hogarth Press to fend for themselves.

At Rodmell, bowls had become Virginia's hobby and into it she creatively channelled her anxieties. Her competitive instincts certainly became mightily aggrieved whenever Leonard bested her. She was also full of animosity about the proximity of Helen Anrep* and her children. 'My present grumble,' she informed Ethel, is that 'friends whom I dislike ... are refuging in the village.' Virginia, who never liked being 'dropped in on', was furious when Helen did this. Cooking became a soothing pastime and Virginia even took to bottling honey. What was agreeable in an odd fashion was the way her neighbours – of every class – were now pulling together. Even the tweed-wearing, dull county women were showing remarkable good sense in the way they organized first aid, 'putting out bombs for practise [*sic*], and jumping out of windows to show us how'. Earlier, while working on the Fry biography and being exposed to the petty jealousies which consumed the art world, she had 'almost lost faith in human beings . . . Now hope revives again.'[35]

Virginia's new project came directly out of this experience. On 12 September, she returned to an idea which had long been simmering: 'a Common History book – to read from one end of literature including biography; & range at will, consecutively'.[36] (Two years before, she had thought of collecting her reading notes together for some kind of book dealing with the entire range of

* 'Earlier, in 1938, Virginia, although ruffled by Helen's outspoken criticism of *Three Guineas*, had offered to pay off her overdraft of £50. She was appalled when £50 turned out to be £150. Virginia disliked Helen, particularly her offhand attitude towards sexuality, but she was also aware of her vitality.

English literature. A bit later, she considered writing a critical book in the form of a diary.) Five days later, on 17 September, she went to the public library in Lewes in order to look for a history of English literature. The next day, she began 'Reading at Random/Notes' in a notebook devoted solely to this new project. From these jottings, she completed a draft of one essay ('Anon') and a small portion of another ('The Reader').

The pageant in *Pointz Hall* centres on four periods in English life and literature (the Renaissance, the eighteenth century, the Victorian era and contemporary life), and Virginia worked on her new novel at the same time as making entries into her new notebook. Although long fascinated with obscure lives in the *Common Readers*, she had obviously decided that the format employed in those two previous books – a series of essays on various aspects of English literature, dealing with the famous and the not so famous – was no longer suitable for the book which would have been her third *Common Reader*.

The clearest idea of the direction in which Virginia intended to turn can be gained from 'Anon', where she celebrates the origins of the English literary tradition and its greatest and most prolific author, Anonymous: 'sometimes man; sometimes woman. He is the common voice singing out of doors. He has no house. He lives a roaming life crossing the fields, mounting the hills, lying under the hawthorn to listen to the nightingale.'[37] Anon is anonymous, definitely not androgynous; she or he lives outside of gender and is in contact with the fundamental needs and desires of society, which seem to be a composite of the best parts of medieval England, where the people are in tune with each other and with nature.

> Anonymity was a great possession. It gave the early writing an impersonality, a generality. It gave us the ballads; it gave us the songs. It allowed us to know nothing of the writer: and so to concentrate upon his song. Anon had great privileges. He was not responsible. He was not self conscious. He is not self conscious. He can borrow. He can repeat. He can say what

> every one feels. No one tries to stamp his own name, to discover his own experience, in his work. He keeps at a distance from the present moment. Anon the lyric poet repeats over and over again that flowers fade; that death is the end. He is never tired of celebrating red roses and white breasts. The anonymous playwright has like the singer this nameless vitality, something drawn from the crowd in the penny seats and not yet dead in ourselves. We can still become anonymous and forget something that we have learnt when we read the plays to which no one has troubled to set a name.[38]

Anon, in touch with the forces of life, was not concerned with her or his own existence and as such created great art, which was both impersonal and communal. The destruction of the oral tradition at the advent of the printed book created a society where people were more self-conscious and, ultimately, selfish. In a time of great calamity, England has to return to the spirit of its ancient lineage in order to endure. This was the task to which Virginia now turned in both her critical writing and her new novel.

At times, however, she was not so sure that she liked the rural community to which she was confined. Before, her existence had been a mix of the urban and the suburban. Now, she felt marooned. In fact, she did not really enjoy the 'lazy life' to which she was reduced.

> Breakfast in bed. Read in bed. Bath. Order dinner. Out to Lodge. After rearranging my room (turning table to get the sun: Church on right; window left; a new very lovely view) tune up, with cigarette: write till 12; stop; visit L.: look at papers; return; type till 1. Listen in. Lunch. Sore jaw. Can't bite. Read papers. Walk to Southease. Back 3. Gather & arrange apples. Tea. Write a letter. Bowls. Type again. Read Michelet [the historian] & write here. Cook dinner. Music. Embroidery. 9.30 read (or sleep) till 11.30. Bed. Compare with the old London day. Three afternoons someone coming. One night, dinner party. Saturday a walk. Thursday shopping. Tuesday

going to tea with Nessa. One City walk. Telephone ringing. L. to meetings.[39]

This passage is deliberately written in a staccato style. Whether she liked it or not, Virginia often took great pleasure in a busy, frenetic life, filled with all sorts of activities, and she became very restless when her London life vanished.

Virginia was stranded. Although she had removed herself from London to protect her life, the countryside was still very dangerous. She might be killed by a bomb at Rodmell. What would this experience be like? She could imagine the sensation of being reduced to a 'suffocating nonentity', one who would suffer the additional indignity of not being able to write about the experience. She could also imagine the bones in her head crushing her 'very active eye & brain: the process of putting out the light'. She would be terrified, then she would swoon, take a few gulps of air in order to remain conscious '& then, dot dot dot'.[40]

Two weeks later, in the middle of October, she became aware of the poignant loveliness of a red admiral butterfly feasting on an apple. 'Who'll be killed tonight?' she immediately asked herself.[41] Later, she was delightfully startled when she beheld a yellow woodpecker nestled in ruby-red willows. Never before in her life had Virginia been so alive to the beauty of the world and in a moment that beauty might be snatched from her.

Her sense of life's precarious imbalance was heightened that October when she visited Tavistock and Mecklenburgh Squares. At the former, she could see a piece of her studio wall standing, but otherwise there was rubble where she had written so many of her books. Her new home was chaos – litter, dust, plaster, glass – even though one of the drawing rooms had survived almost intact. Despite all these sorrows and her growing patriotism, Virginia felt that England had to change its attitude towards its outsiders so that its warriors had something worth defending in place of the oppressive regimes which had long governed the country. This is the theme of 'Thoughts on Peace in an Air Raid', published in the *New Republic* that October:

> We are equally prisoners tonight – the Englishmen in their planes, the Englishwomen in their beds. But if he stops to think he may be killed; and we too. So let us think for him . . . if we are to compensate the young man [after the war] for the loss of his glory and of his gun, we must give him access to the creative feelings. We must make happiness. We must free him from the machine. We must bring him out of his prison into the open air.[42]

Virginia herself could be a bit rigid about maintaining class barriers. She was furious when Mr Freeth, the air-raid warden at Rodmell, gave her a dressing-down: 'Every night you show a light. No other house does.' The next time, he threatened, she would be fined or sent to prison. Virginia tried her 'lady battery' on him.[43] When this proved unavailing, she lamented his lack of manners.

On seemingly more clear-cut issues, Virginia was resolute. She was defiant when Morgan Forster asked if he could propose her name for the London Library Committee. 'I don't want to be a sop – a face saver.'[44]* The Woolfs had other problems: they had to deal with what Virginia called John Lehmann's 'crybaby' attitude towards the Hogarth Press, which had been left largely in the young man's hands. There were other, minor difficulties. One day, while out for a walk, Virginia fell headlong into a 6-foot hole and came home dripping wet like a spaniel. 'How odd,' she reflected, 'to be swimming in a field. Mercifully I was wearing Leonard's old brown trousers.'[45] Now she would have to buy a pair of cords for herself.

Late that November, Virginia completed *Pointz Hall*, which had another working title, *The Pageant*. She felt triumphant. Somehow, this book was more quintessential than the others. Beginning life

* Virginia claimed that Morgan had in 1935 'sniffed about women on Committee', but her diary entry for 9 April of that year gives the impression that he had mentioned her name as a possible new committee member and been snubbed by the other members of the committee.

as an escape from *Roger Fry*, it had allowed her to escape the drudgery of biography. In the future, she again reminded herself, she must have two projects on the go at once: an imaginative book and a factual one. Work on the two should be alternated, allowing her to take full advantage of her poetical and critical sides.

For many years, she had asserted that if they were truly to stake their claim to a place in the literary tradition women must write poetry. She herself had attempted to infuse prose fiction with the flow and intimacy of the lyric. For the pageant in *Pointz Hall*, she wrote poetry, a remarkable turning point in the career of a writer who had never before written or published verse. The form of the book is taken from another genre: drama. Pointz Hall, the home of the Oliver family for 120 years, is the setting of the village pageant, which portrays nothing less than the entire sweep of English history and literature. This entertainment, a composite of songs, tableaux, parody, pastiche and dramatic encounters, takes place between the acts of a drama being enacted among members of the Oliver family.

The Olivers open and close the book and the pageant disrupts the presentation of the troubled marriage of Isa and Giles Oliver. As the book proceeds, it is difficult to know which narrative predominates. This is precisely the point: the life histories of individuals – especially their deep-seated longings and conflicts – are placed in diametric opposition to the story of society. Are the claims of the individual paramount or should the single person give way to the state? Can a resolution be found which allows the claims of both the individual and society to be fused agreeably?

Bart Oliver and Lucy Swithin are brother and sister. Bart, a kindly curmudgeon, embodies many patriarchal attitudes, whereas his sister, a person capable of the occasional brilliant insight, is less forceful and powerful. Giles, Bart's son, is a stockbroker who would rather be living the life of a country squire. He is a thoroughly dissatisfied person who attempts to deal with his emotional conflicts by enacting them sexually. Isa, Giles's wife, is aware of her husband's philandering, which obviously infuriates her. She has strong sexual needs, which her husband is not fulfilling. She too has a roving eye, but she would like to be reconciled with her husband. This is the melodramatic action which the drama of the pageant disrupts. On that day, Isa is particularly angry with her husband because he is openly flirting with Mrs Manresa, a wild, beautiful woman. Despite her anger and her attraction towards other men, Isa retains love and sexual passion for her husband. Her feelings, a composite of love and hate, are a shock even to herself.

More than any other book by Virginia, *Pointz Hall* is filled with sexuality and violence. Many passages in the book are written in a Lawrentian manner, as when Giles's rage is brilliantly brought to life in an encounter with a snake.

> Dead? No, choked with a toad in its mouth. The snake was unable to swallow: the toad was unable to die. A spasm made the ribs contract; blood oozed. It was birth the wrong way round – a monstrous inversion. So, raising his foot, he stamped on them. The mass crushed and slithered. The white canvas on his tennis shoes was bloodstained and sticky. But it was action. Action relieved him.[46]

This is the way men have often dealt with their emotions: Giles directs his fury at the snake because his strong feelings, which are diffuse and repressed, have no real outlet. So the animal suffers because of the man's feelings. This is the real 'monstrous inversion' being described in the above passage.

Miss La Trobe, the impresario of the pageant, partakes of both worlds but is a member of neither. Her sense of individuality makes her an outcast and yet she knows that any hope for the survival of the species lies in a communal sense of shared purpose. She lives between the two worlds of this book. She shuns the company of others, yet is the author of a pageant which demonstrates the value of togetherness. She is the quintessential outsider, whose origins are cloaked in mystery:

> Rumour said that she had kept a tea shop at Winchester; that

> had failed. She had been an actress. That had failed. She had bought a four-roomed cottage and shared it with an actress. They had quarrelled. Very little was actually known about her. Outwardly she was swarthy, sturdy and thick set; strode about the fields in a smock frock; sometimes with a cigarette in her mouth; often with a whip in her hand; and used rather strong language – perhaps, then, she wasn't altogether a lady? At any rate, she had a passion for getting things up.[47]

La Trobe's brand of passion may be a different one from that of Giles or Isa, but it is very real. There is some suggestion of lesbianism in the biographical details provided about Miss La Trobe, who seems in some ways to be a composite of Rose and Elvira from *The Pargiters*.

Early in *Pointz Hall*, there is an oblique reference reminiscent of material in the earlier book. In *The Times*, Isa reads

> 'A horse with a green tail . . .' which was fantastic. Next, 'The guard at Whitehall . . .' which was romantic and then, building word upon word, she read: 'The troopers told her the horse had a green tail; but she found it was just an ordinary horse. And they dragged her up to the barrack room where she was thrown upon a bed. Then one of the troopers removed part of her clothing, and she screamed and hit him about the face . . .'[48]

This is not an imagined event. On 27 April 1938, the day after Virginia had first recorded her Pointz Hall project, a young girl of fourteen was raped by guardsmen, who lured her into their barracks by promising to show her a horse with a green tail. This incident was far more depraved than Rose's encounter with the man in *The Pargiters*, but the episodes are remarkably similar. In each, men impose their sexual wills upon women.

Sexuality in *Pointz Hall* is presented in three vastly different ways. Although fragmented, there is genuine sexual passion between the Olivers; Miss La Trobe has removed herself from the sexual arena; and the soldiers impose their sexual wills upon a young girl. At the very same time that she was composing *Pointz Hall*, Virginia had written for the first time about Gerald Duckworth's misdeeds. In her new novel, the young girl is inveigled into entering the barracks because the soldiers promise something which seems straight out of a fairy-tale. The girl's curiosity is her undoing. Gerald's behaviour as the elder, evil stepbrother who takes advantage of his young sister has a similar kind of aura.

Miss La Trobe, an eccentric cast from the same mould as Rose and Elvira, might possibly have suffered an experience similar to the girl's – or Virginia's. The reader is not given any information on this topic, but La Trobe exists apart from the hall and the village although her pageant is about communal experience. In her final attempt to demonstrate how the past and the present must be integrated, she shows the startled audience its own mirror-image. Her megaphoned voice proclaims: '*Look at ourselves, ladies and gentlemen! Then at the wall; and ask how's this wall, the great wall, which we call, perhaps miscall, civilization, to be built by . . . orts, scraps and fragments like ourselves?*'[49] This is deeply stirring, a timeless moment of being. In writing about Roger Fry, Virginia had been put in touch with his great love of the beauty beyond physical appearances; in 'A Sketch of the Past' she evoked the unseen mysteries hovering at the edge of daily existence. At this point in her new book, the individual is forced to see how he or she is a vital part of the enduring fabric of English life.

At the end, convinced that her vision is not understood, Miss La Trobe skulks off: 'Grating her fingers in the bark, she damned the audience. Panic seized her. Blood seemed to pour from her shoes. This is death, death, death, she noted in the margin of her mind; when illusion fails.'[50] She is confident (wrongly) that she has failed in her attempt to control and move an audience.

After the pageant has ended and their guests have departed, Giles and Isa prepare to confront each other:

> Alone, enmity was bared; also love. Before they slept, they must fight; after they had fought, they would embrace. From that embrace another life might be born. But first they must

> fight, as the dog fox fights with the vixen, in the heart of darkness, in the fields of night . . .
>
> Then the curtain rose. They spoke.[51]

The fight is a piece of drama which the audience is not allowed to witness, but in the showdown between husband and wife there will be anger, love, sex and procreation. Isa and Giles will be at one with nature.

Miss La Trobe's pageant has helped them to become more aware of their individual selves and to once again commit themselves to each other. The book thus ends on a very positive note, but Miss La Trobe, the artist figure whose name is a composite of trope and troubadour, remains a marginalized, lonely figure, one almost outside of gender. In her pageant, she has, like Anon, used the oral tradition to promote her vision of a world united in purpose. And like Anon, she does not seek to have her individual, authorial voice gain supremacy. Her pageant ends with the participants dressed in a wide assortment of costumes from different ages and then the audience sees itself as a part of this heterogeneous mix. Actors and audience are fused together in a single moment, but each epiphany is different for each person; they must obviously cobble together their own visions from ort, scraps and fragments. The artist must not impose her own vision. She has merely provided the opportunity for others to have such an experience. She is invisible.

The Years had been an unnerving, disturbing experience for its author, in large part because she retreated from the frankness so evident in *The Pargiters*. *Pointz Hall* has a direct, naked honesty which Virginia as a writer of fiction had previously avoided. Rose and Sara in *The Years* are difficult characters to understand, in large part because so much vital information about them has been dropped. In contrast, Virginia does little or nothing to make the eccentric Miss La Trobe appealing: she is a woman with a strong vision of the world and, like Virginia in *Three Guineas*, she has strident views on the corrupt nature of patriarchal society. One of the greatest successes of *Pointz Hall* is its unbridled frankness.

However, candour can be bought at a heavy price. With the episode of the horse with the green tail, Virginia showed once again how treacherous men can be and there is certainly betrayal in Giles's behaviour towards his wife. But there is also a great deal of genuine passion, which seems to have found an appropriate outlet at the end of the narrative, which will allow the Oliver marriage to grow. Directness in dealing with sexual matters had been evaded or treated in a low-key manner in Virginia's previous novels. Here, sex between man and woman finds strong, vibrant expression. This is a remarkable change in direction.

Perhaps Virginia finally got in touch with what her marriage could have been but never had because of so many horrible events in her childhood. In her new book, she saw fully into the world of sexuality and became aware in the process of just how outside the cycle of married sexual love her life had been. She might have become more aware of Leonard's sexual needs, to which she, for very understandable reasons, had never been able to respond. There is a heavy sadness in this book. At one point, Isa meditates on the fate of a local woman who drowned herself; later, when contemplating such an end to her own life, she considers the awful consequences of removing herself from the beauty and harmony of the natural world.

Despite the melancholia, *Pointz Hall* is a playful book, one which displays its author's expanded range. Part of the book's brilliance lies in its indeterminacy. At the end, Miss La Trobe, who equates creative failure with death, retreats into silence, whereas Giles and Isa are about to quarrel, perhaps noisily. Each member of the audience has had a vision, but each vision is different. Individuality and communality are both espoused, but Virginia resists the temptation to impose any sort of finality on the orts, scraps and fragments which constitute this brilliantly orchestrated book, which thus has a fragmentary quality. Each piece of the jigsaw is examined, but the pieces are deliberately not joined together.

A similar feeling of incompleteness now invaded the writer, who constantly felt jangled. She was understandably rattled when

Margot Asquith began to deluge her with strange letters about her sex life, as Virginia informed Ethel that November: 'For some reason she writes to me passionately daily. She sent for me in London, and told me the story of her sexual organs. Cold, as you can imagine.'[52] Virginia's disdain for Margot's revelations was twofold. She did not want to hear these confessions, but she also did not wish to learn more about a predicament which bore an uncanny resemblance to her own.

Yet, the pursuit of honesty had been unleashed. When Ethel confided that masturbation was a topic that even she could not write about, Virginia understood. Reticence had always been part of her make-up. But she went on to say: 'as so much of life is sexual – or so they say – it rather limits autobiography if this is blacked out . . . I still shiver with shame at the memory of my half brother, standing me on a ledge, aged about 6, and so exploring my private parts. Why should I have felt shame then? But why should I be writing these sexual speculations now?'[53] Virginia was writing about these emotions because she had at last come directly in touch with them. Those feelings may have liberated her fiction, but the world of Isa and Giles was closed off from her. Her own life had been more like that of Miss La Trobe, the artist who equates creative failure with death.

Virginia had never been able (or allowed) to live an existence which included the procreation of children. Books had been her offspring. Now she realized – well after the menopause – just how removed she had been from one aspect of nature's fecundity. She had been placed – and to a certain extent, placed herself – outside that cycle of reproduction. Her corresponding sense of freedom, which had assisted her to speak with an extraordinary frankness in *Three Guineas* and *Pointz Hall*, was accompanied by a sense of how much of her life had been spoiled for her at a very young age.

Only on 26 February 1941, the day she gave Leonard the typescript, did *Pointz Hall* become *Between the Acts*, a title with many meanings. The book takes place on a mid-June afternoon in 1939, about ten weeks before Britain's declaration of war against Germany. So the action of the book is set on the eve of war but between two world conflicts. The title centres the book on the world of the Olivers, whose lives are described between the acts. 'Acts' obviously refers to sexual intercourse, the action of the book covering a period of time when Isa and Giles have not made love.

When Miss La Trobe leaves the scene of the pageant, she is filled with an overwhelming sadness, very much like the speaker in Yeats's 'The Circus Animals' Desertion'. She has given her life to art but what has life given back to her? She feels that her gift has been either spurned or misunderstood. She retreats into gloomy solitude. These were some of the feelings which invaded Virginia late in 1940. Where was her place? She had devoted herself to the life of writing but had she in the process cut herself off from too many things? Had she ever had a choice in the matter? There was the terror which was never far away: what if she could no longer create? Was anything left? When Desmond rhapsodized about Tom Eliot's *East Coker*, Virginia was consumed with jealousy. She decided to be strict with herself. She had to follow her own path. Significantly, she said: 'That is the only justification for my writing & living.'[54]

Leonard liked *Between the Acts* enormously. He told Virginia the truth: it was one of her best books. Since she had never really recovered from his repudiation of the Fry biography, she found it difficult to believe that her new novel was the masterpiece he rightly claimed. As soon as she completed it, she decided, very much in the manner of Miss La Trobe, it was rubbish.

'Real life',[55] as Virginia labelled it, remained awful. Early in December 1940, the Woolfs had arranged to store the remains of their London belongings in three rooms at the farm of a neighbour, Denny Botten. However, alarmed at what he considered to be inflammable materials, he changed his mind and decided to rent only two rooms. This meant that the couple's books, which arrived by lorry on 7 December, had to be dumped at another nearby location, a storeroom at Mill House, once a shop, belonging to another neighbour, Mr Christian.

Virginia found village life increasingly depressing. Exceedingly small things niggled, as when her cigarette holder needed replacing. The kitchen at Rodmell was penetrated by damp and rationing had begun. 'Our ration of margarine is so small,' she observed, 'that I can't think of any pudding save milk pudding.'[56] Virginia thought of food (or the lack of it) all the time. She even made up imaginary meals. She was ecstatic when Octavia Wilberforce made a 'business proposition': a month's milk and cream in exchange for a copy of what Virginia labelled her 'unborn and as far as I can tell completely worthless book.'[57]

On Christmas Eve 1940, she felt bloody but still very much unbowed: 'We're devilish poor. Lord, what a bill for rent and removal, and no money coming in, and the taxes! I shall have to write and write – till I die – just as we thought we'd saved enough to live, unwriting, till we died! But it's a good thing – being buffeted, and not cosseted.'[58] Such positive emotions were always in danger of eradication. When, early in January, a bomb burst the river bank near Rodmell and caused extensive flooding, Virginia and Leonard saw a large group of moles 'swimming for dear life, only their paws are so short compared with their bodies they didn't get far'.[59] Despite her very real attempts to stay afloat, Virginia felt that she, like the moles, might succumb to the torrents of nature.

James Joyce's death that January recalled the mixture of wonderment, boredom and revulsion that had been her response to *Ulysses*. The Irish author's death revived a memory of Katherine Mansfield, who one day in conversation with Virginia had begun to ridicule him. Then, as she read from the book, Katherine's manner changed completely: 'But,' she told Virginia, 'there's something in this: a scene that should figure I suppose in the history of literature.'[60] Death had cut Katherine away from Virginia and she was also convinced that all her old intimacy with Vita had been destroyed.

In a (lost) letter to Vita, Virginia vented those sentiments but expressed them indirectly by describing her hatred of Hilda Matheson, who had died the previous October and who, Virginia now felt, had stolen Vita from her. In turn, a shocked Vita did not feel that Virginia should dredge up the past. If their friendship was indeed diminished, little purpose would be served in raking the coals for the hint of an old fire: 'I don't feel that any of the foregoing [explanations provided to Virginia] are useful for keeping [our] friendship in repair – if indeed it needs repair – does it? Personally I had quite lost the drifting feeling. All the same, what can I tell you that will evoke a sense of intimacy?'[61]

The problem was that the closeness had long vanished, as Virginia had acknowledged some time before. Yet she could not let go. She wanted to revitalize her friendship with Vita; she wanted an intimacy which had not existed for years, probably because she craved the maternal approbation which had once been at the core of their friendship. She did not tell Vita this. Instead she accused her of bad behaviour in the past and made this teasing reference on 19 January: 'I rather think I've a new lover, a doctor, a Wilberforce . . . ah! does that make you twitch!'[62]

Virginia had become much more anxious than usual. When, in his review of 'The Leaning Tower', Desmond MacCarthy accused her of having cultivated her own ivory-tower mentality, her reply was uncharacteristically sharp.

> No, no, no, my dear Desmond – I really must protest, *I* never sat on top of a tower! Compare my wretched little £150 education with yours, with Lytton's, with Leonard's. Did Eton and Cambridge make no difference to you? Could the Hawk have been so affable and so hawklike without it? Would Lytton have written just as well if he'd spent his youth, as I did mine, mooning among books in a library? I assure you, my tower was a mere toadstool, about six inches high.[63]

That February, the snowdrops were out by the 10th, Vita lectured to the Women's Institute at Rodmell on Persia and Virginia tried to harness her energies. 'Did I tell you,' she asked Ethel, 'I'm reading the whole of English literature through? By the time I've reached Shakespeare the bombs will be falling.'[64] So Virginia imagined herself reading Shakespeare without a gas mask nearby. If that happened, she would simply fade away. As she told Leonard, she could no longer envisage a liveable future.

Civilization was being destroyed. How could she continue to write? To Elizabeth Robins, who had returned to the United States, she wistfully observed: 'No audience. No private stimulus, only this outer roar.'[65] Despite the cacophony, she resolved to go down with her colours flying. She told Ruth Fry, the painter's younger sister, that the reviews of *Roger Fry* which abused the subject gave her great pleasure for they showed just how much bite he still had. Like him, she was a fighter. Yet she was weary and desperately wanted the terrible suspense of war to be over. 'I can't help wishing the invasion would come,' she told a friend. 'It's this standing about in a dentist's waiting room that I hate.'[66]

Recently, as her 'Leaning Tower' essay shows, she had become much more sympathetic to John Lehmann, who had remained a great fan of hers. On 14 March, Leonard and Virginia travelled up to London, in part to discuss Hogarth Press business with their partner. On a day filled with brilliant sunshine, they lunched at St Stephen's Tavern overlooking Parliament Square and Big Ben. Number one on the agenda was Terence Tiller's first volume of verse. Leonard, who was petulant about this poet's retreats into obscurity, deferred to John and Virginia's wish to publish it. This was only a prelude to the real purpose of the meeting.

John noticed that Virginia was unusually nervous. Rather hesitatingly, Leonard broke the news: Virginia had completed a novel. When John turned to congratulate her, she became even more agitated. The book was no good, she claimed. Leonard rebuked her gently and husband and wife began to quarrel. John interrupted by asking if he could see the book. She agreed but six days later wrote to him: 'I've just read my so called novel over; and I really don't think it does. It's much too slight and sketchy. Leonard doesn't agree. So we've decided to ask you if you'd mind reading it and give your casting vote? Meanwhile don't take any steps.'[67]

Lehmann, who had already placed an advertisement for the book in the 'Spring Books' number of the *New Statesman*, was embarrassed. He immediately wrote to Virginia, apologizing for his precipitous behaviour. Then he devoured the book, overcome immediately by its brilliance. To him, it conveyed unparalleled imaginative power. He wrote a second letter to tell her how much he liked it. But Virginia could not share his high opinion of her work: 'I'd decided, before your letter came, that I can't publish that novel as it stands – it's too silly and trivial.'[68]

Virginia felt horribly alone: she could not trust the judgement of either John or Leonard. Her ability to assess her own work had simply disappeared. She had begun to distrust Leonard's sincerity, she felt cut off from Vita and her close friendship with her sister had suffered badly in recent years. On 20 March a very worried Vanessa, whom Leonard had informed of Virginia's increasingly precarious mental state, wrote her sister a letter which is remarkably similar to those of years earlier:

> You must be sensible. Which means you must accept the fact that Leonard and I can judge better than you can. It's true I haven't seen very much of you lately, but I have often thought you looked very tired and I'm sure that if you let yourself collapse and do nothing you would feel tired, and be only too glad to rest a little. You're in the state when one never admits what's the matter – but you must not go and get ill just now. What shall we do when we're invaded if you are a helpless invalid – what should I have done all these last 3 years if you hadn't been able to keep me alive and cheerful. You don't know how much I depend on you . . . Both Leonard and I have always had reputations for sense and honesty so you must believe us . . . I shall ring up sometime and find out what is happening.[69]

The condescension was probably not helpful.

The ascent of Hitler meant that phallic man had triumphed – and that Virginia's island nation would soon be destroyed. England itself seemed incapable of genuine change. Soon there would be no audience for her work even if she could write. Her back was against the wall. By choosing the circumstances of her own death, she could impose her own finality.

In all likelihood Virginia made a suicide attempt on 18 March by trying to drown herself. On that day, she went for a walk in the pouring rain. When she returned soaking wet, she seemed badly shaken and informed her husband that she had fallen into one of the dykes. She had left this letter for Leonard, which she presumably removed from view once the attempt had failed:*

> Dearest,
>
> I feel certain that I am going mad again: I feel we can't go through another of those terrible times. And I shan't recover this time. I begin to hear voices, and can't concentrate. So I am doing what seems the best thing to do. You have given me the greatest possible happiness. You have been in every way all that anyone could be. I don't think two people could be happier till this terrible disease came. I can't fight it any longer, I know that I am spoiling your life . . . What I want to say is that I owe all the happiness of my life to you. You have been entirely patient with me and incredibly good. I want to say that – everybody knows it. If anybody could have saved me it would have been you. Everything has gone from me but the certainty of your goodness. I can't go on spoiling your life any longer.
>
> I don't think two people could have been happier than we have been.[70]

Virginia's letter is filled with love, gratitude and affection, but she is also exonerating Leonard. She also seems consumed by some sort of guilt in her dealings with him, as if she owed him something but is not certain exactly how to express it. That 'something' may be sexual passion, the element in her being which was ripped away from her at a very young age. In her letter, she enumerates all the wonderful things in her marriage but she is also pointing to the wide gulfs between herself and her husband.

If Virginia tried to drown herself on 18 March, the attempt may have been unsuccessful because she wore a light coat and did not weigh her body down. Leonard was suspicious about Virginia's

* This letter was left in Virginia's sitting room and was discovered by Leonard at one in the afternoon of 28 March, the day on which Virginia committed suicide.

explanation that she had fallen into the water; he was all too desperately aware that things had gone badly awry and decided to ask Octavia Wilberforce to see Virginia. Earlier that month, when Octavia had called upon them at Rodmell, Virginia had mentioned her depressed feelings: everything about herself was 'useless . . . the Village wouldn't even allow her to firewatch – could do nothing'. The conversation rambled, but Virginia did blurt out: 'I never remember any enjoyment of my body.'

At a later meeting, Virginia considered the possibility of writing a portrait of Octavia. Then she asked Octavia if she had read *Orlando*. The doctor told her she adored the book. Virginia could not accept the compliment: 'Well, that was a fantastic biography and *Roger Fry* is the other I've attempted and both are failures. And I don't know exactly how I'd do you; probably more like Orlando – but I can't write. I've lost the art. But you are doing more useful work, helping things on.' Octavia stressed Virginia's very real contributions as a writer, but her observations were rejected: 'Yes, but I'm buried down here – I've not the stimulation of seeing people. I can't settle to it.' She also told Octavia that writing was her 'family business', which she felt an abysmal failure in not being able to carry on any longer. She had even taken to scrubbing floors as a distraction from her distress about not being able to work.

On the morning of 27 March, a very agitated Leonard telephoned Octavia at home and asked her to see his wife immediately. Octavia, who was confined to bed with flu, agreed to see the couple at Brighton at 3.15. She decided not to drive to Rodmell because she felt she might be better able to help Virginia if she could 'impress her professionally' in her own surroundings. That afternoon, Octavia met a very withdrawn Virginia, who saw no point in the consultation. She would not answer Octavia's questions and only consented to remove her clothes for examination on one condition.

'Will you promise if I do this not to order me a rest cure?'

'What I promise you is that I won't order you anything you won't think reasonable to do. Is that fair?'

Virginia agreed to this but was petulant and uncooperative. She told Octavia that she was afraid of going mad again. All that Octavia could offer were reassurances which she herself felt were empty. Then she added: 'If you'll collaborate I know I can help you, and there's nobody in England I'd like more to help.'

Virginia seemed to take some consolation from this proposal, but Octavia, when she spoke privately with Leonard, could only give the same advice as all the doctors who had ever treated his wife: 'No writing or criticism for a month. She has been too much nurtured on books. She never gets away from them. Let her be rationed and then she'll come good again. *If* she'll collaborate.' The prognosis was the same as before and, as Leonard was well aware, Virginia had survived previous breakdowns. He badly wanted to believe that he and his wife could get through this new onslaught of mental illness.[71]

But this time the circumstances of despair were overwhelming. On the following morning, Virginia wrote this final letter to Leonard.

> Dearest,
>
> I want to tell you that you have given me complete happiness. No one could have done more than you have done. Please believe that.
>
> But I know that I shall never get over this: and I am wasting your life. It is this madness. Nothing anyone says can persuade me. You can work, and you will be much better without me. You see I can't write this even, which shows I am right. All I want to say is that until this disease came on we were perfectly happy. It was all due to you. No one could have been so good as you have been, from the very first day till now. Everyone knows that.
>
> V.
>
> Will you destroy all my papers?[72]

The sentiments are the same as those in the earlier suicide note, but there are different emphases. The exoneration of Leonard is downplayed and her valediction to her husband is centred on his goodness, on the fact that he had been one of the few men she had ever been able to trust. She also highlights her own inability to work: her identity was so completely wrapped up in the profession of writing that she felt worthless because that talent had been removed from her.

All her life Virginia had battled the forces of death. The evidence of war was everywhere. Her country may have been fighting for survival, but she could no longer wage her own personal fight to stay alive. She felt deeply alienated from Vita, Vanessa and Leonard. She was certain that *Between the Acts*, one of her finest novels, was a failure. Without doubt, she despaired. She could not endure a replay of the depressive illness which had taken over her life in the 1910s, a malady which had taken her a long time to conquer. She was certain that she would not be so fortunate a second time.

However, her determination to end her life should not be seen merely as a decision to withdraw. She carefully chose the time and circumstances of her death, very much in the manner of an artist imposing her will upon life. Her decision was deeply courageous: although she would not be able to write about death, she would actually face the experience itself. This would be another intense and mystical 'moment of being' in which the truth behind appearances would stand revealed. She would confront the hidden force to which she had so long been drawn. The ending of her life was very much in the manner of Septimus Smith in *Mrs Dalloway*, where his suicide was 'defiance. Death was an attempt to communicate . . . There was an embrace in death.'[73]

Friday, 28 March, began quietly enough. At eleven in the morning, Leonard visited Virginia in her writing-room and she accompanied him back to the house, where Louie Everest was dusting in his study. He asked Louie to give his wife a duster so that she could help. Since Virginia had never worked side by side with her, this seemed an odd request, even though the domestic realized that Virginia was deeply agitated and Leonard was looking for a way to keep her mind occupied. After a while, Virginia put down the duster and slipped away. Leonard, who had gone to the garden and worked there until lunch at one, assumed that Virginia was still where he had left her.

Virginia took advantage of her husband's absence to slip away. First, she placed letters to Leonard and Vanessa on the mantelpiece in the sitting-room at Monks House and she left her previous suicide note (from 18 March or thereabouts) in her own sitting-room. Louie was the last person to see Virginia: 'Later in the morning I saw her come downstairs from the sitting-room and go out to her room in the garden. In a few minutes she returned to the house, put on her coat, took her walking-stick and went quickly up the garden to the top gate.' Louie rang the bell for lunch at one. Leonard returned from the garden and told her that he was going upstairs to hear the news on the radio. He would be back in a few minutes. Almost immediately he reappeared: 'Louie! I think something has happened to Mrs Woolf! I think she might have tried to kill herself! Which way did she go – did you see her leave the house?' A very upset Louie told Leonard what she had witnessed and he ran down towards the river.[74]

Virginia had put on her heavy fur coat in preparation for her walk to the Ouse. The water meadows, the brooks and the river bank were part of her favourite trek, but this was a very different, extremely lonely journey. She was not going to see her husband, her friends, her house or her books ever again. She had decided to enter into and become a part of the watery domain which had inspired much of her best writing. In *Between the Acts*, Isa thinks of killing herself but draws back: 'There would the dead leaf fall, when the leaves fall, on the water. Should I mind not again to see may tree or nut tree? Not again to hear on the trembling spray the thrush sing, or to see, dipping and diving as if he skimmed waves in the air, the yellow woodpecker?'[75]

Virginia might well have asked herself such questions as she loaded her pockets with heavy stones, put down her walking-stick and waded into the earth-green water. There, in 'that deep centre, in that black heart',[76] she died quietly but probably not gently, as her body struggled and then surrendered. This well-known woman became invisible – had retreated behind the curtains. Her corpse

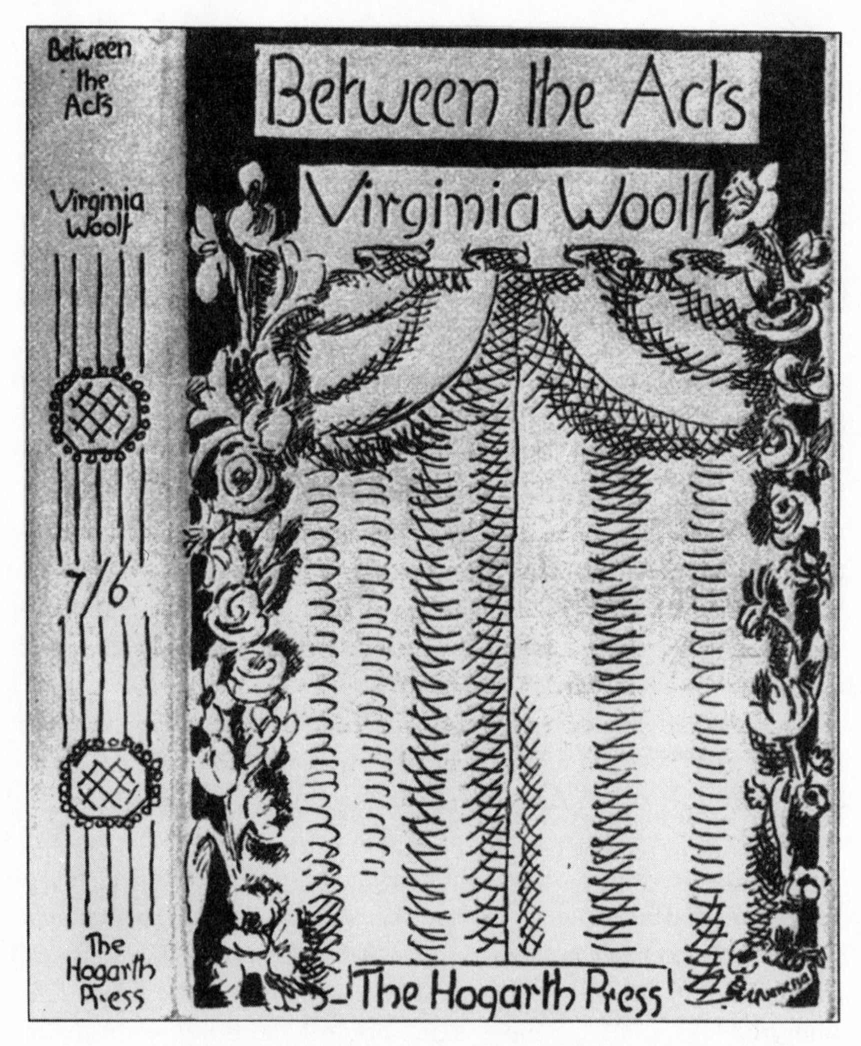

Vanessa Bell. Cover design for Between the Acts *(1941)*

was found three weeks later on the far side of the same stretch of water. In Virginia's writing, water can be a destructive force, but it is also a place of tranquillity, renewal and rebirth.

Notes

All references to Virginia Woolf before her marriage are abbreviated as VS; after her marriage, VW.

MANUSCRIPTS: The material from unpublished sources is indicated by a reference to the collection from which it is derived:

Berg The Virginia Woolf papers in the Berg Collection in the New York Public Library;
BL The British Library;
Sussex The Leonard and Virginia Woolf papers at the University of Sussex;
Tate Tate Gallery Archive.

Further details on manuscripts cited and consulted are given in the Select Bibliography.

VIRGINIA WOOLF'S WRITINGS: Virginia Woolf's letters and 1915–41 diary have been published in magnificent six- and five-volume editions respectively. References to the letters is by name of recipient, date of letter, volume number and page. The 1915–41 diary is referred to as *Diary*, followed by date of the entry, volume number and page. Further details on these two major editions are given in the Virginia Woolf entry in the Select Bibliography. The early diaries are referred to as *Diary*, with the added designation of *Passionate* (*A Passionate Apprentice: The Early Journals, 1897–1909*). References to Virginia Woolf's novels, stories and non-fiction writings are to those editions which I consider the most reliable. Full details on these are given in the Virginia Woolf entry in the Select Bibliography.

In order to make citations more readable, I have occasionally altered the punctuation of printed and manuscript sources.

I have abbreviated the titles of some references which are cited extensively; full details on these titles are supplied in the Select Bibliography.

Autobiography	Leonard Woolf, *An Autobiography*
Bell	Quentin Bell, *Virginia Woolf*
Congenial	*Congenial Spirits: The Selected Letters of Virginia Woolf*
CSF	Virginia Woolf, *The Complete Shorter Fiction*

Essays	Virginia Woolf, *The Essays*
Holroyd	Michael Holroyd, *Lytton Strachey*
LWL	Leonard Woolf, *Letters*
Mausoleum Book	Leslie Stephen, *Mausoleum Book*
Moments	Virginia Woolf, *Moments of Being*
Notes	Vanessa Bell, *Notes on Virginia's Childhood: A Memoir*
Passionate	*A Passionate Apprentice: The Early Journals, 1897–1909*
Recollections	*Recollections of Virginia Woolf*, edited by Joan Russell Noble
Vita–Virginia Letters	*The Letters of Vita Sackville-West to Virginia Woolf*

CHAPTER ONE: STRANGE SOLEMN MUSIC

1. 'A Sketch of the Past', *Moments*, 101.
2. Leslie Stephen to Julia Duckworth, 2 February 1877, MS BL.
3. *Mausoleum Book*, 49.
4. Leslie Stephen to Julia Duckworth, 18 August 1877, MS Berg.
5. Leslie Stephen to Julia Duckworth, 17 August 1877, MS Berg.
6. *Mausoleum Book*, 57.
7. Ibid.
8. *The Winnington Letters*, edited by Van Akin Burd (1969), 150.
9. *Freshwater*, 64–5.
10. Cited in Brian Hill, *Julia Margaret Cameron*. New York: St Martin's Press, 1973, 164–5.
11. 'A Sketch of the Past', *Moments*, 96.
12. Daphne du Maurier, *The Young George du Maurier* (1951), 112.
13. *Mausoleum Book*, 31.
14. 'A Sketch of the Past', *Moments*, 97.
15. 'Reminiscences', *Moments*, 38.
16. *Mausoleum Book*, 35.
17. 'Reminiscences', *Moments*, 39.
18. *To the Lighthouse*, 71.
19. *Mausoleum Book*, 40.
20. Ibid., 9, 11.
21. Ibid., 15, 22.
22. Ibid., 45.
23. Ibid., 47.

CHAPTER TWO: GHOSTS IN THE NURSERY

1. 'Old Bloomsbury', *Moments*, 198–200.
2. 'A Sketch of the Past', *Moments*, 107.
3. Ibid., 74.
4. *Diary*, 4 May 1928, III, 183.
5. Cited in *Bell*, I, 8.
6. See Jean O. Love, *Virginia Woolf: Sources of Madness and Art*, 162–6.
7. Leslie Stephen to Julia Stephen, 20 October 1881, MS Berg.
8. Leslie Stephen to Julia Stephen, 17 October 1881, MS Berg.
9. Leslie Stephen to Julia Stephen, 9 April 1882, MS Berg.
10. Cited in *Bell*, I, 78.
11. VS to George Duckworth, no date, *Congenial*, 2.
12. 'A Sketch of the Past', *Moments*, 84–5.
13. Ibid., 73–4.
14. Ibid., 75.
15. Ibid., 147.
16. See *Bell*, I,33n.
17. 'A Sketch of the Past', *Moments*, 147.
18. Ibid., 148.
19. Ibid., 83.
20. VS to Leslie Stephen, no date, *Congenial*, 2.
21. Leslie Stephen to Julia Stephen, 13 April 1884, MS Berg.
22. Leslie Stephen to Julia Stephen, 22 January 1891, MS Berg.
23. Leslie Stephen to Julia Stephen, 6/7 August 1887, MS Berg.
24. *Notes*, 2.
25. *Diary*, 19 December 1938, V, 192.
26. VS to Julia Stephen, no date, *Congenial*, 3.
27. 'A Sketch of the Past', *Moments*, 79–82.
28. Ibid., 92–3.
29. Ibid., 93.
30. Ibid., 91–2.
31. Ibid., 94.
32. Ibid.
33. Ibid., 93.
34. *Notes*, 8.
35. Ibid., 9.
36. Leslie Stephen and VS to James Russell Lowell, 20 August 1888, I, 2.
37. *Notes*, 9–10.
38. 'A Sketch of the Past', *Moments*, 77.
39. VW to Ethel Smyth, 12 January 1941, VI, 460.
40. MS Harvard.

41. *Notes*, 6–7.
42. 'A Sketch of the Past', *Moments*, 76.
43. Ibid., 78.
44. 'The tea table was the centre . . .': unpublished autobiographical fragment, probably written in October 1940, MS Berg.
45. MS Berg.
46. *Mausoleum Book*, 78.
47. 'A Sketch of the Past', *Moments*, 87.
48. Ibid., 93.
49. 'Old Bloomsbury', *Moments*, 198.
50. Leslie Stephen to Julia Stephen, 29 July 1893, MS Berg.
51. Leslie Stephen to Julia Stephen, 27 July 1893, MS Berg.
52. Leslie Stephen to Julia Stephen, 3 August 1893, MS Berg.
53. Leslie Stephen to Julia Stephen, 25 January 1891, MS Berg.
54. *Notes*, 11.
55. 'A Sketch of the Past', *Moments*, 106.
56. Citations to this text – which is now in the British Library (many entries are evidently in Vanessa Stephen's hand) – are from *Bell*, I, 28–39, and 'A Cockney's Farming Experiences'.
57. Henry James to Theodora Sedgwick, 30 March 1895, *Henry James Letters*, edited by Leon Edel. Cambridge, Mass.: Harvard University Press, 1984, IV, 8.
58. 'Reminiscences', *Moments*, 51.
59. 'A Sketch of the Past', *Moments*, 94.
60. *Mausoleum Book*, 96–7.
61. 'A Sketch of the Past', *Moments*, 102–4.
62. Ibid., 103–5.

CHAPTER THREE: A BROKEN CHRYSALIS

1. 'Reminiscences', *Moments*, 53.
2. Ibid., 54.
3. Ibid., 52.
4. Ibid., 54–5.
5. 'A Sketch of the Past', *Moments*, 108–9.
6. VW to Mary Hutchinson, [15 February 1924], VI, 505.
7. 'Reminiscences', *Moments*, 53.
8. Ibid., 48.
9. VW to Vita Sackville-West, 19 February [1929], IV, 27.
10. 'A Sketch of the Past', *Moments*, 112.
11. Ibid., 115.
12. Ibid., 116.

13. Ibid., 117.
14. Ibid., 114.
15. MS Berg.
16. 'Reminiscences', *Moments*, 58.
17. 'A Sketch of the Past', *Moments*, 112.
18. George Savage, *Insanity and Allied Neuroses*. London: Cassell, 1884, 23.
19. Unpublished autobiographical fragment, MH/MS 5a, MS Sussex.
20. Stella Duckworth's diary, MS Berg.
21. 'Reminiscences', *Moments*, 54.
22. *Diary*, 19 February 1897, *Passionate*, 39.
23. *Diary*, 1 February 1897, *Passionate*, 27.
24. VS to Thoby Stephen, [24 February 1897], I, 6.
25. *Diary*, 27 February 1897, *Passionate*, 44.
26. *Diary*, 26 March 1897, *Passionate*, 60.
27. *Diary*, 27 January 1897, *Passionate*, 23.
28. *Diary*, 28 April 1897, *Passionate*, 77.
29. *Diary*, 4 May 1897, *Passionate*, 80.
30. *Diary*, 6 May 1897, *Passionate*, 82.
31. *Diary*, 8 May 1897, *Passionate*, 82–3.
32. *Diary*, 12 June 1897, *Passionate*, 99.
33. *Diary*, 23 June 1897, *Passionate*, 105.
34. Unpublished autobiographical fragment, MS Berg.
35. Violet Dickinson to Vanessa Bell, 16 June 1942, MS Tate.
36. *Diary*, 9 August and 14 September 1897, *Passionate*, 121, 128.
37. *Diary*, 16 October 1897, *Passionate*, 132.
38. *Diary*, 1 January 1898, *Passionate*, 134.
39. VS to Thoby Stephen, 5 December [1897], I, 12.
40. *Diary*, 12 December 1897, *Passionate*, 133.
41. VS to Emma Vaughan, 23 October [1900], I, 40.
42. VS to Emma Vaughan, [17? June 1900], I, 33–4.
43. *Passionate*, 160.
44. *Diary*, 5 August 1899, *Passionate*, 136.
45. *Diary*, 13 August 1899, *Passionate*, 145.
46. *Diary*, 4 September 1899, *Passionate*, 156.
47. *Diary*, 23 August 1899, *Passionate*, 151.
48. ?8 September and 12 August 1899, *Passionate*, 158, 143.

CHAPTER FOUR: SHELL-LESS

1. 'A Sketch of the Past', *Moments*, 160.
2. See *Bell*, I, 90n.
3. VS to Emma Vaughan, 23 April [1901], I, 41.

4. VS to Emma Vaughan, 23 October [1900], I, 39.
5. VS to Emma Vaughan, 8 August [1901], I, 43.
6. VS to Emma Vaughan, 23 April [1901], I, 42.
7. 'A Sketch of the Past', *Moments*, 139.
8. Unpaginated pamphlet, Virginia Woolf papers, MS Berg.
9. *Moments of Being* (Sussex: The University Press, 1976), 138.
10. Monks House Papers, University of Sussex, A26.
11. Leslie Stephen to Mrs Herbert Fisher, 14 September 1902, cited in *Bell*, I, 82.
12. VS to Violet Dickinson, [4 June? 1903], I, 79.
13. VS to Violet Dickinson, [12 December 1902], I, 62.
14. VS to Violet Dickinson, [7? July 1903], I, 85.
15. VS to Violet Dickinson, [October/November 1902], I, 57.
16. VS to Violet Dickinson, [February? 1903], I, 69–70.
17. VS to Violet Dickinson, [March 1903], I, 71.
18. Vanessa Stephen to VS, 13 April 1905, MS Berg. VW to Vanessa Bell, [24 October 1916], II, 124.
19. '22 Hyde Park Gate', *Moments*, 185–8.
20. VS to Violet Dickinson, 8 June 1903, I, 80.
21. '22 Hyde Park Gate', *Moments*, 191–3.
22. 'Old Bloomsbury', *Moments*, 198.
23. *Diary*, 'Thoughts upon Social Success', 15 July 1903, *Passionate*, 169.
24. *Diary*, 'A Garden Dance', 30 June 1903, *Passionate*, 171.
25. *Diary*, 'Thoughts upon Social Success', 15 July 1903, *Passionate*, 167.
26. *Diary*, 'Miss Case', *Passionate*, 183.
27. VS to Violet Dickinson, [11? October 1903], I, 101.
28. *Diary*, 'An afternoon with the Pagans', *Passionate*, 184.
29. VS to Violet Dickinson, [September 1902], I, 54.
30. *Passionate*, 211–3.
31. VS to Thoby Stephen, [May 1903], I, 77.
32. VS to Violet Dickinson, 2 October [1903], I, 98.
33. VS to Violet Dickinson, [October/November 1903], I, 102.
34. VS to Violet Dickinson, [11? October 1903], I, 100–101.
35. VS to Violet Dickinson, [early October 1903], I, 98–9.
36. VS to Violet Dickinson, [June/July 1903], I, 83–4.
37. VS to Violet Dickinson, [31 December 1903], I, 119–20.
38. VS to Violet Dickinson, [February 1904], I, 127.
39. VS to Violet Dickinson, 28 February 1904, I, 130.
40. VS to Violet Dickinson, 8 March 1904, I, 132.
41. VS to Violet Dickinson, [March 1904], I, 133.
42. Ibid.
43. VS to Emma Vaughan, 25 April 1904, I, 138–9.
44. VS to Violet Dickinson, [6? May 1904], I, 140.

45. VS to Violet Dickinson, [22? September 1904], I, 142.
46. VS to Violet Dickinson, 26 September [1904], I, 143.
47. VS to Violet Dickinson, [22? September 1904], I, 142.
48. VS to Violet Dickinson, [22 October 1904], I, 145.
49. VS to Violet Dickinson, 24 October [1904], I, 146.
50. Vanessa Bell to VW, [22 October 1904], MS Berg.
51. VS to Violet Dickinson, [November 1904], I, 151.
52. VS to Violet Dickinson, 11 November [1904], I, 154.
53. VS to Violet Dickinson, 30 September [1904], I, 144.

CHAPTER FIVE: AN INNER WOMAN

1. Vanessa Stephen to VS, 28 October [1904], MS Berg.
2. 'Phyllis and Rosamond', *CSF*, 24.
3. *Diary*, 23 October 1918, I, 206.
4. *Diary*, 29 January 1905, *Passionate*, 229.
5. *Diary*, 22 January 1905, *Passionate*, 226.
6. *Diary*, 4 February 1905, *Passionate*, 232.
7. VS to Nelly Cecil, 22 December [1904], I, 168.
8. *Guardian*, 25 January 1905, *Essays*, I, 16.
9. *Diary*, 10 January 1905, *Passionate*, 219.
10. VS to Violet Dickinson, [30 December 1904], I, 171.
11. Ibid.
12. *Diary*, 6 January 1905, *Passionate*, 217.
13. VS to Violet Dickinson, [early January 1905], I, 172.
14. 'Report on Teaching at Morley College', cited in *Bell*, I, 202.
15. VS to Violet Dickinson, [May 1905], I, 191.
16. 'Report on Teaching at Morley College', cited in *Bell*, I, 203.
17. VS to Violet Dickinson, [18 June 1905], I, 192.
18. 'Report on Teaching at Morley College', cited in *Bell*, I, 203–4.
19. *Diary*, 15 February 1905, *Passionate*, 237.
20. VS to Violet Dickinson, [24 April 1905], I, 188.
21. *National Review*, March 1905, *Essays*, I, 28.
22. *Diary*, 23 February 1905, *Passionate*, 241–2.
23. VS to Emma Vaughan, 23 February [1905], I, 180.
24. VS to Violet Dickinson, 1 October [1905], I, 208.
25. VS to Violet Dickinson, 5 April [1905], I, 184.
26. VS to Violet Dickinson, 30 April [1905], I, 189.
27. VS to Violet Dickinson, [May 1905], I, 190.
28. *Guardian*, 10 May 1905, *Essays*, I, 40.
29. VS to Violet Dickinson, [July 1905], I, 198.
30. VS to Nelly Cecil, [August 1905], I, 203.

31. *Guardian*, 2 August 1905, *Essays*, I, 55.
32. *Diary*, Cornwall 1905, *Passionate*, 281–99.
33. VS to Nelly Cecil, 10 November [1905], I, 212.
34. VS to Violet Dickinson, [July 1905], I, 201.
35. VS to Violet Dickinson, [3 December 1905], I, 213.
36. VS to Violet Dickinson, [August 1905], I, 205.
37. VS to Nelly Cecil, [July 1905], I, 196.
38. VS to Violet Dickinson, 27 August [1905], I, 205.
39. VS to Violet Dickinson, 1 October [1905], I, 209.
40. VS to Violet Dickinson, [3 December 1905], I, 213.
41. VS to Madge Vaughan, 11 December [1904], I, 166.
42. VS to Nelly Cecil, 10 [November 1905], I, 212.
43. VS to Madge Vaughan, [July 1906], I, 229.
44. *The Speaker*, 21 April 1906, *Essays*, I, 103.
45. VS to Violet Dickinson, [16 April 1906], I, 222.
46. Vanessa Stephen to VS, [15 April 1906], MS Berg.
47. Cited in *Holroyd*, 139.
48. Clive Bell to Lytton Strachey, [20 July 1905], MS BL.
49. VS to Violet Dickinson, [June? 1906], I, 227–8.
50. VS to Violet Dickinson, [6 December 1904], I, 163.
51. VS to Violet Dickinson, [June? 1906], I, 228.
52. VS to Violet Dickinson, 24 August [1906], I, 235.
53. *CSF*, 28.
54. Ibid., 62.
55. VS to Nelly Cecil, [early September 1906], I, 236.
56. *Diary*, Greece 1906, *Passionate*, 333.
57. Ibid., 319.
58. VS to Violet Dickinson, [16 November 1906], I, 245–6.
59. VS to Violet Dickinson, [23? November 1906], I, 249.
60. VS to Violet Dickinson, 25 [November 1906], I, 250–51.
61. VS to Violet Dickinson, [29 November 1906], I, 253.
62. VS to Violet Dickenson, [18 December 1906], I, 266.

CHAPTER SIX: PASSIONATE MAIDEN HEART

1. VS to Violet Dickinson, [18 December 1906], I, 268.
2. VS to Clive Bell, [20 December 1906], I, 268.
3. VS to Violet Dickinson, [30? December 1906], I, 273.
4. VS to Violet Dickinson, [22 December 1906], I, 270.
5. VS to Violet Dickinson, [3 January 1907], I, 276.
6. *Times Literary Supplement*, 9 January 1908, *Essays*, I, 158.
7. VS to Nelly Cecil, [January 1907], I, 278.

8. VS to Violet Dickinson, [15? April 1909], I, 392.
9. Henry James to Mrs W.K. Clifford, 17 February 1907, cited in *Bell*, I, 114.
10. VS to Vanessa Stephen, 6 February 1907, *Congenial*, 38.
11. 'Old Bloomsbury', *Moments*, 213.
12. *Recollections*, 27.
13. Adrian Stephen's 6 June–16 July 1909 diary, cited in *Bell*, I, 146–7.
14. Vanessa Bell to Clive Bell, 25 June 1910, MS Tate.
15. VS to Violet Dickinson, [7 July 1907], I, 298–9.
16. VS to Violet Dickinson, [25 August 1907], I, 306.
17. VS to Violet Dickinson, [1 September 1907], I, 309.
18. VS to Emma Vaughan, [29 September 1907], I, 312.
19. VS to Violet Dickinson, [15? October 1907], I, 316.
20. VS to Violet Dickinson, [December 1907], I, 320.
21. VS to Lytton Strachey, [28 April 1908], I, 328.
22. VS to Clive Bell, [15 April 1908], I, 325.
23. VS to Violet Dickinson, 13 May [1908], I, 331.
24. VS to Clive Bell, [6 May 1908], I, 329–30.
25. VS to Clive Bell, [summer 1908?], I, 336.
26. Vanessa Bell to VS, 2 May [1908], MS Berg.
27. VS to Clive Bell, [3 August 1908], I, 339.
28. VS to Vanessa Bell, [10 August 1908], I, 348.
29. VS to Saxon Sydney-Turner, [14 August 1908], I, 352.
30. Vanessa Bell to VS, 8 August [1908], MS Berg.
31. VS to Nelly Cecil, 14 August [1908], I, 354.
32. VS to Vanessa Bell, [14 August 1908], I, 355.
33. VS to Vanessa Bell, [20 August 1908], I, 358.
34. VS to Clive Bell, 19 August [1908], I, 357, 356.
35. Clive Bell to VS, 3 August 1908, MS Sussex.
36. Vanessa Bell to VS [11 August 1908], MS Sussex.
37. VW to Katharine Furse, printed in Rowena Fowler, 'Virginia Woolf and Katharine Furse: An Unpublished Correspondence [with Appendix]', *Tulsa Studies in Women's Literature*, 9, Fall 1990, 201–28.
38. VS to Clive Bell, [9 August 1908], I, 344.
39. VS to Vanessa Bell, [30 August 1908], I, 366.
40. Vanessa Bell to VS, 25 August 1908, MS Berg.
41. *Diary*, Italy 1908, *Passionate*, 392–3.
42. Ibid., 383.
43. Ibid., 384–90.
44. Clive Bell to VS, 2 September 1908, MS Sussex.
45. VS to Violet Dickinson, [4 October 1908], I, 370.
46. VS to Madge Vaughan, 19 November 1908, I, 373–4.

47. Clive Bell to VS, [?October 1908], MS Sussex.
48. *Times Literary Supplement*, 22 October 1908, *Essays*, I, 221.
49. *Times Literary Supplement*, 12 November 1908, *Essays*, I, 225.
50. VS to Clive Bell, 25 December [1908], I, 376.
51. Cited in *Holroyd*, 447.
52. VS to Madge Vaughan, [May 1909], I, 395.
53. VS to Lytton Strachey, 1 February [1909], I, 382.
54. VS to Clive Bell, 19 February [1909], I, 386.
55. Lytton Strachey to Leonard Woolf, [19 February 1909], cited in *Holroyd*, 405.
56. MS Berg.
57. VS to Madge Vaughan, 21 March [1909], I, 388.
58. VS to Nelly Cecil, [12 April 1909], I, 390.
59. Clive Bell to VS, 9 April 1909, MS Sussex.
60. VS to Clive Bell, [13 April 1909], I, 391.
61. *Diary*, 25 April 1909, *Passionate*, 400.
62. Vanessa Bell to VS, 16 May [1909], MS Berg.
63. *Melymbrosia*, 8.
64. Ibid., 58.
65. Ibid., 60.
66. Ibid., 107.
67. Ibid., 151.
68. Ibid., 198.
69. Ibid., 209.
70. Ibid., 212.
71. Ibid., 225.
72. Ibid., 230.
73. VS to Clive Bell, [7? February 1909], I, 383.
74. *Times Literary Supplement*, 12 August 1909, *Essays*, I, 285.
75. VS to Vanessa Bell, [18 May 1909], I, 395–6.
76. VS to Violet Dickinson, [mid-April 1903], I, 74.
77. Cited in *Holroyd*, 292.
78. Ibid., 144.
79. *The Times*, 21 August 1909, *Essays*, I, 289–90.
80. VS to Vanessa Bell, [12 August 1909], I, 407.
81. *Diary*, 2 January 1923, II, 221.
82. Vanessa Bell to VS, 7 September [1909], MS Berg.
83. VS to Violet Dickinson, [11 October 1909], I, 413.
84. Reginald Smith to VS, 10 November 1909, MS Sussex.
85. VS to Clive Bell, 26 December [1909], I, 417.
86. VS to Saxon Sydney-Turner, [13 June 1910], I, 426–7.
87. Clive Bell, *Old Friends*, 117.

88. Vanessa Bell to VS, 17 July [1910], MS Berg.
89. VS to Vanessa Bell, 28 July [1910], I, 430–31.
90. Vanessa Bell to VS, 29 July [1910], MS Berg.

CHAPTER SEVEN: ALWAYS ALIVE, ALWAYS HOT

1. Vanessa Bell to VS, 5 August [1910], MS Berg.
2. Vanessa Bell to VS, 6 August [1910], MS Berg.
3. VS to Saxon Sydney-Turner, [August 1910], I, 432.
4. VS to Clive Bell, [4 September 1910], I, 434.
5. VS to Ottoline Morrell, [1 January 1911], I, 449.
6. Clive Bell to VS, MS Sussex.
7. VS to Clive Bell, [14? November 1910], I, 439.
8. Clive Bell to VS, [12? January 1911], MS Sussex.
9. VS to Violet Dickinson, [27 November 1910], I, 440.
10. Ibid.
11. VS to Clive Bell, [29 December 1910], I, 446.
12. 'Old Bloomsbury', *Moments,* 214.
13. VS to Molly MacCarthy, [March 1911], I, 455.
14. VS to Violet Dickinson, [27 November 1910], I, 440.
15. VS to Janet Case, [December? 1910], I, 441.
16. VS to Clive Bell, [29 December 1910], I, 446.
17. VS to Molly MacCarthy, [April 1911], I, 456.
18. Cited in Frances Spalding, *Vanessa Bell,* 94.
19. Clive Bell to VS, [3 April 1911], MS Sussex.
20. VS to Violet Dickinson, [25 May 1911], I, 465.
21. Vanessa Bell to Roger Fry, 5 September 1911, MS Tate.
22. Vanessa Bell to Roger Fry, 15 November 1911, MS Tate.
23. VS to Clive Bell, [23 January 1911], I, 449–50.
24. Vanessa Bell to VS, 3 October 1910, MS Berg.
25. VS to Clive Bell, 18 April [1911], I, 461.
26. *Times Literary Supplement*, 8 August 1918, *Essays*, II, 279.
27. VS to Roger Fry, [early September 1911], I, 477.
28. *Diary*, 27 July 1918, I, 172.
29. VS to Vanessa Bell [8? June 1911], I, 466.
30. VS to Violet Dickinson, 1 January [1911], I, 447.
31. VS to Vanessa Bell, [25? July 1911], I, 472–3.
32. *Holroyd*, 169.
33. VS to Vanessa Bell, [21 July 1921], I, 469–70.
34. VS to Vanessa Bell, [25? July 1911], I, 473.
35. VS to Desmond MacCarthy, 4 September [1911], I, 477.
36. VS to Ottoline Morrell, [9 November 1911], I, 480.
37. VS to Violet Dickinson, 20 November 1911, I, 483.

38. VS to Leonard Woolf, 2 December [1911], I, 485.
39. Leonard Woolf to Lytton Strachey, 1 November [1911], *LWL*, 167.
40. Leonard Woolf to Lytton Strachey, 9 April [1901], *LWL*, 15.
41. Cited in *LWL*, 7.
42. Leonard Woolf to Lytton Strachey, 21 March 1906, *LWL*, 115.
43. Leonard Woolf to Lytton Strachey, 4 March 1906, *LWL*, 113.
44. Lytton Strachey to Leonard Woolf, 9 September 1904, *LWL*, 43.
45. Leonard Woolf to Lytton Strachey, 19 May 1907, *LWL*, 128.
46. *Autobiography*, I, 117.
47. 'Old Bloomsbury', *Moments*, 205.
48. *Autobiography*, II, 14.
49. Leonard Woolf to Lytton Strachey, 30 July 1905, *LWL*, 98.
50. Lytton Strachey to Leonard Woolf, 19 February 1909, *LWL*, 147.
51. Lytton Strachey to Leonard Woolf, 21 August 1909, *LWL*, 148–9.
52. Entry for 8 December 1910, MS Berg.
53. VS to Vanessa Bell, [22? August 1911], I, 475.
54. Leonard Woolf to VS, 11 January 1912, *LWL*, 169.
55. VS to Leonard Woolf, [13 January 1912], I, 488.
56. Vanessa Bell to VS, 13 January [1912], MS Berg.
57. VS to Ka Cox, 7 February [1912], I, 488.
58. VS to Violet Dickinson, [7? February 1912], I, 490.
59. VS to Leonard Woolf, [5 March 1912], I, 491.
60. VS to Molly MacCarthy, [March 1912], I, 492.
61. Leonard Woolf to VS, 29 April 1912, *LWL*, 173.
62. VS to Leonard Woolf, 1 May [1912], I, 496–7.
63. MS Sussex.
64. VS to Violet Dickinson, 22 May [1912], I, 499.
65. Leonard Woolf to Lytton Strachey, 2 June 1912, *LWL*, 176.
66. VS to Violet Dickinson, [4 June 1912], I, 500.
67. Clive Bell to VS, [June? 1912], MS Sussex.
68. VS to Violet Dickinson, [July 1912], I, 506.

CHAPTER EIGHT: A WILD SWAN

1. VS to Nelly Cecil, [June 1912], I, 504.
2. VS to Janet Case, [June 1912], I, 502–3.
3. Leonard Woolf, *The Wise Virgins*, 19.
4. VS to Duncan Grant, [8 August 1912], I, 508.
5. VW to Janet Case, [17 August 1912], II, 4.
6. Clive Bell to VW, [Summer 1912], MS Sussex.
7. VW to Clive Bell, [13 August 1912], II, 1.
8. Leonard Woolf to Saxon Sydney-Turner, 1 September 1912, *LWL*, 178.

9. VW to Molly MacCarthy, 28 September 1912, II, 9.
10. VW to Ka Cox, 4 September [1912], II, 6.
11. Gerald Brenan to Rosemary Dinnage, 1967, cited in *LWL*, 162.
12. VW to Vanessa Bell, 25 April [1913], II, 24.
13. Vanessa Bell to Clive Bell, 27 December [1912], MS Tate.
14. Leonard Woolf, *The Wise Virgins*, 41.
15. VW to Violet Dickinson, [29? October 1912], II, 10.
16. VW to Vanessa Bell, [16? October 1928], III, 547.
17. *Melymbrosia*, 45.
18. *The Voyage Out*, 328.
19. *Autobiography*, II, 55–6.
20. Ibid.
21. Ibid.
22. 'Moral Insanity', *Journal of Mental Science*, 27, 1881, 148.
23. Maurice Craig, *Psychological Medicine*. London: J. & A. Churchill, 1905, 24.
24. T. B. Hyslop, 'A Discussion of Occupation and Environment as Causative Factors of Insanity', *British Medical Journal*, 2, 1905, 942.
25. Vanessa Bell to Leonard Woolf, 20 January 1913, MS Sussex.
26. Vanessa Bell to VW, 22 January [1913], MS Berg.
27. Vanessa Bell to VW, [26 January 1913], MS Berg.
28. Vanessa Bell to VW, [2 February 1913], MS Berg.
29. *Autobiography*, II, 408.
30. VW to Violet Dickinson, 11 April [1913], II, 23.
31. VW to Ethel Sands, [9 February 1927], III, 329.
32. *Diary*, 5 September 1926, III, 107.
33. VW to Violet Dickinson, 11 April [1913], II, 23.
34. VW to Molly MacCarthy, 28 May [1913], II, 29.
35. VW's Introductory Letter to *Life as We Have Known It*, xxiii.
36. Leonard Woolf to VW, 27 July [1913], *LWL*, 184–5.
37. VW to Leonard Woolf, [3 August 1913], II, 33.
38. VW to Leonard Woolf, [4 August 1913], II, 34.
39. Vanessa Bell to VW, 28 August [1913], MS Berg.
40. *Autobiography*, II, 113.
41. Marie Woolf to Leonard Woolf, 11 December 1913, *LWL*, 196.
42. Leonard Woolf to Lytton Strachey, 12 December 1913, *LWL*, 197.
43. Leonard Woolf to VW, 4 December 1913, *LWL*, 195–6.
44. VW to Leonard Woolf, [December? 1913], II, 35.
45. VW to Leonard Woolf, [8 March 1914], II, 41.
46. VW to Leonard Woolf, [16 March 1914], II, 45.
47. VW to Violet Dickinson, [mid-April 1914], II, 48.
48. VW to Janet Case, 10 December [1914], II, 55.
49. *Diary*, 2 January 1915, I, 4–5.

50. Ibid., I, 4.
51. *Diary*, 3 January 1915, I, 5.
52. *Diary*, 9 January 1915, I, 13.
53. *Diary*, 15 January 1915, I, 19.
54. *Diary*, 20 January 1915, I, 24.
55. *Diary*, 23 January 1915, I, 26.
56. *Diary*, 25 January 1915, I, 28.
57. *Diary*, 31 January 1915, I, 32.
58. *Diary*, 31 January 1915, I, 31.
59. *Diary*, 13 February 1915, I, 33.
60. *Diary*, 15 February 1915, I, 35.
61. VW to Lytton Strachey, [26 February 1915], II, 61.
62. Vanessa Bell to Roger Fry, 27 May 1915, MS Tate.
63. Vanessa Bell to Roger Fry, 25 July 1915, MS Tate.
64. VW to Margaret Llewelyn Davies, [31 August 1915], II, 63.
65. VW to Lytton Strachey, 22 October 1915, II, 67.
66. E. M. Forster, *Daily News and Leader*, 8 April 1915.
67. Allan Monkhouse, *Manchester Guardian*, 15 April 1915.
68. *Observer*, 4 April 1915.

CHAPTER NINE: THE SHADOW OF THE UNDERGROUND

1. VW to Margaret Llewelyn Davies, [23 January 1916], II, 76.
2. *Diary*, 13 December 1917, I, 91.
3. VW to Leonard Woolf, 17 April [1916], II, 90.
4. VW to Vanessa Bell, 14 May [1916], II, 95.
5. VW to Vanessa Bell, [30 July 1916], II, 109.
6. VW to Lytton Strachey, 25 [July 1916], II, 107.
7. VW to Vanessa Bell, [10 September 1916], II, 115.
8. VW to Vanessa Bell, [24 September 1916], II, 119.
9. VW to David Garnett, [21 October 1916], II, 123.
10. Vanessa Bell to Duncan Grant, [17 October 1916], cited in *Bell*, II, 33.
11. Dora Carrington to Vanessa Bell, [October 1916], cited in *Bell*, II, 34.
12. Vanessa Bell to Lytton Strachey, 24 October 1916.
13. VW to Vanessa Bell, [24 October 1916], II, 124.
14. VW to Saxon Sydney-Turner, [27 November 1916], II, 128.
15. VW to Violet Dickinson, [10 April 1917], II, 147.
16. VW to Vanessa Bell, [11 February 1917], II, 144.
17. *The Collected Letters of Katherine Mansfield*, edited by Vincent O' Sullivan and Margaret Scott. Oxford: The Clarendon Press, 1984, I, 313.
18. VW to Vanessa Bell, [27 June 1917], II, 159.
19. *Diary*, 11 October 1917, I, 58.

20. *Times Literary Supplement*, 13 April 1916, *Essays*, II, 28.
21. *Times Literary Supplement*, 22 February 1917, Essays, II, 85.
22. *CSF*, 86–9.
23. *Diary*, 19 August 1917, I, 43.
24. *Diary*, 18 March 1918, I, 129.
25. VW to Vanessa Bell, 26 April [1917], II, 150.
26. VW to Margaret Llewelyn Davies, [2 May 1917], II, 151.
27. VW to David Garnett, 26 July [1917], II, 167.
28. *Diary*, 23 October 1917, I, 65.
29. VW to Ottoline Morrell, [May 1917], II, 154.
30. VW to Dora Carrington, [5 October 1917], II, 185.
31. *Diary*, 24 June 1918, I, 158–9.
32. *Diary*, 10 November 1917, I, 73.
33. VW to Vanessa Bell, [26 July 1917], II, 169.
34. *Diary*, 2 November 1917, I, 69.
35. VW to Vanessa Bell, [11 June 1918], II, 250.
36. VW to Lytton Strachey, 12 October [1918], II, 281.
37. *Diary*, 12 December 1917, I, 89.
38. *Diary*, 11 January 1918, I, 104.
39. *Diary*, 7 June 1918, I, 153.
40. VW to Saxon Sydney-Turner, 25 February [1918], II, 220–21.
41. *Diary*, 8 March 1918, I, 124.
42. *Diary*, 5 February 1918, I, 118–19.
43. *Diary*, 27 August 1918, I, 186.
44. VW to Vanessa Bell, [22 April 1918], II, 232.
45. *Night and Day*, 106.
46. VW to Ethel Smyth, 16 October [1930], IV, 231.
47. VW to Roger Fry, [21 October 1918], II, 285.
48. *Night and Day*, 323.
49. Ibid., 253.
50. Ibid., 282.
51. *Times Literary Supplement*, 10 April 1919, *Essays*, III, 33.
52. *Diary*, 12 July 1918, I, 167.
53. *Diary*, 7 August 1918, I, 179.
54. VW to Roger Fry, [24 April 1918], II, 234.
55. *Diary*, 18 April 1918, I, 140.
56. VW to Nicholas Bagenal, 15 April 1918, II, 231.
57. VW to Saxon Sydney-Turner, [18 September 1917], II, 181.
58. *Diary*, 19 November 1917, I, 79.
59. *Diary*, 27 July 1918, I, 172.
60. *Diary*, 3 November 1918, I, 212.
61. VW to Barbara Bagenal, 20 September [1918], II, 278.

62. VW to Vanessa Bell, [31 December 1918], II, 312.
63. *Diary*, 26 October 1918, I, 208.
64. MS Tate.
65. *Diary*, 28 October 1918, I, 209.
66. *Diary*, 15 November 1918, I, 217.
67. VW to Vanessa Bell, [13 November 1918], II, 293–4.

CHAPTER TEN: THE SHADOW LINE

1. VW to Vanessa Bell, [12 December 1918], II, 304.
2. VW to Vanessa Bell, [27 February 1919], II, 335.
3. *Diary*, 20 January 1919, I, 234.
4. *Diary*, 22 January 1919, I, 234.
5. VW to Vanessa Bell, [22 January 1919], II, 319.
6. *Diary*, 31 January 1919, I, 238.
7. *Diary*, 10 April 1919, I, 262.
8. VW to Duncan Grant, [17 April 1919], II, 350.
9. *Diary*, 18 February 1919, I, 241.
10. *Diary*, 5 March 1919, I, 247.
11. *Times Literary Supplement*, 6 March 1919, *Essays*, III, 14.
12. 'George Eliot', *The Common Reader. First Series*, 175–6.
13. *Times Literary Supplement*, 13 February 1919, *Essays*, III, 10.
14. VW to Vanessa Bell, [2 April 1920], II, 426.
15. *Diary*, 12 March 1919, I, 252.
16. VW to Vanessa Bell, [23 March 1919], II, 341.
17. *Diary*, 27 March 1919, I, 259.
18. *Diary*, 17 April 1919, I, 264.
19. *Diary*, 20 April 1919, I, 266.
20. 29 May 1919.
21. *Diary*, 9 June 1919, I, 279.
22. VW to Vanessa Bell, [18 June 1919], II, 369.
23. *Diary*, 3 July 1919, I, 286–7.
24. VW to Janet Case, [23 July 1919], II, 379.
25. *Diary*, 12 May 1919, I, 271.
26. *Diary*, 23 June 1919, I, 284.
27. *Diary*, 25 May 1919, I, 277.
28. *Diary*, 12 July 1919, I, 291.
29. *Diary*, 18 February 1919, I, 242–3.
30. *Diary*, 12 September 1919, I, 297.
31. *Diary*, 28 September 1919, I, 302.
32. *Diary*, 7 October 1919, I, 304.
33. *Diary*, 21 October 1919, I, 307.

34. Ford Madox Hueffer, *Piccadilly Review*, 23 October 1919.
35. Katherine Mansfield, *Athenaeum*, 21 November 1919.
36. *Diary*, 28 November 1919, I, 314.
37. *Diary*, 6 November 1919, I, 310.
38. VW to Vanessa Bell, [27 October 1919], II, 393.
39. VW to Janet Case, [19 November 1919], II, 400.
40. *Diary*, 15 November 1919, I, 313.
41. *Diary*, 20 January 1920, II, 10.
42. VW to Margaret Llewelyn Davies, [16 November 1919], II, 400.
43. *Diary*, 6 November 1919, I, 310.
44. VW to Margaret Llewelyn Davies, [16 November 1919], II, 399–400.
45. *Diary*, 5 December 1919, I, 315.
46. VW to Ka Cox, 1 January 1920, II, 410.
47. *Diary*, 6 December 1919, I, 316.
48. VW to Molly MacCarthy, [4 December 1919], II, 407.
49. *Diary*, 28 December 1919, I, 318.
50. *Diary*, 26 January 1920, II, 13–14.
51. *Diary*, 3 March 1920, II, 21.
52. *Diary*, 6 March 1920, II, 23.
53. *Diary*, 4 February 1920, II, 17.
54. *Diary*, 11 May 1920, II, 35.
55. *Diary*, 20 May 1920, II, 40.
56. *Diary*, 26 May 1920, II, 43.
57. *Diary*, 31 May 1920, II, 44–5.
58. *Diary*, 5 June 1920, II, 45.
59. *Diary*, 31 May 1920, II, 45.
60. *Diary*, 8 June 1920, II, 47.
61. *Diary*, 29 June 1920, II, 51.
62. *Diary*, 17 June 1920, II, 48.
63. *Woman's Leader*, 23 July 1920, *Essays*, III, 243.
64. *Diary*, 19 September 1920, II, 67.
65. *Diary*, 13 November 1920, II, 75.
66. VW to Violet Dickinson, 24 November [1920], II, 447.
67. *Diary*, 5 December 1920, II, 77.
68. *Diary*, 19 August 1920, II, 60.
69. VW to Roger Fry, [1 August 1920], II, 438.
70. *Diary*, 2 August 1920, II, 54.
71. *Diary*, 12 December 1920, II, 78–9.
72. *Diary*, 25 August 1920, II, 61.
73. *Diary*, 25 October 1920, II, 73, 72.
74. *Diary*, 19 December 1920, II, 80.

CHAPTER ELEVEN: A PROCESSION OF SHADOWS

1. VW to Vanessa Bell, [7 January 1921], II, 454.
2. VW to Katherine Mansfield, 13 February [1921], *Congenial*, 127–8.
3. VW to Janet Case, 20 March 1922, II, 514–15.
4. VW to Katherine Mansfield, 13 February [1921], *Congenial*, 130.
5. VW to Dora Carrington, 24 August [1922], II, 551.
6. VW to Sydney Waterlow, [19 January 1921], II, 455.
7. *Diary*, 31 January 1921, II, 88.
8. VW to Vanessa Bell, [January 1921], II, 454.
9. VW to Vanessa Bell, 13 May [1921], II, 469.
10. *Diary*, 22 March 1921, II, 103–4.
11. *Diary*, 25 January 1921, II, 87.
12. *Diary*, 1 March 1921, II, 95–6.
13. VW to Saxon Sydney-Turner, [28] March 1921, II, 462.
14. Harold Child, *Times Literary Supplement*, 7 April 1921.
15. *CSF*, 95.
16. *Diary*, 8 April 1921, II, 107.
17. Ibid., II, 106.
18. *New Statesman*, 9 April 1921.
19. VW to Vanessa Bell, 13 May [1921], II, 470.
20. *Diary*, 9 May 1921, II, 117.
21. *Diary*, 2 June 1921, II, 122.
22. Ibid.
23. *Diary*, 23 May 1921, II, 120.
24. *Diary*, 15 May 1921, II, 118.
25. Cited in *Holroyd*, 818.
26. *Diary*, 17 August 1921, II, 131.
27. *Diary*, 18 August 1921, II, 133.
28. *Diary*, 10 September 1921, II, 134.
29. VW to Roger Fry, [29 August 1921], II, 478.
30. *Diary*, 2 November 1921, II, 141.
31. VW to Dorothea Stephen, [28? October 1921], II, 489.
32. *Diary*, 19 December 1921 and 3 January 1922, II, 152, 155.
33. VW to Violet Dickinson, [18 May 1922], II, 528.
34. *Diary*, 16 August 1922, II, 189.
35. VW to Violet Dickinson, [23? January 1923], III, 9.
36. VW to Lytton Strachey, [11] February [1922], II, 503.
37. *Diary*, 12 March 1922, II, 171.
38. Clive Bell to Vanessa Bell, 1 March 1922, MS Tate.
39. *Diary*, 14 February 1922, II, 162.
40. VW to Vanessa Bell, 20 February 1922, II, 505.

41. *Diary*, 18 February 1922, II, 168.
42. *Diary*, 17 February 1922, II, 167.
43. *Diary*, 12 March 1922, II, 171.
44. VW to Roger Fry, [6 May 1922], II, 525.
45. *Diary*, 23 June 1922, II, 178.
46. *Diary*, 18 December 1921, II, 150.
47. *Diary*, 23 June and 28 July 1922, II, 177, 186.
48. VW to Ottoline Morrell, 18 August [1922], II, 548.
49. *Diary*, 14 October 1922, II, 207.
50. *Diary*, 19 July 1922, II, 182.
51. VW to Clive Bell, [14 April 1922], II, 522.
52. VW to Ka Arnold-Forster, 3 June [1922], II, 532.
53. *Diary*, 22 July 1922, II, 185.
54. *Diary*, 16 August 1922, II, 188–9.
55. Ibid., II, 189.
56. *Diary*, 4 October 1922, II, 206.
57. *Diary*, 14 October 1922, II, 208.
58. *Diary*, 26 January 1920, II, 14.
59. Lytton Strachey, *Eminent Victorians*. London: Chatto and Windus, 1966, 7.
60. *Jacob's Room*, 61.
61. Unsigned review, *Times Literary Supplement*, 26 October 1922.
62. Lewis Bettany, *Daily News*, 27 October 1922.
63. Rebecca West, *New Statesman*, 4 November 1922.
64. W. L. Courtney, *Daily Telegraph*, 10 November 1922.
65. *Diary*, 27 November 1922, II, 214.
66. Lytton Strachey to VW, 9 October 1922, *Virginia Woolf–Lytton Strachey Letters*, edited by Leonard Woolf and James Strachey, 144.
67. VW to Lytton Strachey, [10?] October 1922, II, 568–9.
68. VW to David Garnett, 29 October 1922, II, 575.
69. VW to R. C. Trevelyan, 23 November 1922, II, 588.
70. *Diary*, 29 October 1922, II, 209.
71. VW to Nelly Cecil, [12 November 1922], II, 585.
72. VW to Ralph Partridge, [10 November 1922], II, 583.
73. *Diary*, 27 November 1922, II, 213–14.
74. VW to Jacques Raverat, 10 December 1922, II, 592.
75. *Diary*, 2 January 1923, II, 221.
76. *Diary*, 28 January 1923, II, 228.
77. *Diary*, 16 January 1923, II, 225–6.
78. *Diary*, 15 December 1922, II, 216–17.
79. VW to Gerald Brenan, 25 December 1922, II, 600.

CHAPTER TWELVE: THE FORCE FLOWING FULLEST

1. *Diary*, 19 February 1923, II, 235.
2. *Diary*, 6 March 1923, II, 237.
3. VW to Barbara Bagenal, 8 July [1923], III, 56.
4. *Diary*, 15 October 1923, II, 271.
5. *Diary*, 28 June 1923, II, 250.
6. VW to Jacques Raverat, [30 March 1923], III, 23.
7. VW to Vanessa Bell, 1 April [1923], III, 25.
8. Gerald Brenan, *South from Granada*, 139.
9. Ibid., 142.
10. VW to Vanessa Bell, 1 April [1923], III, 26.
11. VW to Roger Fry, 16 April 1923, III, 29.
12. VW to Molly MacCarthy, 22 April 1923, III, 30.
13. VW to Leonard Woolf, [25 April 1923], III, 31.
14. *Diary*, 30 August 1923, II, 263.
15. *Diary*, 13 June 1923, II, 246.
16. *Diary*, 19 June 1923, II, 248.
17. VW to Jacques Raverat, 30 July 1923, III, 59.
18. *Diary*, 27 April 1925, III, 12.
19. *Diary*, 19 February 1923, II, 235–6.
20. VW to Jacques Raverat, 24 January 1925, III, 155.
21. *Portrait of a Marriage*, 116.
22. VW to Gwen Raverat, 11 March [1925], III, 172.
23. Jacques Raverat to VW, 14 September 1923 and [September?] 1924, MS Sussex.
24. VW to Gwen Raverat, 11 March [1925], III, 171.
25. *Diary*, 3 December 1923, II, 277.
26. *Autobiography*, II, 272.
27. *Diary*, 3 January 1924, II, 281.
28. *Diary*, 9 January 1924, II, 283–4.
29. *Diary*, 9 January 1924, II, 283.
30. Ibid.
31. VW to Vanessa Bell, [27 April 1924], III, 104.
32. *Diary*, 23 February 1924, II, 293.
33. Stephen Spender, *World Within World*, 151.
34. May Sarton, *I Knew a Phoenix*, 219.
35. *Diary*, 5 April 1924, II, 298.
36. Ibid., II, 299.
37. *Diary*, 5 May 1924, II, 301.
38. VW to Molly MacCarthy, [22 November 1924], III, 143.
39. *Diary*, 3 February 1924, II, 290.

40. VW to Jacques Raverat, 8 June 1924, III, 115.
41. VW to Marjorie Joad, [20? July 1924], III, 119–20.
42. VW to Vita Sackville-West, 21 May [1924], III, 110.
43. *Diary*, 5 July 1924, II, 306.
44. VW to Jacques Raverat, 26 December 1924, III, 150.
45. *Diary*, 9 February 1924, II, 292.
46. *Diary*, 5 April 1924, II, 299.
47. *Diary*, 3 August 1924, II, 309.
48. *Diary*, 15 September 1924, II, 314.
49. VW to Violet Dickinson, 1 August 1924, III, 124.
50. *Diary*, 17 October 1924, II, 319.
51. VW to Jacques Raverat, 3 October 1924, III, 135.
52. *CSF*, 121.
53. 'Character in Fiction', *Criterion*, July 1924, *Essays*, III, 430.
54. 'Mr Bennett and Mrs Brown', *New York Evening Post*, 17 November 1923, *Essays*, III, 388.
55. *Essays*, III, 487.
56. *Diary*, 17 October 1924, II, 319.
57. *Diary*, 5 June 1925, III, 28.
58. VW to Jacques Raverat, 8 June 1924, III, 115.
59. *Diary*, 17 October 1924, II, 317.
60. VW to Vanessa Bell, 3 April [1925], III, 176.
61. *Diary*, 8 April 1925, III, 7.
62. *Diary*, 15 October 1923, II, 272.
63. *Diary*, 17 October 1924, II, 316.
64. *Diary*, 17 March 1923, II, 239.
65. VW to Pernel Strachey, 3 August [1923], III, 62.
66. Holograph notebook dated 12 March 1922, 153, MS Berg.
67. *Mrs Dalloway*, 34.
68. Ibid.
69. Ibid.
70. Ibid., 38.
71. Ibid., 201–2.
72. Ibid., 204.
73. Ibid., 213.
74. Cited in note 3, *Diary*, 8 April 1925, III, 7.
75. *Diary*, 14 May 1925, III, 18.
76. Ibid., 21.
77. *Diary*, 27 April 1925, III, 12.
78. *Diary*, 9 May 1925, III, 17.
79. Hugh I'Anson Fausset, *Manchester Guardian*, 14 May 1925.
80. 'A Novelist's Experiment', *Times Literary Supplement*, 21 May 1925.

81. P. C. Kennedy, *New Statesman*, 6 June 1925.
82. Vita Sackville-West to VW, 26 May [1925], *Vita–Virginia Letters*, 66.
83. Monks House Papers, Sussex.
84. *Diary*, 17 May 1925, III, 23.

CHAPTER THIRTEEN: WHITE FIRE

1. *Diary*, 16 October 1924, II, 317. See also *Diary*, 6 January 1925, III, 3.
2. *Diary*, 20 July 1925, III, 36.
3. *Diary*, 20 July 1925, III, 37.
4. VW to Roger Fry, 16 September 1925, III, 209.
5. VW to Janet Case, [18 September 1925], III, 211.
6. *Diary*, 27 November 1925, III, 46.
7. VW to Vita Sackville-West, [16 November 1925], III, 221.
8. *Diary*, 7 December 1925, III, 51.
9. *Diary*, 22 September 1925, III, 43.
10. VW to Vita Sackville-West, [1 September 1925], III, 200.
11. VW to Vita Sackville-West, [24 August 1925], III, 198.
12. *Diary*, 27 November 1925, III, 47.
13. Vita Sackville-West to Harold Nicolson, 17 August 1926, *Vita and Harold*, 158–9.
14. *Diary*, 21 December 1925, III, 51–2.
15. *Autobiography*, II, 268–9.
16. VW to Vita Sackville-West, [5 January 1926], III, 226.
17. *Diary*, 19 January 1926, III, 57.
18. Vita Sackville-West to VW, 21 [January 1926], *Vita–Virginia Letters*, 98.
19. VW to Vita Sackville-West, 26 January 1926, III, 231.
20. VW to Vita Sackville-West, [15 September 1925], III, 207.
21. 'On Being Ill', *New Criterion*, January 1926.
22. *Diary*, 23 February 1926, III, 59.
23. *Diary*, 27 February 1926, III, 62–3.
24. *Diary*, 24 February 1926, III, 61.
25. VW to Vita Sackville-West, 16 March 1926, III, 247.
26. VW to Vita Sackville-West, 29 March 1926, III, 251.
27. *Diary*, 24 March 1926, III, 69–70.
28. *Diary*, 9 April 1926, III, 73.
29. *To the Lighthouse*, 57.
30. Ibid., 71.
31. Ibid., 64.
32. Ibid., 90–91.
33. Ibid., 114.
34. *Diary*, 18 April 1926, III, 76.

35. *To the Lighthouse*, 134.
36. Ibid., 145.
37. *Diary*, 12 May 1926, III, 85.
38. *Diary*, 9 May 1926, III, 81.
39. *Diary*, 6 May 1926, III, 78.
40. *Diary*, 9 May 1926, III, 81.
41. *Diary*, 20 May 1926, III, 86–7.
42. *Diary*, 25 May 1926, III, 88.
43. *Diary*, 9 June 1926, III, 89.
44. *Diary*, 25 May 1926, III, 87.
45. VW to Vanessa Bell, 2 June 1926, III, 270–71.
46. VW to Vanessa Bell, 13 June [1926], III, 275.
47. Vanessa Bell to VW, 16 June [1926], MS Berg.
48. *Diary*, 30 June 1926, III, 91.
49. *Diary*, 22 July 1926, III, 95.
50. VW to Vita Sackville-West, [19? July 1926], III, 281.
51. *Diary*, 25 July 1926, III, 96–101.
52. *Diary*, 31 July 1926, III, 103.
53. *Diary*, 3 September 1926, III, 106.
54. VW to Vita Sackville-West, [8 August 1926], III, 285.
55. *Diary*, 5 September 1926, III, 107.
56. *Diary*, 15 September 1926, III, 110.
57. Ibid., III, 110–111.
58. *Diary*, 30 September 1926, III, 113.
59. *To the Lighthouse*, 199.
60. Ibid., 223.
61. Ibid., 188.
62. Ibid., 194.
63. Ibid., 209–210.
64. Ibid., 225–6.
65. Ibid., 57.
66. VW to Vita Sackville-West, 18 February 1927, III, 333.
67. VW to Vita Sackville-West, 31 January [1927], III, 321.
68. *Diary*, 23 November 1926, III, 117.
69. VW to Vita Sackville-West, [19 November 1926], III, 302.
70. *Diary*, 23 November 1926, III, 117.
71. *Diary*, 23 January 1927, III, 125.
72. *Diary*, 14 March 1927, III, 131.
73. VW to Vita Sackville-West, 31 January [1927], III, 320.
74. VW to Vita Sackville-West, 28 February 1927, III, 337.
75. VW to Vanessa Bell, 18 February 1927, III, 334.
76. VW to Vita Sackville-West, 18 February 1927, III, 333.

77. *Diary*, 28 February 1927, III, 129.
78. VW to Vanessa Bell, 5 March 1927, III, 340–41.
79. *Diary*, 21 March 1927, III, 132.
80. VW to Vita Sackville-West, 23 March 1927, III, 352.
81. VW to Vita Sackville-West, 5 April [1927], III, 359.
82. VW to Vanessa Bell, 9 April 1927, III, 360–61.
83. VW to Vanessa Bell, 21 April 1927, III, 365.
84. VW to Vanessa Bell, 26 April 1927, III, 367.
85. Vanessa Bell to VW, [16 April] 1927, MS Berg.
86. VW to Vanessa Bell, 21 April 1927, III, 366.
87. VW to Vanessa Bell, 8 May 1927, III, 369–70.
88. Rachel A. Taylor, *Spectator*, 14 May 1927.
89. Cited in *Diary*, III, 116.
90. Arnold Bennett, 'Another Criticism of the New School', *Evening Standard*, 2 December 1926.
91. 'Am I a Snob?', *Moments*, 211–12.
92. Vita Sackville-West to VW, [12 May 1927], *Vita–Virginia Letters*, 218.
93. Vanessa Bell to VW, [11 May] 1927, MS Berg.
94. VW to Vanessa Bell, 22 May 1927, III, 379.
95. VW to Vita Sackville-West, [13 May 1927], III, 374.
96. VW to Roger Fry, 27 May 1927, III, 385.
97. VW to Vita Sackville-West, [5 June 1927], III, 388.
98. VW to Roger Fry, 27 May 1927, III, 385.
99. Vanessa Bell to VW, 3 May [1927], MS Berg.
100. *Diary*, 6 June 1927, III, 137.
101. *Recollections*, 77.
102. Ibid., 152.
103. Ibid., 78.
104. VW to Vita Sackville-West, [1927], III, 393.
105. *Diary*, 30 June 1927, III, 143–4.

CHAPTER FOURTEEN: A THIN SILVER EDGE

1. VW to Vita Sackville-West, [4 July 1927], III, 395.
2. *Diary*, 4 July 1927, III, 146.
3. *Diary*, [5 September] 1926, III, 106.
4. VW to Vita Sackville-West, [8? July 1927], III, 397.
5. *CSF*, 220.
6. VW to Vanessa Bell, 23 July [1927], III, 401.
7. *Diary*, 21 August 1927, III, 153.
8. *Diary*, 23 July 1927, III, 148–9.
9. *Diary*, 10 August 1927, III, 152.

10. VW to Vita Sackville-West, [7 August 1927], III, 408.
11. VW to Vanessa Bell, [end August 1927], III, 415.
12. VW to Ethel Sands, 2 September [1927], III, 417.
13. E. M. Forster to VW, 5 June 1927, MS copy Sussex.
14. Cited in P. N. Furbank, *E. M. Forster: A Life*, II, 145.
15. Ibid.
16. *Nation and Athenaeum*, 12 November 1927.
17. Cited in Furbank, II. 146.
18. *Diary*, 10 August 1927, III, 152.
19. VW to E. M. Forster, 16 November [1927], III, 437.
20. VW to Vanessa Bell, 23 July [1927], III, 401.
21. VW to Vita Sackville-West, 9 October [1927], III, 427–9.
22. Vita Sackville-West to VW, [11 October 1927], *Vita–Virginia Letters*, 252.
23. VW to Clive Bell, [November 1927], III, 441.
24. VW to Vita Sackville-West, 9 October [1927], III, 428.
25. *Diary*, 22 December 1927, III, 168.
26. *Diary*, 20 December 1927, III, 167.
27. See, for example, *Diary*, 24 November 1936, V, 35.
28. VW to Clive Bell, 21 January [1928], III, 447.
29. VW to Vanessa Bell, 11 February [1928], II, 456–7.
30. VW to Vanessa Bell, 5 March 1928, III, 466–7.
31. VW to Vanessa Bell, 25 March [1928], III, 478.
32. *Orlando*, 181.
33. Ibid., 43.
34. Ibid., 240.
35. Ibid., 94.
36. Ibid., 313–14.
37. *Diary*, 22 March 1928, III, 177.
38. VW to Vita Sackville-West, 31 March 1928, III, 479.
39. VW to Vita Sackville-West, [17 April 1928], III, 484.
40. VW to Clive Bell, 21 April [1928], III, 486–7.
41. VW to Vanessa Bell, 9 May [1928], III, 495.
42. *Diary*, 21 April 1928, III, 181.
43. Richard Kennedy, *A Boy at the Hogarth Press*, 32.
44. Ibid., 39.
45. Ibid., 45.
46. VW to Vanessa Bell, 25 May [1928], III, 501.
47. *Diary*, 31 May 1928, III, 185.
48. *Diary*, 20 June 1928, III, 186.
49. *Diary*, 8 August 1928, III, 188.
50. *Diary*, 3 September 1928, III, 194–5.

51. VW to Vanessa Bell, [2 September 1928], III, 525.
52. VW to Vita Sackville-West, 8 September 1928, III, 529.
53. VW to Vita Sackville-West, [16 September 1928], III, 531.
54. *Diary*, 22 September 1928, III, 197.
55. VW to Leonard Woolf, 28 September [1928], III, 539.
56. See headnote, *Letters*, III, 533.
57. VW to Leonard Woolf, [25 September 1928], III, 535.
58. J. C. Squire, *Observer*, 21 October 1928.
59. Arnold Bennett, 'A Woman's High-Brow Lark', *Evening Standard*, 8 November 1928.
60. MS Sussex.
61. VW to Edward Sackville-West, 21 November [1928], III, 559.
62. *Vita–Virginia Letters*, 304–6.
63. VW to Vita Sackville-West, [12 October 1928], *Congenial*, 241.
64. VW to Vanessa Bell, [16? October 1928], III, 546–7.
65. Cited by S. P. Rosenbaum in *Women & Fiction*, xv–xvi.
66. Ibid., xvi.
67. *Diary*, 27 October 1928, III, 200.
68. *Women & Fiction*, xviii.
69. Ibid., 195.
70. Ibid., 197.
71. Ibid., 198.
72. Ibid., 199.
73. Ibid., 201.
74. VW to Quentin Bell, 1 November 1928, III, 555.
75. *Diary*, 10 November 1928, III, 207.
76. VW to Vita Sackville-West, [14 December 1928], III, 563.
77. *Diary*, 7 November 1928, III, 204.
78. Ibid., II, 203.
79. *Diary*, 27 October 1928, III, 200.
80. *Diary*, 28 November 1928, III, 208–10.
81. *Diary*, 18 December 1928, III, 212.
82. VW to Vita Sackville-West, 29 December 1928, III, 568–9.

CHAPTER FIFTEEN: WRITING FOR WRITING'S SAKE

1. Vita Sackville-West to VW, 12 January [1928], *Vita–Virginia Letters*, 324.
2. VW to Vita Sackville-West, [9? January 1929], IV, 5.
3. VW to Vita Sackville-West, 8 January [1929], IV, 2.
4. VW to Vita Sackville-West, [30 January 1929], IV, 10.
5. Vita Sackville-West to VW, [6 February 1929], *Vita–Virginia Letters*, 336.
6. VW to Vita Sackville-West, 7 February [1929], IV, 17.

7. VW to Vita Sackville-West, [29 January 1929], IV, 9.
8. VW to Vita Sackville-West, 5 April [1929], IV, 36.
9. VW to Vita Sackville-West, 12 February [1929], IV, 21.
10. VW to Dorothy Brett, 8 March 1929, IV, 32.
11. *Diary*, 28 March 1929, III, 219.
12. *Diary*, 31 May 1929, III, 230–31.
13. *Diary*, 23 June 1929, III, 235.
14. VW to Mary Hutchinson, 8 June 1929, *Congenial*, 249.
15. *Diary*, 15 June 1929, III, 232.
16. *Diary*, 23 June 1929, III, 236.
17. *Diary*, 30 June 1929, III, 237.
18. *Diary*, 13 April 1929, III, 221.
19. *A Room of One's Own*, 60–61.
20. Ibid., 62.
21. Ibid., 128.
22. Ibid., 136.
23. Ibid., 90.
24. VW to Ethel Smyth, [6 April 1930], IV, 155.
25. *A Room of One's Own,* 106.
26. Arnold Bennett, *Evening Standard*, 28 November 1929.
27. Vita Sackville-West, *Listener*, 6 November 1929.
28. VW to G. L. Dickinson, 27 October 1931, IV, 397.
29. *The Waves*, 31.
30. VW to Gerald Brenan, 4 October 1929, IV, 97–8.
31. *Diary*, 11 October 1929, III, 260.
32. *Diary*, 4 January 1929, III, 218.
33. *Diary*, 30 September 1926, III, 113.
34. VW to Vita Sackville-West, [13 November 1929], IV, 107.
35. *Diary*, 25 November 1929, III, 267.
36. *Diary*, 14 December 1929, III, 273.
37. *Diary*, 26 December 1929, III, 275.
38. *Diary*, 26 January 1930, III, 285.
39. *Diary*, 16 February 1930, III, 287.
40. VW to Ethel Smyth, 12 October [1940], VI, 439.
41. *New Statesman*, 23 April 1921, *Essays*, III, 299.
42. VW to Ethel Smyth, 30 January 1930, IV, 131.
43. Ethel Smyth to VW, 20 August 1930, MS Berg.
44. VW to Vita Sackville-West, 5 May [1930], IV, 163.
45. Ethel Smyth to VW, 2 May 1930, MS Berg.
46. VW to Ethel Smyth, [16 July 1930], IV, 188.
47. VW to Ethel Smyth, [17 February 1930], IV, 140.
48. *Diary*, 21 February 1930, III, 290–92.

49. VW to Saxon Sydney-Turner, 27 February [1930], IV, 146.
50. VW to Quentin Bell, 14 May 1930, IV, 171.
51. VW to Ethel Smyth, [6 April 1930], IV, 154.
52. *Diary*, 22 February 1930, III, 293.
53. *Diary*, 1 May 1930, III, 303.
54. VW to Vita Sackville-West, 8? May [1930], IV, 165.
55. *Diary*, 16 June 1930, III, 306.
56. VW to Ethel Smyth, [26 July 1930], IV, 192.
57. VW to Ethel Smyth, 2 August [1930], IV, 195–6.
58. VW to Ethel Smyth, 15 August 1930, IV, 200.
59. *Diary*, 6 August 1930, III, 311.
60. *Diary*, 2 September 1930, III, 316.
61. VW to Ethel Smyth, [1 September 1930], IV, 206 and *Diary*, 2 September 1930, III, 315.
62. VW to Ethel Smyth, 19 September 1930, IV, 217.
63. VW to Ethel Smyth, [22] September [1930], IV, 218.
64. *Diary*, [5? November] 1930, III, 329.
65. *Diary*, 12 November 1930, III, 334.
66. VW to Vita Sackville-West, 30 October [1930], IV, 240.
67. VW to Ethel Smyth, 30 October 1930, IV, 242.
68. Cecil Beaton, *The Book of Beauty*, 37.
69. VW to Ethel Sands, [November 1930], IV, 258.
70. *Diary*, 2 December 1930, III, 335.
71. *Diary*, 8 November 1930, III, 329.
72. VW to Ethel Smyth, [14 November 1930], IV, 253.
73. *Diary*, 8 November 1930, III, 331.
74. VW to Vanessa Bell, [22 July 1936], VI, 59.
75. VW to Vita Sackville-West, [6 November 1930], IV, 247.

CHAPTER SIXTEEN: THE SINGING OF THE REAL WORLD

1. *Diary*, 26 January 1931, IV, 7.
2. *Diary*, 2 February 1931, IV, 8.
3. *Diary*, 7 February 1931, IV, 10.
4. VW to Clive Bell, 21 February 1931, IV, 294.
5. *Diary*, 28 March 1931, IV, 16.
6. VW to Roger Fry, 21 February [1931], IV, 295.
7. VW to Clive Bell, 21 February 1931, IV, 293.
8. VW to Ethel Smyth, 11 March 1931, IV, 297–8.
9. VW to Ethel Smyth, 1 April [1931], IV, 302.
10. VW to Ethel Smyth, 7 April [1931], IV, 303.
11. *Diary*, 11 April 1931, IV, 18.

12. VW to Quentin Bell, 24 April 1931, IV, 320.
13. VW to Ethel Smyth, 24 April 1931, IV, 321.
14. *Diary*, 3 May 1931, IV, 25.
15. VW to Ethel Smyth, 12 May [1931], IV, 329.
16. VW to Vanessa Bell, 23 May [1931], IV, 334.
17. VW to Ethel Smyth, [4 July 1931], IV, 352.
18. VW to Vita Sackville-West, [24 May 1931], IV, 337.
19. *Diary*, 19 May 1931, IV, 26.
20. VW to Vita Sackville-West, [8 August 1931], IV, 366.
21. VW to Ethel Smyth, 29 December [1931], IV, 422.
22. VW to Vita Sackville-West, [30 August 1931], IV, 371.
23. VW to Ethel Smyth, 2 September [1931], IV, 372.
24. *The Waves*, 170–71.
25. Ibid., 228.
26. 'The Bubble Reputation', *Life & Letters*, September 1931.
27. VW to Ethel Smyth, [6 September 1931], IV, 375.
28. *Diary*, 22 September 1931, IV, 45.
29. *Diary*, 15 September 1931, IV, 43.
30. VW to John Lehmann, 17 September [1931], IV, 381.
31. VW to Vita Sackville-West, [6 December 1931], IV, 410.
32. *Diary*, 9 October 1931, IV, 47.
33. Lytton Strachey to Topsy Lucas, [4 November 1931], cited in *Holroyd*, 1051.
34. E. M. Forster to VW, 12 November 1931, MS Berg.
35. Ethel Smyth to VW, 8 October 1931, MS Sussex.
36. G. Lowes Dickinson to VW, 23 October 1931, cited in Robin Majumdar and Allen McLaurin (eds.), *Virginia Woolf: The Critical Heritage*, 271.
37. Vanessa Bell to VW, [14 October 1931], cited in *Letters*, IV, 390–91, note 1.
38. Edwin Muir, *Bookman*, December 1931.
39. *Diary*, 23 October? 1931, IV, 51.
40. VW to Ottoline Morrell, 23 February [1933], V, 162.
41. VW to George Rylands, 22 November [1931], IV, 408.
42. VW to Ethel Smyth, [21 November 1931]. IV, 407.
43. VW to Lytton Strachey, 10 December [1931], IV, 412.
44. VW to Ethel Smyth, [19 December 1931], IV, 415.
45. *Diary*, 25 December 1931, IV, 55.
46. *Diary*, 13 January 1932, IV, 63.
47. *Diary*, 22 January 1932, IV, 64–5.
48. *Diary*, 12 March 1932, IV, 82–3.
49. VW to Ottoline Morrell, [25? November 1932], V, 130.
50. VW to Vanessa Bell, 11 April 1932, V, 45.

51. *Diary*, 24 March 1932, IV, 85.
52. VW to William Plomer, [20 March 1932], V, 37.
53. *Diary*, 16 February 1932, IV, 77.
54. *Diary*, 29 February 1932, IV, 79.
55. VW to Clive Bell, 29 February 1932, V, 27.
56. *Diary*, 18 April 1932, IV, 90.
57. VW to Vanessa Bell, 19 April 1932, V, 50.
58. *Diary*, 8 May 1932, IV, 96.
59. *Diary*, 21 April 1932, IV, 90.
60. Ibid., IV, 91.
61. VW to Vanessa Bell, 2 May [1932], V, 57.
62. *Diary*, 8 May 1932, IV, 97.
63. VW to John Lehmann, 8 May [1932], V, 62.
64. *Diary*, 25 May 1932, IV, 102–3.
65. VW to Ethel Smyth, [26 May 1932], V, 67.
66. *Diary*, 1 June 1932, IV, 105.
67. *Diary*, 13 June 1932, IV, 109.
68. *Diary*, 29 June 1932, IV, 113.
69. VW to Ethel Smyth, [12 July 1932], V, 77.
70. VW to Ethel Smyth, [14 July 1932], V, 78.
71. *Diary*, 14 July 1932, IV, 117.
72. VW to Ethel Smyth, [28 July 1932], V, 81–2.
73. VW to Ethel Smyth, 7–8 August [1932], V, 85–6.
74. *Diary*, 5 August 1932, IV, 120.
75. *Diary*, 17 August 1932, IV, 121.
76. VW to Ethel Smyth, 21 August [1932], V, 97.
77. *Diary*, 2 September 1932, IV, 123.
78. VW to Ottoline Morrell, 6 September [1932], V, 98.
79. *Diary*, 2 November 1932, IV, 129.
80. *The Pargiters*, 43.
81. Ibid., 50.
82. Ibid., 154–5.
83. *Diary*, 16 September 1932, IV, 124.
84. *Diary*, 2 October 1932, IV, 125.
85. VW to George Rylands, 29 January 1933, V, 155.
86. VW to Vita Sackville-West, 14 February [1933], V, 157.
87. *Diary*, 10 November 1932, IV, 130.
88. *Diary*, 31 December 1932, IV, 135.
89. *Diary*, 25 March 1933, IV, 148.
90. VW to Vita Sackville-West, 7 January 1933, V, 149.
91. VW to Ethel Smyth, 1 March [1933], V, 164.
92. *Diary*, 29 April 1933, IV, 530.

93. VW to Vanessa Bell, 17 May [1933], V, 185.
94. *Diary*, 11 May 1933, IV, 155.
95. *Diary*, 12 May 1933, IV, 155.
96. *Diary*, 31 May 1933, IV, 161.
97. VW to Ethel Smyth, 18 May [1933], V, 187.
98. VW to Ethel Smyth, 6 June [1933], V, 192.
99. *Diary*, 21 July 1933, IV, 168.
100. VW to Quentin Bell, [26 July 1933], V, 206.
101. VW to Ethel Smyth, 31 July 1933, V, 209.
102. VW to Ethel Smyth, 22 August [1933], V, 217.
103. *Diary*, 24 August 1933, IV, 173.
104. *The Pargiters*, holograph draft, IV, 70, MS Berg.
105. *Diary*, 25 March 1933, IV, 148.
106. *Diary*, 10 September 1933, IV, 178.
107. VW to Quentin Bell, [19 September 1933], V, 226.
108. VW to Quentin Bell, [14 October 1933], V, 234.
109. *Diary*, 5 October 1933, IV, 181.
110. Rebecca West, *Daily Telegraph*, 6 October 1933.
111. Geoffrey Grigson, *Morning Post*, 6 October 1933.
112. *Granta*, 25 October 1933.
113. *Diary*, 29 October 1933, IV, 186.
114. *Diary*, 29 November 1933, IV, 191.
115. *Diary*, 7 December 1933, IV, 192.
116. *Diary*, 17 December 1933, IV, 193.

CHAPTER SEVENTEEN: BETWEEN TWO WORLDS

1. VW to Quentin Bell, 15 February [1934], V, 277.
2. VW to Ethel Smyth, 29 March [1934], V, 285.
3. *Recollections*, 189.
4. *Diary*, 11 July 1934, IV, 224.
5. VW to Ethel Smyth, [26 February 1934], V, 279.
6. *The Pargiters*, holograph draft, V, 65, MS Berg.
7. Ibid., V, 100.
8. Ibid., V, 111.
9. Ibid., V, 126.
10. *Diary*, 18 February 1934, IV, 202.
11. *The Pargiters*, holograph draft, VI, 4, MS Berg.
12. Ibid., VI, 31.
13. VW to Ottoline Morrell, [4 February 1932], V, 14.
14. *Diary*, [24 March] 1932, IV, 86.
15. VW to Vita Sackville-West, 18 [October 1932], V, 111.

16. *Diary*, 19 April 1934, IV, 208.
17. *Recollections*, 62–4.
18. *Diary*, 30 April 1934, IV, 210.
19. *Diary*, 1 May 1934, IV, 211.
20. *Diary*, 3 May 1934, IV, 214.
21. VW to Vanessa Bell, [3 May 1934], V, 299.
22. VW to Vita Sackville-West, [10 May 1934], V, 302.
23. VW to Ethel Smyth, 2 July [1935], V, 409.
24. VW to Ethel Smyth, 25 July 1936, VI, 60.
25. *Diary*, 2 July 1934, IV, 223–4.
26. *Diary*, 7 August 1934, IV, 236.
27. *The Pargiters*, holograph draft, VI, 104, MS Berg.
28. Ibid., VII, 130–31.
29. Ibid., VIII, 12–13.
30. *Diary*, 22 May 1934, IV, 221.
31. *Diary*, 30 September 1934, IV, 245.
32. *Diary*, 12 September 1934, IV, 242.
33. *Diary*, 19 September 1934, IV, 244.
34. VW to Pamela Diamand, [end September 1934], V, 335.
35. *Diary*, 17 October 1934, IV, 253.
36. VW to Ethel Smyth, [8 August 1934], V, 321.
37. VW to Vita Sackville-West, [23 September 1934], V, 333.
38. *Diary*, 11 October 1934, IV, 251.
39. *Diary*, 14 October 1934, IV, 251–2.
40. *Diary*, 15 October 1934, IV, 252.
41. *Diary*, 17 October 1934, IV, 253.
42. VW to Vita Sackville-West, [30 October 1934], V, 342.
43. *Diary*, 26 November 1934, IV, 263.
44. Doris Meyer, *Victoria Ocampo*, 124.
45. *Diary*, 26 November 1934, IV, 263.
46. VW's memoir of Julian Bell, MS Sussex, cited in *Bell.*, II, 256.
47. *Diary*, 27 November 1934, IV, 264.
48. *Diary*, 18 December 1934, IV, 266.
49. Elizabeth Bibesco to VW, 1 January 1935, MS Sussex.
50. *Diary*, 6 January 1935, IV, 273.
51. *Diary*, 9 April 1935, IV, 297–8.
52. *Diary*, 11 March 1935, IV, 287.
53. VW to Ethel Smyth, [25 March 1935], V, 279.
54. VW to Vita Sackville-West, [29 March 1935], V, 380.
55. *Diary*, 15 April 1935, IV, 300.
56. *Diary*, 17 April 1935, IV, 302.
57. *Diary*, 22 April 1935, IV, 304.

58. *Autobiography*, II, 325.
59. VW to Vanessa Bell, 7 May [1935], V, 389.
60. VW to Ethel Smyth, 8 May [1935], V, 391.
61. *Diary*, 9 May 1935, IV, 311.
62. *Autobiography*, II, 330.
63. *Diary*, 4 September 1935, IV, 338.
64. VW to Clive Bell, 15 May [1935], V, 394.
65. *Diary*, 1 June 1935, IV, 318.
66. *Diary*, 5 June 1935, IV, 319.
67. VW to Ethel Smyth, [6 June 1935], V, 399.
68. *Diary*, 6 June 1935, IV, 319.
69. *Diary*, 20 June 1935, IV, 323.
70. *Diary*, 25 June 1935, IV, 326.
71. VW to Vanessa Bell, 3 July [1935], V, 411.
72. VW to Ottoline Morrell, [14 July 1935], V, 415.
73. *Diary*, 17 July 1935, IV, 332.
74. *Diary*, 16 October 1935, IV, 347.
75. *Diary*, 27 October 1935, IV, 348.
76. VW to Ethel Smyth, [26 November 1935], V, 446.
77. *Diary*, 15 September 1935, IV, 342.
78. VW to Vanessa Bell, 17 July [1935], V, 417.
79. VW to Ethel Smyth, [10 August 1935], V, 423.
80. VW to Jane Bussy, [10 August 1935], V, 424.
81. *Diary*, 4 September 1935, IV, 337.
82. *Diary*, 27 October 1935, IV, 348.
83. *Diary*, 15 October 1935, IV, 347.
84. VW to Ethel Smyth, [13 November 1935], V, 442.
85. VW to Ethel Smyth, [26 November 1935], V, 446.
86. Emily Hale's letter to Ruth George describing her encounter with the Woolfs is at Scripps College, Claremont, California. It is cited in note 2, *Letters*, V, 446.
87. VW to Ethel Smyth, [26 November 1935], V, 447.
88. VW to Vita Sackville-West, [10 November 1935], V, 441.
89. *Diary*, 27 November 1935, IV, 355.
90. VW to Julian Bell, 17 December 1935, V, 452.
91. Charlotte Wolff, *Studies in Hand-Reading*, 90.
92. *Diary*, 30 December 1935, IV, 361.

CHAPTER EIGHTEEN: UNDER THE SHADOW

1. *Diary*, 16 March 1936, V, 17.
2. *Diary*, 16 January 1936, V, 8.

3. *Diary*, 7 January 1936, V, 5.
4. VW to Julian Bell, 20 January 1936, VI, 9–10.
5. *Diary*, 20 March 1936, V, 19.
6. VW to Ethel Smyth, [11 January 1936], VI, 4.
7. VW to Julian Bell, 11 March 1936, VI, 20.
8. VW to Ethel Smyth, [25 July 1936], VI, 60.
9. *Recollections*, 110.
10. Cited in note 3, *Letters*, VI, 21.
11. Ethel Smyth to VW, undated letter, MS Berg.
12. *Diary*, 1 April 1936, V, 21.
13. VW to Vita Sackville-West, 14 May [1936], VI, 40.
14. VW to Julian Bell, 21 May 1936, *Congenial*, 372.
15. *Diary*, 11 June 1936, V, 24.
16. VW to Julian Bell, 28 June 1936, 'Some New Woolf Letters', 188.
17. Julian Bell to Vanessa Bell, 20 September 1936, quoted in Peter Stansky and William Abrahams, *Journey to the Frontier*, 278.
18. VW to Julian Bell, 11 March 1936, VI, 20.
19. VW to Ethel Smyth, [22 August 1936], VI, 66.
20. VW to Ottoline Morrell, 9 October [1936], VI, 76.
21. *Diary*, 3 November 1936, V, 29.
22. Ibid., V, 30.
23. *Diary*, 5 November 1936, V, 30.
24. *Autobiography*, II, 301.
25. *Diary*, 24 November 1936, V, 35.
26. 'Am I a Snob?', *Moments*, 224.
27. Ibid., 210–11.
28. Ibid., 220.
29. *Diary*, 30 October 1936, V, 28.
30. *Diary*, 10 December 1936, V, 43.
31. *Diary*, 7 December 1936, V, 39–40.
32. VW to Violet Dickinson, 6 December [1936], VI, 90.
33. VW to Vita Sackville-West, 27 December [1936], VI, 98.
34. *Diary*, 30 December 1936, V, 44.
35. *Diary*, 10 January 1937, V, 47.
36. VW to Janet Case, 24 December 1936, VI, 95.
37. VW to Julian Bell, 30 December 1936, 'Some New Woolf Letters', 196.
38. *Diary*, 22 January 1937, V, 51.
39. *Diary*, 18 February 1937, V, 56.
40. *Diary*, 28 February 1937, V, 62.
41. *Diary*, 1 March 1937, V, 63.
42. *Diary*, 7 March 1937, V, 65.
43. Basil de Selincourt, *Observer*, 14 March 1937.

44. Edwin Muir, *Listener*, 31 March 1937.
45. *Diary*, 2 April 1937, V, 75.
46. *Diary*, 28 March 1937, V, 72–3.
47. VW to Stephen Spender, 7 April [1937], VI, 116.
48. *Diary*, 1 June 1937, V, 91.
49. *Diary*, 9 April 1937, V, 78.
50. *Diary*, 14 March 1937, V, 68.
51. *Diary*, 4 May 1937, V, 86.
52. *Diary*, 21 April 1937, V, 80–81.
53. VW to May Sarton, 16 June [1937], VI, 137.
54. May Sarton, *I Knew a Phoenix*, 217–22.
55. *Diary*, 17 August 1937, V, 108.
56. VW to W. A. Robson, 26 July [1937], VI, 150.
57. VW to Vita Sackville-West, [26? July 1937], VI, 151.
58. VW to Vanessa Bell, [5 August 1937], VI, 153.
59. VW to Vanessa Bell, [31 August 1937], VI, 166.
60. *Diary*, 11 August 1937, V, 106.
61. VW to Vanessa Bell, [17 August 1937], VI, 158.
62. *Diary*, 6 August 1937, V, 105.
63. *Diary*, 22 October 1937, V, 115.
64. VW to Ethel Smyth, 26 October [1937], VI, 185.
65. *Diary*, 12 October 1937, V, 112.
66. *Diary*, 6 August 1937, V, 105.
67. *Diary*, 19 October 1937, V, 114.
68. *Diary*, 18 December 1937, V, 121–2.

CHAPTER NINETEEN: FRESH ADVENTURES, VIOLENT FEELINGS

1. John Lehmann, *Thrown to the Woolfs*, 57.
2. Ibid., 58.
3. *Diary*, 22 October 1937, V, 116.
4. Leonard Woolf to John Lehmann, 2 January 1938. The letter is in VW's hand and is included in the sixth volume of her letters, 201.
5. VW to John Lehmann, [early June 1938], VI, 252.
6. Vanessa Bell to VW, [4 February 1938], MS Berg.
7. VW to Vita Sackville-West, [14 February 1938], VI, 214.
8. *Diary*, 4 February 1938, V, 127.
9. *Diary*, 26 March 1938, V, 132.
10. *Diary*, 22 March 1938, V, 131.
11. *Diary*, 3 May 1938, V, 138.
12. *Diary*, 26 April 1938, V, 135.

13. *Diary*, 25 May 1938, V, 143–4.
14. *Diary*, 24 May 1938, V, 142.
15. *Three Guineas*, 154.
16. Ibid., 261.
17. VW to Vita Sackville-West, 1 June [1938], VI, 231.
18. Theodora Bosanquet, *Time and Tide*, 4 June 1938.
19. Basil de Selincourt, *Observer*, 5 June 1938.
20. Graham Greene, *Spectator*, 17 June 1938.
21. *Diary*, 5 June 1938, V, 148.
22. *Three Guineas*, 179–80.
23. Ibid., 164.
24. Ibid., 180.
25. VW to Ethel Smyth, 7 June [1938], VI, 235.
26. VW to Margaret Llewelyn Davies, 4 July 1938, VI, 250.
27. VW to Vanessa Bell, 25 June [1938], VI, 244.
28. VW to Ethel Smyth, 26 June [1938], VI, 247.
29. VW to Vanessa Bell, 28 [June 1938], VI, 249.
30. *Diary*, 7 July 1938, V, 155.
31. VW to Ethel Smyth, 29 August [1938], VI, 267.
32. *Diary*, 17 September 1938, V, 172.
33. *Diary*, 10 September 1938, V, 167.
34. VW to Sybil Colefax, 2 June 1938, VI, 233.
35. VW to Sybil Colefax, [5 September 1938], VI, 270.
36. *Diary*, 7 August 1938, V, 160.
37. *Diary*, 28 September 1938, V, 174.
38. *Diary*, 17 August 1938, V, 161.
39. *Diary*, 30 September 1938, V, 177.
40. VW to Vanessa Bell, 8 October [1938], VI, 286.
41. VW to Ethel Smyth, [25 November 1938], VI, 303.
42. *Diary*, 9 January 1939, V, 198.
43. *Diary*, 9 December 1939, V, 250.
44. *Diary*, 29 January 1939, V, 202.
45. VW to Ethel Smyth, 24 January [1939], VI, 312.
46. *Diary*, 19 December 1938, V, 193.
47. 'A Sketch of the Past', *Moments*, 109.
48. *Diary*, 22 March 1939, V, 210.
49. *Diary*, 31 January 1939, V, 203.
50. *Diary*, 15 April 1939, V, 215.
51. VW to Victoria Ocampo, 26 June 1939, VI, 342–3.
52. *Diary*, 26 June 1939, V, 221.
53. *Diary*, 13 July 1939, V, 226.
54. *Diary*, 7 August 1939, V, 230.

CHAPTER TWENTY: TRANSFORMATIONS

1. *Diary*, 28 July 1939, V, 228.
2. *Collected Essays*. London: Hogarth Press, 1966, II, 209.
3. Ibid., 215.
4. *Diary*, 20 March 1940, V, 271.
5. *Autobiography*, II, 401.
6. VW to Vita Sackville-West, 29 August [1939], VI, 354.
7. *Diary*, 23 September 1939, V, 237.
8. VW to Angelica Bell, [16 October 1939], VI, 364.
9. VW to Shena, Lady Simon, 22 January [1940], VI, 379.
10. *Diary*, 26 January 1940, V, 261.
11. VW to Ethel Smyth, 1 February 1940, VI, 381.
12. *Diary*, 9 February 1940, V, 266.
13. VW to Vanessa Bell, [15 March 1940], VI, 385.
14. Quoted in *Diary*, 26 March 1940, V, 275.
15. VW to Hugh Walpole, 28 March [1940], VI, 390.
16. *Diary*, 16 February 1940, V, 269.
17. *Diary*, 6 May 1940, V, 282.
18. *Diary*, 11 February 1940, V, 267.
19. *Diary*, 25 April 1940, V, 281.
20. VW to Ethel Smyth, 9 July [1940], VI, 404.
21. *Diary*, 7 August 1939, V, 229.
22. *Diary*, 15 May 1940, V, 285.
23. *Diary*, 25 July 1940, V, 305.
24. *Diary*, 28 July 1940, V, 307.
25. Herbert Read, *Spectator*, 2 August 1940.
26. E. M. Forster, *New Statesman and Nation*, 10 August 1940.
27. VW to Ethel Smyth, 16 August [1940], VI, 418.
28. VW to Violet Dickinson, [8 September 1940], VI, 429.
29. Benedict Nicolson to VW, 6 August 1940, MS Sussex.
30. VW to Benedict Nicolson, 13 August 1940, VI, 413–14.
31. VW to Benedict Nicolson, [24 August 1940], VI, 419–21.
32. *Diary*, 26 October 1940, V, 333.
33. VW to Vita Sackville-West, [30 August 1940], V, 424.
34. VW to Ethel Smyth, 11 September [1940], VI, 429–31.
35. VW to Ethel Smyth, 25 September 1940, VI, 434–5.
36. *Diary*, 12 September 1940, V, 318.
37. 'Anon', 382.
38. Ibid., 397–8.
39. *Diary*, 29 September 1940, V, 325.
40. *Diary*, 2 October 1940, V, 326–7.

41. *Diary*, 17 October 1940, V, 330.
42. 21 October, 551.
43. *Diary*, 3 November 1940, V, 336.
44. *Diary*, 7 November 1940, V, 337.
45. VW to Ethel Smyth, 14 November 1940, VI, 444.
46. *Between the Acts*, 61.
47. Ibid., 37.
48. Ibid., 15.
49. Ibid., 111.
50. Ibid., 107.
51. Ibid., 129–30.
52. VW to Ethel Smyth, 14 November 1940, VI, 444.
53. VW to Ethel Smyth, 12 January 1941, VI, 459–60.
54. *Diary*, 29 December 1940, V, 347.
55. *Diary*, 6 December 1940, V, 342.
56. *Diary*, 19 December 1940, V, 344.
57. VW to Octavia Wilberforce, 31 December 1940, VI, 456.
58. VW to Ethel Smyth, 24 December 1940, VI, 454.
59. VW to Elaine Robson, 10 January 1941, VI, 459.
60. *Diary*, 15 January 1941, V, 353.
61. Vita Sackville-West to VW, 14 January [1941], *Vita–Virginia Letters*, 470.
62. VW to Vita Sackville-West, 19 January [1941], VI, 462.
63. VW to Desmond MacCarthy, 2 February [1941], VI, 467.
64. VW to Ethel Smyth, 1 February 1941, VI, 466.
65. VW to Elizabeth Robins, 13 March 1941, VI, 479.
66. VW to Nelly Cecil, 21 March [1941], VI, 483.
67. VW to John Lehmann, 20 March [1941], VI, 482.
68. VW to John Lehmann, [27? March 1941], VI, 486.
69. Vanessa Bell to VW, 20 March 1941, MS Berg.
70. VW to Leonard Woolf, [18? March 1941], VI, 481.
71. Octavia Wilberforce's treatment of VW in 1940–41 is described vividly in *Octavia Wilberforce: The Autobiography of a Pioneer Woman Doctor*, 160–87.
72. VW to Leonard Woolf, 28 March 1941, VI, 486–7.
73. *Mrs Dalloway*, 202.
74. *Recollections*, 195.
75. *Between the Acts*, 64.
76. Ibid., 28.

Select Bibliography

PRIMARY SOURCES

Manuscripts

Clive Bell to Lytton Strachey	British Library
Clive Bell to Virginia Stephen/ Virginia Woolf	The University of Sussex Library
Vanessa Bell to Clive Bell	Tate Gallery Archive
Vanessa Bell to Roger Fry	Tate Gallery Archive
Vanessa Bell to Virginia Stephen/ Virginia Woolf	Berg Collection, New York Public Library
Stella Duckworth Diary	Berg Collection, New York Public Library
Ethel Smyth to Virginia Woolf	Berg Collection, New York Public Library

Virginia Woolf's Writings

'"Anon" and "The Reader"', edited by Brenda R. Silver, *Twentieth Century Literature*, 25, Fall/Winter 1979, 356–441.

Between the Acts, with an introduction and notes by Gillian Beer, edited by Stella McNichol. Harmondsworth: Penguin Books, 1992.

A Cockney's Farming Experiences and The Experiences of a Pater-familias, edited with an introduction by Suzanne Henig. San Diego: San Diego State University Press, 1972.

Collected Essays, 4 vols. London: The Hogarth Press, 1966–7.

The Common Reader. First Series. New York: Harcourt, Brace & World, 1925.

The Common Reader. Second Series. New York: Harcourt, Brace & World, 1932.

The Complete Shorter Fiction, edited by Susan Dick. London: The Hogarth Press, 1989.

Congenial Spirits: The Selected Letters of Virginia Woolf, edited by Joanne Trautmann Banks. London: The Hogarth Press, 1989.

The Diary, edited by Anne Olivier Bell, assisted by Andrew McNeillie, 5 vols. London: The Hogarth Press, 1977–84.

The Essays, edited by Andrew McNeillie, 3 vols. (to be completed in 6 vols.). London: The Hogarth Press, 1986–.

Flush: A Biography, with an introduction by Margaret Forster. London: The Hogarth Press, 1991.

Freshwater, edited by Lucio P. Ruotolo. New York: Harcourt Brace, Jovanovich, 1976.

'Friendships Gallery', edited by Ellen Hawkes, *Twentieth Century Literature*, 25, Fall/Winter 1979, 273–302.

Jacob's Room, edited by Sue Roe. Harmondsworth: Penguin Books, 1992.

The Letters, edited by Nigel Nicolson and Joanne Trautmann, 6 vols. London: The Hogarth Press, 1975–80.

Introductory letter, *Life as We Have Known It*, edited by Margaret Llewelyn Davies, with a new introduction by Anna Davin. London: Virago, 1977.

Melymbrosia: The Early Version of The Voyage Out, edited with an introduction by Louise A. DeSalvo. New York: The New York Public Library, 1982.

Moments of Being: Unpublished Autobiographical Writings, edited by Jeanne Schulkind, 2nd edn. London: The Hogarth Press, 1985.

Mrs Dalloway, with an introduction and notes by Elaine Showalter, text edited by Stella McNichol. Harmondsworth: Penguin Books, 1992.

Mrs Dalloway's Party: A Short Story Sequence, edited by Stella McNichol. London: The Hogarth Press, 1973.

Night and Day, edited with an introduction and notes by Julia Briggs. Harmondsworth: Penguin Books, 1992.

Orlando: A Biography, edited with an introduction by Rachel Bowlby. Oxford: Oxford University Press, 1992.

The Pargiters: The Novel-Essay Portion of The Years, edited with an introduction by Mitchell A. Leaska. New York: The New York Public Library and Readex Books, 1977.

A Passionate Apprentice: The Early Journals, 1897–1909, edited by Mitchell A. Leaska. London: The Hogarth Press, 1990.

Pointz Hall: The Earlier and Later Typescripts, edited by Mitchell A. Leaska. New York: University Publications, 1983.

A Room of One's Own and *Three Guineas*, edited with an introduction by Morag Shiach. Oxford: Oxford University Press, 1992.

'Some New Woolf Letters', edited by Joanne Trautmann Banks, *Modern Fiction Studies*, 30, 2, Summer 1984, 175–202.

To the Lighthouse, edited by Stella McNichol, with an introduction and notes by Hermione Lee. Harmondsworth: Penguin Books, 1992.

To the Lighthouse: The Original Holograph Draft, edited by Susan Dick. Toronto: University of Toronto Press, 1982.

Virginia Woolf–Lytton Strachey Letters, edited by Leonard Woolf and James Strachey. New York: Harcourt Brace, 1952.

The Voyage Out, edited with an introduction and notes by Jane Wheare. Harmondsworth: Penguin Books, 1992.

The Waves, edited with an introduction and notes by Kate Flint. Harmondsworth: Penguin Books, 1992.

The Waves: The Two Holograph Drafts, edited by J. W. Graham. Toronto: University of Toronto Press, 1976.

Women & Fiction: The Manuscript Version of A Room of One's Own, edited by S. P. Rosenbaum. Oxford: Blackwell, 1992.

SECONDARY SOURCES

Books and articles devoted to Virginia Woolf

Abel, Elizabeth, *Virginia Woolf and the Fictions of Psychoanalysis*. Chicago: University of Chicago Press, 1989.

Alexander, Peter F., *Leonard and Virginia Woolf: A Literary Partnership*. New York and London: Harvester Wheatsheaf, 1992.

Badenhausen, Ingeborg, *Die sprache Virginia Woolfs*. Marburg, 1932.

Bell, Quentin, *Virginia Woolf: A Biography* (*Volume One, Virginia Stephen, 1882–1912*; *Volume Two, Mrs Woolf, 1912–1941*). London: The Hogarth Press, 1972.

Bell, Vanessa, *Notes on Virginia's Childhood: A Memoir*, edited by Richard F. Schaubeck Jr. New York: Frank Hallman, 1974.

Bicknell, John W., 'Mr Ramsay was Young Once', in *Virginia Woolf and Bloomsbury: A Centenary Celebration*, edited by Jane Marcus. London: Macmillan, 1987, 45–89.

Bishop, Edward, 'The Shaping of *Jacob's Room*: Woolf's Manuscript Revisions', *Twentieth Century Literature*, 32, 1, Spring 1986, 115–35.

– *A Virginia Woolf Chronology*. Boston: G. K. Hall & Co., 1989.

– *Virginia Woolf*. New York: St Martin's Press, 1991.

Black, Naomi, 'Virginia Woolf and the Women's Movement', in *Virginia Woolf: A Feminist Slant*, edited by Jane Marcus. Omaha: University of Nebraska Press, 1983, 180–97.

Caramagno, Thomas C., *The Flight of the Mind: Virginia Woolf's Art and Manic-Depressive Illness*. Berkeley: University of California Press, 1992.

Caws, Mary Ann, *Women of Bloomsbury: Virginia, Vanessa and Carrington*. New York and London: Routledge, 1990.

Clarke, Stuart N., 'The Horse with a Green Tail', *Virginia Woolf Miscellany*, 34, 1990, 3–4.

Clements, Patricia and Isobel Grundy (eds.), *Virginia Woolf: New Critical Essays*. London: Vision Press, 1983.

Collins, Millie, *Bloomsbury in Sussex*. Albourne: Albourne Publications, *c*. 1990.

Comstock, Margaret, 'The Loudspeaker and the Human Voice: Politics and the Form of *The Years*', *Bulletin of the New York Public Library*, 80, 2, 1977, 252–75.

Delattre, Floris, *Le roman psychologique de Virginia Woolf*. Paris, 1932.

DeSalvo, Louise A., 'Sorting, Sequencing, and Dating the Drafts of Virginia Woolf's *The Voyage Out*', *Bulletin of Research in the Humanities*, 82, 3, Autumn 1979, 271–93.

– 'Virginia Woolf's Revisions for the 1920 American and English Editions of *The Voyage Out*', *Bulletin of Research in the Humanities*, 82, 3, Autumn 1979, 338–66.

– *Virginia Woolf's First Voyage: A Novel in the Making*. Totowa, New Jersey: Rowman & Littlefield, 1980.

– *Virginia Woolf: The Impact of Childhood Sexual Abuse on Her Life and Work*. Boston: Beacon Press, 1989.

DiBattista, M., *Virginia Woolf's Major Novels: The Fables of Anon*. New Haven: Yale University Press, 1980.

Dunn, Jane, *A Very Close Conspiracy: Vanessa Bell and Virginia Woolf*. London: Jonathan Cape, 1990.

Fleishman, Avrom, *Virginia Woolf: A Critical Reading*. Baltimore and London: The Johns Hopkins University Press, 1975.

Flint, Kate, 'Virginia Woolf and the General Strike', *Essays in Criticism*, 36, October 1986, 319–34.

– 'Revising *Jacob's Room*: Virginia Woolf, Women and Language', *Review of English Studies: A Quarterly Journal of English Literature and the English Language*, 42, 167, August 1991, 361–79.

Forster, E. M., *Virginia Woolf*. Cambridge: Cambridge University Press, 1942 (The Rede Lecture).

Fowler, R., 'Virginia Woolf and Katharine Furse: An Unpublished Correspondence [with appendix]', *Tulsa Studies in Women's Literature*, 9, Fall 1990, 201–28.

Gillespie, D. F., *The Sisters' Arts: The Writing and Painting of Virginia Woolf and Vanessa Bell*. Syracuse: Syracuse University Press, 1988.

Goldensohn, Lorrie, 'Unburying the Statue: The Lives of Virginia Woolf', *Salmagundi*, 74–5, Spring–Summer 1987, 1–41.

Gordon, Lyndall, *Virginia Woolf: A Writer's Life*. Oxford: Oxford University Press, 1984.

Gottlieb, Laura Moss, 'The War between the Woolfs', *Virginia Woolf and Bloomsbury: A Centenary Celebration*, edited by Jane Marcus. London: Macmillan, 1987, 242–52.

Grüber, Ruth, *Virginia Woolf: A Study*. Leipzig, 1935.

Hawkes, Ellen, 'A Form of One's Own', *Mosaic*, 8, 1, 1974, 77–90.

– 'The Virgin in the Bell Biography', *Twentieth Century Literature*, 20, April 1974, 96–113.

Heilbrun, Carolyn G., 'Virginia Woolf in Her Fifties', *Hamlet's Mother and Other Essays*. New York: Columbia University Press, 1990, 78–97.

Heine, Elizabeth, 'The Earlier *Voyage Out*: Virginia Woolf's First Novel', *Bulletin of Research in the Humanities*, 82, 3, Autumn 1979, 294–316.

Hoffman, Charles G., 'Fact and Fantasy in *Orlando*: Virginia Woolf's MS Revisions', *Texas Studies in Literature and Language*, 10, Fall 1968, 435–44.

– 'From Short Story to Novel: the Manuscript Revisions of Virginia Woolf's *Mrs Dalloway*', *Modern Fiction Studies*, 14, Summer 1968, 171–86.

– 'Virginia Woolf's Manuscript Revisions of *The Years*', *PMLA*, 84, 1, January 1969, 79–89.

Holroyd, Michael, 'Virginia Woolf: A Suitable Case for Biography?', in *Unreceived Opinions*. London: Heinemann, 1973, 211–27.

Holtby, Winifred, *Virginia Woolf*. London, 1932.

Hummel, Madeline M., 'From the Common Reader to the Uncommon Critic: *Three Guineas* and the Epistolary Form', *Bulletin of the New York Public Library*, 80, 2, 1977, 151–7.

Hussey, M., *The Singing of the Real World: The Philosophy of Virginia Woolf's Fiction*. Columbus: Ohio State University Press, 1986.

Johnstone, J. K., *The Bloomsbury Group: A Study of E. M. Forster, Lytton Strachey, Virginia Woolf and Their Circle*. London: Secker & Warburg, 1954.

Kenney, Susan M., 'Two Endings: Virginia Woolf's Suicide and *Between the Acts*', *University of Toronto Quarterly*, 44, Summer 1975, 265–89.

Kirkpatrick, B. J., *A Bibliography of Virginia Woolf*, 3rd edn. Oxford: The Clarendon Press, 1980.

Leaska, Mitchell A., *The Novels of Virginia Woolf: From Beginning to End*. New York: The John Jay Press, 1977.

– 'Virginia Woolf, the Pargeter: A Reading of *The Years*', *Bulletin of the New York Public Library*, 80, 2, 1977, 172–210.

– 'The Death of Rachel Vinrace', *Bulletin of Research in the Humanities*, 82, 3, Autumn 1979, 328–37.

Lee, Hermione, *The Novels of Virginia Woolf*. New York: Holmes & Meier Publishers, 1977.

Lehmann, John, *Virginia Woolf and Her World*. London: Thames and Hudson, 1975.

– *Thrown to the Woolfs*. London: Weidenfeld & Nicolson, 1978.

Little, Judy, '*Jacob's Room* as Comedy: Woolf's Parodic Bildungsroman', *New Feminist Essays on Virginia Woolf*, edited by Jane Marcus. London: Macmillan, 1981.

Love, Jean O., *Virginia Woolf: Sources of Madness and Art*. Berkeley and Los Angeles: University of California Press, 1977.

Maika, Patricia, *Virginia Woolf's Between the Acts and Jane Harrison's Conspiracy*. Cambridge, Mass.: UMI Research Press, 1987.

Majumdar, Robin and Allen McLaurin (eds.), *Virginia Woolf: The Critical Heritage*. London: Routledge & Kegan Paul, 1975.

Marcus, Jane, '*The Years* as Greek Drama, Domestic Novel, and Götterdämmerung', *Bulletin of the New York Public Library*, 80, 2, 1977, 276–301.

– 'The Niece of a Nun: Virginia Woolf, Caroline Stephen, and the Cloistered Imagination', in *Virginia Woolf: A Feminist Slant*, edited by Jane Marcus. Lincoln: University of Nebraska Press, 1983, 7–36.

– *Virginia Woolf and the Language of Patriarchy*. Bloomington: Indiana University Press, 1988.

Meisel, Perry, *The Absent Father: Virginia Woolf and Walter Pater*. New Haven: Yale University Press, 1980.

Mepham, John, 'Mourning and Modernism', in *Virginia Woolf: New Critical Essays*, edited by Patricia Clements and Isobel Grundy. London: Vision Press, 1983.

– *Virginia Woolf: A Literary Life*. London: Macmillan, 1991.

– *Virginia Woolf: Criticism in Focus*. London: Bristol Classical Press, 1992.

Middleton, Victoria S., '*The Years*: "A Deliberate Failure"', *Bulletin of the New York Public Library*, 80, 2, 1987, 158–71.

Moers, Ellen, *Literary Women*. New York: Oxford University Press, 1985.

Moore, Madeleine, 'Virginia Woolf's *The Years* and Adverse Male Reviewers', *Women's Studies*, 4, 1977, 247–63.

Nicolson, Nigel, *Portrait of a Marriage*. New York: Athenaeum, 1973.

Noble, Joan Russell (ed.), *Recollections of Virginia Woolf*. London: Sphere, 1975.

Pippett, Aileen, *The Moth and the Star: A Biography of Virginia Woolf*. Boston: Little, Brown, 1955.

Poole, Roger, *The Unknown Virginia Woolf*. Cambridge: Cambridge University Press, 1978; 3rd edn. London: Humanities Press International, 1990.

Radin, Grace, '"Two enormous chunks": Episodes Excluded during the Final Revisions of *The Years*', *Bulletin of the New York Public Library*, 80, 2, 1977, 221–51.

– *Virginia Woolf's The Years: The Evolution of a Novel*. Knoxville: University of Tennessee Press, 1981.

Raitt, Suzanne, '"The Tide of Ethel": Femininity as Narrative in the Friendship of Ethel Smyth and Virginia Woolf', *Critical Quarterly*, 30, 1988, 3–21.

– *Vita & Virginia: The Work and Friendship of Vita Sackville-West and Virginia Woolf*. Oxford: Oxford University Press, 1993.

Richter, Harvena, 'The *Ulysses* Connection: Clarissa Dalloway's Bloomsday', *Studies in the Novel*, 21, Fall 1989, 305–19.

Rose, Phyllis, *Woman of Letters: A Life of Virginia Woolf*. New York: Harcourt, Brace, 1978.

Rosenbaum, S. P. (ed.), *The Bloomsbury Group*. Toronto: University of Toronto Press, 1975.

– 'Virginia Woolf: Beginnings', in *Leon Edel and Literary Art*, edited by Lyall H. Powers, assisted by Clare Virginia Eby. Ann Arbor and London: UMI Research Press, 1988, 43–53.

Rosenman, Ellen Bayuk, *The Invisible Presence: Virginia Woolf and the Mother–Daughter Relationship*. Baton Rouge: Louisiana State University Press, 1986.

Sackville-West, Vita, *The Letters of Vita Sackville-West to Virginia Woolf*, edited by Louise DeSalvo and Mitchell A. Leaska, with an introduction by Mitchell A. Leaska. London: Hutchinson, 1984.

Schlack, Beverly Ann, 'Virginia Woolf's Strategy of Scorn in *The Years* and *Three Guineas*', *Bulletin of the New York Public Library*, 80, 2, 1977, 146–50.

– 'The Novelist's Voyage from Manuscripts to Text: Revisions of Literary Allusions in *The Voyage Out*', *Bulletin of Research in the Humanities*, 82, 3, Autumn 1979, 317–27.

Sears, Sally, 'Notes on Sexuality: *The Years* and *Three Guineas*', *Bulletin of the New York Public Library*, 80, 2, 1977, 211–20.

– 'Theater of War: Virginia Woolf's *Between the Acts*', in *Virginia Woolf: A Feminist Slant*, edited by Jane Marcus. Omaha: University of Nebraska Press, 1983, 212–35.

Silver, Brenda R., *Virginia Woolf's Reading Notebooks*. Princeton: Princeton University Press, 1983.

Spater, George and Ian Parsons, *A Marriage of True Minds: An Intimate Portrait of Leonard and Virginia Woolf*. London: Jonathan Cape, 1977.

Spilka, Mark, *Virginia Woolf's Quarrel with Grieving*. Lincoln: University of Nebraska Press, 1980.

Squier, Susan Merrill, *Virginia Woolf and London: The Sexual Politics of the City*. Chapel Hill: University of North Carolina Press, 1985.

Steele, Elizabeth, *Virginia Woolf's Literary Sources and Allusions: A Guide to the Essays*. New York: Garland, 1983.

Szladits, Lola, 'The Life, Character and Opinions of Flush the Spaniel', *Bulletin of the New York Public Library*, 74, 1970, 211–18.

Trautmann, Joanne, *The Jessamy Brides: The Friendship of Virginia Woolf and V. Sackville-West*. The Pennsylvania State University Studies No. 36, University Park: The Pennsylvania State University, 1973.

Trombley, Stephen, *'All that Summer She was Mad': Virginia Woolf and Her Doctors*. London: Junction Books, 1981.

Willis, J. H. Jr., *Leonard and Virginia Woolf as Publishers: The Hogarth Press 1917–41*. Charlottesville: University Press of Virginia, 1992.

Wilson, Jean Moorcroft, *Virginia Woolf: Life and London, A Biography of Place*. London: Cecil Woolf, 1987.

Wolf, Ernest S. and Ina Wolf, '"We Perished Each Alone": A Psychoanalytical Commentary on Virginia Woolf's *To the Lighthouse*', *International Review of Psycho-Analysis*, 6, 1979, 37–47.

Zwerdling, Alex, *Virginia Woolf and the Real World*. Berkeley and Los Angeles: University of California Press, 1986.

Works with important references to Virginia Woolf, works devoted to friends of Virginia Woolf and Bloomsbury, and works of reference and critical theory

Abrahamsen, David, *Murder & Madness: The Secret Life of Jack the Ripper*, New York: Donald I. Fine, Inc., 1992.

Ackroyd, Peter, *T. S. Eliot*. London: Hamish Hamilton, 1984.

Alexander, Peter F., *William Plomer: A Biography*, Oxford: Oxford University Press, 1989.

Allen, Peter, *The Cambridge Apostles: The Early Years*. Cambridge: Cambridge University Press, 1978.

Annan, Noel, *Leslie Stephen: The Godless Victorian*. New York: Random House, 1984.

Anscombe, Isabelle, *Omega and After*. London: Thames & Hudson, 1981.

Beaton, Cecil, *The Book of Beauty*. London: Duckworth, 1930.

Bell, Clive. *Old Friends: Personal Recollections*. London: Cassell, 1988.

Bell, Julian. *Julian Bell: Essays, Poems and Letters*, edited by Quentin Bell. London: The Hogarth Press, 1938.

Bell, Quentin, *Bloomsbury*. London: Futura, 1974.

Blain, Virginia, Patricia Clements and Isobel Grundy, *The Feminist Companion to Literature in English: Women Writers from the Middle Ages to the Present*. New Haven and London: Yale University Press, 1990.

Boyd, Elizabeth French, *Bloomsbury Heritage: Their Mothers and Their Aunts*. London: Hamish Hamilton, 1976.

Brenan, Gerald, *South from Granada*. London: Hamish Hamilton, 1958.

Cecil, Hugh and Mirabel, *Clever Hearts*. London: Victor Gollancz, 1990.

Darroch, Sandra Jobson, *Ottoline: The Life of Lady Ottoline Morrell*. London: Chatto & Windus, 1976.

David, Hugh, *Stephen Spender: A Portrait with Background*. London: Heinemann, 1992.

Delany, Paul, *The Neo-pagans: Rupert Brooke and the Ordeal of Youth*. New York: The Free Press, 1987.

Edel, Leon, *Bloomsbury: A House of Lions*. London: The Hogarth Press, 1979.

Faderman, Lillian, *Surpassing the Love of Women: Romantic Friendship and Love Between Women from the Renaissance to the Present.* New York: William Morrow, 1981.

Fry, Roger, *Letters*, edited by Denys Sutton. London: Chatto & Windus, 1972.

Furbank, P. N., *E. M. Forster: A Life*, 2 vols. London: Secker & Warburg, 1977, 1978.

Garnett, Angelica, *Deceived with Kindness: A Bloomsbury Childhood.* London: Chatto & Windus, 1984.

Gérin, Winifred, *Anne Thackeray Ritchie.* Oxford: Oxford University Press, 1981.

Gilbert, Sandra M., 'Costumes of the Mind: Transvestism as Metaphor in Modern Literature', in *Writing and Sexual Difference*, edited by Elizabeth Abel. Chicago: University of Chicago Press, 1982, 193–219.

Glendinning, Victoria, *Elizabeth Bowen: Portrait of a Writer.* Weidenfeld & Nicolson, 1977.

– *Vita: The Life of Vita Sackville-West.* Harmondsworth: Penguin Books, 1987.

Hassall, Christopher, *Rupert Brooke: A Biography.* London: Faber & Faber, 1964.

Heilbrun, Carolyn G., *Writing a Woman's Life.* London: The Women's Press, 1988.

Hoare, Philip, *Serious Pleasures: The Life of Stephen Tennant.* London: Hamish Hamilton, 1990.

Holroyd, Michael, *Lytton Strachey: A Biography.* Harmondsworth: Penguin Books, 1987.

Kaplan, Louise A., *Female Perversions: The Temptations of Emma Bovary.* New York: Doubleday Anchor, 1992.

Kennedy, Richard, *A Boy at the Hogarth Press.* Harmondsworth: Penguin Books, 1978.

Keynes, Geoffrey, *The Gates of Memory.* Oxford and New York: Oxford University Press, 1983.

Lehmann, John, *The Whispering Gallery: Autobiography.* London: Longman, 1955.

McQueeney, Maire (ed.), *Virginia Woolf's Rodmell: An Illustrated Guide to a Sussex Village.* Rodmell: Rodmell Village Press, *c.* 1991.

Maitland, Frederic William, *The Life and Letters of Leslie Stephen.* London: Duckworth, 1906.

Meyer, Doris, *Victoria Ocampo: Against the Wind and the Tide.* New York: George Braziller, 1979.

Millgate, Michael, *Thomas Hardy: A Biography.* Oxford: Oxford University Press, 1982.

Rich, Adrienne, 'Compulsory Heterosexuality and Lesbian Existence', in *Women: Sex and Sexuality*, edited by Catharine M. Stimpson and Ethel Spector Person. Chicago: University of Chicago Press, 1980, 62–91.

Rosenbaum, S. P., *Victorian Bloomsbury: The Early Literary History of the Bloomsbury Group, Volume I*. London: Macmillan, 1987.

Sackville-West, Vita and Harold Nicolson, *Vita and Harold: The Letters*, edited by Nigel Nicolson. New York: Putnam, 1992.

St John, Christopher, *Ethel Smyth: A Biography*. London: Longman, Green and Co., 1959.

Sarton, May, *I Knew a Phoenix: Sketches for an Autobiography*. New York: Rinehart & Company, 1959.

Seymour, Miranda, *Ottoline Morrell: Life on the Grand Scale*. London: Hodder & Stoughton, 1992.

Showalter, Elaine, *The Female Malady: Women, Madness and English Culture, 1830–1980*. London: Virago, 1987.

– *A Literature of Their Own: British Women Novelists from Brontë to Lessing*, rev. edn. London: Virago, 1988.

Spalding, Frances, *Roger Fry: Art and Life*. Berkeley: University of California Press, 1980.

– *Vanessa Bell*. London: Papermac, 1984.

Spender, Stephen, *World Within World*. London: Hamish Hamilton, 1951.

Stansky, Peter and William Abrahams, *Journey to the Frontier: A Biography of Julian Bell and John Cornford: Their Lives and the 1930s*. London: Constable, 1966.

Stephen, Adrian, *The 'Dreadnought' Hoax*. London: The Hogarth Press, 1936.

Stephen, Julia Duckworth, *Stories for Children, Essays for Adults*, edited by Diane F. Gillespie and Elizabeth Steele. Syracuse: Syracuse University Press, 1987.

Stephen, Leslie, *Mausoleum Book*, edited by Alan Bell. Oxford: Clarendon Press, 1977.

Tomalin, Claire, *Katherine Mansfield: A Secret Life*. New York: Alfred A. Knopf, 1987.

Tweedsmuir, Susan, *A Winter Bouquet*. London: Duckworth, 1954.

Webb, Beatrice, *Diaries 1924–1932*, edited with an introduction by Margaret Cole. London and New York: Longman, Green and Co., 1956.

Wilberforce, Octavia, *Octavia Wilberforce: The Autobiography of a Pioneer Woman Doctor*, edited by Pat Jalland. London: Cassell, 1989.

Wilson, Duncan, *Leonard Woolf: A Political Biography*. London: The Hogarth Press, 1978.

Wolff, Charlotte, *Studies in Hand-Reading*. London: Chatto & Windus, 1936.

Woolf, Leonard, *The Wise Virgins: A Story of Words, Opinions and a Few Emotions*. London: The Hogarth Press, 1979.

– *An Autobiography*, Vol. I, 1880–1911; Vol. II, 1911–1969. Oxford: Oxford University Press, 1980.

– *Letters*, edited by Frederic Spotts. New York: Harcourt, Brace, Jovanovich, 1989.

Woolmer, J. Howard, *A Checklist of the Hogarth Press, 1917–1938*, with a short history of the Press by Mary E. Gaither. New York: Woolmer/Brotherson, 1976.

Wright, Elizabeth Mary, *The Life of Joseph Wright*. Oxford: Oxford University Press, 1932.

Index

VW = Virginia Stephen/Virginia Woolf